Calculator functions for finance situations:

(2nd)(FIN) Places the calculator in the financial mode.

(N) Enters the number of payment periods or compounding periods.

(%i) Enters the interest rate per compounding period for compound interest calculations. Also, enters the interest rate per payment period for annuities.

(PMT) Enters the payment amount in ordinary annuity or annuity due calculations.

(PV) Enters the present value.

(FV) Enters the future value.

(CPT) Entered with the unknown value key in calculations involving compound interest or ordinary annuities.

(DUE) Entered with the unknown value key in calculations involving annuities due.

In the financial mode, (FIN), three of the values (N), (%i), (PMT), (PV), or (FV), must be entered with the sequence

value, financial key

before the unknown value can be computed by pressing

(CPT), **financial key for unknown value**

for compound interest or ordinary annuity problems, or by pressing

(DUE), **financial key for unknown value**

for annuity due problems.

Mathematics for Management and Finance

2ND CANADIAN EDITION

Gloria E. Mullings, Ph.D.
Teaching Master
Business and Computer Studies Division
Seneca College of Applied Arts and Technology
Willowdale, Ontario

Stephen P. Shao, Ph.D.
Professor of MIS/Decision Science
Old Dominion University
Norfolk, Virginia

This edition is based on the first Canadian edition of *Mathematics for Management and Finance*, Copyright © 1979 Gage Publishing Limited, which was based on *Mathematics for Management and Finance*, Third U.S. Edition, Copyright © 1974 South-Western Publishing Co., Cincinnati, Ohio.

Canadian Cataloguing in Publication Data

Mullings, Gloria E.
　　Mathematics for management and finance

Includes index.
ISBN 0-7715-5596-2

1. Business mathematics.　　I. Shao, Stephen P., 1924-
II. Title.

HF5691.M85 1984　　513'.93'024658　　C83-099120-4

Co-ordinating Editor: Kathy Austin
Editor: Terry-Lee Wheelband

1　　2　　3　　4　　5　　BP　　88　　87　　86　　85　　84

Printed and bound in Canada

More Gage Books in Business

Canadian Business: Its Nature and Environment
Fitzgerald, Chamard, Glos, Steade, Lowry

Accounting Principles, Second Canadian Edition
Parker, Niswonger, Fess

Intermediate Accounting, Second Canadian Edition
Parker, Simons, Smith, Skousen

Communicating With P.O.W.E.R.
Dupuis, Wilson

Business and Government
Fleck, Litvak (forthcoming)

Preface

The Second Canadian Edition of *Mathematics for Management and Finance* has revised many topics which appeared in the previous editions to reflect the current needs of the business student. Chapters One to Five provide a review of the basic concepts of algebra. Break-even analysis is introduced in Chapter Three and the basic concepts of ratio, proportion and percent problems are covered in Chapter Four. The use of calculators to solve problems involving logarithmic functions is introduced in Chapter Five. Chapter Six covers supplemental topics in algebra and Chapter Seven deals with business applications of percent. In Chapters Eight through Seventeen, the presentation of topics reflects the use of electronic calculators. However, special sections are included which illustrate the use of tables and preprogrammed calculators.

The edition is designed for the first course in mathematics for students of business studies. Students who have had little or perhaps no algebra in high school, but who have determination in learning, will find that this text is suited to their capacities. Those who have a strong background in algebra will find challenging material throughout the text. After the completion of this course, the student should be prepared to continue with more advanced work in subjects involving quantitative analysis, such as accounting, statistics, and investment. This leads the authors to believe that, for a student of business studies, this text is more adequate and practical than a one-year course in mathematical analysis or college algebra. The latter courses traditionally emphasize theoretical mathematics, which is less pertinent to the foreseeable needs of a business student.

Experience shows that when students readily know the principles involved in each type of calculation, they usually become better prepared for problem solving and for more advanced work. Throughout this text, the basic principle for each topic in financial problems is illustrated in detail. Every special term is clearly defined and explained before it is applied. Diagrams are frequently employed as aids to illustrate the more complex examples. After the principles have been illustrated, formulae are often used to facilitate computation. However, the number of formulae has been kept to a minimum and they are presented in a simple manner. Proofs for the more complicated formulae are given in footnotes.

Enough number problems (drills) are placed at the beginning of each exercise so that students can quickly learn the mechanics of the new symbols and terms in each new process. In the statement problems that follow, the student has the opportunity to exercise his or her reasoning ability. In addition, ample review problems are provided at the end of certain chapters to give the students an opportunity to solve problems independently without referring to the illustrations in the individual sections of the text.

The problems in each exercise are carefully arranged so that either all odd-numbered or all even-numbered problems can be assigned by the instructor without fear of omitting the material that has been illustrated in the examples. Answers to the odd-numbered problems are placed at the end of the book. Detailed solutions to the odd-numbered and even-numbered problems are given in the instructor's manual.

The material presented in this text is sufficient for a one-year course, offered either in two semesters or in three quarters. The text may also be used as a one-semester course under either one of the following two suggestions:

1. To emphasize general management and financial problems–Chapter Four, Chapters Seven through Twelve, and Chapters Fifteen and Sixteen.
2. To emphasize investment problems–Chapters Eight through Twelve and Chapters Fifteen through Seventeen.

Each of the two suggestions may easily be adjusted for either a one-quarter or a two-quarter course. More detailed assignment suggestions are given in the instructor's manual.

In summary, the Second Canadian Edition of *Mathematics for Management and Finance* incorporates many features in aid of both student and instructor. Each chapter has an introductory section to set the stage for the ideas presented in the chapter. The actual design of the text is an open format for better visual appeal.

The use of calculators is emphasized, however, the use of tables to obtain the compounding factor is also covered, thus providing greater flexibility of the text. A glossary of terms is provided at the end of each chapter as well as a summary of formulae section at the end of each relevant chapter. A summary of the principle formulae is provided in the endpapers for easy access during a test. Also available in the endpapers is a summary of the principle calculator functions and their use, as well as a table with the number of each day of the year. A supplement with compounding interest and annuity tables which include the most commonly used periodic interest rates today is also provided.

It should be noted that when calculators are used for intermediate calculations, these values should be stored in order to reduce rounding error. Also, due to the difference in accuracy provided by different calculators on the market, answers may vary in the value obtained for the last digit. This is due to rounding error.

I am indebted to my colleagues at the Business and Computer Studies Division of Seneca College of Applied Arts and Technology and my colleagues at the other colleges or Applied Arts and Technology for their encouragement and suggestions for revisions to the previous edition of this book. I am especially indebted to Jim Heron, Co-ordinator, Business Mathematics of Niagara College of Applied Arts and Technology who read the draft of the revised manuscript and provided valuable help and insights in updating the content. I am also indebted to Harry J. Rudolph, Business Mathematics Technician at Seneca College who provided the solutions to the problems and to Janifer Chan, a student in the Accounting course at Seneca College and David Mullings who assisted in providing solutions. I am also grateful to friends and relatives for their encouragement and assistance in making this second edition possible.

GLORIA E. MULLINGS
Seneca College of Applied Arts and
Technology, Willowdale, Ontario
February, 1984

Contents

15 Extinction of Debts/532

16 Investment in Bonds/553

PART I

Mathematics in Business Management

1 Review of arithmetic

Introduction

Communication skills are essential to a successful business career. Since numbers are used extensively in business, it is imperative for the business student to possess the number skills necessary in effective business communications.

Technological advances in recent years have provided facilities for communicating efficiently and effectively. The computer allows for the manipulation of numbers to update budgets, to have a tighter control on operations and expenditures, as well as other variables which affect profit. Certain basic mathematical skills are necessary in order to maximize the use of the computer in communications which rely on the use of numbers.

For example, the ability to interpret the correct order in which the fundamental operations are carried out is essential to the effective use of electronic calculators as well as computers. This text provides the student with the mathematical skills regarded as necessary elements in the body of knowledge required for a career in business.

Chapter One concentrates on fundamental operations. While some of the basic procedures may be simple, there is no substitute for a clear and complete understanding of these techniques. Since these techniques are part of an essential base, any weakness in this area will prevent the development of the base into a solid background informational system necessary for advancement in the business community.

1.1 Fundamental Operations with Signed Numbers

The fundamental operations in arithmetic are *addition, subtraction, multiplication*, and *division*. When dealing with signed numbers, the plus and minus signs are used to indicate positive numbers and negative numbers, as well as addition and subtraction.

Numbers containing decimal places are treated as whole numbers in performing the four fundamental operations and in checking answers. However, care must be taken in placing the decimal points during an operation and rounding the decimal places in an answer. A method of rounding decimal places is included in section 1.4C.

A.   OPERATIONS WITH 0 AND 1

The numbers zero and one have certain properties which are explained below:

1. When zero is added to a number, or a number is added to zero the SUM is the number unchanged. Thus,

    $3 + 0 = 3; 0 + 3 = 3; 0 + 0 = 0.$

2. When zero is subtracted from a number, the REMAINDER is the number unchanged. Thus,

    $3 - 0 = 3; 0 - 0 = 0.$

    However, when a number is subtracted from zero, the remainder is the ABSOLUTE VALUE of the number with its sign changed. Thus,

    $0 - 3$ or $0 - (+3) = -3; 0 - (-3) = +3$ or $3.$

3. When zero is multiplied by a number, or a number is multiplied by zero, the PRODUCT is zero. Thus,

    $3 \times 0 = 0; 0 \times 3 = 0; 0 \times 0 = 0.$

4. When zero is divided by any number except zero, the QUOTIENT is zero. Thus,

    $0 \div 3$ or $\dfrac{0}{3} = 0.$

5. Division by zero has no meaning because there is no answer. (This is further illustrated in Section 2.1C.)

6. When a number is multiplied by one, the product is the number unchanged. Thus,

    $6 \times 1 = 6.$

7. When a number is divided by one, the quotient is the number unchanged. Thus,

    $\dfrac{6}{1} = 6.$

B.   ADDITION OF SIGNED NUMBERS

When adding numbers that have the same sign, first find the sum of their absolute values. Second, prefix the common sign to this sum.

Example 1.1a
Add (−5), (−6), and (−3).

SOLUTION:

The sum of the absolute values is $5 + 6 + 3 = 14$.
The common sign is negative. Thus,

$$(−5) + (−6) + (−3) = −14.$$

Example 1.1b
$$(+4) + (+2.16) + (+7.59) = +13.75 = 13.75$$

When adding numbers that have unlike signs, first subtract the smaller absolute value from the larger. Second, prefix the sign of the larger to the remainder.

Example 1.1c
Add (−9) and (+3).

SOLUTION:

The DIFFERENCE between the two absolute values is $9 − 3 = 6$. The sign of the larger number, 9, is negative. Thus,

$$(−9) + (+3) = −6.$$

To obtain the sum of three or more numbers having unlike signs, first add two of the numbers; then add the sum to the third number, and so on.

Example 1.1d
Add $(+14) + (−15) + (+.817\ 9)$.

SOLUTION:

$$(+14) + (−15) + (+.817\ 9) = (−1) + (+.817\ 9) = −.182\ 1$$

Or, first add numbers having the same sign, then combine:

$$(+14) + (−15) + (+.817\ 9) = (+14.817\ 9) + (−15) = −.182\ 1.$$

C. SUBTRACTION OF SIGNED NUMBERS

When subtracting signed numbers, first change the sign of the SUBTRAHEND (the number to be subtracted). Second, add.

Example 1.1e
Subtract (−17) from (−8).

SOLUTION:

$$(−8) − (−17) = (−8) + (+17) = 9$$

Example 1.1f
Subtract (−16) from (+19).

SOLUTION:

$(+19) - (-16) = 19 + (+16) = 35$

Example 1.1g
Subtract (+17.436) from (+12).

SOLUTION:

$(+12) - (+17.436) = 12 + (-17.436) = -5.436$

D. MULTIPLICATION OF SIGNED NUMBERS

When multiplying two numbers having unlike signs, multiply the numerical values and prefix a negative sign to the product.

Example 1.1h

$(+6) \times (-9) = -54$; and $(-6) \times (+3) = -18$

If two numbers have like signs, prefix a positive sign to the product.

Example 1.1i

$(-4)(-5) = +20$

NOTE: If a number appears in a bracket beside another number in a bracket, and there is no sign between them to indicate the operation, the operation implied is multiplication.

$2 \times 4 = 8$
$(2)(4) = 8$
$2(4) = 8$

E. DIVISION OF SIGNED NUMBERS

When dividing one number by another with an unlike sign, divide the numerical values and prefix a negative sign to the quotient.

Example 1.1j

$10 \div (-2) = -5$; $(-18) \div (+3) = -6$

If two numbers have like signs, the quotient is positive.

Example 1.1k

$10 \div 2 = 5$; $(-18) \div (-3) = 6$

EXERCISE 1.1A / REFERENCE SECTIONS: A–E

Add the following signed numbers:

1. $(-7) + (-5)$ -12
2. $(-18) + (-6)$ -24
3. $(-12) + (-18)$ -30
4. $(-15) + (-17)$ -32

5. $(-23) + (-24)$ -47
6. $(-38) + (-2)$ -40
7. $(-15) + (-16)$ -31
8. $(-26) + (-9)$ -35

9. $(+24) + (+7)$ 31
10. $(+45) + (+16)$ 61
11. $(+32) + (+13)$ 45
12. $(+63) + (+41)$ 104

13. $(+52) + (-30)$ 22
14. $(+47) + (-15)$ 32
15. $(+38) + (-13)$ 25
16. $(+44) + (-15)$ 29

17. $(+35) + (-46.23)$ -11.23
18. $(+29) + (-60.15)$ -31.15
19. $(+56) + (-80.37)$ -24.37
20. $(+48) + (-54.49)$ -6.49

21. $(-17.264) + (+30)$ 12.736
22. $(-42.317) + (+46)$ 3.683
23. $(-40.943) + (+64)$ 13.057
24. $(-39.174) + (+50)$ 10.826

25. $(-7) + (-4) + (-12)$ -23
26. $(-18) + (+20) + (+6)$ 8
27. $(+4) + (-8) + (+11)$ 7
28. $(+10) + (-42) + (-41)$ -73

29. $(+6) + (-4) + (-12) + (-17)$ -27
30. $(-2) + (+4) + (-21) + (+6)$ -13
31. $(+4) + (+19) + (+42) + (-63)$ 2
32. $(-41) + (-36) + (-42) + (-7)$ -126

Subtract the following signed numbers:

33. $(+23) - (-4)$ 27
34. $(+24) - (-6)$ 30
35. $(+38) - (-7)$ 45
36. $(+46) - (-5)$ 51
37. $(-3) - (-8)$ 5

38. $(-53) - (-17)$ -36
39. $(-38) - (-12)$ -26
40. $(-26) - (-6)$ -20
41. $(-6.24) - (+11.127\ 8)$ -17.3678
42. $(+3.19) - (-12.465\ 4)$ 15.6554

43. $(-6.145) - (+25.216)$ -31.361
44. $(+8.627) - (-17.354)$ 25.981
45. $(+5) - (-6) - (+4.21)$ 6.79
46. $(+9) - (+6) - (-15.46)$ 18.46
47. $(-10) - (-11) - (-13.83)$ 14.83

48. $(-16) - (+7) - (+2.59)$ -25.59
49. $(-32) + (-4) - (+6) - (-10)$ -32
50. $(+46) - (-3) + (-4) - (-10)$ 55
51. $(-43) + (+7) - (-63) - (+4)$ 23
52. $(+39) + (-30) - (+7) + (-4)$ -2

Multiply the following signed numbers:

53. $(-7)(-6)$ 42
54. $(+8)(+7)$ 56
55. $(-9)(-10)$ 90
56. $(+6)(+9)$ 54

57. $(-6)(-3)$ 18
58. $(+9)(+4)$ 36
59. $(+5)(+7)$ 35
60. $(-3)(-8)$ 24

61. $(-6)(+4)$ -24
62. $(+5)(-7)$ -35
63. $(-8)(+9)$ -72
64. $(-12)(+11)$ -132

65. $(-7)(+2)$ -14
66. $(+10)(-5)$ -50
67. $(+34)(-62)$ -2108
68. $(+14)(-45)$ -630

Divide the following signed numbers:

69. $18 \div (-3)$ ⁻6
70. $14 \div (-2)$ ⁻7
71. $20 \div (-4)$ ⁻5
72. $35 \div (-5)$ ⁻7
73. $(-24) \div 2$ ⁻12
74. $(-45) \div 9$ ⁻5
75. $(-63) \div 3$ ⁻21
76. $(-132) \div 11$ ⁻12
77. $(-36) \div (-2)$ 18

78. $(-44) \div (-11)$ 4
79. $(-92) \div (-4)$ 23
80. $(-48) \div (-12)$ 4
81. $45 \div 3$ 15
82. $104 \div 4$ 26
83. $112 \div (-8)$ ⁻14
84. $-48 \div 12$ ⁻4
85. $-55 \div (-5)$ 11
86. $27 \div -9$ ⁻3

F. SYMBOLS OF GROUPING AND ORDER OF OPERATIONS

Frequently, mathematical problems require a sequence of operations. In such cases, grouping symbols should be used to indicate the groups of the terms in an expression. The most common grouping symbols are parentheses ( ). The terms inside the symbol ( ) are treated as a single number. When a SYMBOL OF GROUPING is required within another symbol of grouping, different symbols, such as brackets [ ], and braces { }, are often used in addition to parentheses to avoid confusion. To perform the indicated operations in an expression including several symbols of groups, it is often convenient to remove the inside symbol first. When this is being done, the following rules should be observed:

1. When a symbol of grouping is preceded by a plus (+) sign, the symbol may be removed without changing the signs of the terms inside the symbol.

Example 1.1l
$24 + [17 + (8 + 3)]$

SOLUTION:

$24 + [17 + 8 + 3] = 24 + 17 + 8 + 3 = 52$
or $= 24 + [17 + (11)] = 24 + [28] = 52$

Example 1.1m
$20 + [42 + (5 - 30)]$

SOLUTION:

$20 + [42 + 5 - 30] = 20 + [17] = 37,$
or $= 20 + [42 + (-25)] = 20 + [17] = 37$

2. When a symbol of grouping is preceded by a minus (−) sign, the symbol may be removed only if the signs of the terms inside the symbol are changed; that is, (+) to (−) and (−) to (+).

Example 1.1n
$7 - [23 - (9 + 4)]$

SOLUTION:

$7 - [23 - 9 - 4] = 7 - [10] = -3$
or $= 7 - [23 - 13] = 7 - [10] = -3$

The following example illustrates expressions which include three symbols. (Remember, it is often more convenient to remove the inside symbol first).

Example 1.1o

$10 \{4 + 3 [5 - \dfrac{2}{3} (8 - 2) + 7] - 9\}$

SOLUTION:

$10 \{4 + 3 [5 - 4 + 7] - 9\}$
$= 10 \{4 + 3 [8] - 9\}$
$= 10 \{4 + 24 - 9\}$
$= 10 \{19\}$
$= 190$

When a sequence of operations must be carried out and no grouping symbols are used, the general rule is, working from left to right, multiplication and division should be completed before addition and subtraction.

Example 1.1p
$1 + 20 \times 12 \div 3$

SOLUTION:

$1 + 240 \div 3 = 1 + 80 = 81$
or,
$1 + 20 \times 4 = 1 + 80 = 81$

(since the priority for multiplication and division is the same)

Example 1.1q
$3 - 6 \div 3 + 8$

SOLUTION:

$3 - 2 + 8 = 9$

Example 1.1r
$30 \div 10 + 7$

SOLUTION:

$3 + 7 = 10$

Example 1.1s
$1 - 30 \times 15 \div 60$

SOLUTION:

$1 - 450 \div 60$
$= 1 - 7.5 = -6.5$

Example 1.1t
$-32 \div (-4) \div 2$

SOLUTION:

$8 \div 2 = 4$
or,
$-32 \div (-4) \div 2$
$= \dfrac{\frac{-32}{-4}}{\frac{2}{1}}$
$= \dfrac{8}{2} = 4$

EXERCISE 1.1B / REFERENCE SECTION: F

Perform the indicated operations in each of the following expressions:

1. $(20 \div 5) \times 2$ 8
2. $(66 \div 11) \times 2$ 12
3. $158 \div (7.9 \times 5)$ 4
4. $89.6 \div (4 \times 7)$ 3.2
5. $(84 \div 3) \div 4$ 7

6. $(126 \div 6) \div 7$ 3
7. $480 \div (5 \div 12)$ 1152
8. $252 \div (9 \div 14)$ 392
9. $(5 + 4) \times 2$ 18
10. $(17 - 88) \div 4$ -1.775

11. $(192 \div 8) \times (4 - 5)$ -24
12. $(252 \div 7) \times (3 + 5)$ 288
13. $62 + [41 + (10 + 5)]$ 118
14. $37 + [30 + (7 + 12)]$ 86
15. $15 + [18 + (9 - 3)]$ 39

16. $42 + [20 + (8 - 15)]$ 55
17. $44 - [29 - (6 + 5)]$ 26
18. $[31 - (22 + 10)]$ -1
19. $82 - [40 - (30 - 7)]$ 79
20. $120 - [67 - (48 - 36)]$ 65

21. $3\{942 - 5[32 + 17(5 + 3)] + 6\} - 15$ 309
22. $40\{87 - 4[45 - 2(8 + 5)] - 9\} - 83$ -3
23. $32 - \{45 + [18 - 6(7 - 2)] + \dfrac{1}{3}(24 - 3)\}$ -8

24. $86 - \{52 + [47 - 12(10 - 4)] + \dfrac{2}{5}(80 - 5)\}$ 29

25. $-5 - 7 \times 9$ -68

26. $-8 \div 2 + 5$ 1
27. $1 + 4 \times 6 \div 8$ 4
28. $1 - 3 \times 8 \div 6$ -3
29. $3 - 16 \div 2 + 9$ 4
30. $84 \div 2 + (-7)$ 36

31. $-82 - 4 \times 16$ -146
32. $-48 \div 3 + 11$ -5
33. $3 \times 2 \div 4 + 11$ 12 1/2
34. $18 \div 3 \div 6$ 1
35. $81 \div 9 \div 3$ 3

1.2 Fractions–Basic Aspects

A. DEFINITION AND TERMINOLOGY

A FRACTION is an INDICATED DIVISION. In a fraction, the DIVIDEND, called the NUMER-ATOR, is written above a line below which the DIVISOR, called the DENOMINATOR is written. The numerator and the denominator are also called the TERMS OF THE FRAC-TION. Thus, $\frac{2}{5}$ is a fraction; 2 is the numerator and 5 is the denominator. The numbers 2 and 5 are the terms of the fraction.

The words "indicated division" are used here to define fractions because division generally means the process of finding how many times the divisor is contained in the dividend. In the example above, although the fraction $\frac{2}{5}$ means $2 \div 5$, the division is not actually carried out to answer the question, "How many fives are there in two?" Rather, the denominator 5 represents the number of equal parts into which the whole of a thing has been divided. The numerator shows the number of equal parts that have been taken out of the whole. If the whole is an apple, $\frac{2}{5}$ of the apple is 2 parts of the apple which has been divided into 5 equal parts. However, when the indicated division is complete, the fraction is referred to as a DECIMAL FRACTION. Thus, $\frac{2}{5} = 2 \div 5$ = .4, which is a decimal fraction.

In addition to decimal fractions, there are also *common fractions*. Three types of common fractions are:

PROPER FRACTION   The numerator is less than the denominator, such as $\frac{1}{3}$ and $\frac{15}{21}$.

IMPROPER FRACTION The numerator is equal to or greater than the denominator, such as $\frac{7}{7}$, $\frac{5}{3}$, and $\frac{17}{6}$.

COMPLEX FRACTION One or more fractions are found in either the numerator or denominator, or in both. The line which separates the numerator from the denominator is usually longer than the lines which are in the numerator or the denominator, such as $\dfrac{\frac{3}{5}}{11}, \dfrac{9}{\frac{2}{5}}, \dfrac{\frac{2}{3}}{\frac{15}{21}}$.

A complex fraction may be converted to a simple form by dividing the numerator by the denominator. For example, $\dfrac{\frac{3}{5}}{11}$ may be written as $\frac{3}{5} \div 11$. When the division is complete, the answer is $\frac{3}{55}$, a proper fraction.

When a number consists of a whole number and a fraction, it is called a MIXED NUMBER. Thus, a mixed number is the sum of a whole number and a fraction, such as the sum of 3 and $\frac{1}{4}$ being written as $3\frac{1}{4}$. A mixed number may be expressed as an improper fraction, such as $3\frac{1}{4}$ being written as $\frac{13}{4}$ because,

$$3\frac{1}{4} = \frac{(3 \times 4) + 1}{4} = \frac{13}{4}.$$

An improper fraction, such as $\frac{17}{6}$, may be expressed as a mixed number by writing it as $2\frac{5}{6}$.

B.   CONVERTING FRACTIONS TO HIGHER AND LOWER TERMS

The terms of a fraction may be converted to either higher or lower terms without changing the value of the fraction. The process of converting a fraction in this manner is called REDUCTION. Thus, the word "reduction" (or reduce) as used in this sense does not mean to reduce a fraction to a smaller or lower value. In division, multiplying or dividing both the dividend and divisor by the same number does not affect the quotient. For example, $6 \div 3 = 2$ and $(6 \times 10) \div (3 \times 10) = 2$; or $(6 \div 3) \div (3 \div 3) = 2$. The principle that multiplying or dividing both the numerator and the denominator by the same number, other than zero, does not affect the value of the fraction is shown in the following examples.

Example 1.2a

Convert $\dfrac{2}{3}$ to higher terms.

SOLUTION:

$$\frac{2}{3} = \frac{2 \times 4}{3 \times 4} = \frac{8}{12}; \qquad \frac{8}{12} = \frac{8 \times 3}{12 \times 3} = \frac{24}{36}$$

There is an unlimited number of higher terms for $\dfrac{2}{3}$.

Example 1.2b

Convert $\dfrac{84}{315}$ to lower terms.

SOLUTION:

$$\frac{84}{315} = \frac{84 \div 3}{315 \div 3} = \frac{28}{105}; \qquad \frac{28}{105} = \frac{28 \div 7}{105 \div 7} = \frac{4}{15}$$

In Example 1.2b, 3 is the common divisor of 84 and 315; 7 is the common divisor of 28 and 105; and there is no common divisor for the terms of the fraction $\frac{4}{15}$. When the numerator and the denominator have no common divisor, the fraction has been converted to its *simplest form*, also called *lowest terms*. The best way to convert a fraction to its lowest terms is to divide both the numerator and the denominator by their GREATEST COMMON DIVISOR. Improper fractions should be reduced to mixed numbers. In Example 1.2b, the product of the two common divisors (3 and 7) equals 21, which is the greatest common divisor of 84 and 315; that is,

$$\frac{84}{315} = \frac{84 \div 21}{315 \div 21} = \frac{4}{15}.$$

C.   *METHOD OF FINDING THE GREATEST COMMON DIVISOR*

When the greatest common divisor (g.c.d.), also called the HIGHEST COMMON FACTOR, of the numerator and the denominator is not apparent, the following procedure is recommended to find the desired divisor:

STEP (1) Divide the larger number by the smaller number.

STEP (2) If there is a remainder in STEP (1), divide the smaller number by the remainder.

STEP (3) If there is a remainder in STEP (2), divide the remainder in STEP (1) by the remainder in STEP (2).

STEP (4) Continue dividing each remainder by its succeeding remainder until there is no remainder (0). The last divisor is the greatest common divisor.

Example 1.2c
Find the g.c.d. of 84 and 315.

SOLUTION:

Here 315 is larger than 84. Thus,

$$
\begin{array}{r}
3 \\
84\overline{)315} \longleftarrow \quad \text{STEP (1)}
\end{array}
$$

$$
\begin{array}{r}
252 \quad 1 \\
\overline{63\,\overline{)84}} \longleftarrow \quad \text{STEP (2)}
\end{array}
$$

Last divisor
$$
\begin{array}{r}
63 \quad 3 \\
\overline{21\,\overline{)63}} \longleftarrow \quad \text{STEPS (3) and (4)}
\end{array}
$$

$$
\begin{array}{r}
63 \\
\overline{0} \text{ (Remainder)}
\end{array}
$$

The g.c.d. is 21

Example 1.2d
Find the g.c.d. of 170 and 9.

SOLUTION:

$$
\begin{array}{r}
18 \\
9\overline{)170}
\end{array}
$$

$$
\begin{array}{r}
162 \quad 1 \\
\overline{8\,\overline{)9}}
\end{array}
$$

Last divisor
$$
\begin{array}{r}
8 \quad 8 \\
\overline{1\,\overline{)8}}
\end{array}
$$

$$
\begin{array}{r}
8 \\
\overline{0}
\end{array}
$$

The g.c.d. is 1

In general, the g.c.d. of two or more numbers is the product of all the prime factors *common* to these numbers. A PRIME FACTOR is a number consisting of no other factors but itself and 1, such as 1, 2, 3, 5, 7, and 11. All other INTEGERS (whole numbers), called COMPOSITE NUMBERS, may consist of two or more prime factors. Thus, the product of all the prime factors of a number is the number itself. For example, the prime factors of the composite number 6 are 2 and 3, and the product of 2 and 3 is 6.

Example 1.2e
Find the g.c.d. of 4, 16, 24, 28, and 36.

SOLUTION:

Since 4 consists of two prime factors, 2 and 2, it may be written:
 $4 = 2 \times 2$.
Hence, the numbers above may be written by their respective prime factors as follows:

 $4 = 2 \times 2$
 $16 = 2 \times 2 \times 2 \times 2$
 $24 = 2 \times 2 \times 2 \times 3$
 $28 = 2 \times 2 \times 7$
 $36 = 2 \times 2 \times 3 \times 3$.

The prime factors common to all of the five numbers are 2 and 2; therefore, the g.c.d. is $2 \times 2 = 4$.

The work is usually done by division and can be conveniently arranged as follows:

$$2\overline{)4, 16, 24, 28, 36}$$
$$2\overline{)2, 8, 12, 14, 18}$$
$$1, 4, 6, 7, 9$$

The common divisors of the five numbers are 2 and 2; thus the g.c.d. is $2 \times 2 = 4$.

Note that the method of finding a g.c.d. of more than two numbers is useful in reducing the terms of a RATIO to the lowest terms, such as the ratio having five terms $4:16:24:28:36 = \frac{4}{4}:\frac{16}{4}:\frac{24}{4}:\frac{28}{4}:\frac{36}{4} = 1:4:6:7:9$. A more complete discussion on the subject of ratios is presented in Chapter Four.

D. METHOD OF FINDING THE LOWEST COMMON DENOMINATOR

In order to compare one fraction with other fractions, there is a need to find a *common denominator* for all of the fractions.

Example 1.2f
Compare the fractions $\frac{2}{3}$ and $\frac{7}{11}$. Which is larger?

SOLUTION:

By visual inspection, it is difficult to know which one of the two fractions is larger. However, when the two fractions are converted to the point that they have a common denominator, the comparison becomes a simple operation.

$$\frac{2}{3} = \frac{2 \times 11}{3 \times 11} = \frac{22}{33} \,, \qquad \frac{7}{11} = \frac{7 \times 3}{11 \times 3} = \frac{21}{33}$$

Since $\frac{22}{33}$ is larger than $\frac{21}{33}$, the fraction $\frac{2}{3}$ is found to be the larger one.

However, in the above example, there are an unlimited number of common denominators of the fractions $\frac{2}{3}$ and $\frac{7}{11}$, such as 33, 33 × 2 or 66, and 33 × 3 or 99; but 33 is the lowest and the simplest one. In adding and subtracting fractions, the work is greatly simplified if the lowest common denominator is used.

The LOWEST COMMON DENOMINATOR (l.c.d.) of a group of fractions is the LEAST COMMON MULTIPLE (l.c.m.) of the denominators of the fractions. A MULTIPLE of a given number is the product of that number and any multiplier.

Thus, 6, 12, and 18 are multiples of 6 since,

$6 \times 1 = 6$
$6 \times 2 = 12$
$6 \times 3 = 18.$

A common multiple of a group of numbers is a number which is a multiple of each of the numbers in the group. For example, 18 is a common multiple of 18, 9, 6, 3, 2, and 1 since,

$18 \times 1 = 18$
$9 \times 2 = 18$
$6 \times 3 = 18.$

Every integer is a multiple of 1, such as 6 × 1 = 6 and 18 × 1 = 18 as illustrated above.

The following methods may be used to find the least common multiple (l.c.m.) of a group of numbers:

METHOD A   When there is no common factor in a group of numbers, the product of the numbers in the group is the l.c.m. Thus,
6 is the l.c.m. of 2 and 3, since 2 × 3 = 6
33 is the l.c.m. of 3 and 11, since 3 × 11 = 33
70 is the l.c.m. of 2, 5 and 7, since 2 × 5 × 7 = 70
There is no common factor in the group of numbers 2 and 3, or 3 and 11, or 2, 5, and 7.

METHOD B   When there are common factors in a group of numbers, the l.c.m. can be determined by division as shown below. In each step of the division, at least *two* of the numbers are divided by their common prime factor. The product of the common prime factors and the final quotients is the l.c.m.

Example 1.2g
Find the l.c.m. of 12, 30, and 56.

SOLUTION:

2) 12, 30, 56
2) 6, 15, 28
3) 3, 15, 14
   1, 5, 14
   The l.c.m. is $2 \times 2 \times 3 \times 1 \times 5 \times 14 = 840$.

NOTE: The first divisor 2 is the common prime factor to all numbers. However, the second divisor 2 is the common prime factor to 6 and 28 only; the number 15 is not divisible by 2 and remains unchanged. The divisor 3 is the prime factor to 3 and 15 only; the number 14 is not divisible by 3 and remains unchanged.

If a divisor is not a common prime factor, there is danger of obtaining a common multiple which is not the *least* common multiple, such as the result of the following division:

6) 12, 30, 56
2) 2, 5, 56
   1, 5, 28

$6 \times 2 \times 1 \times 5 \times 28 = 1680$, which is not the l.c.m. Here, the divisor 6 is not a prime factor since $6 = 2 \times 3$.

Note carefully the distinction between the method used in finding the g.c.d. and the method for finding the l.c.m. when the division method is used. The g.c.d. for a group of numbers is found by multiplying the prime factors which are divisible into *all* of the numbers in the group; whereas, the l.c.m. is found by multiplying the prime factors, which are divisible into at least two of the numbers in each step, *and* the quotients of the division. In the preceding example, 2 (the first divisor common to all three numbers) is the g.c.d. of the group of numbers 12, 30 and 56; whereas, the l.c.m. is 840. The g.c.d. is generally used for reducing a fraction to its lowest terms, whereas the l.c.m. is used for finding the lowest common denominator for a group of fractions.

Example 1.2h

Convert the fractions $\frac{5}{12}$, $\frac{13}{30}$ and $\frac{23}{56}$ to fractions with an l.c.d. Then arrange them in order beginning with the largest.

SOLUTION:

The l.c.m. of the denominators of the three fractions is 840 (see Example 1.2g), or the l.c.d. of the three fractions is 840. When the denominator of a fraction is multiplied by a number, the numerator must also be multiplied by the same number if the value of the fraction is to stay unchanged.

Since $840 \div 12 = 70$,
$840 \div 30 = 28$,
$840 \div 56 = 15$,

then $\dfrac{5}{12} = \dfrac{5 \times 70}{12 \times 70} = \dfrac{350}{840}$

$\dfrac{13}{30} = \dfrac{13 \times 28}{30 \times 28} = \dfrac{364}{840}$

$\dfrac{23}{56} = \dfrac{23 \times 15}{56 \times 15} = \dfrac{345}{840}.$

The order of the three fractions is as follows:

$\dfrac{13}{30}, \dfrac{5}{12}, \dfrac{23}{56}.$

When the l.c.m. of a set of numbers is to be found, any number which is a factor of any other in the set may be omitted in the computation. For example, the l.c.m. of numbers 6, 12, 30 and 56 should be the same as the l.c.m. of numbers 12, 30 and 56, because number 6 is a factor of 12 and 30. Thus, the l.c.m. of 6, 12, 30 and 56 is also 840.

EXERCISE 1.2 / REFERENCE SECTIONS: A–D

Change the following mixed numbers to improper fractions:

1. $2\frac{1}{3}$ $\frac{7}{3}$ 4. $6\frac{4}{15}$ $\frac{94}{15}$ 7. $9\frac{3}{5}$ $\frac{48}{5}$ 10. $26\frac{23}{81}$ $\frac{2129}{81}$

2. $7\frac{2}{5}$ $\frac{37}{5}$ 5. $3\frac{11}{12}$ $\frac{47}{12}$ 8. $20\frac{6}{25}$ $\frac{506}{25}$ 11. $124\frac{19}{325}$

3. $11\frac{3}{8}$ $\frac{91}{8}$ 6. $9\frac{5}{7}$ $\frac{68}{7}$ 9. $45\frac{5}{6}$ $\frac{275}{6}$ 12. $453\frac{235}{311}$

Change the following improper fractions to mixed numbers:

13. $\dfrac{17}{4}$ $4\frac{1}{4}$ 16. $\dfrac{19}{4}$ $4\frac{3}{4}$ 19. $\dfrac{42}{5}$ $8\frac{2}{5}$ 22. $\dfrac{357}{46}$

14. $\dfrac{25}{3}$ $8\frac{1}{3}$ 17. $\dfrac{41}{8}$ $5\frac{1}{8}$ 20. $\dfrac{31}{6}$ $5\frac{1}{6}$ 23. $\dfrac{4\,617}{124}$

15. $\dfrac{11}{8}$ $1\frac{3}{8}$ 18. $\dfrac{38}{5}$ $7\frac{3}{5}$ 21. $\dfrac{214}{31}$ 24. $\dfrac{3\,263}{216}$

Find the g.c.d. of the numerator and the denominator in each of the following and then convert the fraction to its lowest terms:

25. $\dfrac{5}{10}$ $\frac{1}{2}$ 28. $\dfrac{16}{64}$ $\frac{2}{8}$ 31. $\dfrac{847}{1\,331}$ 34. $\dfrac{92}{138}$

26. $\dfrac{6}{24}$ $\frac{1}{4}$ 29. $\dfrac{20}{35}$ $\frac{4}{7}$ 32. $\dfrac{215}{258}$ 35. $\dfrac{308}{374}$

27. $\dfrac{10}{15}$ $\frac{2}{3}$ 30. $\dfrac{42}{28}$ $\frac{6}{4}$ 33. $\dfrac{78}{208}$ 36. $\dfrac{2\,231}{4\,559}$

Arrange the fractions in each group in order beginning with the largest:

37. $\dfrac{5}{7}, \dfrac{3}{4}$ $\dfrac{3}{4}\ \dfrac{5}{7}$

38. $\dfrac{2}{5}, \dfrac{6}{13}$ $\dfrac{6}{13}\ \dfrac{2}{5}$

39. $\dfrac{7}{16}, \dfrac{4}{9}$

40. $\dfrac{14}{15}, \dfrac{22}{25}$

41. $\dfrac{3}{4}, \dfrac{5}{6}, \dfrac{2}{5}$

42. $\dfrac{2}{3}, \dfrac{8}{9}, \dfrac{1}{4}$

43. $\dfrac{1}{2}, \dfrac{2}{7}, \dfrac{3}{5}$

44. $\dfrac{7}{8}, \dfrac{3}{4}, \dfrac{1}{2}, \dfrac{2}{3}$

45. $\dfrac{3}{8}, \dfrac{3}{6}, \dfrac{3}{7}, \dfrac{3}{4}, \dfrac{3}{5}$

46. $\dfrac{12}{15}, \dfrac{2}{3}, \dfrac{3}{5}, \dfrac{12}{5}, \dfrac{1}{3}$

47. $\dfrac{25}{48}, \dfrac{21}{32}, \dfrac{19}{30}, \dfrac{23}{40}$

48. $\dfrac{11}{9}, \dfrac{9}{7}, \dfrac{5}{3}, \dfrac{13}{11}$

1.3 Fractions–Computation

Basically, the principles and the signs used in computations involving fractions are the same as those used in addition, subtraction, multiplication and division of integers. However, there are several special problems relating to computations with fractions which must be discussed.

A.   ADDITION OF FRACTIONS

When fractions are added, all ADDENDS should be reduced to fractions having a lowest common denominator. The sum of the numerators of all addends is the numerator of the required sum; the common denominator is unchanged and is the denominator of the required sum. The required sum will be a proper or an improper fraction. If the sum is an improper fraction, it should be reduced to a mixed number. When mixed numbers are added, it is unnecessary to convert the numbers to improper fractions. It is much easier to add the integers and the fractions separately. The fractional part of an answer should always be converted to its lowest terms.

Example 1.3a

Add $\dfrac{2}{3}, \dfrac{3}{8}, \dfrac{1}{2}$.

SOLUTION:

Here, the least common multiple (l.c.m.) of the denominators 3, 8, and 2 is 24. The three fractions are converted to fractions with the l.c.m. as the common denominator.

$$\frac{2}{3} = \frac{2 \times 8}{3 \times 8} = \frac{16}{24}; \frac{3}{8} = \frac{3 \times 3}{8 \times 3} = \frac{9}{24}; \frac{1}{2} = \frac{1 \times 12}{2 \times 12} = \frac{12}{24}$$

Thus, $\dfrac{2}{3} + \dfrac{3}{8} + \dfrac{1}{2} = \dfrac{16}{24} + \dfrac{9}{24} + \dfrac{12}{24} = \dfrac{16 + 9 + 12}{24} = \dfrac{37}{24} = 1\dfrac{13}{24}$.

Example 1.3b

Add $2\dfrac{1}{3}, 5\dfrac{4}{9}, 7\dfrac{6}{15}$.

SOLUTION:

The l.c.m. of the denominators 3, 9, and 15 is 45.

$$2\frac{1}{3} = 2\frac{15}{45}; \; 5\frac{4}{9} = 5\frac{20}{45}; \; 7\frac{6}{15} = 7\frac{18}{45}$$

Thus, $2\frac{1}{3} + 5\frac{4}{9} + 7\frac{6}{15} = 2\frac{15}{45} + 5\frac{20}{45} + 7\frac{18}{45}$

$$= 2 + 5 + 7 + \frac{15 + 20 + 18}{45}$$

$$= 14 + \frac{53}{45} = 15\frac{8}{45}.$$

Example 1.3c

Add $5\frac{6}{7}, \frac{16}{3}, \frac{232}{21}, 29\frac{3}{7}.$

SOLUTION:

The l.c.m. of the denominators, 7, 3, 21, and 7 is 21.

$$5\frac{6}{7} = 5\frac{18}{21}; \qquad\qquad \frac{232}{21} = 11\frac{1}{21};$$

$$\frac{16}{3} = 5\frac{1}{3} = 5\frac{7}{21}; \qquad 29\frac{3}{7} = 29\frac{9}{21}$$

Thus, $5\frac{6}{7} + \frac{16}{3} + \frac{232}{21} + 29\frac{3}{7} = 5\frac{18}{21} + 5\frac{7}{21} + 11\frac{1}{21} + 29\frac{9}{21}$

$$= 5 + 5 + 11 + 29 + \frac{18 + 7 + 1 + 9}{21}$$

$$= 50 + \frac{35}{21} = 51\frac{14}{21} = 51\frac{2}{3}.$$

Example 1.3d

Fred received dividends on his Alcan Corporation stocks on January 15, April 15, July 15 and October 15. He reinvested his dividends and received the following shares this year:

$$2\frac{1}{3}, 3\frac{1}{5}, 4\frac{1}{6}, 3\frac{1}{9}.$$

How many additional shares did he receive?

SOLUTION:

$$2\frac{1}{3} + 3\frac{1}{5} + 4\frac{1}{6} + 3\frac{1}{9}$$

The l.c.m. of the denominators 3, 5, 6, and 9 is 90.

$$2 + 3 + 4 + 3 + \frac{30 + 18 + 15 + 10}{90}$$

$$= 12 + \frac{73}{90}$$

$$= 12\frac{73}{90}, \text{ therefore, Fred received } 12\frac{73}{90} \text{ additional shares this year.}$$

B.   SUBTRACTION OF FRACTIONS

When fractions are subtracted, both the MINUEND and the subtrahend should be reduced to fractions with a lowest common denominator. The difference between the numerators of the minuend and the subtrahend is the numerator of the required remainder; the common denominator is unchanged and is the denominator of the required remainder. Mixed numbers do not need to be converted to improper fractions before the subtraction is performed unless the fractional part of the minuend is smaller than the fractional part of the subtrahend.

Example 1.3e

Subtract $\frac{2}{7}$ from $\frac{3}{5}$.

SOLUTION:

Here, the l.c.m. of the denominators 7 and 5 is 35.

$$\frac{3}{5} - \frac{2}{7} = \frac{21}{35} - \frac{10}{35} = \frac{11}{35}$$

Example 1.3f

Subtract $\frac{2}{7}$ from $2\frac{3}{5}$.

SOLUTION:

$$2\frac{3}{5} - \frac{2}{7} = 2\frac{21}{35} - \frac{10}{35} = 2\frac{11}{35}$$

Example 1.3g

Subtract $\frac{4}{9}$ from 3.

SOLUTION:

$$3 - \frac{4}{9} = 2\frac{9}{9} - \frac{4}{9} = 2\frac{5}{9}$$

Example 1.3h

Subtract $\frac{4}{9}$ from $3\frac{1}{3}$.

SOLUTION:

$$3\frac{1}{3} - \frac{4}{9} = 3\frac{3}{9} - \frac{4}{9} = 2\frac{9+3}{9} - \frac{4}{9} = 2\frac{12}{9} - \frac{4}{9} = 2\frac{8}{9}$$

C. MULTIPLICATION OF FRACTIONS

When multiplying fractions, there is no need to find a common denominator of the fractions. The product of the numerators is the numerator of the required product, and the product of the denominators is the denominator of the required product.

Example 1.3i

Multiply $\frac{6}{11}$ by $\frac{2}{9}$.

SOLUTION:

$$\frac{6}{11} \times \frac{2}{9} = \frac{6 \times 2}{11 \times 9} = \frac{12}{99} = \frac{4}{33}$$

Since the product of 6×2 is the same as the product of 2×6, the above computation may be written as follows:

$$\frac{6}{11} \times \frac{2}{9} = \frac{2}{11} \times \frac{6}{9} = \frac{2}{11} \times \frac{6 \div 3}{9 \div 3} = \frac{2}{11} \times \frac{2}{3} = \frac{4}{33}$$

For convenience, $\frac{6 \div 3}{9 \div 3} = \frac{2}{3}$ is usually written as $\frac{\overset{2}{\cancel{6}}}{\underset{3}{\cancel{9}}}$. The method of simplifying the fractions should be used in multiplication whenever possible. Thus, multiplication for the above example should be simplified in the following manner:

$$\frac{\overset{2}{\cancel{6}}}{11} \times \frac{2}{\underset{3}{\cancel{9}}} = \frac{4}{33}.$$

In *multiplication involving mixed numbers* a simple method is to convert each mixed number to an improper fraction before multiplying.

Example 1.3j

Multiply $\frac{3}{5}$ by $3\frac{3}{4}$.

SOLUTION:

$$\frac{3}{5} \times 3\frac{3}{4} = \frac{3}{5} \times \frac{(3 \times 4) + 3}{4} = \frac{3}{\underset{1}{\cancel{5}}} \times \frac{\overset{3}{\cancel{15}}}{4} = \frac{9}{4} = 2\frac{1}{4}$$

Example 1.3k

Multiply $5\frac{3}{5}$ by $3\frac{3}{4}$.

SOLUTION:

$$5\frac{3}{5} \times 3\frac{3}{4} = \frac{\overset{7}{\cancel{28}}}{\cancel{5}_1} \times \frac{\overset{3}{\cancel{15}}}{\cancel{4}_1} = 21$$

EXERCISE 1.3A / REFERENCE SECTIONS: A–C

Convert all answers to lowest terms.
Add:

1. $\frac{1}{6} + \frac{1}{3}$ *$\frac{1}{2}$*

2. $\frac{1}{7} + \frac{1}{2}$ *$\frac{9}{14}$*

3. $\frac{1}{4} + \frac{4}{5}$ *$\frac{21}{20}$*

4. $\frac{3}{8} + \frac{3}{4}$ *$\frac{9}{8}$*

5. $9 + \frac{2}{3}$ *$9\frac{2}{3}$*

6. $\frac{2}{5} + \frac{1}{2}$ *$\frac{9}{10}$*

7. $\frac{2}{3} + 5\frac{3}{4}$ *$6\frac{5}{12}$*

8. $2\frac{3}{5} + \frac{1}{2}$

9. $2\frac{2}{5} + \frac{1}{8}$

10. $1\frac{3}{7} + 3\frac{2}{5}$

11. $5\frac{1}{4} + 11\frac{7}{8}$

12. $8\frac{1}{12} + 21\frac{4}{5}$

13. $\frac{3}{7} + \frac{1}{3} + \frac{1}{7}$

14. $\frac{7}{12} + \frac{5}{6} + \frac{1}{5}$

15. $\frac{5}{16} + \frac{3}{8} + \frac{3}{4}$

16. $\frac{4}{21} + \frac{2}{3} + \frac{4}{7}$

17. $\frac{3}{20} + \frac{3}{25} + \frac{7}{10}$

18. $7\frac{1}{6} + 4\frac{2}{3} + 1\frac{5}{12}$

19. $\frac{3}{5} + 2\frac{7}{6} + \frac{19}{3} + \frac{4}{3}$

20. $\frac{3}{2} + 2\frac{1}{4} + \frac{16}{9} + \frac{24}{5}$

21. $\frac{65}{11} + 7\frac{14}{33} + \frac{137}{22} + 3\frac{1}{66}$

22. $3\frac{5}{8} + 4\frac{5}{6} + \frac{7}{12} + \frac{211}{12}$

23. $\frac{17}{4} + \frac{130}{3} + \frac{82}{5} + \frac{19}{6}$

24. $64\frac{1}{2} + 15\frac{1}{3} + 11\frac{1}{6} + 8\frac{2}{5}$

Subtract:

25. $\frac{2}{5} - \frac{1}{4}$

26. $\frac{5}{12} - \frac{1}{4}$

27. $\frac{3}{7} - \frac{1}{3}$

28. $\frac{6}{13} - \frac{2}{7}$

29. $\frac{21}{50} - \frac{87}{300}$

30. $\frac{16}{25} - \frac{29}{60}$

31. $1 - \frac{4}{7}$

32. $3\frac{5}{8} - \frac{3}{8}$

33. $4\frac{5}{9} - 2\frac{2}{9}$

34. $9\frac{13}{15} - \frac{4}{5}$

35. $8\frac{1}{3} - \frac{2}{3}$

36. $7\frac{1}{5} - \frac{5}{7}$

37. $15\frac{2}{3} - 7\frac{8}{9}$

38. $23\frac{1}{3} - 5\frac{1}{2}$

39. $6\frac{7}{11} - \frac{8}{9}$

40. $6 - \frac{7}{9}$

41. $4 - 1\frac{3}{4}$

42. $10\frac{11}{13} - 4\frac{11}{12}$

43. $7\frac{11}{12} - 7\frac{3}{4}$

45. $\frac{12}{5} - \frac{9}{4}$

47. $\frac{436}{45} - 2\frac{4}{9}$

44. $4\frac{3}{5} - \frac{6}{7}$

46. $212\frac{1}{4} - \frac{460}{11}$

48. $\frac{543}{20} - \frac{104}{15}$

Multiply:

49. $\frac{1}{5} \times \frac{1}{3}$

57. $\frac{14}{25} \times \frac{7}{18}$

65. $2\frac{1}{5} \times 3\frac{2}{3}$

50. $\frac{3}{8} \times \frac{6}{7}$

58. $\frac{11}{12} \times \frac{4}{3}$

66. $4\frac{6}{7} \times 7\frac{4}{5}$

51. $\frac{8}{13} \times \frac{7}{16}$

59. $\frac{17}{22} \times \frac{9}{2}$

67. $11\frac{1}{2} \times 13\frac{2}{7}$

52. $\frac{7}{12} \times \frac{6}{11}$

60. $\frac{124}{17} \times \frac{5}{44}$

68. $39\frac{5}{9} \times 20\frac{7}{8}$

53. $\frac{26}{40} \times \frac{20}{39}$

61. $\frac{4}{7} \times \frac{14}{19} \times \frac{5}{36}$

69. $211\frac{4}{5} \times 16\frac{3}{8}$

54. $\frac{21}{25} \times \frac{1}{7}$

62. $\frac{25}{42} \times \frac{3}{5} \times \frac{4}{15}$

70. $250\frac{7}{16} \times 16$

55. $\frac{5}{7} \times \frac{5}{12}$

63. $\frac{6}{7} \times \frac{2}{3} \times \frac{7}{8} \times \frac{4}{9}$

71. $362\frac{1}{7} \times 2\frac{1}{3}$

56. $\frac{12}{19} \times \frac{3}{7}$

64. $\frac{13}{25} \times \frac{3}{14} \times \frac{5}{78} \times \frac{2}{27}$

72. $156\frac{1}{4} \times 111\frac{1}{5}$

D.   DIVISION OF FRACTIONS

Generally, the following three methods are used in division of fractions. Atlhough the first method is relatively popular, it is not superior in every case. Students should be familiar with all the methods in order to perform the division efficiently.

METHOD A   *Multiply the dividend by the reciprocal of the divisor.*

The method may be expressed as follows:

Dividend ÷ Fraction = Dividend × Reciprocal of the Fraction

The RECIPROCAL of a fraction is the fraction inverted. The product of a fraction and its reciprocal is always equal to 1. Thus, the reciprocal of the fraction $\frac{5}{7}$ is $\frac{7}{5}$ and their product is 1; that is, $\frac{5}{7} \times \frac{7}{5} = 1$. The following example is used to illustrate the method.

Example 1.31

Divide 20 by $\frac{3}{4}$.

SOLUTION:

$$20 \div \frac{3}{4} = 20 \times \frac{4}{3} = \frac{80}{3} = 26\frac{2}{3}$$

The above method is derived from the definition of division which gives the following equation:

Dividend ÷ Divisor = Quotient,

                or

Quotient × Divisor = Dividend.

Let the dividend be 20 and the divisor be $\frac{3}{4}$; the above equations become

$$20 \div \frac{3}{4} = \text{Quotient},$$

        or

$$\text{Quotient} \times \frac{3}{4} = 20.$$

If the left side of the above equation is multiplied by $\frac{4}{3}$, the right side of the equation must be multiplied by the same quantity in order to keep both sides equal. Thus,

$$\text{Quotient} \times \frac{3}{4} \times \frac{4}{3} = 20 \times \frac{4}{3}; \text{ Quotient} = 20 \times \frac{4}{3} = \frac{80}{3} = 26\frac{2}{3}.$$

Notice that $\frac{4}{3}$ is the reciprocal of the fraction $\frac{3}{4}$, which is the divisor. Thus, *when a number is to be divided by a fraction, invert the terms of the fraction and then multiply.* The product obtained is the quotient of the division. This method is further illustrated by the following examples:

Common Fractions

Example 1.3m

Divide $\frac{2}{3}$ by $\frac{5}{7}$.

SOLUTION:

$$\frac{2}{3} \div \frac{5}{7} = \frac{2}{3} \times \frac{7}{5} = \frac{14}{15}$$

Example 1.3n

Divide 1 by $\frac{3}{8}$.

SOLUTION:

$$1 \div \frac{3}{8} = \frac{1}{1} \times \frac{8}{3} = \frac{8}{3} = 2\frac{2}{3}$$

NOTE: $\frac{8}{3}$ is the reciprocal of $\frac{3}{8}$. When 1 is divided by a given number, the quotient is the reciprocal of the given number.

Example 1.3o

Divide 5 by $\frac{10}{21}$.

SOLUTION:

$$5 \div \frac{10}{21} = \frac{\overset{1}{\cancel{5}}}{1} \times \frac{21}{\underset{2}{\cancel{10}}} = \frac{21}{2} = 10\frac{1}{2}$$

Example 1.3p

Simplify $\frac{\frac{10}{33}}{\frac{5}{11}}$.

SOLUTION:

This problem means the same as $\frac{10}{33}$ divided by $\frac{5}{11}$.

$$\frac{10}{33} \div \frac{5}{11} = \frac{\overset{2}{\cancel{10}}}{\underset{3}{\cancel{33}}} \times \frac{\overset{1}{\cancel{11}}}{\underset{1}{\cancel{5}}} = \frac{2}{3}$$

Mixed Numbers

A simple method is to convert the mixed numbers to improper fractions; then divide.

Example 1.3q

Divide $26\frac{1}{4}$ by $2\frac{2}{5}$.

SOLUTION:

$$26\frac{1}{4} \div 2\frac{2}{5} = \frac{105}{4} \div \frac{12}{5} = \frac{\overset{35}{\cancel{105}}}{4} \times \frac{5}{\underset{4}{\cancel{12}}} = \frac{175}{16} = 10\frac{15}{16}$$

Example 1.3r

Divide $27\frac{3}{4}$ by 6.

SOLUTION:

$$27\frac{3}{4} \div 6 = \frac{111}{4} \div \frac{6}{1} = \frac{\overset{37}{\cancel{111}}}{4} \times \frac{1}{\underset{2}{\cancel{6}}} = \frac{37}{8} = 4\frac{5}{8}$$

METHOD B *After reducing both the dividend and the divisor to fractions having the lowest common denominator, cancel the common denominators and divide. This method is recommended when the fractions have a common denominator, such as in Example 1.3t.*

Example 1.3s

Divide $\frac{2}{3}$ by $\frac{5}{7}$.

SOLUTION:

The l.c.m. of the denominators 3 and 7 is 21. This division may be written as a complex fraction and divided as follows:

$$\frac{\frac{2}{3}}{\frac{5}{7}} = \frac{\frac{14}{21}}{\frac{15}{21}} = \frac{\frac{14}{21} \times 21}{\frac{15}{21} \times 21} = \frac{14}{15}, \text{ or it may be written}$$

$$\frac{2}{3} \div \frac{5}{7} = \frac{14}{21} \div \frac{15}{21} = 14 \div 15 = \frac{14}{15}.$$

Example 1.3t

Divide $2\frac{7}{30}$ by $\frac{11}{30}$.

SOLUTION:

Here the common denominator is 30.

$$2\frac{7}{30} \div \frac{11}{30} = \frac{67}{30} \div \frac{11}{30} = \frac{67}{11} = 6\frac{1}{11}$$

METHOD C *Divide after converting both the dividend and the divisor to integers.* The conversion may be accomplished by multiplying the dividend and the divisor by the l.c.m. of their denominators. This method is useful when the denominator of one fraction is a factor of the denominator of the other fraction, such as in Example 1.3v.

Example 1.3u

Divide $\frac{2}{3}$ by $\frac{5}{7}$.

SOLUTION:

The l.c.m. of the denominators 3 and 7 is 21.

$$\frac{2}{3} \div \frac{5}{7} = \frac{\frac{2}{3}}{\frac{5}{7}} = \frac{\frac{2}{3} \times \overset{7}{21}}{\frac{5}{7} \times 21_3} = \frac{14}{15}, \text{ or it may be written}$$

$$\frac{2}{3} \div \frac{5}{7} = \left(\frac{2}{3} \times \overset{7}{21}\right) \div \left(\frac{5}{7} \times \overset{3}{21}\right) = 14 \div 15 = \frac{14}{15}$$

Example 1.3v

Divide $6\frac{1}{20}$ by $2\frac{2}{5}$.

SOLUTION:

Here 5 is a factor of 20 since $5 \times 4 = 20$.

$$6\frac{1}{20} \div 2\frac{2}{5} = \frac{121}{20} \div \frac{12}{5} = \left(\frac{121}{\cancel{20}} \times \cancel{20}\right) \div \left(\frac{12}{\cancel{5}} \times \cancel{20}^{4}\right) = 121 \div 48 = 2\frac{25}{48}$$

EXERCISE 1.3B / REFERENCE SECTION: D

Convert all answers to lowest terms.
Write the reciprocal of each number:

1. $\dfrac{1}{8}$ 3. $\dfrac{4}{5}$ 5. $\dfrac{15}{18}$ 7. $3\dfrac{9}{110}$

2. 5 4. $\dfrac{4}{9}$ 6. $2\dfrac{12}{25}$ 8. $2\dfrac{26}{43}$

Divide by using the reciprocal:

9. $\dfrac{3}{7} \div \dfrac{1}{7}$ 13. $25 \div 3\dfrac{2}{7}$ 17. $\dfrac{8}{15} \div 2$ 21. $\dfrac{108}{25} \div \dfrac{54}{205}$

10. $\dfrac{4}{5} \div \dfrac{2}{15}$ 14. $32 \div \dfrac{4}{5}$ 18. $\dfrac{14}{19} \div \dfrac{16}{31}$ 22. $18\dfrac{2}{3} \div 6\dfrac{2}{5}$

11. $\dfrac{4}{7} \div \dfrac{16}{17}$ 15. $\dfrac{8}{9} \div 1\dfrac{1}{7}$ 19. $\dfrac{17}{8} \div \dfrac{9}{4}$ 23. $22\dfrac{6}{7} \div 3\dfrac{5}{9}$

12. $25 \div 2\dfrac{1}{2}$ 16. $\dfrac{11}{12} \div 3\dfrac{5}{12}$ 20. $\dfrac{26}{9} \div \dfrac{13}{8}$ 24. $104\dfrac{3}{8} \div 28\dfrac{7}{11}$

Divide after converting to fractions having a common denominator:

25. $\dfrac{2}{5} \div \dfrac{1}{4}$ 28. $\dfrac{11}{12} \div \dfrac{7}{15}$ 31. $\dfrac{25}{33} \div \dfrac{14}{11}$ 34. $42\dfrac{11}{12} \div 7\dfrac{13}{15}$

26. $\dfrac{2}{3} \div \dfrac{2}{21}$ 29. $\dfrac{14}{15} \div 3$ 32. $\dfrac{98}{99} \div \dfrac{22}{9}$ 35. $\dfrac{5}{12} \div 3\dfrac{1}{3}$

27. $\dfrac{3}{4} \div \dfrac{5}{9}$ 30. $\dfrac{7}{42} \div 2$ 33. $32\dfrac{4}{5} \div 6\dfrac{1}{5}$ 36. $12\dfrac{6}{7} \div 11\dfrac{5}{14}$

Divide after converting both the dividend and the divisor to integers:

37. $\dfrac{4}{7} \div \dfrac{1}{2}$ 40. $\dfrac{13}{14} \div \dfrac{7}{8}$ 43. $\dfrac{24}{33} \div \dfrac{15}{22}$ 46. $32\dfrac{12}{17} \div 5\dfrac{2}{3}$

38. $\dfrac{3}{5} \div \dfrac{2}{3}$ 41. $\dfrac{15}{16} \div 2$ 44. $\dfrac{69}{88} \div \dfrac{15}{8}$ 47. $8\dfrac{4}{9} \div 11\dfrac{1}{3}$

39. $\dfrac{6}{11} \div \dfrac{6}{7}$ 42. $\dfrac{8}{60} \div 3$ 45. $46\dfrac{5}{7} \div 5\dfrac{2}{7}$ 48. $12\dfrac{7}{9} \div 11\dfrac{5}{6}$

1.4 Decimal Fractions and Repetends

A.   DECIMAL FRACTIONS

Common fractions whose denominators are 10 or some power of 10 (that is, the product of 10s, such as 100, 1 000 and 10 000) can be written in a special way by using a decimal point as follows:

$$\frac{1}{10} = .1; \quad \frac{3}{100} = .03; \quad \frac{57}{1\,000} = .057.$$

The above equivalents of the common fractions are called DECIMAL FRACTIONS, or simply DECIMALS. In fact, any common fraction can be written in a decimal fraction form. To change a common fraction to a decimal fraction form, simply divide the numerator by the denominator in the given common fraction.

Example 1.4a

$$\frac{9}{20} = 9 \div 20 = .45$$

Example 1.4b

$$5\frac{3}{15} = 5 + \frac{3}{15} = 5 + .2 = 5.2$$

Example 1.4c

$$12\frac{6}{19} = 12 + \frac{6}{19} = 12.315\,\frac{15}{19}$$

NOTE: When the result in Example 1.4c is rounded to 3 decimal places, the answer is 12.316 since $\frac{15}{19}$ is more than one half of the unit of the last figure retained.

When a decimal fraction is written in a common fraction form, the figures are used as the numerator, and 1 with as many zeros annexed as there are decimal places is used as the denominator. The common fraction is then simplified or converted to its lowest terms.

Example 1.4d

$$.019\,5 = \frac{195}{10\,000} = \frac{39}{2\,000}$$

Example 1.4e

$$6.52 = 6\frac{52}{100} = 6\frac{13}{25}$$

Example 1.4f

$$14.641\frac{2}{7} = 14\,\frac{641\frac{2}{7}}{1\,000} = 14\,\frac{\frac{4\,489}{7}}{\frac{1\,000}{1}} = 14\,\frac{4\,489}{7\,000}$$

NOTE: In Example 1.4f, there are only three decimal places since $\frac{2}{7}$ is a fraction of the thousandth unit.

B.   REPETENDS

When some common fractions are converted to decimals, it may be found that the remainders do not terminate and the decimals continue repeating. For example, when the fraction $\frac{1}{3}$ is reduced to a decimal, the result is .333 3.... Decimals that continue to repeat infinitely are called REPETENDS. They are also known as CIRCULATING or PERIODIC DECIMALS. A repetend may be expressed by placing a dot (.) or dots above the figure or figures that do the repeating.

When any common fraction is expressed in its lowest terms, it may be converted to a FINITE DECIMAL if its denominator contains as prime factors only 2s and/or 5s. If the denominator contains other prime factors as well as 2s and/or 5s, the converted decimal is a mixed one; it is partly finite and partly repeating. If the denominator contains neither 2 nor 5 as a factor, the converted decimal is a purely repeating one.

Thus, $\frac{1}{4}$ and $\frac{1}{20}$ may be converted to finite decimals.

$\frac{1}{4} = .25$; the denominator 4 contains the prime factors 2 and 2.

$\frac{1}{20} = .05$; the denominator 20 contains the prime factors 2, 2, and 5.

$\frac{1}{12}$ and $\frac{1}{70}$ may be converted to partly finite and partly repeating decimals.

$\frac{1}{12} = .083\,333\ldots = .08\dot{3}$; the denominator 12 contains the prime factors 2, 2, and 3.

$\frac{1}{70} = .014\,285\,714\,285\,714\,285\,7\ldots = .0\dot{1}4\,285\,\dot{7}$; the denominator 70 contains the

prime factors 2, 5, and 7.

$\frac{2}{3}$ and $\frac{1}{21}$ may be converted to purely repeating decimals.

$\frac{2}{3} = .666\,666\ldots = .\dot{6}$

$\frac{1}{21} = .047\,619\,047\,619\,047\,619\ldots = .\dot{0}47\,61\dot{9}$; the denominator 21 contains the prime

factors 3 and 7.

A repetend may be converted to a fraction. Use the repeating figures as the numerator and write as many 9s as the number of repeating figures to form the denominator.

Example 1.4g

$$.\dot{6} = \frac{6}{9} = \frac{2}{3}$$

Example 1.4h

$$.\dot{9} = \frac{9}{9} = 1 \ (\text{Thus}, .999\,9\ldots = 1.)^1$$

Example 1.4i

$$.08\dot{3} = .08\frac{3}{9} = \frac{8\frac{3}{9}}{100} = \frac{\frac{75}{9}}{100} = \frac{75}{900} = \frac{1}{12}$$

Example 1.4j

$$.4\dot{1}2\dot{3} = 4\frac{123}{999} = \frac{4\frac{41}{333}}{10} = \frac{1\,373}{3\,330}$$

Example 1.4k

$$5.8\dot{7} = 5.8\frac{7}{9} = \frac{8\frac{7}{9}}{10} = 5\frac{79}{90}$$

A partly finite and partly repeating decimal may be directly reduced to a fraction as follows:

STEP (1) Subtract the finite figures from the overall figures; the remainder is the numerator.

STEP (2) Write as many 9s as there are repeating figures and annex as many zeros as there are finite decimal places to form the denominator.

Example 1.4l

$$.08\dot{3} = \frac{83 - 8}{900} = \frac{75}{900} = \frac{1}{12}$$

---

[1] This relationship, .999 9...= 1, can further be illustrated as follows:

Let $10x = 9.999\,99\ldots(1)$

$\quad x = \ .999\,99\ldots(2)$

$\quad 9x = 9.000\,00\ldots(1)\text{--}(2)$

$\quad\quad x = \tfrac{9}{9} = 1$

Example 1.4m

$$.41\dot{2}\dot{3} = \frac{4\ 123 - 4}{9\ 990} = \frac{4\ 119}{9\ 990} = \frac{1\ 373}{3\ 330}$$

Example 1.4n

$$5.8\dot{7} = 5\frac{87 - 8}{90} = 5\frac{79}{90}$$

C.   ROUNDING DECIMAL PLACES

There are various methods of ROUNDING decimals to a desired number of places for meeting different needs. For example, the rounding method for an engineer is different from the rounding method for a statistician. However, the following rounding method, which is used in this text, does meet most purposes in business.

To round a given number to a desired number of decimal places, the general rule is that *if the portion to be dropped begins with the figure 5* (which is one half of the unit of the last figure retained) *or above, add 1 to the last figure retained; if the portion to be dropped is less than 5, discard it.*

Example 1.4o

The numbers in the left-hand column below have been rounded to two decimal places in the right-hand column:

1.376	1.38
51.245 4	51.25
$ 2.983	$ 2.98 (rounded to the nearest cent)
$32.724 51	$32.72 (rounded to the nearest cent)

NOTE: Refer to the number 1.376. Since 6(thousandths) is more than 5 or one half of the unit of the last figure retained, 7(hundredths), 1 is added to 7 and the answer is 1.38. Now refer to the number $32.724 51. Since the thousandth digit is 4, the places consisting of 4 and thereafter are discarded.

EXERCISE 1.4 / REFERENCE SECTIONS: A–C

Convert the following common fractions to decimal fractions (round to 3 decimal places):

1. $\dfrac{2}{10}$ 3. $\dfrac{6}{17}$ 5. $\dfrac{12}{13}$ 7. $\dfrac{23}{40}$

2. $\dfrac{3}{7}$ 4. $\dfrac{9}{23}$ 6. $\dfrac{15}{22}$ 8. $\dfrac{32}{47}$

9. $\dfrac{40}{13}$ 11. $\dfrac{72}{19}$ 13. $3\dfrac{7}{20}$ 15. $42\dfrac{7}{13}$

10. $\dfrac{56}{11}$ 12. $\dfrac{103}{25}$ 14. $12\dfrac{8}{9}$ 16. $32\dfrac{71}{80}$

Convert the following decimals to common fractions in lowest terms:

17. .32   21. .076   25. 3.002   29. $4.35\dfrac{1}{2}$

18. .45   22. $.085\dfrac{1}{3}$ 26. 1.254   30. $10.42\dfrac{2}{3}$

19. .68   23. 1.75   27. 11.035   31. $2.875\dfrac{1}{4}$

20. .84   24. 5.042   28. 15.005   32. $4.305\dfrac{2}{5}$

Convert the following common fractions to decimal fractions (without the aid of a calculator) and indicate the repetends by placing a dot or dots above the repeating figures:

33. $\dfrac{1}{7}$ 36. $\dfrac{7}{30}$ 39. $\dfrac{14}{27}$ 42. $\dfrac{25}{42}$

34. $\dfrac{4}{9}$ 37. $\dfrac{23}{60}$ 40. $\dfrac{17}{90}$ 43. $\dfrac{17}{150}$

35. $\dfrac{5}{12}$ 38. $\dfrac{11}{45}$ 41. $\dfrac{13}{15}$ 44. $\dfrac{41}{270}$

Convert the following to common fractions or mixed numbers and express in lowest terms:

45. $.\dot{5}$ 48. $.1\dot{6}$ 51. $.04\dot{3}$ 54. $3.5\dot{7}$
46. $.\dot{9}$ 49. $.2\dot{3}$ 52. $.05\dot{6}$ 55. $1.4\dot{5}6\dot{7}$
47. $.2\dot{6}$ 50. $.3\dot{1}$ 53. $4.3\dot{8}$ 56. $5.3\dot{1}2\dot{6}$

Round the following numbers to two decimal places:

57. 32.754 1   60. 73.763   63. 7 362.056 4   66. 5.499 8
58. 568.655 2   61. 2.582 5   64. 8 319.048 6   67. 21.005 1
59. 432.437   62. 0.734 5   65. 1.371 2   68. 57.034 9

1.5 Percent–Basic Concepts and Operations

The word PERCENT is derived from the Latin words per and centum, which indicate "in the hundred." The symbol for percent, %, means $\frac{1}{100}$ or .01 (one hundredth). Thus, percent is a form of fraction and is also a type of RATIO. For example, 5% may be written as $\frac{5}{100}$, which is the ratio of 5 to 100.

Since percent (%) may be written as a fraction ($\frac{1}{100}$) or a decimal (0.1), the following basic operations should be regarded as essential in solving problems involving percent.

A.   CONVERTING A PERCENT TO A DECIMAL OR A WHOLE NUMBER

To convert a percent to a decimal or a whole number, move the decimal point in the percent two places to the left and drop the percent sign (%).

Example 1.5a

$100\% = 1$	$4\ 700\% = 47$	$29\frac{1}{4}\% = .29\frac{1}{4}$
$126\% = 1.26$	$35.52\% = .355\ 2$	$\frac{1}{2}\% = .00\frac{1}{2}$
$2.234\% = .022\ 34$	$4\% = .04$	

B.   CONVERTING A PERCENT TO A COMMON FRACTION

A general way to convert a percent to a common fraction is first to drop the percent sign (%) and then use the number as the numerator and 100 as the denominator. Next, convert the fraction to its lowest terms.

Example 1.5b

$$5\% = \frac{5}{100} = \frac{1}{20} \qquad\qquad 239\% = \frac{239}{100} = 2\frac{39}{100}$$

$$71\% = \frac{71}{100} \qquad\qquad 0.015\% = \frac{.015}{100} = \frac{15}{100\ 000} = \frac{3}{20\ 000}$$

$$6.3\% = \frac{6.3}{100} = \frac{63}{1\ 000} \qquad\qquad .25\% = \frac{.25}{100} = \frac{25}{10\ 000} = \frac{1}{400}$$

The conversion may also be done by changing the percent to a decimal and then changing the decimal to a common fraction in its lowest terms.

Example 1.5c

$$25\% = .25 = \frac{25}{100} = \frac{1}{4}$$

$$.065\% = .000\ 65 = \frac{65}{100\ 000} = \frac{13}{20\ 000}$$

$$1.25\% = .012\ 5 = \frac{125}{10\ 000} = \frac{1}{80}$$

To convert a fractional percent to a common fraction, simply drop the percent sign (%) and then annex two zeros to the denominator.

Example 1.5d

$$\frac{3}{4}\% = \frac{3}{400} \qquad \frac{10}{21}\% = \frac{10}{2\,100} = \frac{1}{210}$$

C.   CONVERTING A DECIMAL OR A WHOLE NUMBER TO A PERCENT

To convert a decimal or a whole number to a percent, move the decimal point two places to the right and annex a percent sign (%).

Example 1.5e

.15 = 15%	.034 = 3.4%
683 = 68 300%	1.2 = 120%
23.4 = 2 340%	.008 9 = .89%

D.   CONVERTING A COMMON FRACTION TO A PERCENT

To convert a common fraction to a percent, convert the fraction to a decimal and then convert the decimal to a percent. Note that the decimals in the illustrations in the next example are carried to two places.

Example 1.5f

$$\frac{2}{5} = .4 = 40\%$$

$$\frac{7}{25} = .28 = 28\%$$

$$\frac{25}{4} = 6\frac{1}{4} = 6.25 = 625\%$$

$$\frac{2}{3} = .66\frac{2}{3} = 66\frac{2}{3}\%, \text{ or rounded to } 67\% \text{ since } \frac{2}{3}\% \text{ is more than one half of the unit to}$$
be retained (% of one unit)

$$\frac{31}{6} = 5\frac{1}{6} = 5.16\frac{2}{3} = 516\frac{2}{3}\%, \text{ or rounded to } 517\%$$

$$\frac{1}{14} = .07\frac{2}{14} = 7\frac{2}{14}\%, \text{ or rounded to } 7\% \text{ since } \frac{2}{14}\% = \frac{1}{7}\%, \text{ which is less than } \frac{1}{2}\%$$

EXERCISE 1.5 / REFERENCE SECTIONS: A–D

To be completed without the aid of a calculator.
Express each of the following as a decimal or a whole number:

1. .24%	4. 3.6%	7. 148%	9. 4 500%
2. .58%	5. 14%	8. 224%	10. 3 400%
3. 6.3%	6. 26%		

Express each of the following as a common fraction in its lowest terms:

11. 8%
12. 25%
13. 375%

14. 6 025%
15. 1.2%
16. 4.8%

17. .024%
18. .062%

19. .004 2%
20. .005%

Express each of the following as a percent: (In problems 31 to 40, carry decimals to two places, then convert the decimals to percents; round the fractional percents, if any.)

21. .38

22. .26

23. .047

24. .132

25. .003 5

26. .000 49

27. 72

28. 62

29. 1.46

30. 2.84

31. $\dfrac{1}{50}$

32. $\dfrac{2}{5}$

33. $3\dfrac{5}{7}$

34. $2\dfrac{3}{8}$

35. $\dfrac{12}{13}$

36. $\dfrac{22}{27}$

37. $16\dfrac{15}{32}$

38. $23\dfrac{71}{82}$

39. $\dfrac{4.5}{8.25}$

40. $\dfrac{5.62}{6.48}$

Glossary

ABSOLUTE VALUE the value of a number without regard to its indicated sign

ADDEND the number or quantity used in addition with another number or quantity

CIRCULATING DECIMAL see *repetends*

COMPLEX FRACTION expressions containing one or more fractions in either the numerator or denominator or both

COMPOSITE NUMBERS numbers consisting of two or more prime factors

DECIMAL a numeral having a decimal point

DECIMAL FRACTION a fraction with 10 or some multiple of 10 as the denominator

DENOMINATOR the divisor in an indicated division

DIFFERENCE the result of a subtraction

DIVIDEND the number to be divided

DIVISOR the number by which another number is to be divided

FINITE DECIMAL a non-repeating decimal number

FRACTION one or more of the equal parts of a whole, a division of one mathematical expression by another

GREATEST COMMON DIVISOR (G.C.D.) the largest number which divides without a remainder into two or more numbers

HIGHEST COMMON FACTOR (H.C.F.) see *greatest common divisor (g.c.d.)*

IMPROPER FRACTION a fraction for which the numerator is equal to or greater than the denominator

INDICATED DIVISION a division written in fractional form

INTEGER any positive or negative whole number or zero

LEAST COMMON MULTIPLE (L.C.M.) the smallest number into which a set of numbers divides evenly

LOWEST COMMON DENOMINATOR (L.C.D.) see *least common multiple (l.c.m.)*

MINUEND a number from which another number is to be subtracted

MIXED NUMBER a number consisting of a whole number and a fraction

MULTIPLE the product of a given number and any multiplier

NUMERATOR the dividend of an indicated division

PERCENT hundredths, part in each hundred

PERIODIC DECIMAL see *repetends*

PRIME FACTOR a number consisting of no other factors but itself and 1

PRODUCT the result of a multiplication

PROPER FRACTION a fraction for which the numerator is less than the denominator

QUOTIENT the result of a division

RATIO a comparison of the relative values of numbers by division

RECIPROCAL the inverted value of a fraction

REDUCTION the process of obtaining equivalent fractions in which the terms have no common factor

REMAINDER see *difference*

REPETENDS decimals that continue to repeat infinitely

ROUNDING the conversion of a decimal to a number with a desired number of decimal places

SUBTRAHEND the number to be subtracted

SUM the result of an addition

SYMBOLS OF GROUPING symbols used to indicate the order in which the sequence of operations should be carried out

TERMS OF A FRACTION the numerator and the denominator

2 Essential algebraic operations

Introduction

This chapter is devoted primarily to reviewing certain basic aspects of algebra.

Algebra adds an important dimension to the student's ability to communicate numerically. In algebra, symbols are used to represent numbers, thus an unknown value can be represented by a symbol and later a particular value can be established that the symbol should assume in order to satisfy the requirements of a problem. Hence, algebra provides a flexibility in numerical communications which is lacking in arithmetic.

As an example, if an hourly employee receives 1.5 times the regular hourly wage for overtime (hours worked in excess of 40 hours) the following expression may be written:

$W = 40R + 1.5(T - 40)R$
W = wage for the week
R = hourly rate
T = total hours worked

This expression may be used to calculate the gross wage of all hourly employees by substituting the correct hourly rate, R, and the total hours worked, T. (See Section 2.6, Example 2.6b). It is possible to instruct a computer to calculate the gross wage of all employees by writing a set of instructions. The instructions are really algebraic expressions and it is necessary to know the order in which the arithmetic operations are carried out so that they may be communicated correctly to the computer.

Chapter Two reviews the fundamental operations of algebra: addition, subtraction, multiplication, and division. Algebraic operations, rules of exponents, symbols of grouping and factoring are presented since these topics are frequently used to facilitate the solution of business problems.

2.1 Fundamental Aspects of Algebra

Students who are familiar with arithmetic operations should enjoy learning algebraic operations. The basic principles of the four fundamental operations of algebra–addition, subtraction, multiplication, and division–are the same as those of arithmetic operations. However, algebra is characterized by the use of letters as symbols for numbers and by the relationships among numbers being expressed in the form of equations. The methods presented in the two sections, symbols of grouping and factoring, are frequently used in algebra to facilitate the performance of fundamental operations.

A. BASIC ARITHMETIC RULES AS APPLIED TO ALGEBRA

Let a, b, c, and d represent numbers:

if $a = b$ and $c = b$, then $a = c$;
if $a = b$ and $c = d$, then $a + c = b + d$;
if $a = b$ and $c = d$, then $a - c = b - d$;
if $a = b$ and $c = d$, then $a \times c = b \times d$;
if $a = b$ and $c = d$; then $a/c = b/d$, provided c is a number other than zero.

Other important arithmetic rules which are accepted for algebra are as follows:

$$a + b = b + a$$

CHECK:

Let a and b represent any two numbers. For example, let $a = 9$ and $b = 7$. Thus, $9 + 7 = 7 + 9 = 16$.

$$a + b + c = (a + b) + c = a + (b + c)$$

CHECK:

Let $a = 9$, $b = 7$, $c = 4$. Thus, $9 + 7 + 4 = (9 + 7) + 4 = 9 + (7 + 4) = 20$.

$$a \times b = b \times a$$

CHECK:

Let $a = 5$, $b = 3$. Thus, $5 \times 3 = 3 \times 5 = 15$.

$$a \times b \times c = (a \times b) \times c = a \times (b \times c)$$

CHECK:

Let $a = 5$, $b = 3$, $c = 2$. Thus, $5 \times 3 \times 2 = (5 \times 3) \times 2 = 5 \times (3 \times 2) = 30$.

Other signs instead of "×" are frequently used in multiplication in algebra. For example, the product of a and c may be written $a \cdot c$, $(a)(c)$, or simply ac. Thus, the two equations above may be written as $ab = ba$, and $abc = (ab)c = a(bc)$, respectively.

Division should be done in the order as indicated. Thus,

$$a \div b \div c = (a \div b) \div c, \text{ or } \frac{\frac{a}{b}}{c} = \frac{a}{b} \cdot \frac{1}{c} = \frac{a}{bc},$$

$$\text{not} = a \div (b \div c), \text{ or } \frac{a}{\frac{b}{c}} = a \cdot \frac{c}{b} = \frac{ac}{b}.$$

$$48 \div 6 \div 2 = (48 \div 6) \div 2 = 8 \div 2 = 4,$$
$$\text{not} = 48 \div (6 \div 2) = 48 \div 3 = 16$$

However, the following order is also permissible:

$$a \div b \div c = (a \div c) \div b, \text{ or } \frac{\frac{a}{c}}{b} = \frac{a}{c} \cdot \frac{1}{b} = \frac{a}{bc},$$

$$48 \div 6 \div 2 = (48 \div 2) \div 6 = 24 \div 6 = 4.$$

Note that in the above division, a is the dividend, and b and c are divisors. The order of divisors may be changed in division.

B.   *TERMINOLOGY IN ALGEBRA*

Algebraic Expression

An ALGEBRAIC EXPRESSION, or simply an EXPRESSION, is any symbol or combination of symbols that represents a number. When an expression consists of several parts that are connected by plus (+) and minus (−) signs, each of the parts, together with the sign preceding it, is called a TERM. If there is no sign expressed preceding a term, the sign is understood to be plus. An expression consisting of one term is called a MONO-MIAL, whereas an expression having more than one term is called a MULTINOMINAL, or a POLYNOMIAL. An expression of two terms is called a BINOMIAL, whereas one of three terms is a TRINOMIAL. For example, $+4ax$ or $4ax$ is an expression and is a monomial; $4ax + 7$ is also an expression but has two terms and is a binomial; and the expression $ax^2 + 4x + 5$ is a trinomial.

Factor and Coefficient

If two or more numbers are multiplied together, each number or the product of any of the numbers is called a FACTOR. Any factor of a term is called the COEFFICIENT of the remaining factors. When a factor is an explicit number, it is called the NUMERICAL COEFFICIENT of the term; other factors are called LITERAL COEFFICIENTS. As an illustration, examine the term $6xy$. Each number and symbol–6, x, and y–or the product of any of these–$6x$, $6y$ and xy–is called a factor. The coefficient of $6x$ is y; y is the literal coefficient. The coefficient of xy is 6; 6 is the numerical coefficient. If no numerical coefficient is indicated in a term, it is understood that the numerical coefficient is one.

Power

The product of equal factors is called a POWER of the factor. Thus, $a \cdot a \cdot a$ is the third power of a and is written a^3; $2 \cdot 2 \cdot 2 \cdot 2$ (=16) is the fourth power of 2 and is written

2^4. The symbol a is called the BASE, and the number 3, which indicates the number of equal factors, is the EXPONENT. The expression of an indicated power of a given symbol or number is called an EXPONENTIAL, such as a^3. The exponent for the first power of a base is 1, which is understood and usually not written; that is, $a^1 = a$. A second power is called a SQUARE, whereas a third power is a CUBE.

+ and − Signs

The plus and minus signs which were used exclusively to indicate addition and subtraction in arithmetic are also used as the indicators of positive numbers and negative numbers. When the concept of positive or negative numbers is disregarded, the value of any number is then called its absolute value and is denoted by the sign $|\ |$. When no sign is written, the number is understood to be a positive one. For example, +3 or 3 is a positive number, whereas −3 is a negative number; $|+3|$ and $|-3|$ indicate the absolute value of 3; that is, $|+3| = |-3| = 3$.

C.   OPERATIONS WITH 0 AND 1

Recall the following properties of zero and one:

1. When zero is added to a number, the sum is the number unchanged. Thus,

    $a + 0 = a; 0 + 0 = 0.$

2. When zero is subtracted from a number, the remainder is the number unchanged. Thus,

    $a - 0 = a; 0 - 0 = 0.$

    However, when a number is subtracted from zero, the remainder is the absolute value of the number with its sign changed. Thus,

    $0 - a = -a; 0 - (-a) = a.$

3. When zero is multiplied by a number, or a number is multiplied by zero, the product is zero. Thus,

    $0 \times 0 = 0; a \times 0 = 0.$

4. When zero is divided by any number except zero, the quotient is zero. Thus,

    $$\frac{0}{a} = 0.$$

5. Division by zero has no meaning because there is no answer. For example, if $\frac{7}{0} = c$, then by multiplying both sides of the equation by 0, we have $\frac{7}{0} \times 0 = c0$, or $7 = c0 = 0$. We know that $7 \neq 0$, or 7 is not equal to 0. When $\frac{0}{0}$, the quotient is meaningless. (Note that the symbol $\neq$ is read "is not equal to.")

6. When a number is multiplied by one, the product is the number unchanged. Thus,

$$6 \times 1 = 6; \; a \times 1 = a.$$

7. When a number is divided by one, the quotient is the number unchanged. Thus,

$$\frac{6}{1} = 6; \; \frac{a}{1} = a.$$

2.2 *Algebraic Operations*

A. *ADDITION OF ALGEBRAIC EXPRESSIONS*

Addition of Monomials

Terms whose literal factors are the same are called LIKE TERMS. To add like terms, add the numerical coefficients. The sum is the coefficient of the common literal factors.

Example 2.2a
Add $5ax$, $9ax$, and $(-20ax)$.

SOLUTION:

The sum of the numerical coefficients is

$$5 + 9 + (-20) = -6. \text{ Thus,}$$
$$5ax + 9ax + (-20ax) = -6ax.$$

The numerical coefficients of UNLIKE TERMS, such as $5a$ and $6b$, cannot be combined; their sum is simply indicated by signs and is written as a polynomial, $5a + 6b$.

Example 2.2b
Add $6xy$, $(-5x)$, $(-3xy)$, and $(-4x)$.

SOLUTION:

$$6xy + (-3xy) = 3xy$$
$$(-5x) + (-4x) = -9x \text{ Thus,}$$
$$6xy + (-5x) + (-3xy) + (-4x) = 3xy + (-9x) = 3xy - 9x.$$

The process of finding the algebraic sum of like terms and unlike terms is sometimes called COLLECTING TERMS.

Addition of Polynomials

Like terms should be combined when two or more polynomials are added. Each set of like terms may be arranged in a vertical column before adding.

Example 2.2c
Add $(3a + 4b + 6)$, $(-4a - 6b - 3)$, and $(7a + 4b - 9)$.

SOLUTION:

$$
\begin{array}{r}
3a + 4b + 6 \\
-4a - 6b - 3 \\
7a + 4b - 9 \\
\hline
6a + 2b - 6
\end{array}
$$

B.   *SUBTRACTION OF ALGEBRAIC EXPRESSIONS*

Subtraction of Monomials

To subtract like terms, subtract the numerical coefficient of the subtrahend from that of the minuend. The remainder thus obtained is the coefficient of the common literal factors.

Example 2.2d
Subtract $5xy$ from $18xy$.

SOLUTION:

$18xy - 5xy = 13xy$, or
$(18 - 5)xy = 13xy$

Example 2.2e
Subtract $-7ab$ from $11ab$.

SOLUTION:

$11ab - (-7ab) = 11ab + 7ab = 18ab$, or
$[11 - (-7)]ab = 18ab$

Subtraction of Polynomials

When one polynomial is subtracted from another, change the sign of each term in the subtrahend and then add.

Example 2.2f

Subtract:
$$
\begin{array}{r}
5a - 2b + 9 \text{ (Minuend)} \\
-2a + 9b - 4 \text{ (Subtrahend)} \\
\hline
\end{array}
$$

SOLUTION:

Minuend $5a - 2b + 9$ (with the same signs)
Subtrahend $2a - 9b + 4$ (signs are changed)
                 $\overline{7a - 11b + 13}$ (add)

Or, written in horizontal form,

$(5a - 2b + 9) - (-2a + 9b - 4)$
$= 5a - 2b + 9 + 2a - 9b + 4$
$= 7a - 11b + 13.$

Example 2.2g
Subtract $(-3a + 4b - 5)$ from $(5a - 8 + 6b)$.

SOLUTION:

$(5a - 8 + 6b) - (-3a + 4b - 5)$
$= 5a - 8 + 6b + 3a - 4b + 5$
$= 8a + 2b - 3$

EXERCISE 2.2 / REFERENCE SECTIONS: A–B

Add the following algebraic terms:

1. $42a + (-16a)$
2. $34bc + (-12bc)$
3. $(-23c) + 5c$
4. $(-36t) + (-2t)$
5. $(-65et) + 7et$
6. $(-27d) + 3d$
7. $(-36f) + (-32f)$

8. $(-24g) + 5g$

9. $14h + 46h + (-17h)$

10. $25v + 13v + 40v$

11. $24w + (-3w) + (7w)$
12. $(-36q) + 3q + (-16q)$
13. $8cd + (-6c) + 4c + (-6cd)$
14. $6xy + 3x + (-15xy) + (-2x)$
15. $4ab + (-a) + 7ab + (-2ab)$
16. $7tb + 5t + 16tb + (-3t)$
17. $(3a + 7b + 4) + (2a + 5b - 2) +$
   $(5a - 2b + 1)$
18. $(6x + 4y + 3) + (3x - 7y - 2) +$
   $(5x + 2y - 6)$
19. $(4xy + 33x + 11y + 1) +$
   $(3xy - 5x - 4y - 1)$
20. $(6abc + 4ab - 3bc + 6) +$
   $(3abc - 2ab + bc - 2)$

Subtract the following algebraic terms:

21. $28xy - 6xy$
22. $16x - (-7x)$
23. $32ab - 6ab$
24. $40t - 2t$
25. $(-9bc) - (-4bc)$
26. $(-60cd) - 7cd$
27. $(-4b) - (-2b)$
28. $(-12ct) - 5ct$

29. $4a - (2a + 7a - 6d)$
30. $(-8t) - (-4t + 3t - 6t)$
31. $(23f - 4f) - (5f + 2f)$
32. $(17g + 4g) - (7g - 3g)$
33. $(14h + 2h) - (3h + 4h)$
34. $(17tb + 2tb) - (-4tb - 7tb)$
35. $(5a + 2b + 7) - (4a + 3b + 6)$
36. $(4xy + 2x + 6) - (2xy - 6x + 4)$

2.3 Rules of Exponents

A. MULTIPLICATION OF EXPONENTIALS

When multiplication involves exponentials, the following laws apply:

LAW(1):   When exponentials have the same base,

$$a^m \cdot a^n = a^{m+n}$$

Illustration:

$$\overbrace{a^m}^{m \text{ factors}} \cdot \overbrace{a^n}^{n \text{ factors}} = (a \cdot a \cdot a \cdot a \cdot \ldots)(a \cdot a \cdot a \cdot a \ldots) = a^{m+n}$$

Example 2.3a
$2^3 \cdot 2^2 = (2 \cdot 2 \cdot 2)(2 \cdot 2) = 2^5$; or $2^3 \cdot 2^2 = 2^{3+2} = 2^5 = 32$

Example 2.3b
$x^3 \cdot x^4 = (x \cdot x \cdot x)(x \cdot x \cdot x \cdot x) = x^7$; or $x^3 \cdot x^4 = x^{3+4} = x^7$

LAW (2):   When exponentials have different bases but have the same exponent:

$$\boxed{a^m \cdot b^m = (ab)^m}$$

Illustration:

$$a^m \cdot b^m = (\overbrace{a \cdot a \cdot a \cdot a \ldots}^{m \text{ factors}})(\overbrace{b \cdot b \cdot b \cdot b \ldots}^{m \text{ factors}})$$
$$= \overbrace{ab \cdot ab \cdot ab \cdot ab \ldots}^{m \text{ products}}$$
$$= (ab)^m$$

Example 2.3c
$5^2 \cdot 4^2 = 5 \cdot 5 \cdot 4 \cdot 4 = (5 \cdot 4)(5 \cdot 4) = 20^2 = 400$; or
$5^2 \cdot 4^2 = (5.4)^2 = 20^2 = 400$

Example 2.3d
$x^3 \cdot y^3 = (x \cdot x \cdot x)(y \cdot y \cdot y) = (xy)(xy)(xy) = (xy)^3$; or $x^3 y^3 = (xy)^3$

LAW (3):   When the base is an exponential:

$$\boxed{(a^m)^n = a^{mn}, \text{ and } (a^{1/m})^n = a^{n/m}}$$

Illustration:

$$(a^m)^n = \overbrace{a^m \cdot a^m \cdot a^m \cdot a^m \cdots}^{n \text{ exponentials}}$$
$$= a^{\overbrace{m+m+m+m \cdots}^{n \text{ times}}}$$
$$= a^{mn}$$

Example 2.3e
$(3^2)^3 = (3 \cdot 3)(3 \cdot 3)(3 \cdot 3) = 3^6 = 729$; or
$(3^2)^3 = 3^{2 \cdot 3} = 3^6 = 729$

Example 2.3f

$(x^3)^2 = (x \cdot x \cdot x)(x \cdot x \cdot x) = x^6$; or $(x^3)^2 = x^{3 \cdot 2} = x^6$

Example 2.3g

$(3^{1/2})^4 = (3^{1/2})(3^{1/2})(3^{1/2})(3^{1/2}) = 3^{1/2+1/2+1/2+1/2} = 3^2 = 9$; or

$(3^{1/2})^4 = (3^{4/2}) = 3^2 = 9$

Example 2.3h

$(x^{1/3})^2 = (x^{1/3})(x^{1/3}) = x^{1/3+1/3} = x^{2/3}$; or $(x^{1/3})^2 = x^{2/3}$

B.   *DIVISION INVOLVING EXPONENTIALS*

When division involves exponentials, the following laws apply:

LAW (1):   When exponentials have the same base:

$$a^m \div a^n = \frac{a^m}{a^n} = a^{m-n}{}^1$$

Example 2.3i

$2^5 \div 2^3 = \dfrac{2 \cdot 2 \cdot 2 \cdot 2 \cdot 2}{2 \cdot 2 \cdot 2} = 2^2 = 4$; or

$2^5 \div 2^3 = \dfrac{2^5}{2^3} = 2^{5-3} = 2^2 = 4$

Example 2.3j

$2^3 \div 2^5 = \dfrac{2 \cdot 2 \cdot 2}{2 \cdot 2 \cdot 2 \cdot 2 \cdot 2} = \dfrac{1}{2 \cdot 2} = \dfrac{1}{2^2} = \dfrac{1}{4}$; or

$2^3 \div 2^5 = \dfrac{2^3}{2^5} = 2^{3-5} = 2^{-2} = \dfrac{1}{2^2} = \dfrac{1}{4}$

Example 2.3k

$x^4 \div x^2 = \dfrac{x^4}{x^2} = \dfrac{x \cdot x \cdot x \cdot x}{x \cdot x} = x \cdot x = x^2$; or

$\dfrac{x^4}{x^2} = x^{4-2} = x^2$

---

[1]$a^m \div a^n = a^{m-n}$ may be provided in the following manner:

$$\frac{a^m}{a^n} = a^m \cdot \frac{1}{a^n}$$

$$= a^m \cdot a^{-n}$$

$$= a^{m-n}.$$

Similarly,

$$a^m \div a^n = \frac{a^m}{a^n} = a^{m-n}, \text{ if } m > n;$$

$$\frac{a^m}{a^n} = a^{m-n} = a^{-(n-m)} = \frac{1}{a^{n-m}}, \text{ if } m < n;$$

$$\frac{a^m}{a^n} = a^{m-n} = a^0 = 1, \text{ if } m = n.$$

NOTE: The sign ">" means greater than; "$m > n$" means m is greater than n. The sign "<" means smaller than; "$m < n$" means m is smaller than n.

When using the exponent zero ($a \neq 0$), the above law gives the following definitions:

I. $\boxed{a^0 = 1}$

Illustration:

$a^m \cdot 1 = a^m$
$a^m \cdot a^0 = a^{m+0} = a^m$

and $a^0 \cdot a^m = a^{0+m} = a^m$

Therefore $\qquad a^0 = 1.$

Thus $\qquad 4^2 \cdot 1 = 4^2$
$\qquad\qquad 4^2 \cdot 4^0 = 4^{2+0} = 4^2$

or $\qquad 4^2 \cdot 4^0 = 4^2 \cdot 1 = 4^2$

and $\qquad 6^3 \cdot 6^0 = 6^{3+0} = 6^3$

or $\qquad 6^3 \cdot 6^0 = 6^3 \cdot 1 = 6^3.$

Thus $\qquad 8^0 = 1$
$\qquad\qquad 256^0 = 1$
$\qquad\qquad .5^0 = 1.$

II. $\boxed{a^{1/m} = a^{-m}}$

Illustration:

$$a^m \cdot \frac{1}{a^m} = \frac{a^m}{a^m} = 1$$

and $\qquad a^m \cdot a^{-m} = a^{m-m}$
$\qquad\qquad\qquad\quad = a^0$
$\qquad\qquad\qquad\quad = 1.$

Therefore $\qquad \frac{1}{a^m} = a^{-m}.$

Thus $\qquad \frac{1}{7^2} = 7^{-2}$

$\qquad\qquad \frac{1}{16^3} = 16^{-3}$

$\qquad\qquad 5^{-2} = \frac{1}{5^2}$

$\qquad\qquad 18^{-3} = \frac{1}{18^3}.$

LAW (2): When exponentials have different bases but have the same exponent:

$$\boxed{\frac{a^m}{b^m} = \left(\frac{a}{b}\right)^m}$$

Illustration:

$$\frac{a^m}{b^m} = \frac{a \cdot a \cdot a \cdot a \ldots (m \text{ factors})}{b \cdot b \cdot b \cdot b \ldots (m \text{ factors})}$$

$$= \frac{a}{b} \cdot \frac{a}{b} \cdot \frac{a}{b} \cdot \frac{a}{b} \ldots (m \text{ factors}) = \left(\frac{a}{b}\right)^m$$

Example 2.3l

$$\frac{6^2}{3^2} = \frac{6 \cdot 6}{3 \cdot 3} = \frac{6}{3} \cdot \frac{6}{3} = \left(\frac{6}{3}\right)^2 = 2^2 = 4; \text{ or}$$

$$\frac{6^2}{3^2} = \left(\frac{6}{3}\right)^2 = 2^2 = 4$$

Example 2.3m

$$x^3 \cdot y^{-3} = \frac{x^3}{y^3} = \left(\frac{x}{y}\right)^3$$

C. EVALUATING EXPONENTIAL EXPRESSIONS

Some expressions often used in business problems involve exponentials. The following problems are intended to be calculated with the aid of an electronic calculator which provides the exponential function.

Example 2.3n
Find the value of $(1 + 16\%)^{15}$ correct to 7 decimal places.

SOLUTION:

action taken	display shows
1. enter 1.16	1.16
2. press the key y^x	1.16
3. enter 15	15
4. press the key $=$	9.2655209

Thus,
$(1 + 16\%)^{15} = 9.265\ 520\ 9.$

Example 2.3o
Find the value of $(1 + 6\%)^{2/5}$ correct to 7 decimal places.

SOLUTION:

$(1 + 6\%)^{2/5} = (1.06)^{.4}$

action taken	display shows
1. enter 1.06	1.06
2. press the key y^x	1.06
3. enter 0.4	0.4
4. press the key $=$	1.0235813

Thus,
$(1 + 6\%)^{2/5} = 1.023\ 581\ 3.$

Example 2.3p

Find the value of $1 - (1 + 8\%)^{-6}$ correct to 7 decimal places.

SOLUTION:

$1 - (1 + 8\%)^{-6} = 1 - (1.08)^{-6}$

action taken	display shows
1. enter 1.08	1.08
2. press the key y^x	1.08
3. enter 6	6
4. press the key $^+/_-$	−6 (change sign)
5. press the key =	0.6301696
6. press the key $^+/_-$	−0.6301696 (change sign)
7. press the key +	−0.6301696
8. enter 1	1
9. press =	.3698304

Thus,
$$1 - (1 + 8\%)^{-6} = 1 - (1.08)^{-6}$$
$$= 1 - .630\ 169\ 6$$
$$= .369\ 830\ 4.$$

Example 2.3q

Find the value of $\dfrac{(1 + .012\ 5)^{40} - 1}{.012\ 5}$.

SOLUTION:

action taken	display shows
1. enter 1.0125	1.0125
2. press the key y^x	1.0125
3. enter 40	40
4. press the key =	1.6436194
5. press the key −	1.6436194
6. enter 1	1
7. press =	0.6436194
8. press ÷	0.6436194
9. enter .0125	.0125
10. press =	51.489552

Thus,

$$\frac{(1 + .012\ 5)^{40} - 1}{.012\ 5} = .643\ 619\ 4.$$

EXERCISE 2.3 / REFERENCE SECTIONS: A - C

Simplify the following:

1. $2^3 \cdot 2^2$
2. $4^3 \cdot 4^0$
3. $5^2 \cdot 5^4$
4. $6^3 \cdot 6^2$
5. $a^4 \cdot a^2$
6. $b^2 \cdot b^{-5}$

7. $c^4 \cdot c^0$
8. $d^5 \cdot d^2$
9. $3^2 \cdot 4^2$
10. $2^3 \cdot 5^3$
11. $x^3 \cdot y^3$
12. $a^4 \cdot b^4 \cdot c^4$

13. $m^a n^a$
14. $t^{7r} p^{7r}$
15. $(5^2)^3$
16. $(4^3)^2$
17. $(p^5)^2$
18. $(x^4)^3$

19. $(y^a)^b$
20. $(ab^2)^3$
21. $(b^{1/x})^y$
22. $(d^{1/p})^q$
23. $(4^{1/2})^6$
24. $(16^{1/2})^4$

Use an electronic calculator to evaluate each of the following expressions:

25. $(1 + 18.75\%)^{20}$
26. $(1 + 18\%)^{-22}$
27. $(1 + 11.25\%)^{\frac{1}{15}}$
28. $1 - (1 + 8\%)^{-22}$
29. $(1 + 11.6\%)^{-28} - 1$

30. $\frac{1 - (1 + 16\%)^{-48}}{16\%}$
31. $(1.065)^{30} - 1$
32. $\frac{(1.087\ 5)^{16} - 1}{.087\ 5}$
33. $\frac{1 - (1.082\ 5)^{-18}}{.082\ 5}$
34. $\frac{1 - (1.031\ 5)^{-24}}{.031\ 5}$

2.4 *Scientific Notation, Significant Digits and Rounding*

A. *SCIENTIFIC NOTATION*

The numbers 10, 100, 1 000, and so on play an important part in calculations involving decimals and are called POWERS OF 10. A convenient way of indicating powers of 10 is by using exponents.

$10^1 = 10$
$10^2 = 100$
$10^3 = 1\ 000$
$10^4 = 10\ 000$
$10^5 = 100\ 000$
$10^6 = 1\ 000\ 000$

Exponents may be used to express numbers in decimal notation.

Example 2.4a
$2\ 586 = 2.586 \times 1\ 000$
$\qquad = 2.586 \times 10^3$

Example 2.4b
$3\ 428\ 763 = 3.428\ 763 \times 1\ 000\ 000$
$\qquad\qquad = 3.428\ 763 \times 10^6$

Example 2.4c

$$.007\ 829 = \frac{7.829}{1\ 000}$$
$$= 7.829 \times 10^{-3}$$

Example 2.4d

$$.000\ 042\ 837\ 15 = \frac{4.283\ 715}{100\ 000}$$
$$= 4.283\ 715 \times 10^{-5}$$

When a number is expressed as a number between one and ten multiplied by a power of ten, the number is said to be given in SCIENTIFIC NOTATION.

A knowledge of scientific notation is helpful in interpreting the results obtained when using an electronic calculator if the calculations involve very large or very small numbers. For example, if the result of a certain computation is .000 082 576, since the display facility is generally limited to eight or nine digits, this result will be displayed on the calculator as 8.2576 − 05, which should be interpreted as $8.257\ 6 \times 10^{-5}$, and 1 000 × 1 000 may be displayed as 1 06, which should be interpreted as $1 \times 10^6 = 1\ 000\ 000$.

B. SIGNIFICANT DIGITS

The numerical value of an observed measurement is an approximation. For example, if a student states that his height is 171 centimetres, he has stated his height to the nearest centimetre. Thus, his height could be more accurately recorded as between 170.5 cm and 171.4 cm. The number of SIGNIFICANT DIGITS in a measurement indicates the degree of accuracy of the measurement. Thus,

    1.028 litres represents 4 significant digits
    1.028 0 litres represents 5 significant digits
171 centimetres represents 3 significant digits
    .002 13 centimetres represents 3 significant digits.

To determine the number of significant digits in a measurement, count the number of recorded digits except zeros which appear as the first digits following the decimal point in numbers less than one. For example,

.002 13 centimetres

has 3 significant digits. The two zeros to the right of the decimal point are not significant digits since they are used to place the decimal. In scientific notation,

$.002\ 13 = 2.13 \times 10^{-3}$

and the number of signficant digits can then be counted directly. Similarly,

$2.13 \times 10^6 = 2\ 130\ 000$

has three significant digits. However,

$2.130\,000 \times 10^6$

has seven significant digits. Therefore, unless written in scientific notation, the number of significant digits in recorded measurements with trailing zeros is not clear.

The recorded amount $10.00 has 4 significant digits since it is assumed that this amount is rounded to the nearest cent. The number of significant digits in the recorded amount $1 000 000 is ambiguous since it may have been rounded to the nearest dollar, the nearest ten dollars, the nearest hundred dollars, etc.

C. ROUNDING

Care should be exercised in rounding calculations, especially when carried out on an electronic calculator. For example, the product,

$\$250.25 \times 10\frac{1}{3}\%$
$= \$250.25 \times .103\,33\ldots.$

In order to obtain the necessary accuracy, at least as many significant digits must be retained in the MULTIPLIER as there are in the MULTIPLICAND. Thus,

  1. $250.25 \times .103$ $= 25.775\,75$
  2. $250.25 \times .103\,3$ $= 25.850\,825$
  3. $250.25 \times .103\,33$ $= 25.858\,333$
  4. $250.25 \times .103\,333$ $= 25.859\,083$
  5. $250.25 \times .103\,333\,3 = 25.859\,158.$

Notice that when these results are rounded to the nearest cent, (1) and (2) above will result in the incorrect amount since the necessary amount of significant digits were not retained.

When a number is rounded to a desired number of significant digits, the rounding convention generally used in business calculations is to drop the digits to the right of the required number of significant digits. If the first digit dropped is 5 or more, add one to the last digit retained.

Calculations done on electronic calculators generally use up to eleven significant digits although only 8 or 9 digits are displayed. For greater accuracy, intermediate results should therefore be stored whenever possible instead of being recorded and then re-entered.

Calculations involving very small or very large numbers may also be completed on electronic calculators by using the function which allows the input of numbers in scientific notation (generally labelled EE).

Example 2.4e
Find the value of 621 032 400 × .008 125.

SOLUTION:

$621\,032\,400 \times .008\,125 = (6.210\,324 \times 10^8)(8.125 \times 10^{-3})$

Basic Calculator		Financial Calculator	
action taken	display shows	action taken	display shows
1. enter 6.210324	6.210324	enter 62103240	62103240
2. press the key EE	6.210324 00	press the key X	62103240
3. enter 8	6.210324 08	enter 10	10
4. press the key X	6.210324 08	press the key =	6.2103 08
5. enter 8.125	8.125	press the key X	6.2103 08
6. press the key EE	8.125 00	enter 8.125	8.125
7. enter 3	8.125 03	press the key ÷	5.0459 09
8. press the key $^+/_-$	8.125 −03	enter 1 000	1 000
9. press the key =	5.0458883 06	press the key =	5045888.3

Thus,

$(6.210\ 324 \times 10^8)(8.125 \times 10^{-3}) = 5.045\ 888\ 3 \times 10^6$

$$= 5\ 045\ 888.3.$$

Example 2.4f

Find the value of $284\ 301\ 600 \div .004\ 215\ 6$.

SOLUTION:

$284\ 301\ 600 \div .004\ 215\ 6 = (2.843\ 016\ 00 \times 10^8) \div (4.215\ 6 \times 10^{-3})$

Basic Calculator		Financial Calculator	
action taken	display shows	action taken	display shows
1. enter 2.8430160	2.8430160	enter 28430160	28430160
2. press the key EE	2.8430160 00	press the key X	28430160
3. enter 8	2.84301600 08	enter 10	10
4. press the key ÷	2.84301600 08	press the key =	2.843 08
5. enter 4.2156	4.2156	press the key ÷	2.843 08
6. press the key EE	4.2156 00	enter 4.2156	4.2156
7. enter 3	4.2156 03	press =	67440364
8. press the key $^+/_-$	4.2156 −03	press X	67440364
9. press the key =	6.7440364 10	enter 1 000	1 000
10.		press =	6.744 10*

Thus,
$$(2.843\ 016\ 00 \times 10^8) \div (4.215\ 6 \times 10^{-3}) = 6.744\ 036\ 4 \times 10^{10}$$
$$= 67\ 440\ 364\ 000.$$

*NOTE: The final answer exceeds the display range and, therefore, it was rounded.

EXERCISE 2.4 / REFERENCE SECTIONS: A - C

(a) Express each of the following in scientific notation:
(b) Indicate the number of significant digits in each of the following:
  1. .000 258   4. 58 264
  2. 6 000 000   5. 63.218
  3. .215 861   6. .214 63

   Find the product or quotient of each of the following and give your answer
   without using scientific notation:
  7. $(2.04 \times 10^2)\,(1 \times 10^4)$ 10. $63.21 \times 10^5 \div 6 \times 10^3$
  8. $(5.02 \times 10^{-3})\,(2 \times 10^{-6})$ 11. $49.44 \times 10^8 \div 3 \times 10^4$
  9. $(7.21 \times 10^6)\,(3 \times 10^3)$ 12. $85.5 \times 10^{-3} \div 5 \times 10^{-2}$

2.5 *Operations with Algebraic Expressions*

A.   *MULTIPLICATION OF ALGEBRAIC EXPRESSIONS*

Multiplication of Monomials

The product of two or more monomials is equal to the product of their numerical
coefficients multiplied by the product of their literal factors.

Example 2.5a
$5ab \cdot 4c = 20abc$

Example 2.5b
$3x^2 \cdot 4x^3y \cdot 5y^2 = (3 \cdot 4 \cdot 5)x^{2+3}y^{1+2} = 60x^5y^3$

Multiplication of a Polynomial by a Monomial

Multiply each term of the polynomial by the monomial. The algebraic sum of the
partial products is the product of the multiplication.

Example 2.5c
Multiply $(4a + 7b)$ by $3c$.

SOLUTION:

$$4a + 7b$$
$$\underline{\times \; 3c}$$
$12ac + 21bc$, or as written:

$$(4a + 7b)3c = (4a \times 3c) + (7b \times 3c) = 12ac + 21bc$$

Multiplication of a Polynomial by Another Polynomial

Multiply each term of the multiplicand by each term of the multiplier. The algebraic sum of the partial products is the product of the multiplication.

Example 2.5d
Multiply $(4a + 7b)$ by $(3c + 5d)$.

SOLUTION:

$$4a + 7b$$
$$\underline{\times \; 3c + 5d}$$
$$12ac + 21bc$$
$$\underline{\quad\quad + 20ad \quad\quad\quad + 35bd \quad\quad}$$
$12ac + 21bc + 20ad + 35bd$, or, as written:

$$(4a + 7b)(3c + 5d) = 12ac + 21bc + 20ad + 35bd$$
Notice that $12ac = (4a)(3c)$; $21bc = (7b)(3c)$; $20ad = (4a)(5d)$; and $35bd = (7b)(5d)$.

The following examples are used to illustrate the multiplication of polynomials involving exponentials.

Example 2.5e
Multiply $(3a - 2)(2a + 5)$.

SOLUTION:

$$3a \;-\; 2$$
$$\underline{2a \;+\; 5}$$
$$6a^2 \;-\; 4a$$
$$\underline{\quad\quad + 15a - 10}$$
$6a^2 + 11a - 10$, or

$$(3a - 2)(2a + 5) = 6a^2 - 4a + 15a - 10 = 6a^2 + 11a - 10$$
Notice that $6a^2 = (3a)(2a)$; $-4a = (-2)(2a)$; $+15a = (3a)(5)$; and $-10 = (-2)(5)$.

Example 2.5f
Multiply $(4bx - 3y)(3b^2 + 2y)$.

SOLUTION:

$$
\begin{array}{r}
4bx - 3y \\
3b^2 + 2y \\
\hline
12b^3x - 9b^2y \\
\end{array}
$$

$$
\begin{array}{r}
+ 8bxy - 6y^2 \\
\hline
\end{array}
$$

$12b^3x - 9b^2y + 8bxy - 6y^2$, or

$(4bx - 3y)(3b^2 + 2y) = 12b^3x - 9b^2y + 8bxy - 6y^2$

B.   DIVISION OF ALGEBRAIC EXPRESSIONS

Division Involving Monomials

When dividing a monomial by another monomial, the quotient of the division is found by multiplying the quotient of the numerical coefficients by the quotient of the literal coefficients.

Example 2.5g
Divide $-45x^3$ by $5x$.

SOLUTION:

$$
\frac{-45x^3}{5x} = \frac{-45}{5} \cdot \frac{x^3}{x} = -9x^2
$$

Example 2.5h
Divide $36x^5y^2z^4$ by $9ax^2y^3$.

SOLUTION:

$$
\frac{36x^5y^2z^4}{9ax^2y^3} = \frac{36}{9} \cdot \frac{1}{a} \cdot \frac{x^5}{x^2} \cdot \frac{y^2}{y^3} \cdot \frac{z^4}{1} = \frac{4x^3z^4}{ay}
$$

Division of a Polynomial by Another Polynomial

The procedure of dividing one polynomial by another is illustrated in the following example.

Example 2.5i
Divide $(15x^3 - 3 + 2x^2)$ by $(3x^2 + 5 - 2x)$.

SOLUTION:

The division is arranged as follows:

(Dividend)

$$15x^3 + 2x^2 \qquad - 3 \qquad\qquad \underline{3x^2 - 2x + 5} \quad \text{(Divisor)}$$
$$\underline{15x^3 - 10x^2 + 25x} \qquad\qquad 5x + 4 \qquad \text{(Quotient)}$$
$$\underline{12x^2 - 25x - 3}$$
$$12x^2 - 8x + 20$$
$$\underline{- 17x - 23} \qquad \text{(Remainder)}$$

The division may also be written in the following form:

$$ 5x + 4 \qquad \text{(Quotient)}$$

(Divisor)
$$3x^2 - 2x + 5 \overline{)15x^3 + 2x^2 \qquad\quad - 3} \quad \text{(Dividend)}$$
$$\underline{15x^3 - 10x^2 + 25x}$$
$$\underline{12x^2 - 25x - 3}$$
$$12x^2 - 8x + 20$$
$$\underline{- 17x - 23}$$
$$\qquad\qquad \text{(Remainder)}$$

Thus, the solution equation is

$$(15x^3 + 2x^2 - 3) \div (3x^2 - 2x + 5) = (5x + 4) + \frac{-17x - 23}{3x^2 - 2x + 5}.$$

The steps in the division above are summarized below:

STEP (1) Arrange the terms of both the dividend and the divisor in descending (or ascending) powers of the same letter.

Dividend: $15x^3 - 3 + 2x^2 = 15x^3 + 2x^2 - 3$
Divisor: $3x^2 + 5 - 2x = 3x^2 - 2x + 5$

STEP (2) Divide the first term of the dividend by the first term of the divisor to obtain the first term of the quotient.

$$15x^3 \div 3x^2 = 5x$$

STEP (3) Multiply the divisor by the quotient term of STEP (2).

$$(3x^2 - 2x + 5)(5x) = 15x^3 - 10x^2 + 25x$$

STEP (4) Subtract the product of STEP (3) from the dividend to obtain a remainder. If the remainder is not zero or is not a lower power than the divisor, continue dividing it by the procedure used in STEPS (2), (3), and (4).

CHECK:

METHOD A Let $x = 2$ (or any number except 0 or 1).
Substitute the value in the solution equation.

$$\text{Left side} = [15(2)^3 + 2(2)^2 - 3] \div [3(2)^2 - 2(2) + 5]$$
$$= (120 + 8 - 3) \div (12 - 4 + 5)$$
$$= 125 \div 13 = 9\frac{8}{13} \text{ or } 9.615\,384\,6$$

$$\text{Right side} = [5(2) + 4] + \frac{-17(2) - 23}{3(2)^2 - 2(2) + 5} = 14 + \frac{-57}{13}$$

$$= 14 - 4\frac{5}{13} = 9\frac{8}{13} \text{ or } 9.615\ 384\ 6$$

METHOD B $\dfrac{\text{Dividend}}{\text{Divisor}} = \text{Quotient} + \dfrac{\text{Remainder}}{\text{Divisor}}$, or

Dividend = Quotient × Divisor + Remainder

Thus,

$$\begin{aligned}
\text{Dividend} &= (5x + 4)(3x^2 - 2x + 5) + (-17x - 23) \\
&= 5x(3x^2 - 2x + 5) + 4(3x^2 - 2x + 5) + (-17x - 23) \\
&= 15x^3 - 10x^2 + 25x + 12x^2 - 8x + 20 - 17x - 23 \\
&= 15x^3 + 2x^2 - 3, \text{ which is correct.}
\end{aligned}$$

EXERCISE 2.5 / REFERENCE SECTIONS: A - B

Multiply the following algebraic expressions:

1. $(6x)(-3y)$
2. $4ab \cdot 7c$
3. $7xy \cdot 56$
4. $(-8ab) \cdot 2b$
5. $5x^2 \cdot 2xy \cdot 3y$
6. $9t \cdot (-3t) \cdot (-4tp)$
7. $(-7pq) \cdot 3p\,q^2 \cdot p^3$
8. $(-6bc) \cdot (-4bcd) \cdot 3b$

9. $2(4a + 3)$
10. $3(2b + 7)$
11. $5(4c - 3)$
12. $-4(3d - b)$
13. $4t(a + b)$
14. $-5c(-4c + 5)$
15. $7b(-3e + 2b)$
16. $3t(-3t - 2p)$

17. $(a + b)(a - b)$
18. $(a + b)(a + b)$
19. $(a - b)(a - b)$
20. $(3m + 2)(4m - 3)$
21. $(-4y + 2)(y - 3)$
22. $(3ab + 2c)(a + 3c)$
23. $(3t^2 - 3a)(2t^3 + 4)$
24. $(-5d^2 + e)(3c^2 - 3)$

Divide the following and check (let $x = 2$):

25. $(12x^2 + 5x - 25) \div (4x - 5)$
26. $(21x^2 - 5x + 23) \div (7x + 3)$
27. $(24x^3 - x^2 - 2x + 42) \div (8x + 5)$
28. $(36x^3 + 2x^2 + x + 4) \div (9x - 4)$

29. $(25x^3 + 5x^2 + 3x - 2) \div (5x^2 - 2x + 3)$
30. $(20x^3 + 3x^2 - 4x + 5) \div (4x^2 + 3x - 7)$
31. $(28x^3 + 2x + 4) \div (7x^2 - 3)$
32. $(30x^3 + 22x^2 - 6) \div (15x^2 - 4x + 3)$

2.6 Symbols of Grouping

A. ORDER OF OPERATIONS

In Chapter One, Section 1.1F, operations involving symbols of grouping were discussed. The rules covered apply equally to algebraic expressions.

    The computer evaluates an arithmetic or algebraic expression in a left to right direction. Terms which are included in parentheses have the highest priority and are calculated first. The order of precedence from highest to lowest is as follows:

Order of Precedence	Symbol	Meaning	Example
	( )	parentheses	$(K - 32)$
	$\updownarrow$	exponentiate	$K \updownarrow 2 = K^2$
	*,/	multiply, divide	$3 * K/5 = \dfrac{3 \times K}{5}$
	+,−	add, subtract	$K + 32 - K$
	=	equals	$B = 3*K/5*(K-32)*K \updownarrow 2$
			$= (3 \times K \div 5)(K - 32)(K^2)$

Example 2.6a

Find the value of B when $B = (3 \times K \div 5)(K - 32)(K^2)$, $K = 12$.

SOLUTION:

STEP (1) Substitute 12 for K in the expression.
$$B = (3 \times 12 \div 5)(12 - 32)(12^2)$$

STEP (2) Complete the operations from left to right.
$$B = (3 \times 12 \div 5)(12 - 32)(12^2)$$
$$= (7.2)(-20)(144)$$
$$= (-144)(144)$$
$$= -20736$$

The steps may be carried out on a basic or financial electronic calculator, which provides the functions (and), as follows:

action taken	display shows
1. press the key (	0
2. enter 3	3
3. press the key X	3
4. enter 12	12
5. press the key ÷	36
6. enter 5	5
7. press the key)	7.2
8. press the key X	7.2
9. press the key (	7.2
10. enter 12	12
11. press the key −	12
12. enter 32	32
13. press the key)	−20
14. press the key X	−144

action taken	display shows
15. press the key (	−144
16. enter 12	12
17. press the key y^x	12
18. enter 2	2
19. press the key)	144
20. press the key =	−20736

Example 2.6b

The weekly wage of an employee is a fixed rate for the first 40 hours worked each week, and 1.5 times the hourly rate for all hours worked in excess of 40 hours.

(a) Write an algebraic expression for the gross income of an employee.
(b) How much will an employee earn if his/her hourly wage is $14.00 and he/she worked 56 hours that week?

SOLUTION:

a. let W = wage for the week
   R = hourly rate
   T = total hours worked

   Wage = 40 times the hourly rate + 1.5 (times the total hours worked minus 40) (times the hourly rate) or,
   $W = 40R + 1.5(T - 40)R$

b. $R = \$14.00$, $T = 56$ hours
   substituting these values in the above expression:
   $W = 40(14) + 1.5(56-40)(14)$
   $= 560 + 336$
   $= \$896.00$

   or the wage for the above employee for a week in which 56 hours were worked is $896.00.

To carry out the indicated operations in an expression including several symbols of grouping, it is often convenient to remove the inside symbols first. When this is being done, the following rules should be observed:

1. When a symbol of grouping is preceded by a plus (+) sign, the symbol may be removed without changing the signs of the terms inside the symbols.

2. When a symbol of grouping is preceded by a minus (−) sign, the symbol may be removed only if the signs of the terms inside the symbol are changed: that is, (+) to (−), and (−) to (+).

EXERCISE 2.6 / REFERENCE SECTION: A

Perform the indicated operations in each of the following expressions:

1. $2x + [3x - \frac{1}{2}(4x + 6)]$

2. $8y + [4y - \frac{1}{6}(6y + 18)]$

3. $4x - [2x - (5x - 4)]$

4. $10y - [11y - (8y - 3)]$

5. $14x - [20x + 9(4x - y)]$

6. $11y - [16y + 7(5x - 2y)]$

7. $2x - \{5y + 4x + [7y - 3(2x - y)] - 2x\}$

8. $16y - \{7x + 3y - [4x + 5(x + y - z) - 3y] + 4z\}$

9. $3a(2W - 1) + 5a(8 - 2W) - 3a(W + 2)$

10. $-6(8b - a) - 5(3a - 6b)$

11. $9a(x - y) - 4a(x + y)$

12. $5\{P - [2(Q - 3) - (11 - P)] + 3(Q + 2P)\}$

2.7 *Factoring*

In arithmetic, the operations of multiplication and division can be greatly simplified when the products of every two of the basic figures from 0 to 9 are memorized. For example, although 5 × 9 means to repeat five nine times, it does not actually have to be repeated. A student should readily know that the product of 5 and 9 is 45. Also, when one is able to recognize the factors of a number, such as the factors of 45 being 5 and 9, or 5, 3, and 3, a great amount of computation in arithmetic is facilitated. Similarly, if one knows certain algebraic expressions and their factors that frequently occur, much work in algebraic operations is reduced. The process of finding the factors in a given expression is called FACTORING. The most common types of factoring are illustrated below.

A.   MONOMIAL FACTOR

Frequently, each term in an expression contains the same or *common* factor which can easily be detected by inspection. When this occurs, the given expression may be written as the product of the common monomial factor and another factor. The other factor is obtained by dividing the given expression by the common factor. In general, the factors can be expressed as follows:

$ax + ay = a(x + y)$.

Factor $(x + y)$ is obtained by dividing $(ax + ay)$ by a; a is the common factor. The left side of the equation is the expanded form, and the right side is the factor form.

Example 2.7a
Factor $7x + 7y$.

SOLUTION:

$7x + 7y = 7(x + y)$

Example 2.7b
Factor $5x - 5y$.

SOLUTION:

$5x - 5y = 5(x - y)$.

Example 2.7c
Factor $12ax - 18ay + 6az$.

SOLUTION:

$12ax - 18ay + 6az = 6a(2x - 3y + z)$

B.   COMMON BINOMIAL FACTORS

In general, this type of factor form is expressed as follows:

$a(x + y) + b(x + y) = (a + b)(x + y)$.

Factor $(a + b)$ on the right side is obtained by dividing $a(x + y) + b(x + y)$ by the common factor $(x + y)$.

Example 2.7d
Factor $3ax - ay + 6cx - 2cy$.

SOLUTION:

$3ax - ay + 6cx - 2cy = a(3x - y) + 2c(3x - y) = (a + 2c)(3x - y)$

C.   DIFFERENCE OF TWO SQUARES

This type of factor form is generally expressed

$x^2 - y^2 = (x + y)(x - y)$.

The above equation is obtained by multiplying the factors on the right side.

$$
\begin{array}{r}
x + y \\
(\times)\ x - y \\
\hline
x^2 + xy \\
-xy - y^2 \\
\hline
x^2 \quad - y^2
\end{array}
$$

Example 2.7e
Factor $25x^2 - 9y^2$.

SOLUTION:

$25x^2 - 9y^2 = (5x)^2 - (3y)^2 = (5x + 3y)(5x - 3y)$

D. TRINOMIALS–PERFECT SQUARES

The general forms of this type are written below:

$$x^2 + 2xy + y^2 = (x + y)^2$$
$$\text{and } x^2 - 2xy + y^2 = (x - y)^2.$$

The above two equations may also be obtained by multiplying the factors on the right side of each equation.

Example 2.7f
Factor $9a^2 + 12ab + 4b^2$.

SOLUTION:

$$9a^2 + 12ab + 4b^2 = (3a)^2 + 2(3a)(2b) + (2b)^2$$
$$= (3a + 2b)^2$$

Example 2.7g
Factor $16a^2 - 24ab + 9b^2$.

SOLUTION:

$$16a^2 - 24ab + 9b^2 = (4a)^2 - 2(4a)(3b) + (3b)^2$$
$$= (4a - 3b)^2$$

E. TRINOMIALS–GENERAL CASE

The general form of this type is written below:

$$ac\,x^2 + (ad + bc)x + bd = (ax + b)(cx + d)$$

because,

$$
\begin{array}{l}
\quad\ ax + b \\
(\times)\quad cx + d \\
\hline
\ ac\,x^2 + bcx \\
\qquad\quad + adx \qquad\quad + bd \\
\hline
ac\,x^2 + (ad + bc)x + bd
\end{array}
$$

The numerical coefficients of each term in a factor form thus may be determined by the trial-and-error method as illustrated in the following examples. This method may be conveniently carried out when the required numbers are arranged in columnar form as shown, so that $(1) = ac$, $(2) = bd$, and $(3) = ad + bc$.

$$
\begin{array}{ccc}
a & & b \\
| & \diagdown \quad \diagup & | \\
(1) & (3) & (2) \\
| & \diagup \quad \diagdown & | \\
c & & d
\end{array}
$$

Example 2.7b
Factor $6x^2 + 23x + 7$.

SOLUTION:

STEP (1) Find a pair of numbers (a and c) whose product is 6. The factors of 6 are 2 and 3 and also 1 and 6.

STEP (2) Find a pair of numbers (b and d), whose product is 7. The factors of 7 are 1 and 7.

STEP (3) Place the 2 pairs of numbers (a, c; b, d) in appropriate positions; that is, the algebraic sum of the products (ad) and (bc) must equal 23.

$$
\begin{array}{ccc}
3 & & 1 \\
a & & b \\
| \quad \searrow \quad \nearrow \quad | & & \\
(1) \quad (3) \quad (2) & & \\
| \quad \nearrow \quad \searrow \quad | & & \\
c & & d \\
2 & & 7
\end{array}
$$

According to the trial-and-error method, the result is that $a = 3$, $b = 1$, $c = 2$, and $d = 7$. Thus, the desired factors are:

$6x^2 + 23x + 7 = (3x + 1)(2x + 7)$.

Example 2.7i
Factor $10x^2 - 21 + 29x$.

SOLUTION:

The trinomial should be arranged in the order of descending powers of x. The expression thus obtained is shown below.

$10x^2 + 29x - 21$

STEP (1) Find a pair of numbers (a and c) whose product is 10. Factors of 10 are 1 and 10; 2 and 5.)

STEP (2) Find a pair of numbers (b and d) whose product is (-21). (Factors of 21 are 1 and 21; 3 and 7; one of the factors in the chosen pair will be negative.)

STEP (3) Place the 2 pairs of numbers (a, c; b, d) in proper positions; that is, the algebraic sum of the products (ad) and (bc) must equal 29.

$$5 \qquad\qquad -3$$
$$a \qquad\qquad b$$
$$|\quad\searrow\quad\diagup\quad|$$
$$(1)\quad(3)\quad(2)$$
$$|\quad\diagup\quad\searrow\quad|$$
$$c \qquad\qquad d$$
$$2 \qquad\qquad 7$$

According to the trial-and-error method, the result is that $a = 5$; $b = (-3)$; $c = 2$; $d = 7$. Thus,

$10x^2 + 29x - 21 = (5x - 3)(2x + 7)$.

The following procedure may also be used to factor a trinomial:

STEP (1) Multiply the coefficient of x^2 by the term not containing x.

STEP (2) Find two numbers whose algebraic sum is the coefficient of x and whose product is equal to the one obtained in STEP (1).

STEP (3) Use the two numbers to replace the coefficient of x in the trinomial and factor the new expression by grouping the terms.

Example 2.7j
Factor $6x^2 + 23x + 7$.

SOLUTION:

STEP (1) $(6)(7) = 42$.

STEP (2) According to the trial-and-error method, $21 + 2 = 23$ and $(21)(2) = 42$.

STEP (3) $6x^2 + (21 + 2)x + 7 = 6x^2 + 21x + 2x + 7$
$$= 3x(2x + 7) + (2x + 7)$$
$$= (3x + 1)(2x + 7)$$

Example 2.7k
Factor $10x^2 + 29x - 21$.

SOLUTION:

STEP (1) $(10)(-21) = -210$

STEP (2) According to the trial-and-error method, $35 + (-6) = 29$ and $(35)(-6) = -210$.

STEP (3) $10x^2 + (35 - 6)x - 21 = 10x^2 + 35x - 6x - 21$
$$= 5x(2x + 7) - 3(2x + 7)$$
$$= (5x - 3)(2x + 7)$$

EXERCISE 2.7 / REFERENCE SECTIONS: A–E

Factor the following:

1. $10a + 5b$
2. $2a - 4b$
3. $6x + 6$
4. $15t - 5$
5. $-18x + 6y - 6z$
6. $24ab + 9ac - 3az$
7. $3ax - ay + 6cx - 2cy$
8. $ax + ay + bx + by$
9. $ax + ay - bx - by$
10. $ax - ay - bx + by$
11. $28ac + 14bc - 4ad - 2bd$
12. $6am - 9an + 4bm - 6bn$

13. $9x^2 - y^4$
14. $x^2 - 1$
15. $25x^2 - 16y^2$
16. $a^2b^2 - 64c^2$
17. $x^4 - 49$
18. $36x^4 - 81y^2$
19. $x^2 + 6x + 9$
20. $x^2 + 8x + 16$
21. $4x^2 + 24x + 36$
22. $9x^2 - 18x + 9$
23. $36y^2 - 60y + 25$
24. $16a^2 - 16a + 4$

25. $9a^2 + 24ab + 16b^2$
26. $25t^2 - 30ts + 9s^2$
27. $x^2 + 3x + 2$
28. $x^2 - 3x + 2$
29. $2y^2 + 5y + 3$
30. $3y^2 + 5y - 2$
31. $2a^2 - a - 3$
32. $12x^2 + 10x + 2$
33. $7x^2 + 20x - 3$
34. $20x^2 + 9x - 18$
35. $21b^2 + 13b - 20$
36. $-15x^2 + 28x - 12$

Glossary

ALGEBRAIC EXPRESSION any symbol or combination of symbols that represent a number

BASE one of the equal factors in a power

BINOMIAL an algebraic expression of two terms

COEFFICIENT any factor of a term is the coefficient of the remaining factors

COLLECTING TERMS the process of finding the algebraic sum of like terms and unlike terms

CUBE a third power of a base

EXPONENT the number of equal factors in a power

EXPONENTIAL the expression of an indicated power of a given symbol or number

EXPRESSION see *algebraic expression*

FACTOR where two or more numbers are multiplied together, each number, or the product of any of the numbers is a factor

FACTORING the process of finding the factors in a given expression

LIKE TERMS terms whose literal factors are the same

LITERAL COEFFICIENT any factor, other than the numerical coefficients in a term

MONOMIAL an algebraic expression consisting of one term

MULTINOMIAL an algebraic expression have more than one term

MULTIPLICAND the number to be multiplied

MULTIPLIER the number by which another number is to be multiplied

NUMERICAL COEFFICIENT a factor which is an explicit number

POLYNOMIAL see *multinomial*

POWER the product of equal factors

POWERS OF 10 the numbers 10, 100, 1 000, etc., involving decimals

SCIENTIFIC NOTATION a number expressed as a number between one and ten multiplied by a power of ten

SIGNIFICANT DIGITS the number of recorded digits, except zeros which appear as the first digits following a decimal point in numbers less than one; trailing zeros (e.g. 7 800), may or may not be significant

SQUARE a second power of a base

TERM one part of an algebraic expression separated from the other parts by a plus or minus sign

TRINOMIAL an algebraic expression consisting of three terms

UNLIKE TERMS terms whose literal factors are not alike

3

Linear systems, fractional equations and break-even analysis

Introduction

Having reviewed a range of basic concepts in arithmetic and algebra in Chapters One and Two, Chapter Three is oriented toward their business application.

The importance of the material on linear equations, covered in the first part of this chapter, deserves emphasis as it provides the opportunity to put into practice the knowledge of the basics in interpreting statements and translating written information into mathematical symbols. The ability to translate information contained in a statement into a logically correct set of symbols is an essential communications skill. The need for this type of skill will grow with the role of the computer in the world of business.

Break-even analysis, which is covered later in the chapter, is a widely applied analytical tool. This topic can be found in several course offerings, such as economics and accounting. Since it is a widely applied technique, it is important to be confident with its use.

3.1. Basic Concepts

A. CONCEPT OF AN EQUATION

An EQUATION is a statement which indicates that two algebraic expressions are equal. The two expressions are called the SIDES or MEMBERS of the equation. There are two types of equations: the identical equation, and the conditional equation.

When the two sides of an equation are equal for any value that may be substituted for the letter or letters involved, the equation is called an IDENTICAL EQUATION, or simply, an IDENTITY. For example, $2x + x = 3x$ is an identity because the two sides are equal when x represents any value. Thus, when $x = 1$, the left side becomes $2(1) + 1 = 3$, and the right side becomes $3(1) = 3$.

When the sides of an equation are equal for only definite values of the letters involved, the equation is called a CONDITIONAL EQUATION, or simply an equation. For example $2x + 1 = 7$ is a conditional equation, because only when x represents 3 are the two sides equal to each other. The value 3, which satisfies the equation is called the SOLUTION or the ROOT. The letter or letters whose value is desired is called the UNKNOWN. When only one letter occurs in an equation, the root is a number; and when letters other than the unknown are included, the root is usually expressed in terms of those letters.

The number of powers of the single unknown value in an equation indicates the DEGREE of an equation. Equations of the first power are called LINEAR EQUATIONS. Thus, $2x + 1 = 7$ is a linear equation because $x = x^1$.

B.   SOLUTION OF EQUATIONS

In solving a linear equation in one unknown, the operations are based on the axiom that if the *same* number is added to, subtracted from, multiplied by, or divided into both sides of an equation, the two sides are still equal; that is, the equality of the equation is not destroyed. By applying this axiom, if an equation is obtained in such a way that the unknown is alone on one side, the other side is the desired solution. The procedure for finding the solution of an equation in one unknown is shown below.

STEP (1) Add (or subtract) the same numbers to (or from) both sides so that the resulting equation will have the term which has the unknown on one side and all other terms on the other.

STEP (2) Divide both sides of the new equation by the coefficient of the unknown to obtain the solution.

Example 3.1a
Solve $4x + 3 = 6x - 15$.

SOLUTION:

STEP (1) Subtract $6x$ from both sides to remove $6x$ at the right:
$4x + 3 - 6x = 6x - 15 - 6x$
Collect the like terms on both sides:
$-2x + 3 = -15$
Subtract 3 from both sides to remove 3 at the left:
$-2x + 3 - 3 = -15 - 3$
Collect the like terms on both sides:
$-2x = -18$

STEP (2) Divide both sides by (-2):
$x = 9$

The operations listed above may be simplified by moving the terms from one side of the equation to the other side after changing their signs, i.e., from + to −, − to +, × to ÷, and ÷ to ×. Usually, all the terms containing the unknown are moved to the left side and all other terms are moved to the right side until the unknown remains alone on the left side. The above example thus may be simplified as follows:

$4x + 3 = 6x - 15$

$4x - 6x = -15 - 3$

$-2x = -18, \; x = \dfrac{-18}{-2}$

$x = 9$

CHECK:

$4(9) + 3 = 6(9) - 15$

$36 + 3 = 54 - 15$

$39 = 39$

Example 3.1b

Solve $4x - 8 = 2x$.

SOLUTION:

$4x - 2x = 8$

$2x = 8$

$x = 4$

CHECK:

$4(4) - 8 = 2(4)$

$16 - 8 = 8$

$8 = 8$

Example 3.1c

Solve $5(x - 2) = x + 18$.

SOLUTION:

$5x - 10 = x + 18$

$5x - x = 10 + 18$

$4x = 28$

$x = 7$

CHECK:

$5[(7) - 2] = (7) + 18$

$5[5] = 7 + 18$

$25 = 25$

Example 3.1d

Solve $2ax + b = 3c$ for x.

SOLUTION:

$$2ax = 3c - b$$

$$x = \frac{3c - b}{2a}$$

CHECK:

$$2a\left(\frac{3c - b}{2a}\right) + b = 3c$$

$$3c - b + b = 3c$$

$$3c = 3c$$

C. SOLUTION OF STATEMENT PROBLEMS INVOLVING ONE UNKNOWN

In solving a statement or word problem, it is necessary to translate the statement into a corresponding mathematical equation. The procedure used may be represented by the following steps:

1. Determine what quantities are unknown.
2. Determine what quantities are known.
3. Represent one of the unknown quantities by a letter, for example x; and express other unknown quantities, if any exist, in terms of x.
4. Determine what relationship exists between the known quantities and the unknown quantities.
5. Translate the relationship into an equation.
6. Solve the equation for the unknown quantity.
7. Check your findings against the statement problem.

Example 3.1e
If 4 is added to 3 times a number, and the sum is 19, what is the number?

SOLUTION:

1. The unknown quantity is the number.
2. The known quantity is 19.
3. Let the unknown number be x.
4. 4 plus 3 times the unknown number is equal to 19.
5. Translate the relationship into an equation: $4 + 3x = 19$.
6. Solve the equation for x:
   $$4 + 3x = 19$$
   $$3x = 19 - 4$$
   $$3x = 15$$
   $$x = 5$$
7. Check your findings against the statement of the problem:
   $$4 + 3(5) = 19$$
   Thus, the answer is correct.

Example 3.1f

A typewriter is sold for $140. The gross profit is computed as (.75) of the cost. Assume that the selling price is equal to the gross profit added to the cost. What are the cost and the gross profit?

SOLUTION:

1. The unknown quantity is the cost.
2. The known quantity is the selling price. Selling price = $140.
3. Let the cost = c, and gross profit = $.75c$.
4. According to the statement:
   gross profit + cost = selling price
5. Translate the relationship into an equation:

   $$.75c + c = 140$$

6. Solve the equation for cost:
   $$.75c + c = 140$$
   $$(.75 + 1)c = 140$$
   $$1.75c = 140$$
   $$c = \$80 \text{ (cost)}$$
   $$\text{gross profit} = .75c$$
   $$= .75(80)$$
   $$= \$60$$

7. CHECK:

   gross profit + cost
   = 60 + 80 = $140 (selling price)

EXERCISE 3.1 / REFERENCE SECTIONS: A–C

Solve the following equations for x:

1. $2x - 7 = 0$
2. $8x + 6 = 22$
3. $3x - 7 = 8$
4. $x - 9 = 5x$
5. $5x - 13 = 7$
6. $12 - 5x = -18$
7. $6x + 3 = 3x + 12$
8. $5x - 4 = 2x + 32$
9. $3(x - 1) = 2x + 9$
10. $5x - 2(2x - 5) = 15$

11. $0.48 + x = 0.26 + 3x$
12. $3x - 0.33 = 0.44 - 4x$
13. $4x = 8a$
14. $4a - 3x = -2a$
15. $2x + 7d = 11d$
16. $7b + 3x = 16b + 6$
17. $3cx + d = 5n$
18. $4y + 2x = 7y$
19. $5(3a - x) - 4(2a - 7x) = -3x$
20. $3(x - 6g) = 5(9x - 2g) - 9g$

Statement Problems:

21. The difference between two numbers is 64 and their sum is 220. What are the numbers?
22. The sum of three numbers is 79. The largest is 11 more than the middle one and the smallest is one-half of the largest one. What are the numbers?
23. If a number is added to 3 times the number, the sum is 72. Find the number.
24. If 7 is subtracted from 4 times a number, the remainder is 93. Find the number.
25. Eight years ago, John was twice as old as his sister. What is the present age of John if the sum of their ages today is 43 years?
26. Divide 138 into two parts. The difference between the two parts should be 12.
27. The profit from the sale of an automobile is $2 946. If the profit is shared among John and his partner Francine, so that John receives $452 less than Francine, how much does John receive?
28. In the Ame Company, the amount budgeted for advertising is 4 times the amount budgeted for customer relations. The difference between the amounts is $27 000. How much is the budget for advertising?
29. Mary would like to change a $10 bill into dimes and quarters. She wants to have 12 more quarters than dimes. How many of each should she receive?
30. The sum of the weekly incomes of Sarah, Brian and Elan is $2 809. Brian earns 5 times as much as Sarah and Elan earns $9 more than Sarah. What are their respective earnings?
31. The cost of two books is $82. If one book costs half as much as the other, what is the cost of each book?
32. A service station has two kinds of gasoline, one selling for 20.5¢ per litre and the other for 22.3¢ per litre. How many litres of each must be used to make 90 litres of a mixture that can be sold for 21.5¢ per litre?
33. A bus which averages 80 kilometres per hour leaves a station 30 minutes before another bus which averages 96 kilometres per hour. If both buses take the same route, how long will it take for the second bus to catch up with the first and how far will the buses have travelled?
34. Two planes leave an airport for Halifax and Vancouver, respectively. The west-bound plane travels 30 kilometres per hour faster than the other. At the end of 3 hours they are 1 440 kilometres apart. What is the average speed of each plane?
35. A car which travels 72 kilometres an hour left Winnipeg 15 minutes after a truck, and was passing it in 2 hours. What was the average speed of the truck?
36. Two cars left Montreal at the same time and headed in the same direction. The average hourly speed of one car is 1.25 times the speed of the other. At the end of 2 hours they are 40 kilometres apart. Find the average speed of each car.
37. A washing machine was sold for $350. The gross profit is computed as .4 of the cost. Assume that the selling price is equal to the gross profit plus the cost. What is the cost?
38. Jack and Peter made $1 400 net profit from their partnership at the end of the year. By agreement, Jack's share is .4 as much as Peter's. How much does Jack receive?

39. In a Mathematics for Finance class, there are 30 students. The number of boys is 4 times the number of girls. How many girls are there?

40. A student made A grades on .2 of his semester's assignments and B grades of .5 of the assignments. The remaining 6 assignments were not handed in. What was the total number of the assignments in the semester?

41. A man has three times as many dimes as quarters and twice as many half dollars as dimes. The total value of his money amounts to $10.65. How many coins of each kind does the man have?

42. A woman has $7.05 in 48 dimes and some quarters. How many quarters does she have?

3.2 Systems of Linear Equations

A.   CONCEPT OF A SYSTEM OF EQUATIONS

A SYSTEM OF EQUATIONS is a group of two or more equations. A linear equation in *one* unknown has only *one* solution, but a linear equation in *two* unknowns has an *unlimited number* of solutions. For example, $x + 2y = 11$ is satisfied by unlimited pairs of numbers such as $x = 1$, $y = 5$; $x = 3$, $y = 4$; and $x = 7$, $y = 2$. If x is equal to any particular numerical value, there is a solution for y in the equation. However, in general, if there are two linear equations in two unknowns, there is only one solution for each unknown that satisfies both equations. The two equations are called INDEPENDENT SIMULTANEOUS EQUATIONS, or simply INDEPENDENT EQUATIONS. If two equations can be reduced to the same form, they are said to be DEPENDENT EQUATIONS. Thus, $x + y = 2$ and $2x + 2y = 4$ are dependent equations because the latter can be reduced to the form of the previous one by dividing by 2; hence there are unlimited pairs of numbers which satisfy the equation. If there is no common solution for two linear equations in two unknowns, they are called INCONSISTENT EQUATIONS. Thus, $x + y = 5$ and $x + y = 7$ are inconsistent equations.

B.   SOLUTION BY ELIMINATION

To solve two independent linear equations simultaneously, first eliminate one of the two unknowns from the two equations and solve the resulting equation in one unknown. The eliminated unknown is then found by substituting the value obtained in either one of the given equations or their derived equivalents. Two methods of elimination are illustrated by the following example. Method A is the simpler method.

Example 3.2a
Solve $3x + y = 5$ (1)
$\quad\quad\ 6x - y = 6$ (2)

METHOD A *Elimination by Addition or Subtraction*

Eliminate y by Addition	Eliminate x by Subtraction		
Add equations (1) and (2)	Multiply equation (1) by 2	$6x + 2y = 10$	(3)
$3x + 6x = 5 + 6$	Rewrite (2)	$6x - y = 6$	(4)
$9x = 11, x = \dfrac{11}{9}$	Subtraction: (3) − (4)	$3y = 4$	(5)
	Solve (5) for y	$y = \dfrac{4}{3}$	
Substitute $x = \dfrac{11}{9}$ in (1)	Substitute $y = \dfrac{4}{3}$ in (2)	$6x - \dfrac{4}{3} = 6$	(6)
$3\left(\dfrac{11}{9}\right) + y = 5$	Solve (6) for x	$6x = 6 + \dfrac{4}{3}$	
$\dfrac{11}{3} + y = 5$		$x = \dfrac{11}{9}$	
$y = 5 - \dfrac{11}{3} = \dfrac{4}{3}$			

CHECK:

Substitute $x = \dfrac{11}{9}$, and $y = \dfrac{4}{3}$ in (1) and (2).

In (1): $3\left(\dfrac{11}{9}\right) + \dfrac{4}{3} = 5, \dfrac{11}{3} + \dfrac{4}{3} = 5, \dfrac{15}{3} = 5, 5 = 5$

In (2): $6\left(\dfrac{11}{9}\right) - \dfrac{4}{3} = 6, \dfrac{22}{3} - \dfrac{4}{3} = 6, \dfrac{18}{3} = 6, 6 = 6$

METHOD B *Elimination by Substitution*

Solve (2) for y in terms of x.
$y = 6x - 6$ (7)

Substitute (7) in (1).   NOTE: Do not substitute in (2)
$3x + (6x - 6) = 5$ (8)   since (7) is derived from (2).

Solve (8) for x.

$3x + 6x - 6 = 5, 9x = 11, x = \dfrac{11}{9}$

Solve for y as in METHOD A when x is found first.

Thus, $y = \dfrac{4}{3}$.

CHECK:

As in METHOD A.

When there are *three* linear equations in *three* unknowns, a solution that satisfies the three equations may be obtained. However, it must be an independent system.

The method of solving a system of three linear equations in three unknowns is an extension of the methods used in solving two equations in two unknowns. Similarly, the methods may be extended to n number of linear equations in n number of unknowns.

C.   SOLUTION OF STATED PROBLEMS INVOLVING TWO UNKNOWNS

The steps discussed in Section 3.1C are also applicable in solving statement problems involving two unknowns. However, two letters and two equations are set up instead of one letter and one equation.

Example 3.2b
The cost of two dozen eggs and five dozen oranges is $6.73. The cost of three dozen eggs and four dozen oranges is $6.63. What is the cost per dozen of each item?

SOLUTION:

1. The unknown quantities are: cost in dollars of one dozen eggs, cost in dollars of one dozen oranges.
2. Known quantities are: the cost of two dozen eggs and five dozen oranges ($6.73), and the cost of three dozen eggs and four dozen oranges ($6.63).
3. Let x = cost in dollars of one dozen eggs.
    Let y = cost in dollars of one dozen oranges.
4. (a) The cost of 2 dozen eggs and 5 dozen oranges is $6.73.
    (b) The cost of 3 dozen eggs and 4 dozen oranges is $6.63.
5. $2x + 5y = 6.73$
    $3x + 4y = 6.63$
    NOTE: In stated problems <u>and</u> is often used to denote (+) and <u>is</u> used to denote (equals).
6. Solve the above two equations simultaneously by eliminating x.
    Multiply (1) by 3 $6x + 15y = \$20.19$ (3)
    Multiply (2) by 2 $6x + \ 8y = \$13.26$ (4)
    (3) − (4) $7y = \$ \ 6.93$

$$y = \frac{\$6.93}{7} = \$0.99$$

Note that 6, the coefficient of x in (3) and (4), is the *lowest common multiple* of 2 and 3, which are the coefficients of x in (1) and (2) respectively.

Substitute $y = .99$ in (1) $2x + 5(.99) = \$6.73$
                                                    $2x + 4.95 = \$6.73$
                                                    $2x = \$6.73 - 4.95 = 1.78$

$$x = \frac{1.78}{2} = \$0.89$$

The cost of one dozen eggs is $.89.
The cost of one dozen oranges is $.99.

7. CHECK:

According to the statement of the problem, the answer gives the following:
The cost of two dozen eggs and five dozen oranges is
$2(.89) + 5(.99) = 1.78 + 4.95 = \$6.73$.
The cost of three dozen eggs and four dozen oranges is
$3(.89) + 4(.99) = 2.67 + 3.96 = \$6.63$.

Example 3.2c
John and Nancy divided $500. If John had received $70 more and Nancy had spent
$30 of her money, they would have equal amounts. How much did each receive?

SOLUTION:

1. The unknown quantities are: John's share in dollars and Nancy's share in dollars.
2. The known quantities are: the total amount of John's share and Nancy's share
   ($500). The relationship between John's share plus $70 and Nancy's share less
   $30.
3. Let $x =$ John's share in dollars.
   Let $y =$ Nancy's share in dollars.
4. The sum of John's share and Nancy's share is $500. If $70 is added to John's
   share it is equal to Nancy's share less $30.
5. $x + y = 500$
   $x + 70 = y - 30$
6. Solve the two equations simultaneously:
   $x = 200$
   $y = 300$
   John received $200. Nancy received $300.

7. CHECK:

   If John had received $70 more, he would have had ($200 + $70) or $270. If
   Nancy had spent $30 of her money, she would have had ($300 − $30) or $270.
   Their shares are $200 and $300, the sum is ($200 + $300) or $500.

Example 3.2d
A typewriter is sold for $140. The gross profit is computed as $\frac{3}{4}$ of the cost. Assume
that the selling price is equal to the gross profit added to the cost. What are the cost
and the gross profit? (This problem is the same as that of Example 3.1f).

SOLUTION:

Let $x =$ cost, and $y =$ gross profit.
Then $x + y = 140$
$$y = \left(\frac{3}{4}\right)x$$

Solve the two equations:

$x = \$80$ (cost) $y = \$60$ (gross profit)

CHECK:

Selling price $= 80 + 60 = \$140$

Gross profit $= \dfrac{3}{4}(80) = \$60$

EXERCISE 3.2 / REFERENCE SECTIONS: A–C

Solve for x and y (elimination by addition or subtraction):

1. $3x + y = 8$
    $2x - y = 7$

2. $x - 2y = 18$
    $x + 3y = 8$

3. $2x + 5y = 32$
    $3x - 2y = 29$

4. $3x - 2y = -13$
    $x + 4y = 19$

5. $5x + 4y = 29$
    $7x + 6y = 41$

6. $3x - 4y = 26$
    $5x - 8y = 46$

7. $x + 2y = -4$
    $2x + y = 1$

8. $2x + 3y = 11$
    $x + 4y = 8$

9. $2x - y = 4$
    $2x + y = 16$

10. $3x - 2y = 1$
    $2x + y = -4$

11. $4x + 2y = -12$
    $x - y = -6$

12. $5x + y = -7$
    $x + 4y = 10$

13. $2x - y = 15$
    $3x + 2y = 40$

14. $3x - 2y = 23$
    $x + 3y = 4$

15. $x + 2y = 19$
    $4x + y = -8$

16. $2x + y = 5$
    $x - 2y = 10$

17. $4x + 3y = 3$
    $2x - 6y = -1$

18. $8x + 3y = 8$
    $4x - 3y = 1$

Solve for x and y (elimination by substitution):

19. $x + y = 5$
    $5x - 2y = 4$

20. $3x - 2y = 7$
    $x + 3y = 6$

21. $x + 2y = 3$
    $4x - 3y = -10$

22. $2x - y = 11$
    $4x + y = 13$

23. $2x + y = -7$
    $3x + 2y = -12$

24. $5x - y = 1$
    $4x - 2y = -4$

25. $5x + 2y = 16$
    $2x + y = 7$

26. $3x - 5y = -31$
    $x + y = 3$

27. $x + 2y = 5$
    $3x + 2y = -1$

28. $3x + 2y = 13$
    $x - y = 1$

29. $x + 5y = -6$
    $3x + y = 10$

30. $2x + 6y = -2$
    $6x + 4y = 1$

31. $4x - y = 13$
    $2x - 3y = 19$

32. $2x + y = 1$
    $5x + 2y = 4$

33. $3x - y = 15$
    $x + y = 1$

34. $2x + 5y = 5$
    $3x + 2y = -9$

35. $2x + 3y = 4$
    $3x + 2y = 11$

36. $3x + 5y = -1$
    $6x + 15y = -5$

State whether each of the following is a dependent or an inconsistent system of equations:

37. $3x + 4y = 11$
    $6x + 8y = 22$

38. $5x - 4y = 20$
    $10x - 8y = 40$

39. $4x + y = 6$
    $4x + y = 16$

40. $8x - 17y = 15$
    $8x - 17y = 19$

41. $2x + 5y = 19$
    $6x + 15y = 57$

42. $3x + y = 7$
    $15x + 5y = 35$

43. $6x + 4y = 22$
     $3x + 2y = 10$

44. $7x + 2y = 14$
     $21x + 6y = 9$

Statement Problems:

45. The cost of a hat and a coat is $64.00, and the cost of 3 hats and 2 coats is $143.50. Find the cost of the hat and the cost of the coat.
46. The sum of A and B is 575. The sum of A times .04 and B times .06 is 30. What is the value of A? of B?
47. The sum of two numbers is 12 and their difference is 2. What are the numbers?
48. Two students made a total of 185 points in a game. One student made 15 points more than the other student. How many points did each student make?
49. A theatre sold 40 tickets amounting to $95 in one evening. The tickets were sold to adults for $2.75 and to children for $1.25. How many of each were sold?
50. A druggist wishes to prepare 450 litres of 45% alcohol. She has two kinds of alcohol solution in stock; one is 55% pure and the other is 30% pure. How many litres of each kind must be used for the mixture?
51. The sum of the ages of a girl and her brother is 20. Four years ago her age was 3 times the age of her brother. Find the girl's age and her brother's age.
52. Two cars start at the same place and the same time but travel in opposite directions. After 6 hours, they are 780 kilometres apart. If one car travels 10 kilometres per hour slower than the other, what are their speeds per hour?
53. The sum of the digits of a two-digit number is 17. The tens' digit is greater than the units' digit by 1. Find the number.
54. Work out Problem 31 of Exercise 3.1 by a system of two equations.
55. A grocer wishes to make 90 kilograms of coffee by mixing two grades of coffee worth $6.40 and $7.00 a kilogram respectively. If the mixed coffee will be sold at $6.65 a kilogram, how many kilograms of each grade of coffee should he use?
56. Work out Problem 32 of Exercise 3.1 by a system of two equations.

3.3. Fractions and Fractional Equations

A. GENERAL STATEMENTS

The rules for computing algebraic fractions are the same as those for computing fractions in arithmetic. However, algebraic fractions are more involved because symbols, as well as numbers, are employed in computation. The principle which indicates that multiplying or dividing both the numerator and the denominator by the same number, other than zero, does not affect the value of the fraction is also important to algebraic fractions. Thus, $\frac{14}{35}$ may be converted to $\frac{2 \times 7}{5 \times 7} = \frac{2}{5}$; likewise, $\frac{ac}{bc}$ may be converted to $\frac{a}{b}$. Furthermore, if the numerator and the denominator of a fraction can be factored and divided by any common factor, it is possible to convert the fraction to a simpler form. If the numerator and the denominator have no common factors, the fraction is in its simplest form. Thus,

$$\frac{x^2 - 9}{x^2 - 8x + 15} = \frac{(x + 3)(x - 3)}{(x - 5)(x - 3)} = \frac{x + 3}{x - 5}, \text{ and}$$

$\dfrac{x + 3}{x - 5}$ is the simpliest form.

When a fraction is converted to its simplest form, the numerator and the denominator in the final answer are usually retained in factored form, as shown in the answer in Example 3.3c.

B.   ADDITION AND SUBTRACTION OF ALGEBRAIC FRACTIONS

Algebraic fractions should have a common denominator if the fractions are to be added or subtracted. If the given fractions do not have the same denominator, it is necessary to convert them to equivalent fractions with the lowest common denominator (l.c.d.) before adding or subtracting. The algebraic sum of the numerators is the numerator of the resulting fraction, and the l.c.d. is its denominator.

Example 3.3a

Combine and simplify: $\dfrac{2x}{3} + \dfrac{x}{5}$.

SOLUTION:

Here the l.c.d. is $3 \times 5 = 15$.

$$\frac{2x}{3} + \frac{x}{5} = \frac{2x \cdot 5}{3 \cdot 5} + \frac{x \cdot 3}{5 \cdot 3} = \frac{10x + 3x}{15} = \frac{13x}{15}$$

Example 3.3b

Combine and simplify: $\dfrac{2}{a} + \dfrac{5}{b}$.

SOLUTION:

Here the l.c.d. is ab.

$$\frac{2}{a} + \frac{5}{b} = \frac{2b}{ab} + \frac{5a}{ab} = \frac{2b + 5a}{ab}$$

Example 3.3c

Combine and simplify: $\dfrac{10}{a^2 - b^2} + \dfrac{3}{a - b}$.

SOLUTION:

Here the l.c.d. is $a^2 - b^2 = (a + b)(a - b)$.

$$\frac{10}{a^2 - b^2} = \frac{10}{(a + b)(a - b)}; \frac{3}{(a - b)} = \frac{3(a + b)}{(a + b)(a - b)}$$

Thus, $\dfrac{10}{a^2 - b^2} + \dfrac{3}{a - b} = \dfrac{10}{(a + b)(a - b)} + \dfrac{3(a + b)}{(a + b)(a - b)} = \dfrac{10 + 3(a + b)}{(a + b)(a - b)}$.

Example 3.3d

Combine and simplify: $\dfrac{a}{a-b} - \dfrac{b}{a+b}$.

SOLUTION:

Here the l.c.d. is $(a-b)(a+b)$.

$$\frac{a}{a-b} - \frac{b}{a+b} = \frac{a(a+b)}{(a-b)(a+b)} - \frac{b(a-b)}{(a+b)(a-b)}$$

$$= \frac{a(a+b) - b(a-b)}{(a+b)(a-b)} = \frac{a^2 + ab - ab + b^2}{(a+b)(a-b)}$$

$$= \frac{a^2 + b^2}{(a+b)(a-b)}$$

Example 3.3e

Combine and simplify: $\dfrac{2}{x+1} + \dfrac{3x+1}{2x^2+5x+3}$.

SOLUTION:

Here the l.c.d. is $(x+1)(2x+3)$ or $2x^2 + 5x + 3$.

$$\frac{2}{x+1} + \frac{3x+1}{2x^2+5x+3} = \frac{2(2x+3)}{(x+1)(2x+3)} + \frac{3x+1}{(x+1)(2x+3)}$$

$$= \frac{4x+6+3x+1}{(x+1)(2x+3)} = \frac{7x+7}{(x+1)(2x+3)} = \frac{7\cancel{(x+1)}}{\cancel{(x+1)}(2x+3)} = \frac{7}{2x+3}$$

C. MULTIPLICATION AND DIVISION OF ALGEBRAIC FRACTIONS

The rules of multiplication and division used in arithmetic also apply in calculations involving algebraic fractions. In some cases, however, the numerators and the denominators of the given fractions may be factored before multiplying.

Example 3.3f

Multiply $\dfrac{10x}{6y}$ by $\dfrac{3y}{15x}$.

SOLUTION:

$$\frac{10x}{6y} \cdot \frac{3y}{15x} = \frac{30xy}{90xy} = \frac{1}{3}$$

Example 3.3g

Multiply $\dfrac{x^2-y^2}{2x^2}$ by $\dfrac{3y}{x+y}$.

SOLUTION:

$$\frac{x^2 - y^2}{2x^2} \cdot \frac{3y}{x + y} = \frac{\cancel{(x + y)}(x - y)}{2x^2} \cdot \frac{3y}{\cancel{x + y}} = \frac{3y(x - y)}{2x^2}$$

Example 3.3h

$$\frac{\frac{x - 1}{x + y}}{\frac{3x + y}{3(x + y)}}$$

SOLUTION:

The problem can be simplified by the method shown below.

METHOD A Multiply the dividend by the reciprocal of the divisor. This complex fraction may be written as follows:

$$\frac{x - 1}{x + y} \div \frac{3x + y}{3(x + y)} = \frac{x - 1}{x + y} \cdot \frac{3(x + y)}{3x + y} = \frac{3(x - 1)}{3x + y}$$

Example 3.3i

Divide $\dfrac{5x + 10}{9x - 9}$ by $\dfrac{5}{3x - 3}$.

SOLUTION:

METHOD A is used for this illustration.

$$\frac{5x + 10}{9x - 9} \div \frac{5}{3x - 3} = \frac{5x + 10}{9x - 9} \cdot \frac{3x - 3}{5}$$

$$= \frac{\cancel{5}(x + 2)}{\underset{3}{\cancel{9}}\cancel{(x - 1)}} \cdot \frac{\cancel{3}\cancel{(x - 1)}}{\cancel{5}}$$

$$= \frac{x + 2}{3}$$

D.   OPERATIONS WITH FRACTIONAL EQUATIONS

When solving an equation involving fractions, first multiply both sides by the lowest common denominator to derive an equation that will contain no fractions. This step is called CLEARING an equation of fractions. Next solve the derived equation for the unknown, as discussed in Section 3.1.

When a fractional equation is being cleared, multiplying by a denominator other than the lowest common denominator may introduce solutions which are not solutions of the original equations. These extra solutions are called EXTRANEOUS ROOTS. When both sides of an equation are multiplied by the same expression containing the unknown, or when both sides of the equation are raised to the same integral power, the resulting equation may also have more solutions than the original equation possessed. The extraneous roots are discarded in solving statement problems. However, when both sides of an equation are divided by an expression containing the unknown, the new equation may have fewer roots than the original equation had. Furthermore, division or multiplication by zero should be excluded.

Example 3.3j

Solve $\dfrac{x}{x-6} = 4$.

SOLUTION:

Clear the equation.

$$\dfrac{x}{\cancel{x-6}} \cdot \cancel{(x-6)} = 4(x-6)$$
$$x = 4(x-6)$$

Solve the derived equation.

$$x = 4x - 24$$
$$x - 4x = -24$$
$$-3x = -24$$
$$x = 8$$

CHECK:

$$\dfrac{x}{x-6} = \dfrac{8}{8-6} = \dfrac{8}{2} = 4$$

Example 3.3k

Solve $\dfrac{7}{x+2} = \dfrac{3}{x-6}$.

SOLUTION:

Here the l.c.d. is $(x+2)(x-6)$.

Clear the equation.

$$\dfrac{7}{\cancel{x+2}} \cdot \cancel{(x+2)}(x-6) = \dfrac{3}{\cancel{x-6}} \cdot (x+2)\cancel{(x-6)},$$
$$7(x-6) = 3(x+2)$$

Solve the derived equation.

$$7x - 42 = 3x + 6$$
$$7x - 3x = 42 + 6$$
$$4x = 48$$
$$x = 12$$

CHECK:

Substitute the x value in the original equation:

$$\text{Left side} = \dfrac{7}{x+2} = \dfrac{7}{12+2} = \dfrac{7}{14} = \dfrac{1}{2}$$
$$\text{Right side} = \dfrac{3}{x-6} = \dfrac{3}{12-6} = \dfrac{3}{6} = \dfrac{1}{2}$$

Example 3.31

A gasoline tank can be filled by one pipe in 2 hours, and drained by another pipe in 5 hours. How long will it take to fill the tank if the drain is left open?

SOLUTION:

Let x = the number of hours needed to fill the tank if the drain is left open.

The one pipe can fill $\frac{1}{2}x$ of the tank in x hours because it can fill $\frac{1}{2}$ of the tank each hour (or it can fill the entire tank in 2 hours). The other pipe can drain $\frac{1}{5}x$ of the tank in x hours because it can drain $\frac{1}{5}$ of the tank each hour (or it can drain the entire tank in 5 hours).

Thus, $\frac{1}{2}x - \frac{1}{5}x = 1$ (the capacity of the tank).
Solve the above equation. Here the l.c.d. is $(2)(5) = 10$.

$$\frac{x}{2} - \frac{x}{5} = 1$$

$$10\left(\frac{x}{2} - \frac{x}{5}\right) = 10(1)$$

$$5x - 2x = 10$$

$$3x = 10$$

$$x = \frac{10}{3} = 3\frac{1}{3} \text{ hours}$$

CHECK:

One pipe will fill $(\frac{1}{2})(3\frac{1}{3})$ tanks of gasoline in $3\frac{1}{3}$ hours, and the other pipe will drain $(\frac{1}{5})(3\frac{1}{3})$ tanks of gasoline in $3\frac{1}{3}$ hours. Thus, the amount which remains in the tank is the difference, or,

$$\left(\frac{1}{2}\right)\left(3\frac{1}{3}\right) - \left(\frac{1}{5}\right)\left(3\frac{1}{3}\right) = \frac{10}{6} - \frac{10}{15} = \frac{50}{30} - \frac{20}{30} = 1,$$

or, one tank full of gasoline.

EXERCISE 3.3 / REFERENCE SECTIONS: A–D

Simplify the following fractions to their lowest terms:

1. $\dfrac{52}{65}$

2. $\dfrac{252}{216}$

3. $\dfrac{4}{4a - 4b}$

4. $\dfrac{a + b}{5a + 5b}$

5. $\dfrac{x + y}{ax + ay + bx + by}$

6. $\dfrac{x^2 - 4}{(x + 2)(x + 1)}$

7. $\dfrac{4x + y^2}{16x^2 - y^4}$

8. $\dfrac{4ab - 32c}{a^2b^2 - 64c^2}$

9. $\dfrac{5x^2 + 35}{x^4 - 49}$

10. $\dfrac{12x - 12}{9x^2 - 18x + 9}$

11. $\dfrac{4x + 12}{x^2 + 6x + 9}$

12. $\dfrac{6a + 8b}{9a^2 + 24ab + 16b^2}$

Perform the following indicated operations and simplify:

13. $\dfrac{3x}{4} + \dfrac{x}{5}$

14. $\dfrac{5y}{7} + \dfrac{2y}{3}$

15. $\dfrac{5}{3x} + \dfrac{2}{4x}$

16. $\dfrac{3}{7y} + \dfrac{5}{4xy}$

17. $1 + \dfrac{a}{a + b}$

18. $\dfrac{4}{x + 2} + \dfrac{7}{x^2 + 3x + 2}$

19. $\dfrac{3}{4x + 2} + \dfrac{3x}{12x^2 + 10x + 2}$

20. $\dfrac{4x}{2 - x} + \dfrac{2}{3x - 4}$

21. $\dfrac{2x}{5} - \dfrac{x}{3}$

22. $\dfrac{5y}{4} - \dfrac{3y}{7}$

23. $\dfrac{3}{4x} - \dfrac{8}{6x}$

24. $\dfrac{4}{9y} - \dfrac{5}{3xy}$

25. $1 - \dfrac{a}{a + c}$

26. $\dfrac{15}{4x - 3} - \dfrac{3x}{20x^2 + 9x - 18}$

27. $\dfrac{-4}{5x - 6} - \dfrac{-9x}{-15x^2 + 28x - 12}$

28. $\dfrac{7}{6x^2 + x - 1} - \dfrac{3}{4x^2 - 1}$

29. $\dfrac{2a^3 b^4}{3x^2 y^4} \cdot \dfrac{9x^3 y^2}{8ab}$

30. $\dfrac{6x^2}{7y^2} \cdot \dfrac{5y}{4z} \cdot \dfrac{2z^2}{3x^3}$

31. $\dfrac{24m^2 n^3}{36x^2 y^3} \cdot \dfrac{12x^2 y^2}{6m^4 n}$

32. $\dfrac{9}{3x - 12} \cdot \dfrac{x - 4}{3}$

33. $\dfrac{x^2 y^3}{x^2 + 2xy + y^2} \cdot \dfrac{x + y}{x^3 y^4}$

34. $\dfrac{x^2 - y^2}{y^4} \cdot \dfrac{4y^2}{x - y}$

35. $\dfrac{6x^2 - 18x}{4x^2 - 1} \cdot \dfrac{4x^2 + 8x + 3}{12x^2 - 30x - 18}$

36. $\dfrac{2x - 8}{x^2 - 16} \cdot \dfrac{x^2 + x - 12}{x - 3}$

37. $\dfrac{4x - 10}{8x - 12} \div \dfrac{2x - 5}{2x - 3}$

38. $\dfrac{5x^2 y^3}{6x^3 y^4} \div \dfrac{4xy}{3xy^3}$

39. $\dfrac{6x^2 + 6xy}{2x - y} \div \dfrac{3x^2 - 3y^2}{6x^2 - y^2}$

40. $\dfrac{4x + 8}{8x - 8} \div \dfrac{8x + 16}{4x - 4}$

41. $\dfrac{10x^2 - 9x + 2}{15x - 6} \div \dfrac{5x^2 + 23x - 10}{3x + 15}$

42. $\dfrac{4 - x^2}{x^2 - 9} \div \dfrac{12 + 6x}{x^2 - 6x + 9}$

43. $\dfrac{x + \frac{2}{y^2}}{\frac{2 + x}{y^2}}$

44. $1 - \dfrac{1}{3 - \dfrac{1}{2 - \frac{1}{3}}}$

Solve for x:

45. $\dfrac{x}{3} + \dfrac{x}{6} = 21$

46. $\dfrac{x}{2} + \dfrac{2x}{5} = 18$

47. $\dfrac{2x}{x - 8} = 4$

48. $\dfrac{x}{x + 5} = \dfrac{3}{4}$

49. $\dfrac{x}{x - 8} = 5$

50. $\dfrac{4}{3 + x} = \dfrac{5}{8 + x}$

51. $\dfrac{6x + 3}{3} = \dfrac{7x - 2}{4}$ 56. $\dfrac{x + 3}{x + 12} = \dfrac{x - 5}{x - 4}$ 59. $\dfrac{a - b}{x} = \dfrac{b - c}{a + b}$

52. $\dfrac{x + 6}{x} = \dfrac{x - 9}{x - 6}$ 57. $\dfrac{x + 10}{x - 2} = \dfrac{x - 1}{x - 3}$ 60. $\dfrac{4}{3x - 3a} = \dfrac{a}{x^2 - a^2}$

53. $\dfrac{x + 1}{x + 3} = \dfrac{4}{3}$ 55. $\dfrac{x - 2}{x + 3} = \dfrac{x - 1}{x + 5}$

54. $\dfrac{x^2}{x - 4} = x - 2$ 58. $S = x(1 + in)$

Statement Problems:

61. The sum of two numbers is 80, and one number is $\frac{7}{9}$ of the other. Find the numbers.

62. Water leaking into an excavation would fill it in 3 hours. Leakage had occurred for $1\frac{1}{4}$ hours before a pump which could empty the entire excavation of water in 2 hours was brought into use. How long would it take the pump to empty the excavation in order to locate the source of the leakage?

63. Steve and Dale together can paint a house in 10 hours. If Dale can paint it by himself in 30 hours, how long would it take Steve to paint it alone?

64. A toy store purchased a shipment of toy guns for $4.20 a dozen. The store sold $\frac{5}{8}$ of the shipment at 48¢ each and the remainder at 3 for $1. The total profit was $9.00. How many of the toy guns were in this shipment?

65. The distances from a plant to Terminals A and B are equal. The driver to Terminal B travels 15 km/h faster than does the driver to Terminal A and takes 20 minutes for the trip. The driver to Terminal A takes 30 minutes for the trip. How far are the terminals from the plant?

66. A student answered correctly 80% of the problems in a test. Thirty-seven correct answers were made in the first 41 problems. Five out of every 8 answers were correct in the remaining problems. How many problems were in the test?

67. A small computer takes 15 hours to complete a set of calculations. Another computer can complete the set in 12 hours. After the two computers have worked on the job for 2 hours, a large computer, which working by itself, would complete the set in 5 hours, is brought into use. How much longer must all 3 computers work to complete the set of calculations?

68. Jack beat Bill by 16 kilometres and George by 32 kilometres in a 1 600 kilometre car race. If Bill and George kept their respective speeds until Bill finished, by how many kilometres did Bill beat George?

3.4. Graphs and Algebraic Equations

The method of graphic presentation of quantitative data is used frequently in analysing business and economic activities. Details of the method are presented in Chapter Six, which describes statistical methods. In this section the discussion concerning graphs emphasizes their use in solving a system of equations.

A. RECTANGULAR CO-ORDINATES

A graph is constructed according to the system of RECTANGULAR CO-ORDINATES. Rectangular co-ordinates are based on two straight reference lines perpendicular to each other in a plane, as shown in Figure 3-1. The horizontal line is usually referred to as the X-AXIS, or the ABSCISSA. The vertical line is referred to as the Y-AXIS, or the ORDINATE. The two lines divide the plane into four parts called QUADRANTS, which are numbered, I, II, III, and IV, as indicated in the chart. The point of intersection of the two lines is called the ORIGIN, which is usually regarded as the zero point. Scales, which begin at the point of origin, are placed along the horizontal and vertical axes. The scale is not necessarily the same for both axes, although use of the same scale is customarily preferred. The abscissas to the right of the origin are conventionally designated as *positive*, whereas those to the left of the origin are *negative*. The ordinates above the origin are positive and those below the origin are negative.

In the plane it is possible to describe the location of any point which refers to two variables. One is called the DEPENDENT VARIABLE and the other, the INDEPENDENT VARIABLE. The dependent variable is so called because its location depends upon the value of the independent variable; that is, once the value of the independent variable is fixed, the corresponding value of the dependent variable is determined from it according to an equation. The independent variable is usually placed on the X-axis and thus is also called the X-variable (or x). The dependent variable is usually placed on the Y-axis and is also called the Y-variable (or y).

Figure 3-1
Rectangular Co-ordinates

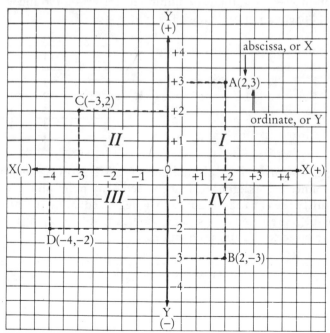

In placing a point on the plane for a set of corresponding X and Y values, first draw a line parallel to the Y-axis, starting at the X-axis at a distance equal to the X-value (abscissa). Second, draw a line parallel to the X-axis, starting at the Y-axis at a distance equal to the Y-value (ordinate), until it intersects the first line. The point of intersection is the desired answer. The abscissa and the ordinate at the point of intersection are called the CO-ORDINATES of the point.

For example, in Quadrant I of Figure 3-1, the abscissa of point A is 2, while the ordinate of A is 3. The values of 2 and 3 constitute the co-ordinates of A. It is customary to write the co-ordinates in parentheses and to separate them by a comma; the abscissa is written before the ordinate. Thus, (2,3) means that 2 is the abscissa and 3 is the ordinate of point A. Notice that the co-ordinates of B, C, and D, are also written in the same manner as those of A.

B.   DRAWING THE GRAPH OF AN EQUATION

The following example is used to illustrate the method of drawing the graph of an equation.

Example 3.4a
Draw a graph for each of the following two equations:
(a) $x + y = 4$ (b) $2x - y = 14$

SOLUTION:

(a)   In the equation $x + y = 4$, there are unlimited answers for x and y. For example, when $x = 1$, the equation becomes $1 + y = 4$, $y = 4 - 1 = 3$.

x	y
1	3
−8	12
10	−6

Here, only three pairs of the answers are arranged at the right side.

The three pairs of answers are plotted in Figure 3-2. Notice that when the three points are connected, straight line A is formed. Any point on the straight line, in turn, will satisfy the equation. Thus, a first-degree equation in one or two unknowns can be represented by a straight line. A first-degree equation is therefore frequently referred to as a linear equation.

(b)   In the equation $2x - y = 14$, there are also unlimited answers for the two unknowns, x and y. For example, when $x = 10$, the equation becomes $2(10) - y = 14$, $y = 20 - 14 = 6$. Theoretically, as illustrated in (a) above, a straight line representing a first-degree equation can be determined by knowing only two points. However, as a checking point, three pairs of answers are listed below.

The three points give the the straight line B in Figure 3-2.

x	y
10	6
8	2
1	−12

Figure 3-2
Graphic Solution of Two Linear Equations
(Example 3.4a)

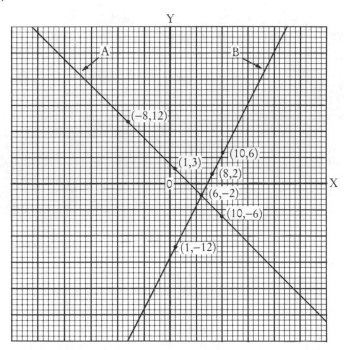

C.   GRAPHIC SOLUTION

Observe that in Figure 3-2 lines A and B intersect at the point (6, −2). The values, $x = 6$ and $y = -2$, thus satisfy both Equations (a) and (b). Therefore, the graphic method can be used to solve the problem of a pair of simultaneous linear equations in two unknowns. The graphic solution of the two equations above is checked as follows:

Substitute $x = 6$ and $y = -2$ in Equations (a) and (b).
Equation (a): $x + y = 4$, $6 + (-2) = 4$, $4 = 4$
Equation (b): $2x - y = 14$, $2(6) - (-2) = 14$, $14 = 14$

EXERCISE 3.4 / REFERENCE SECTIONS: A–C

Solve for x and y graphically:

1. $x + y = 8$	5. $x + 2y = -6$	9. $2x - y = 4$
$\quad 2x - y = 10$	$\quad 2x - y = 8$	$\quad 3x + y = 11$
2. $x - 2y = 9$	6. $x - y = 1$	10. $x + y = 10$
$\quad x + y = 3$	$\quad x + 2y = 13$	$\quad x - 3y = -6$
3. $2x + 3y = 17$	7. $3x + y = 6$	11. $x + y = -5$
$\quad 3x - 2y = 19$	$\quad 5x - y = 2$	$\quad 2x - 3y = 5$
4. $3x - y = 5$	8. $2x + 3y = 5$	12. $x - 2y = 2$
$\quad x + 4y = 19$	$\quad 4x - y = 17$	$\quad 3x + 2y = -18$

3.5. Business Applications: Linear Functions and Break-even Analysis

A. LINEAR FUNCTIONS

Two variables may have a relationship so that when a value is assigned to one variable, the corresponding value of the other variable is determined. For example, the cost of production bears a relationship to the number of units produced. Therefore, the cost of production is said to be a *function* of the number of units produced.

In the cost function,

Total Cost = fixed costs + unit variable cost × number of units produced.

TOTAL COST is the dependent variable since its value depends on the number of units produced, the independent variable.

A linear function in two variables is of the form

$y = a + bx$.

When the cost function is written in this form, y represents the total cost, and x represents the number of units produced (volume). In an analysis of the relationship between cost, profit and production, it is convenient to express cost and profit as a function of the number of units produced and to perform what is called break-even analysis.

In a study of the cost function, the total cost is expressed in terms of fixed cost and variable cost. FIXED COSTS are costs which do not vary when production varies. Among costs which are fixed are rent or lease payments for property or equipment, property taxes and mortgage or loan payments. These costs must be met regardless of the volume of production. VARIABLE COSTS are costs such as labor costs, shipping costs and cost of raw material which generally vary with the volume of production. Total cost is the sum of fixed cost and variable cost since all costs will be considered to fall in either of the two categories.

The relationship between cost, volume of production, and revenue is usually of interest in cost analysis. TOTAL REVENUE is a function of the number of units sold (volume).

The following functional relationships will be used in the discussion of break-even analysis which is presented in the next section:

Total Cost (TC) = fixed cost + unit variable cost × volume
Total Revenue (TR) = unit revenue × volume.

Example 3.5a
The variable cost of production of a toaster is $3.50 per unit and fixed costs for operating the factory are $82 000 per year.
(a)   Express the total cost as a function of the volume of production, and
(b)   find the total cost of producing 250 toasters.

SOLUTION:

(a)   Fixed cost = $82 000
        Variable cost = $3.50 per unit
            let x = number of units (volume)
                TC = total cost
        Then,
                TC = fixed cost + unit variable cost × volume
                TC = $82 000 + 3.50x$

(b)   Volume = 250
        Substitute 250 for x in the above equation:
                TC = $82 000 + $3.50(250)
                    = $82 875.00 (Total Cost)

Example 3.5b
Howard Manufacturing Company sells radial tires at $56 each.
(a)   Express the total annual revenue as a function of the sales volume, and
(b)   find the total revenue when 2 560 tires are sold.

SOLUTION:

(a)   Unit selling price = $56
        let x = sales volume
            TR = total revenue
        Then,
            TR = 56x

(b)   Sales volume = 2 560
        Substitute 2 560 for x in the above equation:
            TR = 56(2 560)
                = $143 360 (Total Revenue)

B.   BREAK-EVEN ANALYSIS

BREAK-EVEN ANALYSIS is a technique used to study the relationship between cost, production and profit. In break-even analysis, the number of units of production for which

Total Revenue = Total Cost

is of interest. At the BREAK-EVEN POINT, the fixed costs have been recovered and sales on units above the break-even point will result in a profit on each unit.

Among the types of decisions for which break-even analysis is used to provide insights are:

1. The number of units which must be produced in order that increase in revenue will be equal to increase in cost of production.
2. The number of units for which sales and production will be equal for two pieces of equipment with different capacity.
3. The time required for net revenue to be equal to investment.

The behavior of fixed cost and volume, variable cost and volume, and total cost and volume are illustrated in Figure 3.3.

Figure 3.3
Break-even charts

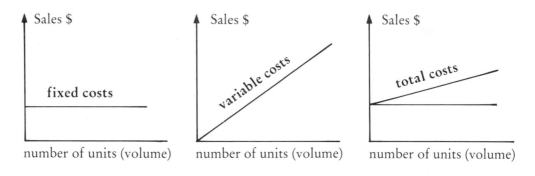

Example 3.5c
A computer manufacturing company must decide if it should introduce a new line of software which will require fixed annual cost allocation of $60 000 for plant facility, etc. Variable cost to cover wages, cost of material, etc., is estimated at $20 per unit. Each unit will sell for $120 and the plant capacity is 1 000 units per year.
(a)   Find the number of units which must be produced and sold in order to just cover cost, and
(b)   find the total revenue and total cost at break-even point.

SOLUTION:

Graphical solution:

Total costs = fixed costs + unit variable costs × number of units
Total revenue = unit price × number of units
Let x = number of units
  TC = total cost
  TR = total revenue
Fixed costs = $60 000
Variable costs = $20 per unit
  TC = $60 000 + 20$x$
  TR = 120x

Find the value of TC and TR for three values of x and graph the lines.

x	TC
200	64 000
400	68 000
700	74 000

x	TR
200	24 000
400	48 000
700	84 000

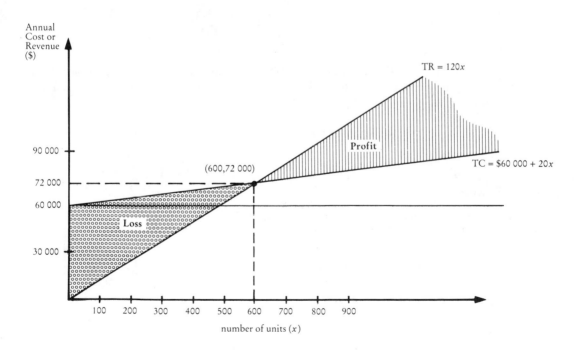

The lines cross at $x = 600$.

(a) The break-even point is at 600 units. That is, if 600 units are sold there is no profit and no loss. If less than 600 units are sold there is a loss and a profit will be realized if more than 600 units are sold.

(b) If 600 units are produced and sold, Total Revenue = Total Cost = \$72 000.

Algebraic solution:

(a) Break-even will occur when
TR = TC
or,
$120x = 60\ 000 + 20x$
$100x = 60\ 000$
$x = 600$

(b) When $x = 600$
$TC = 60\ 000 + 20x$
$= 60\ 000 + 20(600)$
$= \$72\ 000$
$TR = 120x$
$= 120(600)$
$= \$72\ 000$

Therefore, TC = TR.

Example 3.5d

The fixed annual costs of Ace Manufacturing Company are \$20 000 and variable costs are \$10 per unit. Each unit sells for \$30 and plant capacity is x number of units. Find the break-even point

(a) graphically, and (b) algebraically.

SOLUTION:

(a) Let x = number of units
Fixed costs = \$20 000
Variable costs = \$10x
TC = fixed costs + variable costs
$TC = 20\ 000 + 10x$
TR = price per unit × number of units
$TR = 30x$
Find the value of TC and TR for three values of x and graph the points.

x	TC
1 000	30 000
2 000	40 000
3 000	50 000

x	TR
1 000	30 000
2 000	60 000
3 000	90 000

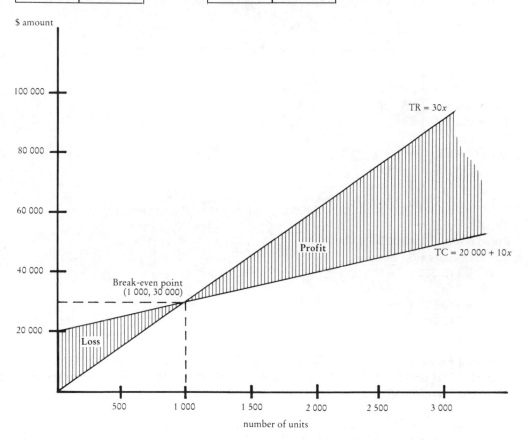

The lines intersect at $x = 1\ 000$. The break-even point is at 1 000 units. When 1 000 units are sold, the total revenue is equal to the total costs ($30 000).

(b)   TR = TC
$$30x = 20\ 000 + 10x$$
$$20x = 20\ 000$$
$$x = 1\ 000$$
For 1 000 units,
$$TR = 30(1\ 000) = \$30\ 000$$
$$TC = 20\ 000 + 10(1\ 000)$$
$$= 20\ 000 + 10\ 000$$
$$= \$30\ 000$$

Example 3.5e

A manager must decide between two packing machines for use in the manufacturing plant of his company. The units produced sell for $20 each and plant capacity is 200 000 units per year. The fixed annual costs for the single packer is $100 000 and variable costs for finishing etc., are $5 per unit. The fixed annual costs for dual packer is $110 000 and variable costs are $2. Which packer has a lower break-even point?

SOLUTION:

Determine which piece of equipment has the lower break-even point:

The single packer–
Fixed costs = $100 000
Variable costs = $5 per unit
$TC = 100\ 000 + 5x$
$TR = 20x$
Let $TC = TR$

$$20x = 100\ 000 + 5x$$
$$15x = 100\ 000$$
$$x = 6\ 666.67 \text{ or } 6\ 667 \text{units}$$

The dual packer–
Fixed costs = $110 000
Variable costs = $2 per unit
$$TC = 110\ 000 + 2x$$
$$TR = 20x$$
$$20x = 110\ 000 + 2x$$
$$18x = 110\ 000$$
$$x = 6\ 111.11 \text{ or at least } 6\ 112 \text{ units}$$

The dual packer has a lower break-even point. That is, 6 112 units must be produced with the dual packer to cover costs, while 6 667 units must be produced with the single packer to cover costs.

C. *FIXED COST AND UNIT CONTRIBUTION*

One method of arriving at the break-even volume of production is to consider the ratio of the fixed cost to the UNIT CONTRIBUTION. The unit contribution is the difference between the unit selling price and the unit variable cost. Thus,

$$\text{break-even quantity} = \frac{\text{fixed costs}}{\text{unit selling price–unit variable cost}}$$

$$= \frac{\text{fixed costs}}{\text{unit contribution}}.$$

Example 3.5f

The fixed costs of introducing a new product are estimated to be $4 200 per year. The variable costs of producing and selling one unit are estimated to be $38. Each unit produced can be sold for $52. Demand is a constant 600 units.

(a)   How many units must be produced to break-even?

(b)   What is the revenue at the break-even point?

SOLUTION:

(a)   Fixed costs = $4 200

Unit variable cost = $38

Unit selling price = $52

Unit contribution = $52 − $38 = $14

Break-even = $\frac{4200}{14}$ = 300 (units)

(b)   Total revenue at break-even = 52(300) = $15 600

CHECK:

Total costs = 4 200 + 38(300) = $15 600

Therefore, TC = TR.

This may be illustrated graphically by:

1.   graphing the line representing fixed costs;
2.   graphing the line representing break-even units;
3.   graphing the line representing revenue at break-even.

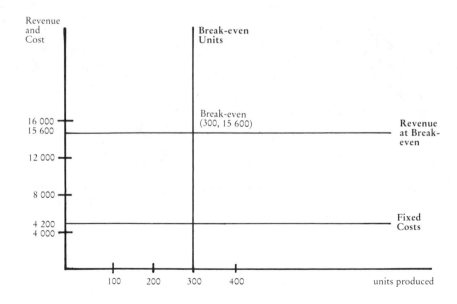

The total cost line can now be drawn by connecting the point (0, 4 200) with the break-even point.

The total revenue line is drawn by connecting (0, 0) with the break-even point.

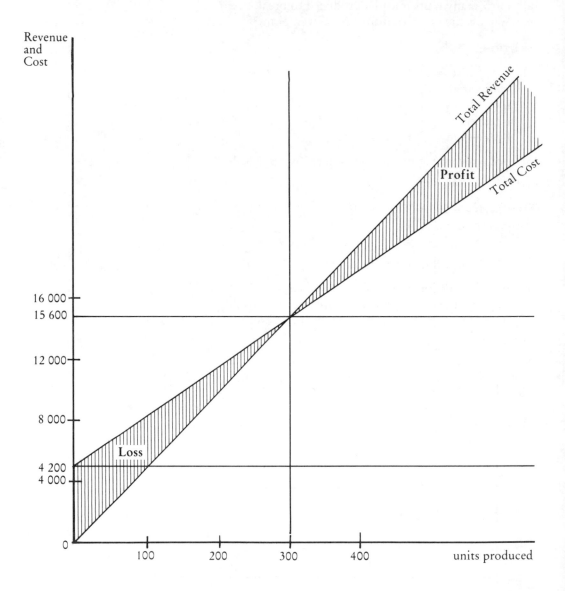

It is often necessary to examine the break-even point at various unit selling prices and unit variable costs.

Example 3.5g
Refer to Example 3.5f. What is the revenue at break-even for the following conditions:

	unit selling price	unit variable cost
(a)	$56	$38
(b)	$52	$40
(c)	$56	$40

SOLUTION:

(a) Fixed costs = $4 200
Unit variable cost = $38
Unit selling price = $56
Unit contribution = 56 − 38 = 18
Break-even = $\frac{4\ 200}{18}$ = 233.$\dot{3}$ (units)
Total revenue at break-even = 56(233.$\dot{3}$) = $13 066.67

(b) Fixed costs = $4 200
Unit variable cost = $40
Unit selling price = $52
Unit contribution = 52 − 40 = 12
Break-even = $\frac{4\ 200}{12}$ = 350 (units)
Total revenue at break-even = 52(350) = $18 200

(c) Fixed costs = $4 200
Unit variable cost = $40
Unit selling price = $56
Unit contribution = 56 − 40 = 16
Break-even = $\frac{4\ 200}{16}$ = 262.5 (units)
Total revenue at break-even = 56(262.5) = $14 700

From Examples 3.5f and 3.5g, the following schedule may be completed:

unit price	unit variable cost	break-even units	revenue at break-even
$52	$38	300	$15 600.00
$56	$38	233.$\dot{3}$	$13 066.67
$52	$40	350	$18 200.00
$56	$40	262.5	$14 700.00

The amount of profit may be found by subtracting the revenue at break-even quantity from the revenue at the demand quantity.

unit price	demand quantity	revenue at demand quantity	PROFIT revenue at demand quantity– revenue at break-even
$52	600	$31 200	$15 600.00
$56	600	$33 600	$20 533.33
$52	600	$31 200	$13 000.00
$56	600	$33 600	$18 900.00

It should be noted that demand may be sensitive to price and thus it is unrealistic to expect a constant demand in many cases. To determine the maximum profit break-even at each unit price must be compared with market demand.

EXERCISE 3.5 / REFERENCE SECTIONS: A–C

For each of the following, express (a) total cost as a function of the number of units produced, and (b) total revenue as a function of the number of units sold:

	Unit Variable Cost	Fixed Costs	Unit Selling Price
1.	$ 8	$ 52 000	$12
2.	$ 7.50	$ 32 000	$11.95
3.	$11.25	$ 62 000	$15.50
4.	$52.00	$168 000	$74.00

For each of the following, calculate the break-even point (a) graphically, (b) algebraically, and (c) using the ratio of fixed costs to unit contribution:

	Unit Variable Cost	Fixed Costs	Unit Selling Price
5.	$5	$18 000	$ 9.50
6.	40% of unit selling price	$14 000	$10.00
7.	60% of unit selling price	$12 000	$18.00
8.	$5	$60 000	$ 8.50

Statement Problems:

9. The variable cost of production of white-wall tires is $16.95 each and the fixed cost of plant operation is $82 000. Express total cost as a function of number of units produced.

10. In Problem 9, the selling price of one tire is $59. Express the total revenue as a function of the number of units sold.

11. Fran's Manufacturing Company sells its desk lamps for $15 each. Variable cost of production is $6 per unit and fixed cost per year is $12 500. The plant capacity is 2 000 units per year. (a) Express total cost as a function of units produced, and (b) express total revenue as a function of units sold.

12. From the following break-even chart, determine:
    (a) total cost at the break-even point.
    (b) total revenue at the break-even point.
    (c) the number of units which must be sold to break-even.
    (d) the new break-even point if fixed costs are increased by $5 000.

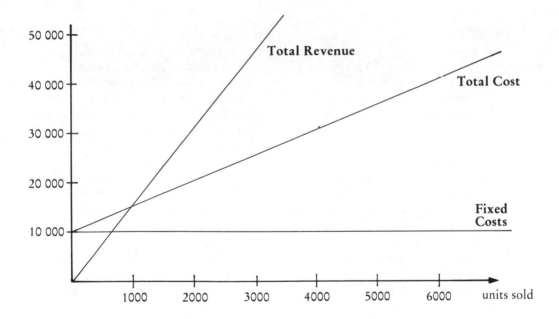

13. The Buildall Company is introducing a new line of stained glass window fittings which will require new equipment and plant facility estimated at $30 000 per year. Variable cost per unit is estimated at $30 and each unit sells for $50. The proposed facility will be able to manufacture 2 000 units per year. How many units must be sold to break even?

14. The recreation committee at St. John's Church is putting on a Christmas dinner to raise funds. They will incur a fixed cost of $500 for the hall and it is estimated that the cost of food, plates and door prizes, etc., will be $5 per dinner. The hall can accommodate 1 000 people. Tickets to the dinner sell at $20 each. How many tickets must they sell to break even?

15. The Jones Company have the following estimates with reference to a jogging suit which they plan to introduce:

Fixed Costs $ 50 000
Variable cost per unit $ 18
Estimated sales volume $100 000
Price per unit $ 40

Find the break-even sales volume.

16. A company has a fixed cost of $28 000 and variable cost of $25 per unit. How many units at $40 each, must be sold in order to break-even.

17. A chair manufacturer has fixed costs of $20 000 and unit variable costs of $20. If the selling price is $50 per chair, how many chairs must he sell to break even?

Glossary

ABSCISSA the *x* co-ordinate of a point

BREAK-EVEN ANALYSIS a technique used to study the relationship between cost, production and profit

BREAK-EVEN POINT the point at which there is neither a loss, nor a profit; the point at which the fixed costs have been recovered; the point at which total cost is equal to total revenue

CLEARING the procedure to derive an equation that will contain no fractions

CONDITIONAL EQUATION an equation for which both sides are equal for only definite values of the letters involved

CO-ORDINATES the abscissa and the ordinate at the point of intersection

DEGREE the number of powers of the single unknown value in an equation

DEPENDENT EQUATIONS two equations that can be reduced to the same form

DEPENDENT VARIABLE a variable whose value depends upon the value of the independent variable

EQUATION a statement which indicates that two algebraic expressions are equal

EXTRANEOUS ROOTS solutions which are not solutions of the original equations

FIXED COSTS costs incurred that do not change when volume of production changes, such as rental costs, property taxes, etc.

INCONSISTENT EQUATIONS two linear equations in two unknowns for which there is no common solution

IDENTICAL EQUATION an equation whose two sides are equal for any value that may be substituted

IDENTITY see *identical equation*

INDEPENDENT EQUATION two linear equations in two unknowns, with only one solution for each unknown that satisfies both equations

INDEPENDENT SIMULTANEOUS EQUATION see *independent equation*

INDEPENDENT VARIABLE the fixed value placed on the X-axis

LINEAR EQUATIONS equations of the first power

MEMBER one part of an equation

ORDINATE the y co-ordinate of a point

ORIGIN the point of intersection of the vertical and horizontal axes in a plane

QUADRANTS the four parts into which a plane is divided by the vertical and horizontal axes

RECTANGULAR CO-ORDINATES co-ordinates based on two straight reference lines perpendicular to each other on a plane

ROOT the value which satisfies an equation

SIDE see *member*

SOLUTION see *root*

SYSTEM OF EQUATIONS a group of two or more equations

TOTAL COST the sum of fixed costs and variable costs

TOTAL REVENUE a function of the number of units sold which equals the unit revenue times the volume

UNIT CONTRIBUTION the difference between the unit selling price and the unit variable cost

UNKNOWN the letter or letters whose value is desired

VARIABLE COSTS costs incurred that are variable, such as costs of material, labor, etc.

X-AXIS see *abscissa*

Y-AXIS see *ordinate*

4 Ratio, proportion, variation and percent

Introduction

In certain business decisions, a comparison of two or more quantities is often involved. It is sometimes convenient to state such a comparison in the form of a RATIO. When the equality of two ratios is expressed, the statement is called a PROPORTION.

A knowledge of the meaning of a ratio and a proportion is essential in business communications. For example, a ratio may be set up to compare the sales volume of one time period to the sales volume of a previous time period. Such a comparison may show an increase or a decrease in sales volume. An index such as the *Consumer Price Index* is essentially a ratio comparing the cost of living in one time period to the cost of living in a previous time period, expressed as a percent.

Business decisions often involve allocation of costs, profits, space and other resources. Distribution of such resources involves the use of proportions.

Chapter Four covers the formulation of ratios, proportions, direct and indirect variation, computations involving percent and percentages and their application to business.

4.1 Ratio

A. MEANING OF RATIO

Numbers may be compared in various ways. One convenient way is to express the comparison according to the relative values of the things being compared instead of stating the actual values. For example, in one city there are 220 000 women and 110 000 men.

Since $\dfrac{220\,000 \text{ women}}{110\,000 \text{ men}} = \dfrac{2 \text{ women}}{1 \text{ man}}$, it is more convenient to state that the number of women compared with the number of men is 2 to 1, which are relatives values, instead of saying 220 000 to 110 000, which are actual values.

Ratio is a way of expressing the relative values of various things. Thus, the comparison above may also be indicated as: "the ratio of the number of women to the number of men in the city is 2 to 1," which may be written $2:1$.

Generally, when two numbers are expressed in ratio form, the ratio is the quotient of the two numbers. When a number, called the *first term*, is divided by another number, called the *second term*, the quotient is the ratio of the first term to the second term. This relationship may be written as follows:

Ratio of the first term to the second term = the first term : the second term

$$= \frac{\text{the first term}}{\text{the second term}}.$$

Thus, the ratio of a to b is expressed as $a:b$, or $\frac{a}{b}$ or $a \div b$. The ratio of b to a is expressed as $b:a$, or $\frac{b}{a}$ or $b \div a$. The ratio of 2 to 10 is $2:10$ or $\frac{2}{10}$; whereas, the ratio of 10 to 2 is $10:2$, or $\frac{10}{2}$.

Since a ratio may be expressed as a fraction, the rules applying to fractions likewise apply to ratios. For convenience, the fraction may be converted to its lowest terms. Thus, $\frac{2}{10}$ may be converted to $\frac{1}{5}$, and the ratio of 2 to 10 is equal to the ratio of 1 to 5, or $2:10 = 1:5$. The quotient of the fraction is sometimes converted to a decimal or a whole number. The quotient then represents the value of the first term, and the value of the second term is always considered to be 1. In the above example, the ratio of 2 to 10 may be expressed as .2, which has the same meaning as the ratio of .2 to 1; and the ratio of 10 to 2 may be expressed as 5, which has the same meaning as the ratio of 5 to 1. A ratio of an improper fraction in its lowest terms is usually not converted to a mixed number.

When more than two relative values are expressed in ratio form, the ratios of the values may be written in separate form or in combined form. For example, assume that the relative values of three things, A, B, and C are 2, 3, and 4 respectively. If A = 2, then B = 3, and C = 4; if one of them is doubled, then the others are also doubled; if one of them is tripled, then the others are also tripled; and so on. Thus, if A = 4 (or 2 × 2), then B = 6 (or 3 × 2), and C = 8 (or 4 × 2). The relationships may be expressed individually as $A:B = 2:3$, $B:C = 3:4$, $A:C = 2:4$, or written in combined form as follows: $A:B:C = 2:3:4$, where

$2:3:4 = (2 \times 2):(3 \times 2):(4 \times 2)$
$\qquad = (2 \times 3):(3 \times 3):(4 \times 3)$ and so on, or
$A:B:C = 2:3:4 = 4:6:8 = 6:9:12$ and so on.

In other words, if each term of the ratio in combined form is multiplied (or divided) by the same number, other than zero, the value of the ratio does not change.

Ratios are important in measurement, for basically every measurement is a ratio; for example, the statement that the length of a desk to the unit of length used, a metre, is $2:1 = \frac{2}{1} = 2$. Here, the answer means that the length of the desk is 2 metres or 2 times 1 metre. However, if the unit of length used is a centimetre, since 2 metres equals 200 centimetres, the ratio thus is $200:1 = \frac{200}{1} = 200$, in which case the length of the desk becomes 200 centimetres and is 200 times the length used.

To determine the ratio of the length of this desk to a book shelf 500 millimetres in length, their measurements must be expressed in the same unit when dividing. If the unit of measurement is a centimetre, the ratio is obtained as follows:

200(centimetres) : 50(centimetres) $= \frac{200}{50} = 4$, since 500 millimetres (the length of the book shelf) equals 50 centimetres (or $\frac{500}{10} = 50$).

If the unit of measurement is a millimetre, the same answer may be obtained by computing as follows:

2 000(millimetres) : 500(millimetres) $= \frac{2\ 000}{500} = 4$, since 2 metres (the length of the desk) equals 2 000 millimetres (or $2 \times 1\ 000 = 2\ 000$).

The answer indicates that the length of the desk is 4 times the length of the book shelf. In these examples, the quantities compared are of the same kind, the length. When numbers of the same kind are compared, the ratio is always ABSTRACT.

There are also ratios of different kinds of quantities. For example, if a carpenter makes 10 chairs in 5 days, the ratio of chairs produced to the time consumed is expressed as 10 chairs : 5 days, which may be written $\frac{10\ \text{chairs}}{5\ \text{days}} = \frac{2\ \text{chairs}}{1\ \text{day}} = 2$ chairs/day, or simply 2. However, when the number 2 is written, it is understood that the ratio indicates the carpenter's average speed; that is, he can make 2 chairs each day during that time.

B.   ALLOCATION OF A NUMBER ACCORDING TO RATIO

To perform the ALLOCATION or division of a number into parts according to a ratio, consider the sum of the terms of the ratio as a unit for dividing. For example, if a number is to be divided into parts A and B according to a ratio of 2 : 3 respectively, consider the sum of the terms of the ratio, 5 (or 2 + 3), as the unit for dividing. From each unit, A gets 2 shares and B gets 3 shares. In other words, A gets 2 out of every 5 and B gets 3 out of every 5. If the number to be divided is 100, the value of A is computed as follows:

100 ÷ 5 = 20 (units); 20 × 2 = 40; or it may be written as

$100 \times \dfrac{2}{5} = 40.$

The value of B is computed as follows:

100 ÷ 5 = 20 (units); 20 × 3 = 60; or it may be written as

$100 \times \dfrac{3}{5} = 60.$

The value of B may also be computed by subtracting the value of A from the number to be divided; thus, 100 − A = 100 − 40 = 60. The answer may be checked as follows:

$A\ :\ B = 40 : 60 = \dfrac{40}{60} = \dfrac{2}{3} = 2 : 3;$

$A + B = 40 + 60 = 100.$

In general, to allocate or divide a number into parts according to ratio, use the following procedure. To obtain the first part, multiply the number by the fraction whose denominator is the sum of the terms of the ratio and whose numerator is the first term of the ratio. To obtain the second part, use the second term of the ratio as the numerator of the fraction. The following examples further illustrate the problems involved in dividing a number according to ratio.

Example 4.1a
Divide 45 into three parts in the ratio $2:3:4$.

SOLUTION:

$2 + 3 + 4 = 9$

$$45 \times \frac{2}{9} = 10$$

$$45 \times \frac{3}{9} = 15$$

$$45 \times \frac{4}{9} = 20$$

The three parts are 10, 15, and 20.

CHECK:

$10 + 15 + 20 = 45$

$$10:15:20 = \frac{10}{5}:\frac{15}{5}:\frac{20}{5}: = 2:3:4$$

Example 4.1b
Five Elements Inc. has an advertising budget of $90 000 for this year. This amount is to be allocated among three departments according to the sales volume for the last month. The sales for last month are as follows:

Department 1	2 000 units
Department 2	3 500 units
Department 3	4 500 units

How much should be allocated to each department?

SOLUTION:

$90 000 must be divided according to the ratio 2 000 : 3 500 : 4 500.

$2\,000 + 3\,500 + 4\,500 = 10\,000$

Department 1 gets: $\dfrac{2\,000}{10\,000} \times 90\,000 = \$18\,000$

Department 2 gets: $\dfrac{3\,500}{10\,000} \times 90\,000 = \$31\,500$

Department 3 gets: $\dfrac{4\,500}{10\,000} \times 90\,000 = \$40\,500$

CHECK:

$18 000 + $31 500 + $40 500 = $90 000
18 000 : 31 500 : 40 500 = 2 000 : 3 500 : 4 500
Note: the ratio 2 000 : 3 500 : 4 500 = 4 : 7 : 9.

Example 4.1c
$510 is to be divided among A, B, and C in the ratio of $\frac{1}{2}$, $\frac{2}{3}$ and $\frac{1}{4}$ respectively. How much should each receive?

SOLUTION:

First, convert each term of the given ratio to have a common denominator. Here the l.c.d. is 12. If each term of the converted ratio is multiplied by 12, the value of the ratio does not change. Thus,

$$\frac{1}{2} : \frac{2}{3} : \frac{1}{4} = \frac{6}{12} : \frac{8}{12} : \frac{3}{12} = 6 : 8 : 3.$$

According to the ratio $6 : 8 : 3$, the amount is divided as follows:

$6 + 8 + 3 = 17.$

A's share $= 510 \times \dfrac{6}{17} = \$180$

B's share $= 510 \times \dfrac{8}{17} = \$240$

C's share $= 510 \times \dfrac{3}{17} = \$\ 90$

CHECK:

$180 + 240 + 90 = 510$

$$180 : 240 : 90 = \frac{180}{30} : \frac{240}{30} : \frac{90}{30} = 6 : 8 : 3$$

Thus, to allocate a number in fractional ratio (such as $\frac{1}{2} : \frac{2}{3} : \frac{1}{4}$), convert the given fractions to fractions with their lowest common denominator ($\frac{6}{12} : \frac{8}{12} : \frac{3}{12}$); then use the numerators ($6 : 8 : 3$) as the ratio in allocating the number.

EXERCISE 4.1 / REFERENCE SECTIONS: A–B

Express the ratios of the following in fractional form and convert them to their lowest terms:

1. 30 to 5
2. 4 to 28
3. 21 to 32
4. 52 to 14
5. $8\frac{2}{3}$ to $5\frac{1}{4}$
6. $6\frac{5}{12}$ to $12\frac{5}{6}$

7. 1.59 to 9.15
8. 6.5 to 2.5
9. 130 kilometres to 4 hours

10. 32 minutes to 8 hours
11. 20 dollars to 5 days
12. 50 grams to 1 kilogram

Statement Problems:

13. Company A has current assets of $26 000 and current liabilities of $16 000. Company B has current assets of $40 000 and current liabilities of $30 000. What is the ratio of the current assets to the current liabilities of Company A? Company B? Which of the two ratios is higher?
14. Last year George's income was $16 000. There were 6 persons in his family. John's income was $18 000. There were 10 persons in his family. (a) Find the ratios of their respective annual income to the size of their families. (b) According to the size of the families, whose income per person was larger?
15. A retail store sold an article for $40. The cost of the article sold is $25, the total amount of other expenses is $5, and the remaining part is the profit. Find the ratios of (a) the cost to the selling price, (b) the total amount of other expenses to the selling price, and (c) the profit to the selling price.
16. Refer to Problem 15. Find the ratios of the following: (a) the total of other expenses to the cost and (b) the profit to the cost.
17. Divide 240 into two numbers in the ratio $1:3$.
18. Divide 300 into two numbers in the ratio $3:5$.
19. Divide 648 into three numbers in the ratio $2:3:7$.
20. Divide 680 into three numbers in the ratio $4:5:8$.
21. Divide 1 020 into four numbers in the ratio $2:3:5:7$.
22. Divide 720 into four numbers in the ratio $1:4:5:8$.
23. Divide 7 688 into three numbers in the ratio $2\frac{3}{4}:\frac{5}{7}:3\frac{2}{5}$.
24. Divide 2 040 into three numbers in the ratio $\frac{2}{7}:\frac{3}{8}:\frac{1}{4}$.
25. A man divides his estate of $38 500 among his four sons in the ratio $\frac{1}{2}:\frac{1}{3}:\frac{1}{4}:\frac{1}{5}$. How much does each son receive?
26. Four partners, A, B, C, and D, agree to share profits in the ratio of $\frac{1}{2},\frac{2}{3},\frac{1}{4}$ and $\frac{2}{5}$ respectively. This year the partnership has a profit of $4 360. How much does each partner receive?
27. The fixed costs of Allen Chemicals were distributed over four departments based on the total of the direct and indirect labor costs for each department. This was done on a monthly basis and for the month of August the relevant data were: Total fixed costs for August, $13 145.

Dept.	$ direct labor	$ indirect labor
A	36 412	1 725
B	28 860	1 214
C	19 720	1 009
D	25 851	1 115

Allocate the fixed costs on the basis indicated above.

28. Swinger Fashions has four plants located in Montreal, Toronto, Winnipeg and Vancouver. The company's head office is located in Toronto and head office costs are allocated to each plant on the basis of inventory plus book value of fixed assets for each plant. The relevant data was as shown:
Total head office costs = $485 000.

Location	Inventory plus book value of fixed assets
Montreal	2 853 200
Toronto	3 418 500
Winnipeg	2 148 100
Vancouver	2 750 000

Allocate the costs of the head office operation over the four plants.

29. Hi Style, which specializes in imported clothing, has three boutique type operations at different locations in Toronto. The overhead costs are allocated to the three boutiques on the basis of average payroll in each store. If the 1983 overhead costs amounted to $128 000, determine how much would be allocated to each store based on the following information:

Store Location	Annual Payroll
Bloor Street	66 500
Sherway Gardens	87 250
Yorkdale Plaza	54 600

30. The fixed costs of Trendwear Ltd. were distributed over four departments based on the sum of the direct and indirect labor cost for each department. This allocation was applied to the fixed costs on a monthly basis. The fixed cost for the month of August was $18 840. Allocate this cost on the basis of this information:

Dept.	Direct Labor	Indirect Labor
Sportswear	41 518	2 015
Ladieswear	39 293	1 908
Menswear	38 430	1 869
Childrenswear	40 093	1 967

4.2 *Proportion*

A. *BASIC COMPUTATIONS*

A proportion is a statement of the equality of two ratios. For example, $2:10 = 1:5$; or $\frac{2}{10} = \frac{1}{5}$, is a proportion. Thus, $a:b = c:d$, or $a/b = c/d$, is also a proportion. It is read

"a is to b as c is to d," or "the ratio of a to b is equal to the ratio of c to d." The letters, a, b, c, and d are the terms of the proportion; a and d are the EXTREMES; b and c are the MEANS.

Since proportions are equations, the rules and operations of equations also apply to proportions. For example, if both sides of the proportion $\frac{a}{b} = \frac{c}{d}$ are multiplied by bd, the common denominator, the answer is $\frac{a}{b} \cdot bd = \frac{c}{d} \cdot bd$, or $ad = bc$. The answer indicates that by cross multiplication of the terms in the proportion, the two products are equal. The answer is diagrammed as follows:

$$\frac{a}{b} \diagdown = \diagup \frac{c}{d}; \ ad = bc.$$

Since the proportion may be written in the form $a : b = c : d$, the answer also indicates that the product of the extremes (ad) equals the product of the means (bc). When any three of the four terms in a proportion are given, the other unknown term can always be found by this relationship. Proportion thus may be used in solving many types of problems in business and is referred to frequently in the forthcoming chapters. The following examples illustrate some uses of proportions in various types of problems.

Example 4.2a
Solve for x. $13 : 4 = 52 : x$

SOLUTION:

Multiply the extremes and the means:
$13 : 4 = 52 : x$
$13x = 4 \cdot 52 = 208$
$x = \dfrac{208}{13} = 16$

Example 4.2b

Solve for x. $\dfrac{28}{7} = \dfrac{x}{5}$

SOLUTION:

Use cross multiplication:
$\dfrac{28}{7} \diagdown = \diagup \dfrac{x}{5}; \ 7x = 28 \cdot 5 = 140;$
$x = \dfrac{140}{7} = 20$

Example 4.2c
Solve for x.
$x : \dfrac{3}{4} = \dfrac{1}{5} : \dfrac{9}{11}$

SOLUTION:

$$\frac{9}{11}x = \left(\frac{3}{4}\right)\left(\frac{1}{5}\right); \ x = \frac{(\frac{3}{4})(\frac{1}{5})}{\frac{9}{11}} = \frac{\frac{3}{20}}{\frac{9}{11}}$$

$$\left(\frac{3}{20}\right)\left(\frac{11}{9}\right) = \frac{11}{60}$$

Example 4.2d

A grocery store charges $2.80 for 5 dozen oranges. How much will it charge for 18 dozen oranges?

SOLUTION:

Let y be the price of the 18 dozen oranges. Thus, the problem may be stated in proportional language as follows:

$2.80 is to 5 dozen as y is to 18 dozen oranges, which may be written:

$$\frac{2.80}{5 \text{ dozen}} = \frac{y}{18 \text{ dozen}}, \text{ or simply,} \frac{2.80}{5} = \frac{y}{18};$$

$$5y = (2.80)(18); \ y = \frac{(2.80)(18)}{5} = \$10.08$$

Example 4.2e

When a tree casts a shadow 730 centimetres long, the shadow of a boy 168 centimetres tall is 250 centimetres long. How high is the tree?

SOLUTION:

The ratio of the boy's height to his shadow equals the ratio of the tree's height to its shadow. Let x = the height of the tree. Thus,

boy   tree

$$\frac{168}{250} = \frac{x}{730}; \ 250x = (168)(730); \ x = \frac{(168)(730)}{250} = 490.56 \text{ (cm)}$$

EXERCISE 4.2 / REFERENCE SECTION: A

Solve for x in each of the following proportions:

1. $\dfrac{x}{6} = \dfrac{7}{12}$

2. $\dfrac{52}{x} = \dfrac{2}{5}$

3. $\dfrac{x}{8} = \dfrac{7}{15}$

4. $\dfrac{2}{7} = \dfrac{x}{34}$

5. $\dfrac{30}{x} = \dfrac{3}{16}$

6. $\dfrac{24.84}{27} = \dfrac{x}{5}$

7. $\dfrac{21.35}{28} = \dfrac{30.5}{x}$

8. $\dfrac{62}{73} = \dfrac{36}{x}$

9. $4:14 = x:9$

10. $15:x = 10:32$

11. $3:15 = x:32$

12. $x:6 = 9:21$

13. $19 : x = 30 : 65$

14. $\dfrac{5}{4} : \dfrac{6}{7} = \dfrac{5}{6} : x$

15. $x : \dfrac{3}{7} = \dfrac{2}{3} : \dfrac{6}{7}$

16. $15 : 5 = 9 : x$

Statement Problems:

17. A car runs 91 kilometres on 13 litres of gasoline. How far will it run on 22.5 litres?
18. A man can plow 6 hectares in 4 days. How much time is needed to plow 30 hectares?
19. If 60 metres of cloth cost $50, what will 210 metres cost?
20. If 130 kilograms of corn cost $52, what will 220 kilograms cost?
21. When a building casts a shadow 1 378 centimetres long, the shadow of a man 182 centimetres tall is 106 centimetres. Find the height of the building.
22. The scale of a map is 1.5 centimetres for 300 kilometres. How many kilometres are represented by 5 centimetres?
23. If a seamstress is paid at the rate of $18.50 per dress completed, how much does she receive after completing 12 dresses?
24. The B. B. Candy Store bought 560 boxes of candy at 45¢ a box. How much is the total cost?
25. If a plane travels 32 kilometres in 16 minutes, how long will it take to travel 200 kilometres?
26. If a field containing 14 hectares yields 1 434 kilograms of wheat, how much will a field containing 42 hectares yield?
27. If 25 men build 30 cubic metres of brick wall in one day, how many men will be needed to build 76.8 cubic metres of brick wall in one day?
28. If a pile of wood containing 8 cubic metres costs $94, how much will a pile containing 140 cubic metres cost?

4.3 Variation

A. DIRECT VARIATION

When the quantity of one thing increases as the quantity of another thing increases, the variation is direct. In DIRECT VARIATION, the ratio of one thing to another is constant and their changes are proportional to each other.

Example 4.3a
Refer to Example 4.2d.

SOLUTION:

The total price for a certain number of dozens of oranges increases as the number of dozens of oranges increases. However, the ratio of the total price to the corresponding number of dozens of oranges sold is a constant:

$$\frac{\$2.80}{5}\text{doz.} = \frac{\$10.08}{18}\text{doz.} = \$\,.56 \text{ per dozen.}$$

If the relationship between two variables, x and y, can be expressed as:

$$\frac{y}{x} = k$$

where k is a constant, or

$$\frac{x_1}{x_2} = \frac{y_1}{y_2}$$

we say that y varies directly as x.

In Example 4.2d,

$$\frac{\text{Selling Price}}{\text{number of dozens}} = \frac{\text{Selling Price}}{\text{number of dozens}} = \$\,.56.$$

This relationship can also be expressed as:

$y = kx$
$y =$ Selling Price, and
$x =$ number of dozens.

Then,

Selling Price = $\$\,.56 \times$ number of dozens
or,
$y = .56x$
and when $x = 5$ dozens, then $y = .56 \times 5 = 2.80$.

The above problem is illustrated below:

x	y
5	2.80
8	4.48
10	5.60

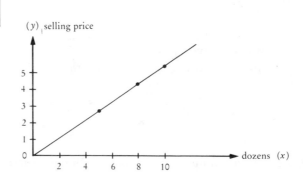

Example 4.3b

Refer to Example 4.2e and find the length of the tree's shadow.

SOLUTION:

Let x = the height of the tree (490.56 cm)

y = the length of the tree's shadow

$$k = \frac{\text{length of shadow of boy}}{\text{height of boy}} = \frac{250}{168} \text{ cm} = 1.488\ 095\ 2$$

$y = kx$

$y = 1.488\ 095\ 2x$

$y = 1.488\ 095\ 2(490.56)$

$y = 730$ cm

The above problem is illustrated below:

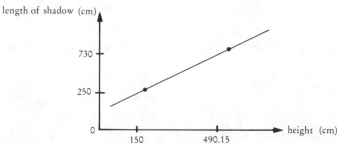

B. **INDIRECT VARIATION**

When the quantity of one thing decreases as the quantity of another thing increases, the variation is indirect or inverse. In INDIRECT VARIATION, the relationship between two variables, x and y, can be expressed as:

$$y = \frac{k}{x} \text{ where } k \text{ is a constant.}$$

In indirect variation, the value of y is some constant value times the value of $\frac{1}{x}$.

That is, $\dfrac{y_2}{y_1} = \dfrac{x_1}{x_2}$ or $y_2 = \dfrac{x_1 y_1}{x_2}$.

Example 4.3c

y varies inversely as x. If $y = 6$ when $x = 4$, what is the value of y when $x = 5$?

SOLUTION:

$x_1 = 4, x_2 = 5; y_1 = 6, y_2 = ?$

$\dfrac{y_2}{y_1} = \dfrac{x_1}{x_2}$

$\dfrac{y_2}{6} = \dfrac{4}{5}$

$y_2 = \dfrac{4(6)}{5} = 4.8$

when $x = 5$, $y = 4.8$

Example 4.3d
If it takes 8 men 12 days to complete a job, how long will it take 15 men to complete the same job?

SOLUTION:

let x = number of men
  y = number of days
then, $x_1 = 8, x_2 = 15$
  $y_1 = 12, y_2 = ?$

$$\frac{y_2}{12} = \frac{8}{15}$$

$$y_2 = \frac{8(12)}{15} = 6.4$$

Example 4.3e
If y varies inversely as x when x is increased by 25%, what change will occur in y?

SOLUTION:

$$x_1 = 100\%, x_2 = 125\%$$

$$\frac{y_2}{y_1} = \frac{x_1}{x_2}$$

$$y_2 = \frac{x_1}{x_2}y_1$$

$$y_2 = \frac{100}{125}y_1$$

$$y_2 = .8y_1$$

or, y_2 is 80% of y_1
therefore, y is decreased by 20%.

EXERCISE 4.3 / REFERENCE SECTIONS: A–B

Solve for the unknown variable and indicate the type of variation:

1. $\dfrac{x_1}{x_2} = \dfrac{y_1}{y_2}$ $x_1 = 2.5, x_2 = 7.2, y_2 = 11$

2. $y = kx$ $k = 3.8, x = 11.2$

3. $\dfrac{x_1}{x_2} = \dfrac{y_2}{y_1}$ $x_1 = 9.3, x_2 = 7.4, y_2 = 15.1$

4. $y = \dfrac{k}{x}$ $x = 19.8, y = 16.2$

Statement Problems:

5. Two workers can complete a job in 116 hours. How long will it take 5 workers working at the same pace?

6. It costs $15 to purchase grapes to make 1.5 litres of juice. How much will it cost to purchase grapes to make 7.8 litres of juice?

7. If the price of a certain item varies directly as the demand, how will the price change if the demand increases by 20%?
8. If 30 men can complete a job in 7 days, how many men will be needed to complete the same job in 11 days?
9. If the volume of stocks traded bears an inverse relationship to a price index, when the price index increases by 10%, what change will occur in the volume of stocks traded?
10. If it takes 16 days to complete a job with 3 machines, how many days will it take with 5 machines of the same type?
11. A study has shown that sick days at a certain plant varies inversely as prevention costs. If the number of sick days reported is 89 when the prevention cost is $33, what will be the prevention cost if sick days are to be reduced to 49?

4.4 Percent–Computation

PERCENT is a term used to denote a type of ratio. The expression 6% means $\frac{6}{100}$. A percent can best be interpreted as a part of the BASE. The base is the number which is regarded as a whole from which a certain number of hundredths is expressed or taken. The statement, "the profit is 18% of $20," means that

$$\frac{\text{Profit}}{\$20} = \frac{18}{100}$$

or, Profit $= \$20 \times \dfrac{18}{100}$

$$= \$20 \times .18 = \$3.60.$$

Thus, $3.60 is 18% of $20.

Here, the number which is regarded as the whole ($20) is the base and the number of hundredths (18%) is the RATE. A rate (percent) has no meaning if a base is not stated. Thus, 18% standing alone has no meaning, but 18% of $20 has a meaning.

A.   FINDING THE PERCENTAGE

The term PERCENTAGE has a two-fold meaning. It is the name used for calculations in which hundredths or percents are involved. It is also the product of the base and the rate. In the statement, "$3.60 is 18% of $20," the rate is 18% which is the number of hundredths of the base which must be taken. The base is the number which is regarded as the whole, in this case, $20. The percentage is the product of the base and the rate.

$$\$20 \times \frac{18}{100} = \$3.60$$

therefore, the percentage is $3.60.

Base = the number regarded as a whole
Rate = the number of hundredths, for example, 18%
Percentage = the product of the base and the rate

This relationship may be expressed as follows:

$$\text{PERCENTAGE} = \text{BASE} \times \text{RATE}.$$

From the above relationship, the following are derived:

$$\text{RATE} = \frac{\text{PERCENTAGE}}{\text{BASE}} \qquad \text{and} \qquad \text{BASE} = \frac{\text{PERCENTAGE}}{\text{RATE}}.$$

The following examples are presented to illustrate the uses of the expression Percentage = Base × Rate.

Example 4.4a
What is 25% of $510?

SOLUTION:

25% is the rate, and $510 is the base from which 25% is taken. Thus,
Percentage = 510 × 25% = 510 × .25 = $127.50.

CHECK:

Since $510 is 100% (base), then 1% should be $\frac{\$510}{100} = \$5.10$, and 25% should be
$5.10 × 25 = $127.50.

Example 4.4b
Charles Taylor sold 10 dozen eggs for $140 for Robert Anderson. If his commission is 6% of the selling price and he paid $6 as selling expense, how much should he remit to Anderson?

SOLUTION:

6% is the rate and $140 is the base from which 6% is taken. Thus, the amount of commission is the percentage.
140 × 6% = 140(.06) = $8.40 (commission)
$140 − $8.40 − $6 = $125.60 (amount Taylor should remit to Anderson)

EXERCISE 4.4A / REFERENCE SECTION: A

Find the percentage in each of the following:

Base	Rate		Base	Rate		Base	Rate		Base	Rate
1. 673	25%	6. 36.25	43%	11. 48	$41\frac{2}{3}\%$	16. 72	$37\frac{1}{2}\%$
2. 426	17%	7. 56.8	$62\frac{1}{2}\%$	12. 56	$14\frac{2}{7}\%$	17. 560	12%
3. 32.12	75%	8. 56	$87\frac{1}{2}\%$	13. 42.60	15%	18. 940	35%
4. 65.48	$16\frac{2}{3}\%$	9. 67.32	16%	14. 145	22%	19. 75	$66\frac{2}{3}\%$
5. 43.20	72%	10. 39.12	24%	15. 90	$\frac{2}{3}\%$	20. 24.60	$83\frac{1}{3}\%$

Statement Problems:

21. What is 45% of $425?
22. What is 70% of $560?
23. A man purchased a radio which was priced at $35. He made a down payment of 20% of the price. (a) How much was the down payment? (b) What percent of the price was the unpaid balance?
24. A retail store sold an article at 25% more than its cost. What was the selling price if the cost of the article was $60?
25. A man's take-home pay is $1 200 a month. His family expenses for each month are as follows: rent, $400; gas and electricity, $48; telephone, $24; food and clothing, 25% and 10% respectively of his monthly pay. Other incidental expenses amount to $2 400 a year. How much can he save in a year?
26. James Kelley and Howard Smith are co-owners of a service station. They have agreed that profits should be divided as follows: 55% to Kelley, 40% to Smith, and the remaining part to a local boys' camp. If the profits amount to $4 500 this year, how much will Kelley and Smith each receive? How much will the boys' camp receive? What percent of the profits will the camp receive?

B. FINDING THE RATE

The following examples are presented to illustrate the uses of the expression

$$Rate = \frac{Percentage}{Base}.$$

Example 4.4c
What percent of $428 is $64.20?

SOLUTION:

$428 is the base from which the percent (rate) is taken, and the part taken is $64.20, which is the percentage. Thus,

$$Rate = \frac{64.20}{428} = .15 = 15\%.$$

CHECK:

1% of $428 is $4.28. $64.20 contains 15 times $4.28 (or $64.20 ÷ $4.28 = 15).
Hence, $64.20 is 15% of $428.

Example 4.4d
In 1982, the total sales of a store were $28 000; in 1983, sales were $34 440. What was
the percent of change in 1983?

SOLUTION:

1. The amount of increase based on the sales of 1982 is $34 400 − $28 000 = $6 440.
    The amount of the 1982 sales must also be the base from which the percent of
    increase is expressed. Thus, the percent of increase is $\dfrac{6\,440}{28\,000} = .23 = 23\%$.
    The sales of 1983 were 23% more than the sales of 1982.
2. This problem may be solved in a different way, as follows:
    First, the following question must be answered: What percent of $28 000 is
    $34 440? Here, $28 000 is the base from which the percent is computed, and
    $34 440 is the percentage. Thus,
    $$\frac{34\,440}{28\,000} = 1.23 = 123\%.$$
    Then $34 440, the amount of 1983 sales, is 123% of $28 000, the amount of 1982
    sales. Since a base is always equal to 100%, the percent of increase of 1983 sales
    over 1982 sales is 123% − 100% = 23%.

CHECK:

23% of 1982 sales is $6 440 (or 28 000 × 23%)
$28 000 + $6 440 = $34 440, the sales of 1983.

C.   FINDING THE BASE

A base may be found in two ways: (a) directly by using the expression Base = $\frac{\text{Percentage}}{\text{Rate}}$,
and (b) by letting x = the base and then solving for x in the translated algebraic equation. Of the two methods, (a) is easier to compute if one understands the relationship
between the percentage and the rate.

When method (a) is applied in finding the base, it is vitally important to know
that the base always corresponds to 100% and the percentage always corresponds to
the rate. The expression has the same meaning as the proportion $\frac{\text{base}}{100\%} = \frac{\text{percentage}}{\text{rate}}$, which
states that "base is to 100% as percentage is to rate." The base is always 100% of
itself. The following examples are used to illustrate the problems in finding the base
by the two methods.

Example 4.4e
If 14% of a number is 112, what is the number?

SOLUTION:

(a) The unknown number is the base, which is equivalent to 100%.

Since, base $= \dfrac{\text{percentage}}{\text{rate}}$, the unknown number $= \dfrac{\text{percentage}}{\text{rate}}$

$$= \dfrac{112}{14\%}$$

$$= 800.$$

CHECK:

1% of the number is $\dfrac{112}{14} = 8$. 100% of the number is $8 \times 100 = 800$.

Or, $800 \times 14\% = 112$.

(b) Let $x =$ the number (base). Then,

$x(14\%) = 112$

$$x = \dfrac{112}{14\%} = 800.$$

Example 4.4f
If 17% of the amount of sales is $150, what is the amount of sales?

SOLUTION:

(a) Sales is the base and 17% is the rate. $150 is a percentage of the base.

base $= \dfrac{\text{percentage}}{\text{rate}}$

$$= \dfrac{150}{17\%} = \$882.35$$

Therefore, sales $= \$882.35$.

CHECK:

$882.35 \times 17\% = \$150$

(b) Let $x =$ the amount of sales (base). Then,

$x(17\%) = 150$

$$x = \dfrac{150}{17\%} = \$882.35.$$

D. FINDING THE BASE WHEN THE RATE IS NOT EXPLICITLY STATED

In cases involving a loss (decrease) or gain (increase), the rate may be stated indi-
rectly. For example, a loss of 7% of an investment implies that the remaining amount
(percentage) is $(100\% - 7\%)$ of the investment. Thus, to find the base

base $= \dfrac{\text{percentage}}{93\%}$.

Also, if a sale results in a profit of 6% of the cost, the selling price (percentage) is (100% + 6%) of the cost (base). Therefore,

$$\text{cost} = \frac{\text{selling price}}{106\%}.$$

Example 4.4g

George Bark had $3 348 at the end of last year after losing 7% of his investment. What was the amount of his investment?

SOLUTION:

(a) The unknown amount is the base (100%) from which 7% has been lost. The remainder, 93% (or 100% − 7%), corresponds to the remaining amount, $3 348. In other words, 93% of investment is equivalent to $3 348. Thus, the value of 100% is computed as follows:

$$\frac{3\ 348}{93\%} = \frac{3\ 348}{.93} = \$3\ 600.$$

(b) Let x = the amount of investment. Then,

$$x - 7\%x = 3\ 348$$
$$x(1 - 7\%) = 3\ 348$$
$$x = \frac{3\ 348}{93\%} = \$3\ 600.$$

CHECK:

$3 600 × 7% = $252
$3 600 − $252 = $3 348

Example 4.4h

A store manager priced his sugar at $9.01 per bag. The price was 6% more than the cost. What was the cost per bag?

SOLUTION:

(a) The cost is the base (100%) from which 6% is computed. The price $9.01 is the percentage which corresponds to 106% (or 100% + 6%). In other words, $9.01 is to 106% as the unknown cost is to 100%.

Thus, the value of 100% is $\dfrac{9.01}{106\%}$ = $8.50 (cost).

(b) Let x = cost. Then,

$$x + 6\%x = 9.01$$
$$x(1 + 6\%) = 9.01$$
$$x = \frac{9.01}{106\%} = \$8.50.$$

CHECK:

$8.50 × 6% = $ .51
$8.50 + $ .51 = $9.01 (price)

Example 4.4i
If a number decreased by 52% is 364.8, what is the number?

SOLUTION:

(a)   364.8 corresponds to 48% (or 100% − 52%). Thus, the value of 100%, the number (base) is

$$\frac{364.8}{48\%} = 760.$$

(b)   Let x = the number
$$x - x \cdot 52\% = 364.8$$
$$x(1 - 52\%) = 364.8$$
$$x = \frac{364.8}{48\%} = 760$$

CHECK:

$760 \cdot 52\% = 395.2$
$760 - 395.2 = 364.8$

Example 4.4j
What number increased by 12% of itself is 296.8?

SOLUTION:

(a)   296.8 corresponds to 112% or (100% + 12%). Thus, the value of 100%, the number (base) is

$$\frac{296.8}{112\%} = 265.$$

(b)   Let x = the number
$$x + 12\%x = 296.8$$
$$112\%x = 296.8$$
$$x = \frac{296.8}{112\%} = \frac{296.8}{1.12} = 265$$

CHECK:

$265 × 12\% = 31.8$
$265 + 31.8 = 296.8$

E.   INCREASE OR DECREASE EXPRESSED AS A RATE

It is often convenient to express an increase or decrease over time as a rate. For example, if the sales volume is 6 840 units in 1982 and 7 258 units in 1983, the increase in the 1983 sales volume is 418 units (7 258 − 6 840) more than the 1982 sales volume.

This increase in sales volume may also be expressed as a percent of the 1982 volume.

$$\text{Percent increase} = \frac{1983 \text{ volume} - 1982 \text{ volume}}{1982 \text{ volume}}$$

or,

$$= \frac{7\ 258 - 6\ 840}{6\ 840} = 6.1\%$$

Thus, the 1983 sales volume shows an increase of 6.1% over the 1982 sales volume.

Example 4.4k

In 1972, Margaret earned $18 000 and in 1984, she earned $24 000. What percent increase is her 1984 income over her 1972 income?

SOLUTION:

$$\text{Percent increase} = \frac{1984 \text{ income} - 1972 \text{ income}}{1972 \text{ income}}$$

$$= \frac{24\ 000 - 18\ 000}{18\ 000}$$

$$= \frac{6\ 000}{18\ 000} = 33.3\%$$

Example 4.4l

Frank's electrical expenses for the month of July were $1 180 and for the month of August, $1 060. By what percent did Frank's electrical expenses decrease?

SOLUTION:

$$\text{Percent decrease} = \frac{\text{July's expenses} - \text{August's expenses}}{\text{July's expenses}}$$

$$= \frac{1\ 180 - 1\ 060}{1\ 180}$$

$$= \frac{120}{1\ 180} = 10.169\%$$

EXERCISE 4.4B / REFERENCE SECTION: B–E

(Round all answers to the nearest tenth of one percent. Example: 2.34% is rounded to 2.3%).

Find the rate in percent (%) of each of the following:

	Rate	Percentage	Base			Rate	Percentage	Base
1.	?	27	36		6.	?	120	560
2.	?	35	20		7.	?	65	50
3.	?	93	31		8.	?	24	48
4.	?	73.5	175		9.	?	30	75
5.	?	56.4	400		10.	?	28.5	57

Statement Problems:
11. What percent of $120 is $9.60?
12. What percent of $45 is $16?
13. $7.50 is what percent of $45?
14. $16 is what percent of $84?
15. $13 is what percent more than $10?
16. $32 is what percent more than $24?
17. $45 is what percent less than $60?
18. $224 is what percent less than $320?
19. A radio bought for $24.50 is sold for $32. What percent of the cost is the profit?
20. In the above problem, what percent of the selling price is the profit?
21. A man pays an employment agency a fee of $273.75 from his first month's salary of $750. What percent of the salary is the fee?
22. A boy gave $15 from his week's pay of $45 to his sister for her birthday party. What percent of his pay did he give?
23. The price of 500 grams of ground beef was $.96 in 1978 and $1.20 in 1979. What was the percent of change in 1979?
24. There were 600 first-year students last year and 800 this year in a Saskatchewan college. Find the percent of increase.
25. A man sold his typewriter for 90% of its cost. (a) What percent did he lose? (b) If the cost was $145, how much did he lose?
26. A retailer has an investment of $5 000 in his store. His net income for last year was 55% of his investment. His net income for this year is $2 200. What is the percent of decrease or increase this year?

Find the base (or 100%) in each of the following:

	Base	Percentage	Rate		Base	Percentage	Rate
27.	?	276	46%	33.	?	740	148%
28.	?	195	39%	34.	?	1 470	245%
29.	?	575	12.5%	35.	?	89.84	112.3%
30.	?	186	62%	36.	?	17 304	432.6%
31.	?	5 264	75.2%	37.	?	514.65	282%
32.	?	588	2.1%	38.	?	247.39	71.5%

Statement Problems:
39. If 29% of a number is 58, what is the number?
40. If 5% of a number is 7, what is the number?
41. 8.4 is 7% of what number?
42. 27 is 12% of what number?
43. What number decreased by 10% of itself is 193.50?
44. What number decreased by 30% of itself is 302.40?
45. What number increased by $5\frac{1}{2}$% of itself is 42.20?

46. What number increased by 9% of itself is 34.88?
47. James Kart received a dividend of $125, which is 5% of his investment. What is the size of the investment?
48. Charles West purchased a car and made a down payment of $270. After the payment, he owes 85% of the purchase price. What is the price of the car?
49. A piece of jewellery was sold for $5.60, which includes a federal tax of 10% and an excise tax of 7%. What is the price excluding the taxes?
50. A man sold a washing machine for $123.50. His profit was 30% of his original purchase price. What was his purchase price?
51. A certain cloth will shrink 2% after washing. If 176.4 centimetres of the cloth are needed, how long should the piece be before washing?
52. A retailer sold an odd lot of ladies' dresses for $232.50, a loss of 7% on his purchase price. What was his purchase price?

REVIEW EXERCISE 4.4C / REFERENCE SECTION: A–E

Statement Problems:
1. A field of 4.8 hectares yields 3 125 kilograms of wheat. How much should a field of 16.8 hectares yield?
2. If it costs $283 750 to build 5.6 kilometres of highway, how much will it cost to build 1.4 kilometres of the same type of highway?
3. If a car runs 504 kilometres on 90.72 litres of gasoline, how many litres of gasoline are needed for going 1 920 kilometres?
4. If 48 kilograms of potatoes cost $9.60, what will 40 kilograms cost?
5. Divide 76 into two parts in the ratio 3:5.
6. Divide 825 into two parts in the ratio 7:8.
7. Divide 686 into three parts in the ratio 2:5:7.
8. Divide 151.2 into three parts in the ratio 1:2:3.
9. How should George Dean and John Mesk divide $1 704 if Dean's share is to exceed Mesk's share by 40%?
10. In Problem 9, if Dean's share is to be 40% less than Mesk's, how much should each of them receive?
11. Find 5% of 100, of 200, of 450, of 620.
12. Find 10% of 13.7, of 42.5, of 63.58, of 65.45.
13. What is 7% of 425?
14. What percent of $260 is $150?
15. 50.60 is 11% of what number?
16. Find 15.5% of 76.
17. 25% of how many dollars is $30?
18. $180 is what percent of $750?
19. What percent of $28 is $42?
20. 180% of $65 is what?
21. How many dollars plus 15% is $414?
22. How many dollars less 20% is $360?

23. A, B, and C started a business as partners. A contributed $15 000; B, $24 000; and C, $32 000. In proportion to their investments, how much should each of the partners receive from a profit of $9 372?

24. In a partnership consisting of three persons, X contributed $23 000; Y, $21 000; and Z, $17 000. At the end of the first year the loss was $7 747. If the partners shared the loss in proportion to their contributions, how much loss did each bear?

25. Thomas bought two cows for $525. He sold one cow at an 8% profit and the other at a 3% loss. His net profit was $20. How much did he pay for each?

26. Nelson has an annual income of $111 from his investments. He invested $\frac{1}{6}$ of his total investments at 6%, $\frac{1}{10}$ at 5%, and the remainder at 3%. Find the amount of his total investments.

27. If unroasted coffee, which is purchased at $1.80 a kilogram, shrinks 10% in weight when roasted, what is the total cost of unroasted coffee needed to secure 6 kilograms of roasted coffee?

28. If 85% of the weight of wheat is made into flour, how many kilograms of wheat are needed to make 316.2 kilograms of flour?

29. Based on his experience, a manufacturer found that the change in the quantity sold is approximately proportional to the change in price. His records show that when the price of television sets was $299.99 each, 1 000 were sold in a one-month period; but only 800 were sold when the price was $319.99. How many television sets should the manufacturer expect to sell in a one-month period when the price is $289.99?

Glossary

ABSTRACT RATIO a ratio involving numbers of the same kind

ALLOCATION the division of a number into parts according to a ratio

BASE the number which is regarded as a whole from which a certain number of hundredths (the rate) is expressed or taken

DIRECT VARIATION a situation in which the quantity of one item increases as the quantity of another increases

EXTREMES outside letters or numbers in a proportion; the product of the extremes equals the product of the means

INDIRECT VARIATION a situation in which the quantity of one item decreases as the quantity of another increases

MEANS inside letters or numbers in a proportion; the product of the means equals the product of the extremes

PERCENT hundredths, parts in each hundred

PERCENTAGE the name used to describe calculations in which percents (hundredths) are involved; also, the product of the base and the rate

PROPORTION a statement of the equality of two ratios

RATE the number of hundredths taken from the base

RATIO an expression of the relative values of two or more things

5 Supplemental algebraic operations

Introduction

Many algebraic techniques exist which may be used to develop formulae to simplify problems encountered in business. This chapter contains several methods which find quite wide business application. This is especially true of logarithms, since all up-to-date electronic calculators are equipped to handle logarithmic calculations. A working knowledge of the rules of logarithms will enhance the understanding of the use of this function.

Problems involving fixed periodic payments may be represented as a series or progression. Operations involving such series are used in the development of formulae which may be used to determine loan rebates, some depreciation schedules and the value of a series of payments. These techniques offer a worthwhile addition to one's capability for communication in numerical terms.

Chapter Five covers quadratic equations, arithmetic progressions and logarithmic operations.

5.1 Quadratic Equations

A QUADRATIC EQUATION in one unknown is an equation which contains up to the second power of the unknown. The standard form of the quadratic equation in x, which represents the unknown, is written as follows:

$$ax^2 + bx + c = 0$$

The left side of the equation is arranged in order of descending powers of the unknown x, and a, b, and c are constants. The letter a may have any value other than zero, and the letters b and c may have any values including zero. If $a = 0$, the equation will convert to the form $bx + c = 0$, which is not quadratic, but linear. A quadratic equation in one unknown has only two roots. Either one of the following three methods may be used to solve a quadratic equation.

A.   SOLUTION BY FACTORING

When the left side of a quadratic equation is readily factored, the roots can be obtained by applying the principle which indicates that if a product equals zero, one or more factors of the product equal zero.

Example 5.1a
Solve $x^2 - x = 6$.

SOLUTION:

Transpose: $x^2 - x - 6 = 0$
Factor: $(x - 3)(x + 2) = 0$
Equate each factor to zero and solve for x:
When $x - 3 = 0$, $x = 3$
When $x + 2 = 0$, $x = -2$

CHECK:

Substitute separately each root in the original equation.
When $x = 3$, $3^2 - 3 = 6$; $9 - 3 = 6$; $6 = 6$
When $x = -2$, $(-2)^2 - (-2) = 6$; $4 + 2 = 6$; $6 = 6$

Example 5.1b
Solve $49x^2 = 81$.

SOLUTION:

$49x^2 = 81$ may be written as $(7x)^2 = 9^2$
Transpose: $(7x)^2 - 9^2 = 0$
Factors: $(7x + 9)(7x - 9) = 0$
Equate each factor to zero and solve for x:

When $7x + 9 = 0$, $x = \dfrac{-9}{7}$

When $7x - 9 = 0$, $x = \dfrac{9}{7}$

CHECK:

Substitute separately each root in the original equation:

When $x = \dfrac{-9}{7}$, $49\left(\dfrac{-9}{7}\right)^2 = 81$; $81 = 81$

When $x = \dfrac{9}{7}$, $49\left(\dfrac{9}{7}\right)^2 = 81$; $81 = 81$

B.   SOLUTION BY COMPLETING THE SQUARES

This method of solving a quadratic equation applies to all quadratic equations whether or not a solution can be found by the factoring method illustrated above.

Example 5.1c
Solve for x. $ax^2 + bx + c = 0$

SOLUTION:

Subtract c from both sides of equation $ax^2 + bx + c = 0$.
$ax^2 + bx = -c$
Divide each side by a.

$$x^2 + \frac{b}{a}x = -\frac{c}{a}$$

Add the square of half the coefficient of x to both sides to make the left side a perfect square.

$$x^2 + \frac{b}{a}x + \left(\frac{b}{2a}\right)^2 = -\frac{c}{a} + \left(\frac{b}{2a}\right)^2; \text{ the right side} = \frac{b^2}{4a^2} - \frac{c}{a} = \frac{b^2 - 4ac}{4a^2}$$

Thus, $\left(x + \frac{b}{2a}\right)^2 = \frac{b^2 - 4ac}{4a^2}$.

Extract the square root of each side.

$$x + \frac{b}{2a}x = \pm\frac{\sqrt{b^2 - 4ac}}{2a}$$

Solve for x.

$$x = \frac{-b \pm \sqrt{b^2 - 4ac}}{2a}$$

C.   SOLUTION BY THE QUADRATIC FORMULA

A FORMULA is a general fact, rule, or principle expressed in algebraic symbols. According to the above example, when

$$ax^2 + bx + c = 0,$$

$$\boxed{x = \frac{-b \pm \sqrt{b^2 - 4ac}}{2a}} \qquad \longleftarrow Formula\ 5\text{-}1$$

The fact thus expressed is a formula and can be used to find the roots of any quadratic equation. When the left side of any quadratic equation is written in the order of descending powers of the unknown and the right side of the equation is a zero, only the values of a, b, and c need to be substituted in the formula. Here a equals the coefficient of the unknown square (x^2), b equals the coefficient of the unknown (x), and c is the constant number.

Example 5.1d
Solve $x^2 - x = 6$ by formula.

SOLUTION:

Transpose: $x^2 - x - 6 = 0$
Hence: $a = 1$, $b = -1$, $c = -6$

Substituting in the formula:

$$x = \frac{-(-1) \pm \sqrt{(-1)^2 - 4(1)(-6)}}{2 \cdot 1} = \frac{1 \pm \sqrt{1 + 24}}{2}$$

$$= \frac{1 \pm \sqrt{25}}{2} = \frac{1 \pm 5}{2}$$

$$x = \frac{1 + 5}{2} = 3$$

$$x = \frac{1 - 5}{2} = -2$$

CHECK:

Substitute the answers in the given equation:

When $x = 3$, $3^2 - 3 = 6$; $6 = 6$
When $x = -2$, $(-2)^2 - (-2) = 6$; $6 = 6$

EXERCISE 5.1 / REFERENCE SECTIONS: A–C

Solve the following by factoring:

1. $4x^2 = 25$
2. $9x^2 = 16$
3. $16x^2 - 49 = 0$
4. $25x^2 - 9 = 0$
5. $15x^2 + 14x - 8 = 0$
6. $6x^2 + 7x + 2 = 0$

7. $8x^2 + 3 = 14x$
8. $8y^2 + 6y = 9$
9. $3y^2 + 17y - 28 = 0$
10. $12y^2 + 3y = 42$
11. $12y^2 + 5 = -23y$

12. $41x - 10 = 21x^2$
13. $x^2 - 5x = -6$
14. $9x^2 - 1 = 0$
15. $3x^2 - 13x + 4 = 0$
16. $15x^2 - x - 2 = 0$

Solve the following by quadratic formula:

17. $6x^2 - 11x + 4 = 0$
18. $10x^2 + 13x - 3 = 0$
19. $4x^2 - 31x + 21 = 0$
20. $x^2 - 64 = 0$
21. $18x^2 - 14 = 9x$
22. $14x^2 - 11x = 15$
23. $9x^2 - 49 = 0$
24. $20x^2 - 76x + 72 = 0$

25. $7m^2 - 19m - 6 = 0$
26. $35y^2 - y - 12 = 0$
27. $24n^2 - 41n + 12 = 0$
28. $4x^2 + 12x - 40 = 0$
29. $35x^2 - 57x = -18$
30. $18x^2 + 25x = 3$
31. $12x^2 - 9 = -23x$
32. $35x^2 - 32 = 36x$

5.2 *Progressions*

A. *DEFINITION AND TERMINOLOGY*

When a set of numbers is arranged in such a manner that there is a first number, a second number, a third number, and so on, the set of numbers is called a SEQUENCE OF

NUMBERS. The successive numbers are called the TERMS OF THE SEQUENCE. The terms of a sequence are generally increased (or decreased) in one of two patterns: the arithmetic progression or the geometric progression.

B.   ARITHMETIC PROGRESSION

An ARITHMETIC PROGRESSION (abbreviated A.P.) is a sequence of numbers in which each term following the first one is obtained by adding the preceding term to a fixed number called the COMMON DIFFERENCE. Thus, 1, 3, 5, 7, 9 is an arithmetic progression with a common difference of 2.

The nth Term of an Arithmetic Progression

According to the above definition of an arithmetic progression, if the first number of a sequence of numbers is 1 and the common difference is 2, the sequence is obtained as follows:

The first term $= 1$
The second term $= 1 + 2 = 3$
The third term $= 1 + (2 \cdot 2) = 5$
The fourth term $= 1 + (3 \cdot 2) = 7$, or $1 + (4 - 1) \cdot 2 = 7$
The fifth term $= 1 + (4 \cdot 2) = 9$, or $1 + (5 - 1) \cdot 2 = 9$
If the number of the terms is n, then
The nth term $= 1 + (n - 1)2$

Furthermore, if the first term of an A.P. is a, the common difference is d, and the nth term is L, then:

The first term $= a$
The second term $= a + d$
The third term $= a + 2d$
The fourth term $= a + 3d$, or $a + (4 - 1)d$
The fifth term $= a + 4d$, or $a + (5 - 1)d$
The nth term

$$L = a + (n - 1)d \qquad \longleftarrow Formula\ 5\text{-}2$$

The Sum of an Arithmetic Progression

Let S_n denote the sum of the first n terms of an arithmetic progression. The sum may be written in both direct and reverse order as follows:

$$S_n = a + (a + d) + (a + 2d) + (a + 3d) + \ldots L$$

$$S_n = L + (L - d) + (L - 2d) + (L - 3d) + \ldots a$$

Add the two equations, then

$$2S_n = (a + L) + (a + L) + (a + L) + (a + L)\ldots(a + L)$$
$$= n(a + L).$$

Thus,

$$\boxed{S_n = \frac{n}{2}(a + L)} \qquad \longleftarrow Formula\ 5\text{-}3$$

According to the two formulae above, if any three of the five quantities, a, d, n, L, and S_n are given, the other two may be found.

Example 5.2a

Find the 25th term and the sum of A.P. 1, 3, 5, 7,...to 25 terms.

SOLUTION:

$$n = 25,\ a = 1,\ d = 3 - 1 = 2$$
$$L = a + (n - 1)d = 1 + (25 - 1)2 = 49$$
$$S_n = \frac{n}{2}(a + L) = \frac{25}{2}(1 + 49) = \frac{25}{2} \cdot 50 = 625$$

Example 5.2b

Given $S_n = 100$, $L = 19$, $n = 10$. Find a and d.

SOLUTION:

$$S_n = \frac{n}{2}(a + L), \qquad 100 = \frac{10}{2}(a + 19), \qquad 100 \cdot \frac{2}{10} = a + 19$$
$$20 = a + 19, \qquad a = 1$$
$$L = a + (n - 1)d, \qquad 19 = 1 + (10 - 1)d, \qquad 18 = 9d$$
$$d = \frac{18}{9}, \qquad d = 2$$

CHECK:

According to the answer, the A.P. is 1, 3, 5, 7, 9, 11, 13, 15, 17, 19 (=L).
The sum is $1 + 3 + 5 + 7 + 9 + 11 + 13 + 15 + 17 + 19 = 100$.

Arithmetic Means

In an A.P., the terms between any two given terms are called the ARITHMETIC MEANS. To insert a given number of arithmetic means between two terms, apply Formula 5-2, where n = the number of terms to be inserted plus 2.

Example 5.2c
Insert five arithmetic means between 4 and 16.

SOLUTION:

$a = 4, L = 16, n = 5 + 2 = 7$

Apply the formula:
$16 = 4 + (7 - 1)d$
$16 = 4 + 6d,$ $12 = 6d$
$d = 2$

Thus, the required means are
$4 + 2 = 6$
$6 + 2 = 8$
$8 + 2 = 10$
$10 + 2 = 12$
$12 + 2 = 14$

CHECK:

The A.P. is 4, 6, 8, 10, 12, 14, 16.

C.   *GEOMETRIC PROGRESSION*

A GEOMETRIC PROGRESSION (abbreviate G.P.) is a sequence of numbers in which each term following the first one is obtained by multiplying the preceding term by a constant factor, called the COMMON RATIO. Thus, 1, 2, 4, 8, 16 is a geometric progression with a common ratio of 2.

The nth Term of a Geometric Progression

According to the above definition of a geometric progression, if the first number of a sequence of numbers is 1 and the common ratio is 2, the sequence is obtained as follows:

The first term $= 1$
The second term $= 1 \cdot 2$
The third term $= 1 \cdot 2^2 = 4$
The fourth term $= 1 \cdot 2^3 = 8$, or $1 \cdot 2^{4-1}$
The fifth term $= 1 \cdot 2^4 = 16$, or $1 \cdot 2^{5-1}$
The *nth* term $= 1 \cdot 2^{n-1}$

Furthermore, if the first term of a G.P. is a, the common ratio is r, the number of terms is n, and the *nth* term is L, then,

The first term $= a$
The second term $= ar$
The third term $= ar^2$

The fourth term $\quad = ar^3$, or ar^{4-1}
The fifth term $\qquad = ar^4$, or ar^{5-1}
Thus,
The *nth* term

$$\boxed{L = ar^{n-1}} \qquad \longleftarrow Formula\ 5\text{-}4$$

The Sum of a Geometric Progression

Let S_n denote the sum of the first n terms of G.P. To derive a formula for the sum, first write the sum as indicated in (1) below, and then multiply (1) by r as indicated in (2).

(1) $S_n = a + ar + ar^2 + ar^3 + \ldots ar^{n-2} + ar^{n-1}$

(2) $rS_n = ar + ar^2 + ar^3 + \ldots ar^{n-2} + ar^{n-1} + ar^n$

Subtract (2) from (1). The answer is,

$S_n - rS_n = a - ar^n$. Factor,

$S_n(1 - r) = a(1 - r^n)$. Solve for S_n,

$$\boxed{S_n = \frac{a(1 - r^n)}{1 - r}} \qquad \longleftarrow Formula\ 5\text{-}5$$

According to the two formulae above, if any three of the five quantities a, r, n, L and S_n are given, the other two may be found.

Example 5.2d
Find L and S_n for G.P. 2, 6, 18,...to 8 terms.

SOLUTION:

Here $a = 2$, $r = \dfrac{6}{2} = 3$, $n = 8$

$L = ar^{n-1} = 2 \cdot 3^{8-1} = 2 \cdot 3^7 = 2 \cdot 2\ 187 = 4\ 374$

$S_n = \dfrac{a(1 - r^n)}{1 - r} = \dfrac{2(1 - 3^8)}{1 - 3} = \dfrac{2(1 - 6\ 561)}{-2}$

$\quad = \dfrac{2(-6\ 560)}{-2} = 6\ 560$

Example 5.2e
Given: $a = 2$, $L = -128$, $S_n = -102$. Find r and n.

SOLUTION:

$$L = ar^{n-1}, \qquad -128 = 2r^{n-1}, \qquad r^{n-1} = -64 \qquad (1)$$

$$S_n = \frac{a(1 - r^n)}{1 - r}, \qquad -102 = \frac{2(1 - r^n)}{1 - r} \qquad (2)$$

Simplifying (2)
$$-102(1 - r) = 2(1 - r^n)$$
$$-102 + 102r = 2 - 2r^n$$
$$2r^n + 102r = 2 + 102 \qquad (3)$$

Factoring (3)
$$r(2r^{n-1} + 102) = 104 \qquad (4)$$

Substituting (1) or $r^{n-1} = -64$ in (4)
$$r[2(-64) + 102] = 104$$
$$-26r = 104$$
$$r = -4$$

Substituting $r = -4$ in (1) $\qquad (-4)^{n-1} = -64$, or $(-4)^{n-1} = (-4)^3$

Since both sides of the equation above have the same base, (-4), their exponents must be equal, or, $n - 1 = 3$,

$n = 3 + 1 = 4$.

CHECK:

According to the answer, the G.P. is 2, −8, 32, −128 (= L).
The sum of the G.P. is $2 + (-8) + 32 + (-128) = -102$ (S_n).

Geometric Means

In a G.P., the terms between any two given terms are called the GEOMETRIC MEANS. To insert a given number of geometric means between two terms, apply Formula 5-4 where n = the number of terms to be inserted plus 2.

Example 5.2f

Insert five geometric means between 3 and 192.

SOLUTION:

$a = 3$, $L = 192$, $n = 5 + 2 = 7$

Apply the formula:
$$192 = 3r^{7-1}$$
$$\frac{192}{3} = r^6, \ 64 = r^6, \ 2^6 = r^6$$
$$r = 2$$

Thus, the required geometric means are

$3 \cdot 2 = 6$
$6 \cdot 2 = 12$
$12 \cdot 2 = 24$
$24 \cdot 2 = 48$
$48 \cdot 2 = 96$

CHECK:

The answer gives a G.P. as follows:
3, 6, 12, 24, 48, 96, 192 $(= L)$

EXERCISE 5.2 / REFERENCE SECTIONS: A–C

Find L and S_n for each of the following A.P.s:

1. 4, 7, 10,...to 9 terms
2. 10, 7, 4,...to 6 terms
3. 2, 4, 6,...to 7 terms
4. $\frac{1}{6}, \frac{1}{4}, \frac{1}{3},$...to 12 terms

5. 0.2, 0.6, 1.0,...to 10 terms
6. 1, 2, 3,...to 30 terms
7. $-2, -4, -6,$...to 16 terms
8. $(a + d), a, (a - d)$...to n terms

Three of the five elements, a, d, n, L and S_n of an A.P. are given below for each problem. Find the remaining elements for each:

9. $L = -11, d = -4, n = 7$
10. $d = -3, L = -12, S_n = -21$
11. $a = 1, n = 9, S_n = 117$
12. $n = 14, L = -29, S_n = -133$

13. $d = \frac{1}{6}, n = 5, S_n = 3\frac{1}{3}$
14. $a = 14, d = -4, S_n = 24$
15. $a = 5, d = -3, S_n = -44$
16. $a = -16, n = 10, S_n = 20$

Find L and S_n for each of the following G.P.s:

17. 3, 6, 12,...to 12 terms
18. 1, 2, 4,...to 25 terms
19. 1, 3, 9,...to 5 terms
20. 54, 18, 6,...to 8 terms

21. 2, 6, 18,...to 7 terms
22. $\frac{1}{3}, -\frac{1}{9}, \frac{1}{27},$...to 6 terms
23. 18, 0.18, 0.001 8,...to 5 terms
24. .2, .04, .008,...to 6 terms

Three of the five elements, a, r, n, L and S_n of a G.P. are given below for each problem. Find the remaining elements for each:

25. $a = -3, n = 3, S_n = -93$
26. $a = 4, L = 324, n = 5$
27. $a = -1, r = -3, S_n = 182$
28. $a = \frac{1}{3}, r = 3, S_n = 364\frac{1}{3}$

29. $a = 2, n = 5, L = 32$
30. $a = 32, L = 1, S_n = 63$
31. $r = 2, L = 96, S_n = 189$
32. $a = 12, r = \frac{1}{2}, L = \frac{3}{8}$

Insert A.P. means and G.P. means between the two given terms:

33. Insert 4 arithmetic means between 2 and $14\frac{1}{2}$.

34. Insert 5 arithmetic means between 2 and 5.

35. Insert 6 arithmetic means between 1 and 15.

36. Insert 3 arithmetic means between 3 and 31.

37. Insert 4 geometric means between 2 and 64.

38. Insert 5 geometric means between 128 and 2.

39. Insert 6 geometric means between 1 and 128.

40. Insert 3 geometric means between 3 and 1 875.

Statement Problems:

41. If a student saves $10 in the first week, $12 in the second week, and continues to increase his savings $2 each week, what will be the total of his savings at the end of 52 weeks?

42. A man plans to give a total of $2 700 to his 6 children. Beginning with the oldest, the man will give each younger child $20 less than the one who precedes him. How much will each child receive?

43. Baxter deposits $10 at the end of January of this year. Thereafter, at the end of every following month, he deposits 20% more than the preceding deposit. Find the sum of his total deposits at the end of December of this year.

44. A married couple has 3 sons. Each son has a wife and 3 boys. Each grandson also has a wife and 3 boys who are married. How many people are there in the family?

5.3 Logarithms–Basic Aspects

A.   GENERAL STATEMENT

Logarithms can be used to simplify the operations of multiplication, division, raising to powers, and extracting roots. In mathematics of finance, logarithms are especially useful in solving some problems that involve compound interest and annuities.

B.   MEANING OF A LOGARITHM

The LOGARITHM of a number is the power (exponent) to which a specified base must be raised in order to yield the number. For example, the logarithm of 100 to the base 10 is 2, since $10^2 = 100$. In exponential form, if $b^x = N$, the exponent x is the logarithm of the number N to the base b. Likewise, since

$2^3 = 8$, the exponent 3 is the logarithm of the number 8 to the base 2
$5^2 = 25$, the exponent 2 is the logarithm of the number 25 to the base 5
$10^3 = 1\ 000$, the exponent 3 is the logarithm of the number 1 000 to the base 10
$e^2 = 7.389\ 056\ 1$, the exponent 2 is the logarithm of the number 7.389 056 1 to the base e.[1]

The above relationships can be written in simpler form as follows:

Since $b^x = N$, then $\log_b N = x$,

where log represents *the logarithm of*.

Since $2^3 = 8$, then $\log_2 8 = 3$.
Since $5^2 = 25$, then $\log_5 25 = 2$.
Since $10^3 = 1\ 000$, then $\log_{10} 1\ 000 = 3$.

Although any positive number greater than one may be a base, in general, base 10 and base e are used in calculations. When base 10 is used, it is customary to omit the subscript that indicates the base; thus, $\log_{10} 1\ 000$ can be written as log 1 000. The logarithms based on 10 are called the COMMON or BRIGGSIAN (Henry Briggs, 1560-1631) system of logarithms. In this system, the following corresponding forms may be written:

Logarithmic Form	Exponential Form
$\log 100\ 000 = 5$	$10^5 = 100\ 000$
$\log\ \ 10\ 000 = 4$	$10^4 = 10\ 000$
$\log\ \ \ \ 1\ 000 = 3$	$10^3 = 1\ 000$
$\log\ \ \ \ \ \ 100 = 2$	$10^2 = 100$
$\log\ \ \ \ \ \ \ \ 10 = 1$	$10^1 = 10$
$\log\ \ \ \ \ \ \ \ \ \ 1 = 0$	$10^0 = 1$
$\log\ \ \ \ \ \ \ .1 = -1$	$10^{-1} = \dfrac{1}{10} = .1$
$\log\ \ \ \ \ .01 = -2$	$10^{-2} = \dfrac{1}{10^2} = \dfrac{1}{100} = .01$
$\log\ \ \ .001 = -3$	$10^{-3} = \dfrac{1}{10^3} = \dfrac{1}{1\ 000} = .001$

[1] $e = \lim\limits_{n \to \infty} \left(1 + \dfrac{1}{n}\right)^n \approx 2.718\ 281\ 8$

In general,

$$\log N = x \qquad\qquad 10^x = N$$

Note that all numbers (N) indicated above have positive values.

From the above explanation, it may be seen that as the number becomes greater, the logarithm of the number also becomes greater. Thus, if N and M are two positive numbers and N is larger than M, then $\log N$ is also larger than $\log M$. This concept is important in finding the logarithm of a number which is not an exact power of 10. For example, if the number is 249, which is larger than 100 (or 10^2), the logarithm of 249 is larger than the logarithm of 100. Further, since the number 249 is smaller than 1 000 (or 10^3), the logarithm of 249 is smaller than the logarithm of 1 000. The relationships may be written as follows:

$\log 100 < \log 249 < \log 1\ 000$

or, $2 < \log 249 < 3$

since, $\log 100 = 2$ and $\log 1\ 000 = 3$.

Thus, $\log 249 = 2 +$ a decimal (since $2 + 1 = 3$), or in exponential form, $10^{2 + \text{a decimal}} = 249$.

Similarly, we may find the logarithm of a positive number which is less than 1, such as .004 5.

Since, $.001 < .004\ 5 < .01$

or, $10^{-3} < .004\ 5 < 10^{-2}$

then, $\log .001 < \log .004\ 5 < \log .01$
or, $-3 < \log .004\ 5 < -2$.

Thus, $\log .004\ 5 = (-3) +$ a decimal (since $(-3) + 1 = (-2)$), or in exponential form, $10^{-3 + \text{a decimal}} = .004\ 5$.

In general, when a number is not an exact power of 10, the logarithm of the number consists of a whole-number part and a decimal part. The whole-number part is called the CHARACTERISTIC of the logarithm, and the decimal part is called the MANTISSA of the logarithm.

> Logarithm of a positive number = Characteristic + Mantissa

Examples of the characteristics of the selected numbers are tabulated in Figure 5.1.

Figure 5.1
Characteristics of Logarithms

Number			Digits in whole number part (1 and above) or Zeros between decimal point and first non-zero digit (less than 1)	Characteristic
10 000	to	99 999.99 (but less than 100 000)	5	4
1 000	to	9 999.99 (but less than 10 000)	4	3
100	to	999.99 (but less than 1 000)	3	2
10	to	99.99 (but less than 100)	2	1
1	to	9.99 (but less than 10)	1	0
.1	to	.99 (but less than 1)	none	−1
.01	to	.099 (but less than .1)	1	−2
.001	to	.009 9 (but less than .01)	2	−3
.000 1 to		.000 99 (but less than .001) etc.	3	−4

This table shows that the characteristic of the logarithm of a number depends only on the position of the decimal point, regardless of the value of the individual digits in the number. The following rules may be used in determining characteristics:

RULE 1: If a number is greater than or equal to 1, the characteristic of its logarithm is positive and is 1 less than the number of digits to the left of the decimal point.

RULE 2: If a number is less than 1, the characteristic of its logarithm is negative and is 1 more than the number of zeros between the decimal point and the first non-zero digit.

Unlike the characteristic, the mantissa of the logarithm of a number is independent of the position of the decimal point in the number. The mantissa is always positive and is determined by the significant digits of the number. The logarithms of numbers which have the same significant digits arranged in the same order thus have the same mantissas. Here the significant digits in a number are the digits which do not include zeros at the left of the first non-zero digit, such as in a decimal, or the zeros at the right of the last non-zero digits, such as in a whole number. Thus, the significant digits of the numbers 3 408 000, 34 080, 34.08, and .003 408 and 3, 4, 0, 8, and the logarithms of the numbers have the same mantissas, although not the same characteristics.

C.   TABLES OF MANTISSAS (BASE 10)

Tables of mantissas are also called tables of logarithms. The mantissas of the logarithms of most numbers are unending decimal fractions, but they can be computed to
any required number of decimal places. Methods of computing most values of
mantissas are developed in advanced algebra. Because they are beyond the scope of
this text, those methods are not introduced here. However, for practical uses, various
tables of mantissas are available; they are known as six-place tables, seven-place
tables, etc., according to the number of digits in the mantissas. It should be noted that
while mantissas are decimal fractions, they are usually given in tables without decimal points. Therefore, a decimal point should always be placed before the first digit
in the mantissa when it is used. A portion of a six-place table is shown in Table 5.1.

How to Determine the Logarithm (base 10) of a Given Number

In general, three operations are required to determine the logarithm of a given number:

1. Determine the characteristic by the rules given above.

2. In the table, find the mantissa corresponding to the significant digits of the given
    number. Two steps are necessary when this is done:

    STEP (1) In Column N, find the first three significant digits of the given number.
              The mantissa required is in the row horizontal with these digits.
    STEP (2) In this row locate the required mantissa in the column headed by the
              fourth significant digit of the given number.

3. Place a decimal point before the first digit of the mantissa, and add the mantissa
    to the characteristic. The sum is the required logarithm of the given number.

Example 5.3a
Find log 82.46.

SOLUTION:

1. The characteristic is +1 since there are two digits to the left of the decimal point.

2. STEP (1) The first three significant digits 824 are found in Column N in Table
              5.1.
    STEP (2) Opposite the finding in STEP (1), the required mantissa is found in the
              column which has 6 at the top. The mantissa is 916 243.[2]

---

[2] The first two digits of each mantissa are not printed in every column in the tables of mantissas. They are printed only in the columns which have 0 at the top. However, when the mantissas have the same first two digits, only the digits for the line having the smallest mantissa and
the line having the largest mantissa of the group are printed in the 0 column. In order to secure

3. The logarithm of 82.46 is 1 + .916 243 = 1.916 243, or
      log 82.46 = 1.916 243.

   In exponential form, the logarithm is written as

      $10^{1.916\ 243} = 82.46$.

How to Determine the Number From a Given Logarithm (Finding the Antilogarithm)

In general, the process of finding the number from a given logarithm is the inverse of the process of finding the logarithm of a number. The number found is called the ANTILOGARITHM (ANTILOG) of the given logarithm. The steps in this process are as follows:

1. Find the given mantissa in the table.
2. Determine the significant digits from the location of the mantissa.
3. The required number is determined by placing a decimal point in the significant digits according to the given characteristic.

Example 5.3b

If log N = 2.926 445, find N.

SOLUTION:

1. In Table 5.1, find the mantissa 926 445 (the mantissa is located in the row labelled 844 under N and the column headed 2).

2. The significant digits are 8442.

3. The required number is 844.2 since the characteristic is 2.

Thus,

$$10^{2.926\ 445} = 844.2.$$

---

a six-place mantissa, the first two digits must be prefixed to each entry on the same line and the lines below it until the two digits change. The first two digits of an entry marked by * are located on the line below the entry in the 0 column. Thus, in Example 5.3a, STEP (2), the first two digits 91 are prefixed to 6243, or written as 916243. On the same page in the tables, the first two digits 92 must be prefixed to entry *0019, or written as 920019.

Table 5.1
Logarithms of numbers 8 000-8 499
Six-Place Mantissas

N	0	1	2	3	4	5	6	7	8	9	D
800	90 3090	3144	3199	3253	3307	3361	3416	3470	3524	3578	55
01	3633	3687	3741	3795	3849	3904	3958	4012	4066	4120	55
02	4174	4229	4283	4337	4391	4445	4499	4553	4607	4661	55
03	4716	4770	4824	4878	4932	4986	5040	5094	5148	5202	54
04	5256	5310	5364	5418	5472	5526	5580	5634	5688	5742	54
05	5796	5850	5904	5958	6012	6066	6119	6173	6227	6281	54
06	6335	6389	6443	6497	6551	6604	6658	6712	6766	6820	54
07	6874	6927	6981	7035	7089	7143	7196	7250	7304	7358	54
08	7411	7465	7519	7573	7626	7680	7734	7787	7841	7895	54
09	7949	8002	8056	8110	8163	8217	8270	8324	8378	8431	54
810	8485	8539	8592	8646	8699	8753	8807	8860	8914	8967	54
11	9021	9074	9128	9181	9235	9289	9342	9396	9449	9503	54
12	90 9556	9610	9663	9716	9770	9823	9877	9930	9984	*0037	54
13	91 0091	0144	0197	0251	0304	0358	0411	0464	0518	0571	54
14	0624	0678	0731	0784	0838	0891	0944	0998	1051	1104	54
15	1158	1211	1264	1317	1371	1424	1477	1530	1584	1637	54
16	1690	1743	1797	1850	1903	1956	2009	2063	2116	2169	54
17	2222	2275	2328	2381	2435	2488	2541	2594	2647	2700	54
18	2753	2806	2859	2913	2966	3019	3072	3125	3178	3231	54
19	3284	3337	3390	3443	3496	3549	3602	3655	3708	3761	53
820	3814	3867	3920	3973	4026	4079	4132	4184	4237	4290	53
21	4343	4396	4449	4502	4555	4608	4660	4713	4766	4819	53
22	4872	4925	4977	5030	5083	5136	5189	5241	5294	5347	53
23	5400	5453	5505	5558	5611	5664	5716	5769	5822	5875	53
24	5927	5980	6033	6085	6138	6191	6243	6296	6349	6401	53

N	0	1	2	3	4	5	6	7	8	9	D
25	6454	6507	6559	6612	6664	6717	6770	6822	6875	6927	53
26	6980	7033	7085	7138	7190	7243	7295	7348	7400	7453	53
27	7506	7558	7611	7663	7716	7768	7820	7873	7925	7978	53
28	8030	8083	8135	8188	8240	8293	8345	8397	8450	8502	53
29	8555	8607	8659	8712	8764	8816	8869	8921	8973	9026	53
830	9078	9130	9183	9235	9287	9340	9392	9444	9496	9549	53
31	91 9601	9653	9706	9758	9810	9862	9914	9967	*0019	*0071	53
32	92 0123	0176	0228	0280	0332	0384	0436	0489	0541	0593	53
33	0645	0697	0749	0801	0853	0906	0958	1010	1062	1114	53
34	1166	1218	1270	1322	1374	1426	1478	1530	1582	1634	52
35	1686	1738	1790	1842	1894	1946	1998	2050	2102	2154	52
36	2206	2258	2310	2362	2414	2466	2518	2570	2622	2674	52
37	2725	2777	2829	2881	2933	2985	3037	3089	3140	3192	52
38	3244	3296	3348	3399	3451	3503	3555	3607	3658	3710	52
39	3762	3814	3865	3917	3969	4021	4072	4124	4176	4228	52
840	4279	4331	4383	4434	4486	4538	4589	4641	4693	4744	52
41	4796	4848	4899	4951	5003	5054	5106	5157	5209	5261	52
42	5312	5364	5415	5467	5518	5570	5621	5673	5725	5776	52
43	5828	5879	5931	5982	6034	6085	6137	6188	6240	6291	52
44	6342	6394	6445	6497	6548	6600	6651	6702	6754	6805	52
45	6857	6908	6959	7011	7062	7114	7165	7216	7268	7319	52
46	7370	7422	7473	7524	7576	7627	7678	7730	7781	7832	52
47	7883	7935	7986	8037	8088	8140	8191	8242	8293	8345	52
48	8396	8447	8498	8549	8601	8652	8703	8754	8805	8857	52
49	8908	8959	9010	9061	9112	9163	9215	9266	9317	9368	52

D.   *LOGARITHMS BASED ON* e (2.718 281 8)

The logarithms based on e are called NATURAL or NAPERIAN logarithms. Natural logarithms are denoted by ln. Thus, $\log_e 2$ is written as ln 2. In the system of natural logarithms, the following corresponding forms may be written:

Logarithmic Form	Exponential Form
ln 54.598 148 = 4	e^4 = 54.598 148
ln 20.085 536 = 3	e^3 = 20.085 536
ln 7.388 905 59 = 2	e^2 = 7.388 905 59
ln 2.718 281 8 = 1	e^1 = 2.718 281 8
ln 1 = 0	e^0 = 1
ln .367 879 4 = −1	e^{-1} = .367 879 4
ln .135 335 3 = −2	e^{-2} = .135 335 3

A simple relationship exists between common logarithms and natural logarithms.[3]

$$\log x = \frac{\ln x}{\ln 10} = 0.434\ 294\ 5 \ln x$$

Thus,
$$\log 1\ 000 = \frac{\ln 1\ 000}{\ln 10} = \frac{6.907\ 755\ 3}{2.302\ 585\ 1}$$
$$= 0.434\ 294\ 5(6.907\ 755\ 3)$$
$$= 3$$

and,
$$\ln x = \frac{\log x}{\log e} = 2.302\ 585\ 1 \log x.$$

Thus,
$$\ln 2.718\ 281\ 8 = 2.302\ 585\ 1 \log 2.718\ 281\ 8$$
$$= 2.302\ 585\ 1(0.432\ 945)$$
$$= 1.$$

---

[3]

Let $y = \log_{10} x$ (a)
Thus $x = 10^y$ (b)

Taking the logarithm base e of both sides of equation (b):
$\log_e x = y \log_e 10$

Solve for y:
$$y = \frac{\log_e x}{\log_e 10}.$$

Substitute the value for y from equation (a):
$$\log_{10} x = \frac{\log_e x}{\log_e 10}$$
or, $\log x = \dfrac{\ln x}{\ln 10}$.

Notice that

$$\log e = \frac{1}{\ln 10}$$

$$= \frac{1}{2.302\ 585\ 1}$$

$$= 0.434\ 294\ 5$$

and,

$$\ln 10 = \frac{1}{\log e}$$

$$= \frac{1}{0.434\ 294\ 5}$$

$$= 2.302\ 585\ 1.$$

5.4 Using Calculators to Determine the Logarithm of a Number and the Number of a Given Logarithm

Most calculators now on the market are equipped with the $\ln x$ or $\log x$ function. Therefore discussion in this section will not include the use of tables of mantissas since the value displayed on calculators usually includes characteristic and mantissa.

Example 5.4a
Find $\log x$ if $x = 82.46$.

SOLUTION:

To find the logarithm base 10 of a number from a calculator, the following action should be taken:

$\log x = .434\ 294\ 5\ \ln x$

Basic Calculator		Financial Calculator	
action taken	display shows	action taken	display shows
enter 82.46	82.46	enter 82.46	82.46
press logx	1.9162433	press 2nd lnx	4.4123133
		press x	4.4123133
		enter .4342945	.4342945
		press =	1.9162434

In exponential form, the logarithm is written as:

$10^{1.916\ 243\ 3} = 82.46.$

NOTE: It may be necessary to use a function such as *2nd* or *INV* in order to get $\log x$ and/or 10^x, also $\ln x$ and/or e^x.

Example 5.4b
If log of $x = 1.542\ 775\ 6$, find x correct to 3 decimal places.

SOLUTION:

Basic Calculator		Financial Calculator	
action taken	display shows	action taken	display shows
enter 1.5427756	1.5427756	enter 10	10
press 10^x	34.895996	press y^x	10
		enter 1.5427756	1.5427756
		press $=$	34.895996

Thus,
$10^{1.542\ 775\ 6} = 34.896$.

Example 5.4c
Find the natural logarithm of 82.46 (i.e., $\ln x$).

SOLUTION:

Basic Calculator		Financial Calculator	
action taken	display shows	action taken	display shows
enter 82.46	82.46	enter 82.46	82.46
press $\ln x$	4.4123133	press 2nd $\ln x$	4.4123133

Therefore,
$\ln 82.46 = 4.412\ 313\ 3$.
In exponential form, the logarithm is:
$e^{4.412\ 313\ 3} = 82.46$.

Example 5.4d
If $\ln x = 8.185\ 071\ 5$, find x.

SOLUTION:

Basic Calculator		Financial Calculator	
action taken	display shows	action taken	display shows
enter 8.1850715	8.1850715	enter 8.1850715	8.1850715
press e^x	3 587	press 2nd e^x	3 587

Therefore,
$e^{8.185\ 071\ 5} = 3\ 587$

Example 5.4e

Find the logarithm base 10 and base *e* of .007 964.

SOLUTION:

Let $x = .007\ 964$

$\ln x = -4.832\ 823\ 9$

$\log x = -2.098\ 868\ 8$

Example 5.4f

Express in exponential form:
(a) $\ln x = -4.354\ 411\ 5$
(b) $\log x = -1.891\ 096\ 5.$

SOLUTION:

(a) $e^{-4.354\ 411\ 5} = .012\ 85$
(b) $10^{-1.891\ 096\ 5} = .012\ 85$

EXERCISE 5.4 / REFERENCE SECTION: 5.3 A–D, 5.4

Write the following in logarithmic form:
1. $58 = 10^{1.763\ 428}$
2. $6 = 10^{0.778\ 151}$
3. $0.003\ 25 = e^{-5.729\ 100\ 3}$
4. $0.025\ 13 = e^{-3.683\ 629}$

5. $5\ 683 = 10^{3.754\ 578}$
6. $136 = 10^{2.133\ 539}$
7. $10\ 253 = e^{9.235\ 325\ 6}$
8. $0.010\ 492 = e^{-4.557\ 142\ 2}$

Write the following in exponential form:
9. $\log 10.6 = 1.025\ 306$
10. $\log 147 = 2.167\ 317$
11. $\ln 2\ 452 = 7.804\ 659\ 9$
12. $\ln 2.603 = 0.956\ 646$

13. $\log .003\ 559 = -2.448\ 672$
14. $\log .063\ 4 = -1.197\ 910\ 7$
15. $\ln .005\ 42 = -5.217\ 659\ 5$
16. $\ln .694\ 3 = -0.364\ 851\ 1$

Use an electronic calculator or a table of mantissas to find (a) $\log x$ (b) $\ln x$ for each of the following:
17. 285
18. 0.002 85
19. 3.823
20. 43.25
21. 4 328
22. 624

23. 0.000 395 2
24. 0.687
25. 2 374
26. 453.6
27. 10.452
28. 102 830

Find x if $\log x$ is:

29.	2.201 670	36.	1.700 184
30.	3.176 959	37.	0.162 564
31.	0.445 604	38.	5.652 489 2
32.	−1.568 315	39.	−3.729 701 4
33.	−2.399 572	40.	6.541 03
34.	−2.005 22	41.	−5.179 645 8
35.	4.691 081	42.	9.197 862 9

Refer to problems 29 - 42. Use an electronic calculator to find x if $\ln x$ is the value given.

5.5 *Logarithms–Computation*

In order to use logarithms in computation, the laws of multiplication, division and powers must be understood. The following laws are stated using log which is usually associated with base 10. If base e is used, ln should be substituted. However, the rule is unchanged.

Law of Multiplication: $\log MN = \log M + \log N$

Law of Division: $\log \dfrac{M}{N} = \log M \div \log N$

Law of Powers: $\log M^p = p \log M$

$$\log M^{1/p} = \frac{1}{p} \log M$$

A.   *SOLVING EQUATIONS*

To solve an equation by using logarithms, first equate the logarithms of both sides of the equation; then solve the unknown from the new logarithmic equation.

Example 5.5a
If $(1 + i)^{69} = 2.794$, find i.

SOLUTION:

First, equate the logarithms of both sides.
$$\log (1 + i)^{69} = \log 2.794$$
$$69 \log (1 + i) = 0.446\ 226$$
$$\log (1 + i) = \frac{0.446\ 226}{69}$$
$$= 0.006\ 467$$
$$1 + i = 10^{0.006\ 467} = 1.015$$
$$i = 1.015 - 1 = 0.015, \text{ or } 1\tfrac{1}{2}\%$$

Example 5.5b
If $(1 + i)^{-46} = 0.287\ 1$, find i.

SOLUTION:

First, equate the logarithms of both sides.
$\ln(1 + i)^{-46} = \ln 0.287\ 1$
$(-46)\ln(1 + i) = -1.247\ 924\ 7$

$\ln(1+i) = \dfrac{-1.247\ 947}{-46} = .027\ 128\ 8$

$1 + i = e^{.027\ 128\ 8} = 1.027\ 5$

$\quad i = 1.027\ 5 - 1 = 0.027\ 5$ or $2\frac{3}{4}\%$

Example 5.5c
If $(1 + 2\frac{1}{2}\%)^n = 2.15$, find n.

SOLUTION:

First, equate the logarithms of both sides.
$\log(1 + 2\frac{1}{2}\%)^n = \log 2.15$
$n(\log 1.025) = \log 2.15$

$$n = \frac{\log 2.15}{\log 1.025} = \frac{0.332\ 438}{0.010\ 724} = 31$$

Example 5.5d
If $(1 + 6.5\%)^n = 26.435\ 018$, find n.

SOLUTION:

First, equate the logarithms of both sides.
$n = \ln(1.065) = \ln 26.435$

$n = \dfrac{\ln 26.435}{\ln 1.065}$

$n = \dfrac{3.274\ 688\ 9}{.062\ 974\ 8}$

$n = 52$

EXERCISE 5.5 / REFERENCE SECTION: A

Solve the following equations:
1. If $(1 + i)^{46} = 1.771$, find i.
2. If $(1 + i)^{25} = 1.45$, find i.
3. If $(1 + i)^{2/5} = 1.008$, find i.
4. If $(1 + i)^{1/6} = 1.004\ 9$, find i.
5. If $(1 + i)^{-20} = .311\ 8$, find i.
6. If $(1 + i)^{-4} = .854\ 8$, find i.
7. If $(1 + i)^{-1/4} = .995\ 1$, find i.
8. If $(1 + i)^{-1/2} = .971\ 3$, find i.
9. If $(1 + 1\frac{1}{2}\%)^n = 4.432$, find n.
10. If $(1 + 4\%)^n = 1.947\ 9$, find n.
11. If $(1 + 4\frac{1}{2}\%)^{-n} = .267$, find n.
12. If $(1 + 5\%)^{-n} = .010\ 7$, find n.

Summary of Formulae

Formula 5-1	$x = \dfrac{-b \pm \sqrt{b^2 - 4ac}}{2a}$	Used to find the roots of any quadratic equation.
Formula 5-2	$L = a + (n - 1)d$	Used to insert a given number of arithmetic means between two terms, where n = the number of terms to be inserted plus 2.
Formula 5-3	$S_n = \dfrac{n}{2}(a + L)$	Used if any three of the five quantities, a, d, n, L, and S_n are given to find the other two quantities in an arithmetic progression.
Formula 5-4	$L = ar^{n-1}$	Used to insert a given number of geometric means between two terms where n = the number of terms to be inserted plus 2.
Formula 5-5	$S_n = \dfrac{a(1 - r^n)}{1 - r}$	Used if any three of the five quantities, a, r, n, L, and S_n are given to find the other two quantities in a geometric progression.

Glossary

ANTILOGARITHM the number found from a given logarithm

ARITHMETIC MEANS the terms between any two given terms in an arithmetic progression

ARITHMETIC PROGRESSION (A.P.) a sequence of numbers in which each term following the first one is obtained by adding the preceding term to a fixed number (the common difference)

BRIGGSIAN LOGARITHMS see *common logarithms*

CHARACTERISTIC the whole-number part of a logarithm

COMMON DIFFERENCE the fixed number to which each term in an arithmetic progression is added

COMMON LOGARITHMS logarithms based on 10

COMMON RATIO the constant factor by which a geometric progression is multiplied

FORMULA a general fact, rule, or principle expressed in algebraic symbols

GEOMETRIC MEANS the terms between any two given terms in a geometric progression

GEOMETRIC PROGRESSION (G.P.) a sequence of numbers in which each term following the first one is obtained by multiplying the preceding term by a constant factor

LOGARITHM the power (exponent) to which a specified base must be raised in order to yield a number

MANTISSA the decimal part of a logarithm

NAPERIAN LOGARITHMS see *natural logarithms*

NATURAL LOGARITHMS logarithms based on e

QUADRATIC EQUATION an equation which contains up to the second power of an unknown; an equation of this type in one unknown has only two roots

QUADRATIC FORMULA a general rule which can be used to find the roots of any quadratic equation

SEQUENCE OF NUMBERS a set of numbers arranged so that there is a first number, second number, third number and so on

TERMS OF THE SEQUENCE the successive numbers in a sequence

Modern algebra–supplemental topics 6

Introduction

While the topics in this chapter are introductory in nature, they are important from an applications point-of-view.

Contained in the chapter are basic concepts and operations involving matrix algebra and linear programming, as well as the binary number system. All of these topics are relevant and their appropriateness has been greatly enhanced by the significance of their roles in relation to the computer. Matrix algebra can be applied to a wide variety of business problems, due in part to the ease with which data stored in matrix form can be accessed and manipulated by the computer. The computer is ideally suited to deal with the calculations involved with linear programming where the computational requirements involved in handling large numbers of equations would be overwhelming if handled by any other means.

Since the functioning of computers involves one or the other of two voltage levels, called "high" (represented by 1) and "low" (represented by 0), the binary numbering system, which involves only 1s or 0s, finds wide application in computer operations.

Chapter Six covers matrix algebra, linear programming, and the binary number system.

6.1 Vectors

A VECTOR is an ordered collection of numbers. The numbers may be arranged either in a row or in a column and enclosed in brackets [   ] or in boldfaced parentheses ( ). In general vectors are represented by lower-case letters, such as a, b, c, and so on.

For example, vectors a and b are ROW VECTORS:
$$a = [1, 7] \qquad b = [6, 4]$$
and c and d are COLUMN VECTORS:

$$c = \begin{bmatrix} 2 \\ 5 \\ 9 \end{bmatrix} \qquad d = \begin{bmatrix} 3 \\ 8 \\ 4 \end{bmatrix}$$

The above vectors may be applied to a practical problem as follows:

Company R has two plants: No.1 and No.2. Each plant manufactures products X and Y. The production of the products during a given period by each plant is shown in Table 6-1. (See vectors a and b.) Each product is made of three types of raw material, M-1, M-2, and M-3. The material required by each product is shown in Table 6-2. (See vectors c and d.)

Table 6-1
Company R
Production by plants
Row vectors a and b

Product	Plant	
	No. 1	No. 2
X	1 unit	7 units
Y	6	4
Total	7 units	11 units

Table 6-2
Company R
Material requirements by products
Column vectors c and d

Type of material	Product		
	X	Y	Total
M-1	2 kg	3 kg	5 kg
M-2	5	8	13
M-3	9	4	13

The numbers in the rows or columns are also known as the COMPONENTS of the vectors. Thus, a and b are two-component row vectors, and c and d are three-component column vectors. The concept of components is important in the basic vector operations: addition, subtraction, and multiplication.

A. ADDITION

Vectors with the same number of components and the same arrangement may be added. The corresponding components of the vectors are added to obtain the components of the sum of the addition. The sum is also a vector with the same arrangement as the given vectors.

Example 6.1a
(a) Add the two-component row vectors a and b:

SOLUTION:

$a + b = [1, 7] + [6, 4] = [1 + 6, 7 + 4] = [7, 11]$ (See the total row of Table 6-1.)

(b) Add the three-component column vectors c and d:

SOLUTION:

$$c + d = \begin{bmatrix} 2 \\ 5 \\ 9 \end{bmatrix} + \begin{bmatrix} 3 \\ 8 \\ 4 \end{bmatrix} = \begin{bmatrix} 2+3 \\ 5+8 \\ 9+4 \end{bmatrix} = \begin{bmatrix} 5 \\ 13 \\ 13 \end{bmatrix}$$ (See the total column of Table 6-2.)

B. SUBTRACTION

Vectors with the same number of components and the same arrangement may be subtracted. The corresponding components of the vectors are subtracted to obtain the components of the remainder of the subtraction. The remainder is also a vector with the same arrangement as the given vectors.

Example 6.1b
(a) Subtract vector b from vector a:

SOLUTION:

$$a - b = [1, 7] - [6, 4] = [1 - 6, 7 - 4] = [-5, 3]$$

(b) Subtract vector d from vector c:

SOLUTION:

$$c - d = \begin{bmatrix} 2 \\ 5 \\ 9 \end{bmatrix} - \begin{bmatrix} 3 \\ 8 \\ 4 \end{bmatrix} = \begin{bmatrix} 2-3 \\ 5-8 \\ 9-4 \end{bmatrix} = \begin{bmatrix} -1 \\ -3 \\ 5 \end{bmatrix}$$

C. MULTIPLICATION

Multiplication involving vectors is presented under two different cases below.

Case I. Scalar Multiplication

Any real number, called a SCALAR (as opposed to an IMAGINARY NUMBER), may be multiplied by a vector. The number must be multiplied by each component of the vector to obtain the components of the product. The product thus is also a vector with the same number of components and the same arrangement as the vector multiplied.

Example 6.1c
(a) Multiply 7 by vector $e = \begin{bmatrix} 3 \\ 5 \end{bmatrix}$.

SOLUTION:

$$7 \cdot e = 7 \begin{bmatrix} 3 \\ 5 \end{bmatrix} = \begin{bmatrix} 7 \times 3 \\ 7 \times 5 \end{bmatrix} = \begin{bmatrix} 21 \\ 35 \end{bmatrix}$$

(b) Multiply 2 by vector $f = [1, 3, 7]$.

SOLUTION:

$2 \cdot f = 2[1, 3, 7] = [2 \times 1, 2 \times 3, 2 \times 7] = [2, 6, 14]$

Case II. Multiplication of Two Vectors

In multiplying two vectors, a row vector is multiplied by a column vector with the same number of components. Each component of the row vector is multiplied by the corresponding component of the column vector to obtain the partial product. The sum of all partial products, called the INNER PRODUCT, or DOT PRODUCT, of the two vectors multiplied, is a *number*, not a vector.

Example 6.1d
(a) Multiply the row vector a by the column vector e.

SOLUTION:

$$a \cdot e = [1, 7]\begin{bmatrix} 3 \\ 5 \end{bmatrix} = (1 \times 3) + (7 \times 5) = 38$$

(b) Multiply the row vector f by the column vector c.

SOLUTION:

$$f \cdot c = [1, 3, 7]\begin{bmatrix} 2 \\ 5 \\ 9 \end{bmatrix} = (1 \times 2) + (3 \times 5) + (7 \times 9)$$

$$= 2 + 15 + 63 = 80$$

Note that the row vector is always written first and the column vector second. Vectors may be shown graphically. A two-component vector, such as

$a = [1, 7]$ or its *transposed* column vector $a' = \begin{bmatrix} 1 \\ 7 \end{bmatrix}$, may be represented by a point ($X = 1$, $Y = 7$) in a 2-dimensional space based on the system of rectangular co-ordinates. Figure 6-1, for example, shows the points representing vectors a, b, and $a + b$ on a 2-dimensional space. Likewise, a three-component column vector, such as

$c = \begin{bmatrix} 2 \\ 5 \\ 9 \end{bmatrix}$ or its transposed row vector $c' = [2, 5, 9]$ may be represented by a point

(2, 5, 9) in a 3-dimensional space.

Figure 6-1
Two-Component Vectors a, b, and a + b
as shown in a two-dimensional space

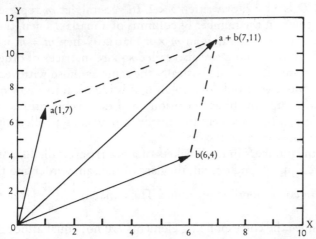

The lines drawn from the origin (0) to the three points (a, b, and $a + b$) show the geometric interpretation of vectors. Vectors may be interpreted as lines representing direction and length.

Note that two vectors are said to be equal if, and only if, both vectors are arranged in the same form (both in rows or both in columns) and their corresponding components are equal. Thus, row vector a is not equal to column vector a', although they are represented by the same point on a graph. This concept is consistent with matrices presented in the next sections.

Additional illustration: $a = [1, 7]$, $a' = \begin{bmatrix} 1 \\ 7 \end{bmatrix}$,

$$g = [7, 1], h = [1, 7]$$

We have, $a = h$, $a \neq a'$, $a \neq g$, $g \neq h$, $a' \neq h$ and ag. ($\neq$ represents "is not equal to.")

6.2 Matrices

A MATRIX is a rectangular array of numbers enclosed in brackets or in boldfaced parentheses. In general, matrices are represented by capital letters, such as A, B, C, and D as shown below:

$$A = \begin{bmatrix} 1 & 7 \\ 6 & 4 \end{bmatrix}, \qquad B = \begin{bmatrix} 3 & 2 \\ 5 & 8 \end{bmatrix}, \qquad C = \begin{bmatrix} 2 & 3 \\ 5 & 8 \\ 9 & 4 \end{bmatrix}, \qquad D = \begin{bmatrix} 6 & 1 \\ 4 & 2 \\ 9 & 7 \end{bmatrix}$$

A matrix is usually described first by its number of rows and then by its number of columns. This type of description is referred to as the *order* of a matrix. In the above illustrations, the order of matrices A and B is 2 by 2, or written 2×2, and that of matrices C and D is 3 by 2, or written 3×2. In general, let m represent the number of rows and n represent the number of columns of a matrix. Then, the order of a matrix is $m \times n$ and we may call it an $m \times n$ matrix. When $m = n$, it is called a SQUARE MATRIX. Thus, A and B are also called square matrices of order 2.

   Operations with matrices are basically the same as those with vectors. When a matrix has only one row or only one column, it is identical to a row or a column vector. Thus, in performing the basic operations–addition, subtraction, and multiplication–with matrices, it is convenient to consider a matrix as a collection of vectors of the same number of components.

   However, the numbers in the brackets of a matrix are called ELEMENTS. Note that two matrices are equal if, and only if, they are of the same order and they consist of equal elements in corresponding positions. Thus, matrix $\begin{bmatrix} 1 & 7 \\ 6 & 4 \end{bmatrix}$ is not equal to

matrix $\begin{bmatrix} 6 & 4 \\ 1 & 7 \end{bmatrix}$ since the corresponding elements are not equal although the two

matrices are of the same order, but $\begin{bmatrix} 1 & 7 \\ 6 & 4 \end{bmatrix} = \begin{bmatrix} 3-2 & 8-1 \\ 6 \times 1 & 2+2 \end{bmatrix}$.

A.   ADDITION

The corresponding elements of two matrices with the same order (the same number of rows and the same number of columns) may be added. The sum is a matrix with the same order as the given matrices.

Example 6.2a
(a)   Add the 2×2 matrices A and B.

   SOLUTION:

$$A + B = \begin{bmatrix} 1 & 7 \\ 6 & 4 \end{bmatrix} + \begin{bmatrix} 3 & 2 \\ 5 & 8 \end{bmatrix} = \begin{bmatrix} 1+3 & 7+2 \\ 6+5 & 4+8 \end{bmatrix} = \begin{bmatrix} 4 & 9 \\ 11 & 12 \end{bmatrix}$$

(b)   Add the 3×2 matrices C and D.

   SOLUTION:

$$C + D = \begin{bmatrix} 2 & 3 \\ 5 & 8 \\ 9 & 4 \end{bmatrix} + \begin{bmatrix} 6 & 1 \\ 4 & 2 \\ 9 & 7 \end{bmatrix} = \begin{bmatrix} 2+6 & 3+1 \\ 5+4 & 8+2 \\ 9+9 & 4+7 \end{bmatrix} = \begin{bmatrix} 8 & 4 \\ 9 & 10 \\ 18 & 11 \end{bmatrix}$$

B.   SUBTRACTION

Like addition, the corresponding elements of two matrices of the same order may be subtracted. The remainder is a matrix with the same order as the given matrices.

Example 6.2b

(a) Subtract matrix B from matrix A.

SOLUTION:

$$A - B = \begin{bmatrix} 1 & 7 \\ 6 & 4 \end{bmatrix} - \begin{bmatrix} 3 & 2 \\ 5 & 8 \end{bmatrix} = \begin{bmatrix} 1-3 & 7-2 \\ 6-5 & 4-8 \end{bmatrix} = \begin{bmatrix} -2 & 5 \\ 1 & -4 \end{bmatrix}$$

(b) Subtract matrix D from matrix C.

$$C - D = \begin{bmatrix} 2 & 3 \\ 5 & 8 \\ 9 & 4 \end{bmatrix} - \begin{bmatrix} 6 & 1 \\ 4 & 2 \\ 9 & 7 \end{bmatrix} = \begin{bmatrix} 2-6 & 3-1 \\ 5-4 & 8-2 \\ 9-9 & 4-7 \end{bmatrix} = \begin{bmatrix} -4 & 2 \\ 1 & 6 \\ 0 & -3 \end{bmatrix}$$

C. MULTIPLICATION

Multiplication involving matrices is also presented under two different cases below.

Case I. Scalar Multiplication

When a real number (scalar) is multiplied by a matrix, the number must be multiplied by each element of the matrix. The product thus is also a matrix with the same order of the matrix multiplied.

Example 6.2c

(a) Multiply 4 by the 2×3 matrix $E = \begin{bmatrix} 1 & 3 & 6 \\ 2 & 5 & 7 \end{bmatrix}$

$$4 \cdot E = 4 \begin{bmatrix} 1 & 3 & 6 \\ 2 & 5 & 7 \end{bmatrix} = \begin{bmatrix} 4 \times 1 & 4 \times 3 & 4 \times 6 \\ 4 \times 2 & 4 \times 5 & 4 \times 7 \end{bmatrix} = \begin{bmatrix} 4 & 12 & 24 \\ 8 & 20 & 28 \end{bmatrix}$$

(b) Multiply $\frac{1}{2}$ by the 2×2 matrix A.

SOLUTION:

$$\frac{1}{2} \cdot A = \frac{1}{2} \begin{bmatrix} 1 & 7 \\ 6 & 4 \end{bmatrix} = \begin{bmatrix} \frac{1}{2} \times 1 & \frac{1}{2} \times 7 \\ \frac{1}{2} \times 6 & \frac{1}{2} \times 4 \end{bmatrix} = \begin{bmatrix} \frac{1}{2} & 3\frac{1}{2} \\ 3 & 2 \end{bmatrix}$$

Case II. Multiplication of Two Matrices

A matrix may be multiplied by another matrix if, and only if, the number of columns in the first matrix is equal to the number of rows in the second matrix. Thus, an $m \times n$ matrix may be multiplied by an $n \times p$ matrix. The product of the two matrices is an $m \times p$ matrix.

Multiplication of Two Matrices

First matrix		Second matrix	
Rows	Columns	Rows	Columns
m	$\times$ n	n	$\times$ p

$$m \times p \text{ matrix}$$
(product)

Let A be the first matrix and B be the second matrix. Each row vector of A is multiplied by each column vector of B to obtain the corresponding element of the product matrix $A \cdot B$. Or, more generally, the element in the ith row and jth column in the product is obtained by multiplying the ith row vector in the first matrix by the jth column vector in the second matrix.

Example 6.2d

(a) Multiply matrix A by matrix B. The order of each matrix is written directly under the matrix for checking the answer. Since A and B are 2×2 matrices, the product $A \cdot B$ should be a 2×2 matrix also.

SOLUTION:

$$A \cdot B = \begin{bmatrix} 1 & 7 \\ 6 & 4 \end{bmatrix} \cdot \begin{bmatrix} 3 & 2 \\ 5 & 8 \end{bmatrix} = \begin{bmatrix} [1 \ 7]\begin{bmatrix}3\\5\end{bmatrix} & [1 \ 7]\begin{bmatrix}2\\8\end{bmatrix} \\[2mm] [6 \ 4]\begin{bmatrix}3\\5\end{bmatrix} & [6 \ 4]\begin{bmatrix}2\\8\end{bmatrix} \end{bmatrix}$$

$$= \begin{bmatrix} (1 \times 3) + (7 \times 5) & (1 \times 2) + (7 \times 8) \\ (6 \times 3) + (4 \times 5) & (6 \times 2) + (4 \times 8) \end{bmatrix} = \begin{bmatrix} 38 & 58 \\ 38 & 44 \end{bmatrix}$$

NOTE: It can easily be verified that $A \cdot B \neq B \cdot A$.

Example 6.2e

(b) Multiply matrix C by matrix A.

SOLUTION:

Since C is a 3×2 matrix and A is a 2×2 matrix, the product $C \cdot A$ will be a 3×2 matrix.

$$C \cdot A = \begin{bmatrix} 2 & 3 \\ 5 & 8 \\ 9 & 4 \end{bmatrix} \cdot \begin{bmatrix} 1 & 7 \\ 6 & 4 \end{bmatrix} = \begin{bmatrix} [2 \ 3]\begin{bmatrix}1\\6\end{bmatrix} & [2 \ 3]\begin{bmatrix}7\\4\end{bmatrix} \\[2mm] [5 \ 8]\begin{bmatrix}1\\6\end{bmatrix} & [5 \ 8]\begin{bmatrix}7\\4\end{bmatrix} \\[2mm] [9 \ 4]\begin{bmatrix}1\\6\end{bmatrix} & [9 \ 4]\begin{bmatrix}7\\4\end{bmatrix} \end{bmatrix}$$

$$= \begin{bmatrix} (2 \times 1) + (3 \times 6) & (2 \times 7) + (3 \times 4) \\ (5 \times 1) + (8 \times 6) & (5 \times 7) + (8 \times 4) \\ (9 \times 1) + (4 \times 6) & (9 \times 7) + (4 \times 4) \end{bmatrix} = \begin{bmatrix} 20 & 26 \\ 53 & 67 \\ 33 & 79 \end{bmatrix}_{3 \times 2}$$

Note that since the number of columns in A (2 columns) is not equal to the number of rows in C (3 rows), we could not multiply A by C (or $A \cdot C$). Also, Example 6.2e may be written in a practical problem as shown in Table 6-3. This table is constructed from the information given in Section 6.1 (Tables 6-1 and 6-2). It shows the total amount of each type of raw material required by each plant. The totals shown in the table are the same as the elements in the product matrix $C \cdot A$.

Table 6-3
Company R
Material requirements by plants

| Material | Plant No. 1 | | | | | | | Plant No. 2 | | | | | | |
| | Product X | | | Product Y | | | | Product X | | | Product Y | | | |
	For each unit	Units of X	Sub-total	For each unit	Units of Y	Sub-total	Total	For each unit	Units of X	Sub-total	For each unit	Units of Y	Sub-total	Total
M-1	2 kg	1	2 kg	3 kg	6	18 kg	20 kg	2 kg	7	14 kg	3 kg	4	12 kg	26 kg
M-2	5	1	5	8	6	48	53	5	7	35	8	4	32	67
M-3	9	1	9	4	6	24	33	9	7	63	4	4	16	79

First column vector of matrix $C \cdot A$ Second column vector of matrix $C \cdot A$

SOURCE: Computed from Tables 6-1 and 6-2. See Example 6.2e for matrix $C \cdot A$.

EXERCISE 6.2 / REFERENCE SECTIONS: A-C

Operations with vectors.

Let $u = [6,2]$; $v = [4,5]$; $w = \begin{bmatrix} 3 \\ 7 \end{bmatrix}$; $x = \begin{bmatrix} 1 \\ 6 \\ 5 \end{bmatrix}$; $y = \begin{bmatrix} 2 \\ 3 \\ 7 \end{bmatrix}$; and $z = [4, 8, 9]$.

Perform the indicated operations in each of the following expressions:

1. $u + v$
2. $x + y$
3. $x - y$
4. $u - v$
5. $y - x$
6. $v - u$
7. $5u$
8. $\frac{2}{3}v$
9. $3w$
10. $6z$
11. $4x$
12. $\frac{1}{5}y$
13. $u \cdot w$
14. $v \cdot w$
15. $z \cdot x$
16. $z \cdot y$

Operations with matrices.

Let $A = \begin{bmatrix} 3 & 9 \\ 2 & 4 \end{bmatrix}$; $B = \begin{bmatrix} 5 & 6 \\ 1 & 7 \end{bmatrix}$; $C = \begin{bmatrix} 1 & 2 \\ 3 & 9 \\ 8 & 4 \end{bmatrix}$; $D = \begin{bmatrix} 5 & 1 \\ 2 & 7 \\ 3 & 6 \end{bmatrix}$; $E = \begin{bmatrix} 4 & 6 & 3 \\ 1 & 5 & 8 \end{bmatrix}$;

and $F = \begin{bmatrix} 2 & 4 & 7 \\ 5 & 3 & 1 \end{bmatrix}$.

Perform the indicated operations in each of the following expressions:

17. $A + B$	23. $\frac{1}{4}C$	29. $A \cdot F$	35. $F \cdot C$
18. $C + D$	24. $\frac{1}{3}E$	30. $B \cdot E$	36. $E \cdot D$
19. $C - D$	25. $A \cdot B$	31. $E \cdot C$	37. $C \cdot E$
20. $A - B$	26. $B \cdot A$	32. $F \cdot D$	38. $D \cdot F$
21. $3A$	27. $A \cdot E$	33. $C \cdot A$	39. $C \cdot F$
22. $2B$	28. $B \cdot F$	34. $D \cdot B$	40. $D \cdot E$

6.3 Determinants

A DETERMINANT is a number which determines whether or not there is an *inverse* of a square matrix. The details concerning the inverse of a square matrix are presented in the next section. This section introduces the basic operations with determinants.

A determinant is written in a manner similar to its associated square matrix except that two vertical lines instead of brackets are used. For example, if the 2 × 2 square matrix

$A = \begin{bmatrix} 2 & 5 \\ 1 & 3 \end{bmatrix}$, the determinant of A, denoted by $|A|$, is

$|A| = \begin{vmatrix} 2 & 5 \\ 1 & 3 \end{vmatrix}$, which is also called a determinant of order 2.

The value of a determinant may be computed in two ways: (1) by cross multiplying the elements, and (2) by finding the minors. Each of these methods is discussed in more detail below.

A.   EVALUATING DETERMINANTS BY CROSS MULTIPLICATION

We shall evaluate only the determinants of orders 2 and 3 by this method.
    If the 2 × 2 square matrix

$A = \begin{bmatrix} a_{11} & a_{12} \\ a_{21} & a_{22} \end{bmatrix}$, then the determinant of A is

$$|A| = \begin{bmatrix} a_{11} & a_{12} \\ a_{21} & a_{22} \end{bmatrix} = a_{11}a_{22} - a_{12}a_{21}.$$

secondary   primary
diagonal   diagonal

Observe that the letter a represents the elements of the matrix A, with the first subscript indicating the location of the row and the second subscript indicating the location of the column. The positive product $(+a_{11}a_{22})$ consists of the elements on the primary diagonal and the negative product $(-a_{12}a_{21})$ consists of the elements on the secondary diagonal of the determinant; also, each product has only one element from each row and each column.

Example 6.3a

Evaluate the determinant of the matrix A if

(a) $A = \begin{bmatrix} 2 & 5 \\ 1 & 3 \end{bmatrix}$, and (b) $A = \begin{bmatrix} 3 & 1 \\ 6 & -1 \end{bmatrix}$.

SOLUTION:

(a)
$$|A| = \begin{vmatrix} 2 & 5 \\ 1 & 3 \end{vmatrix} = (2 \times 3) - (5 \times 1) = 6 - 5 = 1$$

(b)
$$|A| = \begin{vmatrix} 3 & 1 \\ 6 & -1 \end{vmatrix} = (3 \times (-1)) - (1 \times 6) = -3 - 6 = -9$$

Likewise, the determinant of order 3 is associated with a 3×3 matrix, or written

$$|A| = \begin{vmatrix} a_{11} & a_{12} & a_{13} \\ a_{21} & a_{22} & a_{23} \\ a_{31} & a_{32} & a_{33} \end{vmatrix}$$
$$= a_{11}a_{22}a_{33} + a_{12}a_{23}a_{31} + a_{13}a_{21}a_{32} - a_{13}a_{22}a_{31} - a_{12}a_{21}a_{33} - a_{11}a_{23}a_{32}$$

The three positive products are obtained from the primary diagonals as shown below:

The three negative products are obtained from the secondary diagonals as shown below:

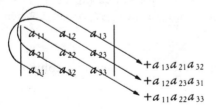

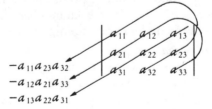

Note that the cross multiplication method as shown above does not work for determinants of order higher than 3. Determinants of higher order should be evaluated by the minors, as shown below.

Example 6.3b
Evaluate the determinant $|A|$.

SOLUTION:

$$|A| = \begin{vmatrix} 2 & -3 & 4 \\ 1 & 5 & -2 \\ 4 & 2 & 6 \end{vmatrix} = (2 \times 5 \times 6) + [(-3) \times (-2) \times 4] + (4 \times 1 \times 2) - (4 \times 5 \times 4) - [(-3) \times 1 \times 6] - [2 \times (-2) \times 2]$$

$$= 60 + 24 + 8 - (80) - (-18) - (-8) = 38$$

The positive and negative products may be computed in the following manner. Note that the first two columns of the determinant are written as the 4th and 5th columns respectively to facilitate the computation.

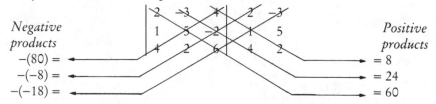

Negative products
$-(80) = \quad = 8$
$-(-8) = \quad = 24$
$-(-18) = \quad = 60$

Positive products

B.   EVALUATING DETERMINANTS BY MINORS

A MINOR is a determinant of order $(n - 1)$ obtained from a determinant of order n. Thus, in a 3×3 determinant, we may have 2×2 minors. A minor is specified by an element. The minor of the element a_{ij}, located in the ith row and jth column in a determinant, is denoted by A_{ij}. Minor A_{ij} is obtained by deleting both the ith row and jth column of the determinant. Thus, in the 2×2 determinant

$$|A| = \begin{vmatrix} a_{11} & a_{12} \\ a_{21} & a_{22} \end{vmatrix}, \text{ minor } A_{11} = \begin{vmatrix} a_{11} & a_{12} \\ a_{21} & a_{22} \end{vmatrix} = |a_{22}|,$$

and in the 3×3 determinant

$$|A| = \begin{vmatrix} a_{11} & a_{12} & a_{13} \\ a_{21} & a_{22} & a_{23} \\ a_{31} & a_{32} & a_{33} \end{vmatrix}, \text{ minor } A_{21} = \begin{vmatrix} a_{11} & a_{12} & a_{13} \\ a_{21} & a_{22} & a_{23} \\ a_{31} & a_{32} & a_{33} \end{vmatrix} = \begin{vmatrix} a_{12} & a_{13} \\ a_{32} & a_{33} \end{vmatrix}.$$

(The element a_{ij} (a_{11} and a_{21}) is circled in each illustration.)

A minor should be prefixed by a sign when it is used for evaluating a determinant. When $i + j$ is an even number, the sign of the minor is positive, or $+A_{ij}$. When $i + j$ is an odd number, the sign is negative, or $-A_{ij}$.

Illustrations:
The minor of element a_{11} is $+A_{11}$ since it appears in the first row and first column and $1 + 1 = 2$, an even number.

$$\text{If } |A| = \begin{vmatrix} 2 & 5 \\ 1 & 3 \end{vmatrix}, a_{11} = 2 \text{ and } + A_{11} = \begin{vmatrix} 2 & 5 \\ 1 & 3 \end{vmatrix} = +|3|.$$

The minor of element a_{21} is $-A_{21}$ since it appears in the second row and first column and $2 + 1 = 3$, an odd number.

$$\text{If } |A| = \begin{vmatrix} 2 & -3 & 4 \\ 1 & 5 & -2 \\ 4 & 2 & 6 \end{vmatrix}, a_{21} = 1 \text{ and } -A_{21} = - \begin{vmatrix} 2 & -3 & 4 \\ 1 & 5 & -2 \\ 4 & 2 & 6 \end{vmatrix}$$

$$= - \begin{vmatrix} -3 & 4 \\ 2 & 6 \end{vmatrix}.$$

NOTE: A signed minor is also called a COFACTOR of the element a_{ij}.

A determinant may be evaluated by signed minors as follows:

STEP (1): Multiply each element of *any* column (or any row) by its signed minor.

STEP (2): Add the n products obtained above. The sum is the value of the determinant.

Thus, for a 2×2 determinant $|A|$, we may express the value in terms of the elements of the *first column* and their signed minors:

$$|A| = a_{11}A_{11} - a_{21}A_{21}.$$

Example 6.3c
Evaluate the determinants in Example 6.3a by minors.

SOLUTION:

(a) $|A| = \begin{vmatrix} 2 & 5 \\ 1 & 3 \end{vmatrix} = 2 \begin{vmatrix} 2 & 5 \\ 1 & 3 \end{vmatrix} - 1 \begin{vmatrix} 2 & 5 \\ 1 & 3 \end{vmatrix} = 2|3| - 1|5|$

$$= 6 - 5 = 1$$

(b) $|A| = \begin{vmatrix} 3 & 1 \\ 6 & -1 \end{vmatrix} = 3 \begin{vmatrix} 3 & 1 \\ 6 & -1 \end{vmatrix} - 6 \begin{vmatrix} 3 & 1 \\ 6 & -1 \end{vmatrix} = 3|-1| - 6|1|$

$$= (-3) - 6 = -9$$

For a 3×3 determinant $|A|$, we may also express the value in terms of the elements of the *first column* and their signed minors:

$$|A| = a_{11}A_{11} - a_{21}A_{21} + a_{31}A_{31}$$

Example 6.3d
Evaluate the determinant in Example 6.3b by minors.

SOLUTION:

$$|A| = \begin{vmatrix} 2 & -3 & 4 \\ 1 & 5 & -2 \\ 4 & 2 & 6 \end{vmatrix} = 2 \begin{vmatrix} 2 & -3 & 4 \\ 1 & 5 & -2 \\ 4 & 2 & 6 \end{vmatrix} - 1 \begin{vmatrix} 2 & -3 & 4 \\ 1 & 5 & -2 \\ 4 & 2 & 6 \end{vmatrix} + 4 \begin{vmatrix} 2 & -3 & 4 \\ 1 & 5 & -2 \\ 4 & 2 & 6 \end{vmatrix}$$

$$= 2 \begin{vmatrix} 5 & -2 \\ 2 & 6 \end{vmatrix} - 1 \begin{vmatrix} -3 & 4 \\ 2 & 6 \end{vmatrix} + 4 \begin{vmatrix} -3 & 4 \\ 5 & -2 \end{vmatrix}$$

$$= 2[30 - (-4)] - 1[(-18) - 8] + 4(6 - 20)$$

$$= 68 + 26 - 56 = 38$$

Determinants of higher order may be evaluated by repeating the process of finding the products of the elements of the first column and their signed minors as illustrated in Example 6.3d. For instance, a 4×4 determinant may be evaluated from its 3×3 signed minors. Each of the 3×3 signed minors is then evaluated from its 2×2 signed minors.

EXERCISE 6-3 / REFERENCE SECTIONS A–B

Evaluate each of the following determinants by (a) the cross multiplication method, and (b) finding the signed minors of the first column elements:

1. $\begin{vmatrix} 3 & 8 \\ 5 & 6 \end{vmatrix}$ 3. $\begin{vmatrix} -2 & 8 \\ 4 & -9 \end{vmatrix}$ 5. $\begin{vmatrix} 1 & -2 & 3 \\ 4 & 5 & -6 \\ 7 & 8 & 9 \end{vmatrix}$ 7. $\begin{vmatrix} 1 & 2 & 0 \\ -1 & 1 & 2 \\ 2 & 1 & 0 \end{vmatrix}$

2. $\begin{vmatrix} 2 & -3 \\ 5 & 4 \end{vmatrix}$ 4. $\begin{vmatrix} -3 & 12 \\ -7 & 8 \end{vmatrix}$ 6. $\begin{vmatrix} 3 & 5 & -1 \\ 2 & -7 & 8 \\ 4 & 1 & 6 \end{vmatrix}$ 8. $\begin{vmatrix} 1 & 3 & 2 \\ 2 & -1 & 0 \\ 3 & 2 & 1 \end{vmatrix}$

Evaluate each determinant by the signed minors of the elements of the row or column indicated:

9. The determinant given in Problem 1–Use the elements in the first row.
10. The determinant given in Problem 2–Use the elements in the first row.
11. The determinant given in Problem 5–Use the elements in the 2nd row.
12. The determinant given in Problem 6–Use the elements in the 2nd column.

6.4 The Inverse of a Square Matrix

In algebra, the INVERSE or RECIPROCAL of the number a is a^{-1} (or $\frac{1}{a}$); the product of the number and its inverse is always equal to 1, or $a \cdot a^{-1} = 1$. A similar relationship between a matrix and its inverse may be expressed.

Let A = a square matrix, and
   A^{-1} = the inverse of A.
Then,
$A^{-1} \cdot A = A \cdot A^{-1} = I$,
where I = an identity matrix of the same order as A and A^{-1}.

An IDENTITY MATRIX or UNIT MATRIX is a square matrix with all elements on its PRINCIPAL DIAGONAL (the line from the upper left corner to the lower right corner) equal to 1 and all other elements 0, such as

the 2×2 identity matrix $I = \begin{bmatrix} 1 & 0 \\ 0 & 1 \end{bmatrix}$, and the 3×3 identity matrix $I = \begin{bmatrix} 1 & 0 & 0 \\ 0 & 1 & 0 \\ 0 & 0 & 1 \end{bmatrix}$.

An identity matrix acts in matrix algebra in the same ways as 1 in the ordinary algebra concerning multiplication. Thus, the expression

$A \cdot I = I \cdot A = A$ is true for all matrices A.

Example 6.4a

Let the 2×2 matrix $A = \begin{bmatrix} 2 & 5 \\ 1 & 3 \end{bmatrix}$ and $I = \begin{bmatrix} 1 & 0 \\ 0 & 1 \end{bmatrix}$.

SOLUTION:

$$A \cdot I = \begin{bmatrix} 2 & 5 \\ 1 & 3 \end{bmatrix} \cdot \begin{bmatrix} 1 & 0 \\ 0 & 1 \end{bmatrix} = \begin{bmatrix} (2 \times 1) + (5 \times 0) & (2 \times 0) + (5 \times 1) \\ (1 \times 1) + (3 \times 0) & (1 \times 0) + (3 \times 1) \end{bmatrix}$$

$$= \begin{bmatrix} 2 & 5 \\ 1 & 3 \end{bmatrix} = A$$

$$I \cdot A = \begin{bmatrix} 1 & 0 \\ 0 & 1 \end{bmatrix} \cdot \begin{bmatrix} 2 & 5 \\ 1 & 3 \end{bmatrix} = \begin{bmatrix} (1 \times 2) + (0 \times 1) & (1 \times 5) + (0 \times 3) \\ (0 \times 2) + (1 \times 1) & (0 \times 5) + (1 \times 3) \end{bmatrix}$$

$$= \begin{bmatrix} 2 & 5 \\ 1 & 3 \end{bmatrix} = A$$

There are various methods of finding the inverse of a square matrix. We shall introduce two methods: (1) the basic method, and (2) the short method by using determinants.

A. BASIC METHOD

This method is illustrated by the example below.

Example 6.4b

Find the inverse of the square matrix $A = \begin{bmatrix} 2 & 5 \\ 1 & 3 \end{bmatrix}$. Let $I = \begin{bmatrix} 1 & 0 \\ 0 & 1 \end{bmatrix}$.

SOLUTION:

If A^{-1}, the inverse of A, exists, then we may write $A \cdot A^{-1} = I$ as

$$\begin{bmatrix} 2 & 5 \\ 1 & 3 \end{bmatrix} \cdot A^{-1} = \begin{bmatrix} 1 & 0 \\ 0 & 1 \end{bmatrix}.$$

Since A is a 2×2 square matrix and the product I is a 2×2 square matrix, the unknown matrix A^{-1} must also be a 2×2 square matrix. Let b represent the elements of the matrix A^{-1}, with the first and second subscripts indicating the locations of rows and columns in the matrix respectively, or

$$A^{-1} = \begin{bmatrix} b_{11} & b_{12} \\ b_{21} & b_{22} \end{bmatrix}.$$

We then have

$$\begin{bmatrix} 2 & 5 \\ 1 & 3 \end{bmatrix} \cdot \begin{bmatrix} b_{11} & b_{12} \\ b_{21} & b_{22} \end{bmatrix} = \begin{bmatrix} 1 & 0 \\ 0 & 1 \end{bmatrix}.$$

Multiply the left side,

$$\begin{bmatrix} (2b_{11} + 5b_{21}) & (2b_{12} + 5b_{22}) \\ (1b_{11} + 3b_{21}) & (1b_{12} + 3b_{22}) \end{bmatrix} = \begin{bmatrix} 1 & 0 \\ 0 & 1 \end{bmatrix}.$$

Equate corresponding elements of the matrices on both sides. We have a system of four equations:

$$\begin{cases} 2b_{11} + 5b_{21} = 1 & \text{(1)} \\ 1b_{11} + 3b_{21} = 0 & \text{(2)} \end{cases} \qquad \begin{cases} 2b_{12} + 5b_{22} = 0 & \text{(3)} \\ 1b_{12} + 3b_{22} = 1 & \text{(4)} \end{cases}$$

Solve equations (1) and (2) for b_{11} and b_{21}:

$(2) \times 2 \quad 2b_{11} + 6b_{21} = 0 \qquad (2)'$

$(2)' - (1) \qquad\qquad b_{21} = -1$

Substitute $b_{21} = -1$ in (2),

$\qquad b_{11} + 3(-1) = 0,$

$\qquad\qquad b_{11} = 3.$

Solve equations (3) and (4) for b_{12} and b_{22}:

$(4) \times 2 \quad 2b_{12} + 6b_{22} = 2 \qquad (4)'$

$(4)' - (3) \qquad\qquad b_{22} = 2$

Substitute $b_{22} = 2$ in (4),

$\qquad b_{12} + 3(2) = 1,$

$\qquad\qquad b_{12} = -5.$

Thus,

$$A^{-1} = \begin{bmatrix} b_{11} & b_{12} \\ b_{21} & b_{22} \end{bmatrix} = \begin{bmatrix} 3 & -5 \\ -1 & 2 \end{bmatrix}.$$

CHECK:

$$A \cdot A^{-1} = \begin{bmatrix} 2 & 5 \\ 1 & 3 \end{bmatrix} \cdot \begin{bmatrix} 3 & -5 \\ -1 & 2 \end{bmatrix} = \begin{bmatrix} 6 + (-5) & (-10) + (10) \\ 3 + (-3) & (-5) + 6 \end{bmatrix}$$

$$= \begin{bmatrix} 1 & 0 \\ 0 & 1 \end{bmatrix} = I$$

Also, $A^{-1} \cdot A = \begin{bmatrix} 3 & -5 \\ -1 & 2 \end{bmatrix} \cdot \begin{bmatrix} 2 & 5 \\ 1 & 3 \end{bmatrix} = \begin{bmatrix} 6 + (-5) & 15 + (-15) \\ (-2) + 2 & (-5) + 6 \end{bmatrix}$

$$= \begin{bmatrix} 1 & 0 \\ 0 & 1 \end{bmatrix} = I.$$

The results from the checking show that $A^{-1} \cdot A = A \cdot A^{-1} = I$.

B. SHORT METHOD

The process of finding the inverse of a square matrix can be simplified when determinants are used. Observe the procedures illustrated in Example 6.4b. Let the 2×2 square matrix A be written in a general form, or

$A = \begin{bmatrix} a_{11} & a_{12} \\ a_{21} & a_{22} \end{bmatrix}$. If A^{-1} exists, we may write $A \cdot A^{-1} = I$ as

$$\begin{bmatrix} a_{11} & a_{12} \\ a_{21} & a_{22} \end{bmatrix} \cdot \begin{bmatrix} b_{11} & b_{12} \\ b_{21} & b_{22} \end{bmatrix} = \begin{bmatrix} 1 & 0 \\ 0 & 1 \end{bmatrix}.$$

After multiplying the matrices on the left side of the above equation, equating corresponding elements to obtain the four equations, and solving the four equations, we have[1]

---

[1]Multiply the left side:
$$\begin{bmatrix} a_{11}b_{11} + a_{12}b_{21} & a_{11}b_{12} + a_{12}b_{22} \\ a_{21}b_{11} + a_{22}b_{21} & a_{21}b_{12} + a_{22}b_{22} \end{bmatrix} = \begin{bmatrix} 1 & 0 \\ 0 & 1 \end{bmatrix}$$

Equate corresponding elements:
$$\begin{cases} a_{11}b_{11} + a_{12}b_{21} = 1 \dots\dots(1) \\ a_{21}b_{11} + a_{22}b_{21} = 0 \dots\dots(2) \end{cases} \qquad \begin{cases} a_{11}b_{12} + a_{12}b_{22} = 0 \dots\dots(3) \\ a_{21}b_{12} + a_{22}b_{22} = 1 \dots\dots(4) \end{cases}$$

Solve equations (1) and (2) for b_{11} and b_{21}:

$(1) \times a_{21} \qquad a_{21}a_{11}b_{11} + a_{21}a_{12}b_{21} = a_{21} \dots\dots (1)'$

$(2) \times a_{11} \qquad \underline{a_{11}a_{21}b_{11} + a_{11}a_{22}b_{21} = 0 \dots\dots(2)'}$

$(1)' - (2)' \qquad a_{21}a_{12}b_{21} - a_{11}a_{22}b_{21} = a_{21}$

$\qquad\qquad\quad b_{21}(a_{21}a_{12} - a_{11}a_{22}) = a_{21}$

$$b_{21} = \frac{a_{21}}{a_{21}a_{12} - a_{11}a_{22}}$$

$$= \frac{a_{21}}{-(a_{11}a_{22} - a_{21}a_{12})} = \frac{-a_{21}}{|A|}$$

Substitute b_{21} value in (2):

$$a_{21}b_{11} + a_{22}\left(\frac{a_{21}}{a_{21}a_{12} - a_{11}a_{22}}\right) = 0$$

$$b_{11} = -\frac{a_{22}a_{21}}{a_{21}a_{12} - a_{11}a_{22}} \cdot \frac{1}{a_{21}} = \frac{a_{22}}{|A|}$$

We may solve equations (3) and (4) in a similar manner to obtain the values of b_{12} and b_{22}.

$$b_{11} = \frac{a_{22}}{|A|}, \qquad\qquad b_{12} = \frac{-a_{12}}{|A|},$$

$$b_{21} = \frac{-a_{21}}{|A|}, \qquad\qquad b_{22} = \frac{a_{11}}{|A|};$$

$$\text{and } A^{-1} = \begin{bmatrix} b_{11} & b_{12} \\ b_{21} & b_{22} \end{bmatrix} = \begin{bmatrix} \dfrac{a_{22}}{|A|} & \dfrac{-a_{12}}{|A|} \\ \dfrac{-a_{21}}{|A|} & \dfrac{a_{11}}{|A|} \end{bmatrix} = \frac{1}{|A|} \begin{bmatrix} a_{22} & -a_{12} \\ -a_{21} & a_{11} \end{bmatrix},$$

$$\text{where } |A| = \begin{vmatrix} a_{11} & a_{12} \\ a_{21} & a_{22} \end{vmatrix} = a_{11}a_{22} - a_{12}a_{21} \neq 0.$$

Thus, the determinant $|A|$ determines the existence of the inverse of a square matrix A. If, and only if, $|A| \neq 0$, the inverse A^{-1} exists.

Example 6.4b now may be solved by the short method as follows:

$$A = \begin{bmatrix} a_{11} & a_{12} \\ a_{21} & a_{22} \end{bmatrix} = \begin{bmatrix} 2 & 5 \\ 1 & 3 \end{bmatrix} \qquad |A| = \begin{vmatrix} 2 & 5 \\ 1 & 3 \end{vmatrix} = (2 \times 3) - (5 \times 1) = 1.$$

Since $|A| \neq 0$, A has an inverse.

$$A^{-1} = \frac{1}{|A|} \begin{bmatrix} a_{22} & -a_{12} \\ -a_{21} & a_{11} \end{bmatrix} = \frac{1}{1} \begin{bmatrix} 3 & -5 \\ -1 & 2 \end{bmatrix} = \begin{bmatrix} 3 & -5 \\ -1 & 2 \end{bmatrix}$$

In summary, to write the inverse of a 2×2 square matrix A for which $|A| \neq 0$, we may interchange the elements on the principal diagonal, prefix each of the other two elements with a negative sign, and multiply the resulting matrix by $\frac{1}{|A|}$.

The inverse of a 2×2 square matrix may also be written in terms of signed minors as follows:

$$A^{-1} = \frac{1}{|A|} \begin{bmatrix} A_{11} & -A_{21} \\ -A_{12} & A_{22} \end{bmatrix}, \text{ since } \begin{cases} A_{11} = a_{22}, & -A_{21} = -a_{12}, \\ -A_{12} = -a_{21}, & A_{22} = a_{11}. \end{cases}$$

Observe that the signed minors in the above matrix are in *transposed order*. For example, the subscripts 21 in element a_{21} indicate that the element is in the second *row* and the first *column*. Now, the subscripts 21 in the signed minor $-A_{21}$ indicate the location of the minor being in the second *column* and the first *row*.

Similarly, the inverse of a 3×3 square matrix may be written in terms of signed minors:

$$A^{-1} = \frac{1}{|A|} \begin{bmatrix} A_{11} & -A_{21} & A_{31} \\ -A_{12} & A_{22} & -A_{32} \\ A_{13} & -A_{23} & A_{33} \end{bmatrix}.$$

Again observe the transposed subscripts, such as 31 in the signed minor A_{31} indicating the location of the minor in the third column and the first row. Note that the minor of element a_{31} is $+A_{31}$ (a positive determinant) since the sum of the subscripts

$3 + 1 = 4$ is an even number. The minors A_{12}, A_{21}, A_{23}, and A_{32} have negative signs since the sums of their subscripts are odd numbers, such as $1 + 2 = 3$, and $2 + 3 = 5$.

Example 6.4c

Find the inverse of the 3×3 square matrix $A = \begin{bmatrix} 2 & -3 & 4 \\ 1 & 5 & -2 \\ 4 & 2 & 6 \end{bmatrix}$.

SOLUTION:

$$|A| = \begin{vmatrix} 2 & -3 & 4 \\ 1 & 5 & -2 \\ 4 & 2 & 6 \end{vmatrix} = 38 \text{ (See Example 6.3d.)}$$

Since $|A| \neq 0$, A^{-1} or the inverse of A exists.

$$A^{-1} = \frac{1}{38} \begin{bmatrix} \begin{vmatrix} 5 & -2 \\ 2 & 6 \end{vmatrix} & -\begin{vmatrix} -3 & 4 \\ 2 & 6 \end{vmatrix} & \begin{vmatrix} -3 & 4 \\ 5 & -2 \end{vmatrix} \\ -\begin{vmatrix} 1 & -2 \\ 4 & 6 \end{vmatrix} & \begin{vmatrix} 2 & 4 \\ 4 & 6 \end{vmatrix} & -\begin{vmatrix} 2 & 4 \\ 1 & -2 \end{vmatrix} \\ \begin{vmatrix} 1 & 5 \\ 4 & 2 \end{vmatrix} & -\begin{vmatrix} 2 & -3 \\ 4 & 2 \end{vmatrix} & \begin{vmatrix} 2 & -3 \\ 1 & 5 \end{vmatrix} \end{bmatrix}$$

See the formula for A^{-1} on page 168.

$$= \frac{1}{38} \begin{bmatrix} 34 & 26 & -14 \\ -14 & -4 & 8 \\ -18 & -16 & 13 \end{bmatrix}$$

CHECK:

$$A^{-1} \cdot A = \frac{1}{38} \begin{bmatrix} 34 & 26 & -14 \\ -14 & -4 & 8 \\ -18 & -16 & 13 \end{bmatrix} \cdot \begin{bmatrix} 2 & -3 & 4 \\ 1 & 5 & -2 \\ 4 & 2 & 6 \end{bmatrix} = \begin{bmatrix} 1 & 0 & 0 \\ 0 & 1 & 0 \\ 0 & 0 & 1 \end{bmatrix}$$

EXERCISE 6.4 / REFERENCE SECTIONS: A–B

Let $A = \begin{bmatrix} 5 & -2 \\ 3 & 4 \end{bmatrix}$, $B = \begin{bmatrix} 3 & 4 \\ 2 & 6 \end{bmatrix}$, and $I = \begin{bmatrix} 1 & 0 \\ 0 & 1 \end{bmatrix}$:

1. Show that $A \cdot I = A$ and $I \cdot A = A$.
2. Show that $B \cdot I = B$ and $I \cdot B = B$.

Find the inverse of each matrix A if the inverse exists by (a) the basic method, and (b) the short method. Also, check your answers by the relationship $A \cdot A^{-1} = I$:

3. $A = \begin{bmatrix} 3 & 3 \\ 5 & 5 \end{bmatrix}$ 4. $A = \begin{bmatrix} -4 & 2 \\ -1 & \frac{1}{2} \end{bmatrix}$ 5. $A = \begin{bmatrix} 4 & 5 \\ 9 & 7 \end{bmatrix}$ 6. $A = \begin{bmatrix} 1 & -6 \\ 2 & 3 \end{bmatrix}$

Find the inverse of each matrix A if the inverse exists by the short method. Also, check your answers by the relationship $A \cdot A^{-1} = I$:

7. $A = \begin{bmatrix} 1 & -2 & 3 \\ 4 & 5 & -6 \\ 7 & 8 & 9 \end{bmatrix}, |A| = 240$

8. $A = \begin{bmatrix} 3 & 5 & -1 \\ 2 & -7 & 8 \\ 4 & 1 & 6 \end{bmatrix}, |A| = -80$

6.5 Solving Linear Equations by Matrix Algebra

A system of linear equations may be solved by the usual algebraic operations as presented in Chapter 3. However, the work of solving a system of three or more linear equations becomes increasingly difficult by the ordinary method. Matrix algebra offers a simplified and systematic method of solving the equations. The systematic steps may also be conveniently programmed for electronic computers to speed the calculations.

There are various methods of solving a system of n linear equations in n unknowns by matrix algebra. We shall introduce two methods below: (1) using the inverse of a square matrix, and (2) using determinants.

A.   USING THE INVERSE OF A SQUARE MATRIX IN SOLVING EQUATIONS

This method is illustrated by Example 6.5a. Example 6.5a uses only 2 equations, although this method is applicable to a system of more than 2 linear equations.

Example 6.5a
Solve the following equations simultaneously:
$$\begin{cases} 3x + y = 5 \\ 6x - y = 6 \end{cases}$$

SOLUTION:

The two equations can be written in matrix form as follows:

$$\begin{bmatrix} 3 & 1 \\ 6 & -1 \end{bmatrix} \cdot \begin{bmatrix} x \\ y \end{bmatrix} = \begin{bmatrix} 5 \\ 6 \end{bmatrix}$$

The first matrix on the left side is formed by the coefficients of unknowns x and y, the second matrix by the unknowns, and the matrix on the right side by the constants.

Let A be the coefficient matrix, or $A = \begin{bmatrix} 3 & 1 \\ 6 & -1 \end{bmatrix}$. Then,

$$A \cdot \begin{bmatrix} x \\ y \end{bmatrix} = \begin{bmatrix} 5 \\ 6 \end{bmatrix}.$$

Multiply both sides by A^{-1}, the inverse of the 2×2 square matrix A,

$$A^{-1} \cdot A \cdot \begin{bmatrix} x \\ y \end{bmatrix} = A^{-1} \cdot \begin{bmatrix} 5 \\ 6 \end{bmatrix}.$$

Since $A^{-1} \cdot A = I$ and $I \cdot \begin{bmatrix} x \\ y \end{bmatrix} = \begin{bmatrix} x \\ y \end{bmatrix}$, we obtain

$$\begin{bmatrix} x \\ y \end{bmatrix} = A^{-1} \cdot \begin{bmatrix} 5 \\ 6 \end{bmatrix}.$$

Thus, the problem of solving a system of linear equations now becomes a problem of finding the inverse of the coefficient matrix, A^{-1}. The value of A^{-1} is computed first:

$$|A| = \begin{vmatrix} 3 & 1 \\ 6 & -1 \end{vmatrix} = (3 \times (-1)) - (1 \times 6) = -9.$$

Since $|A| \neq 0$, A has an inverse.

$$A^{-1} = \frac{1}{-9} \begin{bmatrix} -1 & -1 \\ -6 & 3 \end{bmatrix}$$

Substitute the value of A^{-1} in the above obtained equation,

$$\begin{bmatrix} x \\ y \end{bmatrix} = \frac{1}{-9} \begin{bmatrix} -1 & -1 \\ -6 & 3 \end{bmatrix} \cdot \begin{bmatrix} 5 \\ 6 \end{bmatrix} = \frac{1}{-9} \begin{bmatrix} (-5) + (-6) \\ (-30) + 18 \end{bmatrix}$$

$$= \begin{bmatrix} -11/-9 \\ -12/-9 \end{bmatrix} = \begin{bmatrix} 11/9 \\ 4/3 \end{bmatrix}.$$

Thus, $x = \dfrac{11}{9} = 1\dfrac{2}{9}$;

$$y = \dfrac{4}{3} = 1\dfrac{1}{3}.$$

B.   CRAMER'S RULE: USING DETERMINANTS IN SOLVING EQUATIONS

Let $|A|$ = the determinant formed by coefficients of unknowns in a system of linear equations. The following rule, called *Cramer's Rule* in honor of Gabriel Cramer of Geneva (1704-1752), has been established:

> A system of n linear equations in n unknowns has a single solution if, and only if, the determinant formed by the coefficients of the unknowns is not equal to zero; that is, $|A| \neq 0$. Each unknown is equal to the product of $1/|A|$ and the determinant obtained from $|A|$ by replacing the column of coefficients of this unknown by the column of constants.

The application of this rule is illustrated in the examples below.

Example 6.5b

Solve: $\begin{cases} 3x + y = 5 \\ 6x - y = 6 \end{cases}$ (Same as Example 6.5a.)

SOLUTION:

Let $|A|$ = the determinant of the coefficients of the unknowns in the two equations, or

$$|A| = \begin{vmatrix} 3 & 1 \\ 6 & -1 \end{vmatrix} = -9.$$

The coefficients of x in $|A|$ are replaced by the constants.

$$x = \frac{1}{|A|} \begin{vmatrix} 5 & 1 \\ 6 & -1 \end{vmatrix} = \frac{1}{-9}[5(-1) - 1(6)] = \frac{11}{9} = 1\frac{2}{9}$$

The coefficients of y in $|A|$ are replaced by the constants.

$$y = \frac{1}{|A|} \begin{vmatrix} 3 & 5 \\ 6 & 6 \end{vmatrix} = \frac{1}{-9}[3(6) - 5(6)] = \frac{12}{9} = \frac{4}{3} = 1\frac{1}{3}$$

Example 6.5c

Solve: $\begin{cases} 2x - 3y + 4z = -4 \\ x + 5y - 2z = 15 \\ 4x + 2y + 6z = 10 \end{cases}$

SOLUTION:

Let $|A|$ = the determinant of the coefficients of the unknowns in the three equations, or

$$|A| = \begin{vmatrix} 2 & -3 & 4 \\ 1 & 5 & -2 \\ 4 & 2 & 6 \end{vmatrix} = 38. \text{ (See Example 6.3d.)}$$

The coefficients of x in $|A|$ are replaced by the constants.

$$x = \frac{1}{|A|} \begin{vmatrix} -4 & -3 & 4 \\ 15 & 5 & -2 \\ 10 & 2 & 6 \end{vmatrix} = \frac{1}{38}\left(-4\begin{vmatrix} 5 & -2 \\ 2 & 6 \end{vmatrix} - 15\begin{vmatrix} -3 & 4 \\ 2 & 6 \end{vmatrix} + 10\begin{vmatrix} -3 & 4 \\ 5 & -2 \end{vmatrix}\right)$$

$$= \frac{1}{38}(114) = 3$$

The coefficients of y in $|A|$ are replaced by the constants.

$$y = \frac{1}{|A|} \begin{vmatrix} 2 & -4 & 4 \\ 1 & 15 & -2 \\ 4 & 10 & 6 \end{vmatrix} = \frac{1}{38}\left(2\begin{vmatrix} 15 & -2 \\ 10 & 6 \end{vmatrix} - 1\begin{vmatrix} -4 & 4 \\ 10 & 6 \end{vmatrix} + 4\begin{vmatrix} -4 & 4 \\ 15 & -2 \end{vmatrix}\right)$$

$$= \frac{1}{38}(76) = 2$$

The coefficients of z in $|A|$ are replaced by the constants.

$$z = \frac{1}{|A|} \begin{vmatrix} 2 & -3 & -4 \\ 1 & 5 & 15 \\ 4 & 2 & 10 \end{vmatrix} = \frac{1}{38}\left(2\begin{vmatrix} 5 & 15 \\ 2 & 10 \end{vmatrix} - 1\begin{vmatrix} -3 & -4 \\ 2 & 10 \end{vmatrix} + 4\begin{vmatrix} -3 & -4 \\ 5 & 15 \end{vmatrix} \right)$$

$$= \frac{1}{38}(-38) = -1$$

CHECK:

Substitute $x = 3$, $y = 2$, and $z = -1$ in the given equations:
$2x - 3y + 4z = 2(3) - 3(2) + 4(-1) = -4,$
$x + 5y - 2z = (3) + 5(2) - 2(-1) = 15,$
$4x + 2y + 6z = 4(3) + 2(2) + 6(-1) = 10.$

NOTES:
1. If there are 3 unknowns, we must have 3 equations in order to have a single solution. If one of the 3 given equations includes only 2 unknowns, we may change it to an equation with 3 unknowns by adding the third unknown with a zero coefficient, such as $3x + 4y = 17$ is equal to $3x + 4y + 0z = 17$. This addition of a zero coefficient is necessary if we wish to have a square determinant $|A|$.

2. If $|A| = 0$ and $1/|A| = 1/0$ for a system of linear equations, there will be no single solution. That is, the system either has an infinitely large number of solutions, such as for dependent equations
$\begin{cases} x + y = 2 \\ 2x + 2y = 4, \end{cases}$ $|A| = \begin{vmatrix} 1 & 1 \\ 2 & 2 \end{vmatrix} = 0$, or has no solution, such as for inconsistent

equations $\begin{cases} x + y = 5 \\ x + y = 7, \end{cases}$ $|A| = \begin{vmatrix} 1 & 1 \\ 1 & 1 \end{vmatrix} = 0.$

3. The symbol $|A|$ used in the Cramer's Rule above is sometimes written as Δ (delta).

EXERCISE 6.5 / REFERENCE SECTIONS: A–B

Solve each of the following systems of equations by (a) using the inverse of a square matrix, and (b) using determinants:

1. $x + y = 8$ 2. $3x - y = 5$ 3. $x + 2y = -4$ 4. $5x + y = -7$
   $2x - y = 10$ $x + 4y = 19$ $2x + y = 1$ $x + 4y = 10$

Solve each of the following systems of equations by using determinants:

5. $3x + y + z = 4$ 6. $3x + 2y - z = 1$ 7. $2x + y + 2z = 3$ 8. $x - 3y + 3z = -2$
   $2x + 2y + 3z = 1$ $2x + z = 13$ $x - 2y - 3z = 1$ $2x + y - 2z = 3$
   $3x - y - 2z = 7$ $x + y + 2z = 11$ $3x + 2y + 4z = 5$ $3x - y + z = 2$

6.6 *Inequalities and Linear Programming*

This section introduces the basic concepts of inequalities and linear programming. We shall first present the concept of inequalities since it is needed in the illustrations of linear programming problems.

A. *INEQUALITIES*

An INEQUALITY is a statement which indicates that one algebraic expression is *greater than* (>) or *less than* (<) another. Let a, b, and c be real numbers. Then, the statement "a is greater than b" or written symbolically

$$a > b$$

is an inequality. Also, the statement "a is less than c" or

$$a < c$$

is an inequality. The rules for dealing with inequality operations are as follows:

1. If the same number is added to, or subtracted from, both sides of an inequality, the same inequality sign is used for the new inequality. Thus, let

    $15 > 2$. Then, $15 + 8 > 2 + 8$, or $23 > 10$.
    Also, $15 < 25$. Then, $15 - 8 < 25 - 8$, or $7 < 17$.

2. If both sides of an inequality are multiplied or divided by the *same positive number*, the same inequality sign is used for the new inequality. Thus, let

    $6 < 12$. Then, $6 \times 3 < 12 \times 3$, or $18 < 36$,
        and $6 \div 3 < 12 \div 3$, or $2 < 4$.

3. If both sides of an inequality are multiplied or divided by the *same negative number*, the reversed inequality sign is used for the new inequality. Thus, let

    $8 > 3$. Then, $8(-4) < 3(-4)$, or $-32 < -12$,
        and $8 \div (-2) < 3 \div (-2)$, or $-4 < -1\frac{1}{2}$.

The signs representing equality (=) and inequality (> or <) may also be written together. The sign $\geq$ represents "is equal to or greater than," and the sign $\leq$ represents "is equal to or less than." Thus,

$X \geq 20$ means that X is equal to 20 or is greater than 20, and
$Y \leq 30$ means that Y is equal to 30 or less than 30.

Note that the = part of a combined sign indicates the limit of the inequality, such as 20 being the lower limit of the inequality $X \geq 20$ and 30 being the upper limit of the inequality $Y \leq 30$.

Inequalities may be presented graphically according to the system of rectangular coordinates.

Example 6.6a
Graph each of the following statements:
(a) $X \geq 0$,   (b) $Y \geq 0$,   (c) $3X + Y \leq 15$, and
(d) $2X + 4Y \leq 20$.

SOLUTION:

The four graphs are shown in Figure 6-2. Note the following:
(a) The graph of $X = 0$ is the set of points on the Y-axis. The graph of $X > 0$ is the set of points on the right side of the Y-axis. The graph of $X = 0$ and $X > 0$, or $X \geq 0$ is shown by the shaded area on graph (a) of the chart. Check: Point K (in the shaded area) has $X = 3$ and $X > 0$.
(b) The graph of $Y = 0$ is the set of points on the X-axis. The graph of $Y > 0$ is the set of points above the X-axis. The graph of $Y = 0$ and $Y > 0$, or $Y \geq 0$ is shown by the shaded area on graph (b). Check: Point K has $Y = 2$ and $Y > 0$.
(c) The graph of equation $3X + Y = 15$ is determined by the points representing the following three pairs of X and Y values:

The three points are on a straight line as shown on graph (c). The two points representing $(X = 0, Y = 15)$ and $(X = 5, Y = 0)$ are called *terminal points*.

X	Y
0	15
5	0
2	9

The graph of the inequality $3X + Y < 15$ is the set of the points below the straight line as indicated by the shaded area on graph (c). Check: Point K on the graph has $X = 2$ and $Y = 4$. $3X + Y = 3(2) + 4 = 10$, which is smaller than 15.

(d) The graph of equation $2X + 4Y = 20$ is determined by the points representing the following three pairs of X and Y values:

X	Y
0	5
10	0
2	4

The three points are on a straight line as shown on the graph (d). The two terminal points represent $(X = 0, Y = 5)$ and $(X = 10, Y = 0)$. The graph of the inequality $2X + 4Y < 20$ is the set of the points below the straight line as indicated by the shaded area on graph (d). Check: Point K in the graph has $X = 3$ and $Y = 2$. $2X + 4Y = 2(3) + 4(2) = 14$, which is smaller than 20.

Figure 6-2 / (Example 6.6a)

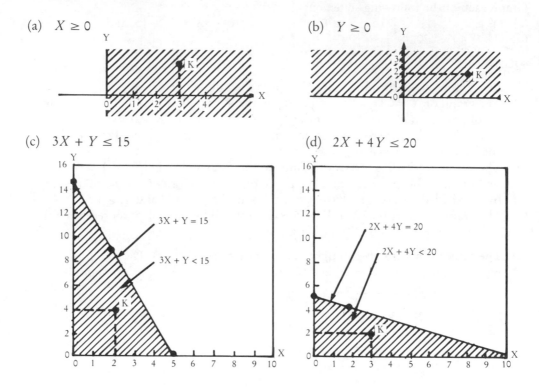

(a) $X \geq 0$

(b) $Y \geq 0$

(c) $3X + Y \leq 15$

3X + Y = 15

3X + Y < 15

(d) $2X + 4Y \leq 20$

2X + 4Y = 20

2X + 4Y < 20

B. LINEAR PROGRAMMING

Linear programming is a mathematical technique for finding the best or *optimum* solution from a set of possible solutions to a given problem. It can be used to solve various complicated business problems, such as maximizing profits and minimizing costs. The basic steps for solving a problem by the linear programming technique are:

1. Derive a group of linear equations and inequalities under certain restraining conditions given by the problem.
2. Solve the group of linear equations and inequalities for an optimum solution.

There are various methods for solving a group of linear equations and inequalities in linear programming. The simplex method, which is derived by the use of matrix algebra, is commonly used. The chief advantage of the simplex method is that its systematic steps in computation can be programmed conveniently on an electronic computer to solve very complicated problems. In this section, the graphic method is used to introduce the basic concept of linear programming.

  Note that the example illustrated below involves only two variables (X and Y).

Two variables can easily be shown on a two-dimensional space (Figure 6-3). Drawing a three-dimensional space is more difficult but is occasionally used with the graphic method. However, the graphic method becomes impracticable when a linear programming problem involves more than three variables.

Example 6.6b

A toy factory is planning to produce two types of toys: boats and cars. Each boat requires 3 hours on machine I and 2 hours on machine II. Each car requires 1 hour on machine I and 4 hours on machine II. Machine I has a maximum of 15 hours available. Machine II has a maximum of 20 hours available. The profit on each boat is $7. The profit on each car is $9. Determine the best combination of boats and cars that should be produced in order to maximize profit.

SOLUTION:

Let X = the optimum number of boats to be produced, and
  Y = the optimum number of cars to be produced.

Then, the equation representing the objective of our study, called the *objective function*, is:

Maximize the profit: Profit = $\$7X + \$9Y$.
(X boats at $7 each and Y cars at $9 each)
The inequalities based on the restraining conditions, called *restraints*, are:

Restraint on machine I:
1. $3X + 1Y \leq 15$ (Each boat requires 3 hours on the machine and each car requires 1 hour on the machine. The total number of hours on the machine should be equal to or less than 15 hours.)

Restraint on machine II:
2. $2X + 4Y \leq 20$ (Each boat requires 2 hours on the machine and each car requires 4 hours on the machine. The total number of hours on the machine should be equal to or less than 20 hours.)

Other restraints:
3. $X \geq 0$, and   (The values of X and Y must be positive. We cannot pro-
4. $Y \geq 0$.   duce a negative number of boats or cars.)

The four straight lines, (1) AB, (2) CD, (3) Y-axis, and (4) X-axis, representing the four equations of the above restraints respectively are plotted in Figure 6-3. Lines AB and CD may be determined by finding the two terminal points for each equation represented. Details concerning the construction of the four lines were presented in Example 6.6a. Observe the four straight lines on the chart. The lines form a four-sided polygon, $OCEB$, the shaded area. The polygon also represents the four inequalities stated above. Any point K within the polygon will satisfy the four restraints and thus is a possible solution.

However, our problem is to maximize the objective function, the profit. Thus, we should select a point in the shaded area that will give the highest profit. This point must be located on an extreme far position of the polygon. There are four extreme points on the polygon: O, C, E, and B. The profits based on the four points are computed from the profit equation as follows:

Objective function: Profit = $7X + $9Y.

Point O:$X = 0$ and $Y = 0$:   Profit = $7(0) + $9(0) = $0.
Point C:$X = 0$ and $Y = 5$:   Profit = $7(0) + $9(5) = $45.
Point E:$X = 4$ and $Y = 3$:   Profit = $7(4) + $9(3) = $55.
Point B:$X = 5$ and $Y = 0$:   Profit = $7(5) + $9(0) = $35.

The graph of the profit function is shown in Figure 6-4.

Figure 6-3 / (Example 6.6b)

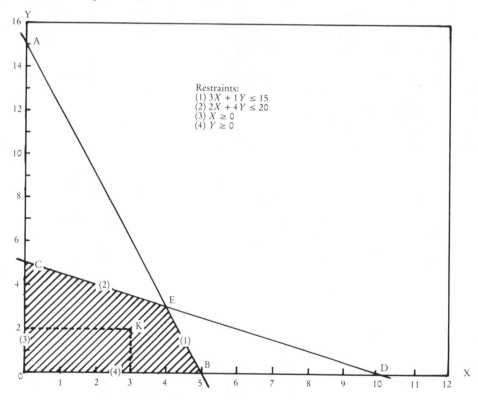

Restraints:
(1) $3X + 1Y \le 15$
(2) $2X + 4Y \le 20$
(3) $X \ge 0$
(4) $Y \ge 0$

Point E, which gives the highest profit ($55), is the optimum solution, or the best solution from all possible solutions indicated by the points in the shaded area. Thus, the toy factory should produce 4 boats and 3 cars by using the available hours of machines I and II.

CHECK:

The four restraints are satisfied by the optimum solutions $X = 4$ and $Y = 3$ since

1. $3X + 1Y = 3(4) + 1(3) = 15$ (hours available on machine I).
2. $2X + 4Y = 2(4) + 4(3) = 20$ (hours available on machine II).
3. $X = 4$, which is larger than 0.
4. $Y = 3$, which is larger than 0.

Also, select any point in the shaded area, say point K, which has $X = 3$ and $Y = 2$. Substitute the X and Y values in the profit equation:

Profit = $7(3) + $9(2) = 39, which is smaller than the profit based on the optimum solution.

It is possible to have more than one optimum solution. This fact is illustrated in the example below.

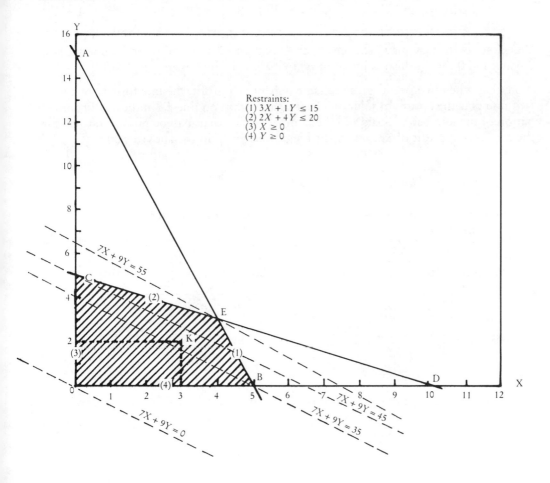

Example 6.6c

Refer to Example 6.6b. Find the answer if the profit of each boat is $18 and that of each car is $6.

SOLUTION:

Here, the objective function is to maximize: Profit = $18X + $6Y.

The profits based on the four points in Figure 5-3 are computed from the new profit equation as follows:

Objective function: Profit = $18X + $6Y.
Point O:X = 0 and Y = 0:   Profit = $18(0) + $6(0) = $0.
Point C:X = 0 and Y = 5:   Profit = $18(0) + $6(5) = $30.
Point E:X = 4 and Y = 3:   Profit = $18(4) + $6(3) = $90.

Point B:X = 5 and Y = 0:   Profit = $18(5) + $6(0) = $90.

Thus, the toy factory may produce either 4 boats and 3 cars (indicated by point E) or 5 boats and 0 cars (indicated by point B) to realize the highest profit, $90.

Note that when two points give the same maximized profit, the line formed by the two points is the optimum solution. That is, any point on line EB indicates a combination of the number of boats and the number of cars that may be produced to obtain the maximized profit of $90 under the conditions given in the above example.

EXERCISE 6.6 / REFERENCE SECTIONS A–B

1. Graph each of the following statements: (Shade areas representing the statements.)
   (a) $X \geq 2$ (b) $Y \geq 3$ (c) $4Y + 3X \leq 12$ (d) $5Y + 2X \leq 10$

2. Graph each of the following statements: (Shade areas representing the statements.)
   (a) $X \leq 1$ (b) $Y \leq 2$ (c) $4Y + 5X \geq 20$ (d) $2Y + X \geq 6$

3. Restraints: $X + Y \leq 7$
   $\qquad\qquad\quad 2X + 5Y \leq 20$
   $\qquad\qquad\quad X \geq 0, Y \geq 0$

   Use the graphic method to find the values of X and Y which maximize the objective function F:
   (a) $F = 3X + 8Y$, and (b) $F = 3X + 4Y$.

4. Refer to Problem 3. Find the answers if
   (a) $F = 10X + 8Y$, and (b) $F = 7X + 7Y$.

5. Restraints: $X + \frac{1}{2}Y \leq 6$
$$2X + 3Y \leq 24$$
$$X \geq 0, \, Y \geq 0$$

   Use the graphic method to find the values of X and Y which maximize the objective function F:
   (a) $F = 8X + 7Y$, and (b) $F = 16X + 6Y$.

6. Refer to Problem 5. Find the answers if
   (a) $F = 8X + 16Y$, and (b) $F = 8X + 4Y$.

7. Smith Company makes chairs and tables among other products. The company can realize a profit of \$5 on each chair and \$10 on each table. Each chair requires 1 hour on the machine and 2 hours of skilled labor. Each table requires 3 hours on the machine and 1 hour of skilled labor. The company has a maximum of 9 hours on the machine available and a maximum of 8 hours of skilled labor available. Determine the units of chairs and tables that should be produced in order to maximize profit. Use the graphic method.

8. Find the answer to Problem 7 if the company can realize a profit of
   (a) \$5 on each chair and \$15 on each table, and
   (b) \$5 on each chair and \$20 on each table.

6.7 Linear Programming-Computation

A.   MATRIX NOTATION

The linear programming problem may be expressed in matrix notation. Consider the toy factory problem in Section 6.6B, if we let x_1 = boats and x_2 = cars, the problem is defined as follows:

Maximize: Profit $= 7x_1 + 9x_2$

Subject to $\begin{cases} 3x_1 + x_2 \leq 15 \\ 2x_1 + 4x_2 \leq 20 \\ x_1, x_2 \geq 0 \end{cases}$

Then, in matrix notation, the restraints are:

$$X = \begin{bmatrix} x_1 \\ x_2 \end{bmatrix} \qquad A = \begin{bmatrix} 3 & 1 \\ 2 & 4 \end{bmatrix} \qquad R = \begin{bmatrix} 15 \\ 20 \end{bmatrix}$$

or, $\begin{bmatrix} 3 & 1 \\ 2 & 4 \end{bmatrix} \begin{bmatrix} x_1 \\ x_2 \end{bmatrix} \leq \begin{bmatrix} 15 \\ 20 \end{bmatrix}$

$$\begin{bmatrix} x_1 \\ x_2 \end{bmatrix} \geq \begin{bmatrix} 0 \\ 0 \end{bmatrix}$$

The objective function is

$$P = \begin{bmatrix} 7 & 9 \end{bmatrix} \begin{bmatrix} x_1 \\ x_2 \end{bmatrix}$$

and we wish to maximize profit, PX subject to the restraints
AX≤R,   X≥0
where AX≤R are the requirements and X≥0 states that the number of production units must be non-negative.

B.   THE DUAL PROBLEM

Generally, the Simplex Method of solving linear programming problems requires that in a case where the objective function is to be minimized (for example, cost) the *dual* or maximum function must be written.

For each linear programming problem, a dual problem may be written. The dual problem may be found by the use of matrix algebra.

Example 6.7a
Refer to the toy factory problem.
Maximize: PX

$$\text{Subject to} \begin{cases} AX \leq R \\ X \geq 0 \end{cases}$$

SOLUTION:

The dual is:
Minimize: $R^T z$

$$\text{Subject to} \begin{cases} \underline{A^T z \geq P^T} \\ z \geq 0 \end{cases}$$

where A^T means take the transpose of matrix A. The transpose of a matrix A is found by interchanging the rows and columns of A. Rows 1, 2,...m of A become respectively columns 1, 2,...m of A^T. Or, more generally, the ith row of A becomes the ith column of A^T.

$$A = \begin{bmatrix} 3 & 1 \\ 2 & 4 \end{bmatrix}$$

$$A^T = \begin{bmatrix} 3 & 2 \\ 1 & 4 \end{bmatrix}$$

$$P = \begin{bmatrix} 7 & 9 \end{bmatrix}$$

$$P^T = \begin{bmatrix} 7 \\ 9 \end{bmatrix}$$

$$R = \begin{bmatrix} 15 \\ 20 \end{bmatrix}$$

$$R^T = \begin{bmatrix} 15 & 20 \end{bmatrix}$$

Thus, minimize: $15z_1 + 20z_2$

Subject to $\begin{cases} 3z_1 + 2z_2 \geq 7 \\ z_1 + 4z_2 \geq 9 \\ z_1, z_2 \geq 0 \end{cases}$

The general linear programming problem can be illustrated by a factory which produces m different products requiring n different machine operations. Let a_y be the number of units of product i produced on machine j. Then,

	Machine 1	Machine 2		Machine n
Product 1	a_{11}	a_{12}	$\cdots$	a_{1-n}
Product 2	a_{21}	a_{22}	$\cdots$	a_{2n}
	.			.
	.		.	.
	.		.	.
Product 3	a_{m1}	a_{m2}	$\cdots$	a_{mn}

The factory must meet certain daily minimum production requirements. These requirements are:

$$R = \begin{bmatrix} r_1 \\ r_2 \\ \vdots \\ r_m \end{bmatrix}$$

The cost of production is:

$$C = [C_1\ C_2 \ldots C_n]$$

The number of days of operation for the machines can be expressed as:

$$x = \begin{bmatrix} x_1 \\ x_2 \\ \vdots \\ x_n \end{bmatrix} \quad x_1, x_2, \ldots x_n \geq 0$$

The primal problem is:
minimize: $\text{Cost} = Cx$

Subject to $\begin{cases} Ax \geq R \\ x \geq 0 \end{cases}$

and the *dual* or maximization problem is:
maximize: $R^T z$

Subject to $\begin{cases} A^T z \leq C \\ z \leq 0 \end{cases}$

Example 6.7b
Write the dual of the following problem:
minimize: $C = 200x_1 + 160x_2$

Subject to $\begin{cases} 6x_1 + 2x_2 \geq 12 \\ 2x_1 + 2x_2 \geq 8 \\ 4x_1 + 12x_2 \geq 24 \\ x_1, x_2 \geq 0 \end{cases}$

SOLUTION:

$$A = \begin{bmatrix} 6 & 2 \\ 2 & 2 \\ 4 & 12 \end{bmatrix} \qquad A^T = \begin{bmatrix} 6 & 2 & 4 \\ 2 & 2 & 12 \end{bmatrix} \qquad C^T = \begin{bmatrix} 200 \\ 160 \end{bmatrix} \qquad R^T = [12 \quad 8 \quad 24]$$

Therefore,
maximize: $12z_1 + 8z_2 + 24z_3$

Subject to $\begin{cases} 6z_1 + 2z_2 + 4z_3 \leq 200 \\ 2z_1 + 2z_2 + 12z_3 \leq 160 \\ z_1, z_2, z_3 \geq 0 \end{cases}$

C.   *SOLUTION BY THE SIMPLEX METHOD*

When the number of unknowns, for example, the number of products, exceeds three, a geometric solution of the linear programming problem is not possible. The simplex method is used to obtain an algebraic solution to such problems. In this section, we will introduce the computational aspect of the simplex method. Our discussion will be limited to the cases where the objective function has positive entries only and where the requirements are stated as inequalities. For problems where the objective function has negative entries, or the requirements are stated as equalities, a text on linear programming should be consulted.[1]

Example 6.7c
Refer to the toy factory problem.

maximize: $7x_1 + 9x_2$

Subject to $\begin{cases} 3x_1 + x_2 \leq 15 \\ 2x_1 + 4x_2 \leq 20 \\ x_1, x_2 \geq 0 \end{cases}$

---

[1]   Dantzig, G.B. *Linear Programming and Extensions*. Princeton University Press, Princeton, New Jersey, 1963.

SOLUTION:

First, we introduce two *slack variables*, x_3 and x_4 having non-negative values so that the constraints may be written as equalities. Thus,

$$3x_1 + x_2 + x_3 + 0x_4 = 15$$

$$2x_1 + 4x_2 + 0x_3 + x_4 = 20$$

In matrix notation, this is now

$$\begin{bmatrix} 3 & 1 & 1 & 0 \\ 2 & 4 & 0 & 1 \end{bmatrix} \begin{bmatrix} x_1 \\ x_2 \\ x_3 \\ x_4 \end{bmatrix} = \begin{bmatrix} 15 \\ \\ \\ 20 \end{bmatrix}$$

Notice that columns three and four are an identity matrix. We augment the above matrix with a column representing the column matrix R.
Thus,

$$\begin{bmatrix} 3 & 1 & 1 & 0 & \vdots & 15 \\ 2 & 4 & 0 & 1 & \vdots & 20 \end{bmatrix}$$

We then add a row representing the row matrix P.

$$\begin{bmatrix} 3 & 1 & 1 & 0 & 15 \\ 2 & 4 & 0 & 1 & 20 \\ \hline 7 & 9 & 0 & 0 & P \end{bmatrix}$$

The last entry in row three represents the value of the objective function which is now equal to zero if $x_1 = 0$, $x_2 = 0$, $x_3 = 15$, and $x_4 = 20$. This corresponds to the point $(0,0)$ on the graph in Figure 6-3.

The value which maximizes the objective function, Profit, is obtained by performing elementary row operations on the matrix until all the elements in the last row are equal to or less than zero. The elementary row operations to be carried out are:

(a) add or subtract a multiple of one row to another,
(b) divide all elements in a row by an element in that row.

Next, we arbitrarily select a column with a value greater than zero in the last row. Divide each non-zero element of the chosen column into the corresponding element of the last column. The element for which the ratio is the smallest non-negative number is the PIVOT ELEMENT.

Our next step is to use the row in which the pivot element falls to perform elementary row operations on the other rows in such a way that all other elements in the pivot column are equal to zero. Repeat this operation until all elements in the last row are equal to or less than zero.

STEP (1) Let us choose column 1 to start the process.

$$\frac{15}{3} = 5 \text{ and } \frac{20}{2} = 10$$

Since $5 < 10$, three is the pivot element and row one is the pivot row. We indicate the pivot element with an asterisk below:

$$\begin{bmatrix} 3^* & 1 & \vdots & 1 & 0 & \vdots & 15 \\ 2 & 4 & \vdots & 0 & 1 & \vdots & 20 \\ 7 & 9 & \vdots & 0 & 0 & \vdots & P \end{bmatrix}$$

STEP (2) Make all other elements in column 1 equal to 0 by adding $-\frac{2}{3}$ row one to row 2 and $-\frac{7}{3}$ row one to row three. (Note: watch how you round these numbers in your calculations). The new matrix is:

$$\begin{bmatrix} 3 & 1 & \vdots & 1 & 0 & \vdots & 15 \\ 0 & 3.\dot{3} & \vdots & -.\dot{6} & 1 & \vdots & 10 \\ 0 & 6.\dot{6} & \vdots & -2.\dot{3} & 0 & \vdots & P-35 \end{bmatrix}$$

We now select another column with a pivot element in row three which is greater than zero and repeat the above steps. Column two is the only column with element in row three greater than zero. Since $\frac{10}{3.3} < \frac{15}{1}$ the pivot element is 3.3 and the pivot row is row two. Make all elements in column two equal to zero. That is, add $\frac{-1}{3.3}$ row two to row one and -2 times row two ($\frac{-6.6}{3.3} = -2$) to row three. The new matrix is now:

$$\begin{bmatrix} 3 & 0 & \vdots & .8 & -.3 & \vdots & 12 \\ 0 & 3.\dot{3}^* & \vdots & -.\dot{6} & 1 & \vdots & 10 \\ 0 & 0 & \vdots & -1 & -2 & \vdots & P-55 \end{bmatrix}$$

The final tableau is obtained by dividing the elements of row one by 3 and the elements of row two by 3.3 and is:

	x_1	x_2		x_3	x_4		
z_1	1	0	⋮	.2\dot{6}	-.1	⋮	4
z_2	0	1	⋮	.\dot{2}	.3	⋮	3
z_3	0	0	⋮	-1	-2	⋮	P-55

The values of x_1 and x_2 which will maximize the function can now be read from the last tableau. The identity matrix is in rows one and two of the tableau. In matrix notation:

$$\begin{bmatrix} 1 & 0 \\ 0 & 1 \end{bmatrix} \begin{bmatrix} x_1 \\ x_2 \end{bmatrix} = \begin{bmatrix} 4 \\ 3 \end{bmatrix}.$$

That is, $x_1 = 4$, $x_2 = 3$. The value of P can be found by letting $P - 55 = 0$. Thus profit is equal to \$55, when $x_1 = 4$, and $x_2 = 3$, and this is the optimal solution found graphically in Section 6.6B, Figure 6-3.

The solution for the dual problem can also be found from the last tableau.

$$
\begin{array}{c}
z_1 \\
z_2 \\
z_3
\end{array}
\left[
\begin{array}{cc:cc:c}
1 & 0 & .26 & -.1 & 4 \\
0 & 1 & .2 & .3 & 3 \\
\hline
0 & 0 & -1 & -2 & P\text{-}55
\end{array}
\right]
$$

Since the dual problem is the transpose of the problem solved, the solution for the dual can be obtained from the transpose of the last row of the above tableau.

$$z = \begin{bmatrix} z_1 \\ z_2 \end{bmatrix}$$

$$-z^T = [-1 \quad -2]$$

Thus, $z = \begin{bmatrix} 1 \\ 2 \end{bmatrix}$

or, $z_1 = 1$, $z_2 = 2$

and the objective function

$$15z_1 + 20z_2 = 15(1) + 20(2)$$
$$= 55.$$

Example 6.7d

Maximize: $P = 3x + 2y$

Subject to $\begin{cases} 2x_1 + x_2 \le 5 \\ x_1 + x_2 \le 3 \\ x_1, x_2 \ge 0 \end{cases}$

GRAPHICAL SOLUTION:

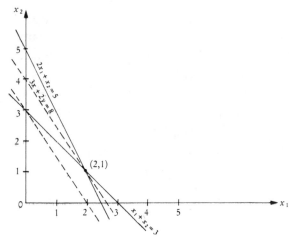

The shaded region represents all of the feasible solutions to the problem. The function $P = 3x_1 + 2x_2$ achieves a maximum value at $(2,1)$. At this point, $3x_1 + 2x_2 = 8$.

SIMPLEX SOLUTION:

Write the augmented matrix as follows:

$$\left[\begin{array}{cc|cc|c} 2^* & 1 & 1 & 0 & 5 \\ 1 & 1 & 0 & 1 & 3 \\ \hline 3 & 2 & 0 & 0 & P \end{array}\right]$$

STEP (1) Arbitrarily select column one to start the process.

STEP (2) Form the ratios and select the pivot element. Since $\frac{5}{2} < \frac{3}{1}$ the pivot element is 2 in row one, column one.

STEP (3) Perform the elementary row operations. Subtract $\frac{1}{2}$ row one from row two and $\frac{3}{2}$ row one from row three. ($R_2 - \frac{1}{2}R_1$ and $R_3 - \frac{3}{2}R_1$). The new matrix is:

$$\left[\begin{array}{cc|cc|c} 2 & 1 & 1 & 0 & 5 \\ 0 & .5^* & -.5 & 1 & .5 \\ \hline 0 & .5 & -1.5 & 0 & P\text{-}7.5 \end{array}\right]$$

STEP (4) Select the next column with element in the last row greater than zero. The ratios are:

$$\frac{5}{1}, \frac{.5}{.5}.$$

Since $\frac{5}{.5} < \frac{5}{1}$ the pivot element is .5 and row two is the pivot row.

STEP (5) Using row two as the pivot, perform elementary row operations to make all other entries in column two equal to zero. Subtract 2 times row two from row one and row two from row three ($R_1 - 2R_2$, $R_3 - R_2$). The new matrix is:

$$\left[\begin{array}{cc|cc|c} 2 & 0 & 2 & -2 & 4 \\ 0 & .5 & -.5 & 1 & .5 \\ \hline 0 & 0 & -1 & -1 & P\text{-}8 \end{array}\right]$$

STEP (6) For the final matrix divide row one by 2 and row two by .5.

$$\left[\begin{array}{cc|cc|c} 1 & 0 & 1 & -1 & 2 \\ 0 & 1 & -1 & 2 & 1 \\ \hline 0 & 0 & -1 & -1 & P\text{-}8 \end{array}\right]$$

The solution is:

$$x = \begin{bmatrix} x_1 \\ x_2 \end{bmatrix} = \begin{bmatrix} 2 \\ 1 \end{bmatrix}$$

$P - 8 = 0$

$P = 8$

PROOF: $P = 3x_1 + 2x_2$, therefore substituting in variables $x_1 = 2$ and $x_2 = 1$, we get:

$\quad P = 3(2) + 2(1)$

$\quad\quad = 6 + 2$

$\quad\quad = 8$ (as above).

The dual is:

minimize: $C = 5z_1 + 3z_2$

$\quad$ Subject to $\begin{cases} 2z_1 + z_2 \geq 3 \\ z_1 + z_2 \geq 2 \\ z_1, z_2 \geq 0 \end{cases}$

The solution to the dual problem is:

$$z = \begin{bmatrix} z_1 \\ z_2 \end{bmatrix} = \begin{bmatrix} 1 \\ 1 \end{bmatrix}$$

$C = 5z_1 + 3z_2 = 8$

EXERCISE 6.7 / REFERENCE SECTIONS A–C

Express each of the following in matrix notation and write the dual of each:

1. Minimize: $C = x_1 + x_2$

$\quad$ Subject to $\begin{cases} x_1 + 2x_2 \geq 12 \\ x_1 + 0x_2 \geq 6 \\ 0x_1 + x_2 \geq 8 \\ x_1, x_2 \geq 0 \end{cases}$

2. Maximize: $P = 2x_1 + x_2$

$\quad$ Subject to $\begin{cases} x_1 + x_2 \leq 1 \\ x_1 - x_2 \leq 6 \\ x_1 + x_2 \leq 4 \\ x_1, x_2 \geq 0 \end{cases}$

3. Maximize: $P = 3x_1 + 5x_2 + 4x_3$

$\quad$ Subject to $\begin{cases} 2x_1 + 3x_2 \leq 8 \\ 2x_2 + 5x_3 \leq 10 \\ 3x_1 + 2x_2 + 4x_3 \leq 15 \\ x_1, x_2, x_3 \geq 0 \end{cases}$

4. Minimize: $70x_1 + 80x_2 + 90x_3 + 100_4$

$\quad$ Subject to $\begin{cases} 3x_1 + 0x_2 + 3x_3 + 4x_4 \geq 9 \\ 7x_1\, 2x_2\, 4x_3\, 6x_4 \geq 18 \\ 4x_1\, 4x_2\, 0x_3\, 5x_4 \geq 14 \\ 0x_1\, 6x_2\, 5x_3\, 3x_4 \geq 11 \\ x_1, x_2, x_3, x_4 \geq 0 \end{cases}$

5. Maximize: $3x_1 + 2x_2$

$$\text{Subject to} \begin{cases} 2x_1 + x_2 \le 5 \\ x_1 + x_2 \le 3 \\ x_1, x_2 \ge 0 \end{cases}$$

6. The Hunt Company is a small woodwork shop which manufactures two products, A and B, which require finishing by a special machine. The machine is available for fifteen hours each day and sixty units of product A and fifty units of product B can be finished in one hour. Before the products are finished on the machine, they must be hand assembled. Each worker can assemble twelve units of product A and fifteen units of product B in one hour, and sixty man hours are available each day. A profit of $4.00 can be made on each unit of product A and $6.00 on each unit of product B. Express the constraints and the objective function in matrix notation.

Solve the following problems by the simplex method:

7. Maximize: $z = 5x_1 + 3x_2$

$$\text{Subject to} \begin{cases} 3x_1 + 5x_2 \le 15 \\ 5x_1 + 2x_2 \le 10 \\ x_1, x_2 \ge 0 \end{cases}$$

8. Minimize: $C = 800x_1 + 400z_2 + 200z_3$

$$\text{Subject to} \begin{cases} z_1 + z_2 + z_3 \ge 2 \\ z_1 + z_2 + 2z_3 \ge 1 \\ z_1 + z_3 \ge 4 \\ z_1, z_2, z_3 \ge 0 \end{cases}$$

9. Minimize : $C = 80z_1 + 60x_2 + 80x_3$

$$\text{Subject to} \begin{cases} x_1 + 2x_2 + 3x_3 \ge 4 \\ 2x_1 + 3x_3 \ge 3 \\ 2x_1 + 2x_2 + x_3 \ge 4 \\ 4x_1 + x_2 + x_3 \ge 6 \\ x_1, x_2, x_3 \ge 0 \end{cases}$$

10. Maximize: $P = 2x_1 + x_2$

$$\text{Subject to} \begin{cases} 4x_1 + 3x_2 \le 24 \\ 3x_1 + 5x_2 \le 15 \\ x_1, x_2 \ge 0 \end{cases}$$

11. Maximize: $z = 11x_1 + 4x_2$

$$\text{Subject to} \begin{cases} 7x_1 + 6x_2 \le 84 \\ 2x_1 + x_2 \le 16 \\ x_1, x_2 \ge 0 \end{cases}$$

12. Minimize: $y_0 = 15y_1 + 120y_2 + 100y_3$

$$\text{Subject to} \begin{cases} y_1 + 7y_2 + 3y_3 \ge 6 \\ y_1 + 5y_2 + 5y_3 \ge 5.5 \\ y_1 + 3y_2 + 10y_3 \ge 9 \\ y_1 + 2y_2 + 15y_3 \ge 8 \\ y_1, y_2, y_3 \ge 0 \end{cases}$$

13. Maximize: $z = 3x_1 + 2x_2$

Subject to $\begin{cases} x_1 + x_2 \leq 4 \\ x_1 - x_2 \leq 2 \\ x_1, x_2 \geq 0 \end{cases}$

14. Minimize: $g = 3w_1 + 4w_2$

Subject to $\begin{cases} 2w_1 + 4w_2 \geq 1 \\ 3w_1 + w_2 \geq 2 \\ w_1, w_2 \geq 0 \end{cases}$

15. Maximize: Profit $= 3x_1 + 2x_2$

Subject to $\begin{cases} x_1 + x_2 \leq 4 \\ x_1 - x_2 \leq 2 \\ x_1, x_2 \geq 0 \end{cases}$

Statement Problems:

16. The Northern Manufacturing Company uses machine and labor hours in the manufacture of its products. The manager of the wigit department makes three kinds of wigits and has 200 machine hours and 300 labor hours available. The requirements and potential profit for one unit of each kind of wigit are as follows:

	Labor Hours	Machine Hours	Profit
wigit 1	10	15	$ 5
wigit 2	25	10	$10
wigit 3	20	10	$12

Unused labor and machine hours will be allocated to another department. How many units of each kind of wigit should the manager of the wigit department make in order to maximize profit. (Assume that all units manufactured will be sold.)

17. An oil company sells two types of gasoline. Type 1 is a mixture of 25% grade 1, 25% grade 2 and 50% grade 3. Type 2 is 50% grade 1, 25% grade 2 and 25% grade 3. Type 1 sells at a profit of 25¢ per litre and type 2 sells at a profit of 30¢ per litre. The company has available 150 litres of grade 1, 600 litres of grade 2 and 600 litres of grade 3. How many units of each grade should be made in order to maximize profit?

18. A company has two machines which manufacture a certain article. The article is manufactured in three sizes; large, medium and small. The company has contracts to supply 800 large, 600 medium and 900 small. In one day, machine 1 produces 200 large, 100 medium and 100 small, while machine 2 produces 100 large, 100 medium and 200 small. It costs $1 000 per day to operate machine 1 and $2 000 per day to operate machine 2. How many days should each machine operate to fill the order at the least cost?

19. Use the CalcStar spread sheet in Appendix I to solve the following problems:

(a) Maximize:

Profit = $3x_1 + 4x_2 + x_3 + 7x_4$

Subject to $\begin{cases} 8x_1 + 3x_2 + 4x_3 + x_4 \leq 7 \\ 2x_1 + 6x_2 + x_3 + 5x_4 \leq 3 \\ x_1 + 4x_2 + 5x_3 + 2x_4 \leq 8 \\ x_1, x_2, x_3, x_4 \geq 0 \end{cases}$

(b) Minimize: Cost = $15x_1 + 90x_2 + 100x_3$

Subject to $\begin{cases} x_1 + 5x_2 + 3x_3 \geq 7 \\ x_1 + 5x_2 + 4x_3 \geq 6 \\ x_1 + 4x_2 + 10x_3 \geq 9 \\ x_1 + 3x_2 + 12x_3 \geq 7 \\ x_1, x_2, x_3 \geq 0 \end{cases}$

6.8 Binary Number System

The number systems discussed in this section concern the methods of expressing numbers. A number system usually has a *base*. The base may consist of any fixed number of symbols, such as two (BINARY SYSTEM), ten (DECIMAL SYSTEM), and twelve (DUODECIMAL SYSTEM).

The decimal system is by far the most popular one among the various number systems. Perhaps the popularity is mainly due to the fact that human beings have ten fingers. It is rather convenient for humans to count by tens. The ten symbols used in the decimal system are Arabic figures or digits 0, 1, 2, 3, 4, 5, 6, 7, 8 and 9. The decimal system was used in the previous sections and also will be used in illustrations of later chapters throughout this text.

Among other number systems, the binary system is more frequently mentioned in many areas during recent years. The binary system uses the two symbols 0 and 1. This system can be used conveniently to represent data within modern high-speed electronic computers, although other number systems may also be used. Data within a computer are indicated by electronic signals in two possible conditions, *on* (or the presence of the electrical pulse) and *off* (or the absence of the electrical pulse). This is the same principle as turning an electric light bulb on or off. We may assign the symbol 1 to indicate *on* and the symbol 0 to indicate *off*.

After a base is selected for a system, the principle of place value is usually employed in expressing numbers larger and smaller than the values of basic symbols. The PRINCIPLE OF PLACE VALUE is that the value of a symbol varies according to its location in a number. In the decimal system, the value of any digit is *ten* times the value of a *like* digit placed in a position immediately to its right. For example, the value of 9 in the three-digit number 900 is ten times the value of 9 in the two-digit number 90.

Table 6-4 further illustrates the place values of basic symbols in the decimal system.

Table 6-4

Illustration of Place Value in Decimal System (Base 10)

Place Value	$10^6 =$ 1 000 000	$10^5 =$ 100 000	$10^4 =$ 10 000	$10^3 =$ 1 000	$10^2 =$ 100	$10^1 =$ 10	$10^0 =$ 1*	$\frac{1}{10} =$ .1	$\frac{1}{100} =$ .01
Value of each digit	millions	hundred thousands	ten thousands	thousands	hundreds	tens	ones	tenths	hundredths
	8	2	6	7	9	4	3	2	1

*By definition any number raised to zero power is equal to 1 (see page 45).

Note that whole numbers are separated from decimal fractions by a decimal point. For convenience, in reading large numbers the digits are usually divided by commas or by extra spaces into groups of three to the left of the decimal point. The number 8 267 943.21 should be read as "eight million, two hundred and sixty-seven thousand, nine hundred and forty-three, and twenty-one hundredths."

In the binary system, the principle of place value means that the value of the digit 1 is two times the value of the like digit placed in a position immediately to its right. For example, the value of 1 in the three-digit number 100 ($1 \times 2^2 + 0 \times 2^1 + 0 \times 2^0 = 4$ with base 10) is two times the value of 1 in the two-digit number 10($1 \times 2^1 + 0 \times 2^0 = 2$ with base 10). With the understanding of the principle of place value, a binary number can easily be changed to its equivalent decimal number, and vice versa. Also, the fundamental arithmetic operations for binary numbers can be performed in a manner similar to those for decimal numbers.

A. CHANGING A BINARY NUMBER TO ITS EQUIVALENT DECIMAL NUMBER

A number with base 2 (a binary number) may be changed to its equivalent number with base 10 (a decimal number) by adding the place values of individual digits of the binary number. The steps of the change are illustrated in Example 6.8a.

Example 6.8a

Change the number 1 010 111.11 with base 2 to its equivalent number with base 10.

SOLUTION:

The base value of each digit of the given binary number is listed in Table 6-5:

Table 6-5
Illustration of Place Value in Binary System (Base 2)

Place Value	$2^6 = 64$	$2^5 = 32$	$2^4 = 16$	$2^3 = 8$	$2^2 = 4$	$2^1 = 2$	$2^0 = 1$	$2^{-1} = \frac{1}{2} = .5$	$2^{-2} = \frac{1}{2} = .25$
Binary digit	1	0	1	0	1	1	1	1	1
Value of each digit	64	0	16	0	4	2	1	.5	.25

Since $64 + 0 + 16 + 0 + 4 + 2 + 1 + .5 + .25 = 87.75$, the number 1 010 111.11 with base 2 is equivalent to the number 87.75 with base 10.

B.   *CHANGING A DECIMAL NUMBER TO ITS EQUIVALENT BINARY NUMBER*

A number with base 10 may be changed to its equivalent number with base 2 by reversing the steps illustrated above.

Example 6.8b
Change the number 53 with base 10 to its equivalent number with base 2.

SOLUTION:

First, subtract successively the place values as listed in the first row of Table 6-5, from the given number 53 until the remainder is zero:

```
  53
- 32
────
  21        Observe that the first place value 32 in the subtraction is the largest number
- 16        that is smaller than the given number 53. Also, since the remainder after sub-
────        tracting 16 is only 5 and that after subtracting 4 is only 1, the place values 8
   5        and 2 are omitted respectively in the successive subtractions.
-  4
────
   1
-  1
────
   0
```

Next, write 1s under the place values used in the subtractions and 0s under the place values omitted as follows:

Place value	32	16	8	4	2	1
Binary figure	1	1	0	1	0	1

Thus, the number 53 with base 10 is equivalent to the number 110 101 with base 2.

The following table shows 0 to 16 with base 10 and their equivalent numbers with base 2 for the purpose of further comparison of the two systems:

Table 6-6
Decimal Numbers 0 to 16 as Compared to Equivalent Binary Numbers

Decimal numbers (Base 10)	Binary numbers (Base 2)	Decimal numbers (Base 10)	Binary numbers (Base 2)
0	0	9	1 001
1	1	10	1 010
2 (= 2^1)	10 (= 10^1)	11	1 011
3	11	12	1 100
4 (= 2^2)	100 (= 10^2)	13	1 101
5	101	14	1 110
6	110	15	1 111
7	111	16 (= 2^4)	10 000 (= 10^4)
8 (= 2^3)	1 000 (= 10^3)		

C. PERFORMING FUNDAMENTAL ARITHMETIC OPERATIONS

The methods of performing the four fundamental operations–addition, subtraction, multiplication and division–in the binary system are basically the same as those in the decimal system. However, we should remember that the binary system has only two digits, 0 and 1. Keep the place value of the binary digits in mind as you look at the examples below.

Example 6.8c
Addition:

SOLUTION:

(a)
Base 2	Base 10
1	1
+ 1	+ 1
10 =	2

(b)
Base 2	Base 10
1 011 =	8 + 0 + 2 + 1 = 11
+ 110 =	4 + 2 + 0 = 6
10 001 =	16 + 0 + 0 + 0 + 1 = 17

Detailed steps for the addition with base 2 of (b), adding columns from right to left are:

$$
\begin{array}{r}
1\ 011 \\
+\quad 110 \\
\end{array}
$$

1 = 1 + 0 (add 1st column)
10 = 1 + 1 (add 2nd column)
1 = 0 + 1 (add 3rd column)
1 = 1 (add 4th column)

$$
\begin{array}{r}
01 \\
10 \\
1 \\
\hline
10\ 001
\end{array}
$$

Example 6.8d
Subtraction:

SOLUTION:

(a) Base 2   Base 10   (b) Base 2   Base 10
      1 000 = 8 + 0 + 0 + 0 = 8   110 111 = 32 + 16 + 0 + 4 + 2 + 1 = 55
      −   11 =   2 + 1 = 3   −   1 101 =   8 + 4 + 0 + 1 = 13
         101 =   4 + 0 + 1 = 5   101 010 = 32 +   0 + 8 + 0 + 2 + 0 = 42

Detailed steps for each subtraction with base 2 may be illustrated in two ways:

1. *Borrowing Method.* This method may be used when 1 is subtracted from 0 in a
    column. Since 0 is smaller than 1, the value in a higher place-value column must
    be borrowed for the subtraction. The borrowing process can be done in two
    steps:

    First, move to the left of the given 0 in the minuend until finding a 1.
    Second, change the found 1 to 0, each 0 (if any) between the found 1 and the
    given 0 to 1, and the given 0 to 10 (two).
    The detailed steps for (a) and (b) are as follows:

(a)   0 1 1 10   (b)   0 10
        1̸ 0̸ 0̸ 0̸   (Minuend)   1 1̸ 0̸ 1 1 1   (Minuend)
      −   1 1   (Subtrahend)   −   1 1 0 1   (Subtrahend)
             1 0 1   (Remainder)   1 0 1 0 1 0   (Remainder)

2. *Complementing Method.* The complement of a binary number is obtained by
    replacing each 0 by 1 and each 1 by 0 in the number. Subtraction by the comple-
    menting method involves three steps:

    First, add zeros to the left of the subtrahend until there are the same number of
    digits as there are in the minuend and find the complement of the new subtra-
    hend.

    Second, add the minuend, the complement of the new subtrahend, and 1.
    Third, cancel the 1 in the far-left position of the sum obtained in the second step.
    The detailed steps for (a) and (b) by the complementing method are as follows:

(a)   1 000   (Minuend)   (b)   110 111   (Minuend)
       + 1 100   (Complement of   110 010   (Complement of
                     subtrahend 0 011)   subtrahend 001 101)
       ――――――   ――――――――
        10 100   1 101 001
       +   1   +   1
        1̸0 101   (Answer: 101)   1̸ 101 010   (Answer: 101 010)

NOTES:

1. There are 4 digits in the minuend 1 000 of (a). The subtrahend is therefore prefixed by two zeros to obtain the 4 digit binary number 0 011. There are 6 digits in the minuend 110 111 of (b). The subtrahend 1 101 is written as the 6 digit binary number 001 101.

2. The complementing method is based on the fact that the sum of a binary number, its complement, and 1 is always equal to 1 with as many zeros annexed as there are digits in the binary number, such as

$$
\begin{array}{ll}
\ 0\ 011 & \text{(a binary number)} \\
+\ \ 1\ 100 & \text{(complement of 0 011)} \\
\hline
\ 1\ 111 & \\
+\ \ \ \ \ \ 1 & \\
\hline
10\ 000 & \text{(1 with 4 zeros)}
\end{array}
$$

Subtraction (a) in Example 6.8d above thus may be written in a more complicated form as shown below:

$$
\left.
\begin{array}{r}
1\ 000 \\
-\ \ \ 11
\end{array}
\right\} =
\left\{
\begin{array}{ll}
+\ \ 1\ 000 & \text{(Minuend)} \\
-\ \ 0\ 011 & \text{(Subtrahend)} \\[6pt]
+\ \ 0\ 011 & \text{(Same as the subtrahend)} \\
+\ \ 1\ 100 & \text{(Complement of 0 011)} \\
+\ \ \ \ \ \ \ 1 & \\
-\ 10\ 000 & \\
\hline
\not{1}0\ 101 &
\end{array}
\right.
$$

(Same as the subtrahend) (Complement of 0 011) $\Big\} = 0$

The sum of the two subtrahends (−0011 and +0011) is zero. Thus, the complicated form may be simplified as the arrangement presented in the complementing method above.

Example 6.8e
Multiplication:

SOLUTION:

Base 2   Base 10

$$
\begin{array}{ll}
\ 1\ 101 = & 8+4+0+1 = 13 \\
\times\ \ \ 111 = & 4+2+1 = \underline{\ 7} \\
\hline
\ 1\ 101 & 20 \\
1\ 10\ 1 & \\
1\ 01\ & \\
\hline
1\ 011\ 011 = & 64+0+16+8+0+2+1 = \overline{91}
\end{array}
$$

The multiplication with base 2 may be arranged for ease in addition as follows:

$$
\begin{array}{r}
1101 \\
\times\ \ 111 \\
\hline
1101 \\
+\ \ 1101 \\
\hline
100111 \\
+\ \ 1101 \\
\hline
1011011
\end{array}
$$

Example 6.8f
Division:

SOLUTION:

(a)
Base 2	Base 10

$$101 = 4 + 0 + 1 = 5$$

$$110 \overline{) 11110} \qquad 6 \overline{) 30}$$

$$\begin{array}{r} 110 \\ \hline 110 \\ 110 \end{array} \qquad \begin{array}{r} 30 \\ \hline \end{array}$$

(b)
Base 2	Base 10

$$1101 = 13$$

$$111 \overline{) 1011011} \qquad 7 \overline{) 91}$$

$$\begin{array}{r} 111 \\ \hline 1000 \\ 111 \\ \hline 111 \\ 111 \end{array} \qquad \begin{array}{r} 7 \\ \hline 21 \\ 21 \end{array}$$

CHECK:

	Base 2	Base 10
Dividend	$11110 =$	$16 + 8 + 4 + 2 + 0 = 30$
Divisor	$110 =$	$4 + 2 + 0 = 6$

CHECK:

See Example 6.8e

EXERCISE 6.8 / REFERENCE SECTIONS: A–C

Convert each of the following numbers with base 2 to its equivalent number with base 10:

1. 1 110   3. 1 101   5. 10 111   7. 111 101   9. 1 111 101   11. 11 101 111
2. 1 010   4. 1 001   6. 11 011   8. 101 111   10. 1 101 101   12. 11 101 110

Convert each of the following numbers with base 10 to its equivalent number with base 2:

13. 14   15. 26   17. 42   19. 49   21. 78   23. 336
14. 18   16. 30   18. 57   20. 38   22. 82   24. 448

The following numbers are expressed with base 2. Perform each indicated operation for the numbers (a) with base 2, and (b) after converting them to base 10:
Addition:

25.   10   27.   101   29.   1 110   31.   11 001
     + 11   + 100   + 1 011   + 100 111

26.   11   28.   110   30.   1 101   32.   1 101 110
     + 1   + 111   + 1 011   + 110 101

Subtraction–Use the borrowing method to compute and the complementing method to check your answers for the numbers with base 2:

33.   1 001   35.   1 110   37.   111 110   39.   1 100 011
     −   11   − 101   − 10 010   − 1 011 101

34.   110   36.   1 100   38.   101 101   40.   1 100 000
     − 100   − 111   − 11 011   − 100 010

Multiplication:

41.	111	43.	1 100	45.	10 100	47.	11 111
	× 110		× 1 010		× 1 010		× 1 100

42.	101	44.	1 101	46.	11 011	48.	11 111
	× 101		× 1 001		× 1 101		× 1 001

Division:

49. 10$)\overline{110}$ 51. 11$)\overline{1\ 100}$ 53. 111$)\overline{100\ 011}$ 55. 110$)\overline{111\ 100}$

50. 11$)\overline{110}$ 52. 101$)\overline{1\ 111}$ 54. 1001$)\overline{110\ 110}$ 56. 101$)\overline{1\ 100\ 100}$

Glossary

BINARY SYSTEM a number system based on two fixed numbers (0,1)

COFACTOR the cofactor of an element a_{ij} is the signed minor of the element a_{ij}, the sign of the element a_{ij} is −1 raised to the $i+j$, $(-1)^{i+j}$

COLUMN VECTORS vectors situated vertically in a column

COMPONENTS the numbers in the rows/columns of vectors

DECIMAL SYSTEM a number system based on ten fixed numbers

DETERMINANT a number which determines whether or not there is an inverse of a square matrix

DOT PRODUCT see *inner product*

DUODECIMAL SYSTEM a number system based on twelve fixed numbers

ELEMENTS the numbers in the brackets of a matrix

IDENTITY MATRIX a square matrix with all elements on its principal diagonal equal to one and all other elements equal to zero

IMAGINARY NUMBER the square root of −1 ($\sqrt{-1}$) is defined to be i, and is called an imaginary number, thus $\sqrt{i}$ is equal to −1

INEQUALITY a statement which indicates that one algebraic expression is greater than or less than another

INNER PRODUCT the sum of all partial products of two vectors

INVERSE a number a^{-1} which, when multiplied by its inverse, a, yields a product of one

MATRIX a rectangular array of numbers enclosed in brackets or boldfaced parentheses

MINOR a determinant of order $n - 1$ obtained from a determinant of order n; the minor of the element a_{ij} is obtained by deleting the ith row and jth column

PIVOT ELEMENT the element found during solution by the simplex method for which the ratio of the element in the last column to the non-zero element of a chosen column is the smallest non-negative number

PRINCIPAL DIAGONAL the line from the upper-left-hand corner to the lower-right-hand corner (matrix)

PRINCIPLE OF PLACE VALUE the principle which state that the value of a symbol varies according to its location in a number

RECIPROCAL see *inverse*

ROW VECTORS vectors situated horizontally in a row

SCALAR any real number, as opposed to an imaginary number

SQUARE MATRIX a matrix in which the number of rows equals the number of columns

UNIT MATRIX see *identity matrix*

VECTOR an ordered collection of numbers

7 *Income statement analysis and other business applications of percent*

Introduction

Chapter Seven provides the student with an opportunity to apply, in a variety of practical situations, what was covered earlier in the text on percents.

Before starting a topic-by-topic review of the contents of the chapter, it is suggested that the student carry out a very brief review of the chapter's contents. What is noteworthy in such a brief examination is the wide variety of topics to which your knowledge of percents may be applied.

The importance of calculations involving percents or related material deserves extra emphasis because of its applicability to a wide range of topics in business. When we are studying number-based communication skills, it is wise to emphasize those with a wide range of applications in business situations.

Chapter Seven covers income statements, markup, markdown, trade discount, cash discount, commissions and fees, sales, excise and payroll taxes.

7.1 *Income Statement Analysis*

The INCOME STATEMENT, sometimes called the PROFIT AND LOSS STATEMENT, is one of the most important types of financial reports of a business. The profit or loss is obtained as a result of comparison between the revenue and the expenses listed in the statement for a designated period of operation. When the total revenue exceeds the total expenses, there is a profit; otherwise, there is a loss. The period of operation may be a month, a year, or any other unit of time, depending on the intention of the management or the accounting system of the business. Since the income statement shows the result of operation, the arrangement of the items listed in the statement provides a logical order in discussing the common percentage problems in business.

The income statement, shown on this page, is that of a trading business whose major activity is purchasing merchandise for resale, e.g. Eaton's, The Bay, Robinson's, etc. In the income statement, the total revenue obtained during the period from the sale of goods, is shown as the net revenue figure of $10 000. The cost of the goods which were sold during the period (cost of goods sold) was $5 300 and the costs involved in operating the stores (total operating expenses) were $3 700. Together, the cost of goods sold and the total operating expenses make up the total expenses, which were $9 000 in this case. Thus, the net income from operations, or net profit, before income taxes, for the period was $1 000.

Because of their simplicity, not all of the income statement items need a detailed mathematical discussion. A brief explanation of the items and the plan for discussing them are presented.

Figure 7-1
Income Statement of a Trading Business
W.R. Grace Furniture
Income Statement for the month ended June 30, 19—

REVENUE FROM SALES:

Sales (or selling price)		$10 200
Less: Sales discount (or cash discount)		200
Net sales		$10 000
Cost of goods sold (or cost)		5 300
Gross profit on sales (or gross profit)		$ 4 700

OPERATING EXPENSES:

Delivery expenses	$ 400	
Store supplies expenses	200	
Store rent expense	450	
Sales staff salaries	1 800	
Sales commissions and fees	400	
Taxes expense (other than income tax)	300	
Interest expense	50	
Depreciation expense–office furniture and equipment	100	
Total operating expenses		3 700
Net income from operations (net profit)		$ 1 000
Estimated income tax		250
Net income after income tax		$ 750

A.   SALES (SELLING PRICE)

In a trading business, the transactions which involve the delivery of merchandise in exchange for cash or promises to pay are called SALES. The amount recorded by an accountant under this title is the actual selling price at which the seller agrees to sell and the buyer agrees to buy. Thus, the selling price is the buyer's purchase price.

In some cases, the company sold goods at a price which was less than the price at which the company listed the goods in its sales catalogue. The difference between the listed price and the price at which the goods were sold is known as a TRADE DISCOUNT. The sales figure is based on the price at which the W.R. Grace Company sold the goods in question, not on the list price of these goods.

As an example, consider a lamp which is listed in W.R. Grace's catalogue at $100 but sells at a trade discount of 20%. Since trade discounts are based on list price (100%) then the selling price or sales resulting from the sale of this lamp will be derived as follows:

List price	$100	
Less: trade discount	$ 20	(20% × $100)
Selling price (or sales)	$ 80	

Thus, W.R. Grace's sales for the month will be credited with $80 for this transaction.

B.   SALES DISCOUNTS (OR CASH DISCOUNTS)

SALES DISCOUNTS are also called CASH DISCOUNTS. The W.R. Grace Company gives some of its customers a cash discount. If the customer elects to take the cash discount the amount which they will pay on a bill from W.R. Grace Company will be less than the amount shown on the bill by the amount of the cash discount. Thus, for the period in question, all cash discounts must be subtracted from the amount of sales made in order to establish the net sales amount. Details concerning cash discounts are discussed in Section 7.4.

The difference between the selling price and the sales discount is the NET SALES. The seller collects the net sales as revenue.

C.   COST OF GOODS SOLD (OR COST)

The COST OF GOODS SOLD is the total COST of purchase of the merchandise which has been sold. The cost of purchases includes not only the net purchase price but also the incidental costs relating to merchandise acquisition, preparation, and placement for sale. Examples of the incidental costs are transportation charges, duties, taxes, insurance and storage.

D.   GROSS PROFIT ON SALES (OR GROSS PROFIT)

As shown in the income statement, the GROSS PROFIT ON SALES, or GROSS PROFIT, is the excess of the net sales over the cost of goods sold. It is called gross profit because the operating expenses of the business must be deducted from gross profit before the net income from operations is obtained.

E.   OPERATING EXPENSES

In a large business the various types of OPERATING EXPENSES may be classified into a number of groups. As shown in the income statement in Figure 7-1, however, only the common types of operating expenses are listed and these have been classified in a single group in order to simplify the discussion. The mathematical operations required to determine the delivery expenses, store supplies expenses, store rent and sales staff salaries are not discussed because their calculation is relatively simple. Other operating expenses are discussed as follows:

Sales commissions and fees are discussed in Section 7.5. Taxes expense (other than income tax) is discussed in Sections 7.6 through 7.8. Only the taxes that frequently affect every business are discussed in these sections. These taxes are: sales taxes (7.6), excise taxes (7.7) and payroll taxes (7.8). If a tax is imposed upon the business, the tax payment is classified as an operating expense. However, if the business is required by law to collect the tax and to transfer the tax collected to a government agency at a later date, the amount is not listed as an income statement item.

The calculations necessary to determine interest expense require a detailed discussion. From Chapter Eight to the end of this text, almost all of the discussion is devoted to the mathematics of interest computation.

Depreciation expense can be computed in various ways. Some of the methods of computing depreciation expense require a knowledge of compound interest and annuity. For convenience and uniformity, the discussion of methods of computing depreciation expense is deferred until Chapter Seventeen.

F.   NET INCOME FROM OPERATIONS (NET PROFIT)

As shown in the income statement, the excess of the gross profit on sales over the total operating expenses is the NET INCOME FROM OPERATIONS, or, as it is commonly called, NET PROFIT.

G.   ESTIMATED INCOME TAX

INCOME TAXES are levied on a taxpayer's annual income by the federal government, and by the province in which the taxpayer resided on December 31 of that year. Net income from business operations is subject to tax under income tax laws. The tax rate usually increases as the taxable income increases. In the above income statement, it is assumed that the net income from operations, $1 000, is a portion of the business owner's taxable income of the year and that the tax rate applied to the portion is 25%.

H.   NET INCOME AFTER INCOME TAX

The NET INCOME AFTER INCOME TAX is the actual income that the owner of a business may use as desired.

The income statement items mentioned above, from sales through net income after income tax, give complete financial information about the business operations. However, if the information is further analysed, the use of the statement can be increased and thus a more intelligent business policy may be achieved. An analysis of the relative relationships among the individual income statement items may be performed in a manner similar to that presented in the next section.

7.2 Relationships Among Income Statement Items with Percents

A.   BASIC CONCEPTS

Buying and selling are basic business activities. A business person usually buys merchandise at a lower cost but sells it at a higher price. The difference between the selling price and buying cost is called gross profit (MARKUP) on sales. From the gross profit, the operating expenses, such as store supplies and rents, are deducted to obtain the net profit or net loss.

From an operating point-of-view, there are certain widely applied relationships which can be derived from the income statement. Before stating these relationships, the symbols used will be explained; and the following three points noted:

1. (a)   The meaning of the term "markup rate." This is the gross profit expressed as a percent of the cost price, i.e.,

$$\text{MARKUP RATE} = \frac{\text{GROSS PROFIT IN DOLLARS}}{\text{COST PRICE IN DOLLARS}} \times 100.$$

(b)   The meaning of the term "margin rate." This is the gross profit expressed as a percent of the selling price, i.e.,

$$\text{MARGIN RATE} = \frac{\text{GROSS PROFIT IN DOLLARS}}{\text{SELLING PRICE IN DOLLARS}} \times 100.$$

2.   Whenever a percent figure is mentioned in such a problem, pay particular attention to whether such a figure is associated with a selling price or a cost price, since whichever of these two prices is mentioned will be treated as the base or 100% in the solution to the problem.

3.   Note the method of solution employed here, where a table is set up in which the relationships contained in the problem are expressed in terms of percents and/or

dollars. This approach may simplify the calculations involved and is worth experimenting with.

The symbols used for the terms in an income statement are as follows:

SP = selling price of an item
CP = cost price of an item
GP = gross profit on sale of an item
OE = operating expenses incurred on sale of an item
NP = net profit on sale of an item

The first relationship is that involving the selling price, cost price and gross profit and it may be symbolized as follows:

①   SP = CP + GP, or SP − CP = GP   ②

This relationship indicates that the difference between the selling price and the cost price is the gross profit.

A further relationship involves the gross profit, the operating expenses and the net profit:

③   GP = OE + NP, or GP − OE = NP   ④

This relationship shows that when the operating expenses are deducted from the gross profit, the result is the net profit.

If OE + NP are substituted for GP in ① the relationship between selling price, cost price, operating expenses and net profit is established as follows:

SP = CP + OE + NP

These basic relationships are worth understanding and committing to memory. The use of these income statement relationships is illustrated in the following examples.

Example 7.2a

The Canadian Automotive Stores buys radial tires at $80 each. The current markup rate used by the store is 25% of cost. What should be the selling price of the tires?

SOLUTION:

The cost price is the base or 100%. The markup rate expresses the gross profit as a percent of the cost price and the basic relationship may be set up in the following form:

	$	% of CP
SP	?	125
CP	80	100
GP		25

If the known values are located in the table, the answer can be obtained readily. Note that the gross profit is 25% of the cost price (i.e., the markup rate is 25%), thus we can locate the value 25 in the column headed "% of CP." If CP is the base then opposite the cost price in the same column we can enter the value 100.

Knowing that SP = CP + GP, then the figure to be entered in the column headed "% of CP" opposite the selling price will be the sum of the two percents which represent GP and CP, i.e., SP = 125% of CP.

Knowing from the table that the selling price is 125% of the cost price and knowing that the cost price is $80, it is a simple matter to find the selling price:

$$SP = 125\% \text{ of } CP = \frac{125}{100} \times 80 = \$100$$

Example 7.2b

B.C. Record Shop sells a record player for $250. The cost of the record player is $200 and the operating expenses are 4% of the selling price. What would be the gross profit (markup) and the net profit?

SOLUTION:

In this problem, we know the selling price of the record player is $250, the cost of this unit is $200, and the operating expenses are 4% (or $10, as $250 × .04 = $10). We wish to find the gross profit and the net profit, therefore, a table may be set up and the known values located:

	$	% of SP
SP	250	100
CP	200	
GP	?	
OE		4
NP	?	

The gross profit may be established quickly in both dollar and percent terms. Since the gross profit = selling price − cost price, we can obtain the gross profit as $50. This figure can be converted to a percent of the selling price, GP as % of SP = $\frac{50}{250} \times 100 =$ 20%.

This figure can now be entered into the table:

	$	% of SP
SP	250	100
CP	200	
GP	50	20
OE		4
NP	?	

Since we know that GP = OE + NP, we can rearrange the equation to find NP, i.e., NP = GP − OE. Using this information, we establish that,

$$NP = (20 − 4)\% \text{ of SP, or } 16\% \text{ of SP}$$

therefore, $NP = \dfrac{16}{100} \times 250 = \$40.$

The five items–selling price, cost, gross profit, operating expenses and net profit–usually constitute the major parts of an income statement. The income statement reports in dollar amounts for periodic results of the business operation. It gives important information to the business concern in reviewing its operations during the period and thus assists management in making policies for the future. Detailed discussion concerning individual items of an income statement is presented in further sections. This section is devoted to the methods of analysing the relationships among the major items with percents.

To express in percents the relationships among the items, a BASE (or 100%) must first be selected. Theoretically, any one of the items may be selected as the base. However, in most business concerns, either the cost or the selling price is used as the base. Many businesses, such as manufacturers, that keep inventory records at cost, usually find that the cost is a convenient figure to be used as a basis for computing selling price, gross profit, operating expenses and net profit. On the other hand, some business concerns find that the selling price is the most convenient figure to be used as a basis for computing cost, gross profit, operating expenses and net profit. In these firms, sales commissions and bonuses are often expressed as a certain percent of the selling price instead of the cost.

The relative values in percent form for Example 7.2b are computed as shown in the following table.

Table 7-1
Relative Values of Income Statement Items in Percent Form

Actual Values		Relative Values	
		Selling price as the base	Cost as the base
Selling Price	$250	$100\% \left(\text{or } \dfrac{250}{250} \right)$	$125\% \left(\text{or } \dfrac{250}{200} \right)$
Cost	200	$80\% \left(\text{or } \dfrac{200}{250} \right)$	$100\% \left(\text{or } \dfrac{200}{200} \right)$
Gross Profit	50	$20\% \left(\text{or } \dfrac{50}{250} \right)$	$25\% \left(\text{or } \dfrac{50}{200} \right)$
Operating Expenses	10	$4\% \left(\text{or } \dfrac{10}{250} \right)$	$5\% \left(\text{or } \dfrac{10}{200} \right)$
Net Profit	40	$16\% \left(\text{or } \dfrac{40}{250} \right)$	$20\% \left(\text{or } \dfrac{40}{200} \right)$

The rates (in percent form) for the above computation are calculated from the formula

$$\boxed{\text{RATE} = \frac{\text{PERCENTAGE}}{\text{BASE}}} \quad \longleftarrow Formula\ 7\text{-}1$$

The base is always 100% of itself. Thus, when the selling price is the base, the selling price is 100% of itself. The cost is 80% of the base, gross profit margin is 20%, operating expenses are 4%, and net profit is 16% of the base. These percentages may be proved as follows:

$$\text{Cost} = 250(\text{selling price}) \times 80\% = \$100$$
$$\text{Gross profit} = 250 \times 20\% = \$50$$
$$\text{Operating expenses} = 250 \times 4\% = \$10$$
$$\text{Net profit} = 250 \times 16\% = \$40$$

When the cost is the base, the cost is 100% of itself. The selling price is 125% of the base, gross profit is 25%, operating expenses are 5% and net profit is 20% of the base. These percentages may be proved as follows:

$$\text{Selling price} = 200(\text{cost}) \times 125\% = \$250$$
$$\text{Gross profit} = 200 \times 25\% = \$50$$
$$\text{Operating expenses} = 200 \times 5\% = \$10$$
$$\text{Net profit} = 200 \times 20\% = \$40$$

When the dollar amounts are reduced to relative values, preferably in percent form, the relationships among the income statement items may easily be analysed. Thus, the 'reduced' statement may serve as a more powerful guide to management. For example, it should be an easier task in pricing various articles if the relative values, in percents of the gross profit and the base cost are known. Also, management would be more alert if it were informed that operating expenses were 4% of the selling price this year and the rate was only 2% last year.

The following examples illustrate additional problems that involve the use of cost and selling price as the basis for computation.

B.   FINDING THE SELLING PRICE FROM THE COST AND VICE VERSA

The Value of a Base is Given

The base may be the selling price or the cost. When the value of a base is given, the required item can easily be computed by the formula

$$\boxed{\text{PERCENTAGE} = \text{BASE} \times \text{RATE}} \quad \longleftarrow Formula\ 7\text{-}2$$

Example 7.2c
The U.I.B. Unisex Sweater Shop sells a sweater for $90. The net profit rate used by the shop is 20% of the selling price, and the operating expenses are 10% of the selling price. What is the cost of the sweater?

SOLUTION:

	$	% of SP
SP	90	100
CP		70
GP		30
OE		10
NP		20

The cost of the sweater is 70% of SP $= \dfrac{70}{100} \times 90 = \$63$.

The cost price of the sweater is $63.

Example 7.2d

Victoria Shoe Company must reduce the selling price of a certain type of shoes which presently sells for $85. The markup on cost is 45%. What is the lowest price at which the shoes can be sold in order to recover the cost?

SOLUTION:

	$	% of CP
SP	85	145
CP		100
GP		45

Therefore, CP $= \dfrac{100}{145} \times 85 = \$58.62$. The lowest price at which the shoes can be sold in order to recover cost is $58.62.

The Value of a Base is Not Given

Under this condition, the value of an item related to the base and the percent rate representing the item must be given or can be determined. When a given value and its percent rate are known, the base can be obtained by dividing the given value by its corresponding percent rate, or

$$\boxed{\text{BASE} = \frac{\text{PERCENTAGE}}{\text{RATE}}} \quad \longleftarrow \textit{Formula 7-3}$$

Example 7.2e

Lucy's Hat Shop buys a certain line of hats at $70 each. For how much must Lucy's Hat Shop sell the hats if the shop wants to make a gross profit of 35% of the selling price?

SOLUTION:

	$	% of SP
SP		100
CP	70	65
GP		35

Therefore, $SP = \dfrac{70}{65\%} = \$107.69$. Lucy's Hat Shop must sell the hats for $107.69 each in order to make a gross profit of 35%.

EXERCISE 7.2A / REFERENCE SECTIONS: A–B

Find the selling price in each of the following problems:

	Cost	Gross Profit based on Cost		Cost	Gross Profit based on Selling Price
1.	$ 28.00	10%	7.	$ 72.00	10%
2.	6.25	12%	8.	39.60	12%
3.	8.20	7%	9.	41.73	22%
4.	36.00	15%	10.	42.00	25%
5.	24.30	6%	11.	227.15	30%
6.	57.52	8%	12.	204.90	20%

Find the cost in each of the following problems:

	Selling Price	Gross Profit based on Cost		Selling Price	Gross Profit based on Selling Price
13.	$ 22.76	42%	19.	$ 24.00	40%
14.	31.50	26%	20.	30.00	25%
15.	287.76	32%	21.	46.50	38%
16.	524.40	52%	22.	53.40	26%
17.	331.16	36%	23.	267.42	55%
18.	2 461.69	15%	24.	654.14	45%

Statement Problems:

25. A dealer bought ten T.V. sets at $450 each. The dealer sold the T.V. sets at a markup of 45% on the cost. What is (a) the amount of gross profit on each set, and (b) the selling price of each set?

26. A jewellery store wishes to price a watch that costs $65 to yield a gross profit of 52% of the cost. What should the selling price be?

27. The cost of a mattress is $95, the operating expenses are 20% of the cost, and the net profit is 5% of the cost. What should be the selling price?

28. The cost of a comb and brush set is $1.30, the operating expenses are 15% of the cost, and the retailer wishes to gain 7% net profit of the cost. What should be the selling price of the set?

29. Harvey's appliance store sells electric mixers at a gross profit of 35% of the selling price. The last shipment of mixers received cost $22 each. For how much will the store sell each mixer?

30. A department store bought 25 women's handbags for $487.50. At what price should the store sell each handbag if it is to have a gross profit of 22% of the selling price?

31. A retail store owner purchased windbreaker jackets at $22.75 each. He knows from past experience that the operating expenses are 20% of the selling price. If he wishes to gain 15% of the selling price as the net profit, what is the lowest price at which he should sell each windbreaker?

32. The cost of a dozen neckties is $18, the operating expenses are 18% of the selling price, and the net profit is 7% of the selling price. What is the selling price for each necktie?

33. A hardware store sells at markup of 30% of cost. A handsaw sells for $39. (a) What is the cost of the handsaw and (b) what is the amount of the gross profit on a handsaw?

34. A dress shop figures its gross profit at 45% of cost. What are (a) the cost and (b) the gross profit of a dress that sells for $13.95?

35. The selling price of a watch is $75.60, the operating expenses are 20% of the cost, and the net profit is 15% of the cost. What is the cost?

36. The selling price of a fan is $49, the operating expenses are 28% of the cost, and the retailer wishes to have a net profit of 12% of the cost. What is the cost?

37. The gross profit of a women's apparel store is 45% of the selling price. What are (a) the gross profit and (b) the cost of a scarf that sells for $4.98?

38. A shoe store owner plans to buy gloves for a line that sells for $8.50 per pair. What is the highest price that he can afford to pay for this line if his gross profit must be 38% of the selling price?

39. A dealer needs a camera that sells for $96. He knows from past experience that the operating expenses are 35% of the selling price. If he wishes to gain 20% of the selling price as the net profit from the sale, what is the highest price that he can afford to pay for the purchase of the camera?

40. A clothier sells a dozen sweaters for $150. If his operating expenses are 32% of the selling price and his net profit is 16% of the selling price, what is the cost of each sweater?

C.   FINDING THE GROSS PROFIT RATES FROM THE SELLING PRICE AND THE COST, AND VICE VERSA

Finding the Gross Profit Rates

Example 7.2f indicates how the gross profit rate based on the selling price (margin rate) and the gross profit based on cost (markup rate) are determined when the selling price and the cost are given.

Example 7.2f
Winnipeg Cycle Shop sells a men's 10-speed cycle which costs $81 for $108. What is (a) the markup rate, and (b) the margin rate?

SOLUTION:

GP = SP − CP
$\quad$ = 108 − 81
$\quad$ = $27

(a)$\quad$ markup rate $= \dfrac{GP}{CP} = \dfrac{27}{81} = 33.3\%$

(b)$\quad$ margin rate $= \dfrac{GP}{SP} = \dfrac{27}{108} = 25\%$

$\qquad$ Therefore, the markup rate is 33.3% and the margin rate is 25%.

Finding the Selling Price and the Cost

Examples 7.2g and 7.2h illustrate how the selling price and the cost are determined when the gross profit and its rate on the selling price and on the cost are given.

Example 7.2g
A hardware store makes a gross profit of $35 on a snowblower which is 17% of the selling price. What is (a) the selling price and (b) the cost price?

SOLUTION:

(a)$\quad$ GP = $35
$\qquad$ GP = 17% of SP
$\qquad$ SP $= \dfrac{GP}{17\%} = \dfrac{\$35}{.17} = \$205.88$

(b)$\quad$ CP = SP − GP

	$	% of SP
SP	205.88	100
GP	35.00	17
CP	170.88	83

CHECK:

CP = 83% of SP
CP = 83% × $205.88
CP = $170.88

Example 7.2h
The gross profit of an item is $25 and the gross profit rate is 20% of the cost. What are the selling price and the cost?

SOLUTION:

The cost is the base, 100%. Since $25 is equivalent to 20% of the cost, or

$$CP \times 20\% = \$25$$

$$CP = \frac{\$25}{20\%} = \$125$$

	$	% of CP
SP		
CP	125	100
GP	25	20

$$SP = CP + GP = 125 + 25 = 150$$

CHECK:

$$SP = 120\% \text{ of } CP$$
$$SP = 120\% \times 125$$
$$SP = \$150$$

EXERCISE 7.2B / REFERENCE SECTION: C

In each of the following problems, find (a) the gross profit, (b) the margin rate, and (c) the markup rate:

	Selling Price	Cost			Selling Price	Cost
1.	$80.00	$60.00		6.	$ 9.45	$ 8.30
2.	20.50	15.00		7.	88.20	65.10
3.	37.25	28.10		8.	76.24	55.40
4.	12.50	10.50		9.	128.50	86.20
5.	6.50	5.80		10.	456.46	384.72

In each of the following problems find (a) the selling price, and (b) the cost:

	Gross Profit	Markup Rate	Margin Rate
11.	$ 25.00	10%	
12.	42.00		15%
13.	1.95		5%
14.	43.80	12%	
15.	16.80	32%	
16.	18.99		45%
17.	12.71		50%
18.	15.26	35%	
19.	761.42	55%	
20.	313.45		25%
21.	987.51		30%
22.	529.06	20%	

Statement Problems:

23. A dealer bought a piano for $590.40 and sold it for $820. (a) What was the gross profit? (b) What was the gross profit rate on the cost? (c) What was the gross profit rate on the selling price?

24. A furniture store bought a chair for $48 less 15% and sold it for $52.80. (a) What was the gross profit? (b) What was the gross profit rate on the cost? (c) What was the gross profit rate on the selling price?

25. A jewellery store buys a dozen watches for $540 less 12% and sells them at $52 each. What is the gross profit rate (a) on the cost? (b) on the selling price?

26. A grocery store sold 1.4 kilograms of dried fruit for $3.50. The cost of the fruit was $36 per box containing 18 kilograms. What was the gross profit rate (a) on the cost? (b) on the selling price?

27. The gross profit of a furniture store for last year was $5 600. The store manager figured the gross profit rate on all pieces of furniture at 40% of cost. What was (a) the total cost of sales? (b) the amount of sales?

28. A department store made a gross profit of 32% of the selling price on all merchandise sold. The gross profit for last month was $39 580. What was (a) the total amount of sales? (b) the total cost of sales?

29. On March 1, a shoe store had merchandise on hand worth $1 400 at cost. Merchandise worth $2 200 had been purchased during March. The net sales at selling price during the month amounted to $1 000. The gross profit was estimated to be 40% of the selling price. At the end of the month, the store was destroyed by fire. At the time of the fire, what was the value of the inventory at cost?

30. On June 1, a hardware store had merchandise on hand worth $1 200 at cost. The selling price of the merchandise was $2 000. Later the store sold a part of it for $750. What is the value of the remaining merchandise at cost?

D.   CONVERTING ONE BASE TO ANOTHER BASE

In converting the base on cost to the base on selling price or vice versa, first set up the Selling Price-Cost-Gross Profit relationship according to the base (100%) of the gross profit rate. Then find the desired answer from the relationship as illustrated in the following examples.

Example 7.2i
The markup rate on an item is 60%. What is the margin rate?

SOLUTION:
Since the known rate is based on the cost, the cost is the original base and is 100% of itself. Thus,

	% of CP
CP	100
+ GP	60
SP	160

SP = 160% of CP

$$\text{margin rate} = \frac{\text{GP (or rate)}}{\text{SP (or rate)}}$$

$$= \frac{60\%}{160\%} = 37.5\%$$

CHECK:

Let CP be any amount, such as $300. Then GP is $300 \times 60\% = \$180$. SP is $300 + 180 = \$480$. When GP on selling price is 37.5%, the margin should be $\$480 \times 37.5\% = \$180$.

Example 7.2j
The gross profit of an item is 20% of the selling price. What is the gross profit rate based on cost?

SOLUTION:

The selling price is the original base and is 100% of itself since the given rate is based on the selling price. Thus,

	% of SP
SP	100
−CP	80
GP	20

$$\text{Markup} = \frac{\text{GP}}{\text{CP}} = \frac{20\%}{80\%} = 25\%$$

CHECK:

Let SP be any amount, such as $200. Then, GP on SP is $200 \times 20\% = \$40$. The CP is $200 - 40 = \$160$. GP on CP is $160 \times 25\% = \$40$.

Example 7.2k
The gross profit rate of an item is 10% of the selling price and the operating expenses are 7.2% of the selling price. What percent of the cost are the operating expenses?

SOLUTION:

The selling price is the original base and is 100% of itself, since the given gross profit rate is based on the selling price. Thus,

	% of SP
SP	100
−CP	90
GP	10

Since the operating expenses are also based on the selling price and the operating expenses rate on cost = $\frac{\text{OPERATING EXPENSES}}{\text{COST}}$, the new converted operating expenses on cost is

$$\frac{7.2\%}{90\%} = \frac{7.2}{90} = .08 = 8\%.$$

CHECK:

Let SP by any amount, such as $200. Then GP is 200 × 10% = $20. CP is 200 − 20 = $180. OE based on SP are 200 × 7.2% = $14.40. OE based on CP are 180 × 8% = $14.40.

Example 7.21

What percent of the selling price is equal to 34% of the cost if the gross profit is 26% of the selling price?

SOLUTION:

This type of problem can be broken down into three steps. First, split the statement of the problem into two parts, Then, establish from one of these parts the basic relationship which exists, and finally, take the remaining part of the problem which asks the question and answer the question using the relationship established in the second step.

(a) The two parts would read:
     The gross profit is 26% of the selling price, and what percent of the selling price is equal to 34% of the cost (or, 34% of the cost is what percent of the selling price)?

(b) The statement of the basic relationship reads GP is 26% of SP. Since CP + GP must be 100% of SP, then CP must be 74% of SP.

	% of SP
SP	100
−CP	74
GP	26

(c) Now address the statement which asks the question:
     What percent of the selling price is equal to 34% of the cost? Since we know that CP = 74% of SP, we also know that 100% of CP is 74% of SP.
     Therefore, finding 34% of CP in terms of SP is given by 100% of CP = 74% of SP. 34% of CP = $\left(\frac{74}{100} \times \frac{34}{100} \right)$% of SP = 25.16% of SP.

CHECK:

Let SP be any amount, such as $200. Then GP is 200 × 26% = $52. The CP is 200 − 52 = $148. The value of 34% of CP is 148 × 34% = $50.32. The value of 25.16% of the SP is 200 × 25.16% = $50.32.

EXERCISE 7.2C / REFERENCE SECTION: D

Convert each of the following markup rates to a margin rate:

1. 10%	4. 30%	7. 65%	10. 140%
2. 20%	5. 45%	8. 70%	11. 150%
3. 25%	6. 50%	9. 80%	12. 200%

Convert each of the following margin rates to a markup rate:

13. 15%	16. 40%	19. 75%	22. 45%
14. 20%	17. 56%	20. 85%	23. 10%
15. 30%	18. 62%	21. 90%	24. 50%

Statement Problems:

25. If the gross profit rate on the sale of a watch is 26% of the cost, what is the gross profit rate based on the selling price?

26. If the gross profit rate on the sale of a radio is 28% of the selling price, what is the gross profit rate based on the cost?

27. The gross profit rate on the sale of a table is 55% of the selling price and the operating expenses are 15% of the selling price. What percent of the cost are the operating expenses?

28. For the sale of a typewriter, the operating expenses are 22% of the selling price, and the gross profit is 40% of the selling price. What percent of the cost are the operating expenses?

29. If the gross profit rate is 65% of the selling price, what percent of the selling price is equal to 30% of the cost?

30. What percent of the selling price is equal to 38% of the cost if the gross profit is 48% of the cost?

31. When the gross profit is 65% of the selling price, what percent of the selling price is equal to 54% of the cost?

32. What percent of the selling price is equal to 36% of the cost if the gross profit rate based on cost is 25%?

33. If the gross profit is 75% of the cost, what percent of the cost is equal to 42% of the selling price?

34. What percent of the cost is equal to 26% of the selling price if the gross profit is 32% of the cost?

35. If the gross profit rate on the sale of a television set is 36% of the cost, what is the gross profit rate based on the selling price?

36. When the gross profit is 52% of the selling price, what percent of the cost is 35% of the selling price?

37. If the gross profit rate on the sale of a book is 45% of the selling price, what is the gross profit rate based on the cost?

38. The gross profit rate on the sale of a fan is 25% of the cost and the operating expenses are 12% of the cost. What percent of the selling price are the operating expenses?

REVIEW EXERCISE / REFERENCE SECTIONS: 7.2 A–D

Statement Problems:

1. If the cost of an item is $25 and the gross profit is 20% of the cost, what is the selling price?

2. A man bought a chair for $125. If he wishes to sell it and to realize a gross profit equal to 15% of the cost, what should the selling price be?

3. The cost of an electric drill is $48. If the operating expenses are 16% of the cost and the net profit is 12% of the cost, find the selling price?

4. The cost of a refrigerator is $550. The company wants to sell it so as to cover 28% of the cost as the operating expenses and to earn 15% of the cost as the net profit. What should the selling price be?

5. Canadian Automotive Store received a shipment of 100 tires and was invoiced for $6 000. The store operates on a markup (gross profit) of 45% of cost. (a) For how much must each tire be sold? and (b) what is the amount of the gross profit on each tire?

6. The cost of a table is $51.60 and the gross profit is 14% of the selling price. What is the selling price?

7. The cost of a radio is $35.20 and the gross profit is 12% of the selling price. What is the selling price?

8. The cost of a trailer is $385, the operating expenses are 35% of the selling price, and the net profit is 10% of the selling price. Find the selling price.

9. What is the selling price of a pair of shoes that costs $10.98 if the operating expenses are 24% of the selling price and the net profit is 15% of the selling price?

10. The selling price of a kilogram of beef is $4.20 and the gross profit is 30% of the cost. What is the cost?

11. The selling price of a box of candy is $4.35 and the gross profit is 45% of the cost. Find the cost.

12. An electric sewing machine sells for $650 and the gross profit is 30% of the selling price. What is the cost of the machine?

13. Honest Joe's Men's Wear is having a sale of men's suits which were originally priced at $250. The gross profit rate (margin) based on the selling price is 30%. What is the lowest price at which Honest Joe can sell the suits and clear cost?

14. A bottle of perfume sells at a price to give a gross profit of $2.50, which is also 40% of cost. What is the selling price?

15. A shoe store manager figures that her operating expenses are 34% of cost and that she needs a net profit of 13% of cost. What is the cost of a pair of shoes that sells for $6.

16. An office equipment store manager buys some typewriters for $168 each. His operating expenses are 33% of the selling price and his net profit is 22% of the selling price. At what price should he mark the typewriters?

17. The selling price of a bag of sugar is $7.37, the operating expenses are 14% of the cost, and the net profit is 20% of the cost. What is the cost of a bag of sugar?

18. In a retail store, the manager computed the operating expenses at 22% of the cost and the net profit at 15% of the cost. What is the cost of a handbag that sells for $36.85?

19. A pair of scissors sells for $5 and the gross profit is 40% of the selling price. What is the cost?

20. The selling price of an electric coffee maker is $38 and the gross profit is 45% of the selling price. What is the cost?

21. Bad Girl's Furniture Store sells wall units for $565, which represents a 45% markup on cost. For quick sale, the walls units were marked down 20% based on the selling price. (a) What is the cost of each unit? (b) What is the sale price of each unit? (c) What is the gross profit rate based on the sale price?

22. The selling price of a box of cookies is $1.60 and the cost is $1.20. What is the amount of gross profit and its rate (a) based on the selling price, (b) based on the cost?

23. The cost of a portable typewriter is $150 and it sells for $180. Find the amount of gross profit and the gross profit rate based on (a) the cost, and (b) the selling price.

24. The gross profit on the sale of a clock is $6 which is 40% of the cost. What are (a) the cost and (b) the selling price?

25. A company computed its gross profit rate as 25% of cost. If the gross profit on the sale of a cabinet is $60, find (a) the cost and (b) the selling price of the cabinet.

26. The gross profit on the sale of a book is $4.20 which is 35% of the selling price. What are (a) the selling price and (b) the cost?

27. A company computed its gross profit as 42% of the selling price. Find (a) the cost and (b) the selling price of a boy's jacket if the gross profit on the sale of the jacket is $2.10?

28. Radio Shed is having a spring clearance of Hi Fi speakers. The speakers were originally sold for $69.95 each, which represented a 45% markup on cost. The speakers were marked down to $49.95 each. (a) What was the cost of each speaker? (b) What is the amount of gross profit realized on each speaker? (c) What is the gross profit rate realized on each?

29. The gross profit rate on the sale of a bag of potatoes is 35% of the cost. What is the gross profit rate based on the selling price?

30. The gross profit rate on the sale of a set of tools is 55% of the cost. What is the gross profit rate based on the selling price?

31. The gross profit rate on the sale of a machine is 30% of the cost and the operating expenses are 26% of the cost. What percent of the selling price are the operating expenses?

32. On the sale of a handsaw, the operating expenses are figured at 30% of the cost and the gross profit rate is 42% of the cost. What percent of the selling price are the operating expenses?

33. What percent of the selling price is 65% of the cost if the gross profit is 30% of the selling price?

34. What percent of the selling price is 52% of the cost if the gross profit is 35% of the selling price?

35. If the gross profit rate on the sale of an item is 38% of the selling price, what is the gross profit rate based on cost?

36. If the gross profit rate on the sale of a truck is 28% of the selling price, what is the gross profit rate based on the cost of the truck?

37. The gross profit rate on the sale of a mirror is 15% of the selling price and the operating expenses are 6% of the selling price. What percent of the cost are the operating expenses?

38. The operating expenses are 14% of the selling price for a desk and the gross profit rate is 24% of the selling price. Find the operating expense rate based on the cost?

39. What percent of the cost is 42% of the selling price if the gross profit is 35% of the cost?

40. What percent of the cost is 58% of the selling price if the gross profit is 30% of the cost?

7.3 Trade Discount

A. GENERAL CONCEPT AND COMPUTATION

Generally speaking, there are two types of merchants in the trading business: the wholesaler and the retailer. The WHOLESALE MERCHANT usually purchases goods from manufacturers and producers and sells them to retailers and large consumers. The RETAIL MERCHANT purchases goods from several sources including wholesalers, producers, manufacturers, and agent middlemen, such as brokers and manufacturer's agents. The retailer mainly sells the goods to ultimate consumers.

Wholesalers normally tend to buy in larger amounts than retailers, and retailers tend to buy in larger amounts than consumers. Manufacturers, wholesalers, or other types of sellers therefore frequently grant substantial reductions from the list price quoted in their catalogues to allow for price differentials among different classes of customers. Such reductions, usually based on list price, are called trade discounts. For example, a manufacturer may offer the following selling prices to customers:

Type of Customer	Selling Price
Ultimate consumer	list (as quoted in catalogue)
Retailer and large consumer	10% off list
Wholesaler	10% and 5% off list

One reason for using trade discounts is to facilitate the movement of goods through what are referred to as the CHANNELS OF DISTRIBUTION. A simple illustration of the type of channel of distribution which may exist between a manufacturer and an ultimate consumer is shown in Figure 7-2.

Figure 7-2
Channels of Distribution

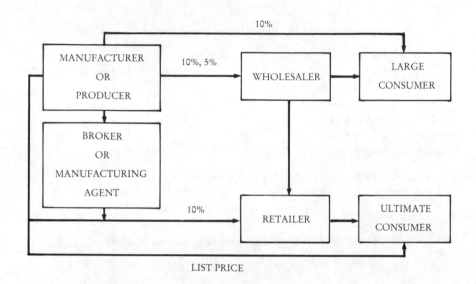

LIST PRICE

Trade discounts are sometimes used to make a revision in list prices without reprinting the catalogue. As prices fluctuate, new schedules of trade discounts are issued. For example, as market prices decrease, a manufacturer may offer a 5% discount from all prices listed in the catalogue for the purpose of establishing new prices for the consumer. When market prices increase, the discounts might be reduced or dropped. Other reasons for granting trade discounts are the location of the customer, and the size of the order, and the customer's credit rating.

If there are two or more trade discounts applying to a list price, the discounts are known as DISCOUNT SERIES or as CHAIN DISCOUNTS. When chain discounts are allowed, each succeeding discount is deducted from the remainder of the preceding discount.

Example 7.3a
The price of a typewriter listed in a catalogue at $150 is subject to a discount of 10%. What are the trade discount and the selling price?

SOLUTION:

Trade discount = List price × Discount rate
            = 150 × 10% = $15
    Selling price = List price − Trade discount
            = 150 − 15 = $135

Example 7.3b

The list price of $400 for a television set is subject to discounts of 10%, 5% and 2%. What is the selling price?

SOLUTION:

This problem may be computed in the following two ways:

(a) $400.00   List price   (b) $400.00
   − 40.00   10% of $400   ×   .90   100% − 10% = 90%
   $360.00   1st remainder $360.00
   − 18.00   5% of $360   ×   .95   100% − 5% = 95%
   $342.00   2nd remainder $342.00
   − 6.84   2% of $342   ×   .98   100% − 2% = 98%
   $335.16   Selling price $335.16

Chain discounts may be converted to a single equivalent discount. In Example 7.3b, the total amount of trade discounts is:

400.00 − 335.16 = $64.84.

If the amount $64.84 is considered as a single trade discount, since

LIST PRICE × DISCOUNT RATE = TRADE DISCOUNT, then

400 × discount rate = 64.84

$$\text{Discount rate} = \frac{64.84}{400} = .162\ 1, \text{ or } 16.21\%$$

The answer indicates that the single discount rate 16.21% is equivalent to the discounts of 10%, 5%, and 2%. The single discount rate is *not* equal to the sum of the chain discounts, since 10% + 5% + 2% = 17%. It is important to remember that each succeeding discount is applied to a *diminishing* balance of the list price. The result is used to check the answer in Example 7.2b as follows:

400 × 16.21% = 64.84
400 − 64.84 = $335.16

B. CALCULATION BY FORMULA

The computation of the solution in Example 7.3b, may be written in the following manner:

Selling price = 400(100% − 10%)(100@ − 5%)(100% − 2%)
             = 400(90%)(95%)(98%)
             = 400 × .837 9
             = $335.16

According to this method, the following formula may be developed in computing chain discounts:

SELLING PRICE = LIST PRICE$(1 -$ First discount rate)$(1 -$ Second discount rate)$(1 -$ Third discount rate) $(\ldots)$

NOTE: $1 = 100\%$

Let S = Selling price

   L = List price

   r_1 = 1st discount rate

r_2 = 2nd discount rate

r_3 = 3rd discount rate

r_n = nth discount rate

The above formula can be simplified as follows:

$$S = L(1 - r_1)(1 - r_2)(1 - r_3)\ldots(1 - r_n)$$ $\longleftarrow$ *Formula 7-4*

NOTE: The order in which the individual discount rates in a chain are multiplied does not affect the results. For example, the result of 400 (90%)(95%)(98%) is the same as the result of 400 (95%)(98%)(90%), or 400 (98%)(90%)(95%). In other words, the result of any one of the calculations equals 335.16.

Example 7.3c

The list price of $300 for a refrigerator is subject to discounts of $33\frac{1}{3}\%$, 25%, and 10%. Find (a) the selling price, and (b) the total amount of trade discount.

SOLUTION:

(a)   L = $300, $r_1 = 33\frac{1}{3}\%$, $r_2 = 25\%$, $r_3 = 10\%$

    Substituting the values in Formula 7-4:

    $S = 300(1 - 33\frac{1}{3}\%)(1 - 25\%)(1 - 10\%)$

      $= 300(.\dot{6})(.75)(.9)$

      $= 300(.45)$

      $= \$135$

(b)   Trade discount $= 300 - 135 = \$165$

    NOTE: Watch the rounding in the above example $(1 - 33\frac{1}{3}\% = .66\frac{2}{3}\% = .666\ldots)$

When the selling price and the trade discounts are known, the list price may be found by Formula 7.4 as shown in the following example.

Example 7.3d

The selling price of a hat is $27.36. At what price should the hat be listed if a series of discounts 20%, 10% and 5% is allowed?

SOLUTION:

S = $27.36, $r_1 = 20\%$, $r_2 = 10\%$, $r_3 = 5\%$

Substituting the values in Formula 7-4:

$27.36 = L(1 - 20\%)(1 - 10\%)(1 - 5\%)$

$27.36 = L(.8)(.9)(.95) = L(.684)$

$$L = \frac{27.36}{.684} = \$40$$

CHECK:

$$
\begin{array}{ll}
\$40.00 & \\
-\ 8.00 & \text{20\% of \$40} \\
\hline
\$32.00 & \\
-\ 3.20 & \text{10\% of \$32} \\
\hline
\$28.80 & \\
-\ 1.44 & \text{5\% of \$28.80} \\
\hline
\$27.36 & \text{Selling price}
\end{array}
$$

Or,

$$
\begin{aligned}
S &= 40(1 - 20\%)(1 - 10\%)(1 - 5\%) \\
&= 40(.8)(.9)(.95) = 40(.684) \\
&= \$27.36
\end{aligned}
$$

Chain discounts may be converted to a single equivalent discount rate by Formula 7.5, as shown, without referring to the list price or the selling price.

Let r = the single discount rate which is equivalent to a series of discounts, $r_1, r_2, r_3. \ldots$

Formula 7.4 becomes

$$\boxed{S = L(1 - r)} \quad \longleftarrow Formula\ 7\text{-}5$$

Equate the right sides of the above equation and Formula 7-5.
The following equation is obtained:

$$L(1 - r) = L(1 - r_1)\,(1 - r_2)(1 - r_3)\ldots(1 - r_n)$$

Divide both sides by L and solve for r. Then,

$$\boxed{r = 1 - (1 - r_1)(1 - r_2)(1 - r_3)\ldots(1 - r_n)} \quad \longleftarrow Formula\ 7\text{-}6$$

Example 7.3e

What is the single trade discount rate which is equivalent to chain discounts of 10%, 5% and 2%?

SOLUTION:

$r_1 = 10\%,\ r_2 = 5\%,\ r_3 = 2\%$

Substituting the values in Formula 7-6 the single equivalent discount rate r is computed as follows:

$$
\begin{aligned}
r &= 1 - (1 - 10\%)(1 - 5\%)(1 - 2\%) \\
&= 1 - (90\%)(95\%)(98\%) \\
&= 1 - (.9)(.95)(.98) \\
&= 1 - .8379 \\
&= .1621,\ \text{or } 16.21\%
\end{aligned}
$$

This answer may be used to check the solution in Example 7.3b, as shown:

Selling price, $S = L(1 - r) = 400(1 - 16.21\%) = 400 \times .8379$
$$= \$335.16$$

EXERCISE 7.3 / REFERENCE SECTIONS: A–B

Find (a) the selling price, (b) the total amount of the trade discount, and (c) the single equivalent discount rate:

	List Price	Discount Rates		List Price	Discount Rates
1.	$ 500	20%, 10%, 5%	6.	$2 500	15%, 30%, 20%
2.	$ 600	$12\frac{1}{2}\%$, 8%, 4%	7.	$ 30	40%, 40%, 40%
3.	$ 300	10%, $12\frac{1}{2}\%$, 15%	8.	$ 80	50%, 50%, 50%
4.	$ 400	5%, 10%, 20%	9.	$ 15.20	2%, 1%
5.	$1 000	25%, 20%, $16\frac{2}{3}\%$	10.	$ 35.50	5%, 3%

Statement Problems:

11. The list price of an electric clock is $8.50 and the trade discount rate is 26%. Find the net price (selling price).
12. If the list price of a chair is $25.40 and the trade discount is 5%, what is the selling price?
13. The list price of a fountain pen is $12, and the discount rate listed on the discount sheet for this item is 15%. Find the selling price.
14. If the list price of an electric fan is $45 and the discount rate is 12%, what is the selling price?
15. A wholesaler ordered a dozen kitchen ranges listed at $250 each less discounts of 10%, 5%, and 2%. What is the net price of the entire order?
16. What is the net price of a sewing machine listed at $340, less discounts of 20%, 12% and 10%?

Find (a) the selling price and (b) the total amount of trade discount:

	List Price	Rates of Trade Discounts		List Price	Rates of Trade Discounts
17.	$ 50	10%, 7%, 5%	20.	$ 75	20%, 22%, 35%
18.	$ 20	12%, 15%, 18%	21.	$125.70	$33\frac{1}{3}\%$, $37\frac{1}{2}\%$, $88\frac{8}{9}\%$
19.	$ 48	15%, 20%, 45%	22.	$434	$66\frac{2}{3}\%$, 75%, $28\frac{4}{7}\%$

Find the list price:

Selling Price	Rates of Trade Discounts		Selling Price	Rates of Trade Discounts
23. $ 30.24	10%, 20%, 30%	26.	$1 365.00	20%, 25%, 30%, 35%
24. $828.75	15%, 25%, 35%	27.	$ 500.65	5%, 15%
25. $168.00	30%, 40%, 50%, 60%	28.	$ 132.30	2%, 10%

Find the equivalent rate of trade discount:

29. 20%, 10%, 2%   31. 5%, 10%, 20%   33. 25%, $28\frac{4}{7}$%, $37\frac{1}{2}$%

30. 25%, 20%, 10%   32. 10%, 12%, 15%   34. $12\frac{1}{2}$%, $18\frac{2}{11}$%, $8\frac{1}{3}$%

Statement Problems:

35. A furniture dealer can buy an armchair from manufacturer X for $20 less discounts of 15% and 10%, or from manufacturer Y for $25 less discounts of 20%, 5% and 15%. (a) Which manufacturer has offered the lower price? (b) What is the difference between the two prices?

36. Company A offers a retailer trade discounts of $33\frac{1}{3}$%, 25%, and 1%. Company B offers the retailer trade discounts of 30%, 20%, and 15%. Which company offers the lower price on an article if the list price is the same at both companies?

37. A manufacturer of hosiery offers to ship 500 pairs of ladies' hose to a retailer at $1.50 per pair less discounts of 10%, 5%, and 2%. If the 2% discount is later removed, by what amount will the retailer's cost be affected?

38. Two television manufacturers offer similar products at prices as follows: Manufacturer C offers a list price less 20%, 8% and 2%. Manufacturer D offers a list price less 15%, 10% and 5%. Which manufacturer has the lower net price on his item if the list price is the same for both manufacturers?

39. A refrigerator which sold for $581.40 net has been subject to discounts of 5%, 10%, and 15%. What is the list price?

40. A wholesaler paid $54 in cash for an electric sander which was bought at trade discounts of 20%, 25%, and 10%. What was the list price?

41. The selling price of a washing machine is $327.60. At what price should the machine be listed if a series of discounts 10%, 20% and 30% is allowed?

42. The selling price of a used car is $3 633.75. At what price should the car be listed if the list price is subject to discounts of 25%, 15%, and 5%?

43. A manufacturer can cover his expenses and make a fair profit if he sells his tape recorder for $136.89. What should the list price of the item be in his catalogue so that his customers can be allowed a series of discounts of 35% and 22%?

44. An invoice shows that the net price of an electric saw is $106.19 after discounts of 30% and 18% have been taken. Find the list price.

45. The list price of an electric fan is $28.80 less a discount of 10%. The wholesaler later allowed an additional discount to make the selling price of $19.44. (a) What was the additional discount rate? (b) What single discount rate will give the same new selling price?

46. The list price of an electric coffee pot is $18.60 less discounts of 15% and 12%. Because of rising costs, the company changed the 12% discount to 10%. (a) What is the net change in the selling price? (b) What single discount rate will give the same new selling price?

47. The Northern Manufacturing Company uses a markup rate of 30%. At what price should they list an article which costs $265 if they want to offer their wholesale customers trade discounts of 10%, 25%, 5%?

48. A manufacturer of leather goods has a line of ladies' coats which cost $75 to make. The coats are to be sold at a price which will yield a gross margin of 60%. At what price should the coats be listed so that the retailer may be given trade discounts of 22% and 10% and still allow the manufacturer to make his desired gross margin?

49. A manufacturer of trophies makes some trophies which list at $45 each. If the manufacturer wishes to have a gross markup of 30% and offers retailers of the trophies discounts of 15% and 8%, (a) what is the highest cost at which he can manufacture the trophies, and (b) what will his selling price be?

7.4 *Cash Discount*

A. CONCEPT AND COMPUTATION

There is considerable variation in the methods of payment among different types of businesses. Some firms require immediate payment, but others allow their customers to pay their bills within a specified period of time known as the CREDIT PERIOD. Many companies offer their customers a discount from the selling price called a CASH DISCOUNT. A cash discount is also called a SALES DISCOUNT by the seller, and a PURCHASE DISCOUNT by the buyer. A cash discount, which is usually stated on the invoice, is generally used to encourage an early payment before the expiration of the credit period. For example, the seller may offer his debtor cash discount terms of "2/10, $n/30$." These terms mean that if payment is made within 10 days from the date of the invoice, a 2% cash discount is allowed, although the debtor is permitted a period of 30 days to pay the bill. However, if the bill is paid after the end of 10 days but on or before the end of the 30-day period, the net amount of the invoice must be paid. After 30 days, the bill will be considered overdue and may be subject to an interest charge.

Although cash discount rates are small in comparison to trade discount rates, most buyers are eager to pay their bills in time to earn cash discounts. The discount terms 2/10, $n/30$, actually provides the buyer with a high annualized rate or return on the funds used to settle the account on or before the tenth day. The time from the last day of the discount to the due date is 20 days ($30 - 10 = 20$). Thus 2% interest may be earned for 20 days, which is equivalent to a high annual rate of return.

When an invoice states credit terms in a form such as 2/10, 1/20, $n/30$, the number at the left in each term is the discount rate in percent; the number at the right is the allowed credit period in number of days; and n indicates the net amount in the invoice, or the selling price.

The amount of cash discount is determined as follows:

CASH DISCOUNT = INVOICE AMOUNT (or selling price) × CASH DISCOUNT RATE (%)

Example 7.4a

An invoice of $600 was dated May 1 with credit terms of 2/10, 1/20, n/30. What amount should the buyer pay if he pays in full on (a) May 8? (b) May 15? (c) May 31?

SOLUTION:

(a) It is 7 days from May 1 to May 8. Thus, 2% cash discount is allowed.
    600 × 2% = 12   600 − 12 = $588

(b) It is 14 days from May 1 to May 15. Thus, 1% cash discount is allowed.
    600 × 1% = 6   600 − 6 = $594

(c) It is 30 days from May 1 to May 31. Thus, no cash discount is allowed. The debtor must pay the entire bill of $600.

Example 7.4b

An invoice dated April 6 states that the selling price for merchandise is $620.50; the freight charge is $12.60; and the terms are 2/10, n/30. Find the total payment if the bill is paid on (a) April 12, (b) April 20.

SOLUTION:

(a) It is 6 days from April 6 to April 12. Thus, a discount of 2% of the selling price is allowed. However, discount is not taken on the freight charges.
    620.50 × 2% = 12.41
    620.50 − 12.41 + 12.60 = $620.69

(b) It is 14 days from April 6 to April 20. Thus, no cash discount is allowed. The total amount of the payment for the invoice is the selling price plus the freight charge.
    620.50 + 12.60 = $633.10

B. RECEIPT OF GOODS AND END OF THE MONTH DATING

Although the credit period generally begins with the date of the invoice, it may begin on the day of RECEIPT OF GOODS (ROG). The ROG DATING is particularly useful when a considerable amount of time is required for transportation. Or, it may begin at the END OF THE MONTH (EOM) following the date of the invoice, such as "2/10 EOM."

"2/10 EOM" means that if the invoice is paid during the first ten days following the end of the month of the invoice date, the buyer is entitled to a 2% cash discount. If the invoice is not paid during the cash discount period, an additional 20-day period is usually allowed to pay the net amount.

Example 7.4c

Etonia Sportwear received an invoice dated June 6 for 20 tweed jackets purchased at $45 each. The credit terms on the invoice were 3/10, n/30 EOM. How much will settle the account on July 3?

SOLUTION:

EOM means *end of month*. The credit terms start at the end of the month in which the invoice is dated (June). The last date on which 3% discount may be taken is July 10.

Amount of Invoice = 45×20

$= \$900$

$100\% - 3\% = 97\%$

Amount Paid $= 900(.97)$

$= \$873$

Example 7.4d

On September 15, Harvey's Furniture Outlet received a shipment of mirrors. The invoice dated August 5, was in the amount of $1 892 with credit terms 4/10, $n/30$ ROG. When is the last date on which Harvey's Furniture Outlet may take the 4% discount? How much will settle the account on that date?

SOLUTION:

(a) The last date on which the account may be taken is 10 days after the receipt of the goods (ROG):

September 15 + 10 = September 25

(b) The discount is 4%

$100\% - 4\% = 96\%$

Amount paid $= 1 892(.96)$

$= \$1 816.32$

C. PARTIAL PAYMENTS

Sometimes the buyer makes a partial payment on the invoice. If the partial payment is made within the discount period, the purchaser is entitled to a discount on the portion of the amount paid.

Example 7.4e

An invoice of $400 dated September 25 with credit terms of 2/10 EOM was issued to G.D. Miller. He paid $245 on the invoice on October 7. What is (a) the amount credited to Miller's account by the seller? (b) the cash discount? (c) the balance due? Assume that cash discount is allowed on partial payment.

SOLUTION:

(a) The credit period begins at the end of September. It is 7 days from the end of September to October 7. Thus, Miller is entitled to a 2% cash discount on the amount he pays. Since $245 is equivalent to 98% (or 100% – 2%), the base (100%) must be

245 ÷ 98% = $250

The amount credited to Miller's account is $250, which is the partial payment before the 2% discount is taken.

(b) Cash discount is 250 – 245 = $5

CHECK:

$250 \times 2\% = \$5$

(c)   Balance due is $400 - 250 = \$150$

In Example 7.4e, the statement "he paid $245 on the invoice on October 7" is very often not fully appreciated for its significance in determining cash discounts. To try to clarify the significance of this type of statement, let us compare two situations.

If Miller had paid the $400 bill in full on October 7, he would have calculated the discount as follows:

$\$400 \times .02 = \$8,$

and remitted to his creditor the discounted amount of $400 - $8 or $392, i.e. Miller would have calculated the discount first and forwarded the balance. Compare this situation to what actually happened. Miller sent a cheque for $245 on October 7. He remitted a cheque for the discounted amount as was done in the first case.

In order to credit Miller properly for the $245, which he forwarded, we have to take the approach that for every 98 cents paid by Miller, his account is credited with $1.00. Thus, to establish the credit to his account for the $245, which he sent to his creditor, we must proceed as follows:

$$\text{Amount credited to Miller's account} = \frac{245}{.98} = 250$$

Note that the 2% discount earns Miller an extra $5 of credit here. Had we tried to obtain the answer by taking 2% of $245, we would have obtained an amount of

$245 \times 2\% = \$4.90,$

which is incorrect.

EXERCISE 7.4 / REFERENCE SECTIONS: A–C

In each of the following cases find: (a) the amount of cash discount, and (b) the amount paid. Assume that the invoice date and the date of payment are for the same year.

	Invoice Amount	Invoice Date	Terms	Payment Date
1.	$550	January 6	2/10, n/30	January 16
2.	$478	February 2	2/10, n/30	February 12
3.	$456.20	March 10	4/10, 2/30, n/60	March 26
4.	$725.60	April 7	4/10/ 2/30, n/60	April 20
5.	$ 65.16	May 20	3/10, 2/20, n/30	May 24
6.	$ 38.58	June 3	3/10, 2/20, n/30	June 9
7.	$ 24.30	July 5	5/10, 2/30, n/60	August 10
8.	$ 15.50	August 4	5/10, 2/30, n/60	September 29
9.	$ 29.65	September 21	2/10 EOM	October 8
10.	$ 62.28	October 26	3/10 EOM	November 7

Statement Problems:

11. The Metro Company received a cheque from a customer who took the company's usual 2% cash discount on an invoice for $1 582. What was the amount received?

12. What is the amount of the cheque sent in payment of an invoice for $236.40; terms 3/10, n/30; dated November 16 and paid November 21?

13. An invoice for $850 was issued on September 10 with credit terms of 3/10, 2/20, n/30. What amount should the buyer pay if he makes the payment in full on: (a) September 15? (b) September 22? (c) October 6?

14. An invoice for $522.40 dated October 16 has the terms 2/10, 1/15, n/30, EOM. Find the amount of payment if the bill is paid on (a) November 20, (b) November 28, and (c) November 10.

15. Billy Meyer, a wholesaler, made a sale of merchandise having a list price of $750 and a trade discount of 25%. He prepared the sales invoice on Februrary 16 and included a freight charge of $16.50. The credit terms are 2/10, n/20. How much should the customer pay if the bill is paid on (a) February 24? (b) February 28?

16. An invoice dated June 25 has terms 3/15, 2/20, n/30 ROG. The goods were received on July 5. (a) What is the last date on which the 3% discount may be taken? (b) What is the last date on which the 2% discount may be taken?

17. John Parker, a retailer, received an invoice which gives the following information:

    Date of invoice June 16, 19—
    Item 1: 2 kitchen sinks; list price, $125 each, less trade discounts of 5% and 10%
    Item 2: 12 radios, list price, $22 each, less trade discounts of 15% and 8%
    Freight charges: $25.20
    Credit terms: 2/10 EOM

    Determine: (a) the last day on which the cash discount may be taken, and (b) the total amount of the payment for the bill if it is paid on that day.

18. An invoice for $500 dated June 2 with credit terms of 2/10, n/30 was received by George Sanders. He paid $196 on June 6 and $162 on June 15. (a) What was the total cash discount on the two payments? (b) What was the balance due after the payments were made? Assume that cash discount is allowed on partial payment.

19. On an invoice for $650 with credit terms of 5/10, 2/20, n/30, dated May 24, the partial payments were made as follows: $285 cash on June 1; $260 cash on June 5. Find (a) the total cash discount on the two payments, and (b) the balance due after the payments were made. Assume that the cash discount is allowed on partial payment.

20. Newlife Incorporated received a shipment of vitamins on August 19. The invoice was dated August 5 with terms 4/20, 3/25, n/30 ROG. How much will settle the account on September 9?

21. Fairview Hardware Ltd. received a shipment of twenty washing machines. The washing machines were listed at $650 each, with trade discounts of 15%, 10%. The invoice was dated May 18 and had credit terms of 3/10, 11/20, n/30, EOM. Determine: (a) the single equivalent discount rate, (b) the amount that will settle the account on June 15 if a partial payment of $1 500 was made on June 9 (assume that cash discounts are applied to partial payments), and (c) for how much Fairview Hardware Ltd. should sell the washing machines if the company uses a markup rate of 30%?

7.5 *Commissions and Fees*

A.   BASIC CONCEPTS

Wholesalers and retailers are merchant middlemen who take title to the goods they handle and assume complete responsibility for the risks involved in their trade. Their profits, if any, are obtained by subtracting the cost of goods sold and the operating expenses from the net sales. However, there are other types of middlemen known as agents or agent middlemen, who do not actually buy, sell or take title to goods themselves. They only negotiate or assist in purchasing or selling for people, called PRINCIPALS, who wish to buy or sell merchandise. Agent middlemen generally receive their remuneration in the form of commissions or fees. The most important types of agent middlemen are brokers, commission merchants, manufacturers' agents, sales agents, purchasing agents, auction companies, and resident buyers.

Commissions and fees are usually expressed as a certain percent of the selling price if the agents represent sellers. If the agents represent buyers, the commissions and fees are usually expressed as a certain percent of the purchase price, known as the PRIME COST. The prime cost includes the price paid to a seller but excludes the amount which is paid for other incidental costs of the purchase, such as the cost of assembling and shipping. As explained below, the computation of commissions and fees is the same as that of percentage problems.

Commission for selling = Selling price × Commission rate
Commission for buying = Prime cost × Commission rate
Selling price − Commission − Expenses = Net proceeds (the amount received by the principal from the agent who sells for the principal)
Prime cost + Commission + Expenses = Net purchase cost (the amount paid by the principal to the agent who buys for the principal)

Example 7.5a

John Kramer, a farmer, shipped a carload of tomatoes to Harry Baum, a commission merchant. Baum sold the shipment for $350 and paid $15 for freight charges. If Baum charges 4% commission, how much will Kramer receive from the shipment?

SOLUTION:
Commission for the sale is

$350 × 4\% = \$14.$

Net proceeds that Kramer will receive are

350 (selling price) − 14 (commission) − 15 (expenses) = $321.

Example 7.5b
George Larson, a purchasing agent for Mary Rice, bought 200 crates of apples. He paid $2.45 per crate and $35 for shipping costs. If he charged 5% commission, how much should Larson receive from Rice?

SOLUTION:

Commission for the purchase is computed below:

2.45 × 200 = $490   (prime cost)
490 × 5% = $24.50   (commission)

The total amount that Larson should receive from Rice is

490 (prime cost) + 24.50 (commission) + 35 (expenses) = $549.50.

EXERCISE 7.5 / REFERENCE SECTION: A

Statement Problems:
1. John Hanson, a commission merchant, received a shipment of 260 cases of bananas from Jack Todd. He stored the entire shipment in a warehouse for 3 days at a cost of 2 cents a case per day. He then sold the shipment for $10.50 per case. If he charged 10% of the selling price as his commission, how much should he remit to Jack Todd?
2. A sales clerk made sales totalling $12 256 with sales returns and allowances of $516. The clerk receives a 5.25% commission on net sales. What would her wages be?
3. The Food Market, a sales agent, received a shipment of 600 cases of eggs. Each case contained 30 dozen eggs, but some of them were broken. They were sorted and repacked at a cost of 7¢ per case. The remaining 575 cases and 2 dozen were sold at $.55 per dozen. If the commission charged was 2.5% of the selling price, what amount did the principal receive?
4. A collection agency charged $293 as its fee for securing payment on some outstanding accounts. If the agency charges a fee of 11.25% of the amount collected, how much was collected?
5. George Martin, a salesman in a shoe store, made sales as follows: $2 500 in January, $4 300 in February, and $3 650 in March. His monthly salary is $150 plus 6% commission on the amount of sales exceeding $2 000 each month. How much did he receive for each of the three months?
6. A salesperson for a company which makes sporting goods is allowed a drawing account of $940 per month and is paid on commission as follows: $3\frac{1}{2}$% on the first $5 000 of sales; $5\frac{1}{2}$% on the next $10 000 of sales and 7% on all additional sales. If the individual's sales for the month in question were $28 520, (a) what

was the total commission and (b) assuming that the drawing account was used to
its limit, how much additional pay was due for the month?

7. Lisa Valle, a saleswoman for a company offering day trips in a resort area, earned
$305.72 last week. Lisa is paid on the basis of a weekly salary of $96 plus 4.375%
of sales. What were Lisa's sales last week?

8. Merle Wiser manages a branch of a travel agency. Her salary is $135 per week
plus a 5.5% commission on her sales in excess of $1 200. She also receives a
0.75% override on the sales of the other employees. If Merle's sales last week
were $3 440 and the sales of the other clerks totalled $17 315, what was her salary for the week?

9. John Brise was in charge of making the arrangements for business functions for a
large Toronto hotel. He was paid a weekly salary of $115 plus $\frac{1}{2}$% commission on
the invoiced cost of these functions. What was his salary for a week when the
invoiced cost of such functions was $53 271?

10. A salesman receives a salary of $800 a month plus 8% commission on all sales
over $2 000 to $2 500 during the month. He also receives 10% commission on all
sales over $2 500 during the month. What must be the amount of his sales each
month in order to earn a total monthly income of $2 500?

7.6 Provincial Sales Taxes

All provinces except Alberta, rely on sales taxes as one of their main sources of revenue. PROVINCIAL SALES TAXES are levied on retail sales and are therefore direct taxes.
RETAIL SALES are sales of tangible personal property at retail prices to the consumer.
Retail sales also include the sales of specified services, such as amusement, restaurant
meals, hotel rooms, and public utility services. Certain commodities, for example,
children's clothing and medical prescriptions are exempt from provincial sales taxes,
as is gasoline, which is subject to special taxes.

The rate of retail sales taxes presently ranges from five to nine percent
among the provinces. The tax is calculated as follows:

Sales tax = Selling price × Sales tax rate

However, when the selling price is less than one dollar, or exceeds a whole number of
dollars, the tax on the fraction of a dollar is usually based on a published list or guide.

Example 7.6a
The sales tax schedule used in a certain province is shown below:

Amount of Sale	Amount of Tax (7%)
$ .21 or less	$.01
.22 to .35	.02
.36 to .49	.03
.50 to .64	.04
.65 to .78	.05
.79 to .92	.06

Amount of Sale	Amount of Tax (7%)
$ .93 to 1.07	.07
1.08 to 1.21	.08
1.22 to 1.35	.09

Find the amount of tax that a furniture store should charge on the sales of a chair priced at $10.50.

SOLUTION:

Tax on $10	70¢ (10 × 7¢)
Tax on .50	4¢ (per schedule, 50¢ to 64¢)
Tax on $10.50	74¢

The seller is required by law to collect the tax, file returns, and remit the required percentage of sales to the appropriate tax authority. Generally, the actual sales total and the sales tax collections are recorded separately at the time of the sale. However, if the combined amount of taxable sales and the sales tax are recorded, the tax liability may be computed from the total amount of sales.

Example 7.6b

During the month of June, a store collected $2 520, which includes sales and sales taxes. If the sales tax rate is 5%, (a) what is the amount of the sales? (b) the sales tax? Assume that all sales are taxable.

SOLUTION:

(a)   The sales tax is 5% of the sales. Therefore, the sales are the base (100%). The amount $2 520 is equivalent to

100% + 5% = 105% (of the sales).

Thus, the amount of the sales during the month is

$2 520 ÷ 105% = $2 400.

(b)   The tax is 2 520 − 2 400 = $120.

CHECK:

	$2 400	Sales
$2 400 × 5% =	120	Tax
	$2 520	Total amount collected

7.7 Federal Sales and Excise Taxes

The federal sales and excise taxes are levied by the federal government under the *Excise Tax Act*.

A.   FEDERAL SALES TAX

The FEDERAL SALES TAX is levied on sale of tangible personal property and services. Until recently, the federal sales tax was levied against the manufacturer or importer, who then charged the customer at the time of the sale. On April 30, 1982, draft amendment to the *Excise Tax Act* was tabled in the House of Commons which shifted the federal sales tax from the manufacturer level to the wholesale trade level. The proposed revision reduces the federal sales tax rate on most items to 8% in order to offset the effective increase in the amount of the sales tax when levied on the price paid by the retailer. Figure 7-3 illustrates the points in the flow of goods at which the federal sales tax is payable under the new provision.

Figure 7-3
Payment of Federal Sales Tax Under the 1982 Provision

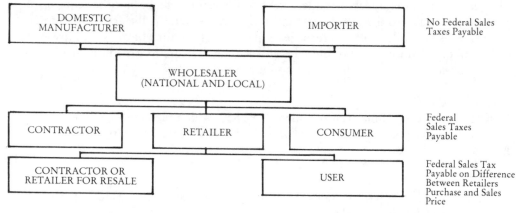

B.   EXCISE TAXES

The term EXCISE TAX is used to refer to a special additional tax imposed on the manufacture or importation of certain specified goods or services. Table 7-2 is a partial list of the items shown in Schedules I and II of the *Excise Tax Act*.

Table 7-2
Excerpt from the Excise Tax Act

Article	Tax Rate
Air conditioners (automobile)	$100
Amusement devices	10%
Cigarette holders	10%
Cigars	$20\frac{1}{2}$%
Jewellery	10%
Gasoline	1.5¢ per litre
Wines (1.2% to 7% alcohol by volume)	19.30¢ per litre
Wines (more than 7% alcohol by volume)	40.21¢ per litre

Under the new provisions of the Act, alcohol and tobacco will continue to be taxed at the manufacturer level while other items will be taxed at the wholesale level.

EXERCISE 7.7 / REFERENCE SECTIONS: 7.6, 7.7 A–B

Use the schedule in Example 7.6a to compute the amount of provincial sales tax for each of the following sales:

1. $ .45	4. $ .08	7. $4.75	10. $1.05
2. $ .25	5. $2.10	8. $4.65	11. $6.15
3. $ .38	6. $3.15	9. $5.60	12. $1.50

Statement Problems:

13. Bill Becker purchased the following articles at Gray's Department Store: a shirt for $2.50, a tie for $1.10, and a belt for $1.78. (a) How much sales tax must he pay on the total amount if the sales tax rate is 10%? (b) What is the total cost of the purchase?

14. Mary Jennings bought a mop for $2.25, a broom for $1.98 and a dust pan for $2.50 from a hardware store. (a) How much is the sales tax if the tax rate is 9%? (b) What is the total amount that she had to pay?

15. A retail store received $14.42 in cash from a sale that included 7% sales tax. (a) What is the price of the article sold? (b) How much is the sales tax?

16. A department store received $25.50 in cash, which included a sales tax of 5%, from the sale of a coat. (a) What is the price of the coat? (b) How much is the sales tax?

Use the rates given in Table 7-2, Section 7.7B to solve the following:

Article	Price
17. Find the amount of excise tax:	
(a) Jewellery	$ 35.20 (tax included)
(b) Cigarette holder	$ 25.00 (tax included)
18. Find the total cost of purchase:	
(a) 16 litres of gasoline	$ 0.32 per litre (plus tax)
(b) 5 litres of wine (over 7% alcohol)	$ 18.00 per litre (plus tax)
19. Find the amount of excise tax and the total cost of purchase:	
(a) Jewellery	$ 82.50 (plus tax)
(b) Air conditioner (automobile)	$600.00 (tax included)
20. Find the amount of excise tax and the cost before tax:	
(a) 38 litres of gasoline	$ 0.40 per litre (tax included)
(b) 1½ litres of wine (under 7% alcohol)	$ 6.80 per litre (tax included)

7.8 *Payroll Taxes*

A **PAYROLL** is a schedule which gives information regarding the earnings of employees for a certain period of time. When a payroll is made, payroll taxes are imposed upon either the employees or the employer, or, in some instances, upon both the employees and the employer. In general, the payroll taxes imposed upon employees are those levied under the *Unemployment Insurance Act* and the *Canada Pension Plan*. In addition, payroll taxes are levied upon employees under the *Income Tax Act*.

A. EMPLOYEES' PAYROLL TAXES

Unemployment Insurance

The new *Unemployment Insurance Act*, which was enacted in 1971, provides assistance for loss of earnings because of unemployment, including unemployment as a result of illness, but excluding worker's compensation claims. Under the Act, most employment in Canada and certain employment outside Canada, covered by an expressed or implied contract, are classified as insurable employment. The law requires contribution from both employer and employee. At present, the employee's premium is 2.3% of insurable earnings with maximum insurable earnings of $385 per week and minimum insurable earnings of $77 per week. Insurable earnings included items such as bonuses, gratuities, retroactive pay increases, share of profit, overtime pay, lump sum vacation payment, and sick pay credits.

The amount of premiums to be withheld from each employee's earnings is generally determined by using the Unemployment Insurance Premium Tables, which are provided by the Department of National Revenue. Tables are available for hourly, daily, weekly, bi-weekly, semi-monthly, and monthly pay periods. If employment commences after January 1, the maximum insurable earnings must be prorated.

A portion of the table for bi-weekly and monthly pay period is following.

Canada and Quebec Pension Plan

Under the Canada Pension Plan, all individuals between the ages of 18 and 70, employed or self-employed, must make contributions to the Plan. Contributions are based on earnings and the rate of contribution at the present time is 1.8% of insurable income with a maximum annual contribution of $300.60. The maximum annual insurable income is $16 700 with an annual exemption of $1 800. The maximum insurable income and exemption must be prorated if any of the following occur after January 1:

(a) A person becomes 18 (use number of months after month of birth).
(b) A person becomes 70 (use number of months prior to and including month of birth).
(c) A person receives a retirement or disability pension (use number of months in that year in which pension was not payable).
(d) A person dies (use the number of months prior to and including month of death).

To prorate, the amount is divided by 12 and multiplied by the number of months obtained above. For example, if an individual becomes 18 on March 1, the maximum insurable income is: $\frac{9}{12}(\$18\ 470 - \$1\ 800)$.

For self-employed individuals, the required contribution is 3.6% of insurable income.

The employer sends the withheld contribution with an equal amount as his own share to the Receiver General for Canada.

The provisions of the Quebec Pension Plan are similar to the provisions of the Canada Pension Plan. However, the Province of Quebec levies and collects its own premiums.

Example 7.8a

The Webb Company prepares a bi-weekly payroll. The total amount of wages earned by Alan Taylor, an employee, during the sixteenth pay period is $800. The record of the employee's earnings for the current year shows that Alan Taylor has cumulative earnings of $4 000 prior to the sixteenth pay period.

(a) How much Canada Pension Plan contribution, and (b) how much Unemployment Insurance premium should the employer (The Webb Company) withhold from Taylor's wages for the sixteenth pay period?

SOLUTION:

(a) The sum of $4 000 and $800 is $4 800, which is less than the maximum insurable amount, $16 700. The basic bi-weekly exemption is $1 800/26 = $69.23. Thus, the insurable income is $800 − 69.23 = $730.77. The contribution is $730.77 × 1.8% = $13.15.

(b) The maximum insurable bi-weekly income is $385 × 2 = $770. Thus, the premium is $770 × 2.3% = $17.71.

Example 7.8b

In Example 7.3a, assume that Alan Taylor's total earnings for the year prior to the sixteenth pay period were $17 000. (a) How much Canada Pension Plan contribution, and (b) how much Unemployment Insurance premium should be withheld from his wages in the sixteenth pay period?

SOLUTION:

(a) His earnings prior to the pay period exceeded the maximum insurable amount of $16 700, therefore, there is no deduction for Canada Pension Plan.

(b) The deduction for Unemployment Insurance premium is the same as in Example 7.8a.

Federal and Provincial Income Tax

The law requires that, except for certain types of employment, employers withhold a portion of each employee's earnings to be used in payment of the employee's income tax liability. Each employee is required to certify the amount of exemptions claimed by filing the Employee's Tax Deduction Return form, TD1, with his employer. The amount to be withheld is computed on the net earnings, which are arrived at by subtracting personal exemptions from the total gross earnings for the pay period.

Personal exemptions vary from one year to the next since exemptions are indexed. Personal exemptions for 1983 are as follows:

Single	$ 3 770
Married (with net income not exceeding $570)	$ 3 300
Child–under age 18 (with net income not exceeding $2 450)	$ 710
–age 18 or over (with net income not exceeding $2 570	$ 1 300
Age and disability	$ 2 300

Withholding tables are provided for weekly, bi-weekly, semi-monthly, monthly and daily payroll periods. A portion of the income tax withholding table based on a bi-weekly and monthly payroll period is presented on the following page.

Exact computation of the income tax to be withheld is based on the percentage method. The method requires a set of tables with progressive tax ranging from 7.37% to 51.13%. The tables can be obtained from the *Income Tax Deductions at Source*, issued by Revenue Canada. Exact computation is required for quarterly, semi-annual or annual payroll periods. The percentage method is not illustrated here since the method involves only simple mathematical operations.

Example 7.8c
Refer to Example 7.8a. The "net claim code" for the employee, Alan Taylor, is 6. How much income tax should be withheld from his wages by the employer?

SOLUTION:

The bi-weekly income tax withholding table shows that $800 is in the bracket $796 to $805.99 of the table. When the "net claim code" is 6, the amount of tax to be withheld as shown in the table is $127.45.

B.   EMPLOYER'S PAYROLL TAXES

Employers are required by law to make contributions to Unemployment Insurance and Canada or Quebec Pension Plan based on the earnings of their employees. The employer must remit deductions withheld from each employee's earnings plus the employer's contribution. Remittance must be made by the 15th of the month following the month in which deductions were made from the employee's earnings.

Unemployment Insurance Premium

The *Unemployment Insurance Act* requires, at present, that the employer contribute 1.4 times the contribution of each employee. This amount of premium may be reduced if the employer maintains a wage-loss plan which reduces Unemployment Insurance benefits payable under certain circumstances.

Canada or Quebec Pension Plan

The employer must contribute an amount equal to the contribution of each employee.

Example 7.8d

Refer to Example 7.8a. For what amount of Canada Pension Plan contributions is the employer liable to the government for Taylor's employment in the sixteenth pay period?

SOLUTION:

(a) The employer must pay his share of the Canada Pension Plan contribution, $13.15, the same as Taylor's contribution.
(b) The employer is liable to the government for his own contribution and for the contribution withheld from Taylor's wage. The total amount of the Canada Pension Plan contribution for which the employer is liable for the employment period is $26.30, or
$13.15 + $13.15 = $26.30.

Example 7.8e

Refer to Example 7.8a. Assume that the employer's Unemployment Insurance premium rate is 1.4 times the employee's premium. How much Unemployment Insurance premium should the employer pay for Taylor's employment during the sixteenth pay period?

SOLUTION:

The employee's premium is $17.71.
The employer's premium is $1.4 \times 17.71 = \$24.79$.

To summarize, under the present laws and regulations, the payroll taxes in a calendar year for eligible employers and employees are as follows:

Table 7-3

Payroll Taxes	Imposed upon Employers	Imposed upon Employees
Canada Pension Plan	Same as employee's premium	1.8% of taxable earnings
Unemployment Insurance Premium	Generally, 1.4 times employee's contribution	2.3% of taxable earnings
Federal and Provincial income tax	None for the payroll	Based on earnings, payroll period, and exemption claimed

CANADA PENSION PLAN CONTRIBUTIONS / COTISATIONS AU RÉGIME DE PENSIONS DU CANADA
Bi-Weekly Pay Period / Période de paie de deux semaines $708.96–$2,126.72

Remuneration / Rémunération From-de	To-à	C.P.P. R.P.C.	Remuneration / Rémunération From-de	To-à	C.P.P. R.P.C.	Remuneration / Rémunération From-de	To-à	C.P.P. R.P.C.	Remuneration / Rémunération From-de	To-à	C.P.P. R.P.C.
708.96 –	709.50	11.52	1046.73 –	1051.72	17.64	1406.73 –	1411.72	24.12	1766.73 –	1771.72	30.60
709.51 –	710.06	11.53	1051.73 –	1056.72	17.73	1411.73 –	1416.72	24.21	1771.73 –	1776.72	30.69
710.07 –	710.61	11.54	1056.73 –	1061.72	17.82	1416.73 –	1421.72	24.30	1776.73 –	1781.72	30.78
710.62 –	711.17	11.55	1061.73 –	1066.72	17.91	1421.73 –	1426.72	24.39	1781.73 –	1786.72	30.87
711.18 –	711.72	11.56	1066.73 –	1071.72	18.00	1426.73 –	1431.72	24.48	1786.73 –	1791.72	30.96
711.73 –	716.72	11.61	1071.73 –	1076.72	18.09	1431.73 –	1436.72	24.57	1791.73 –	1796.72	31.05
716.73 –	721.72	11.70	1076.73 –	1081.72	18.18	1436.73 –	1441.72	24.66	1796.73 –	1801.72	31.14
721.73 –	726.72	11.79	1081.73 –	1086.72	18.27	1441.73 –	1446.72	24.75	1801.73 –	1806.72	31.23
726.73 –	731.72	11.88	1086.73 –	1091.72	18.36	1446.73 –	1451.72	24.84	1806.73 –	1811.72	31.32
731.73 –	736.72	11.97	1091.73 –	1096.72	18.45	1451.73 –	1456.72	24.93	1811.73 –	1816.72	31.41
736.73 –	741.72	12.06	1096.73 –	1101.72	18.54	1456.73 –	1461.72	25.02	1816.73 –	1821.72	31.50
741.73 –	746.72	12.15	1101.73 –	1106.72	18.63	1461.73 –	1466.72	25.11	1821.73 –	1826.72	31.59
746.73 –	751.72	12.24	1106.73 –	1111.72	18.72	1466.73 –	1471.72	25.20	1826.73 –	1831.72	31.68
751.73 –	756.72	12.33	1111.73 –	1116.72	18.81	1471.73 –	1476.72	25.29	1831.73 –	1836.72	31.77
756.73 –	761.72	12.42	1116.73 –	1121.72	18.90	1476.73 –	1481.72	25.38	1836.73 –	1841.72	31.86
761.73 –	766.72	12.51	1121.73 –	1126.72	18.99	1481.73 –	1486.72	25.47	1841.73 –	1846.72	31.95
766.73 –	771.72	12.60	1126.73 –	1131.72	19.08	1486.73 –	1491.72	25.56	1846.73 –	1851.72	32.04
771.73 –	776.72	12.69	1131.73 –	1136.72	19.17	1491.73 –	1496.72	25.65	1851.73 –	1856.72	32.13
776.73 –	781.72	12.78	1136.73 –	1141.72	19.26	1496.73 –	1501.72	25.74	1856.73 –	1861.72	32.22
781.73 –	786.72	12.87	1141.73 –	1146.72	19.35	1501.73 –	1506.72	25.83	1861.73 –	1866.72	32.31
786.73 –	791.72	12.96	1146.73 –	1151.72	19.44	1506.73 –	1511.72	25.92	1866.73 –	1871.72	32.40
791.73 –	796.72	13.05	1151.73 –	1156.72	19.53	1511.73 –	1516.72	26.01	1871.73 –	1876.72	32.49
796.73 –	801.72	13.14	1156.73 –	1161.72	19.62	1516.73 –	1521.72	26.10	1876.73 –	1881.72	32.58
801.73 –	806.72	13.23	1161.73 –	1166.72	19.71	1521.73 –	1526.72	26.19	1881.73 –	1886.72	32.67
806.73 –	811.72	13.32	1166.73 –	1171.72	19.80	1526.73 –	1531.72	26.28	1886.73 –	1891.72	32.76
811.73 –	816.72	13.41	1171.73 –	1176.72	19.89	1531.73 –	1536.72	26.37	1891.73 –	1896.72	32.85
816.73 –	821.72	13.50	1176.73 –	1181.72	19.98	1536.73 –	1541.72	26.46	1896.73 –	1901.72	32.94
821.73 –	826.72	13.59	1181.73 –	1186.72	20.07	1541.73 –	1546.72	26.55	1901.73 –	1906.72	33.03
826.73 –	831.72	13.68	1186.73 –	1191.72	20.16	1546.73 –	1551.72	26.64	1906.73 –	1911.72	33.12
831.73 –	836.72	13.77	1191.73 –	1196.72	20.25	1551.73 –	1556.72	26.73	1911.73 –	1916.72	33.21
836.73 –	841.72	13.86	1196.73 –	1201.72	20.34	1556.73 –	1561.72	26.82	1916.73 –	1921.72	33.30
841.73 –	846.72	13.95	1201.73 –	1206.72	20.43	1561.73 –	1566.72	26.91	1921.73 –	1926.72	33.39
846.73 –	851.72	14.04	1206.73 –	1211.72	20.52	1566.73 –	1571.72	27.00	1926.73 –	1931.72	33.48

Pay		Tax	Pay		Tax	Pay		Tax	Pay		Tax
851.73	– 856.72	14.13	1211.73	– 1216.72	20.61	1571.73	– 1576.72	27.09	1931.73	– 1936.72	33.57
856.73	– 861.72	14.22	1216.73	– 1221.72	20.70	1576.73	– 1581.72	27.18	1936.73	– 1941.72	33.66
861.73	– 866.72	14.31	1221.73	– 1226.72	20.79	1581.73	– 1586.72	27.27	1941.73	– 1946.72	33.75
866.73	– 871.72	14.40	1226.73	– 1231.72	20.88	1586.73	– 1591.72	27.36	1946.73	– 1951.72	33.84
871.73	– 876.72	14.49	1231.73	– 1236.72	20.97	1591.73	– 1596.72	27.45	1951.73	– 1956.72	33.93
876.73	– 881.72	14.58	1236.73	– 1241.72	21.06	1596.73	– 1601.72	27.54	1956.73	– 1961.72	34.02
881.73	– 886.72	14.67	1241.73	– 1246.72	21.15	1601.73	– 1606.72	27.63	1961.73	– 1966.72	34.11
886.73	– 891.72	14.76	1246.73	– 1251.72	21.24	1606.73	– 1611.72	27.72	1966.73	– 1971.72	34.20
891.73	– 896.72	14.85	1251.73	– 1256.72	21.33	1611.73	– 1616.72	27.81	1971.73	– 1976.72	34.29
896.73	– 901.72	14.94	1256.73	– 1261.72	21.42	1616.73	– 1621.72	27.90	1976.73	– 1981.72	34.38
901.73	– 906.72	15.03	1261.73	– 1266.72	21.51	1621.73	– 1626.72	27.99	1981.73	– 1986.72	34.47
906.73	– 911.72	15.12	1266.73	– 1271.72	21.60	1626.73	– 1631.72	28.08	1986.73	– 1991.72	34.56
911.73	– 916.72	15.21	1271.73	– 1276.72	21.69	1631.73	– 1636.72	28.17	1991.73	– 1996.72	34.65
916.73	– 921.72	15.30	1276.73	– 1281.72	21.78	1636.73	– 1641.72	28.26	1996.73	– 2001.72	34.74
921.73	– 926.72	15.39	1281.73	– 1286.72	21.87	1641.73	– 1646.72	28.35	2001.73	– 2006.72	34.83
926.73	– 931.72	15.48	1286.73	– 1291.72	21.96	1646.73	– 1651.72	28.44	2006.73	– 2011.72	34.92
931.73	– 936.72	15.57	1291.73	– 1296.72	22.05	1651.73	– 1656.72	28.53	2011.73	– 2016.72	35.01
936.73	– 941.72	15.66	1296.73	– 1301.72	22.14	1656.73	– 1661.72	28.62	2016.73	– 2021.72	35.10
941.73	– 946.72	15.75	1301.73	– 1306.72	22.23	1661.73	– 1666.72	28.71	2021.73	– 2026.72	35.19
946.73	– 951.72	15.84	1306.73	– 1311.72	22.32	1666.73	– 1671.72	28.80	2026.73	– 2031.72	35.28
951.73	– 956.72	15.93	1311.73	– 1316.72	22.41	1671.73	– 1676.72	28.89	2031.73	– 2036.72	35.37
956.73	– 961.72	16.02	1316.73	– 1321.72	22.50	1676.73	– 1681.72	28.98	2036.73	– 2041.72	35.46
961.73	– 966.72	16.11	1321.73	– 1326.72	22.59	1681.73	– 1686.72	29.07	2041.73	– 2046.72	35.55
966.73	– 971.72	16.20	1326.73	– 1331.72	22.68	1686.73	– 1691.72	29.16	2046.73	– 2051.72	35.64
971.73	– 976.72	16.29	1331.73	– 1336.72	22.77	1691.73	– 1696.72	29.25	2051.73	– 2056.72	35.73
976.73	– 981.72	16.38	1336.73	– 1341.72	22.86	1696.73	– 1701.72	29.34	2056.73	– 2061.72	35.82
981.73	– 986.72	16.47	1341.73	– 1346.72	22.95	1701.73	– 1706.72	29.43	2061.73	– 2066.72	35.91
986.73	– 991.72	16.56	1346.73	– 1351.72	23.04	1706.73	– 1711.72	29.52	2066.73	– 2071.72	36.00
991.73	– 996.72	16.65	1351.73	– 1356.72	23.13	1711.73	– 1716.72	29.61	2071.73	– 2076.72	36.09
996.73	– 1001.72	16.74	1356.73	– 1361.72	23.22	1716.73	– 1721.72	29.70	2076.73	– 2081.72	36.18
1001.73	– 1006.72	16.83	1361.73	– 1366.72	23.31	1721.73	– 1726.72	29.79	2081.73	– 2086.72	36.27
1006.73	– 1011.72	16.92	1366.73	– 1371.72	23.40	1726.73	– 1731.72	29.88	2086.73	– 2091.72	36.36
1011.73	– 1016.72	17.01	1371.73	– 1376.72	23.49	1731.73	– 1736.72	29.97	2091.73	– 2096.72	36.45
1016.73	– 1021.72	17.10	1376.73	– 1381.72	23.58	1736.73	– 1741.72	30.06	2096.73	– 2101.72	36.54
1021.73	– 1026.72	17.19	1381.73	– 1386.72	23.67	1741.73	– 1746.72	30.15	2101.73	– 2106.72	36.63
1026.73	– 1031.72	17.28	1386.73	– 1391.72	23.76	1746.73	– 1751.72	30.24	2106.73	– 2111.72	36.72
1031.73	– 1036.72	17.37	1391.73	– 1396.72	23.85	1751.73	– 1756.72	30.33	2111.73	– 2116.72	36.81
1036.73	– 1041.72	17.46	1396.73	– 1401.72	23.94	1756.73	– 1761.72	30.42	2116.73	– 2121.72	36.90
1041.73	– 1046.72	17.55	1401.73	– 1406.72	24.03	1761.73	– 1766.72	30.51	2121.73	– 2126.72	36.99

SOURCE: Revenue Canada Taxation, *Income Tax Deductions at Source* (Ottawa, 1983), p. 32

CANADA PENSION PLAN CONTRIBUTIONS / COTISATIONS AU RÉGIME DE PENSIONS DU CANADA

Monthly Pay Period / Période de paie de deux semaines $949.73–$1,109.72

Remuneration Rémunération From-de	To-à	C.P.P. R.P.C.	Remuneration Rémunération From-de	To-à	C.P.P. R.P.C.	Remuneration Rémunération From-de	To-à	C.P.P. R.P.C.	Remuneration Rémunération From-de	To-à	C.P.P. R.P.C.
949.73 –	950.27	14.40	989.73 –	990.27	15.12	1029.73 –	1030.27	15.84	1069.73 –	1070.27	16.56
950.28 –	950.83	14.41	990.28 –	990.83	15.13	1030.28 –	1030.83	15.85	1070.28 –	1070.83	16.57
950.84 –	951.38	14.42	990.84 –	991.38	15.14	1030.84 –	1031.38	15.86	1070.84 –	1071.38	16.58
951.39 –	951.94	14.43	991.39 –	991.94	15.15	1031.39 –	1031.94	15.87	1071.39 –	1071.94	16.59
951.95 –	952.49	14.44	991.95 –	992.49	15.16	1031.95 –	1032.49	15.88	1071.95 –	1072.49	16.60
952.50 –	953.05	14.45	992.50 –	993.05	15.17	1032.50 –	1033.05	15.89	1072.50 –	1073.05	16.61
953.06 –	953.61	14.46	993.06 –	993.61	15.18	1033.06 –	1033.61	15.90	1073.06 –	1073.61	16.62
953.62 –	954.16	14.47	993.62 –	994.16	15.19	1033.62 –	1034.16	15.91	1073.62 –	1074.16	16.63
954.17 –	954.72	14.48	994.17 –	994.72	15.20	1034.17 –	1034.72	15.92	1074.17 –	1074.72	16.64
954.73 –	955.27	14.49	994.73 –	995.27	15.21	1034.73 –	1035.27	15.93	1074.73 –	1075.27	16.65
955.28 –	955.83	14.50	995.28 –	995.83	15.22	1035.28 –	1035.83	15.94	1075.28 –	1075.83	16.66
955.84 –	956.38	14.51	995.84 –	996.38	15.23	1035.84 –	1036.38	15.95	1075.84 –	1076.38	16.67
956.39 –	956.94	14.52	996.39 –	996.94	15.24	1036.39 –	1036.94	15.96	1076.39 –	1076.94	16.68
956.95 –	957.49	14.53	996.95 –	997.49	15.25	1036.95 –	1037.49	15.97	1076.95 –	1077.49	16.69
957.50 –	958.05	14.54	997.50 –	998.05	15.26	1037.50 –	1038.05	15.98	1077.50 –	1078.05	16.70
958.06 –	958.61	14.55	998.06 –	998.61	15.27	1038.06 –	1038.61	15.99	1078.06 –	1078.61	16.71
958.62 –	959.16	14.56	998.62 –	999.16	15.28	1038.62 –	1039.16	16.00	1078.62 –	1079.16	16.72
959.17 –	959.72	14.57	999.17 –	999.72	15.29	1039.17 –	1039.72	16.01	1079.17 –	1079.72	16.73
959.73 –	960.27	14.58	999.73 –	1000.27	15.30	1039.73 –	1040.27	16.02	1079.73 –	1080.27	16.74
960.28 –	960.83	14.59	1000.28 –	1000.83	15.31	1040.28 –	1040.83	16.03	1080.28 –	1080.83	16.75
960.84 –	961.38	14.60	1000.84 –	1001.38	15.32	1040.84 –	1041.38	16.04	1080.84 –	1081.38	16.76
961.39 –	961.94	14.61	1001.39 –	1001.94	15.33	1041.39 –	1041.94	16.05	1081.39 –	1081.94	16.77
961.95 –	962.49	14.62	1001.95 –	1002.49	15.34	1041.95 –	1042.49	16.06	1081.95 –	1082.49	16.78
962.50 –	963.05	14.63	1002.50 –	1003.05	15.35	1042.50 –	1043.05	16.07	1082.50 –	1083.05	16.79
963.06 –	963.61	14.64	1003.06 –	1003.61	15.36	1043.06 –	1043.61	16.08	1083.06 –	1083.61	16.80
963.62 –	964.16	14.65	1003.62 –	1004.16	15.37	1043.62 –	1044.16	16.09	1083.62 –	1084.16	16.81
964.17 –	964.72	14.66	1004.17 –	1004.72	15.38	1044.17 –	1044.72	16.10	1084.17 –	1084.72	16.82
964.73 –	965.27	14.67	1004.73 –	1005.27	15.39	1044.73 –	1045.27	16.11	1084.73 –	1085.27	16.83
965.28 –	965.83	14.68	1005.28 –	1005.83	15.40	1045.28 –	1045.83	16.12	1085.28 –	1085.83	16.84
965.84 –	966.38	14.69	1005.84 –	1006.38	15.41	1045.84 –	1046.38	16.13	1085.84 –	1086.38	16.85
966.39 –	966.94	14.70	1006.39 –	1006.94	15.42	1046.39 –	1046.94	16.14	1086.39 –	1086.94	16.86
966.95 –	967.49	14.71	1006.95 –	1007.49	15.43	1046.95 –	1047.49	16.15	1086.95 –	1087.49	16.87
967.50 –	968.05	14.72	1007.50 –	1008.05	15.44	1047.50 –	1048.05	16.16	1087.50 –	1088.05	16.88
968.06 –	968.61	14.73	1008.06 –	1008.61	15.45	1048.06 –	1048.61	16.17	1088.06 –	1088.61	16.89

From	To	Tax	From	To	Tax	From	To	Tax	From	To	Tax
968.62 –	969.16	14.74	1008.62 –	1009.16	15.46	1048.62 –	1049.16	16.18	1088.62 –	1089.16	16.90
969.17 –	969.72	14.75	1009.17 –	1009.72	15.47	1049.17 –	1049.72	16.19	1089.17 –	1089.72	16.91
969.73 –	970.27	14.76	1009.73 –	1010.27	15.48	1049.73 –	1050.27	16.20	1089.73 –	1090.27	16.92
970.28 –	970.83	14.77	1010.28 –	1010.83	15.49	1050.28 –	1050.83	16.21	1090.28 –	1090.83	16.93
970.84 –	971.38	14.78	1010.84 –	1011.38	15.50	1050.84 –	1051.38	16.22	1090.84 –	1091.38	16.94
971.39 –	971.94	14.79	1011.39 –	1011.94	15.51	1051.39 –	1051.94	16.23	1091.39 –	1091.94	16.95
971.95 –	972.49	14.80	1011.95 –	1012.49	15.52	1051.95 –	1052.49	16.24	1091.95 –	1092.49	16.96
972.50 –	973.05	14.81	1012.50 –	1013.05	15.53	1052.50 –	1053.05	16.25	1092.50 –	1093.05	16.97
973.06 –	973.61	14.82	1013.06 –	1013.61	15.54	1053.06 –	1053.61	16.26	1093.06 –	1093.61	16.98
973.62 –	974.16	14.83	1013.62 –	1014.16	15.55	1053.62 –	1054.16	16.27	1093.62 –	1094.16	16.99
974.17 –	974.72	14.84	1014.17 –	1014.72	15.56	1054.17 –	1054.72	16.28	1094.17 –	1094.72	17.00
974.73 –	975.27	14.85	1014.73 –	1015.27	15.57	1054.73 –	1055.27	16.29	1094.73 –	1095.27	17.01
975.28 –	975.83	14.86	1015.28 –	1015.83	15.58	1055.28 –	1055.83	16.30	1095.28 –	1095.83	17.02
957.84 –	976.38	14.87	1015.84 –	1016.38	15.59	1055.84 –	1056.38	16.31	1095.84 –	1096.38	17.03
976.39 –	976.94	14.88	1016.39 –	1016.94	15.60	1056.39 –	1056.94	16.32	1096.39 –	1096.94	17.04
976.95 –	977.49	14.89	1016.95 –	1017.49	15.61	1056.95 –	1057.49	16.33	1096.95 –	1097.49	17.05
977.50 –	978.05	14.90	1017.50 –	1018.05	15.62	1057.50 –	1058.05	16.34	1097.50 –	1098.05	17.06
978.06 –	978.61	14.91	1018.06 –	1018.61	15.63	1058.06 –	1058.61	16.35	1098.06 –	1098.61	17.07
978.62 –	979.16	14.92	1018.62 –	1019.16	15.64	1058.62 –	1059.16	16.36	1098.62 –	1099.16	17.08
979.17 –	979.72	14.93	1019.17 –	1019.72	15.65	1059.17 –	1059.72	16.37	1099.17 –	1099.72	17.09
979.73 –	980.27	14.94	1019.73 –	1020.27	15.66	1059.73 –	1060.27	16.38	1099.73 –	1100.27	17.10
980.28 –	980.83	14.95	1020.28 –	1020.83	15.67	1060.28 –	1060.83	16.39	1100.28 –	1100.83	17.11
980.84 –	981.38	14.96	1020.84 –	1021.38	15.68	1060.84 –	1061.38	16.40	1100.84 –	1101.38	17.12
981.39 –	981.94	14.97	1021.39 –	1021.94	15.69	1061.39 –	1061.94	16.41	1101.39 –	1101.94	17.13
981.95 –	982.49	14.98	1021.95 –	1022.49	15.70	1061.95 –	1062.49	16.42	1101.95 –	1102.49	17.14
982.50 –	983.05	14.99	1022.50 –	1023.05	15.71	1062.50 –	1063.05	16.43	1102.50 –	1103.05	17.15
983.06 –	983.61	15.00	1023.06 –	1023.61	15.72	1063.06 –	1063.61	16.44	1103.06 –	1103.61	17.16
983.62 –	984.16	15.01	1023.62 –	1024.16	15.73	1063.62 –	1064.16	16.45	1103.62 –	1104.16	17.17
984.17 –	984.72	15.02	1024.17 –	1024.72	15.74	1064.17 –	1064.72	16.46	1104.17 –	1104.72	17.18
984.73 –	985.27	15.03	1024.73 –	1025.27	15.75	1064.73 –	1065.27	16.47	1104.73 –	1105.27	17.19
985.28 –	985.83	15.04	1025.28 –	1025.83	15.76	1065.28 –	1065.83	16.48	1105.28 –	1105.83	17.20
985.84 –	986.38	15.05	1025.84 –	1026.38	15.77	1065.84 –	1066.38	16.49	1105.84 –	1106.38	17.21
986.39 –	986.94	15.06	1026.39 –	1026.94	15.78	1066.39 –	1066.94	16.50	1106.39 –	1106.94	17.22
986.95 –	987.49	15.07	1026.95 –	1027.49	15.79	1066.95 –	1067.49	16.51	1106.95 –	1107.49	17.23
987.50 –	988.05	15.08	1027.50 –	1028.05	15.80	1067.50 –	1068.05	16.52	1107.50 –	1108.05	17.24
988.06 –	988.61	15.09	1028.06 –	1028.61	15.81	1068.06 –	1068.61	16.53	1108.06 –	1108.61	17.25
988.62 –	989.16	15.10	1028.62 –	1029.16	15.82	1068.62 –	1069.16	16.54	1108.62 –	1109.16	17.26
989.17 –	989.72	15.11	1029.17 –	1029.72	15.83	1069.17 –	1069.72	16.55	1109.17 –	1109.72	17.27

SOURCE: Revenue Canada Taxation, *Income Tax Deductions at Source* (Ottawa, 1983) p. 45

UNEMPLOYMENT INSURANCE PREMIUMS / PRIMES D'ASSURANCE-CHÔMAGE
Monthly Pay Period / Période mensuelle de paie

$1,025.87–$1,151.08

Remuneration / Rémunération From-de	To-à	U.I. Premium / Prime d'a.-c.	Remuneration / Rémunération From-de	To-à	U.I. Premium / Prime d'a.-c.	Remuneration / Rémunération From-de	To-à	U.I. Premium / Prime d'a.-c.	Remuneration / Rémunération From-de	To-à	U.I. Premium / Prime d'a.-c.
1025.87	1026.30	23.60	1057.17	1057.60	24.32	1088.48	1088.90	25.04	1119.78	1120.21	25.76
1026.31	1026.73	23.61	1057.61	1058.03	24.33	1088.91	1089.34	25.05	1120.22	1120.64	25.77
1026.74	1027.16	23.62	1058.04	1058.47	24.34	1089.35	1089.77	25.06	1120.65	1121.08	25.78
1027.17	1027.60	23.63	1058.48	1058.90	24.35	1089.78	1090.21	25.07	1121.09	1121.51	25.79
1027.61	1028.03	23.64	1058.91	1059.34	24.36	1090.22	1090.64	25.08	1121.52	1121.95	25.80
1028.04	1028.47	23.65	1059.35	1059.77	24.37	1090.65	1091.08	25.09	1121.96	1122.38	25.81
1028.48	1028.90	23.66	1059.78	1060.21	24.38	1091.09	1091.51	25.10	1122.39	1122.82	25.82
1028.91	1029.34	23.67	1060.22	1060.64	24.39	1091.52	1091.95	25.11	1122.83	1123.25	25.83
1029.35	1029.77	23.68	1060.65	1061.08	24.40	1091.96	1092.38	25.12	1123.26	1123.69	25.84
1029.78	1030.21	23.69	1061.09	1061.51	24.41	1092.39	1092.82	25.13	1123.70	1124.12	25.85
1030.22	1030.64	23.70	1061.52	1061.95	24.42	1092.83	1093.25	25.14	1124.13	1124.56	25.86
1030.65	1031.08	23.71	1061.96	1062.38	24.43	1093.26	1093.69	25.15	1124.57	1124.99	25.87
1031.09	1031.51	23.72	1062.39	1062.82	24.44	1093.70	1094.12	25.16	1125.00	1125.43	25.88
1031.52	1031.95	23.73	1062.83	1063.25	24.45	1094.13	1094.56	25.17	1125.44	1125.86	25.89
1031.96	1032.38	23.74	1063.26	1063.69	24.46	1094.57	1094.99	25.18	1125.87	1126.30	25.90
1032.39	1032.82	23.75	1063.70	1064.12	24.47	1095.00	1095.43	25.19	1126.31	1126.73	25.91
1032.83	1033.25	23.76	1064.13	1064.56	24.48	1095.44	1095.86	25.20	1126.74	1127.16	25.92
1033.26	1033.69	23.77	1064.57	1064.99	24.49	1095.87	1096.30	25.21	1127.17	1127.60	25.93
1033.70	1034.12	23.78	1065.00	1065.43	24.50	1096.31	1096.73	25.22	1127.61	1128.03	25.94
1034.13	1034.56	23.79	1065.44	1065.86	24.51	1096.74	1097.16	25.23	1128.04	1128.47	25.95
1034.57	1034.99	23.80	1065.87	1066.30	24.52	1097.17	1097.60	25.24	1128.48	1128.90	25.96
1035.00	1035.43	23.81	1066.31	1066.73	24.53	1097.61	1098.03	25.25	1128.91	1129.34	25.97
1035.44	1035.86	23.82	1066.74	1067.16	24.54	1098.04	1098.47	25.26	1129.35	1129.77	25.98
1035.87	1036.30	23.83	1067.17	1067.60	24.55	1098.48	1098.90	25.27	1129.78	1130.21	25.99
1036.31	1036.73	23.84	1067.61	1068.03	24.56	1098.91	1099.34	25.28	1130.22	1130.64	26.00
1036.74	1037.16	23.85	1068.04	1068.47	24.57	1099.35	1099.77	25.29	1130.65	1131.08	26.01
1037.17	1037.60	23.86	1068.48	1068.90	24.58	1099.78	1100.21	25.30	1131.09	1131.51	26.02
1037.61	1038.03	23.87	1068.91	1069.34	24.59	1100.22	1100.64	25.31	1131.52	1131.95	26.03
1038.04	1038.47	23.88	1069.35	1069.77	24.60	1100.65	1101.08	25.32	1131.96	1132.38	26.04
1038.48	1038.90	23.89	1069.78	1070.21	24.61	1101.09	1101.51	25.33	1132.39	1132.82	26.05
1038.91	1039.34	23.90	1070.22	1070.64	24.62	1101.52	1101.95	25.34	1132.83	1133.25	26.06
1039.35	1039.77	23.91	1070.65	1071.08	24.63	1101.96	1102.38	25.35	1133.26	1133.69	26.07
1039.78	1040.21	23.92	1071.09	1071.51	24.64	1102.39	1102.82	25.36	1133.70	1134.12	26.08

Pay		Tax	Pay		Tax	Pay		Tax	Pay		Tax
1040.22 –	1040.64	23.93	1071.52 –	1071.95	24.65	1102.83 –	1103.25	25.37	1134.13 –	1134.56	26.09
1040.65 –	1041.08	23.94	1071.96 –	1072.38	24.66	1103.26 –	1103.69	25.38	1134.57 –	1134.99	26.10
1041.09 –	1041.51	23.95	1072.39 –	1072.82	24.67	1103.70 –	1104.12	25.39	1135.00 –	1135.43	26.11
1041.52 –	1041.95	23.96	1072.83 –	1073.25	24.68	1104.13 –	1104.56	25.40	1135.44 –	1135.86	26.12
1041.96 –	1042.38	23.97	1073.26 –	1073.69	24.69	1104.57 –	1104.99	25.41	1135.87 –	1136.30	26.13
1042.39 –	1042.82	23.98	1073.70 –	1074.12	24.70	1105.00 –	1105.43	25.42	1136.31 –	1136.73	26.14
1042.83 –	1043.25	23.99	1074.13 –	1074.56	24.71	1105.44 –	1105.86	25.43	1136.74 –	1137.16	26.15
1043.26 –	1043.69	24.00	1074.57 –	1074.99	24.72	1105.87 –	1106.30	25.44	1137.17 –	1137.60	26.16
1043.70 –	1044.12	24.01	1075.00 –	1075.43	24.73	1106.31 –	1106.73	25.45	1137.61 –	1138.03	26.17
1044.13 –	1044.56	24.02	1075.44 –	1075.86	24.74	1106.74 –	1107.16	25.46	1138.04 –	1138.47	26.18
1044.57 –	1044.99	24.03	1075.87 –	1076.30	24.75	1107.17 –	1107.60	25.47	1138.48 –	1138.90	26.19
1045.00 –	1045.43	24.04	1076.31 –	1076.73	24.76	1107.61 –	1108.03	25.48	1138.91 –	1139.34	26.20
1045.44 –	1045.86	24.05	1076.74 –	1077.16	24.77	1108.04 –	1108.47	25.49	1139.35 –	1139.77	26.21
1045.87 –	1046.30	24.06	1077.17 –	1077.60	24.78	1108.48 –	1108.90	25.50	1139.78 –	1140.21	26.22
1046.31 –	1046.73	24.07	1077.61 –	1078.03	24.79	1108.91 –	1109.34	25.51	1140.22 –	1140.64	26.23
1046.74 –	1047.16	24.08	1078.04 –	1078.47	24.80	1109.35 –	1109.77	25.52	1140.65 –	1141.08	26.24
1047.17 –	1047.60	24.09	1078.48 –	1078.90	24.81	1109.78 –	1110.21	25.53	1141.09 –	1141.51	26.25
1047.61 –	1048.03	24.10	1078.91 –	1079.34	24.82	1110.22 –	1110.64	25.54	1141.52 –	1141.95	26.26
1048.04 –	1048.47	24.11	1079.35 –	1079.77	24.83	1110.65 –	1111.08	25.55	1141.96 –	1142.38	26.27
1048.48 –	1048.90	24.12	1079.78 –	1080.21	24.84	1111.09 –	1111.51	25.56	1142.39 –	1142.82	26.28
1048.91 –	1049.34	24.13	1080.22 –	1080.64	24.85	1111.52 –	1111.95	25.57	1142.83 –	1143.25	26.29
1049.35 –	1049.77	24.14	1080.65 –	1081.08	24.86	1111.96 –	1112.38	25.58	1143.26 –	1143.69	26.30
1049.78 –	1050.21	24.15	1081.09 –	1081.51	24.87	1112.39 –	1112.82	25.59	1143.70 –	1144.12	26.31
1050.22 –	1050.64	24.16	1081.52 –	1081.95	24.88	1112.83 –	1113.25	25.60	1144.13 –	1144.56	26.32
1050.65 –	1051.08	24.17	1081.96 –	1082.38	24.89	1113.26 –	1113.69	25.61	1144.57 –	1144.99	26.33
1051.09 –	1051.51	24.18	1082.39 –	1082.82	24.90	1113.70 –	1114.12	25.62	1145.00 –	1145.43	26.34
1051.52 –	1051.95	24.19	1082.83 –	1083.25	24.91	1114.13 –	1114.56	25.63	1145.44 –	1145.86	26.35
1051.96 –	1052.38	24.20	1083.26 –	1083.69	24.92	1114.57 –	1114.99	25.64	1145.87 –	1146.30	26.36
1052.39 –	1052.82	24.21	1083.70 –	1084.12	24.93	1115.00 –	1115.43	25.65	1146.31 –	1146.73	26.37
1052.83 –	1053.25	24.22	1084.13 –	1084.56	24.94	1115.44 –	1115.86	25.66	1146.74 –	1147.16	26.38
1053.26 –	1053.69	24.23	1084.57 –	1084.99	24.95	1115.87 –	1116.30	25.67	1147.17 –	1147.60	26.39
1053.70 –	1054.12	24.24	1085.00 –	1085.43	24.96	1116.31 –	1116.73	25.68	1147.61 –	1148.03	26.40
1054.13 –	1054.56	24.25	1085.44 –	1085.86	24.97	1116.74 –	1117.16	25.69	1148.04 –	1148.47	26.41
1054.57 –	1054.99	24.26	1085.87 –	1086.30	24.98	1117.17 –	1117.60	25.70	1148.48 –	1148.90	26.42
1055.00 –	1055.43	24.27	1086.31 –	1086.73	24.99	1117.61 –	1118.03	25.71	1148.91 –	1149.34	26.43
1055.44 –	1055.86	24.28	1086.74 –	1087.16	25.00	1118.04 –	1118.47	25.72	1149.35 –	1149.77	26.44
1055.87 –	1056.30	24.29	1087.17 –	1087.60	25.01	1118.48 –	1118.90	25.73	1149.78 –	1150.21	26.45
1056.31 –	1056.73	24.30	1087.61 –	1088.03	25.02	1118.91 –	1119.34	25.74	1150.22 –	1150.64	26.46
1056.74 –	1057.16	24.31	1088.04 –	1088.47	25.03	1119.35 –	1119.77	25.75	1150.65 –	1151.08	26.47

SOURCE: Revenue Canada Taxation, *Income Tax Deductions at Source* (Ottawa, 1983) p. 90

ONTARIO
Bi-Weekly Tax Deductions / Déductions D'impôt de Deux Semaines
Basis—26 Pay Periods per Year / Base—26 périodes de paie par année

IF THE EMPLOYEE'S "NET CLAIM CODE" ON FORM TD1 is–SI LE «CODE DE RÉCLAMATION NETTE» DE L'EMPLOYÉ SELON LA FORMULE TD1 EST DE

DEDUCT FROM EACH PAY–DÉDUISEZ SUR CHAQUE PAIE

BI-WEEKLY PAY / Use appropriate bracket — PAIE DE DEUX SEMAINES / Utilisez le palier approprié	1	2	3	4	5	6	7	8	9	10	11	12	13	See note on page 24. / Voir remarque p.24 / Column A / Colonne A
$ 666.00 – 675.99	120.40	116.35	109.15	102.30	95.15	89.30	85.50	79.85	72.10	63.75	55.10	47.15	40.15	7.00
676.00 – 685.99	123.40	119.35	112.15	105.15	98.00	92.15	88.35	82.70	74.95	66.60	57.95	49.85	42.85	7.00
686.00 – 695.99	126.40	122.35	115.15	108.10	100.90	95.00	91.20	85.55	77.80	69.45	60.80	52.55	45.55	7.00
696.00 – 705.99	129.45	125.40	118.15	111.10	103.75	97.85	94.05	88.40	80.65	72.30	63.65	55.30	48.30	7.00
706.00 – 715.99	132.45	128.40	121.15	114.10	106.60	110.70	96.90	91.25	83.50	75.15	66.55	58.20	51.00	7.20
716.00 – 725.99	135.45	131.40	124.15	117.10	109.60	103.55	99.80	94.10	86.35	78.00	69.40	61.05	53.70	7.35
726.00 – 735.99	138.45	134.40	127.20	120.10	112.50	106.45	102.65	97.00	89.25	80.85	72.25	63.90	56.55	7.35
736.00 – 745.99	141.45	137.40	130.20	123.15	115.60	109.40	105.50	99.85	92.10	83.75	75.10	66.75	59.40	7.35
746.00 – 755.99	144.45	140.40	133.20	126.15	118.60	112.40	108.45	102.70	94.95	86.60	77.95	69.60	62.25	7.35
756.00 – 765.99	147.50	143.45	136.20	129.15	121.60	115.45	111.45	105.55	97.80	89.45	80.80	72.45	65.10	7.35
766.00 – 775.99	150.50	146.45	139.20	132.15	124.65	118.45	114.45	108.50	100.65	92.30	83.70	75.30	67.95	7.35
776.00 – 785.99	153.50	149.45	142.20	135.15	127.65	121.45	117.45	111.50	103.50	95.15	86.55	78.20	70.80	7.40
786.00 – 795.99	156.50	152.45	145.20	138.15	130.65	124.45	120.45	114.50	106.35	98.00	89.40	81.05	73.70	7.40
796.00 – 805.99	159.50	155.45	148.25	141.15	133.65	127.45	123.45	117.50	109.35	100.90	92.25	83.90	76.55	7.40
806.00 – 815.99	162.70	158.45	151.25	144.20	136.65	130.45	126.50	120.50	112.35	103.75	95.10	86.75	79.40	7.40
816.00 – 825.99	166.20	161.50	154.25	147.20	139.65	133.50	129.50	123.55	115.35	106.60	97.95	89.60	82.25	7.40
826.00 – 835.99	167.65	165.00	157.25	150.20	142.70	136.50	132.50	126.55	118.40	109.60	100.80	92.45	85.10	7.40
836.00 – 845.99	173.10	168.45	160.25	153.20	145.70	139.50	135.50	129.55	121.40	112.60	103.70	95.35	87.95	7.40
846.00 – 855.99	176.55	171.90	163.60	156.20	148.70	142.50	138.50	132.55	124.40	115.60	106.55	98.20	90.80	7.40
856.00 – 865.99	180.00	175.35	167.05	159.20	151.70	145.50	141.50	135.55	127.40	118.60	109.55	101.05	93.70	7.40

866.00 – 875.99	183.50	178.80	170.50	162.40	154.70	148.50	144.55	138.55	130.40	121.60	112.55	103.90	96.55	7.40
876.00 – 885.99	186.95	182.30	173.95	165.85	157.70	151.55	147.55	141.60	133.40	124.65	115.55	106.75	99.40	7.40
886.00 – 895.99	190.40	185.75	177.40	169.30	160.75	154.55	150.55	144.60	136.45	127.65	118.55	109.75	102.25	7.50
896.00 – 905.99	193.85	189.20	180.90	172.75	164.10	157.55	153.55	147.60	139.45	130.65	121.55	112.75	105.10	7.65
906.00 – 915.99	197.30	192.65	184.35	176.20	167.60	160.55	156.55	150.60	142.45	133.65	124.55	115.80	108.05	7.75
916.00 – 925.99	200.75	196.10	187.80	179.70	171.05	163.90	159.55	153.60	145.45	136.65	127.60	118.80	111.05	7.75
926.00 – 935.99	204.25	199.55	191.25	183.15	174.50	167.40	162.80	156.60	148.45	139.65	130.60	121.80	114.05	7.75
936.00 – 945.99	207.70	203.05	194.70	186.60	177.95	170.85	166.25	159.65	151.45	142.70	133.60	124.80	117.05	7.75
946.00 – 955.99	211.15	206.50	198.20	190.05	181.40	174.30	169.70	162.85	154.50	145.70	136.60	127.80	120.05	7.75
956.00 – 965.99	214.60	209.95	201.65	193.50	184.85	177.75	173.15	166.30	157.50	148.70	139.60	130.80	123.05	7.75
966.00 – 975.99	218.05	213.40	205.10	197.00	188.35	181.20	176.60	169.75	160.50	151.70	142.60	133.85	126.10	7.75
976.00 – 985.99	221.55	216.85	208.55	200.45	191.80	184.65	180.10	173.25	163.85	154.70	145.65	136.85	129.10	7.75
986.00 – 995.99	225.05	220.35	212.00	203.90	195.25	188.15	183.55	176.70	167.30	157.70	148.65	139.85	132.10	7.75
996.00 – 1005.99	228.80	223.80	215.45	207.35	198.70	191.60	187.00	180.15	170.75	160.75	151.65	142.85	135.10	7.75
1006.00 – 1015.99	232.55	227.50	218.95	210.80	202.15	195.05	190.45	183.60	174.25	164.10	154.65	145.85	138.10	7.75
1016.00 – 1035.99	238.20	233.15	224.10	216.00	207.35	200.25	195.65	188.80	179.40	169.30	159.15	150.35	142.60	7.75
1036.00 – 1055.99	245.70	240.65	231.60	222.90	214.30	207.15	202.55	195.70	186.35	176.20	165.80	156.40	148.65	7.75
1056.00 – 1075.99	253.25	248.20	239.15	230.30	221.20	214.10	209.50	202.65	193.25	183.15	172.70	162.60	154.65	7.95
1076.00 – 1095.99	260.75	255.70	246.65	237.85	228.45	221.00	216.40	209.55	200.15	190.05	179.60	169.50	160.65	8.85
1096.00 – 1115.99	268.30	263.20	254.20	245.35	235.95	228.20	223.30	216.45	207.10	197.00	186.55	176.40	167.50	8.90

SOURCE: Revenue Canada Taxation, *Canada Pension Plan Contribution and Unemployment Insurance Premium Tables* (Ottawa, 1983) p. 32

ONTARIO
Monthly Tax Deductions / Déductions D'impôt par Mois
Basis–12 Pay Periods per Year / Base–12 périodes de paie par année

BI-WEEKLY PAY — Use appropriate bracket
PAIE DE DEUX SEMAINES — Utilisez le palier approprié

IF THE EMPLOYEE'S "NET CLAIM CODE" ON FORM TD1 is–SI LE «CODE DE RÉCLAMATION NETTE» DE L'EMPLOYÉ SELON LA FORMULE TD1 EST DE

DEDUCT FROM EACH PAY–DÉDUISEZ SUR CHAQUE PAIE

Pay range	1	2	3	4	5	6	7	8	9	10	11	12	13	Column A / Colonne A
$ 953.00 – 962.99	114.20	106.30	92.20	78.45	63.85	52.45	45.10	34.15	19.10	—	—	—	—	—
963.00 – 972.99	117.00	109.10	95.00	81.20	66.55	55.10	47.75	36.75	21.75	—	—	—	—	—
973.00 – 982.99	119.90	111.85	97.75	84.00	69.35	57.70	50.35	39.40	24.35	2.15	—	—	—	—
983.00 – 992.99	122.85	114.65	100.55	86.80	72.15	60.35	53.00	42.05	27.00	9.75	—	—	—	—
993.00 – 1002.99	125.80	117.45	103.35	89.60	74.90	63.00	55.65	44.65	29.65	13.60	—	—	—	—
1003.00 – 1012.99	128.75	120.40	106.15	92.35	77.70	65.65	58.25	47.30	32.25	16.10	—	—	—	—
1013.00 – 1022.99	131.70	123.35	108.90	95.15	80.50	68.45	60.90	49.95	34.90	18.70	—	—	—	—
1023.00 – 1032.99	134.65	126.30	111.70	97.95	83.30	71.20	63.55	52.55	37.55	21.35	—	—	—	—
1033.00 – 1042.99	137.55	129.25	114.50	100.75	86.10	74.00	66.20	55.20	40.15	24.00	—	—	—	—
1043.00 – 1052.99	140.50	132.20	117.30	103.55	88.85	76.80	69.00	57.85	42.80	26.60	7.10	—	—	—
1053.00 – 1062.99	143.45	135.15	122.25	106.30	91.65	79.60	71.80	60.45	45.45	29.25	12.75	—	—	—
1063.00 – 1072.99	146.40	138.05	123.20	109.10	94.45	82.35	74.60	63.10	48.05	31.90	15.20	—	—	—
1073.00 – 1082.99	149.35	141.00	126.15	111.90	97.25	85.15	77.40	65.75	50.70	34.50	17.80	—	—	—
1083.00 – 1092.99	152.30	143.95	129.05	114.70	100.00	87.95	80.15	68.55	53.35	37.15	20.40	—	—	—
1093.00 – 1102.99	155.25	146.90	132.00	117.45	102.80	90.75	82.95	71.35	55.95	39.80	23.05	—	—	—
1103.00 – 1112.99	158.20	149.85	134.95	120.45	105.60	93.50	85.75	74.10	58.60	42.40	25.70	5.95	—	—
1113.00 – 1122.99	161.10	152.80	137.90	123.40	108.40	96.30	88.55	76.90	61.25	45.05	28.30	12.35	—	—
1123.00 – 1132.99	164.05	155.75	140.85	126.30	111.15	99.10	91.30	79.70	63.85	47.70	30.95	14.85	—	—
1133.00 – 1142.99	167.00	158.65	143.80	129.25	113.95	101.90	94.10	82.50	66.60	50.30	33.60	17.40	—	—
1143.00 – 1152.99	169.95	161.60	146.75	132.20	116.75	104.70	96.90	85.30	69.35	52.95	36.20	20.05	—	—

See note on page 24. / Voir remarque p. 24

Income range														
1153.00 – 1162.99	172.90	164.55	149.70	135.15	119.65	107.45	99.70	88.05	72.15	55.60	38.85	22.65	2.75	2.75
1163.00 – 1172.99	175.85	167.50	152.60	138.10	122.60	110.25	102.45	90.85	74.95	58.20	41.50	25.30	10.35	10.35
1173.00 – 1182.99	178.80	170.45	155.55	141.05	125.55	113.05	105.25	93.65	77.75	60.85	44.10	27.95	13.80	13.80
1183.00 – 1192.99	181.70	173.40	158.50	144.00	128.50	115.85	108.05	96.45	80.55	63.50	46.75	30.55	16.30	14.25
1193.00 – 1202.99	184.65	176.35	161.45	146.90	131.45	118.60	110.85	99.20	83.30	66.15	49.40	33.20	18.90	14.30
1203.00 – 1212.99	187.60	179.30	164.40	149.85	134.40	121.65	113.65	102.00	86.10	68.95	52.00	35.85	21.55	14.30
1213.00 – 1232.99	192.05	183.70	168.80	154.30	138.80	126.05	117.80	106.20	90.30	73.15	55.95	39.80	25.50	14.30
1233.00 – 1252.99	197.90	189.60	174.70	160.15	144.70	131.95	123.75	111.75	95.85	78.70	61.25	45.05	30.75	14.30
1253.00 – 1272.99	203.80	195.45	180.60	166.05	150.60	137.85	129.60	117.35	101.45	84.30	66.60	50.30	36.05	14.30
1273.00 – 1292.99	209.70	201.35	186.45	171.95	156.45	143.70	135.50	123.25	107.00	89.85	72.15	55.60	41.30	14.30
1293.00 – 1312.99	215.55	207.25	192.35	177.85	162.35	149.60	141.40	129.15	112.60	95.45	77.75	60.85	46.55	14.30
1313.00 – 1332.99	221.45	213.10	198.25	183.70	168.25	155.50	147.30	135.00	118.15	101.00	83.30	66.15	51.85	14.30
1333.00 – 1352.99	227.35	219.00	204.15	189.60	174.10	161.40	153.15	140.90	124.10	106.60	88.90	71.75	57.10	14.65
1353.00 – 1372.99	233.35	224.90	210.00	195.50	180.00	167.25	159.05	146.80	130.00	112.20	94.45	77.30	62.35	14.95
1373.00 – 1392.99	239.50	230.80	215.90	201.35	185.90	173.15	164.95	152.70	135.90	117.75	100.05	82.90	67.80	15.10
1393.00 – 1412.99	245.60	236.80	221.65	207.15	191.65	178.90	170.70	158.45	141.65	123.55	105.50	88.35	73.25	15.10
1413.00 – 1432.99	251.60	242.85	227.40	212.85	197.40	184.65	176.40	164.15	147.35	129.25	110.90	93.80	78.65	15.15
1433.00 – 1452.99	257.65	248.85	233.20	218.55	203.10	190.35	182.15	169.85	153.10	135.00	116.35	99.20	84.05	15.15
1453.00 – 1472.99	263.65	254.85	239.20	224.30	208.80	196.05	187.85	175.60	158.80	140.70	122.00	104.60	89.50	15.15
1473.00 – 1492.99	269.65	260.90	245.20	230.00	214.50	201.80	193.55	181.30	164.50	146.40	127.70	110.00	94.90	15.15

SOURCE: Revenue Canada Taxation, *Canada Pension Plan Contribution and Unemployment Insurance Premium Tables* (Ottawa, 1983) p. 39

EXERCISE 7.8 / REFERENCE SECTIONS: A–B

Assume that the 1983 rates apply to the following problems:
In Problems 1 through 10, find:
(a)   the employee's payroll taxes:
   (1)   Federal income tax (if not given in the problem)
   (2)   Canada Pension Plan contribution
   (3)   Unemployment Insurance Premium
(b)   the employee's take-home pay
(c)   the employer's payroll taxes:
   (1)   Canada Pension Plan contribution
   (2)   Unemployment Insurance Premium
(d)   the total employer's cost for the employment during the current period
(e)   the distribution of the employer's cost

	Earnings in the Current Period	Payroll Period	Cumulative Earnings Prior to Current Period	Net Claim Code	Income Tax[1]
1.	$1 100	Monthly	$ 4 100	2	$?
2.	180	Weekly	6 000	3	10.35
3.	807	Bi-weekly	8 000	4	?
4.	250	Weekly	3 500	5	23.00
5.	710	Bi-weekly	1 500	2	89.80
6.	200	Weekly	0	3	15.70
7.	900	Weekly	0	4	172.75
8.	780	Bi-weekly	4 200	2	?
9.	1 065	Monthly	11 800	3	?
10.	1 106	Monthly	7 000	5	?

[1] The given taxes are obtained from the tables in 1983 Income Tax Deductions at Source, issued by Revenue Canada.

Statement Problems:
11.   The total amount of J.D. Kener's wages for this year up to July 31 was $4 100. He earned $1 095 in August. Assume that the employer prepared the monthly payroll on August 31 and that Kener's "net claim code" is 4. How much Unemployment Insurance premium, Canada Pension Plan contribution and federal income tax should the employer withhold from Kener's wages for the month of August?
12.   Refer to Problem 11. For how much payroll tax is the employer subject?
13.   The earnings record for the current week shows that C.T. Olson worked 42 hours at the rate of $5.20 per hour for the first 40 hours and $1\frac{1}{2}$ times $5.20 for all

additional hours. His Canada Pension Plan contribution withheld prior to the current week is $169.20. Find (a) Olson's earnings for the current week, (b) the Unemployment Insurance premium to be withheld.

14. Refer to Problem 13. Find the payroll taxes imposed upon the employer.

15. The total salary and wage expense of a retail store for a year was $400 000. The payroll taxes imposed upon the store were Unemployment Insurance premium, $7 200.00 and Canada Pension Plan contribution, $6 894.00. (a) How much of the total salary and wages was exempt from Unemployment Insurance Premium? (b) from the Canada Pension Plan contribution?

16. The November monthly payroll of J.D. Fuller's Department Store indicated that the total salary and wage expense was $20 000. During that month, $2 000 was exempt from Unemployment Insurance premium and $6 000 was exempt from Canada Pension Plan contribution. Find the employer's payroll taxes in November. Assume that the employer's Unemployment Insurance premium rate is 1.4 times the employee's premium.

Summary of Formulae

$\text{RATE} = \dfrac{\text{PERCENTAGE}}{\text{BASE}}$	*Formula 7-1*	Used to determine the rate when the percentage is known.
$\text{PERCENTAGE} = \text{BASE} \times \text{RATE}$	*Formula 7-2*	Used to find the percentage when the value of the base is known.
$\text{BASE} = \dfrac{\text{PERCENTAGE}}{\text{RATE}}$	*Formula 7-3*	Used to find the base when its value is not given.
$S = L(1 - r_1)(1 - r_2)(1 - r_3)\ldots(1 - r_n)$	*Formula 7-4*	Used to calculate chain discounts.
$S = L(1 - r)$	*Formula 7-5*	*Formula 7-4* converted to a single equivalent discount rate, without referring to the list price or the selling price.
$r = 1 - (1 - r_1)(1 - r_2)(1 - r_3)\ldots(1 - r_n)$	*Formula 7-6*	*Formula 7-5* converted after dividing both sides of the equation by the list price, L.

Glossary

BASE the item or number which is considered as 100%

CASH DISCOUNT a discount from the selling price granted to buyers for paying their bills within a specified period of time

CHAIN DISCOUNT two or more trade discounts applied in succession to a list price

CHANNELS OF DISTRIBUTION independent business organizaitons which directly aid the flow of products or services between a company and its market and between a company and its supplier

COST total cost of purchase of merchandise

COST OF GOODS SOLD see *cost*

CREDIT PERIOD time allowed for the payment of outstanding bills

DISCOUNT SERIES see *chain discount*

END OF THE MONTH DATING (EOM) payment terms based on last day of the month in which the invoice is dated

EXCISE TAX a special additional tax imposed on the manufacture or importation of certain specified goods and services

FEDERAL SALES TAX tax levied by the federal government on the sale of tangible personal property and services

GROSS PROFIT the difference between the net selling price and the cost of the merchandise

GROSS PROFIT ON SALES see *gross profit*

INCOME STATEMENT a financial report detailing the comparison between revenue and expenses over a given period of time

INCOME TAX a tax levied on a taxpayer's annual income by the government (federal and provincial)

MARKUP the difference between the selling price and the cost price of an item

NET INCOME AFTER INCOME TAX the actual income available for use

NET INCOME FROM OPERATIONS the excess of the gross profit on sales over total operating expenses

NET PROFIT see *net income from operations*

NET SALES the difference between the selling price and the sales discount

OPERATING EXPENSES expenses incurred in the operation of a business

PAYROLL a schedule which provides information regarding the earnings of employees for a certain period of time

PRIME COST the purchase price, excluding incidental costs

PRINCIPALS people who buy or sell merchandise using an agent or agent middleman

PROFIT AND LOSS STATEMENT see *income statement*

PROVINCIAL SALES TAX taxes levied by the provincial government on retail sales; direct taxes

PURCHASE DISCOUNT see *cash discount*

RECEIPT OF GOODS DATING (ROG) payment terms based on the date of the receipt of goods

RETAIL MERCHANT a business enterprise that sells primarily to household consumers for non-business use

RETAIL SALES sales of goods or services to the ultimate consumer for personal, non-business use

SALES transactions which involve the delivery of merchandise in exchange for cash or promises to pay

SALES DISCOUNT see *cash discount*

TRADE DISCOUNT a reduction from the list price offered to buyers

WHOLESALE MERCHANT someone who usually purchases goods from manufacturers and producers and sells to retailers and consumers who order in large quantities

PART II

Mathematics
in Investment
–Basic Topics
and Applications

Simple interest and simple discount   8

Introduction

Having covered a range of arithmetic and algebraic techniques, which are applied in business, the coverage of what may be called *money* mathematics is now examined. The remainder of the text therefore concentrates on the mathematics used in financial calculations.

The concept and operation of simple interest and simple discount are essential in the study of compound interest and discount, as well as topics based on the principle of compounding of interest, such as annuities, sinking funds, and amortization schedules.

Since no one appreciates errors in financial dealings, especially if their money is involved, the need for precision when working in the area of financial mathematics should be self-evident. From a communications point-of-view, there is no room for ambiguity when dealing with financial mathematics, thus care should be taken to ensure accuracy at all times. Accuracy to the cent is usually required.

Chapter Eight covers simple interest, simple discount and partial payment.

8.1 Simple Interest

A. BASIC CONCEPT AND COMPUTATION

When a person borrows money, he usually pays INTEREST as a fee for the use of the money. The money borrowed is called the PRINCIPAL. The sum of the principal and the interest due is called the AMOUNT. The RATE OF INTEREST is usually expressed as a percent of the principal for a specified period of time, which is generally one year. Interest paid only on the principal borrowed is called SIMPLE INTEREST. When the interest for each period is added to the principal in computing the interest for the next period, it is called COMPOUND INTEREST. Simple interest is usually charged for short-term borrowing, whereas compound interest is commonly employed in long-term obligations. SHORT-TERM BORROWING involves obligations undertaken for the purpose of buying goods or to obtain cash for everyday services. Short-term obligations are usually for a period of less than a year but may run up to five years. LONG-TERM BORROWING are obligations such as a mortgage which are extended over a long period of time.

In this chapter, only simple interest is involved. Compound interest problems are discussed in more detail in Chapter Eleven.

The basic formula for computing simple interest is:

$$\text{INTEREST} = \text{PRINCIPAL} \times \frac{\text{INTEREST RATE}}{\text{PER PERIOD}} \times \frac{\text{NUMBER OF INTEREST}}{\text{PERIODS (OR TIME)}}.$$

The formula may be simply written:

$$\boxed{I = Pin} \qquad \longleftarrow Formula\ 8\text{-}1$$

Formula 8-1 may be regarded as a general formula for calculating the simple interest I. However, when the time involved is in months, a modification is used by some people as indicated,

$$I = Pi\frac{m}{12} \text{ where } m \text{ is the number of months involved.}$$

In a situation where time is measured in days, the modification used may be,

$$I = Pi\frac{d}{365} \text{ where } d \text{ is the number of days involved.}$$

The values of rate and time *must* correspond to each other. If the rate is an annual rate, the time must be expressed in years; whereas, if the rate is a quarterly rate, the time must be stated in quarters. *Hereafter unless otherwise specified, the annual interest rate will be used in computing simple interest problems.* When the unit of time is one year, the formula is explained as follows:

$I = Pin$, where I = interest
$\qquad\qquad\qquad P$ = principal
$\qquad\qquad\qquad i$ = interest rate per year
$\qquad\qquad\qquad n$ = number of years, or a fraction of one year

Example 8.1a
What is the simple interest on $100 at 15% (a) for three years, (b) for two months, and (c) for 30 days?

SOLUTION:

(a) $P = 100$, $i = 15\%$ (per year), $n = 3$ years
    Substituting the values in Formula 8-1:
    $I = Pin = 100 \times 15\% \times 3 = \$45$

(b) $n = \dfrac{2}{12}$, since 2 months is $= \dfrac{2}{12}$ years.

$I = Pin = 100 \times 15\% \times \dfrac{2}{12} = \$2.50$

(c) $n = \dfrac{30}{365}$, since 30 days is $\dfrac{30}{365}$ years.

$I = Pin = 100 \times 15\% \times \dfrac{30}{365} = 1.23$

B.   DETERMINING THE NUMBER OF DAYS

When the dates involved in a transaction are given, the number of days must be determined before the interest can be computed. Count the number of days between the two given dates, counting either the beginning date or the ending date, but *not* both. In this text, the practice of counting the ending date will be followed. The table found on the inside front cover of the book may be used to find the number of days between two dates. Since this table lists 365 days for the year, in the case of a leap year, an additional day must be added for February, therefore the number of each day from March 1 is one greater than the number given.

Exact Time

When calculating simple interest for a fraction of a year, the exact number of days is used. When the time is expressed as a fraction of a year, the numerator is the EXACT TIME (t) and the denominator is 365, thus $\frac{t}{365}$ years. In the case of a leap year, the denominator is also 365. LEAP YEARS are those years divisible by 4, such as 1980, 1984 and 1988 in which the month of February has 29 days instead of 28 days as in other years. But the last year of a century, although it is divisible by 4, is not a leap year unless it is divisible by 400. Thus, 1700, 1800 and 1900 were not leap years, but 2000 will be a leap year.

When the number of months is given and the exact number of days cannot be found, the number of months is used as the numerator and 12 as the denominator, thus $\frac{m}{12}$.

NOTE: In some international transactions, ORDINARY INTEREST is used. Each month is assumed to have 30 days and the year 360 days.

Example 8.1b
(a)   Find the exact time from June 24, 1984 to September 27, 1984.
(b)   Express the time as a fraction of a year.

SOLUTION:

(a)   June   6 days (30 − 24 = 6 days remaining)
      July   31 days
      August   31 days
      September $\underline{27\ days}$
                      95 days

Or, according to the table, June 24 is the 175th day of the year and September 27 is the 270th day of the year.

270 − 175 = 95 days

(b) When expressing time as a fraction of the year, use 365 as the denominator.

$$n = \frac{95}{365} \text{ (years)}$$

Example 8.1c

Find the exact time from November 14, 1980 to April 24, 1981, and express it in years.

SOLUTION:

1980	November	16 days (remainder, or 30 − 14 = 16)
	December	31 days
1981	January	31 days
	February	28 days
	March	31 days
	April	24 days
	Total	161 days

Or, according to the table, which shows the exact number of days, November 14 is the 319th day of year 1980. The number of days remaining in 1980 is 366 − 319 = 47 days. April 24 is the 114th day of year 1981. Thus, the total number of days between the two given dates is 47 + 114 = 161 days. (1980 is a leap year).

$$n = \frac{161}{365} \text{ years (use 365 as the denominator even for a leap year)}$$

Example 8.1d

Find the exact time from January 22, 1980 to March 12, 1980, and express it in years.

SOLUTION:

January	9 days (remainder of 31 − 22 = 9)
February	29 days (leap year)
March	12 days
	50 days

$$n = \frac{50}{365} \text{ years}$$

Example 8.1e

Find the simple interest on $1 450 at 18% from May 23 to June 22.

SOLUTION:

May 23 to June 22 = 30 days

$P = 1\ 450,\ i = 18\%,\ n = \dfrac{30}{365}$ years

$I = 1\ 450(18\%)\dfrac{30}{365}$

$\quad = \dfrac{1\ 450(.18)(30)}{365}$

$\quad = \dfrac{\$7\ 830}{365}$

$\quad = \$21.45$

Review the order of operations using a calculator to solve Example 8.1e:

Action Taken	Display Shows
enter 1450	1450
press X	1450
enter 18	18
press %	.18
press X	261
enter 30	30
press ÷	7830
enter 365	365
press =	21.45

Rounding

In carrying out operations in which non-terminating decimal fractions appear, care must be taken in rounding. Generally, if an answer is to be computed correct to the nearest cent, it is necessary to retain as many significant digits as there are in dollars and cents in the principal.

Example 8.1f
Katrina borrowed $1 426.00 and agreed to pay $15\tfrac{1}{3}\%$ interest. How much interest must she pay at the end of one year?

SOLUTION:

$I = Pin$
$\ = 1\ 426.00(.153333)(1)$
$\ = \$218.65$

NOTE: If $15\tfrac{1}{3}\%$ was rounded to .1533, the answer would be $218.61, four cents less than the correct answer.

Daily Interest Accounts

Many DAILY INTEREST savings accounts now exist on which interest is paid on the minimum daily balance and credited to the account at the end of the month.

Example 8.1g
Marlene has a daily interest savings account which pays 8.5% interest. Her account showed the following balances for May:

May 1 $1 200
May 5 $ 890
May 19 $1 324
May 30 $ 759

(a) How much interest will be credited to her account at the end of May? (b) If interest was calculated on the minimum monthly balance, how much interest would Marlene receive for May?

SOLUTION:

(a) Daily Interest May 1 to May 31:

Time Period	Principal	Number of Days	Interest
May 1–May 5	1 200	4	$I = 1\ 200(0.85)\left(\dfrac{4}{365}\right) = 1.118$
May 5–May 19	890	14	$I = 890(.085)\ \left(\dfrac{14}{365}\right) = 2.902$
May 19–May 30	1 324	11	$I = 1\ 324(.085)\left(\dfrac{11}{365}\right) = 3.392$
May 30–May 31	759	1	$I = 759(.085)\ \left(\dfrac{1}{365}\right) = \underline{0.177}$
			7.589

Interest, May 1 - May 31 = $7.59

(b) May 1 - May 31 minimum monthly balance was $759.
$P = 759$, $i = 8.5\%$, $n = 30$ days
$$I = 759(.085)\left(\frac{30}{365}\right) = \$5.30$$

The interest on the minimum daily balance is $2.29 more than the interest on the minimum monthly balance.

EXERCISE 8.1 / REFERENCE SECTIONS: A–B

Find the simple interest in each of the following problems:

	Principal	Rate of Interest	Time
1.	$ 550.30	17.25%	7 months
2.	1 307.20	15.5 %	5 months
3.	1 208.50	14.25%	1 year
4.	975.25	18.75%	2 years
5.	2 450.00	12.00%	60 days
6.	1 500.00	24.00%	25 days
7.	900.00	20.00%	290 days

For each of the following problems, (a) determine the number of days, and (b) find the simple interest.

	Principal	Rate of Interest	Time
8.	$ 3 180.00	15.00%	June 6 to September 28
9.	4 080.25	12.25%	July 10 to November 12
10.	42 200.32	19.00%	May 21, 1984 to February 21, 1985
11.	2 972.84	17.5 %	September 5, 1986 to February 9, 1987
12.	892.00	18.3 %	November 8, 1985 to June 3, 1986
13.	652.38	17.5 %	March 4 to August 9
14.	1 066.33	19.5 %	November 18, 1983 to March 11, 1984
15.	330.27	16.25%	October 31, 1987 to September 1, 1988

8.2 Amount, Rate and Time

A.   FINDING THE AMOUNT

The amount is the sum of the principal and the interest. Let S denote the amount. The formula below is based on this definition:

$S = P + I$, or
$S = P + Pin$, or factoring P,

$$\boxed{S = P(1 + in)}\quad \longleftarrow \text{Formula 8-2}$$

Example 8.2a
(a)   What is the simple interest on $700 for 125 days at 15%, and
(b)   what is the amount?

SOLUTION:

(a) Since the number of days is given in the problem, the simple interest is computed by Formula 8-2 as follows:

$$I = Pi\left(\frac{t}{365}\right) = 700(.15)\left(\frac{125}{365}\right) = \$35.96$$

(b) Substituting the interest and the principal in Formula 8-2:

$$S = P + I$$
$$= 700 + 35.96 = \$735.96$$

Example 8.2b

Susan McKay borrowed $2 000 to buy a car. How much must she repay at the end of 3 months if 18% interest is charged?

SOLUTION:

Since the number of months is given in the problem, the simple interest is computed by expressing three months as $\frac{3}{12}$ or .25 of a year and by substituting the given values in Formula 8-2 as follows:

$$S = \$2\ 000\ [1 + (.18)(.25)]$$
$$= \$2\ 000\ (1.045)$$
$$S = \$2\ 090.00$$

Example 8.2c

On May 24, 1984, John Harrison borrowed $1 900 and agreed to repay the loan together with interest at 18.5% in 90 days. What amount must he repay? On what date?

SOLUTION:

$$S = 1\ 900\left[1 + (.185)\left(\frac{90}{365}\right)\right]$$
$$S = 1\ 900\ (1.0456164) = \$1\ 986.67$$

May	7 days (31 − 24 = 7)
June	30 days
July	31 days
	68 days
August	22 days
	90 days

The amount $1 986.67 must be repaid on August 22, 1984.

B. FINDING THE RATE

An interest rate (i) is obtained by dividing the interest by the product of the principal and the time. This is based on Formula 8-1. When both sides of the formula $I = Pin$ are divided by Pn, the following result is obtained:

$$i = \frac{I}{Pn} = \frac{\text{INTEREST}}{\text{PRINCIPAL} \times \text{TIME}}$$

⟵ *Formula 8-3*

Note that the interest rate and the time must correspond to each other. In other words, when the given time is expressed in months, the interest rate found is expressed in a monthly rate; when the time is expressed in years, the rate found is a yearly rate. In computing simple interest, the time should be expressed in years since the rate is usually expressed in a yearly rate in such a problem.

Example 8.2d
At what rate of interest will $680 yield $251.60 in two years?

SOLUTION:

Substituting $P = 680$, $I = 251.60$, and $n = 2$ (years) in the formula

$$i = \frac{I}{Pn}$$

$$i = \frac{251.60}{680(2)} = \frac{251.60}{1\,360} = .185 \text{ or } 18\tfrac{1}{2}\%$$

Example 8.2e
Find the rate of interest charged on a loan of $289 if the amount paid in settlement after 20 days is $292.64.

SOLUTION:

$$P = 289, \ S = 292.64, \ n = \frac{20}{365} \text{ years}$$

$$I = S - P = 292.64 - 289 = \$3.64$$

$$i = \frac{I}{Pn}$$

$$i = \frac{3.64}{(289)(\frac{20}{365})} = .229\,861\,6 \text{ or } 22.986\%$$

Example 8.2f
Mary's statement from Visa for the month of July showed an interest charge of $10.60. She was billed on June 3 for $489 and the last date on which she could make payment without interest penalty was June 28. Visa received her payment on June 30. What rate of interest was she charged?

SOLUTION:

Since the bill was paid after the due date, interest charges will begin on the date of billing.

$P = 489$, $I = 10.60$
June 3 to June 30 = 27 days

$$n = \frac{27}{365}$$

$$i = \frac{I}{Pn} = \frac{10.60}{489(\frac{27}{365})} = .293\ 039\ 5 \text{ or } 29.3\%$$

Example 8.2g

Marty's Hardware received an invoice dated May 15 in the amount of $1 296 with terms 2/15, 1/20, n/30. If Marty's Hardware borrowed to pay the bill on May 30 and repaid the loan on June 14, what is the highest rate of interest they can afford to pay?

SOLUTION:

On May 30, 2% cash discount is allowed.
Amount of discount: 1 296(.02) = $25.92
Amount borrowed: 1 296 − 25.92 = $1 270.08
May 30 to June 14 = 15 days

$P = 1\ 270.08$

$I = 25.92$

$$n = \frac{15}{365}$$

$$i = \frac{I}{Pn}$$

$$= \frac{25.92}{1\ 270.08(\frac{15}{365})}$$

$$= .496\ 598\ 6, \text{ or } 49.66\%$$

Marty's Hardware could afford to borrow $1 270.08 at the rate of 49.66% per year for 15 days. The cash discount of $25.92 would pay the interest expense.

C. FINDING THE TIME

The time (n) of a loan is obtained by dividing the interest by the product of the principal and the interest rate. This is also based on Formula 8-1. When both sides of the formula $I = Pin$ are divided by Pi, the following result is obtained:

$$\boxed{n = \frac{I}{Pi} = \frac{\text{INTEREST}}{\text{PRINCIPAL} \times \text{RATE}}}$$ ⟵ *Formula 8-4*

Example 8.2b
How long will it take $1 000 to yield $150 interest at 16%?

SOLUTION:

Substituting $I = 150$, $P = 1 000$, and $i = 16\%$

$$n = \frac{150}{1\ 000(.16)} = \frac{150}{160} = .9375 \text{ (years)}$$

The answer may be converted to months as .9375(12) = 11.25 months. It may also be converted to days, as .9375(365) = 342.19 days.

EXERCISE 8.2 / REFERENCE SECTIONS: A–C

In each of the following cases, find the unknown values:

	Principal	Annual Interest Rate	Time	Interest	Amount
1.	$3 000	19.5%	30 days	$? 48.08	$? 3048.08
2.	2 500	? 4.1%	45 days	? 12.50	2 512.50
3.	4 500	17.5%	? days	56.25	?
4.	345	?	120 days	9.20	?
5.	720	8%	? months	?	739.20
6.	640	?	6 months	16.00	?
7.	570	?	4 months	?	577.60
8.	860	21.2%	? months	17.20	?
9.	1 200	15.25%	? years	96.00	?
10.	2 250	?	$2\frac{1}{2}$ years	?	2 587.50
11.	3 460	?	3 years	519.00	?
12.	4 280	7%	? years	?	4 729.40

Statement Problems:
13. (a) Find the simple interest on $72 400 at 7% for 45 days. (b) What is the amount?
14. (a) Harriet borrowed $290 at 16.5%. How much must she repay at the end of two years? (b) How much is the interest?
15. A man borrowed $650 at 11% for five months. How much must he repay?
16. Anna borrowed $900 at 14.5% on July 4. How much must she repay on December 11 of the same year.
17. If $540 is borrowed for three years at 10.5%, what is the amount due at the end of the third year?
18. If $820 is borrowed for eight months at 19.25%, what is the amount due at the end of the period?

19. On July 10, 1979, Jim Tedd borrowed $950 and agreed to repay it with interest at 11% in 120 days. (a) What amount must he repay, and (b) on what date?

20. On May 21, 1981, Jack Herbert borrowed $1 200 at 11.5% interest for 45 days. (a) What amount must he repay and (b) when?

21. Margaret deposited $950 in an account which pays interest on the minimum daily balance. At the end of 30 days she received $11.71 interest. What rate of interest did she receive?

22. At what interest rate will $450 yield $9 interest in (a) three months and (b) one year?

23. A man borrowed $1 350 and paid $1 399.50 after four months. What was the interest rate charged for the debt?

24. A note for $2 400 was repaid after 120 days in the amount of $2 471.01. What was the interest rate on the note?

25. Taylor's Furniture Store received an invoice for the purchase of coat racks costing $500. The terms were 3/15, n/30. If the store were to borrow money to pay the bill in 15 days, and repay the loan in 30 days from the date of invoice, what is the highest interest rate at which the store could afford to borrow?

26. Hansel's Hardware Store received an invoice for $2 875 dated August 19 with terms, 2.5/10, 1/20, n/30, EOM. If the store borrowed to pay the invoice on September 10 and repaid the loan on September 20, what was the maximum rate of interest which it could afford to pay?

27. Georgian Marine Supplies received an invoice for $4 876 dated May 27 with terms 2/10, 1/20, n/30 ROG. If the goods were received on July 2 and the company borrowed to pay the invoice on July 12 and repaid the loan on August 1, what was the maximum rate of interest which it could afford to pay?

28. Everet borrowed $2 460 at 13% simple interest and repaid $2 523.96. For how long did he borrow the money?

29. How many years will be required for $55 to yield $8.80 interest at 8%?

30. Michelle deposited $800 in an account which pays 12% interest on the daily balance. She received $7.89 interest. For how many days did she leave the deposit in the account?

31. How many days are needed for $380 to (a) amount to $389.50 at 5%, and (b) yield $1.90 interest at 3%?

32. The Moore Drug Store received an invoice of $250, terms 3/10, 1/20, n/30. If the store borrows money in 10 days to pay the bill and repays the loan in 20 days from the date of invoice, what is the highest interest rate at which the store can afford to borrow?

33. A man has part of his money invested at 10% and the remainder at 16%. His annual income from the investment is $1 780. If he had received 1% less interest on each of his two investments, his income would have been $1 650 annually. How much did he invest at each interest rate?

34. A man borrows $3 000 and agrees to pay $500 on the principal plus the simple interest at 7% on the principal outstanding at the end of each six-month period. Find the total amount that must be paid to discharge the debt.

8.3 Principal, Present Value, and Simple Discount

A. FINDING THE PRINCIPAL

The principal may be obtained in the following ways:

1. by formula $I = Pin$:

when both sides of the formula $I = Pin$ are divided by in, the following result is obtained:

$$P = \frac{I}{in}$$ ← *Formula 8-5*

Example 8.3a

Diane receives $225 interest in 90 days from an investment which pays 18% interest. What is the principal that she invested?

SOLUTION:

Substituting $I = 225$, $i = 18\%$, $n = \dfrac{90}{365}$

Solving for P:

$$P = \frac{I}{in} = \frac{\$225}{(.18)(\frac{90}{365})} = \frac{\$255(365)}{(.18)(90)} = \$5\,069.44$$

2. by formula $S = P + I = P + Pin = P(1 + in)$ ← *Formula 8-6*

Example 8.3b

Lois paid a debt with a $280 cheque which included $30 interest. Find the principal.

SOLUTION:

Substituting $S = 280$ and $I = 30$ in the formula $P = S - I$, since $S = P + I$:
$P = 280 - 30 = \$250$

When both sides of the formula $S = P(1 + in)$ are divided by $(1 + in)$, the following result is obtained:

$$P = \frac{S}{1 + in} = \frac{S}{\text{AMOUNT OF 1}}$$ ← *Formula 8-7*

The numerator, S, is the total amount, while the denominator is the amount of 1 unit; that is, when the principal is $1 and is invested at i for n periods, the amount is $\$(1 + in)$.

Example 8.3c

How much money must Jack Jones invest today at 12% simple interest if he is to receive $1 416, the amount, in two years?

SOLUTION:

Substituting $S = 1\ 416$, $i = 12\%$, and $n = 2$ (years), in the formula $S = P(1 + in)$:

$$P = \frac{S}{1 + in}$$

$$= \frac{1\ 416}{1 + (.12)(2)} = \frac{1\ 416}{1.24} = \$1\ 141.94$$

In the above example, 1.24 is the amount of a principal of 1 (dollar) plus its interest at 12% for two years.

Review the order of operations using a calculator to solve Example 8.3c:
1. Calculate the denominator.
2. Use the store function or $\frac{1}{x}$ function to complete the division.

Action Taken	Display Shows
1. enter 12	12
2. press the key %	.12
3. press the key X	.12
4. enter 2	2
5. press the key +	.24
6. enter 1	1
7. press the key =	1.24
8. press the key $\frac{1}{x}$	0.8064516
9. press the key X	0.8064516
10. enter 1416	1416
11. press the key =	1141.9355

OR

8. store the result (1.24) (use STO or M M, specify register if necessary)	1.24
9. enter 1416	1416
10. press the key ÷	1416
11. recall the result (1.24) (use RCL or R and specify register if necessary)	1.24
12. press the key =	1141.9355

B.   PRESENT VALUE

PRESENT VALUE *is the value at the time of investment, such as the principal, or at any time before the maturity date (due date).* Example 8.3c indicates that if Jack Jones invests $1 141.94 today at 12% simple interest, he will get $1 416 in two years. In other words, the present value of $1 416 which is due in two years and includes 12% interest is $1 141.94. Thus, the method of finding the present value of a given amount which is due in the future, is the same as the method used in Example 8.3c in finding the principal.

This is illustrated in the following diagram:

P = $1 141.94 S = $1 416

0   1   2 Years

C.   SIMPLE DISCOUNT

The process of finding the present value of a given amount which is due on a future date is called DISCOUNTING AT SIMPLE INTEREST, or as commonly called, the SIMPLE DISCOUNT METHOD. In other words, to discount an amount by the simple interest process is to find its present value.

When interest is involved, the amount must be larger than its present value. The difference between the amount and its present value is called the SIMPLE DISCOUNT. Thus, the simple discount on the amount is the same as the simple interest on the principal or the present value. There are numerous occasions in business when it becomes necessary to discount an amount which is due on a future date. The principle of simple discount is important to compound discount problems dealing with long-term investments, although the bank discount method is used widely in discounting short-term loans.

Discounting a Non-Interest-Bearing Debt

The following examples are given to illustrate the discounting of a non-interest-bearing debt.

Example 8.3d

What is the present value of $3 270 which is due at the end of six months if the interest rate is 18%. What is the simple discount?

SOLUTION:

S = 3 270, i = 18%, and n = $\dfrac{6}{12}$, or .5 (years)

Substituting the values in

$S = P(1 + in)$, or $P = \dfrac{S}{1 + in}$:

$$P = \frac{3\ 270}{1 + (.18)(.5)} = \frac{3\ 270}{1.09} = \$3\ 000$$

$I = 3\ 270 - 3\ 000 = \$270$ (simple discount)

CHECK:

According to the answer, the amount due at the end of six months should be:
$S = P(1 + in) = \$3\ 000\ [1 + (.18)(.5)] = \$3\ 000(1.09) = \$3\ 270.00$

NOTE: The simple discount on the amount \$3 270 is the same as the simple interest on the present value \$3 000. In other words, I has a twofold meaning: it is the simple interest on the principal or the present value; and it is also the simple discount on the amount. This is illustrated in the following diagram.

$I = Pin = \$270$

$P = \$3\ 000$ $S = \$3\ 270$

0 6 Months

Example 8.3e
Discount \$3 270 for six months at simple interest rate 18%. What is the present value and the simple discount?

SOLUTION:

The answer in this example is the same as that in Example 8.3d, since the two examples have the same meaning.

Example 8.3f
Gina owes \$988 which is due 3 months from today. How much will settle the debt today if the simple interest rate of 16% is allowed? What is the simple discount?

SOLUTION:

Substituting: $S = 988$, $i = 16\%$, and $n = \frac{3}{12}$ or .25 (years)

$P = \dfrac{S}{1 + in}$, then the present value is

$$P = \frac{988}{1 + (.16)(.25)} = \frac{988}{1.04} = \$950$$

The simple discount is:
$I = S - P = 988 - 950 = \$38$

CHECK:

$950(.16)(.25) = \$38$

Discounting an Interest-Bearing Debt

To find the present value of an interest-bearing debt (or to discount the amount by the simple discount method), take the following steps:

STEP (1) Find the MATURITY VALUE (the amount) according to the original interest rate and the time stipulated for the debt. Use the formula $S = P(1 + in)$, where S is the maturity value and P is the original debt.

STEP (2) Find the present value (the value on the date of discount) of the maturity value according to the interest rate for discounting and the discount period. The discount period is the period from the date of discount to the maturity date. Use the formula in the form, $P = \frac{S}{1 + in}$, where P is the present value and S is the maturity value. However, the values of i and n in this step are often different from the values of i and n in STEP (1).

Example 8.3g

Arne borrowed $1 000 on May 1, 1983, and agreed to repay the money plus 18% interest in 146 days. Sixty days after the money was borrowed, the creditor agreed to settle the debt by discounting it at the simple interest rate of 17.75%. How much did the creditor receive when the debt was discounted?

SOLUTION:

STEP (1) Find the maturity value of the debt according to the original stipulation of the debt. $P = 1\ 000$, $i = 18\%$, $n = \frac{146}{365}$, or .4 (years)
Substituting these values in the formula:
$S = P(1 + in) = 1\ 000[1 + 18\%(.4)]$
$= 1\ 000(1.072) = \$1\ 072.00$ (amount on September 24, 1983)

STEP (2) Find the present value of the maturity value according to the discounting terms. $S = 1\ 072$, $i = 17.75\%$, $n = \frac{86}{365}$ (year), or $146 - 60 = 86$ (days)
Substituting these values in the formula:
$$P = \frac{S}{1 + in} = \frac{1\ 072}{1 + 17.75\%(\frac{86}{365})} = \frac{1\ 072}{1.041\ 821\ 9}$$
$= \$1\ 028.97$ (value on June 30, 1983)

This example may be diagrammed as follows:

STEP (1) Maturity Value–Accumulate the principal at 18% for 146 days

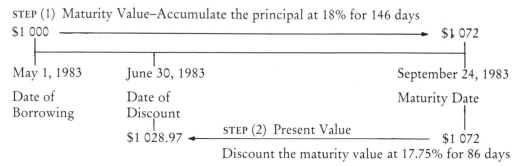

Example 8.3h

In Example 8.3g, assume that the simple interest rate for discounting is also 18%. How much would the creditor receive when the debt was discounted?

SOLUTION:

STEP (1) The maturity value is the same, $1 072.

STEP (2) The present value of the maturity value is found as follows:

$$S = \$1\ 072,\ i = 18\%,\ n = \frac{86}{365}\ (\text{years})$$

$$P = \frac{S}{1 + in} = \frac{1\ 072}{1 + (.18)(\frac{86}{365})} = \frac{1\ 072}{1.042411} = \$1\ 028.39$$

NOTE: Even when the interest rate for computing the maturity value is the same as the interest rate for discounting, the two steps are still required. Refer to Example 8.3h. The sum of the principal and the interest for 60 days (the period between the date of borrowing and the date of discounting) at a rate of 18% is

$$S = P + Pin = 1\ 000 + \left(1\ 000 \times .18 \times \frac{60}{365}\right)$$
$$= 1\ 000 + 29.59$$
$$= \$1\ 029.59$$

The sum is not the same as the present value $1 028.39 obtained by the method used in Example 8.3h.

EXERCISE 8.3 / REFERENCE SECTIONS: A–C

In each of the following cases, find the principal:

	Interest Rate	Time	Interest	Amount
1.	–	–	$16.42	$ 344.82
2.	12%	2 years	38.40	–
3.	8%	6 months	–	5 720.00
4.	18%	2 years	52.00	–
5.	15%	$2\frac{1}{2}$ years	–	258.75
6.	8%	120 days	–	3 542.00
7.	19%	25 days	42.50	–
8.	–	–	24.38	487.60
9.	14%	60 days	20.00	–
10.	8%	90 days	–	4 030.00

Statement Problems:

11. What principal will yield $134 interest for 61 days at 15.5%?

12. How much must be deposited in an account at 17% in order to yield $242.28 in 180 days?

13. Pierre paid $525 to settle a loan for 2 years with interest at 17.5%. How much was the loan?

14. What principal will amount to $839.70 in 73 days at 17% simple interest?

15. How much money must J.D. Gooch invest at 16.5% interest for two years in order to receive $2 552 at the end of the second year?

16. B.C. Dodge will receive $543.60 on June 30. How much can he borrow at 11% on May 1, if he uses his receipts to repay the loan?

17. (a) What is the present value of $1 000 due in two years if the money is worth 17.25%? (b) How much is the simple discount?

18. (a) What is the present value of $640 due at the end of four months if the money is worth 16.25%? (b) How much is the simple discount?

19. A debt of $1 800 is due in 1 year and 3 months. If the debt is settled now and the simple interest rate of 17.25% is allowed, what are, (a) the present value and (b) the simple discount?

20. A debt of $2 500 is due eight months from now. (a) What is the present value of the debt if 19% simple interest is allowed? (b) What is the simple discount on the debt if it is settled now?

21. Mrs. J.A. Outen purchased a refrigerator and made a down payment of $150. She agreed to pay $250 after one month and $200 after two months. If the rate of interest is 24%, what is the cash price of the refrigerator?

22. Mrs. W.R. Wages plans to purchase a television set. She is offered the option of paying $200 down and $500 in four months, or of paying $350 down and $350 in five months. If the rate of interest is 21%, which option would be a better offer for her?

23. Mr. Green borrowed $5 000 on June 1 of this year and agreed to repay the principal plus 19.5% interest in 120 days. On July 1, he wishes to pay the loan by discounting it at the simple interest rate of 19%. How much should he pay according to the discount?

24. Refer to Problem 23. If the debt is discounted at the simple interest rate of 20%, how much should he pay?

25. On May 1, J.D. Taylor borrowed $1 000 from Ms Bennett and agreed to pay the debt plus 18% simple interest in 90 days. If the debt is settled on May 31 at 18.5% simple interest, how much did Ms Bennett receive?

26. In Problem 25, if the debt is settled at an interest rate of 17.5%, how much did Ms Bennett receive?

8.4 Partial Payments

If PARTIAL PAYMENTS are made on a debt before it is due, there should be an agreement between the creditor and the borrower regarding the interest on each partial payment. Some creditors may agree to reduce the interest when partial payments on the debt are made. One method often used is to calculate the interest on the declining balance.

A.   THE DECLINING-BALANCE METHOD

Under the DECLINING-BALANCE method, each partial payment must first be applied to the accumulated interest up to the date of the payment. Any remainder is then credited as a deduction from the principal. Therefore, the successive interest is computed from a declining balance each time a payment is made. A debtor may thus know the actual amount of his unpaid balance immediately after each payment. The following steps may be employed:

STEP (1)   Find the interest on the principal for the period from the date of borrowing to the date of the first partial payment.

STEP (2)   Subtract the interest from the first payment. If there is a remainder, subtract the remainder from the principal to obtain the unpaid balance. If the partial payment is not sufficient to cover the interest due, the partial payment is then held and is included in the next payment.

STEP (3)   If there are further partial payments, the processes in STEPS (1) and (2) are repeated, *but the interest is computed on the declining unpaid balance*. Each payment must be first applied to the ACCRUED INTEREST which has accumulated up to the date of each payment. *The final balance is the sum of the unpaid principal and the accumulated interest up to the date of the final settlement*.

Example 8.4a

On July 1, Ms Zito borrowed $2 000 at 17.5%. She paid $500 on August 30, and $600 on September 29. Find the balance on October 29 of the same year.

SOLUTION:

Original debt (7/1)		$2 000.00
Deduct:		
First payment (8/30)	$500.00	
Deduct interest on **$2 000** for 60 days (7/1–8/30)	57.53	
Remainder applied to principal	442.47	442.47
Balance on 8/30		$1 557.53
Deduct:		
Second payment (9/29)	600.00	
Deduct interest on **$1 557.53** for 30 days (8/30–9/29)	22.40	
Remainder applied to principal	577.60	577.60
Balance on 9/29		$ 979.93
Add interest on **$979.93** for 30 days (9/29–10/29)		14.09
		$ 994.02

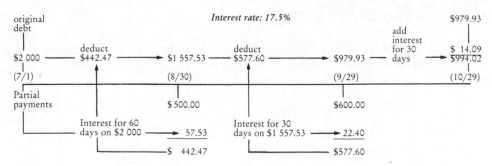

The balance on October 29 is $994.02.

NOTE: After each payment is made, it is the balance of the principal which is used to calculate the next value of accrued interest, and the interest calculated on the final balance of the principal is *added* to that balance to determine the value of the debt on the due date.

Example 8.4b

On June 2, Mr. Schmidt received a loan of $4 000 on which interest is charged at 15.5%. He made the following payments: $1 000 on August 5, $25 on September 10, and $1 500 on October 10. How much will settle the debt on November 3?

SOLUTION:

Original debt (June 2)		$4 000.00
Deduct:		
First payment (August 5)	$1 000.00	
Deduct interest for 64 days (6/2–8/5)	108.71	
Remainder applied to principal	891.29	891.29
Balance on August 5		$3 108.71
Deduct:		
Second payment (September 10)	25.00*	
Third payment (October 10)	1 500.00	
Total payment (October 10)	1 525.00	
Deduct interest for 66 days (8/5–10/10)	87.13	
Remainder applied to principal	1 437.87	1 437.87
Balance on October 10		1 670.84
Add interest on $1 670.84 for 24 days (10/10–11/3)		17.03
Balance on November 3		$1 687.87

* Interest on $3 108.71 is $47.52, which is larger than the partial payment of $25. Thus, the payment is held and is included in the payment of October 10.

The debt could be settled on November 3 with $1 687.87.

EXERCISE 8.4 / REFERENCE SECTION: A

In each of the following problems, find the unpaid balance on the indicated date by the declining-balance method:

Date of Loan	Principal	Rate of Interest	First Partial Payment Date	Amount	Second Partial Payment Date	Amount	Date of Unpaid Balance
1. 4/1/83	$1 000	19.5%	5/1	$ 300	6/30	$ 500	7/30/83
2. 6/10/83	2 500	15%	7/11	500	10/8	800	12/7/83
3. 1/19/84	560	16.5%	2/8	200	–	–	3/20/84
4. 9/24/84	840	18.5%	11/3	300	–	–	12/23/84
5. 8/15/84	1 600	16.25%	10/12	40	11/13	1 000	1/12/85
6. 7/6/84	2 800	24%	7/21	1 000	8/20	1 200	9/19/84
7. 11/15/85	4 200	14%	1/14	3 000	–	–	4/8/86
8. 10/2/85	3 500	20%	12/1	2 000	–	–	1/10/86
9. 3/25/86	3 700	18.5%	6/23	1 000	8/22	2 000	10/21/86
10. 5/6/86	4 800	17.3%	6/5	2 400	11/2	1 800	1/31/87

Statement Problems:

11. On January 12, 1983, Jack Southerland purchases a lot for $5 000. He makes a partial payment of $1 000 once every 30 days, beginning February 11. On June 11, he plans to make the last payment plus the interest. If the rate of interest is 18%, what is the amount due?

12. A note for $6 000 with an interest rate of 17.3%, dated March 18, 1984, has the following partial payments: May 17, $2 000; July 1, $2 000, and September 14, $1 000. Find the balance due on December 13, 1984.

13. On April 25, 1985, a man borrowed $4 000 at 10.5% interest. He paid $1 000 on June 24, $500 on July 24, $5 on August 23, and $2 000 on September 22. Find the balance due November 21, 1985.

14. Bill Farr borrowed $3 000 on May 7, 1985. Partial payments were made as follows: $500 on June 6, $15 on July 21, $1 000 on September 4, and $800 on November 3. On December 3, 1985, he wishes to settle his obligation. If the interest charged is 13.5%, what is the total amount due?

8.5 *Equivalent Values*

A. *SIMPLE INTEREST*

Occasionally there arises the need to replace a single debt or a set of debts by another set of debts due at different times. In order to satisfy both the creditor and the debtor, the values of the new debts should be equivalent to the values of the original ones.

For example, if a debt of $100 due now is to be replaced by a new debt due in one year and the money is worth 15.5%, the new debt is computed as follows:

$$S = P(1 + in) = 100(1 + 15.5\% \times 1) = \$115.50$$

The computation indicates that $100 due now is *equivalent* to $115.50 due in one year if the money is worth 15.5%. Thus, the creditor may allow his debtor to repay his $100 now or $115.50 in a year. This is illustrated in the following diagram:

$P = \$100$	$S = \$115.50$

15.5%

0(Now)   1 Year

On the other hand, if a debt of $231.00 due in a year is to be replaced by a new debt now, and the interest rate agreed on by the creditor and the debtor is 15.5%, the new debt is computed as follows:

$$P = \frac{S}{1 + in} = \frac{231.00}{1 + (15.5\%)(1)} = \$200$$

This is illustrated in the following diagram:

$200	$231

15.5%

0 (Now)   1 Year

The computation indicates that $231 due in a year is equivalent to $200 due now if the rate of interest is 15.5%. Thus, the creditor and the debtor may agree to settle the debt now by the debtor's payment of only $200.

When interest is involved, a sum of money has different values at various times. For convenience, a COMPARISON DATE, also called a FOCAL DATE, should first be chosen in comparing the values of old debts with the values of new debts. An EQUATION OF VALUE, which gives the equivalent values of original debts and new debts on the comparison date at the specified interest rate, should then be arranged for obtaining the required equivalent values. The answer for a required equivalent value may vary slightly in simple interest problems depending on the selection of the comparison date, but it does not vary in compound interest problems. The following examples are used to illustrate problems in equivalent values involving simple interest.

Example 8.5a
A debt of $200 is due in six months. If the rate of interest is 15.5%, what is the value of the debt if it is paid (a) two months hence, (b) six months hence, or (c) nine months hence?

SOLUTION:

According to the problem, $200 is the maturity value or the amount due at the end of six months, and the interest rate agreed upon by both creditor and debtor for settlement of the debt is 15.5%.

(a) If the $200 debt is paid two months hence, which is four months before the original due date, the required equivalent value is less than $200. Thus, the present value formula $P = S/(1 + in)$ should be used to compute the required value. In other words, the value is obtained by discounting the maturity value at a simple interest rate for the advance time of the payment. $S = 200$, $i = 15.5\%$, $n = \frac{4}{12} = \frac{1}{3}$ (year). Substituting the values in the formula:

$$P = \frac{200}{1 + (15.5\%)(\frac{1}{3})} = \frac{200}{1.051\ 666\ 7} = \$190.17$$

If the debt is paid two months hence, the payment is $190.17.

(b) If the debt is paid in six months, at which time the debt is due, the payment is $200, unchanged.

(c) If the debt of $200 is paid nine months from now, which is three months after the due date, the required equivalent value is more than $200. Thus, the amount formula $S = P(1 + in)$ should be used to compute the required value. In other words, the value is obtained by accumulating the original debt $200 for the extended time.

$$P = 200, \quad i = 15.5\%, \quad n = \frac{3}{12}, \text{ or } \frac{1}{4} \text{ (year)}$$

Substituting the values in the formula:

$$S = 200\left[1 + (15.5\%)\left(\frac{1}{4}\right)\right] = 200(1.03875) = \$207.75$$

When the debt is paid at the end of nine months, the payment is $207.75.

This example may be diagrammed as follows:

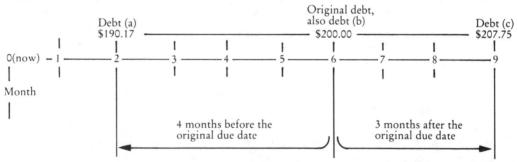

Example 8.5b

A man owes (1) $100 due in two months and (2) $400 due in eight months. His creditor has agreed to settle the debts by 2 equal payments in four months and ten months, respectively. Find the size of each payment if the rate of interest is 18% and the comparison date is four months hence.

SOLUTION:

Let x represent each equal payment. The values as of the comparison date are computed as follows:

(a) The value of the old debt of $100 becomes $103 on the comparison date. The value is computed as follows:
$P = 100$, $i = 18\%$, $n = \frac{2}{12} = \frac{1}{6}$ (year) since the comparison date is two months after the due date

$$S = 100\left[1 + (18\%)\left(\frac{1}{6}\right)\right] = \$100(1.03) = \$103$$

(b) The value of the old debt of $400 becomes $377.36 on the comparison date. The value is computed as follows:
$S = 400$, $i = 18\%$, $n = \frac{4}{12} = \frac{1}{3}$ (year) since the comparison date is four months before the due date

$$P = \frac{400}{1 + (18\%)(\frac{1}{3})} = \$377.36$$

(c) The value of the first new debt, which is due in four months, does not change and is x since the comparison date is also in four months.

(d) The value of the second new debt, which is due in ten months, becomes $x/1.09$ on the comparison date. It is computed as follows:
$S = x$, $i = 18\%$, $n = \frac{6}{12} = \frac{1}{2}$ (year) since the comparison date is six months before the due date

$$P = \frac{x}{1 + (18\%)(\frac{1}{2})} = \frac{x}{1.09}$$

The values are diagrammed in the following manner.

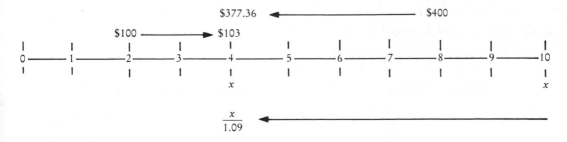

new debts = old debts

$$x + \frac{x}{1.09} = 103 + 377.36$$

Solve for x:

$$x\left(1 + \frac{1}{1.09}\right) = 480.36$$
$$x(1 + .917\ 431\ 2) = 480.36$$
$$1.917\ 431\ 2x = 480.36$$
$$x = \frac{480.36}{1.917\ 431\ 2}$$
$$= \$250.522$$
$$= \$250.52$$

The two original debts may be discharged by paying $250.52 in four months and $250.52 in ten months.

CHECK:

On the comparison date,

$$\text{New debts} = 250.522 + \frac{250.522}{1 + 18\%(\frac{1}{2})} = 250.52 + 229.837 = \$480.36$$

$$= \text{Old debts}$$

Example 8.5c

In the above example, what is the size of each equal payment if the comparison date is set ten months hence?

SOLUTION:

Let x represent each payment. The values as of the comparison date are computed as follows:

(a) The value of the old debt (1), $100, becomes

$$S = 100\left[1 + (18\%)\left(\frac{8}{12}\right)\right] = \$112$$

(b) The value of the old debt (2), $400, becomes

$$S = 400\left[1 + (18\%)\left(\frac{2}{12}\right)\right] = \$412$$

(c) The value of the first new debt, which is due in four months becomes

$$S = x\left[1 + (18\%)\left(\frac{6}{12}\right)\right] = 1.09x$$

(d) The value of the second new debt, which is due in ten months, does not change and is x since the comparison date is also in ten months.

The values are diagrammed as follows:

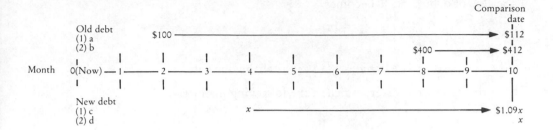

The equation of value based on the comparison date is given below:

New Debts   Old Debts

$x + x(1.09) = 412 + 112$

$x(1 + 1.09) = 524$

$2.09x = 524$

$$x = \frac{524}{2.09}$$

$= \$250.72$

This answer may be compared with that given on page 282. The difference is only $0.20(or \$250.72 – \$250.52)$ which is due to the selection of the comparison date.

NOTE: When the due date of the last new debt is selected as the comparison date, division in the discounting process may be avoided.

Example 8.5d

A man owes (a) \$500 in 146 days and (b) \$1 000 plus 10% interest due in 73 days. If money is worth 9%, what single payment 219 days hence will be equivalent to the two original debts?

SOLUTION:

Let x represent the unknown single payment. The comparison date is 219 days hence. Since debt (b) is interest bearing, its maturity value, having a 10% interest rate for 73 days, should be computed first. The maturity value plus 9% interest for 146 days is the value of debt (b) on the comparison date.
The maturity value of debt (b) is

$$1\ 000 \left[1 + (10\%)\left(\frac{73}{365} \right) \right] = 1\ 000(1.02) = \$1\ 020,$$

and its value on the comparison date becomes

$$1\ 020 \left[1 + (9\%)\left(\frac{146}{365} \right) \right] = 1\ 020(1.036) = \$1\ 056.72.$$

The value of debt (a) $500 becomes

$$500\left[1 + 9\%\left(\frac{73}{365}\right)\right] = \$509$$

on the comparison date, which is $\frac{73}{365}$ year after the due date.

The entire problem is diagrammed in the following manner:

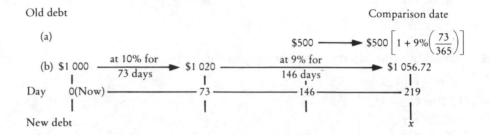

The equation of value based on the comparison date is written below:

$x = 1\ 056.72 + 509$
$\quad = \$1\ 565.72$

The single payment at the end of 219 days is $1 565.72.

EXERCISE 8.5 / REFERENCE SECTION: A

Find the value of the new obligations in each of the following problems:

	Original Debt	Worth of Money (%)	New debt and Comparison Date
1.	$2 000 due in 2 months	17%	All in 5 months
2.	$3 000 due in 3 months	13.5%	All in 1 month
3.	$3 040 due in 6 months	16.25%	All in 2 months
4.	$1 200 due in 4 months	19%	All in 6 months
5.	(a) $5 000 due in 4 months	20%	All in 6 months
	(b) $2 400 due in 1 month		
6.	(a) $2 200 due in 1 month	19.5%	All in 4 months
	(b) $4 600 due in 9 months		
7.	(a) $1 000 in 5 months	18%	Two equal payments, one in 2 months, the other in 9 months. Comparison date, 2 months hence.
	(b) $1 800 in 8 months		
8.	(a) $1 000 in 5 months	18%	Same as Problem 7, except the comparison date is 9 months hence.
	(b) $1 800 in 8 months		

Statement Problems:

9. A debt of $1 000 is due in four months. If money is worth 14%, what is the value of the debt if it is paid (a) one month hence, (b) four months hence, and (c) six months hence?

10. A debt of $2 000 is due at the end of six months. If money is worth 17.3%, what is the value of the debt (a) at the end of five months, (b) at the end of six months, and (c) at the end of ten months?

11. A man owes (a) $1 000 due in three months and (b) $2 000 due in eight months. He and his creditor agree to settle the obligations by 2 equal payments, one in five months and the other in eleven months. Find the size of each payment if money is worth 16.5% and the comparison date is five months hence.

12. Answer the questions in Problem 11 if the comparison date is 11 months hence.

13. A debt of $2 400 due in two months is to be paid by 3 equal payments due three, five and seven months hence. Money is worth 18.5%. What is the size of each payment? Let the comparison date be five months hence.

14. Answer the questions in Problem 13 if the comparison date is two months hence.

15. A man owes (a) $1 000 due in four months and (b) $3 000 plus interest at 9.5% due in six months. If money is worth 13.25%, what single payment ten months hence will be equivalent to the two original debts?

16. In Problem 15, if money is worth 16.75%, what single payment three months hence will be equivalent to the two original debts?

17. Jack Simpson owes Dale Peterson (a) $1 000 which is four months overdue, (b) $2 000 which is three months overdue, and (c) $1 500 which is due today. Simpson wishes to sign a three-month non-interest-bearing note to cover all the debts. If an 18.3% interest rate is used to compute the obligations, what should be the face value of the note?

18. In Problem 17, assume that Simpson wishes to sign two non-interest-bearing notes of equal amounts with one note due in one month and the other due in two months. The 18.3% interest rate is used throughout. What should be the face value for each note if the comparison date is (a) now, and (b) two months hence?

EXERCISE / CHAPTER REVIEW

1. What is the simple interest on $500 at 15% for (a) four years, (b) three months?

2. Find the simple interest on $650 at 17.5% for (a) two years, (b) five months.

3. What is the exact time from March 10 to July 24?

4. Find the exact time from May 2, 1982 to February 8, 1983.

5. Determine the number of days by the exact time method from January 14, 1983 to June 10, 1984.

6. Find the number of days by the exact time method from July 8, 1984 to February 15, 1985.

7. Find (a) the exact interest and (b) the ordinary interest on $2 000 at 4% for 45 days.

8. What is (a) the exact interest and (b) the ordinary interest on $3 500 at 17.8% for 60 days?

9. Tara made the following deposits in a daily interest account. March 1, $500; March 12, $200; March 29, $100. How much interest will she receive on March 31 if (a) interest is payable on the daily balance and (b) interest is payable on the minimum monthly balance? Assume an interest rate of 8.25%.

10. Find the exact interest on $396 at 19.2% for 78 days.

11. How much must be paid to settle a loan of $2 000 for 9 months at 18%?

12. On May 1, Jina deposited $900 in an account which pays 8% interest on the minimum monthly balance at the end of each month. How much does she have in the account on May 31?

13. A debt of $1 260 is to be repaid in 120 days at 14%. How much will settle the debt?

14. Find the amount if $1 500 is invested for 95 days at 6%.

15. On June 30, 1984, Jack Horner borrowed $600 and agreed to repay the loan in 60 days. The interest rate is 12%. (a) What is the simple interest? (b) What amount must he repay? (c) On what date?

16. If $800 is borrowed at 16.4% simple interest for two years, what will be the amount due?

17. At what interest rate will $360 yield $54 in 1.5 years?

18. Mary borrowed $320 two years ago. She paid $448 today to discharge the loan. What was the interest rate charged?

19. Bill borrowed $240 seventy days ago. He has to pay $247.20 now to settle the debt. What is the interest rate?

20. A payment of $702 was made to discharge a six-month loan of $650. What was the interest rate?

21. How many months will it take $1 500 to yield $37.50 interest at 16% simple interest.

22. Angela took a cash advance of $2 000 on her credit card for which the interest rate is 24%. She was charged $78.90 interest. For how many days did she receive the advance?

23. Mark lent a friend $420 at 10% and received $24.80 interest. For how long did he make the loan?

24. How many months are necessary for $500 to yield $5 interest at 6.5% simple interest?

25. Sarah receives $50 every two months from an investment which pays 18% interest. What was the principal that she invested?

26. Denton paid $650 for discharging a debt which includes $60 interest. What is the principal?

27. How much money should Eaton invest now at 14.5% simple interest if he is to receive $5 350 in two years?

28. What is the present value of $6 300 which is due at the end of ten months? The interest rate is 15.25% .

29. Discount $810 for three months at the simple interest rate of 12.5%. What are (a) the present value and (b) the simple discount?

30. Arlene promises to pay Jack $750 nine months from now. (a) If the debt is settled now and the simple interest rate of 12% is allowed, how much should Arlene pay now? (b) What is the simple discount?

31. Gray borrowed $800 and agreed to repay the loan plus 16.3% interest at the end of the year. Four months after the loan had been made, his creditor agreed to settle the debt by discounting it at the simple interest rate of 14.5%. (a) How much should Gray pay? (b) What is the simple discount?

32. On April 10, Herbert borrowed $1 200 and agreed to pay the loan plus 13.5% simple interest in 60 days. If the debt is settled on May 25 at 14%, simple interest, how much should he pay?

33. Sherwood borrowed $4 500 on February 6, 1984 at 12%. He paid $600 on February 21, and $1 400 on March 23. Find the balance on April 22, 1984 by the declining-balance method.

34. On May 2, 1983, a man borrowed $2 400 at 16%. He paid $800 on June 1, $8 on July 1, and $1 000 on July 16. Find the balance due on August 15, 1983 by the declining-balance method.

35. A debt of $600 is due in eight months. If the rate of interest is 15%, what is the value of the debt if it is paid (a) three months hence, (b) eight months hence, and (c) ten months hence?

36. A debt of $1 500 is due at the end of five months. If money is worth 17.25% what will be the value of the debt if it is settled at the end of (a) three months, (b) five months, and (c) nine months?

37. A man owes $600 due in three months and $900 due in nine months. His creditor has offered to settle the debts by two equal payments in five months and in eleven months respectively. If the man were to accept the offer, what would be the size of each payment, assuming the interest rate is 16% and the comparison date is five months from now?

38. Bill bought a truck for $8 000. He paid $1 000 down and agreed to make two equal payments, one due in four months and one due in seven months. What should the amount of these payments be if the interest charged is 18%? The comparison date is four months from now.

39. A man owes $700 due in eight months and $1 200 plus 10% interest due in two months. If money is worth 12% now, what single payment ten months hence will be equivalent to the two original debts?

40. Janis owes $2 000 due in three months from now and $4 000 due seven months from now. She has agreed to pay $1 000 two months from now. How much will the balance be six months from now if money is worth 14%?

Summary of Formulae

$I = Pin$	*Formula 8-1*	Used to calculate the simple interest.
$S = P(1 + in)$	*Formula 8-2*	Used to calculate the amount, which is the sum of the principal and the interest.
$i = \dfrac{I}{Pn}$	*Formula 8-3*	Based on Formula 8-1, used to calculate the interest rate.
$n = \dfrac{I}{Pi}$	*Formula 8-4*	Based on Formula 8-1, used to calculate the time.
$P = \dfrac{I}{in}$	*Formula 8-5*	Based on Formula 8-1, used to calculate the principal.
$S = P + I = P + Pin = P(1 + in)$	*Formula 8-6*	Based on Formula 8-2, used to calculate the amount.
$P = \dfrac{S}{1 + in}$	*Formula 8-7*	Based on Formula 8-2, used to calculate the principal.

Glossary

ACCRUED INTEREST the interest on the debt which has accumulated up to a specific date

AMOUNT the sum of the principal and interest due at maturity

COMPARISON DATE a date on which the value of an original debt or debts is compared to a new debt or set of debts

COMPOUND INTEREST interest accumulated when the interest for each period is added to the principal before computing the interest for the next period

DAILY INTEREST interest calculated on the minimum daily balance and credited to the account at the end of the month

DECLINING BALANCE after each partial payment is made, it is the balance of the principal which is used to calculate the next value of accrued interest

DISCOUNTING AT SIMPLE INTEREST see *simple discount method*

EQUATION OF VALUE an equation which gives equivalent values between the original debts and the new debts on the comparison date at the specified interest rate

EXACT TIME the exact number of days used to express time as a fraction of a year

FOCAL DATE see *comparison date*

INTEREST the amount paid as a fee for borrowing money

LEAP YEARS those years which are divisible by 4, except for centuries, which must be divisible by 400; a year in which February has 29 days

LONG-TERM BORROWING obligations such as mortgages which are extended over a long period of time

MATURITY VALUE see *amount*

ORDINARY INTEREST used in international transactions, where each month is assumed to have 30 days and the year 360 days

PARTIAL PAYMENT the amount paid in partial settlement of a debt

PRESENT VALUE the value at the time of investment, such as the principal, or at any time, before the maturity date (due date)

PRINCIPAL the money borrowed

RATE OF INTEREST the percent of the principal which is paid as a fee for borrowing money, generally for one year

SHORT-TERM BORROWING obligations undertaken to obtain goods or cash for everyday services

SIMPLE DISCOUNT the difference between the amount and its present value; the same as simple interest

SIMPLE DISCOUNT METHOD the process of finding the present value of a given amount which is due on a future date

SIMPLE INTEREST interest paid only on the principal borrowed

9 Demand loans, discounted loans and negotiable instruments

Introduction

The topics covered in this chapter are relevant to the personal finance of the individual as well as to the finance of a business. An individual should be capable of comparing different types of loans which are available in order to make accurate decisions when alternatives exist.

A demand loan, for example, applies equally to personal and corporate finance. Since a demand loan is fully secured by suitable collateral, there is very little risk to the lending institutions and the rate is more favorable than that on other loans.

The late seventies and early eighties has seen many cases of bankruptcy of large and small companies. The high cost of finance has been blamed in many cases.

As we move into the late eighties, the need to exercise care in the structure of the financial obligations of a company or individual will become even more important.

Chapter Nine covers demand loans, discounted loans and negotiable instruments.

9.1 Demand Loans

A. BASIC CALCULATIONS

A DEMAND LOAN is a SECURED LOAN for which the security (bonds, term deposits, shares, etc.) is in the possession of the bank or financial institution giving the loan. Demand loans are issued at a lower rate than unsecured loans. The rate charged on demand loans depends on the credit worthiness of the borrower. Generally, the rate is 1% higher than the chartered bank prime rate. Interest is calculated on the daily balance and is payable monthly.

Since the chartered bank prime rate is subject to change, the rate of interest on a demand loan may change during the term of the loan. A demand loan is due whenever the payee decides to call it. However, repayment is usually arranged to suit the borrower who may pay all or part of the loan without notice or penalty.

Example 9.1a

A demand loan for $1 000 at 15% was made on June 1. On June 8, the rate was changed to 16%. If the loan is settled on June 23, how much interest is due?

NOTE: Interest is payable on the first day and not on the last day of the term.

SOLUTION:

Using Formula 8-1 $I = Pin$:
June 1 to June 8: 7 days

$$I = 1\ 000(.15)\left(\frac{7}{365}\right) = 2.877$$

June 8 to June 23: 15 days

$$I = 1\ 000(.16)\left(\frac{15}{365}\right) = 6.575$$

Total interest due = $9.45

Example 9.1b

On March 3, Sylvia Limited obtained a demand loan in the amount of $2 000 at 14%. On March 31, a payment of $500 was made and on April 6, the rate of interest was changed to 15%. (a) How much interest is due on April 3? (b) How much will settle the debt on April 23? (c) What is the total cost of financing the loan?

SOLUTION:

(a) On April 3, interest is calculated on the daily balance from March 3 to April 3.

March 3 to March 31 (28 days):
$P = \$2\ 000$
$i = 14\%$
$n = \dfrac{28}{365}$

$$I = Pin = 2\ 000(.14)\left(\frac{28}{365}\right)$$
$$= \$21.48$$

March 31 to April 3 (3 days):
$P = \$1\ 500\ (\$2\ 000 - \$500)$ (outstanding balance)
$i = 14\%$

$n = \dfrac{3}{365}$

$I = Pin = 1\ 500(.14)\left(\dfrac{3}{365}\right)$

        $= \$1.73$

Total amount of interest $= 21.48 + 1.73$
                        $= \$23.21$

(b) If the debt is settled on April 23, the outstanding balance plus interest from April 3 to April 23 is due.

April 3 to April 6 (3 days):
$P = \$1\ 500$ (outstanding balance)
$i = 14\%$

$n = \dfrac{3}{365}$

$I = Pin = 1\ 500(.14)\left(\dfrac{3}{365}\right)$

        $= \$1.73$

April 6 to April 23 (17 days):
$P = \$1\ 500$
$i = 15\%$ (rate changed April 6)

$n = \dfrac{17}{365}$

$I = Pin = 1\ 500(.15)\left(\dfrac{17}{365}\right)$

        $= \$10.48$

April 3 to April 23:
Interest expense $= 1.73 + 10.48 = \$ \quad 12.21$
Outstanding balance $= \quad \underline{1\ 500.00}$
                                   $\$1\ 512.21$
On April 23, $\$1\ 512.21$ will settle the debt.

(c) Total cost of financing March 3 to April 23:
March 3 to April 3 $\$23.21$
April 3 to April 23 $\underline{12.21}$
                             $\$35.42$

EXERCISE 9.1 / REFERENCE SECTION: A

In each of the following cases involving demand loans, find the unknown values:

Amount of loan	Interest rate	Period of loan	Amount of interest	Amount paid
1. $5 000	15.25%	30 days	$?	$?
2. ?	16.4%	16 days	21.57	?
3. 2 500	?	21 days	?	2 524.81
4. 3 000	18.25%	?	28.50	?

Statement Problems:

5. Alberta Gas has a demand loan for $25 000. During the month of June, the following rates were charged:

   June 1   16.25%
   June 7   16.5 %
   June 14   17   %
   June 21   16.75%
   June 28   17   %

   Find the amount of interest due on June 30th.

6. Refer to Problem 5. If Alberta Gas paid $5 000 on June 17, what is the total amount, principal plus interest, due on June 30th?

7. Mama's Pizza received a demand loan for $20 000 on June 1. What is the amount of the interest due on June 23 if the interest rate was 17% on June 1 and was changed to 16.75% on June 10?

8. Harry's Enterprise Limited borrowed $100 000 on demand on May 1. The rate of interest charged on that day was 17.5%. On May 11, the rate was changed to 18%. How much interest is due on May 23?

9. Ernie's Hardware Limited received a demand loan from Toronto-Dominion Bank on October 6, in the amount of $3 500. Ernie's Hardware agreed to have the interest expense deducted from a current account on the 6th of each month. What is the total interest expense incurred on December 6 if the interest rates were as follows:

   October 6   16.5%
   October 20   16.75%
   November 10   15.8%
   December 2   16.25%

10. Refer to Problem 9, and assume the interest rates are unchanged. Ernie's Hardware made the following payments:
    October 22 $ 200.00
    November 3 $1 000.00
    (a) What is the total interest expense on December 6, and (b) what is the balance due on December 6?

9.2 Discounted Loans—Interest Deducted in Advance

A. INTRODUCTION

When a discounted loan is made, the interest is usually computed on the basis of the maturity value, the final amount of the loan on the due date. The interest rate used in computing the loan is called the BANK DISCOUNT RATE, or simply the DISCOUNT RATE. The time used in computing is called the PERIOD OF DISCOUNT, which is the period from the date of discount to the maturity date. The interest thus computed is deducted immediately from the maturity value of the loan. This deduction is known as the BANK DISCOUNT, or INTEREST DEDUCTED IN ADVANCE. The value received by the borrower after the deduction is called the PROCEEDS.

Although discounted loans are rarely made today, the principle of bank discount is important in the discounting of negotiable instruments.

B. GENERAL COMPUTATION

In general, bank discount and proceeds may be expressed as follows:

BANK DISCOUNT = MATURITY VALUE × DISCOUNT RATE × PERIOD OF DISCOUNT
PROCEEDS = MATURITY VALUE − BANK DISCOUNT

In computing bank discount, the rate and the time must correspond to each other. The discount rate is usually stated as a yearly rate. Since the bank discount method is generally used for short-term borrowing, the period of discount normally is a fraction of a year. In practice, it will therefore be necessary to state the time in days when computing interest for short-term borrowing. When a fraction is expressed, the exact interest method, as discussed in Chapter Eight, Section 8.1, is followed.

Let P' = proceeds
$\quad S$ = maturity value
$\quad I'$ = bank discount or the interest in advance
$\quad d$ = annual discount rate
$\quad n$ = period of discount expressed in years

The above expressions may be written as follows:

$$\boxed{I' = Sdn} \qquad\qquad \longleftarrow Formula\ 9\text{-}1$$

$P' - S = I'$, or
$\quad = S - Sdn$, or factoring S,

$$\boxed{P' = S(1 - dn)} \qquad\qquad \longleftarrow Formula\ 9\text{-}2$$

Finding the Value of Bank Discount and Proceeds

To find the value of bank discount and proceeds, Formulas 9-1 and 9-2 are used as illustrated in Example 9.2a.

Example 9.2a

Bing Enterprise Limited obtained a discounted loan for 65 days with maturity value of $100 000. If the discount rate is 14.5%, (a) what is the discount amount, and (b) how much did Bing Enterprise Limited receive as the proceeds of the loan?

SOLUTION:

$S = \$100\ 000$
$d = 14.5\%$
$n = \dfrac{65}{365}$ (years)

$I' = Sdn = 100\ 000(.145)\left(\dfrac{65}{365}\right)$
$\qquad = \$2\ 582.19$ (discount)
$P' = S - I' = 100\ 000 - 2\ 582.19$
$\qquad\quad = \$97\ 417.81$ (proceeds received)

Or, $P' = S(1 - dn)$
$\qquad = 100\ 000\left[1 - (.145)\left(\dfrac{65}{365}\right)\right]$
$\qquad = 100\ 000(1 - .0258219)$
$\qquad = 100\ 000(.9741781)$
$\qquad = \$97\ 417.81$ (proceeds)
$I' = S - P'$
$I' = 100\ 000 - 97\ 417.81$
$\qquad = \$2\ 582.19$ (discount)

The solution is illustrated below:

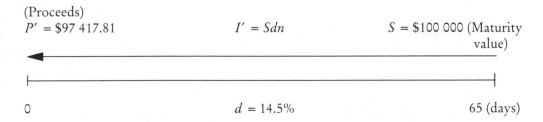

(Proceeds)
$P' = \$97\ 417.81$ $\qquad\qquad\qquad I' = Sdn \qquad\qquad\qquad S = \$100\ 000$ (Maturity value)

0 $\qquad\qquad\qquad\qquad\qquad d = 14.5\% \qquad\qquad\qquad\qquad$ 65 (days)

Finding the Maturity Value

To find the MATURITY VALUE, select either Formula 9-1 or 9-2. Examples 9.2b and 9.2c illustrate this selection.

Example 9.2b

Shelley's Footware Limited negotiated a discounted loan for which the discount charged was $476.71 for 60 days at 14.5% How much must Shelley's Footware repay?

SOLUTION:

$I' = \$476.71$

$d = 14.5\%$

$n = \dfrac{60}{365}$

$I' = Sdn$

$S = \dfrac{I'}{dn}$

$= \dfrac{476.71}{.145\left(\frac{60}{365}\right)}$

$= \$19\ 999.90$

Example 9.2c

Johnson wants \$2 450 in cash as the proceeds of a 146-day discounted loan from a bank which charges 10% discount. What is the loan that Johnson must pay on the maturity date?

SOLUTION:

$P' = 2\ 450$

$d = 10\%$

$n = \dfrac{146}{365}$

Substituting the values in Formula 9-2:

$P' = S(1 - dn)$

$2\ 450 = S\left[1 - (.10)\left(\dfrac{146}{365}\right)\right] = S(.96)$

$S = \dfrac{2\ 450}{.96}$

$= \$2\ 552.08$

NOTE: When both sides of the formula $P' = S(1 - dn)$ are divided by $(1 - dn)$, the following result is obtained:

$S = \dfrac{P'}{1 - dn}.$

The above result may be used directly in finding the maturity value for Example 9.2c.

Finding the Annual Discount Rate

To find the annual discount rate, d, or the rate of interest charged in advance, divide the discount I' by the product of the final amount S and the discount period n. This is based on Formula 9-1. When both sides of the formula $I' = Sdn$ are divided by Sn, the following result is obtained:

$$d = \frac{I'}{Sn}.$$

Example 9.2d

A man received a 73-day discounted loan of $550 from a bank. The proceeds were $539. What is the discount rate?

SOLUTION:

$S = 550$
$P' = 539$
$n = \dfrac{73}{365}$
$I' = S - P = 550 - 539 = \$11$

Substituting the values in Formula 9-1:
$I' = Sdn$

$$11 = 550(d)\left(\frac{73}{365}\right)$$

$$d = \frac{11}{550\left(\frac{73}{365}\right)} = \frac{1}{50\left(\frac{1}{5}\right)} = 10\%$$

Finding the Period of Discount

To find the period of discount n (in years), divide the discount I' by the product of the final amount S and the discount rate d. This is also based on Formula 9-1. When both sides of the formula $I' = Sdn$ are divided by Sd, the following result is obtained:

$$n = \frac{I'}{Sd}.$$

Example 9.2e

A man borrowed $800 from a bank which charged 12% interest in advance. He received $775.54. When will the loan be due?

SOLUTION:

$S = \$800$
$P' = \$775.54$
$d = 12\%$
$I' = S - P' = 800 - 775.54 = \$24.46$

Substituting the values in Formula 9-1:

$I' = Sdn$

$n = \dfrac{I'}{Sd}$

$n = \dfrac{24.46}{800(.12)} = .255$ years, or

$.255 \times 365 = 93$ days after the date of borrowing.

EXERCISE 9.2 / REFERENCE SECTIONS: A–B

In each of the following cases involving discounted loans, find the unknown values:

	Maturity Value (S)	Discount Rate (d)	Period of Discount (n)	Bank Discount (I')	Proceeds (P')
1.	$60 000	15%	60 days	?	?
2.	20 000	10%	? days	$200.00	?
3.	?	?	146 days	12.00	$ 788.00
4.	3 000	?	60 days	80.00	?
5.	2 400	12%	? days	?	2 342.40
6.	?	9%	? days	98.01	4 367.99
7.	9 000	?	75 days	225.00	?
8.	1 800	?	73 days	?	1 773.00
9.	?	8%	216 days	?	844.95
10.	?	11%	? days	5.97	894.00

Statement Problems:

11. On July 15, K.C. King received a discounted loan and paid $3 500 for the loan on October 16. If the rate charged is 18% interest in advance, how much were the proceeds?

12. On April 1, James Timer obtained a 60-day discounted loan of $4 200 at 22% interest in advance. How much did Timer receive from the loan? On what date does he have to pay his loan?

13. Jeannette needs $65 000 in cash. If a bank lends her the money and charges 17% interest in advance, how much must she pay after 45 days?

14. Todd desires $3 650 in cash as the proceeds of a discounted loan from a bank which charges 18.5% discount. What is the loan that Todd must pay after 150 days?

15. A woman borrowed $780 for 73 days. The proceeds were $760. What was the discount rate?

16. Shaw received $1 200 in cash as the proceeds from a discounted loan. After 120 days he paid $1 248. What was the interest rate charged by the bank in advance?

17. Helen paid $3 600 for a discounted loan from a bank which charged 10% interest

in advance. The proceeds were $3 546. In how many days after the borrowing did she repay the loan?

18. Frank received $2 723 in cash as the proceeds from a discounted loan of $2 800. The discount rate was 16%. Find the discount period in years.

19. Dixon and Sons Limited is negotiating a loan of $100 000 for 30 days. They have been offered the following alternatives: (a) a 20% demand loan, or (b) a discounted loan at 14.5%. Assuming that the conditions for receiving these loans are the same, which of these alternatives should they choose?

20. Fairview Limited is seeking a loan of $200 000 for 20 days. They can obtain either (a) a demand loan for the $200 000 at 19%, or (b) a demand loan for $100 000 at 18.75% and a discounted loan for the remaining $100 000 at 16.5% interest in advance. Which of these alternatives should they select if the conditions for receiving credit are the same?

9.3 Nature of Negotiable Instruments

NEGOTIABLE INSTRUMENTS are written promises or orders to pay money. They are transferable or saleable by one person to another person or to a bank. Frequently, negotiable instruments are discounted by the bank discount method. Generally speaking, there are two types of negotiable instruments, promissory notes and bills of exchange.

A.   PROMISSORY NOTES

PROMISSORY NOTES, or simply NOTES, have two parties, the MAKER, who makes the promise to pay, and the PAYEE, to whom the promise is made. (See Figure 9-1).

Figure 9-1
A Promissory Note

$ 2 500 | Yonge & Sheppard Ave., Toronto | October 2 19 84

Address of Branch

FOR VALUE RECEIVED, I promise to pay to The Toronto-Dominion Bank or order at the ABOVE BRANCH the sum of

Two Thousand Five Hundred   00 /100 Dollars

(hereinafter called the "principal") with interest at ___17.5___% per annum calculated and payable monthly, not in advance, as well after as before maturity and both before and after default, in instalments of _____ /100 Dollars each (to be applied first in payment of interest due and the balance, if any, of such instalment to be applied in reduction of principal) on the _____ day of each and every month in each and every year from and including the _____ day of _____, 19_____ up to and including the ___4th___ day of _____December_____, 19 84 when the balance, if any, of the principal and interest thereon shall also become due and payable. In case said instalments, or any of them, are not paid as the same become due, the whole unpaid principal and interest accrued shall forthwith become due and payable at the option of the holder of this note. In the event that the undersigned shall fail to make any of the payments above provided for, the undersigned promises to pay interest at the nominal annual percentage rate expressed above as the cost of borrowing in this transaction on each such defaulted payment from the date of default until payment.

When not in default the undersigned shall have the right to prepay all or any of the principal of this note at any time without notice or bonus, provided that any partial prepayment(s) shall be applied in inverse order of maturity.

CONSUMER LOAN NOTE
(AMOUNT $50,000 OR LESS
NOT SECURED BY COLLATERAL
LAND MORTGAGE)

11440 (4–83)   No. _____

Courtesy Toronto-Dominion Bank

The following information is found in this promissory note:

Face value: $2 500
Date of Note: October 2, 1984
Term of the Note: 60 days
Interest Rate: 17.5%
Maturity Date: 60 days after October 2, 1984 or December 1, 1984
Legal Due Date: December 4, 1984 (maturity date plus 3 days grace)
Maturity Value: $2 500 + 2 500(17.5) $\left(\frac{63}{365}\right)$
                      = $2 500 + 75.51 = $2 575.51

Promissory notes may also be payable on demand (see Figure 9-2). A demand note is due whenever the payee decides to call it. However, repayment is usually arranged to suit the maker. Interest is calculated on the daily balance and is payable once per month.

Figure 9-2
A Demand Promissory Note

$\$$ __5 000.00__   July 1   19 84

ON DEMAND after date for value received _____ I _____ promise to pay to
_____ Margaret Telfor _____ or order at **THE ROYAL BANK OF CANADA**
____ Winnipeg, Manitoba ____ the sum of _____ Five Thousand _____ 00/100 **DOL-**
LARS with interest thereon calculated and payable monthly at a rate equal to The Royal Bank of Canada's Prime Interest Rate per annum in effect from time to time plus ___2___% per annum as well after as before maturity, default and judgment, with interest on overdue interest at the same rate as the principal. At the date of this note such Prime Interest Rate is ___10___% per annum.
Prime Interest Rate is the annual rate of interest announced from time to time by The Royal Bank of Canada as a reference rate then in effect for determining interest rates on Canadian dollar commercial loans in Canada.
This note is given for an advance by the said Bank to the undersigned pursuant to the application for credit and promise to give security made by the undersigned to the said Bank and dated the _____ First _____ day of
_____ July _____ 19 84 ____, and any application(s) for credit and promise(s) to give security supplemental thereto. The undersigned hereby promise(s) and agree(s) to give to the said Bank from time to time and as often as requested by the said Bank warehouse receipts and/or bills of lading covering the property described in the said application(s) for credit and promise(s) to give security or any part thereof which is now or may hereafter be covered by warehouse receipts or bills of lading, as security for the said advance. No such security shall be merged in any subsequent security or be taken to be substituted for any security previously acquired.

NAME:
LOAN ACCT. NO.
CR. ACCT. NO.   CASUAL
REN.$ DISCOUNT
LOAN NO.   MGR. INIT.   ✓

Courtesy Royal Bank of Canada

The following information is found on this note:

Face Value: $5 000.00
Date of Note: July 1, 1984
Monthly Interest: Prime Rate + 2% (12% when prime rate is 10%)
Legal Due Date: On demand
Maturity Value: $5 000 plus any outstanding interest

B.   *BILLS OF EXCHANGE*

A **BILL OF EXCHANGE** has three parties: the **DRAWER**, the person who draws the bill; the

DRAWEE, the person to whom the bill is addressed and who is ordered to pay the bill; and the PAYEE, the person to whom the payment is made. The drawee is not bound to pay the bill unless he accepts the order of payment from the drawer. When the bill is accepted by the drawee, he immediately becomes the ACCEPTOR and is liable for the bill.

The most frequently used bills of exchange in commercial practice are CHEQUES and DRAFTS. A cheque is always drawn upon a bank by the drawee and is always payable upon demand. Drafts are classified as sight drafts or time drafts. A draft which is payable at sight is called a SIGHT DRAFT. Cheques and sight drafts are demand bills of exchange; that is, they are payable as soon as they are presented for payment. There is no need for a discount process in making payments with demand bills. A TIME DRAFT, however, is payable at a future time, either within a certain number of days *after sight*, *after date* (see Figure 9-3) or on a specified date (see Figure 9-4).

Maturity Date

The MATURITY DATE is the date on which the note or draft is due. The maturity date of an after-sight draft is determined by counting the days after the date on which the drawee accepts the draft. The maturity date of an after-date draft or note is determined by counting the number of days after the date on which the instrument is drawn.

Days of Grace

Except for demand notes and notes marked 'no grace,' three days called DAYS OF GRACE are allowed on all negotiable instruments. The three days are included in the number of days used when computing interest or discount on notes or drafts.

Legal Due Date

When days of grace apply, the LEGAL DUE DATE of a note or draft is three days after the maturity date. If the note is marked 'no grace,' the legal due date and the maturity date are the same. Demand notes are due on demand and no days of grace apply.

Figure 9-3
An After-Date Time Draft

248 WHARNCLIFFE RD. N. & OXFORD STREET
P.O. BOX 216
LONDON, ONTARIO
N6A 4V8

$ 3 500.00 PRINCIPAL — DUE July 20, 1985 D
$ INTEREST — June 20 19 85
$ TOTAL
Thirty days — AFTER DATE FOR VALUE RECEIVED I

PROMISE
TO PAY TO THE TORONTO-DOMINION BANK OR ORDER AT THE TORONTO-DOMINION BANK HERE,

THE SUM OF Thirty-five hundred -----------------00/100 DOLLARS
WITH INTEREST AT THE RATE OF %PER ANNUM AS WELL AFTER AS BEFORE MATURITY

Mia Low

SAMPLE

Courtesy Toronto-Dominion Bank

The following information is found in this after-date time draft:

Face Value: $3 500
Date of the Draft: June 20, 1985
Term of the Note: 30 days after date
Interest Rate: None
Maturity Date: 30 days after June 20, 1985 or July 20, 1985
Maturity Value: $3 500
Legal Due Date: July 23, 1985 (maturity date plus 3 days grace)

Figure 9-4
A Trade Acceptance (A Type of Draft)

No. 36	**Toronto** October 12	**19** 85
To S. P. Simpson	Horton, Alberta	
On December 3,1985 (no grace) **Pay to the order of** Ourselves		
Nine hundred and eighty 00/100 -------------- **Dollars, ($** 980.00 **)**		

The obligation of the acceptor hereof arises out of the purchase of goods from the drawer. The drawee may accept this bill payable at any bank, banker, or trust company in Canada which such drawee may designate.

Accepted at Horton,Alberta on Oct.18 19 85

Payable at The Unity **Bank** The Grover Co.

Bank Location Horton, Alberta

Buyers Signature *S.P.Simpson*

By Agent or Officer _____ By *D.C.Fort* Manager

(TRADE ACCEPTANCE) — SAMPLE

The following information is found on this trade acceptance:

Face Value: $980
Date of Draft: October 12, 1985
Accepted Date: October 18, 1985
Term of the Draft: 46 days (from October 18, 1985 to December 3, 1985)
Interest Rate: None
Maturity Date: December 3, 1985
Maturity Value: $980
Legal Due Date: December 3, 1985 (no days grace)

A promissory note may or may not bear interest, but a draft generally bears none. If no interest is mentioned in the note, it is assumed to be non-interest-bearing, and the face value is the maturity value. However, the omission of a stated interest rate does not necessarily indicate that the original debt bears no interest. The interest, if any, might have been added to the original debt when the face value was determined.

C. *BORROWING IN THE CANADIAN MONEY MARKET*

The CANADIAN MONEY MARKET is a meeting place for suppliers and users of short-term capital. The *Bank of Canada*, the chartered banks and the investment dealers play a special role in the money market. However, all levels of government, financial institutions of all types, non-financial corporations and individual investors use and supply short-term capital.

Corporations wishing to raise short-term funds on the money market use commercial paper or banker's acceptance drafts.

COMMERCIAL PAPER is an unsecured promissory note issued by corporations and sold in the open market to institutional investors. Commercial paper is normally available in a minimum amount of $100 000 and may be interest-bearing or priced at a discount. Commercial paper has a maximum term of 365 days however, most notes are issued to mature in 30 to 90 days. Commercial paper allows corporations to borrow at a more favorable rate than the bank prime rate.

A BANKER'S ACCEPTANCE is a negotiable time draft drawn on a chartered bank by a corporate borrower (Figure 9-5). An investor who purchases the banker's acceptance is investing in the credit of the bank accepting the bill of exchange. Banker's acceptances are usually issued in the amount of $100 000 or multiples thereof, for terms ranging from 30 to 90 days. These instruments are eligible for re-discount at the *Bank of Canada* as collateral for day loans, with the chartered banks. Banker's acceptances allow corporations to borrow at a lower rate than at a bank but at a higher rate than for issuing commercial paper.

Figure 9-5
Banker's Acceptance

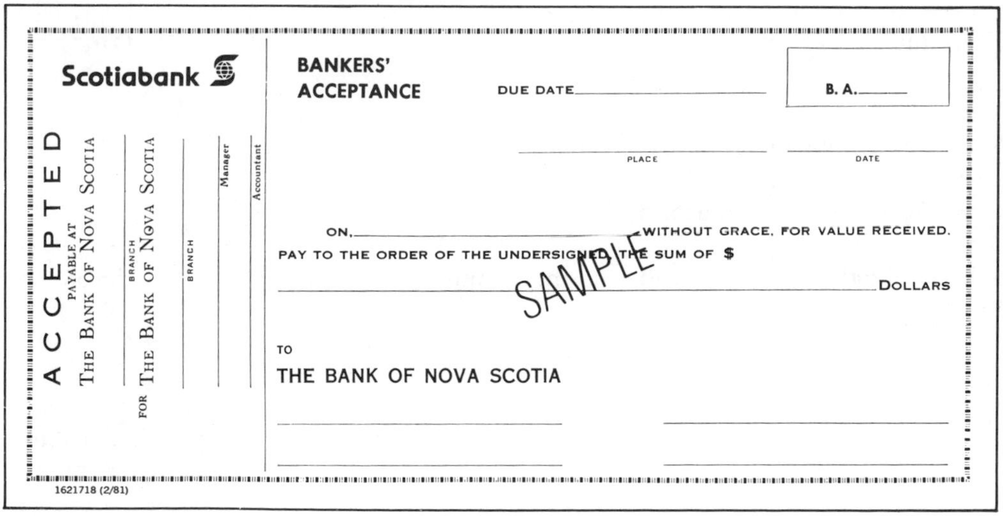
Scotiabank
BANKERS' ACCEPTANCE
DUE DATE
B. A.
PLACE
DATE
ACCEPTED
PAYABLE AT THE BANK OF NOVA SCOTIA
BRANCH
FOR THE BANK OF NOVA SCOTIA
BRANCH
Manager
Accountant
ON, WITHOUT GRACE, FOR VALUE RECEIVED.
PAY TO THE ORDER OF THE UNDERSIGNED THE SUM OF $
DOLLARS
SAMPLE
TO
THE BANK OF NOVA SCOTIA
1621718 (2/81)

Courtesy Bank of Nova Scotia

9.4 Discounting Negotiable Instruments

The basic principles of discounting a note or a draft at a bank are the same as those of obtaining a discounted loan, that is, a loan on which interest is deducted in advance. The following examples are used to illustrate the problems involved in discounting negotiable instruments by the bank discount method. Observe that when the term of a note or a draft is stated in *days*, the *exact time* is used in determining the maturity date and the period of discount (see Example 9.4a). However, when the term is stated in *months*, the corresponding date in the *due month* is used in determining the maturity date. If there is no date in the due month corresponding to the date of issue, the last date of the due month is used. The legal due date is then the maturity date plus three days of grace.

A.   DISCOUNTING NON-INTEREST-BEARING NOTES

Example 9.4a
After Harry Jones had accepted the draft for $3 500 (refer to Figure 9-3), Mia Low discounted the draft at the Bank of Nova Scotia on June 20. How much did Low receive if the draft was discounted at 17.5%.

SOLUTION:

The maturity value of the note: $S = \$3\ 500$. The discount rate $d = 17.5\%$.

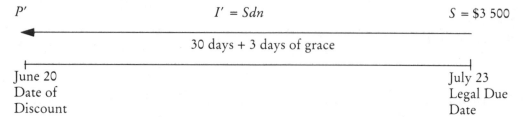

Substituting these values in the formula $I' = Sdn$:

$$I' = 3\ 500(.175)\left(\frac{33}{365}\right) = \$55.38.$$

Substituting the values of S and I' in the formula $P' = S - I'$: $P' = 3\ 500 - 55.38 = \$3\ 444.62$.

Example 9.4b
A three-month, non-interest-bearing note dated on March 2, 1984, was discounted in a bank on March 24 at 18.25%. The proceeds were $1 470. Find the face value of the note.

SOLUTION:

The face value of the non-interest-bearing note is the maturity value S on the legal due date. The maturity date is June 2, or the corresponding date three months after March 2. The legal due date is June 5. The period of discount is 73 days, from March 24 to June 5.

$P' = 1\ 470$

$d = 18.25\%$

$n = \dfrac{73}{365}$

Thus, $\dfrac{1\ 470}{1 - (18.25\%)(\frac{73}{365})} = \dfrac{1\ 470}{1 - .036\ 5}$

$= \dfrac{1\ 470}{.963\ 5}$

$= \$1\ 525.69$

B.   DISCOUNTING INTEREST-BEARING NOTES

In Example 9.4a, the discount is computed from the maturity value, which is given. However, the maturity value is usually not given on an interest-bearing note. Thus, in discounting an interest-bearing note, take the following two steps:

STEP (1) Find the maturity value:
Add the interest to the face value of the note. Compute the interest according to the rate and the time stipulated on the note. (Use the formula $S = P(1 + in)$, where S is the maturity value and P is the face value).

STEP (2) Find the proceeds:
Discount the maturity value. Compute the interest in advance (or the discount) according to the discount rate charged by the buyer (or the bank) and the period of discount, which is from the date of discount to the legal due date. (Use the formula $P' = S - I' = S - Sdn$).

Example 9.4c

Bartelier and Sons Limited had a note for $2 500 with interest at 17.5%. The note was dated October 2, 1984, and the maturity date was 60 days after date (refer to Figure 9-1). If on October 31, 1984, the note was discounted at a bank at a discount rate of 18%, how much will Bartelier and Sons Limited receive for the note?

SOLUTION:

STEP (1) Find the maturity value according to the face value, the rate, and the time stipulated on the note.

$P = 2\ 500$

$i = 17.5\%$

$$n = \frac{63}{365} \text{ (60 days + 3 days of grace)}$$

Substituting the values in the formula $S = P(1 + in)$:

$$S = 2\ 500 \left[1 + (17.5\%)\left(\frac{63}{365}\right)\right] = \$2\ 575.51$$

STEP (2) Find the proceeds. Discount the maturity value according to the discount rate and the period of discount.

$S = 2\ 575.51$ (the maturity value of the note)
$d = 18\%$ (the discount rate charged by the bank)
$n = 34$ days (from October 31, 1983, the date of discount, to December 4, 1983, the legal due date)

Substituting these values in the formula $I' = Sdn$:

$$I' = 2\ 575.51\ (.18)\left(\frac{34}{365}\right) = \$43.18$$

Substituting the values of S and I' in the formula $P' = S - I'$:
$P' = 2\ 575.51 - 43.18 = \$2\ 532.33$

This computation may be tabulated as follows:

Face value of note	$2 500.00
ADD: Interest on note	
(63 days at 17.5%)	75.51
Maturity value of note	$2 575.51
LESS: Discount on the maturity value	
(34 days at 18%)	43.18
Proceeds of note discounted	$2 532.33

This example is diagrammed as follows:

(1) Maturity Value—Accumulate the face value at 17.5% for 63 days

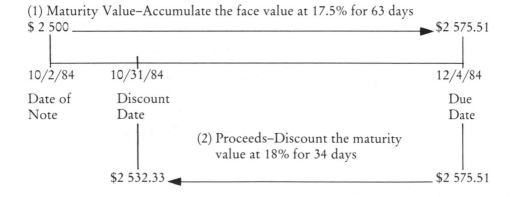

EXERCISE 9.4 / REFERENCE SECTIONS: A–B

For each of the following promissory notes, find the (a) legal due date, (b) maturity value, (c) discount period, (d) discount, and (e) proceeds:

	Date of Note	Face Value	Interest Rate On Note	Term	Date of Discount	Bank Discount Rate
1.	1/6/83	$2 000	12%	30 days	1/16/83	10%
2.	2/10/83	1 200	15%	45 days	2/25/83	14.5%
3.	4/18/83	1 800	None	2 months	4/29/83	16.2%
4.	6/14/84	570	15.3%	120 days	7/14/84	15%
5.	8/5/84	4 200	17%	90 days	9/4/84	16.25%
6.	9/16/84	1 540	13.25%	3 months	11/16/84	12%
7.	10/1/85	2 500	14.5%	2 months	11/1/85	15.25%
8.	1/15/85	880	12.5%	180 days	5/15/85	13.5%
9.	3/24/86	1 620	17%	150 days	6/7/85	17.5%
10.	4/12/86	630	None	4 months	7/2/86	16%

Statement Problems:

11. On July 3, Herbert discounted a 90-day non-interest-bearing note for $1 500, dated June 5, at a bank which charges 14.6% discount. How much should Herbert receive as the proceeds of the note?

12. On June 30, 1985, the draft in Figure 9.3 was discounted at 15%. What are the discount and the proceeds?

13. Johnson receives $4 455 in cash as the proceeds of a 45-day, non-interest-bearing note from a bank that charges 16.25% discount. What is the face value of the note? (Assume no grace).

14. A non-interest-bearing note (no grace) is discounted at 14.25%, 180 days before maturity. The proceeds were $3 600. What is the face value of the note?

15. On November 2, 1985, the trade acceptance in Figure 9-4 was discounted by the Grover Co. at a local bank which charged a discount of 15.5%. What are the discount and the proceeds?

16. J.K. Osbourne has a 90-day (no grace) note dated May 16, with face value of $2 800 and bearing interest at 15.4%. When should he discount it at 16% in order to receive $2 853.28 as the proceeds?

17. A.C. Tent received a 90-day, 13.25% note dated March 6, for $2 400 from B.F. Rice. Tent discounted the note at 14.5% at a bank on March 16. What are the (a) legal due date, (b) maturity date, (c) discount period, (d) discount, and (e) proceeds?

18. A 60-day, 15% interest-bearing note of $1 500 is discounted at 15.5% 30 days before maturity. What are the (a) maturity value, (b) discount, and (c) proceeds? (Assume no grace).

19. A note for $2 100 at 16% for 180 days is discounted at 16.5% in a bank 120 days before maturity. What is the discount? What are the proceeds? (Assume no grace).

20. D.H. Wilson has a 60-day note for $2 500 at 17% interest. The maturity date is May 6. If the note is discounted on March 17 at 17.5%, how much will Wilson receive?

21. A 120-day note bearing 18.25% interest is discounted at 17% 90 days before maturity. If the discount is $573.75, what is the face value? (Assume no grace).

22. Johnson signed a 60-day, no grace, non-interest-bearing note for $2 000 and discounted it at 16% at the Royal Bank. If the note was immediately rediscounted by the bank at 15% at the Bank of Canada, what is the profit of the Royal Bank?

23. A 180-day (no grace) note dated August 5 and bearing interest at 16.25% is discounted on December 8 at 17%. The proceeds are $3 600. What is the face value?

EXERCISE / CHAPTER REVIEW

1. The Abby Warehouse Company must raise funds in the amount of $600 000, which they expect to repay in 90 days. Which of the following methods of obtaining the funds will generate less interest expense and by how much? (a) A demand loan at 16.75%. (b) A banker's acceptance draft at 16.5% discount (no grace).

2. Company A and Company B must each raise $200 000 for 60 days for expansion. Company A negotiated a demand loan at 17.3% while Company B issued commercial paper (no grace) at 17.25% discount. Which one will have the higher interest expense and by how much?

3. Karl and Company paid $500 000 to settle a 30-day loan discounted at 17.25%. What were the proceeds?

4. Katrina Hardware paid $300 000 to settle a 60-day discounted loan at 16.5%. What were the proceeds?

5. A man received a 90-day discounted loan of $200 000. The proceeds were $191 986.31. What is the discount rate?

6. Find the bank discount rate on a discounted note if the amount is $300 000, the discount is $6 000, and discount time is 60 days. (Assume no grace).

7. Lynn borrowed $1 000 from a bank which charged 10% interest in advance. She received $980 from the loan. For how long did she borrow the money?

8. Margaret received $671.50 in cash as the proceeds from a discounted loan of $680. The discount rate was 10%. Find the discount period in days.

9. A non-interest-bearing note was discounted in a bank 45 days before maturity at 12%. The proceeds were $597. What was the face value of the note? (Assume no grace).

10. A non-interest-bearing note was discounted in a bank 90 days before maturity at 15.3%. Find the face value of the note if the proceeds were $197.50. (Assume no grace).

11. Nancy had a note for $800 with an interest rate of 16.25%. It was dated on April 7, 1984 and the maturity date was 60 days after date. On April 22, 1984, the note was discounted at a discount rate of 17.5%. How much did Nancy receive as the proceeds from the discounting?
12. A 90-day note (no grace) bearing 17.25% interest is discounted 30 days before it is due at 18%. If the discount is $8.20, what is the face value of the note? What are the proceeds?
13. Discount $2 000 for 90 days at 18% by using (a) the bank discount method, and (b) the simple interest method. What are the discount and the proceeds by method (a)? What are the present value and the discount by method (b)? How much difference exists between the two types of discounts?
14. Otis borrowed $800 in cash but paid $815 at the end of 45 days to the lender. (a) Consider the difference of $15 as the interest deducted in advance from the maturity value of $815. Find the bank discount rate. (b) Consider the $15 as the interest added to the principal of $800. Find the simple interest rate.

Summary of Formulae

$I' = Sdn$	*Formula 9-1*	Used to find the bank discount where interest is deducted in advance.
$P' = S(1 - dn)$	*Formula 9-2*	Used to find the proceeds.

Glossary

ACCEPTOR the drawee, having accepted the bill of exchange, who is immediately liable for its payment

BANK DISCOUNT the interest computed on a discounted loan, deducted at time of discount from the maturity value

BANK DISCOUNT RATE see *discount rate*

BANKER'S ACCEPTANCE negotiable time draft drawn on a chartered bank by a corporate borrower

BILLS OF EXCHANGE cheques and drafts

CANADIAN MONEY MARKET a meeting place for users and suppliers of short-term capital

CHEQUE a bill of exchange drawn on a commercial bank and payable on demand

COMMERCIAL PAPER an unsecured promissory note issued by corporations and sold in the open market to institutional investors

DAYS OF GRACE three days allowed on all negotiable instruments, except demand notes or notes marked 'no grace'; days of grace are included in the number of days used in computing interest on discount

DEMAND LOAN a secured loan for which the security (bonds, term deposits, etc.) is in the possession of the lending institution

DISCOUNT RATE the interest rate used in computing discounted loans (interest in advance)

DRAFT a bill of exchange which occurs in two classifications; see *sight draft* and *time draft*

DRAWEE the person to whom a bill of exchange is addressed and who is ordered to pay

DRAWER the person who draws a bill of exchange

INTEREST DEDUCTED IN ADVANCE see *bank discount*

LEGAL DUE DATE the date a note or draft is legally due when 'days of grace' is involved; if 'no grace' allowed, same as maturity date

MAKER the person making the promise to pay

MATURITY DATE the date on which a note or draft is due

MATURITY VALUE the final amount of a note or loan on the legal due date or the maturity date

NEGOTIABLE INSTRUMENTS written promises or orders to pay money which are transferable

NOTES see *promissory notes*

PAYEE the person to whom a payment is made

PERIOD OF DISCOUNT the time used in computing discounted loans; the period from the date of discount to the legal due date

PROCEEDS the value of a loan received by the borrower after the bank discount has been deducted

PROMISSORY NOTES written promises to pay

SECURED LOAN a loan for which collateral has been put up

SIGHT DRAFT demand bills of exchange; payable as soon as they are presented for payment

TIME DRAFT draft payable at a future time; either within a certain number of days after sight, after date or on a specified date

Consumer credit 10

Introduction

In the past decade, many factors have influenced the increased demand for credit for personal use, called CONSUMER CREDIT. Among these are the rapid increase in population and the changing trends in employment, incomes and spending and saving patterns.

By the late seventies, if you were in the eighteen to thirty-five age group, were head of a family with children in their teens or younger, and were earning $10 000 to $30 000 per year, the probability of your having some debt obligation was very high.

The changing attitude towards debt should not necessarily be viewed in a negative way. There are certain advantages to planned debt. After all, planned debt is simply paying for the use of someone elses money. Planned debt results from the desire of the CONSUMERS of today to satisfy their aspirations; that is to satisfy their wants as well as their needs. Another factor which has influenced the trend towards increase in debt obligations is a greater sense of financial security. Many of the items for which the consumer saved in the past are now taken care of by certain plans. For example, there are health insurance plans, pension plans, social insurance plans and unemployment insurance plans, to name a few. The working wife has also resulted in greater economic stability for the family. The two income family can now afford much more than the single income family of the past.

The shift towards service industries rather than agrarian industries has resulted in more workers with regular paycheques and has thus contributed to attaining aspirations through borrowing or instalment buying. An additional factor may be the security provided by financial assets, such as the equity built up in one's home. The easy availability of credit cards has also been a contributing factor.

The late seventies and early eighties has seen a change in attitudes towards debt. There is now less emphasis on total ownership and more emphasis on services. This trend makes it essential that the consumer be aware of the credit options which are available and knowledgeable about the different types of loans and the costs which are associated with these loans.

Chapter Ten covers credit regulations and credit rating, variable credit, consumer loans, interest rate calculations, instalment loan schedules, rebates–the Rule of 78, and credit do's and don'ts. The glossary includes not only credit terms discussed in this chapter, but also numerous other credit terms the student should be aware of.

10.1 Credit Regulations and Credit Rating

A.   CREDIT REGULATIONS

Consumer credit is generally provided by the chartered banks, trust companies, credit unions, caisses populaires, consumer loan companies, sales finance companies, retailers and department stores. The federal government has jurisdiction over banks, bills of exchange, interest rates and bankruptcy. The provincial governments have jurisdiction over property and civil rights and contractual agreements. Regulations governing credit are therefore set at two levels of government.

Under existing legislation, lending institutions are required to state the cost of credit in dollars and cents as well as the corresponding annual rate of interest. Banks are regulated under the *Bank Act*[1], while loan and trust companies are regulated by the *Loan and Trust Company Act*. Other pieces of legislation affecting consumer credit are the *Bills of Exchange Act* and the *Consumer Protection Act*.

B.   CREDIT RATING

Your CREDIT RATING is a record of your credit history. This record includes most of your credit transactions. Information about how much you borrow, from whom, the date of the transaction and how you meet your payments may be included. Each credit item listed may be given a rate.

Under the *Consumer Reporting Act*, you have the right to examine your record. In order to examine your record, you should visit the CREDIT BUREAU nearest you, during business hours. The *Consumer Reporting Act* also specifies the type of information which may be reported. Under the act, you have the right to correct false or misleading information.

10.2 Variable Credit

One of the most widely used forms of credit is VARIABLE CREDIT. Variable credit is provided when a LENDER makes credit available to the borrower from time to time for the purchase of goods and services. Bank credit cards, charge cards and charge accounts are examples of variable credit. The *Consumer Protection Act* requires those who offer variable credit to provide the borrower, before credit is granted, with a written statement of the finance charges (cost of borrowing) which are assessed on any unpaid balance, stated both as an annual rate and in dollars and cents. The lender is also required to provide the borrower with a statement at the end of each payment period showing

---

[1] Canada. Laws, Statutes, etc. *The Banks and Banking Law Revision Act, 1980*. 29 Eliz. II, 1980-83, c. 40.

(a)   the outstanding balance at the beginning of the period (previous balance)
(b)   the amount of credit extended to the account and the date of such credit (purchases/charges)
(c)   the finance charges for the period (credit service charge)
(d)   the outstanding balance for the period (new balance).

The following is an example of such a statement.

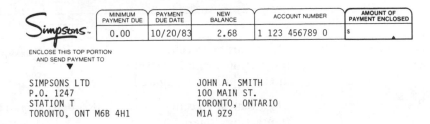

MINIMUM PAYMENT DUE	PAYMENT DUE DATE	NEW BALANCE	ACCOUNT NUMBER	AMOUNT OF PAYMENT ENCLOSED
0.00	10/20/83	2.68	1 123 456789 0	$

ENCLOSE THIS TOP PORTION
AND SEND PAYMENT TO
▼

SIMPSONS LTD   JOHN A. SMITH
P.O. 1247   100 MAIN ST.
STATION T   TORONTO, ONTARIO
TORONTO, ONT M6B 4H1   M1A 9Z9

PLEASE WRITE YOUR ACCOUNT NUMBER ON THE
BACK OF YOUR CHEQUE OR MONEY ORDER.

ACCOUNT NUMBER	CREDIT LINE	AVAILABLE CREDIT	STATEMENT DATE	PAYMENT DUE DATE	PAST DUE AMOUNT	MINIMUM PAYMENT DUE
1 123 456789 0	2000	1997	09/25/83	10/20/83	0.00	0.00

DATE MO. DAY	REFERENCE	DESCRIPTION	AMOUNT *
0826	0826P907T000046VU	PAYMENT - THANK YOU CREDIT SERVICE CHARGE	44.21- 0.06

PREVIOUS BALANCE	PAYMENTS	RETURNS AND CREDITS	PURCHASES / CHARGES	CREDIT SERVICE CHARGE	NEW BALANCE
46.83 −	44.21 −	0.00 +	0.00 +	0.06 =	2.68

* PLEASE NOTE THAT A MINUS SIGN (−) FOLLOWING AN AMOUNT SIGNIFIES A PAYMENT, RETURN OR CREDIT.

SEND INQUIRIES TO:
   SIMPSONS ONTARIO
   P.O. BOX 67 STATION A SCARBOROUGH, M1K 5B9   416-111-0000
02912 (0383)   PLEASE SEE REVERSE FOR IMPORTANT INFORMATION

Courtesy Simpsons Ltd.

Up to May 31, 1983, there was no service charge to the consumer for the use of bank credit cards. Revenue for the use of these cards was obtained from

(a) the interest paid by users who did not pay by the due date
(b) the merchants who accept these credit cards; these merchants pay 2.5% to 6% discount for the service.

The following charges were instituted by the banks and trust companies during 1983:

Issuer	User Fee	Interest on Balance
Canadian Imperial Bank of Commerce Visa	$12 a year, or 15 cents per transaction with 50-cent per month minimum; August 1	18.6 percent; August 1
Royal Bank Visa	$12 a year or 15 cents per transaction; June 1	18.6 percent; June 1
Toronto-Dominion Bank Visa	$12 a year or $6 a year plus 10 cents per transaction; August 1	18.6 percent; August 1
Bank of Nova Scotia Visa	15 cents per transaction to a maximum of $1 per month; September 1	18.6 percent; August 1
Bank of Montreal MasterCard	None, no decision made to introduce them	21 percent
Canada Trust MasterCard	$1 for every month a statement is issued	18.45 percent

A.   *VARIABLE CREDIT INTEREST CHARGES*

The rate of interest charged for credit by the use of bank cards, charge cards and CHARGE ACCOUNTS varies among the companies and the types of accounts. However, this type of credit is generally more expensive that other types of credit available to the consumer. Monthly interest charges are generally based on the previous month's BALANCE and may be calculated daily or monthly.

Example 10.2a
Francine's statement from Visa showed the following:
Statement date: June 16
Payment due date: July 7
Previous balance: $ 0.00
New balance: $359.00
Interest: .05095% daily rate or 18.6% annual rate
If Francine pays the full amount on July 10, what amount of credit service charge will appear on her next statement dated July 14?

CANADIAN IMPERIAL BANK OF COMMERCE **BANQUE CANADIENNE IMPÉRIALE DE COMMERCE**

CENTRE CHARGEX CENTRE

PAYMENT DUE DATE DATE D'ÉCHÉANCE DU VERSEMENT	MONTH MOIS	DAY JOUR	YEAR AN

ENTER AMOUNT OF PAYMENT INSCRIRE LE MONTANT DU VERSEMENT	$

ACCOUNT NUMBER
NUMÉRO DU COMPTE

YOUR NEW BALANCE
VOTRE NOUVEAU SOLDE

MINIMUM PAYMENT DUE
VERSEMENT MINIMUM ÉCHU

CANADIAN IMPERIAL BANK OF COMMERCE **BANQUE CANADIENNE IMPÉRIALE DE COMMERCE**

CENTRE CHARGEX CENTRE

STATEMENT DATE DATE DU RELEVÉ		ACCOUNT NUMBER NUMÉRO DU COMPTE
06 . 16 . 83 M-M D-J Y-A	P. O. Box 4058, Terminal A TORONTO, ONT. M5W 1L8	123 456 789

FOR STATEMENT INQUIRIES - PLEASE CALL
POUR DE PLUS AMPLES DÉTAILS CONCERNANT
LE RELEVÉ, VEUILLEZ TÉLÉPHONER AU

DATE MTH/DAY MOIS/JOUR	REFERENCE NO. RÉFÉRENCE Nº	PARTICULARS DÉTAILS	AMOUNT MONTANT
05 19	01D090525	SIMON'S RESTAURANT TORONTO ON	40.82
06 06	02A000608	PAYMENT THANK YOU – PAIEMENT MERCI	375.01
06 08	03D930608	IMPERIAL OIL LIMITED/ESSO	302.18
06 08	04D930608	IMPERIAL OIL LIMITED/ESSO	16.00

REDUCE OR AVOID INTEREST CHARGES BY MAKING YOUR VISA
PAYMENT PRIOR TO 3:00 P.M. ON THE PAYMENT DUE DATE AT
ANY COMMERCE BRANCH DISPLAYING THE INTERBRANCH BANKING
SIGN.

CX 103B-83 (AUG)

CREDIT LIMIT	BALANCE ON LAST STATEMENT	TOTAL CREDITS	TOTAL DEBITS	TOTAL INTEREST	YOUR NEW BALANCE
1 500	375.01	375.01	359.00		359.00
LIMITE DE CRÉDIT	SOLDE DU RELEVÉ PRÉCÉDENT	TOTAL DES CRÉDITS	TOTAL DES DÉBITS	TOTAL DES INTÉRÊTS	VOTRE NOUVEAU SOLDE

ANNUAL INTEREST RATE	DAILY INTEREST RATE	PAYMENT DUE DATE MONTH DAY YEAR	PAST DUE	CURRENT DUE	MINIMUM PAYMENT DUE
18.60%	0.05095%	07. 07. 83		17.00	17.00
TAUX D'INTÉRÊT ANNUEL	TAUX D'INTÉRÊT QUOTIDIEN	DATE D'ÉCHÉANCE DU VERSEMENT	ARRÉRAGES	DÛ POUR MOIS COURANT	VERSEMENT MINIMUM ÉCHU

IMPORTANT
PLEASE RETURN THE TOP PORTION OF THIS
STATEMENT WITH YOUR PAYMENT, THE BOTTOM
PORTION SHOULD BE RETAINED AS YOUR
PERMANENT RECORD.

IMPORTANT
VEUILLEZ RETOURNER LA PARTIE SUPÉRIEURE DE CE
RELEVÉ AVEC VOTRE VERSEMENT ET CONSERVER LA
PARTIE INFÉRIEURE POUR VOS DOSSIERS.

OPTIONS

SOLUTION:

Francine paid the account after the due date therefore interest is charged on the daily balance from the statement date on which the item was first listed.

June 16 to July 10 = 24 days

$P = \$359$

$i = 18.6\%$

$n = \dfrac{24}{365}$

$I = Pin$

$\quad = 359(.186)\left(\dfrac{24}{365}\right)$

$\quad = \$4.39$

or, using the daily rate $I = 359(.000\ 595)(24)$

$$= \$4.39$$

Example 10.2b

Brian's statement from Simpsons dated June 25 showed the following:

Previous balance: $63.22
Service charges: $ 1.52
Plus purchases: $44.21
Service charge: 2.4% per month (28.8% per annum)
Payment: $63.22

(a) How much must Brian pay to settle the account?
(b) If payment is made on August 6, how much service charge will appear on the August 25 statement?
(c) What is the effective rate of interest charged?
(d) If interest was calculated daily what would be the amount of service charge?

SOLUTION:

(a)

Previous balance		63.22
Plus purchases	44.21	
Plus service charge	1.52	
	45.73	45.73
		108.95
Less payments		63.22
		45.73

Balance payable = $45.73

(b) Interest is payable monthly on the previous month's balance.
Previous month's balance =45.73
(purchases plus previous month's service charge)
Monthly rate = 2.4%
Service charge = 45.73(.024) = $1.10

(c) If payment was made by July 25, there was no service charge.
Therefore, time of credit is from July 25 to August 6 = 12 days.

Using $i = \dfrac{I}{Pn}$:

$$i = \frac{1.10}{(45.73)\left(\dfrac{12}{365}\right)}$$

= .7316 495 or 73.164 95%

(d) $P = 45.73$
$i = 28.8\%$

$$n = \frac{12}{365}$$

$$I = 45.73(.288)\left(\frac{12}{365}\right)$$

= 0.43 or 43¢

EXERCISE 10.2 / REFERENCE SECTION: A

For each of the following problems involving variable credit, find (a) the finance charge that will appear on the next month's statement and (b) the balance that will appear on the next month's statement. (Interest is charged on the outstanding daily balance at the annual rate of 18.6% (.050 95% daily).

Statement Date	Payment Due Date	Previous Balance	Amount Paid	Date Paid	Purchases
1. June 25	July 15	$156.22	$156.22	July 20	$ 85.00
2. November 12	November 23	285.00	50.00	November 23	0.00
3. October 17	November 7	560.00	560.00	November 6	290.61
4. October 25	November 19	800.65	400.00	November 19	100.25
5. March 3	March 29	420.00	0.00		
6. August 5	September 1	385.21	385.21	September 1	230.00

Statement Problems:

7. Marge received a statement from the T. Eaton Company which showed the following: Previous balance: $654.21, Purchases: $85.00, Payment: $62.00. If interest is charged at 28.8% per annum on the previous month's balance, find (a) the credit service charge, (b) the new balance, and (c) the credit service charge that will appear on the next month's statement.

8. Victor's statement from Visa showed the following: Statement date: July 8, Payment due date: August 2, Previous balance: $0.00, New balance: $869.21, Interest: 18.6% annual rate (.050 95% daily). If Victor pays the full amount on August 9, what amount of service charge will appear on his next month's statement?

10.3 Consumer Loans

CONSUMER LOANS may be classified according to the TERMS of payment. In some cases the consumer has the option to pay the amount of the loan in a single payment or in a series of partial payments, while in other cases the terms of the loan require that regular instalments be paid for the life of the loan. Consumer loans may be obtained from banks, trust companies, credit unions, sales finance companies and life insurance companies, if the consumer has a life insurance policy.

A.   INSTALMENT LOANS

An instalment loan is a loan for which the consumer has signed an agreement to pay a specified amount at regular intervals, usually weekly or monthly, for a specified length of time. The amount of each payment is determined as follows:

(a) the cost of the loan is determined and added to the principal
(b) the amount of principal and interest is divided by the number of payments to determine that amount of each payment.

Generally, the amount and number of payments are fixed for the term of the loan. However, the trend is now towards variable interest rates and as a result either the term or the amount of each payment may vary.

Example 10.3a
Louis bought a television set for $869.00. He made a down payment of $100.00 and agreed to pay the balance plus interest in twelve equal payments of $69.41 each. What are the finance charges?

SOLUTION:

Cost Price	$869.00
Down payment	100.00
Balance	$769.00
Total amount paid in instalments (69.41 × 12)	832.92
Less amount financed	769.00
Finance charge (C)	$ 63.92

B.   CONDITIONAL SALES CONTRACTS

When a product is purchased from a retailer on INSTALMENTS a conditional sales contract and PROMISSORY NOTE may be signed. The retailer may then sell the contract and note to a lender. The consumer will then make the payments agreed upon to the lender who owns the contract. At one time, consumers were forced to continue payments to the lender even if a difficulty arose between the consumer and the retailer over the quality of the product. However, the lender now has the same obligations as the seller of the product.

Cooling-off-Period

On a contract which was entered into as a result of a door-to-door sale, the consumer has the right to cancel the contract within three days–THE COOLING-OFF PERIOD–without penalty and with full refund of all deposits made.

C.   DEMAND LOANS

A consumer may obtain a demand loan from banks, trust companies, credit unions or caisses populaires if the consumer has enough COLLATERAL to back up the loan. The lender may require repayment of the loan at any time, however, repayment is usually made according to the agreement made at the time of borrowing. Demand loans provide two advantages:

(a)   partial or full payment may be made at any time without penalty
(b)   the interest rate is tied to the prime lending rate and is therefore usually lower than that on other consumer loans. (Demand loans were discussed in Section 9.1.)

D.   LIFE INSURANCE LOANS

A consumer who has a life insurance policy may obtain a loan against the cash surrender value of the policy. The face value of the policy is then reduced by the amount of the loan until it is paid. Such loans may be obtained at a rate which is much lower than the rate of other consumer loans.

Example 10.4b

Fran wants to buy a new washer and dryer set priced at $900.00. She can (a) buy the set on the instalment plan by making a down payment of $100 and six equal payments of $139.23, or (b) borrow the balance of $800 on demand at the bank at 12.5% and repay $139.23 plus interest accrued at the end of each month. Which plan will result in a lower finance charge?

SOLUTION:

(a) Total instalment payments (6 × 139.23) $835.38

      Amount financed (900 − 100)   <u>800.00</u>

      Finance charge (C)   35.38

(b) $i = 12.5\%$

    $n = \dfrac{1}{12}$ (year)

    (i) for each month calculate the interest on the outstanding principal using the formula $I = Pin$

    (ii) add the interest values calculated in (i) to obtain the finance charge:

Payment Number	Balance Owing (P)	Interest $I = Pin$
1	$800.00	$ 8.33
2	800.00 − 139.23 = 660.77	6.88
3	660.77 − 139.23 = 521.24	5.43
4	521.54 − 139.23 = 382.31	3.98
5	382.31 − 139.23 = 243.08	2.53
6	243.08 − 139.23 = 103.85	1.08
		$28.23
	The finance charges =	28.23

The finance charges (interest) = $28.23. Fran should get the demand loan and pay for the washer. NOTE: The last payment is $103.85, balance owing.

EXERCISE 10.3 / REFERENCE SECTIONS: A–D

For each of the following problems, determine the total cost of credit:

Original Amount of Loan	Amount of Each Payment	Number of Payments
1. $2 000	$180.52	12
2. 1 500	262.16	6
3. 2 500	120.62	24
4. 895	94.50	10

Statement Problems:

5. Steve received a demand loan of $1 000 from his bank. He authorized the bank to deduct $250 plus interest on the outstanding balance from his account at the end of each month for four months. If the interest rate charged was 15.5% per annum, what is the total amount of finance charges?

6. On July 1, Arlene borrowed $2 500 on demand with interest at 16.25% per annum payable at the end of each month. If she repays the loan on November 1, (a) what is the total amount of finance charge and (b) what is the total amount of the finance charge if the interest rate was changed to 16.75% on September 1?

7. On March 3, May signed a demand note for $2 500 plus interest at 14.25% per annum payable at the end of each month. On April 3, and each month thereafter for five months, she paid $500 and the outstanding interest. What is the total amount of finance charge paid?

8. Which of the following options will result in a lower finance charge: (a) A demand loan of $1 500 repaid in six monthly instalments of $250 plus the monthly interest on the outstanding balance at the rate of 14.5% per annum. Or, (b) A loan of $1 500 repaid in six instalments of $262.16 each?

9. Marlene borrowed $1 500 and agreed to make six equal payments of $271.57 each. Her friend Fred took a demand loan for $1 500 at 14% per annum. At the end of each month for six months he paid $250 plus the monthly interest on the outstanding balance. Which one paid the lower finance charge and by how much?

10.4 Instalment Loan Repayment Schedules

A. PAYMENT SCHEDULE

When a payment is made on an instalment loan a part of each payment is used to pay off the interest obligation and the remainder of the payment is used to reduce the outstanding principal. This method of repaying a loan is referred to as the AMORTIZA-TION METHOD. When this method is used the interest at each payment is calculated on the DECLINING BALANCE of the principal.

Example 10.4a
Mr. Wise borrowed $1 200 and agreed to repay the loan and interest charges of $99.72 in twelve equal monthly payments of $108.31. If the interest rate charged is 15% calculated on the unpaid monthly balance, construct a payment schedule.

SOLUTION:

STEP **(1)**   When each payment is made calculate the interest on the outstanding balance of the previous period and deduct this from the payment. (Table 10-1)
Interest = Outstanding balance from Column 1 × monthly rate.

STEP **(2)**   Subtract the remainder of the payment from the outstanding balance to obtain the principal for the next period. (Table 10-1)
Column 5 = Previous value in Column 5 − Column 4.

Payment Number 1
Column 3:   Outstanding balance = $1 200
Monthly rate = 1.25%
I = $1 200 (.012 5) = $15
(Column 1 × monthly rate)

Column 4:   Amount credited to principal = Payment − Interest
Column 2 − Column 3
108.31 − 15 = $93.31

Column 5:   Balance before payment − Amount credited to principal
Column 1 − Column 4
1 200 − 93.31 = $1 106.69

Column 1:   Enter the value from the previous Column 5.

Payment Number 2
Column 3:   Outstanding balance × Monthly rate
= 1 106.69 × .0125 = $13.83

Column 4:   Amount credited to principal
= Payment − Interest
= 108.31 − 13.83
= $94.48

Column 5:   Balance before payment − Amount credited to principal
= Column 1 − Column 4
= 1 106.69 − 94.48 = $1 012.21

Column 1:   Enter the value from the previous Column 5.
The values for payments one to twelve are shown in Table 10-1.

Table 10-1
Amortization Schedule

annual rate   = 15%
monthly rate = 1.25%

| | | | amount credited to: | | |
| | 1 | 2 | 3 | 4 | 5 |
Payment Number	Balance Before Payment	Payment	Interest	Principal	Balance After Payment
0					$1 200.00
1	$1 200.00	$ 108.31	$15.00	$ 93.31	1 106.69
2	1 106.69	108.31	13.83	94.48	1 012.21
3	1 012.21	108.31	12.65	95.66	916.55
4	916.55	108.31	11.46	96.85	819.70
5	819.70	108.31	10.25	98.06	721.64
6	721.64	108.31	9.02	99.29	622.35
7	622.35	108.31	7.78	100.53	521.82
8	521.82	108.31	6.52	101.79	420.03
9	420.03	108.31	5.25	103.06	316.97
10	316.97	108.31	3.96	104.35	212.62
11	212.62	108.31	2.66	105.65	106.97
12	106.97	108.31	1.34	106.97	0.00
TOTAL		1 299.72	99.72	1 200.00	

B.   USE OF A FINANCIAL CALCULATOR TO COMPLETE THE PAYMENT SCHEDULE

A payment schedule may be completed by using the special keys on a financial calculator. The following steps should be taken:

STEP (1)   Enter the value for the present value of the loan (PV), the future value (FV), interest rate per payment period ($\%i$), the amount of payment (PMT).
STEP (2)   Enter the payment number (N).
STEP (3)   Press *2nd/BAL*.
STEP (4)   Repeat steps (2) and (3) for each payment period for which the balance is to be found.

Example 10.4b
Refer to Example 10.4a.

SOLUTION:

$$PV = 1\ 200$$
$$FV = 108.31 \times 12 = 1\ 299.72$$

$$\%i = \frac{15\%}{12} = 1.25$$

$$PMT = 108.31$$

The steps are shown below:

Enter	Press	Display Shows
1200	*PV*	1200
1299.72	*FV*	1299.72
1.25	*%i*	1.25
108.31	*PMT*	108.31
1	*2nd/BAL*	1106.69
2	*2nd/BAL*	1012.2136
3	*2nd/BAL*	916.55631
4	*2nd/BAL*	819.70326
5	*2nd/BAL*	721.63956
6	*2nd/BAL*	622.35006
7	*2nd/BAL*	521.81943
8	*2nd/BAL*	420.03217
9	*2nd/BAL*	316.97258
10	*2nd/BAL*	212.62474
11	*2nd/BAL*	106.97255
12	*2nd/BAL*	−0.0002976

Compare the values with those found in Example 10.4a.

Example 10.4c

Muriel bought a stereo system priced at $1 700. She made a down payment of $200 and agreed to pay the balance plus interest at 15% in 15 equal payments of $110.29 each made at the end of the month. How much does she owe after (a) the 6th payment, and (b) the 11th payment?

SOLUTION:

(a) Down payment = $200
$$PV = \$1\ 700 - 200 = \$1\ 500$$
$$FV = 110.29 \times 15 = \$1\ 654.35$$
$$\%i = \frac{15\%}{12} = 1.25\%$$

Enter	Press	Display Shows
1500	<u>PV</u>	1500
1654.35	<u>FV</u>	1654.35
1.25	<u>%i</u>	1.25
6	<u>2nd/BAL</u>	945.56501

The balance after the 6th payment is $945.57.

(b) With the above values already entered:

Enter	Press	Display Shows
11	<u>2nd/BAL</u>	450.89981

The balance after the 11th payment is $450.10.

EXERCISE 10.4 / REFERENCE SECTIONS: A–B

For each of the following problems construct a loan repayment schedule (interest is calculated on the unpaid monthly balance):

Amount of Loan	Monthly Payment	Number of Payments	Annual Rate of Interest
1. $1 500	$ 261.05	6	15%
2. 3 000	270.07	12	14.5%
3. 2 500	263.96	10	12%
4. 6 500	481.75	15	16.25%
5. 2 000	348.32	6	15.25%
6. 1 500	200.74	8	18.5%

Statement Problems:

7. Mr. DeVito received a loan of $2 500 and agreed to repay the loan by making 12 equal payments of $229.80. The interest rate charged is 18.5% per annum calculated on the unpaid monthly balance. (a) Set up a partial payment schedule for the first six payments. (b) What is the outstanding balance of the principal after the 6th payment?

8. Ms Barrett borrowed $1 900 at 17.25% per annum calculated on the unpaid monthly balance. She agreed to repay the loan in 12 equal monthly payments of $173.51. Set up a payment schedule for the 12 payments.

10.5 Interest Rate Charges

Legislation at the federal and provincial levels require that the lender disclose the cost of credit in the form of dollars and cents as well as the simple annual rate of interest. The purpose of this legislation is to make consumers aware of the cost of borrowing. It is hoped that the consumer will then be in a position to compare credit from several sources. Among the costs which are included in the finance charges (C) are interest charges, insurance costs, service charge where applicable and fees to register chattel mortgages.

Although the lender is required to state the finance charges as a simple annual rate of interest a knowledge of how this is calculated for different types of loans will assist consumers in comparing the cost of credit. For loans involving a single payment of the principal the simple annual rate of interest (nominal rate) is:

$$i = \frac{C}{Pn}$$ ←——— *Formula 10-1*

where i = simple annual interest rate
   C = total amount of finance charge
   P = the original amount of the loan
   n = time in years.

For instalment purchases and instalment loans, a simple interest charge is calculated by applying a rate or percent payment period. Department stores, commercial banks, credit card agencies and others offering variable credit (REVOLVING CREDIT) calculate the interest on the outstanding balance and add it to the minimum monthly payment. Thus, as the balance decreases the finance charge decreases.

Since consumers and CREDITORS usually find it easier to handle regular equal payments in settling instalment loans the trend is to pre-compute the charge for each period. The finance charge is pre-computed by the method which will be discussed in Chapter Twelve. The rate of interest charged may be estimated by the constant ratio method. In this method:

P = original amount of the loan
M = number of payment periods in one year
C = total amount of finance charge
N = number of payments.

$$i = \frac{2MC}{P(N + 1)}$$ ←——— *Formula 10-2*[2]

The **CONSTANT RATIO METHOD** assumes that the amount borrowed is paid off in equal amounts at each payment period. Thus, a principal of $1 200 to be paid off in 12 instalments would require a payment of $100 at each instalment or $\frac{P}{N}$. Thus, the length of time for which each instalment is owed is as follows:

Instalment 1: 1 period
2: 2 periods
3: 3 periods
. . .
Instalment N: N periods

Example 10.5a

Mr. Loaner lent $1 200 to a friend who paid him $99.72 in interest. What rate of interest did Mr. Loaner receive if (a) the total amount of the loan was repaid one year from the time of borrowing (nominal rate) and (b) the loan and interest was repaid in twelve equal monthly instalments of $108.31?

SOLUTION:

(a)   The total amount is borrowed for one year:
$P = 1\ 200$
$C = 99.72$
$n = 1$ (year)

The nominal rate is $i = \dfrac{C}{Pn}$

$$= \frac{99.72}{1\ 200(1)}$$

$$= .083\ 1 \text{ or } 8.31\%$$

---

[2] Proof of Formula 10-2

$$i = \frac{C}{\dfrac{P}{N}\left[\dfrac{1 + 2 + 3 + \ldots + N}{M}\right]}$$

$$1 + 2 + 3 + \ldots + N = \frac{N}{2}(N + 1)$$

$$i = \frac{C}{\dfrac{P}{N}\left[\dfrac{\dfrac{N}{2}(N + 1)}{M}\right]}$$

$$i = \frac{C}{\dfrac{P}{2M}(N + 1)}$$

$$i = \frac{2MC}{P(N + 1)}$$

(b) The loan is repaid in instalments. Interest is charged on the declining balance.
Total amount paid = 108.31 × 12 = $1 299.72

$P = 1\ 200$

$C = 1\ 299.72 - 1\ 200 = 99.72$ (finance charge)

$M = 12$ (number of payments in one year)

$N = 12$ (number of payments)

Substituting the values in Formula 10-2:

$$i = \frac{2MC}{P(N+1)}$$

$$= \frac{2(12)(99.72)}{1\ 200(12+1)}$$

$$= .1534154, \text{ or } 15.34\%$$

The constant ratio method overestimates the simple annual rate of interest. The exact value of the simple annual rate of interest may be found from an annuity table to be 15%. (See Chapter Twelve.) The constant ratio method provides a reasonably accurate estimate of the rate of interest only if payments are made according to schedule. If there are any deviations in the amount of payment or the time between payments this method will not provide a good estimate of the simple annual rate of interest.

EXERCISE 10.5 / REFERENCE SECTION: A

For each of the following find (a) the nominal rate, (b) the simple annual rate using the constant ratio method:

	Amount of Loan	Monthly Payment	Number of Monthly Payments
1.	$ 3 000	$ 270.07	12
2.	6 500	531.75	15
3.	2 000	348.32	6
4.	1 500	200.74	8
5.	4 000	157.50	36
6.	1 500	180.00	12

Statement Problems:

7. Nadia bought a washing machine priced at $890 on the instalment plan. She made a down payment of $60 and agreed to pay the balance in 12 equal monthly payments of $86.24. Find (a) the total amount of the finance charge and (b) the simple annual rate of interest using the constant ratio method.

8. You bought a stereo priced at $1 600 on the instalment plan. You made a down payment of $50 and agreed to pay the balance plus interest in 15 equal monthly payments of $123. Find (a) the total finance charge, and (b) the simple annual rate of interest using the constant ratio method.
9. A refrigerator is advertised for $1 200. It can be bought for $50 down plus 12 equal monthly payments of $120. Find (a) the total finance charge and (b) the simple annual rate of interest using the constant ratio method.
10. Ms Zito bought a color television set with no down payment and agreed to pay $30 per month for 24 months. (a) What is the total cost to Ms Zito and (b) if the list price is $540, what is the amount of the carrying charges and (c) what is the simple annual rate of interest using the constant ratio method?

10.6 Unearned Finance Charges (Rebates)–Rule of 78

When a payment is made on an instalment plan a part of the payment is used to pay the interest and the remainder to decrease the amount of the loan. The amount of interest owing at each payment is calculated on the declining balance of the principal. A schedule called an amortization schedule may be set up to determine the balance due after each payment. (See Section 10.4A.)

Some chartered banks, trust companies and finance companies use what is called the RULE OF 78, or the SUM-OF-THE-DIGITS RULE to determine the unpaid balance of the instalment loan.

A.   RULE OF 78

With a pre-computed loan the borrower's liability at the time the loan is contracted is the principal and the total amount of the finance charge. The outstanding balance at any payment date is UNPAID BALANCE of the principal plus a part of the unearned interest.

In the case of a twelve-month loan the borrower has the use of the full amount (12 parts or digits) of the loan for the first month. The number of parts or digits of the loan is decreased by one for each succeeding month. (See Table 10-2, column (2)).

The sum-of-the-digits in the arithmetic progression:
$12 + 11 + 10 + 9 + 8 + 7 + 6 + 5 + 4 + 3 + 2 + 1 = 78$
or,

$$\boxed{\text{Sum} = \frac{N}{2}(N + 1)} \quad \longleftarrow Formula\ 10\text{-}3$$

where N = the number of items in the progression.

Table 10-2 shows the number of parts of the loan outstanding after each payment, the corresponding fraction of the interest attributed to that month and the frac-

tion of the interest allowed as a REBATE if the debt is paid off on a payment date.
    To calculate the unearned finance charge (rebate):

$$\text{Rebate} = \frac{\text{Sum-of-the-digits of outstanding payments}}{\frac{N}{2}(N+1)} \times C \qquad \longleftarrow \textbf{\textit{Formula 10-4}}$$

Table 10-2
Rebate Fractions for a Twelve-Month Loan

Payment Number	Parts of Principal	Interest Owed	Fraction of Interest Allowed as a Rebate
1	12	$\dfrac{12}{78}$	$\dfrac{66}{78}$
2	11	$\dfrac{11}{78}$	$\dfrac{55}{78}$
3	10	$\dfrac{10}{78}$	$\dfrac{45}{78}$
4	9	$\dfrac{9}{78}$	$\dfrac{36}{78}$
5	8	$\dfrac{8}{78}$	$\dfrac{28}{78}$
6	7	$\dfrac{7}{78}$	$\dfrac{21}{78}$
7	6	$\dfrac{6}{78}$	$\dfrac{15}{78}$
8	5	$\dfrac{5}{78}$	$\dfrac{10}{78}$
9	4	$\dfrac{4}{78}$	$\dfrac{6}{78}$
10	3	$\dfrac{3}{78}$	$\dfrac{3}{78}$
11	2	$\dfrac{2}{78}$	$\dfrac{1}{78}$
12	1	$\dfrac{1}{78}$	$\dfrac{0}{78}$

Example 10.6a
Calculate the sum-of-the-digits of the payments for (a) a 12-month loan, (b) a 15-month loan, and (c) a 24-month loan.

SOLUTION:

(a) $N = 12$

$$\text{Sum} = \frac{12}{2}(12 + 1)$$

$$= 6(13)$$

$$= 78$$

(b) $N = 15$

$$\text{Sum} = \frac{15}{2}(15 + 1)$$

$$= \frac{15}{2}(16)$$

$$= 120$$

(c) $N = 24$

$$\text{Sum} = \frac{24}{2}(24 + 1)$$

$$= 12(25)$$

$$= 300$$

Example 10.6b
Express the rebate as a fraction of the total interest charges for each of the following:

Length of Loan	Payments Outstanding
(a) 15 months	6
(b) 24 months	9

SOLUTION:

(a) Sum-of-the-digits for 15 months $= \frac{15}{2}(15 + 1) = 120$

Sum-of-the-digits for 6 outstanding payments $= \frac{6}{2}(6 + 1) = 21$

Fraction of interest charges $= \frac{21}{120}$

(b) Sum-of-the-digits for 24 months $= \frac{24}{2}(25) = 300$

Sum-of-the-digits for 9 outstanding payments $= \frac{9}{2}(9 + 1) = 45$

Fraction of interest charges $= \frac{45}{300}$

Example 10.6c

Marian took out an instalment loan of $2 000 and agreed to make 12 payments of $180.52. (a) What are the finance charges and (b) how much rebate will she receive if she repays the loan when 8 payments are outstanding?

SOLUTION:

(a) Finance charge $= (12 \times 180.52) - 2\ 000$

$$= 2\ 166.24 - 2\ 000$$

$$= \$166.24$$

(b) Sum-of-the-digits for 12 months:

$$\text{Sum} = \frac{N}{2}(N + 1)$$

$$= \frac{12}{2}(12 + 1)$$

$$= 78$$

Sum-of-the-digits for 8 outstanding payments:

$$\frac{8}{2}(8 + 1) = 36$$

The rebate is:

$\frac{36}{78} \times$ finance charge

$\frac{36}{78} \times 166.24$

$= \$76.73$

Example 10.6d

Sylvia bought a stereo set for $1 100. She made a down payment of $100 and agreed to make 15 monthly payments of $73.53. If she paid off the debt when the 7th payment was due (a) how much rebate will she receive and (b) how much must she pay?

SOLUTION:

(a) The sum-of-the-digits $= \frac{15}{2}(15 + 1) = 120$

Total payment = 73.53 × 15 = 1 102.95
Finance charge = 1 102.95 – 1 000 = 102.95
Number of remaining payments = 15 – 7 = 8

Sum-of-the-digits of outstanding payments = $\frac{8}{2}(8 + 1) = 36$

Rebate fraction $= \frac{36}{120}$

Rebate $= \frac{36}{120} \times 102.95$ 30.88

(b) Amount of debt $1 102.95
     Amount paid (73.53 × 6)   441.18
     Balance   661.77
     Rebate   30.88
     Pay off Amount   630.89

Example 10.6e

Harrison took out a loan for $1 200 to pay for his tuition. He agreed to pay $108.31 a month for twelve months. (a) What are the total finance charges? (b) What would he receive as a rebate if he pays off the debt after the fifth payment? (c) How much would settle the debt after the fourth payment?

SOLUTION:

(a) Total amount to be paid (108.31 × 12)   1 299.72
Original amount of loan   1 200.00
Finance charges   99.72

(b) Payments made:

Month	Fraction of Finance Charge Earned at Payment
1	12/78
2	11/78
3	10/78
4	9/78
5	8/78
	50/78

Unearned fraction of finance charge: $\frac{78}{78} - \frac{50}{78} = \frac{28}{78}$

Rebate: $\frac{28}{78} \times 99.72 = \$35.80$

(c) Total amount to be paid   1 299.72
     Total amount paid (4 payments)   433.24
     Balance   866.48
     Rebate   35.80
Payment of $830.68 will settle the debt.   830.68

EXERCISE 10.6 / REFERENCE SECTION: A

For each of the following problems involving instalment payments use the Rule of 78 to find the missing items:

	Amount of Debt	Finance Charge	Required Number of Payments	Number of Payments Outstanding	Balance Owed	Finance Rebate if Paid Off
1.	$20 000	$ 2 500	12	7	?	?
2.	5 000	1 960	48	21	?	?
3.	12 000	2 000	24	10	?	
4.	18 000	3 600	15	12	?	
5.		7 200	12	4	9 720	?
6.		1 500	18	6	7 850	?

Statement Problems:

7. A debt of $2 500 is to be repaid in 15 instalments of $200. How much will settle the debt just after the 8th payment? (Use the Rule of 78.)

8. Carmen bought a washing machine for $800. She made a down payment of $50 and agreed to pay the balance plus interest in 12 instalments of $70. When the 6th payment was due she settled the debt. If the balance due was calculated using the Rule of 78, how much did she pay?

9. Sam bought a car listed for $10 500. He received a trade-in allowance of $2 000 and made a down payment of 10% of the list price. He then signed an agreement to pay the balance in 36 equal monthly payments of $225.00. By the Rule of 78, how much does he owe just after making his 17th payment?

10. You bought a snowmobile for $15 000 and agreed to settle the debt plus a finance charge of $2 100 in 18 equal monthly payments. (a) What is the amount of each payment? (b) By the Rule of 78, how much must you pay if you pay off the loan when the 7th monthly payment is due? (c) Set up a schedule of the payments to determine the balance outstanding on the 7th month by the declining balance method.

10.7 Some Do's and Don'ts of Credit

1. When taking out a long term loan *do* ask for a clause which allows early repayment (pre-payment) at the smallest possible penalty or at no penalty to you. This will allow you to renegotiate if the rates drop.

2. *Do* use free credit before borrowing. For example, use the free credit period on your credit card and charge account (usually 25 to 30 days) where possible. If you shop just after the billing date you will not receive the bill for about 30 days thus you will have free credit for about 55 days.

3. When negotiating a loan *do* offer the best security (collateral) you can in order to get the lowest possible rates.
4. Before buying on the instalment plan *do* ask yourself if you would buy the product or service if you had to pay cash.
5. *Do* save a percent of your monthly income even if it is a small amount.
6. Except for home mortgages, *do not* owe more than one-third of your discretionary income.
7. *Do not* use instant cash such as credit card or automatic line of credit before comparing the cost to the cost of a traditional loan.
8. *Do not* borrow more than you need to borrow.
9. *Do not* cosign for someone's debt unless you are willing to assume the obligation in case of default of payment.
10. *Do not* buy on credit just because credit is easily available.

EXERCISE / CHAPTER REVIEW

1. Ms Browne received a statement from Sears which showed the following: Previous balance: $231.47; Purchases: $161.80; Payment: $120.00.
    If the interest rate charged is 22.5% per annum calculated on the monthly balance find (a) the credit service charge, (b) the new balance and (c) the credit service charge that will appear on the next statement.
2. Mr. John Gray borrowed $1 200 from Forcier Credit Union. He agreed to settle the loan by 6 equal monthly payments plus the monthly interest calculated on the unpaid balance at 18.5%. Find the total interest charge.
3. A loan of $2 500 is to be repaid by 12 equal monthly payments of $229.80. The interest charged is 18.5% per annum calculated on the unpaid monthly balance. Determine the outstanding balance of the principal after the 8th payment. (Use the declining balance method.)
4. Use the constant ratio method to find the rate of interest charged if a debt of $1 200 is to be settled by 12 equal monthly payments of $120.
5. A debt of $2 500 is to be repaid by 15 monthly instalments of $200 each. How much will settle the debt just after the 10th payment?
6. A man borrowed $2 000 at 12% compounded monthly and promised to repay the loan and interest in 36 equal monthly payments. The total cost of the loan is $391.48. Find the outstanding balance after the 12th payment (a) by the Rule of
7. The Payoff Company borrowed $10 000 at 12% compounded monthly and promised to repay the loan and interest in 60 equal monthly payments. The total cost of the loan is $3 346.59. Find the outstanding balance after the 36th payment (a) by the Rule of 78 and (b) by the declining balance method. Use a financial calculator.
8. You borrowed $5 000 at 18.5% per annum calculated on the unpaid monthly balance and agreed to repay the loan plus interest in equal monthly payments of $250.83. Use the CalcStar spread sheet in Appendix II to set up a repayment schedule.

Summary of Formulae

$i = \dfrac{C}{Pn}$	*Formula 10-1*	To find the interest rate.
$i = \dfrac{2MC}{P(N+1)}$	*Formula 10-2*	To find the interest rate of an instalment loan.
$\text{Sum} = \dfrac{N}{2}(N+1)$	*Formula 10-3*	To find the sum-of-the-digits.
$\text{Rebate} = \dfrac{\text{Sum-of-the-digits of outstanding payments}}{\frac{N}{2}(N+1)} \times C$	*Formula 10-4*	To find the unearned finance charge (rebate).

Glossary

ACCRUED INTEREST the amount of interest that has accumulated

AMORTIZATION METHOD repayment of an instalment loan whereby part of each payment is used to pay off the interest obligation and the remainder of the payment is used to reduce the outstanding principal

BALANCE the amount owed by the borrower on a loan at any given time

BILLING DATE the date of the month on which credit accounts and monthly bills are calculated; payments or new charges made after this date will show on the next month's statement

CHARGE ACCOUNT an account held with a bank or service or company whereby purchases are made against an account number to be settled at a later date and in a variety of ways

COLLATERAL anything of value owned against which one may borrow money

CO-MAKER see *co-signer*

CO-SIGNER the other signer of a note when two people jointly guarantee to pay a loan

CONSOLIDATE to bring together several financial obligations under one agreement, contract or note

CONSTANT RATIO METHOD where an amount borrowed is paid off in equal amounts at each payment period

CONSUMER any person who uses goods and/or services for personal, household or family use

CONSUMER CREDIT credit extended to a person primarily for personal or family purposes, for which a finance charge is payable, and which is payable in instalments; consumer credit is usually short-term or intermediate term debt

CONSUMER LOANS loans to individuals or families, the proceeds of which are used for personal as opposed to business purposes

COOLING-OFF PERIOD the right to cancel a contract under certain circumstances within three business days without penalty and with full refund of deposits made; used in home improvement contracts and door-to-door sales

CREDIT BUREAU a company which keeps a credit record on a borrower

CREDIT CONTRACT a written agreement that states how, when, and how much must be paid

CREDIT RATING an evaluation of your qualification to receive credit based largely on your past record of meeting credit payments

CREDITOR see *lender*

CREDIT-WORTH one who is given a favorable credit rating and therefore entitled to use credit facilities

DECLINING BALANCE the decreasing amount owed on a debt as one makes payments

DEFERRED PAYMENT future payments or payments on a contract entered into sometime before the payments are due

DELINQUENT a credit account that is past due for which the borrower has made no satisfactory arrangements with the lender

DOLLAR COST the cost of credit stated as the difference between what you must pay back and what you receive as merchandise or a loan

DUE DATE see *maturity date*

FACE AMOUNT the total amount which you agree to repay before finance charges are deducted

INSTALMENT one of a series of payments to pay off a debt

INTERMEDIATE CREDIT credit extended for a period ranging from three to ten years

LENDER the person, persons, or organization to whom the borrower owes money

LOAN RATE the rate of interest you pay for borrowing money on a specific date at a specific rate

MATURITY DATE the date on which the final payment on a cash loan or instalment purchase is due

NON-INSTALMENT CREDIT credit that is repaid as a lump sum

NOTE a written promise to pay which lists details of the agreement: where, when, what size of instalments, rate of interest; a note may be transferred to a third party

PRE-PAYMENT PRIVILEGE the privilege stated in a loan, which allows the payment of part or all of a loan in advance of the dates stated in the contract

PROCEEDS the actual amount received by a borrower

PROMISSORY NOTE the note signed by a borrower promising to repay the total amount on a specified date

REBATE return of a portion of the payment required in a loan contract if payments are made in advance of the date or dates due

REFINANCE revision of a payment timetable often involving revision of interest rate charged

REPOSSESSION the taking back of goods bought on an instalment sales contract for which payments are overdue

REVOLVING CREDIT see *variable credit*

RULE OF 78 used with a pre-computed loan where the borrower's liability at the time of the loan is contracted as the principal and the total amount of the finance charge

SECURED LOAN a loan for which some collateral is pledged

SHORT-TERM CREDIT credit extended for a period of up to five years

SUM-OF-THE-DIGITS RULE see *Rule of 78*

TERM the prescribed time in which to make instalment or other payments under a loan or credit contract

TIME LOAN a single payment loan that has a fixed maturity date

UNPAID BALANCE the outstanding principal at any payment date

VARIABLE CREDIT credit extended by a lender to a borrower from time to time for the purchase of goods and services

11 *Compound interest– computing basic values*

Introduction

Many financial transactions in real life involve the technique of compounding interest. For example, compound interest is calculated on a deposit made at a credit union, bank or trust company where the interest on the deposit is credited to the account on some regular basis, such as monthly or semi-annually. Interest is also compounded on deposits made to a Registered Retirement Savings Plan (RRSP) or a Registered Home Ownership Savings Plan (RHOSP). Mortgage contracts also involve compounding of interest.

A sound foundation in the topics covered in this chapter will therefore facilitate communication skills in financial mathematics. Moreover, the concepts covered are employed in the development of formulae in subsequent chapters.

Chapter Eleven covers the method of computing interest and related values based on the concept of compounding interest.

11.1 Terminology

The compound interest method is generally used in long-term borrowing. There is usually more than one period for computing interest during the borrowing time. The interest for each period is added (compounded or converted) to the principal before the interest for the next period is computed. The final sum at the end of the period of borrowing is called the COMPOUND AMOUNT.

The process of accumulating a principal to obtain a compound amount is called COMPOUND ACCUMULATION. COMPOUND INTEREST is the difference between the original principal and the compound amount. The period for computing interest, usually at regularly stated intervals such as annually, semi-annually, quarterly, or monthly, is called the CONVERSION PERIOD, or the INTEREST PERIOD. The interest rate per conversion period is equal to the stated annual interest rate divided by the number of conversion periods in one year. The stated annual interest rate is called the NOMINAL

ANNUAL RATE, or simply the NOMINAL RATE. Thus, if the nominal rate is 16%, the interest rate for the annual conversion period is also 16%, but, if the conversion period is semi-annually, the interest rate for a period of six months is 16%/2, or 8%.

11.2 Computing Compound Interest

A. BASIC METHOD

The basic method of computing compound interest for *each* conversion period is the same as the method of computing simple interest. Thus, if there is only one conversion period, compound interest is the same as simple interest. The following example illustrates the method of computing interest in general.

Example 11.2a

What are the compound amount and the compound interest at the end of three months if $10 000 is borrowed at 12% compounded monthly?

SOLUTION:

The original principal is $10 000.
The conversion period is one month.

The number of conversion periods in three months is $\dfrac{3 \text{ months}}{1 \text{ month}} = 3$.

The interest rate per conversion period is

$$\frac{\text{Annual interest rate}}{\text{Number of conversion periods in one year}} = \frac{12\%}{12} = 1\%.$$

The computation is written as follows:

Original principal	$10 000.00
ADD: Interest for the 1st month	100.00 = $10 000 × 1%
Principal at the end of 1st month	$10 100.00
ADD: Interest for the 2nd month	101.00 = $10 100 × 1%
Principal at the end of 2nd month	$10 201.00
ADD: Interest for the 3rd month	102.01 = $10 201 × 1%
Principal at the end of 3rd month, or the compound amount	$10 303.01

Compound Interest = Compound Amount − Original Principal
        = 10 303.01 − 10 000 = $303.01

The simple interest at 12% on $10 000 for three months is:

$10 000 \times 12\% \times \dfrac{3}{12} = \$300.$

The compound interest is greater than the simple interest by:

303.01 − 300 = $3.01.

EXERCISE 11.2 / REFERENCE SECTION: A

Find the compound amount and the compound interest in each of the following problems:

1. $1 000 for $1\frac{1}{2}$ years at 17.5% compounded semi-annually.
2. $5 000 for one year at 21% compounded quarterly.
3. $10 000 for three months at 13.5% compounded monthly.
4. $8 000 for 9 months at 21% compounded quarterly.
5. $4 000 for 6 months at 15% compounded quarterly.
6. $100 for one year at 15.5% compounded semi-annually.
7. $500 for two months at 12% compounded monthly.
8. $2 000 for two months at 18% compounded monthly.

Statement Problems:

9. (a) Find the simple interest on $4 000 for 6 months at 15%. (b) What is the difference between the simple interest and the interest in Problem 5?
10. (a) What is the simple interest on $100 for one year at 15.5% interest rate? (b) Compare the simple interest with the compound interest in Problem 6, and find the difference.
11. (a) What is the simple interest on $500 for two months at a simple interest rate of 12%? (b) Compare the simple interest with the compound interest in Problem 7, and find the difference.
12. (a) Find the simple interest on $2 000 for two months at 18%. (b) What is the difference between the simple interest and the interest in Problem 8?

11.3 *The Compound Amount*

A.   *FINDING THE COMPOUND AMOUNT BY FORMULA*

To find the compound amount by formula, we shall use the following symbols:

Let P = original principal
   i = interest rate per conversion period
   n = number of conversion periods
   S = compound amount, or the principal at the end of the nth period

The compound amount formula is:

$$\boxed{S = P(1 + i)^n} \quad \longleftarrow Formula\ 11\text{-}1^1$$

---

[1]Proof–Formula 11-1

In Example 11.2a, let
the original principal $10 000 = P$, and
the interest rate per month (conversion period) = i

This formula serves as a basis in establishing more complex formulae used later in the text. It is therefore essential that the relationship between P, i, n and S be understood. The relationship is diagrammed as follows:

P $\qquad\qquad\qquad$ $I = S - P$ $\qquad\qquad\qquad$ $S = P(1 + i)^n$

0 (Now) $\qquad\qquad\qquad\qquad\qquad\qquad$ n (Number of Conversion Periods)

Example 11.3a

What is the compound amount at the end of three months if $10\ 000 is borrowed at 12% compounded monthly?

SOLUTION:

$P = 10\ 000$
$i = 1\%$ (per month)
$n = 3$ (months)

Substituting these values in the compound amount formula:
$$S = P(1 + i)^n = 10\ 000(1 + 1\%)^3$$
$$= 10\ 000(1.030301)$$
$$= \$10\ 303.01$$
The answer may be compared with the answer in Example 11.2a.

The value for $(1 + i)^n$ may be obtained by the use of an electronic calculator which has the function y^x, or from a set of tables. The use of tables is covered in Section 11.8.

The computation in Example 11.2a may be written symbolically as follows:

Original principal	P
ADD: Interest (1st month)	$(+)\ Pi$
Principal (1st month end)	$P(1 + i)$
ADD: Interest (2nd month)	$(+)\ P(1 + i)i$
Principal (2nd month end)	$P(1 + i)(1 + i) = P(1 + i)^2$
ADD: Interest (3rd month)	$(+)\ P(1 + i)^2 i$
Principal (3rd month end)	$P(1 + i)^2 (1 + i) = P(1 + i)^3$

When this idea is extended, the compound amount at the end of the nth period may be expressed as:

$$S = P(1 + i)^n.$$

B.   USE OF AN ELECTRONIC CALCULATOR TO CALCULATE $(1 + i)^n$

Example 11.3b

What is the compound amount of $2 500 invested for 5 years and 6 months at 17% compounded semi-annually?

SOLUTION:

$P = 2\ 500$

$i = \dfrac{17\%}{2} = 8.5\% = .085$ (semi-annually)

$n = 5.5 \times 2 = 11$ (semi-annual periods)
$S = P(1 + i)^n = 2\ 500(1 + .085)^{11}$

First, calculate the value of $(1.085)^{11}$, then multiply by the principal, $2 500. Following are the steps:

Action Taken	Display Shows
1. enter 1.085	1.085
2. press the key y^x	1.085
3. enter 11	11
4. press the key $=$	2.453167
5. press the key $\underline{X}$	2.453167
6. enter 2500	2500
7. press the key $=$	6132.9176

Thus, $(1.085)^{11} = 2.453167$
and, $S = 2\ 500(2.453167)$
            $= \$6\ 132.92.$

The answer is diagrammed as follows:

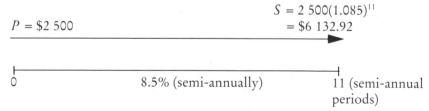

$P = \$2\ 500$

$S = 2\ 500(1.085)^{11}$
$= \$6\ 132.92$

0

8.5% (semi-annually)

11 (semi-annual periods)

NOTE:
1. Hereafter, unless otherwise specified, the words "interest" and "amount" mean compound interest and compound amount respectively, and the interest rate expressed by % means the nominal annual rate.
2. Where possible, intermediate calculations such as the value of $(1 + i)^n$ should not be cleared from the register of the calculator and re-entered, as this may affect

the accuracy of the final result. Where necessary, such values should be stored using the store function on the calculator.

3. If an answer is to be accurate to the nearest cent, the minimum number of decimal places to be multiplied is equal to the number of digits in the multiplicand, including dollars and cents.

Example 11.3c

A note having a face value of $3 500 and bearing interest at 14.5% compounded quarterly will mature in 10.5 years. What is the maturity value?

SOLUTION:

$P = 3\ 500$

$i = \dfrac{14.5\%}{4} = 3.625\%$

$n = 10.5 \times 4 = 42 \text{ (quarters)}$

$S = 3\ 500\left(1 + \dfrac{14.5\%}{4}\right)^{42} = 3\ 500(4.461\ 807\ 5)$

$\qquad\qquad\qquad\qquad = \$15\ 616.33$

Steps using an electronic calculator:

Action Taken	Display Shows
1. enter 14.5	14.5
2. press the key %	.145
3. press the key ÷	.145
4. enter 4	4
5. press the key =	.03625
6. press the key +	.03625
7. enter 1	1
8. press the key =	1.03625
9. press the key y^x	1.03625
10. enter 42	42
11. press the key =	4.4618075
12. press the key X	4.4618075
13. enter 3500	3500
14. press the key =	15616.326

Thus, the maturity value, $S = \$15\ 616.33$.

This is diagrammed as follows:

$P = \$3\ 500$ $S = \$15\ 616.33$

0   3.625% (per quarter)   42 (quarters)

C.   INTEREST RATE CHANGES DURING COMPOUND ACCUMULATION

If the interest rate changes during compound accumulation, the compound amount is the product of the principal and the several ACCUMULATION FACTORS which are at different interest rates for respective given periods.

Example 11.3d

On August 1, 1984, Marvin bought a cash-and-carry certificate for $5 000 earning interest at 9.5% compounded monthly. On July 1, 1985, the interest rate was changed to 10.25% compounded semi-annually. What is the compound amount on July 1, 1986?

SOLUTION:

The values for compounding the interest from August 1, 1984 to July 1, 1985 are:

$P = 5\ 000$

$i = \dfrac{9.5\%}{12}$ (per month)

$n = 11$ (months)

$$\begin{aligned}
S &= 5\ 000\left(1 + \frac{9.5\%}{12}\right)^{11} \\
&= 5\ 000(1.007\ 916\ 7)^{11} \\
&= 5\ 000(1.090\ 613\ 6) \\
&= \$5\ 453.07
\end{aligned}$$

The values for computing the compound amount from July 1, 1985 to July 1, 1986 are:

$P = 5\ 453.07$ (the new principal on July 1, 1985)

$i = \dfrac{10.25\%}{2}$ (per six months)

$n = 12$ (months)

$$\begin{aligned}
S &= 5\ 453.07\left(1 + \frac{10.25\%}{2}\right)^{2} \\
&= 5\ 453.07(1.051\ 25)^{2} \\
&= 5\ 453.07(1.105\ 126\ 6) \\
&= \$6\ 026.33
\end{aligned}$$

Thus, the compound amount on July 1, 1986 is $6 026.33, or

$$S = 5\,000\left(1 + \frac{9.5\%}{12}\right)^{11}\left(1 + \frac{10.25\%}{2}\right)^{12}$$
$$= 5\,000(1.090\ 613\ 6)(1.105\ 126\ 6)$$
$$= \$6\,026.33$$

D. CONVERSION PERIODS INCLUDING A FRACTIONAL PART

When the conversion periods include a fractional part, one of the methods illustrated below may be used in computing the compound amount. The method used may depend on the terms of the contract.

METHOD A Use the formula $S = P(1 + i)^n$, where n is a whole number representing the total number of whole conversion periods. The computed value, S, is further computed by the simple interest method for the remaining fractional period.

METHOD B Use the formula $S = P(1 + i)^n$, where n is a mixed number which equals the entire time.

Example 11.3e
$1 000 is invested at 12.9% compounded monthly on April 6, 1984. What is the amount on May 3, 1986, if the contract states that (a) interest for a fraction of a month is calculated at the simple interest rate, and (b) compound interest is calculated for a fraction of a month?

SOLUTION:

(a) $P = 1\,000$

$$i = \frac{12.9\%}{12} = 1.075\% \text{ (monthly)}$$

April 6, 1984 to May 3, 1986 = 2 years and 27 days
$n = 2 \times 12$ (months) + 27 (days)

Thus, the compound interest at the end of 24 conversion periods is

$$S = 1\,000(1 + 1.075\%)^{24}$$
$$= 1\,000(1.292\ 557\ 9)$$
$$= \$1\,292.557\ 9$$

The simple interest for the remaining 27 days is

$$1\,292.557\ 9(12.9\%)\left(\frac{27}{365}\right) = \$12.334\ 2$$

The compound amount is
$1\,292.557\ 9 + 12.334\ 2 = \$1\,304.89$

This method is diagrammed below:

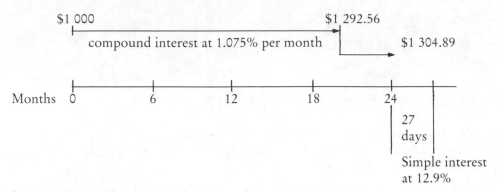

(b) $P = 1\ 000$
     $i = 1.075\%$ (monthly)

$$n = 24 + \frac{27}{365}\ (12) = 24.887\ 671 \text{ (months)}$$

$$S = 1\ 000(1.010\ 75)^{24.887671}$$
$$= 1\ 000(1.304\ 884\ 7)$$
$$= \$1\ 304.88$$

Example 11.3f

Manny bought \$2 500 in Canada Savings Bonds which paid interest at 12.5% compounded annually with interest accruing at the simple interest rate for each month before November 1. How much will she receive for the bonds if they are cashed in four years and seven months after the date of issue?

SOLUTION:

$P = 2\ 500$
$i = 12.5\%$ (annually)

$$n = 4\frac{7}{12} \text{ (years)}$$

Interest for the fraction of a year is payable at simple interest. The compound interest for the 4 years is:

$S = 2\ 500(1.125)^4$
    $= 2\ 500(1.601\ 806\ 6)$
    $= \$4\ 004.52$

The simple interest for 7 months is:

$$I = \$4\ 004.516\ 6(.125)\left(\frac{7}{12}\right)$$
$$= \$291.996$$

The amount for 4 years and 7 months is:

$S = 4\ 004.516\ 6 + 291.996$

$\quad = \$4\ 296.51$

Example 11.3g

If the contract in Example 11.3f required the use of compound interest for the fractional part of a conversion period, what would be the amount?

SOLUTION:

$P = 2\ 500$

$i = 12.5\%$ (annually)

$n = 4\dfrac{7}{12} = 4.583\ 333\ 3$ (years)

The compound amount is:

$S = 2\ 500(1.125)^{4.583\ 333\ 3}$

$\quad = 2\ 500(1.715\ 730\ 5)$

$\quad = \$4\ 289.33$

Notice that the answer obtained when METHOD A is used is greater than the amount obtained when METHOD B is used. When the investment time is a fraction of the conversion period, the use of the compound interest method will generally give less interest than the simple interest method.

EXERCISE 11.3 / REFERENCE SECTIONS: A–D

Find the compound amount in each of the following problems:

	Principal (P)	Interest Rate	Time
1.	$1 200	12% compounded monthly	$3\frac{1}{2}$ years
2.	500	18% compounded monthly	$1\frac{1}{2}$ years
3.	650	19.5% compounded semi-annually	$12\frac{1}{2}$ years
4.	4 200	15% compounded quarterly	$4\frac{1}{2}$ years
5.	3 500	$6\frac{1}{2}$% compounded monthly	20 years
6.	220	21% compounded quarterly	10 years
7.	800	19% compounded semi-annually	6 years
8.	2 000	14% compounded annually	15 years
9.	1 000	18% compounded semi-annually	10 years, 2 months
10.	5 000	15% compounded quarterly	6 years, 1 month

Statement Problems:

11. Accumulate $2 500 for $3\frac{2}{3}$ years at 18% compounded monthly. How much is the interest?

12. Carl Johnson deposits $550 in the Provincial Bank which pays 12.5% compounded semi-annually. What amount will he have at the end of 11 years?

13. What will be the amount after one year if $1 000 is invested at 15% compounded (a) monthly? (b) quarterly? (c) semi-annually? (d) annually?

14. What will the amount be after ten years is $500 is invested at 12% compounded (a) monthly? (b) quarterly? (c) semi-annually? (d) annually?

15. On January 2, 1983, Vito deposited $2 000 in a savings account which paid 15.5% compounded monthly. Effective January 2, 1984, the bank changed the interest rate to 14% compounded semi-annually. How much does he have in the account on January 2, 1986?

16. Five Elements Limited made the following investments: on January 1, 1983, $1 000 at 15% compounded quarterly; on April 1, 1984, $15 000 at 12% compounded monthly. What is the total value of these investments on April 1, 1986?

17. On March 1, 1984, Katrina deposited $2 500 in an account which paid 15% compounded monthly. On August 1, the rate was changed to 16% compounded monthly. How much will she have in the account on December 1, 1988?

18. The B.F. Kitch Company deposited $10 000 in an account which paid 18% compounded quarterly. How much will be in the account 5 years and 1 month later? (Use both methods).

19. Ms Wiggan invested $25 000 at 17.5% compounded semi-annually. What is the value of the investment at the end of 6 years and 2 months? How much is the interest? (Use both methods).

20. Harriet borrowed $20 000 at 18% compounded monthly on October 1, 1983. How much does she owe on December 1, 1984?

21. You bought $1 500 in Canada Savings Bonds on November 1, 1984. How much will you receive on March 3, 1986 if the bonds pay interest at 12% compounded annually? (Use METHOD A).

22. The Liberty Bank offers $1 000 guaranteed investment certificates at $12\frac{1}{8}$% compounded semi-annually. You deposit $1 000 in your credit union which pays 12% compounded monthly. Which investment pays more interest and by how much?

23. Refer to Problem 22. If the certificates are compounded quarterly, which investment pays more and by how much?

11.4 Finding the Present Value and Compound Discount

As stated in the previous chapter, there are numerous occasions in business when it becomes necessary to discount an amount which is due on a future date. "To discount a given compound amount due in the future" means to find its present value on the date of discount. The difference between the value of the compound amount and its present value is called COMPOUND DISCOUNT. Therefore, the compound discount on the compound amount is the same as the compound interest on the present value.

For instance, in Example 11.3b, the amount of $2 500 invested at 17% compounded semi-annually and due at the end of $5\frac{1}{2}$ years is $6 132.92. The compound interest is $6 132.92 – $2 500 = $3 632.92. This example may be stated in a different way. The present value of $6 132.92 due at the end of $5\frac{1}{2}$ years at 17% compounded semi-annually is $2 500, and the compound discount is $3 632.92. In other words, $2 500 is equivalent to $6 132.92 after $5\frac{1}{2}$ years according to the compound interest rate. The amount is found by applying the formula $S = P(1 + i)^n$. From the relationship, the present value (P) is obtained as follows:

$$\boxed{P = S(1 + i)^{-n}} \quad \longleftarrow Formula\ 11\text{-}2$$

or,

$$\boxed{P = \frac{S}{(1 + i)^n}} \quad \longleftarrow Formula\ 11\text{-}2A$$

This is diagrammed as follows:

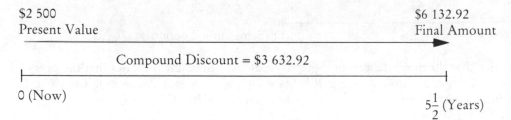

$2 500
Present Value

$6 132.92
Final Amount

Compound Discount = $3 632.92

0 (Now)

$5\frac{1}{2}$ (Years)

The value of $(1 + i)^{-n}$ may be obtained by the use of the $\underline{y^x}$ function on an electronic calculator or from a set of tables. The use of tables is covered in Section 11.8.

A.   USE OF AN ELECTRONIC CALCULATOR TO CALCULATE $(1 + i)^{-n}$

Example 11.4a
What is the present value of $4 745.74 due at the end of five years and six months if money is worth 12% compounded semi-annually?

SOLUTION:

$S = 4\ 745.75$
$i = 6\%$ (semi-annually)
$n = 5\frac{1}{2} \times 2 = 11$ (semi-annual periods)
$P = S(1 + i)^{-n}$
$\quad = 4\ 745.75(1.06)^{-11}$

First calculate the value of $(1.06)^{-11}$, then multiply by the amount, 4 745.75.

Action Taken	Display Shows
1. enter 1.06	1.06
2. press the key y^x	1.06
3. enter 11	11
4. press the key $^+/_-$	−11
5. press the key $=$	0.5267875
6. press the key X	0.5267875
7. enter 4745.75	4745.75
8. press the key $=$	2500.0019

Thus, $P = 4\ 745.75(1.06)^{-11}$
$\qquad = 4\ 745.75(.5267875)$
$\qquad = \$2\ 500.00$

This is diagrammed as follows:

P $S = \$4\ 745.75$

0 (Now)   11 (Semi-annual periods)

Notice that the movement from right to left along a time line indicates that the present value should be found, that is $P = S(1 + i)^{-n}$, while movement from left to right indicates that the amount should be found, that is $S = P(1 + i)^n$.

EXERCISE 11.4A / REFERENCE SECTION: A

Find the present value in each of the following problems:

	Amount (S)	Interest Rate	Time
1.	$2 000	15% compounded monthly	$1\frac{2}{3}$ years
2.	600	18% compounded monthly	2 years
3.	400	17.5% compounded annually	10 years
4.	3 500	19% compounded quarterly	$3\frac{1}{2}$ years
5.	1 500	13.5% compounded annually	4 years
6.	800	16% compounded quarterly	6 years
7.	4 000	19.5% compounded semi-annually	20 years
8.	700	15.5% compounded semi-annually	$7\frac{1}{2}$ years

Statement Problems:

9. Find the present value of $1 400 due at the end of nine years if money is worth (a) 25% compounded quarterly, (b) 23.5% compounded semi-annually. How much is the compound discount in each case?

10. Find the present value of $2 500 due at the end of three years if money is worth (a) 15% compounded monthly, (b) 16.25% compounded annually. How much is the compounded discount in each case?

11. Jane Harrison has $1 500 at the end of three years in her savings account. The interest rate is 21% compounded quarterly. How much did she deposit in the account three years ago?

12. How much money does R.T. White need if he can invest the money at 15% compounded monthly for 2 years and receive $5 000 at the end of the period?

13. If $3 600 is due seven years from now and money is worth 13.5% compounded annually, find the present value and the compound discount.

14. Find the present value and the compound discount if $1 800 is due five years from now and money is worth 18% compounded quarterly.

15. What principal will accumulate to $3 200 in $1\frac{1}{3}$ years at 12% compounded monthly?

16. What principal will accumulate to $4 300 in 12 years at 11.5% compounded annually?

17. A man paid a two-year debt with $1 690.74. The interest charged was at 18% compounded monthly. What was the principal?

18. A man borrowed some money for five years. When the debt was due, he paid $5 200 for the money borrowed and the interest charged. The interest rate was 17% compounded quarterly. How much did he borrow?

B   COMPOUND DISCOUNT ON NOTES

If a note is non-interest-bearing, the present value of its face value is the PROCEEDS. Here, the word "proceeds" represents the value received by the seller of the note, which is discounted at a compound interest rate. The method of finding the present value of a note is the same as that explained above. However, the word "present" usually is referred to here as the date of discount. Example 11.4a may be stated in the following manner:

A non-interest-bearing note of $4 745.74 is due $5\frac{1}{2}$ years from now. If the note is now discounted at 12% compounded semi-annually, what are the proceeds and the compound discount? The answers: proceeds = $2 500.00, and compound discount = $4 745.74 − 2 500.00 = 2 245.74.

If a note is interest bearing, the proceeds is the present value on the date of discount computed from the maturity value of the note. The maturity value includes the face value of the note and the interest. Thus, two steps are required in finding the proceeds:

STEP (1)　Find the compound amount of the face value of the note according to the rate and the time stipulated on the note. The compound amount is the maturity value. (Use formula $S = P(1 + i)^n$.)

STEP (2)　Find the present value (on the date of discount) of the maturity value, according to the rate and the time of discount. (Use the formula $P = S(1 + i)^{-n}$.)

Example 11.4b

A note of \$1 000 dated January 1, 1984, at 18% compounded monthly for three years and four months was discounted on May 1, 1984. What are the proceeds and the compound discount if the note was discounted at 16% compounded quarterly?

SOLUTION:

STEP (1)　Find the maturity date value on May 1, 1987, according to the rate and the time stipulated on the note. $P = \$1\ 000$ (face value), $i = 18\%/12 = 1\frac{1}{2}\%$ (per month), $n = 3\frac{1}{3} \times 12 = 40$ (months).

$$\begin{aligned}
\text{Maturity value } (S) &= P(1 + i)^n \\
&= 1\ 000(1 + 1\tfrac{1}{2}\%)^{40} \\
&= 1\ 000(1.814\ 018) \\
&= \$1\ 814.02
\end{aligned}$$

STEP (2)　Find the present value (as of May 1, 1984, the date of discount, or three years before the maturity date).
$S = \$1\ 814.02$, $i = 16\%/4 = 4\%$ (per quarter), $n = 3 \times 4 = 12$ (quarterly periods)

$$\begin{aligned}
\text{Proceeds (or present value } P) &= S(1 + i)^{-n} \\
&= 1\ 814.02(.624\ 597) \\
&= \$1\ 133.03
\end{aligned}$$

$$\begin{aligned}
\text{Compound discount} &= 1\ 814.02 - 1\ 133.03 \\
&= \$680.99
\end{aligned}$$

This example is diagrammed as follows:

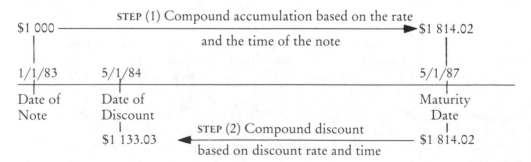

C.   DISCOUNT TIMES INCLUDING A FRACTION OF A CONVERSION PERIOD

When the discount time includes a fraction of a conversion period, the proceeds may be computed by either of the following methods:

METHOD **A** Use the formula $P = S(1 + i)^{-n}$, where n is a whole number representing the total number of whole conversion periods plus 1. The computed value P is then accumulated by the simple interest method for the extra fractional part included in n to obtain the proceeds.

METHOD **B** Use the formula $P = S(1 + i)^{-n}$, where n is a mixed number which equals the entire discount time.

Theoretically speaking, METHOD B is more reasonable than the other because the compound discount method is used throughout. However, the method used may depend on the terms of the agreement.

Example 11.4c
A non-interest-bearing note of $1 000 is discounted at 12% compounded quarterly for one year and seven months. Find the proceeds and the compound discount.

SOLUTION:

METHOD A: $S = 1\ 000$

$i = 12\%/4 = 3\%$ (per quarter)

$n = 6 + 1 = 7$ (quarters) (1 year 7 months = $1\frac{1}{2}$ years + 1 month)

$P = S(1 + i)^{-n}$

$\quad = 1\ 000\ (1 + 3\%)^{-7}$

$\quad = 1\ 000(.813\ 092)$

$\quad = \$813.09$

By the simple interest method, accumulate P for the extra fractional period of two months (7 quarterly periods, or 1 year and 9 months, minus 1 year and 7 months) at 12% as follows:

Simple interest $= 813.09 \times 12\% \times \frac{2}{12} = \$16.26$

The proceeds are: $813.09 + 16.26 = \$829.35$

Compound discount $= 1\ 000 - 829.35 = \$170.65$

Method A is diagrammed as follows:

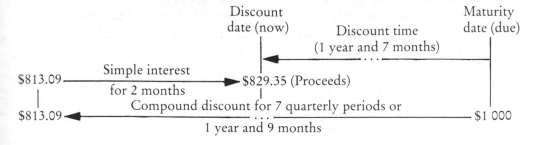

METHOD B: $S = 1\ 000$

$i = 12\%/4 = 3\%$ (quarterly)

$n = 1\dfrac{7}{12} \times 4 = 6\dfrac{1}{3}$ (quarterly periods)

$P = S(1 + i)^{-n}$

$= 1\ 000(1 + 3\%)^{-6\frac{1}{3}}$

$= 1\ 000(1 + 3\%)^{-6}(1 + 3\%)^{6\frac{1}{3}}$

$= 1\ 000 \times \dfrac{(1 + 3\%)^{-4}}{(1 + 3\%)^{\frac{1}{3}}}$

$= 1\ 000 \times \dfrac{.837484}{1.009\ 902}$

$= \$829.27$

Compound discount $= 1\ 000 - 829.27 = \$170.73$

NOTE: The proceeds in METHOD A are larger than those in METHOD B. Such a condition is always true when the discount time includes a fraction of the conversion period.

EXERCISE 11.4B / REFERENCE SECTIONS: B–C

Find (a) the proceeds, and (b) the compound discount in each of the following problems:

	Date of Note	Face Value	Compound Interest Rate of Note	Term of Note	Date of Discount	Discount Rate
1.	7/1/84	$1 000	none	4 years	7/1/85	19.5% semi-annually
2.	8/1/84	6 000	none	12 years	2/1/87	18% quarterly
3.	5/1/85	2 500	none	7 years	5/1/88	17.5% annually
4.	4/1/85	3 000	none	$2\frac{1}{4}$ years	7/1/85	15% monthly
5.	1/2/86	1 500	10% semi-annually	10 years	1/2/89	17% quarterly
6.	2/1/86	1 200	9% monthly	5 years	2/1/87	$17\frac{1}{4}\%$ annually
7.	3/1/86	2 400	12% monthly	2 years	9/1/86	15% quarterly
8.	5/1/86	8 000	6% annually	8 years	5/1/89	22.5% monthly

Statement Problems:

9. A non-interest-bearing note of $1 800 is discounted at 13.5% compounded annually for 20 years. Find the proceeds.

10. A non-interest-bearing note of $5 000 is discounted at 17% compounded quarterly for five years before it is due. Find the proceeds.

11. A note of $4 500 dated June 1, 1984 at 15% compounded quarterly for $6\frac{1}{2}$ years is discounted on October 1, 1986. Find the proceeds if the note is discounted at 22.5% compounded monthly.

12. A note of $400 dated May 1, 1984 at 13.5% compounded monthly for four years is discounted on February 1, 1987. Find the proceeds if the note is discounted at 14.5% compounded quarterly.

13. Gina Power received a seven-year, 12% compounded annually, $5 000 note dated April 1, 1985. Power discounted the note at 15% compounded semi-annually, on February 1, 1986. Find the proceeds. Use METHOD A.

14. F.W. Bondson has a $4\frac{1}{2}$-year note of $3 600 at 12% compounded monthly. The maturity date is February 1, 1985. If the note is discounted on January 1, 1983 at 13.5% compounded annually, how much will Bondson receive? Use METHOD A.

15. A nine-year note bearing interest at 14.5% compounded semi-annually is discounted at 15% compounded quarterly. The face value of the note is $7 200 and the discount period is five years and two months. Find the proceeds. Use METHOD A.

16. Jack. H. Kelley received a non-interest-bearing note for $4 200. He discounted the note at 16.5% compounded semi-annually one year and 7 months before it was due. How much proceeds did he receive? Use METHOD A.

17. Mary Dolton signs a note for $7 000 due in $1\frac{3}{4}$ years to a bank that charges 17.5% compounded semi-annually. What should Dolton receive as the proceeds from the bank? Use METHOD B.

18. John Edwards has a note that will pay him $2 000 at the end of $5\frac{1}{2}$ years. He sells the note three years and one month before it is due at 15.5% compounded quarterly. How much proceeds does he receive from the sale? Use METHOD B.

11.5 The Interest Rate

A. FINDING THE INTEREST RATE

When finding the interest rate solve for $(1 + i)^n$ from the formula $S = P(1 + i)^n$. Thus,

$$\boxed{(1 + i)^n = \frac{S}{P}} \quad \longleftarrow Formula\ 11\text{-}3$$

The value of i can be obtained by taking the nth root of both sides of the equation.

$$(1 + i) = \left(\frac{S}{P}\right)^{1/n}$$

$$\boxed{i = \left(\frac{S}{P}\right)^{1/n} - 1} \quad \longleftarrow Formula\ 11\text{-}3A$$

Example 11.5a

If $1 000 will accumulate to $1 947.90 in $4\frac{1}{4}$ years, what is the nominal interest rate compounded quarterly?

SOLUTION:

$P = \$1\ 000$
$S = \$1\ 947.90$
$n = 4\frac{1}{4} \times 4 = 17$ (quarterly periods)

Substituting these values into Formula 11-3,

$$(1 + i)^{17} = \frac{1\ 947.90}{1\ 000.00} = 1.947\ 90$$

And using Formula 11-3A,

$i = (1.947\ 90)^{1/17} - 1$
$\quad = 1.04 - 1$
$\quad = .04,$ or 4%

The nominal interest rate is therefore 4% × 4 = 16%.

The steps may be performed on a calculator as follows:

Action Taken	Display Shows
1. enter 1.94790	1.94790
2. press the key y^x	1.9479
3. enter 17	17
4. press the key $\frac{1}{x}$	0.0588236
5. press the key $=$	1.04

B.   EFFECTIVE ANNUAL INTEREST RATE

The EFFECTIVE ANNUAL INTEREST RATE is commonly abbreviated as the EFFECTIVE RATE. If the principal is $1, the value of the compound interest for a one-year period is the effective rate. In general, the effective rate is the ratio of the compound interest earned for a one-year period to the principal, as shown:

$$\text{EFFECTIVE RATE} = \frac{\text{COMPOUND INTEREST FOR A ONE-YEAR PERIOD}}{\text{PRINCIPAL}}.$$

In other words, an effective rate is an interest rate compounded annually.

Example 11.5b

If $1 is invested at 12.5% compounded quarterly for one year, what is the effective rate?

SOLUTION:

$P = 1$

$i = 12.5\%/4 = 3.125\%$ or $3\frac{1}{8}\%$ (per quarter)

$n = 4$ (quarters)

The compound amount is computed as follows:
$$\begin{aligned} S &= P(1 + i)^n \\ &= 1(1 + 3.125\%)^4 \\ &= 1(1.130\ 982\ 4) \\ &= 1.130\ 982\ 4 \end{aligned}$$
The compound interest is $1.130\ 982\ 4 - 1 = .130\ 982\ 4$.
The effective rate is $.130\ 982\ 4$, which may be rounded to 13.098%.
Thus, 13.098% compounded annually is equivalent to an interest rate of 12.5% compounded quarterly.

   Normally, the effective rate is greater than the nominal rate (stated annual rate).

In Example 11.5b, the effective rate is greater than the nominal rate by $.598\%$ (or $13.098\% - 12.5\%$).
   To obtain a formula for the effective rate, the following assumptions are made:
Let j = nominal rate
   m = number of conversion periods for one year
   $i = j/m$ (per conversion period)
   f = effective rate
   These values are then substituted in the compound amount formula (11-1). Thus, in a one-year period:

According to the nominal rate, $S = P(1 + j/m)^m$.

According to the effective rate, $S = P(1 + f)$.

The right sides of the two equations above are equated as follows:

$$P(1 + f) = P(1 + j/m)^m, \qquad \text{or} \qquad 1 + f = (1 + j/m)^m$$

$$\boxed{f = \left(1 + \frac{j}{m}\right)^m - 1} \qquad \longleftarrow Formula\ 11\text{-}4$$

or,

$$\boxed{f = (1 + i)^m - 1} \qquad \longleftarrow Formula\ 11\text{-}4A$$

Example 11.5c
Find the effective rate if money is worth 12.5% compounded quarterly on the investment market.

SOLUTION:

$j = 12.5\%$
$m = 4$

Substituting these values in Formula 11-4:

$$f = \left(1 + \frac{12.5\%}{4}\right)^4 - 1$$
$$= (1 + 3.125\%)^4 - 1$$
$$= 1.130\ 982\ 4 - 1$$
$$= .130\ 982\ 4, \text{ or } 13.098\%$$

NOTE: The above effective rate, 13.098% is computed from Formula 11-4 without mentioning the values of S and P. The answer may be compared with that in Example 11.5b.

    The effective rate is frequently used as a device to compare one interest rate with another rate compounded at different time intervals. It is especially useful to those who invest or borrow money from various sources. By comparing the effective rates of the various sources, a person may select the one having the lowest effective rate for borrowing and the one having the highest effective rate for investing.

Example 11.5d
Bank A offers its depositors an interest rate of 24% compounded monthly, while Bank B gives its depositors an interest rate of 24.5% compounded semi-annually. Which of the two banks makes the better offer?

SOLUTION:

The effective rate based on the interest rate of Bank A is:

$$f = \left(1 + \frac{24\%}{12}\right)^{12} - 1$$

$$= (1 + 2\%)^{12} - 1$$
$$= 1.268\ 241\ 8 - 1$$
$$= .268\ 241\ 8, \text{ or } 26.824\ 18\%$$

The effective rate based on the interest rate of Bank B is:

$$f = \left(1 + \frac{24.5\%}{2}\right)^2 - 1$$

$$= (1 + 12.25\%)^2 - 1$$
$$= 1.260\ 006\ 3 - 1$$
$$= .260\ 006\ 3, \text{ or } 26.000\ 63\%$$

The effective rate of Bank A is greater than that of Bank B by .564174% (or 26.824 18% − 26.000 63%); that is, Bank A offers a better interest rate to its depositors.

NOTE:
1. If there is only one conversion period in one year ($m = 1$), the value of f in Formula 11-4 becomes:

$$f = (1 + j/1)^1 - 1 = j.$$

Also, when $m = 1$, $i = j/m = j/1 = j$; and $f = j = i$. The relationships may be stated as follows: If there is only one conversion period in one year, the effective rate equals the nominal rate, which in turn equals the interest rate per conversion period.

2. If the number of conversion periods per year (m) is increased while the value of the nominal rate (j) remains constant, the value of the effective rate (f) is also increased. For example, the effective rates for the nominal rate 24% compounded annually, semi-annually, quarterly, monthly, semi-monthly, weekly and daily are shown below. The values of f are computed by substituting the respective values of m in Formula 11-4 as illustrated in Example 11.5c, above.

	Annually	Semi-Annually	Quarterly	Monthly	Semi-Monthly	Weekly	Daily
$m =$	1	2	4	12	24	52	365
$f =$	.24	.254 4	.262 477	.268 241 8	.269 734 6	.270 547 4	.271 148 9

The table indicates that the effective rate (f) increases as the number of conversion periods (m) increases. However, the increases of the rate are rather moderate.

EXERCISE 11.5 / REFERENCE SECTIONS: A–B

Find the interest rate per conversion period in each of the following problems:

	Principal	Amount	Term	Interest Rate Compounded
1.	$1 000	$ 1 599.77	$3\frac{1}{2}$ years	monthly
2.	2 500	4 771.20	$4\frac{1}{2}$ years	quarterly
3.	4 000	19 688.66	$9\frac{1}{2}$ years	semi-annually
4.	3 000	5 911.02	11 years	annually
5.	2 500	8 736.00	$1\frac{1}{3}$ years	monthly
6.	5 000	13 491.18	6 years	semi-annually
7.	200	739.00	15 years	semi-annually
8.	3 600	5 600.00	7 years	monthly

Statement Problems:

9. At what nominal interest rate compounded quarterly for $5\frac{1}{2}$ years will $1 200 accumulate to the amount of $1 700?

10. If $2 800 amounts to $4 200 in four years with interest compounded quarterly, what is the nominal interest rate?

11. What is the effective rate if $1 is invested for one year at 13.5% compounded (a) annually? (b) semi-annually? (c) quarterly? (d) monthly?
12. What is the effective rate if money is worth 18% compounded (a) annually? (b) semi-annually? (c) quarterly? (d) monthly?
13. Harry invested his money at 16.5% compounded monthly, while Betty invested her money at 17% compounded annually. Who receives the better interest rate?
14. Which is the higher interest rate in the following cases: (a) 15.5% compounded semi-annually, (b) 16% compounded annually?

11.6 Finding the Number of Conversion Periods

The number of conversion periods may be obtained by electronic calculator by use of the logarithmic function, $\ln x$ or $\log x$.

$$(1+i)^n = \frac{S}{P}$$

$$\ln(1 + i)^n = \ln\frac{S}{P}$$

$$\boxed{n = \frac{\ln S/P}{\ln(1 + i)}} \quad \longleftarrow Formula\ 11\text{-}5$$

Example 11.6a
How long will it take $1 000 to accumulate to at least the amount of $1 105 at 8% compounded quarterly?

SOLUTION:

$S = 1\ 105$
$P = 1\ 000$
$i = 8\%/4 = 2\%$ (per quarter)

Substituting these values in Formula 11-5:

$$(1 + i)^n = \frac{S}{P}$$

$$(1 + 2\%)^n = \frac{1\ 105}{1\ 000} = 1.105$$

$$n = \frac{\ln 1.105}{\ln 1.02} = \frac{.099\ 845\ 3}{.019\ 802\ 6} = 5.04.$$

n is greater than 5 and less than 6. Since the principal must amount to at least $1 105, 6 conversion periods are required. Therefore, $n = 6$ quarterly periods, or $1\frac{1}{2}$ years.

CHECK:

$1\ 000(1 + 2\%)^5 = 1\ 000(1.104\ 081) = \$1\ 104.08$, which is \$.92 less than the required amount.
$1\ 000(1 + 2\%)^6 = 1\ 000(1.126\ 162) = \$1\ 126.16$, which is \$21.16 more than the required amount.

EXERCISE 11.6

Find the number of conversion periods in each of the following problems:

	Principal	Amount	Interest Rate	Compounded
1.	\$2 000	\$ 2 300	16%	monthly
2.	3 000	3 475	15%	quarterly
3.	8 000	9 552	12%	semi-annually
4.	5 000	12 828.92	12.5%	annually
5.	5 000	5 700	16%	monthly
6.	7 500	12 000	14%	semi-annually
7.	4 000	9 000	12%	semi-annually
8.	7 200	11 200	15%	monthly

Statement Problems:

9. How long will it take \$1 000 to accumulate to the amount of \$1 166 at 16% compounded annually?
10. How much time is required for \$1 500 to yield \$1 000 interest if the interest rate is 15% compounded monthly?
11. How many years are needed for \$4 000 to yield \$1 375.66 interest if the interest rate is 12% compounded semi-annually?
12. How long will it take \$3 000 to amount to \$8 753.27 at 13.5% effective rate?
13. On January 1, 1984, James Horton borrowed \$1 200 and agreed to repay it with \$1 247.11 interest. If the interest is at 19% compounded quarterly, what amount must he repay and on what date?
14. On July 1, 1985, Albert Todd borrowed \$2 800 at 10% compounded quarterly. He repaid \$4 156.61 on the due date. Find the due date.

11.7 Using a Financial Calculator

Where a financial calculator (preprogrammed) is available, the task of calculating the amount, present value, interest per conversion period and the number of conversion periods may be simplified by use of the special keys provided.

On most financial calculators, the keys used in compounding interest are:

Press key	to enter a value
2nd/FIN	to enter financial mode
FV	future value (S)
PV	present value (P)
%i	interest rate per conversion period (i)
N	the number of conversion periods (n)

To retrieve a value press CPT followed by one of the above (FV, PV, %i, N).

When DEC appears in the display, the decimal point is fixed at two places. To change to a floating decimal point or vice versa, press 2nd/DECIMAL.

Example 11.7a

Marjorie invested $2 500 at 13.5% compounded semi-annually for five years and three months. What amount will she receive at the end of five years and three months?

SOLUTION:

$P = 2\ 500$

$i = \dfrac{13.5}{2}$ (semi-annual rate)

$n = 5.25 \times 2 = 10.5$ (semi-annual periods)

The steps are shown below:

Enter	Press	Display Shows
	2nd/FIN	FIN
2500	PV	2500
6.75	%i	6.75
10.5	N	10.5
	CPT/FV	4963.6687

Thus, $S = 2\ 500\left(1 + \dfrac{13.5\%}{2}\right)^{10.5}$

$\qquad = \$4\ 963.67$

Example 11.7b
A debt of \$8 297.63 is due $9\frac{1}{2}$ years from now. How much will settle the debt now if the discount rate allowed is 15.75% compounded quarterly?

SOLUTION:

$S = 8\ 297.63$

$i = \dfrac{15.75}{4}$ (quarterly rate)

$n = 9\frac{1}{2} \times 4 = 38$ (quarters)
$P = ?$

	Enter	Press	Display Shows
1.		2nd/FIN	FIN
2.	8297.63	FV	8297.63
*3.	15.75	÷	15.75
4.	4	=	3.9375
*5.		%i	3.9375
6.	38	N	38
7.		CPT/PV	1912.5286

Thus, $P = S(1 + i)^{-n}$

$$= 8\ 297.63\left(1 + \frac{15.75\%}{4}\right)^{-38}$$

$$= \$1\ 912.53$$

* NOTE: the order in which steps 3 and 5 are carried out is very important.

Example 11.7c
For how many years must \$3 872.49 be invested at 15.88% compounded quarterly in order to amount to \$9 269.76?

SOLUTION:

$P = 3\ 872.49$
$i = 3.97$ (quarterly rate)
$n = ?$
$S = 9\ 269.76$

Enter	Press	Display Shows
1.	2nd/FIN	FIN
2. 3872.49	PV	3872.49
3. 3.97	%i	3.97
4. 9269.76	FV	9269.76
5.	CPT/N	22.42

Thus, $n = 22.42$, number of years $= 22.42 \div 4 = 5.605$ years.

Example 11.7d
At what nominal rate of interest compounded monthly must $2 500 be invested in order to amount to $17 519.93 in 12.25 years?

SOLUTION:

$P = 2\ 500$
$i = ?$
$n = 12.25 \times 12 = 147$ (months)
$S = 17\ 519.93$

Enter	Press	Display Shows
1.	2nd/FIN	FIN
2. 2500	PV	2500
3. 147	N	147
4. 17519.93	FV	17519.93
5.	CPT/%i	1.3333333

Thus, $i = 1.333\ 333\ 3\%$ (monthly rate),
nominal rate $= 1.333\ 333\ 3\% \times 12$
$\qquad\qquad = 16\%$.

EXERCISE 11.7 / REFERENCE SECTION: 11.7

For each of the following problems use a financial calculator to calculate the missing item:

	Principal	Time	Interest Rate	Amount
1.	$2 000	6 years, 2 months	12.5% compounded quarterly	$?
2.	896	2 years, 6 months	$15\frac{1}{2}$% compounded monthly	?
3.	?	3 years, 1 month	13.5% compounded semi-annually	6 240
4.	?	2 years, 8 months	$12\frac{1}{4}$% compounded quarterly	1 628
5.	3 260	?	$11\frac{1}{2}$ compounded annually	4 279.62
6.	1 482	?	12.25% compounded monthly	1 725.89

Statement Problems:

7. Beulah invested $5 000 in a Guaranteed Investment Certificate paying interest at $11\frac{7}{8}$% compounded monthly. How much will she receive at the end of 5 years?

8. Bill invested $3 500 in a three-year retirement term deposit paying $8\frac{1}{2}$% compounded semi-annually. How much will the deposit amount to at the end of three years?

9. A note for $6 500 dated June 1, 1986 is discounted on May 1, 1984. What are the proceeds if the note is discounted at 12.5% compounded monthly.

10. Eclair Limited estimates that a new car will cost $9 560 by September 1, 1986. How much must the corporation put aside on September 1, 1984 in an account which pays interest at 13.5% compounded quarterly in order to have the required amount on September 1, 1986?

11. For how long must $1 963 be invested at 16.6% compounded monthly in order to amount to $4 476.25?

12. John discounted a five-year note for $6 600 at 11.5% compounded quarterly. If he received $6 461.31 as the proceeds, how long was the discount period?

13. Marlene invested $4 960 on June 1, 1984 and received $6 500 on October 1, 1986. What rate of interest compounded quarterly did she receive?

14. Harry bought a lot of land for $10 000. Three years later he sold it for $15 000. What rate of interest compounded monthly did he receive on his investment? (Ignore cost of purchase and tax expense).

11.8 Using a Table of Values

A. FINDING THE AMOUNT

A table of values of $(1 + i)^n$ may be used to find the amount. For convenience, the most common values of $(1 + i)^n$ are tabulated in Tables 1 and 1A in the supplement. In Table 1, the numbers of the conversion periods are whole numbers; that is, n is a round number, such as 1, 2, 3, and so on. In Table 1A, the numbers of conversion periods are fractional numbers; that is, n is a fraction, such as $\frac{1}{2}, \frac{1}{3}, \frac{1}{4}$ and is generally represented by $\frac{1}{m}$. Each of the values (entries) in the tables is the compound amount when the principal is 1.

Symbolically, let s = the compound amount S when the prinicpal is 1. Then, the formula becomes:

$s = S = P(1 + i)^n = 1(1 + i)^n$, or $s = (1 + i)^n$.

The unit value of each entry may best be represented by a dollar, although it may be represented by any other unit. Thus, each entry in the tables becomes the compound amount in dollars when the principal is $1. The factor $(1 + i)^n$ is also frequently referred to as the ACCUMULATION FACTOR in computing a compound amount.

The methods of computing a compound amount by using the compound amount formula and the tables are illustrated below.

B.   USE OF TABLE 1

When Table 1 is used, Formula 11-1 may be written as follows:

COMPOUND AMOUNT (S) = PRINCIPAL (P) × AN ENTRY IN TABLE 1.

(The entry is at the interest rate i per conversion period for n conversion periods).

Tables 1 through 4 (the compound interest and annuity tables) provide eight decimal places for each entry. It is obvious that it would be a waste of time if all eight places were employed in multiplying a multiplicand of a small value. In most financial problems, the answers are required to contain dollars and cents. In order to avoid unneccessary multiplication and at the same time to obtain a result close enough to the exact value, a simple rule may be used:

If an answer is to be computed to the nearest cent, the minimum number of decimal places to be multiplied is equal to the number of digits in the multiplicand, including dollars and cents.

For example, in finding a compound amount if the principal is $250.10, which has three dollar-digits (250) and two cent-digits (.10), an entry in Table 1 containing five decimal places is employed in multiplication.

Example 11.8a
Find the amount if $5 000 is invested at 12% compounded semi-annually for six years.

SOLUTION:

$P = 5\ 000$

$i = \dfrac{12\%}{2} = 6\%$ (semi-annually)

$n = 6 \times 2 = 12$ (semi-annual periods)

The value of the factor $(1 + i)^n = (1 + 6\%)^{12}$ is found to be 2.012 196 47 in the 6% column opposite $n = 12$ in Table 11-1.

The compound amount $S = 5\ 000(1 + 6\%)^{12}$
$$= 5\ 000(2.012\ 196\ 47)$$
$$= \$10\ 060.98$$

Example 11.8b

Ms Jones signed a note for $2 000 on March 1, 1985 with interest at 18% compounded monthly. What amount is due on March 1, 1990?

SOLUTION:

$P = 2\ 000$

$$i = \frac{18\%}{12} = 1.5\% \text{ (monthly)}$$

March 1, 1985 to March 1, 1990 = 5 years
$n = 5 \times 12 = 60$ (months)
The value of the factor $(1 + 1.5\%)^{60}$ is found to be 2.443 219 78 in the $1\frac{1}{2}\%$ column opposite $n = 60$ in Table 11-1.
The compound amount $S = 2\ 000(1 + 1.5\%)^{60}$

$$= 2\ 000(2.443\ 219\ 78)$$
$$= \$4\ 886.44$$

When the value of $(1 + i)^n$ is obtained from a table, additional calculations are sometimes required.

C. THE NUMBER OF CONVERSION PERIODS (n) IS GREATER THAN THE HIGHEST NUMBER IN TABLE 1

When the number of conversion periods is greater than that given in Table 1, the number of conversion periods may be divided into several smaller numbers which are listed in the table. The product of the corresponding entries of the smaller numbers is the desired accumulation factor. For example,

$$(1 + 4\%)^{239} = (1 + 4\%)^{100}(1 + 4\%)^{100}(1 + 4\%)^{39};$$

$$(1 + 3\%)^{126} = (1 + 3\%)^{100}(1 + 3\%)^{26}.$$

Although these values on the left sides of the equations are not listed in the table, the values of the expanded factors on the right sides of the equations are included in the table. Thus, the entries in the table may be used in computing the accumulation factor $(1 + i)^n$ when the value of n is greater than the highest number in the table.

Example 11.8c

Laura deposited $1 200 in an account which paid 18% compounded monthly. If the interest rate remained unchanged, how much does she have in the account at the end of fifteen years?

SOLUTION:

$P = 1\ 200$

$i = \dfrac{18\%}{12} = 1\frac{1}{2}\%$ (monthly)

$n = 15 \times 12 = 180$ (months)
$S = 1\ 200(1 + 1\frac{1}{2}\%)^{180}$

$(1 + 1\frac{1}{2}\%)^{180} = (1 + 1\frac{1}{2}\%)^{100}(1 + 1\frac{1}{2}\%)^{80}$
$\phantom{(1 + 1\frac{1}{2}\%)^{180}} = (4.43204565)(3.29066279)$
$\phantom{(1 + 1\frac{1}{2}\%)^{180}} = 14.584367$

Thus, $S = 1\ 200(14.584367)$
$ = \$17\ 501.24.$

EXERCISE 11.8A / REFERENCE SECTIONS: A–C

Use a table of values to find the compound amount in each of the following problems:

	Principal (P)	Interest Rate (i)	Time (n)
1.	$ 2 500	12% compounded monthly	6 years
2.	5 000	15% compounded semi-annually	8 years
3.	21 000	13.5% compounded annually	7 years
4.	11 500	12% compounded quarterly	$1\frac{1}{2}$ years
5.	2 300	18% compounded monthly	10 years
6.	1 600	16% compounded quarterly	30 years

Statement Problems:

7. How much will settle a debt of $3 500 with interest at 12% compounded monthly for 11 years?

8. A condominium corporation has set aside $10 000 in an account which will be used to cover major repairs. The account earns 16% compounded quarterly. How much will be in the account if it remains untouched for 30 years?

9. On the day that Margaret was born, her aunt deposited $2 000 in an account which paid 15% compounded monthly. How much does Margaret receive if her aunt gives her the amount in the account on her twenty-first birthday?

10. Stephan deposited $1 000 in a trust fund on his daughter's tenth birthday. The fund is to be available to his daughter on her twentieth birthday. How much will she receive if the rate of interest is 18% compounded monthly?

D.   FINDING THE PRESENT VALUE

A table of values of $(1 + i)^{-n}$ may be used to find the present value of a given amount.

For convenience, the most common values of $(1 + i)^{-n}$ are tabulated in Table 2 of the supplement. The values (entries) in the table may best be considered as the present values in dollars when the compound amount is $1, although each entry may be considered as the value in a unit other than a dollar.

Let p = the present value P when the compound amount is 1. Then, the formula becomes:

$$p = P = S(1 + i)^{-n} = 1(1 + i)^{-n}, \text{ or } p = (1 + i)^{-n}.$$

The factor $(1 + i)^{-n}$ is frequently referred to as the DISCOUNT FACTOR in discounting a compound amount. The methods of finding the present value of a given amount that is due on a future date are presented below.

E. USE OF TABLE 2

When Table 2 is used, Formula 11-2 may be expressed as follows:

PRESENT VALUE (P) = COMPOUND AMOUNT (S) × AN ENTRY IN TABLE 2.

(The entry is at the interest rate i per conversion period and for n conversion periods).

Example 11.8d
Find the present value of $2 479.27 due at the end of $8\frac{1}{2}$ years if money is worth 6% compounded semi-annually.

SOLUTION:

The amount (S) = $2 479.27, the interest rate per semi-annual period (i) = 6%/2 = 3%, and the number of conversion periods (n) = $8\frac{1}{2} \times 2 = 17$ (semi-annual periods). The discount factor $(1 + i)^{-n} = (1 + 3\%)^{-17} = .605\ 016\ 45$ (Table 11-2).

Substituting these values in Formula 11-2:
$$P = S(1 + i)^{-n}$$
$$= 2\ 479.27(1 + 3\%)^{-17}$$
$$= 2\ 479.27(.605\ 016)$$
$$= \$1\ 500$$

Example 11.8e
If $1 000 is due $1\frac{2}{3}$ years from now and money is worth 12% compounded monthly, find its present value and the compound discount.

SOLUTION:

The given amount (S) = $1 000, $i = \frac{12\%}{12} = 1\%$ (per month), $n = 1\frac{2}{3} \times 12 = 20$ (months), and the factor $(1 + 1\%)^{-20} = .819\ 544\ 47$ (Table 11-2).

Present value $P = 1\ 000(1 + 1\%)^{-20}$
$$= 1\ 000(.819\ 544)$$
$$= \$819.54$$

Compound discount = Compound Amount − Present Value
$$= 1\ 000 - 819.54$$
$$= \$180.46$$

The value of P may be obtained by using Formula 11-2A, but division is involved:

$$P = \frac{S}{(1 + i)^n} = \frac{1\ 000}{(1 + 1\%)^{20}} = \frac{1\ 000}{1.220\ 19} = \$819.54 \text{ (Table 11-1).}$$

The solution may also be stated as follows:

If \$819.54 is invested now at 12% compounded monthly for $1\frac{2}{3}$ years, the compound amount at the end of $1\frac{2}{3}$ years is \$1 000.

CHECK:

$$S = P(1 + i)^n$$
$$= 819.54(1 + 1\%)^{20}$$
$$= 819.54(1.220\ 19)$$
$$= \$999.99, \text{ or rounded to } \$1\ 000$$

EXERCISE 11.8B / REFERENCE SECTIONS: D–E

Use a table of values to find the present value in each of the following problems:

	Amount (S)	Interest Rate (i)	Time (n)
1.	\$ 2 800	15% compounded semi-annually	4 years
2.	6 900	12% compounded monthly	$5\frac{1}{2}$ years
3.	2 400	8.5% compounded annually	16 years
4.	16 000	16% compounded quarterly	15 years
5.	9 800	18% compounded monthly	12 years
6.	10 000	20% compounded quarterly	25 years

Statement Problems:

7. What is the present value now of a debt of \$4 850 due 3 years from now if the discount rate is 15% compounded semi-annually?

8. A condominium corporation estimates that major repairs will be required to the building in 10 years at a cost of \$15 000. If funds may be invested at 12% compounded semi-annually, how much should the corporation invest now in order to have the required amount 10 years from now?

9. John would like to have \$4 000 on December 27, 1990 for a vacation in Hawaii. How much must he set aside in a fund on March 27, 1984 if the fund pays interest at 16% compounded monthly?

10. On Mary's tenth birthday, her aunt set up a trust fund for Mary. On her twenty-first birthday, Mary received the amount of \$6 859 from the fund. If the fund earned interest at 12% compounded semi-annually, how much did Mary's aunt deposit in the fund?

F. THE INTEREST RATE PER CONVERSION PERIOD (i) IS NOT GIVEN IN THE TABLE

When the interest rate is not given in the table, the interpolation method may be used to obtain an approximate entry which is accurate enough for most purposes.

Example 11.8f

Find the compound amount if $1 000 is invested at 8.5% compounded quarterly for $2\frac{1}{2}$ years.

SOLUTION:

$P = 1\ 000$

$i = 8.5\%/4 = 2\frac{1}{8}\%$ (per quarter)

$n = 2\frac{1}{2} \times 4 = 10$ (quarterly periods)

There is no $2\frac{1}{8}\%$ column in Table 11-1. However, the rate which is just above and that which is just below the rate $2\frac{1}{8}\%$ may be found in the table, and the accumulation factor for $2\frac{1}{8}\%$ may be obtained through interpolation. When the interpolation method is used, it is assumed that the differences between the values of $(1 + i)^n$ are proportional to the differences between the values of i in the table.

The factor $(1 + 2\frac{1}{8}\%)^{10}$ is obtained by the interpolation method as follows:

	i	$(1 + i)^{10}$	
	$2\frac{1}{4}\%$	1.249 203 43	(1)
	$2\frac{1}{8}\%$	x	(2)
	2%	1.218 994 42	(3)
(2) − (3)	$\frac{1}{8}\%^1$	$x -$ 1.218 994 42	(4)
(1) − (3)	$\frac{1}{4}\%_2$	0.030 209 01	(5)

The differences on line (4) are obtained by subtracting the values on line (3) from the corresponding values on line (2), or

$\frac{1}{8}\% = 2\frac{1}{8}\% - 2\%$, and $x -$ 1.218 994 42 (= unknown).

The differences on line (5) are obtained in a similar manner, or

$\frac{1}{4}\% = 2\frac{1}{4}\% - 2\%$, and 0.030 209 01 = 1.249 203 43 − 1.218 994 42.

The differences on lines (4) and (5) give the proportion which indicates that $\frac{1}{8}\%$ is to $(x - 1.21899442)$ as $\frac{1}{4}\%$ is to 0.030 209 01. The proportion is also expressed in equation form on these two lines.

Solve for x in the equation. First, the fraction at the left side of the equation is simplified by multiplying both numerator and denominator by 800, or

$$\frac{\frac{1}{8}\% \times 800}{\frac{1}{4}\% \times 800} = \frac{1}{2}, \text{ and } \frac{1}{2} = \frac{x - 1.218\ 994\ 42}{0.030\ 209\ 01}.$$

Then, $x -$ 1.218 994 42 = 0.030 209 01 $\cdot \frac{1}{2}$,

$x =$ 1.218 994 42 + 0.015 104 505 = 1.234 098 925, or

$(1 + 2\frac{1}{8}\%)^{10} =$ 1.234 098 925.

Thus, $S = 1\ 000(1 + 2\frac{1}{8}\%)^{10} = 1\ 000(1.234\ 099) = \$1\ 234.10$.

NOTE:

1. In the above arrangement, the larger values are placed on the top line in order to facilitate subtraction.

2. The order of the subtraction, either by first subtracting line (3) from line (2) or by first subtracting line (3) from line (1), does not affect the answer. The value of x in the proportion

$$\frac{\frac{1}{8}\%}{\frac{1}{4}\%} = \frac{x - 1.218\ 994\ 42}{0.030\ 209\ 01}$$

is the same as in the reversed-term proportion,

$$\frac{\frac{1}{4}\%}{\frac{1}{8}\%} = \frac{0.030\ 209\ 01}{x - 1.218\ 994\ 42}.$$

However, the former proportion does simplify the operation in solving for x.

3. According to the rule of the number of decimal places in a multiplier, only 6 decimal places are required in multiplying the 6-digit number 1 000.00. Thus, the result in the above interpolation would be a satisfactory one if the value of $(1 + i)^n$ included only 7 decimal places. The one extra place provides for safety in rounding to the 6-place requirement.

EXERCISE 11.8C / REFERENCE SECTION: F

Find the compound amount in each of the following problems. (Use the interpolation method to find each accumulation factor):

Principal (P)	Interest Rate (i)	Time (n)
1. $1 000	$15\frac{3}{4}\%$ compounded monthly	1 year
2. 1 500	$18\frac{1}{4}\%$ compounded semi-annually	10 years
3. 900	21% compounded monthly	7 months
4. 850	$17\frac{1}{4}\%$ compounded semi-annually	12 years
5. 2 200	$16\frac{1}{2}\%$ compounded quarterly	6 years
6. 3 400	22% compounded monthly	10 months

G. FINDING THE INTEREST RATE

When finding the interest rate, Table 1 in the supplement may be used as explained below:

Solve $(1 + i)^n$ from the formula $S = P(1 + i)^n$. Thus,

$$\boxed{(1 + i)^n = \frac{S}{P}} \quad \longleftarrow Formula\ 11\text{-}6$$

Formula 11-5 may be expressed as follows:

$$\text{AN ENTRY IN TABLE } 1 = \frac{\text{COMPOUND AMOUNT}}{\text{PRINCIPAL}}.$$

Formula 11-6 contains four values. If the values of S, P, and n are known, an entry which is equal to $\frac{S}{P}$ may be found in the n row of Table 1. The value of the interest rate (i) is thus found in the column containing the entry. If the exact entry cannot be found in the table, the interpolation method may be used to find an approximate value of i.

Example 11.8g

If \$1 000 will accumulate to \$1 947.90 in $8\frac{1}{2}$ years, what is the nominal interest rate compounded semi-annually?

SOLUTION:

$P = 1\ 000$
$S = 1\ 947.90$
$n = 8\frac{1}{2} \times 2 = 17$ (semi-annual periods)

Substituting these values in Formula 11-6:

$$(1 + i)^{17} = \frac{1\ 947.90}{1\ 000.00} = 1.947\ 9.$$

In the $n = 17$ row of Table 11-1, the entry 1.947 9 is found in the 4% column. Thus, $i = 4\%$, and the nominal interest rate is $4\% \times 2 = 8\%$.

Example 11.8h

At what nominal interest rate compounded semi-annually for ten years will \$300 accumulate to \$890?

SOLUTION:

$P = 300$
$S = 890$
$n = 10 \times 2 = 20$ (semi-annual periods)

Substituting these values in Formula 11-6:

$$(1 + i)^{20.} = \frac{890}{300} = 2.966\ 7.$$

There is no entry 2.966 7 in the row $n = 20$ in Table 11-1. However, an entry which is just above and one which is just below the value of 2.9667 may be found in the table and the interest rate may be obtained through interpolation. When the interpolation method is used, it is assumed that the differences between the values of i are proportional to the differences between the values of $(1 + i)^n$ in the table. The findings are arranged for interpolation as follows:

	i		$(1 + i)^{20}$	
	6%		3.207 1	(1)
	x		2.966 7	(2)
	$5\frac{1}{2}\%$		2.917 8	(3)
(2) − (3)	$x - 5\frac{1}{2}\%$	=	0.048 9	(4)
(1) − (3)	$\frac{1}{2}\%$		0.289 3	

Solve for x from the proportion formed by the differences on lines (4) and (5):

$$x - 5\frac{1}{2}\% = \frac{1}{2}\%\left(\frac{0.048\ 9}{0.289\ 3}\right) = \frac{1}{200} \cdot \frac{489}{2893} = .000\ 845$$

$x = 5\frac{1}{2}\% + .000\ 845 = .055 + .000\ 845 = .055\ 845$, or $i = .055\ 845$ (interest rate per semi-annual period).

The nominal interest rate is .055 845 × 2 = .111 690
$$= 11.169\%, \text{ or rounded to } 11.17\%.$$

NOTE:

1. The values of $(1 + i)^n$ include four decimal places in the above interpolation. This practice may be followed in solving the problems in the following exercises. In most cases, the accuracy of the result of an interpolation will not be any greater if the values include more than four decimal places.

2. The time unit of n should always agree with the time unit of i in computing compound interest problems. For instance, in the above example, n represents the number of semi-annual periods and i represents the interest rate per semi-annual period.

EXERCISE 11.8D / REFERENCE SECTION: G

Find the nominal interest rate in each of the following problems:

	Principal	Amount	Term	Interest Rate
1.	$ 1 000	$ 1 233	$3\frac{1}{2}$ years	compounded monthly
2.	2 500	3 220	$4\frac{1}{2}$ years	compounded quarterly
3.	4 000	7 690	$4\frac{1}{4}$ years	compounded semi-annually
4.	3 000	5 406	$5\frac{1}{2}$ years	compounded annually
5.	6 500	10 800	6 years	compounded quarterly
6.	3 942	7 916	$6\frac{1}{2}$ years	compounded semi-annually

H. FINDING THE NUMBER OF CONVERSION PERIODS

In Formula 11-6, $(1 + i)^n = \frac{S}{P}$, if the values of S, P, and i are known, an entry which is equal to the value of $\frac{S}{P}$ may be found in the i column in Table 11-1. The value of n, the number of conversion periods, is thus found in the row containing the entry. If the value of $\frac{S}{P}$ cannot be found in the table, the interpolation method may be used for finding the value of n. However, most long-term investors are not interested in a fraction of a conversion period. Therefore, it is generally unnecessary to carry out the interpolation.

Example 11.8i
How long will it take $1 000 to accumulate to the amount of $1 105 at 8% compounded quarterly?

SOLUTION:

$S = 1\ 105$
$P = 1\ 000$
$i = 8\%/4 = 2\%$ (per quarter)

Substituting these values in Formula 11-6:
$$(1 + i)^n = \frac{S}{P}$$

$$(1 + 2\%)^n = \frac{1\ 105}{1\ 000} = 1.105$$
$n = 6$ quarterly periods, or $1\frac{1}{2}$ years

In the 2% column in Table 11-1, the value 1.105 is between the entries 1.104 080 80 (where $n = 5$) and 1.126 162 42 (where $n = 6$). Since the nearest value to 1.105 is 1.104 080 80, the required time is slightly over 5 conversion periods, or $1\frac{1}{4}$ years. The finding may be written: $5 < n < 6$; that is, n is greater than 5 but is smaller than 6.

However, the sixth conversion period is necessary for the principal to accumulate to at least $1 105. For simplicity in this text, the larger value of n is hereafter regarded as the answer to this type of problem.

CHECK:

$1\ 000(1 + 2\%)^5 = 1\ 000(1.104\ 081) = \$1\ 104.08$, which is $.92 less than the required amount.
$1\ 000(1 + 2\%)^6 = 1\ 000(1.126\ 162) = \$1\ 126.16$, which is $21.16 more than the required amount.

EXERCISE 11.8E / REFERENCE SECTION: H

Find the number of conversion periods in each of the following problems:

	Principal	Amount	Interest Rate	Compounded
1.	$ 2 000	$ 2 300	8%	monthly
2.	3 000	5 310	5%	quarterly
3.	8 000	9 552	6%	semi-annually
4.	5 000	10 580	$5\frac{1}{2}$%	annually

Table 11-1
Compound Amount
when principal is 1 $s = (1 + i)^n$

n	$\frac{2}{3}$%	$\frac{3}{4}$%	$\frac{7}{8}$%	1%	n
15	1.1048 0422	1.1186 0259	1.1396 0203	1.1609 6896	15
16	1.1121 6958	1.1269 9211	1.1495 7355	1.1725 7864	16
17	1.1195 8404	1.1354 4455	1.1596 3232	1.1843 0443	17
18	1.1270 4794	1.1439 6039	1.1697 7910	1.1961 4748	18
19	1.1345 6159	1.1525 4009	1.1800 1467	1.2081 0895	19
20	1.1421 2533	1.1611 8414	1.1903 3980	1.2201 9004	20
21	1.1497 3950	1.1698 9302	1.2007 5527	1.2323 9194	21
22	1.1574 0443	1.1786 6722	1.2112 6188	1.2447 1586	22
23	1.1651 2046	1.1875 0723	1.2218 6042	1.2571 6302	23
24	1.1728 8793	1.1964 1353	1.2325 5170	1.2697 3465	24

n	$1\frac{1}{8}$%	$1\frac{1}{4}$%	$1\frac{3}{8}$%	$1\frac{1}{2}$%	n
57	1.8920 6684	2.0300 9713	2.1780 0780	2.3364 9259	57
58	1.9133 5259	2.0554 7335	2.2079 5541	2.3715 3998	58
59	1.9348 7780	2.0811 6676	2.2383 1480	2.4071 1308	59
60	1.9566 4518	2.1071 8135	2.2690 9163	2.4432 1978	60
61	1.9786 5744	2.1335 2111	2.3002 9164	2.4798 6807	61
62	2.0009 1733	2.1601 9013	2.3319 2065	2.5170 6609	62
63	2.0234 2765	2.1871 9250	2.3639 8456	2.5548 2208	63
77	2.3665 0358	2.6026 6011	2.8620 4710	3.1469 1674	77
78	2.3931 2675	2.6351 9336	2.9014 0024	3.1941 2050	78
79	2.4200 4942	2.6681 3327	2.9412 9450	3.2420 3230	79
80	2.4472 7498	2.7014 8494	2.9817 3730	3.2906 6279	80
81	2.4748 0682	2.7352 5350	3.0227 3618	3.3400 2273	81
82	2.5026 4840	2.7694 4417	3.0642 9881	3.3901 2307	82
83	2.5308 0319	2.8040 6222	3.1064 3291	3.4409 7492	83
97	2.9599 0559	3.3367 0716	3.7609 2021	4.2384 4057	97
98	2.9932 0452	3.3784 1600	3.8126 3287	4.3020 1718	98
99	3.0268 7807	3.4206 4620	3.8650 5657	4.3665 4744	99
100	3.0609 3045	3.4634 0427	3.9182 0110	4.4320 4565	100

Table 11-1 (Continued)
Compound Amount
when principal is 1 $s = (1 + i)^n$

n	1⅝%	1¾%	1⅞%	2%	n
1	1.0162 5000	1.0175 0000	1.0187 5000	1.0200 0000	1
2	1.0327 6406	1.0353 0625	1.0378 5156	1.0404 0000	2
3	1.0495 4648	1.0534 2411	1.0573 1128	1.0612 0800	3
4	1.0666 0161	1.0718 5903	1.0771 3587	1.0824 3216	4
5	1.0839 3388	1.0906 1656	1.0973 3216	1.1040 8080	5
6	1.1015 4781	1.1097 0235	1.1179 0714	1.1261 6242	6
7	1.1194 4796	1.1291 2215	1.1388 6790	1.1486 8567	7
8	1.1376 3899	1.1488 8178	1.1602 2167	1.1716 5938	8
9	1.1561 2563	1.1689 8721	1.1819 7583	1.1950 9257	9
10	1.1749 1267	1.1894 4449	1.2041 3788	1.2189 9442	10
11	1.1940 0500	1.2102 5977	1.2267 1546	1.2433 7431	11

n	2¼%	2½%	2¾%	3%	n
5	1.1176 7769	1.1314 0821	1.1452 7334	1.1592 7407	5
6	1.1428 2544	1.1596 9342	1.1767 6836	1.1940 5230	6
7	1.1685 3901	1.1886 8575	1.2091 2949	1.2298 7387	7
8	1.1948 3114	1.2184 0290	1.2423 8055	1.2667 7008	8
9	1.2217 1484	1.2488 6297	1.2765 4602	1.3047 7318	9
10	1.2492 0343	1.2800 8454	1.3116 5103	1.3439 1638	10
11	1.2773 1050	1.3120 8666	1.3477 2144	1.3842 3387	11

n	3¼%	3½%	3¾%	4%	n
13	1.5155 5180	1.5639 5606	1.6137 8387	1.6650 7351	13
14	1.5648 0723	1.6186 9452	1.6743 0076	1.7316 7645	14
15	1.6156 6347	1.6753 4883	1.7370 8704	1.8009 4351	15
16	1.6681 7253	1.7339 8604	1.8022 2781	1.8729 8125	16
17	1.7223 8814	1.7946 7555	1.8698 1135	1.9479 0050	17
18	1.7783 6575	1.8574 8920	1.9399 2928	2.0258 1652	18
19	1.8361 6264	1.9225 0132	2.0126 7662	2.1068 4918	19
20	1.8958 3792	1.9897 8886	2.0881 5200	2.1911 2314	20
21	1.9574 5266	2.0594 3147	2.1664 5770	2.2787 6807	21

n	4½%	5%	5½%	6%	n
10	1.5529 6942	1.6288 9463	1.7081 4446	1.7908 4770	10
11	1.6228 5305	1.7103 3936	1.8020 9240	1.8982 9856	11
12	1.6958 8143	1.7958 5633	1.9012 0749	2.0121 9647	12
13	1.7721 9610	1.8856 4914	2.0057 7390	2.1329 2826	13
14	1.8519 4492	1.9799 3160	2.1160 9146	2.2609 0396	14
15	1.9352 8244	2.0789 2818	2.2324 7649	2.3965 5819	15
16	2.0223 7015	2.1828 7459	2.3552 6270	2.5403 5168	16
17	2.1133 7681	2.2920 1832	2.4848 0215	2.6927 7279	17
18	2.2084 7877	2.4066 1923	2.6214 6627	2.8543 3915	18
19	2.3078 6031	2.5269 5020	2.7656 4691	3.0255 9950	19
20	2.4117 1402	2.6532 9771	2.9177 5749	3.2071 3547	20
21	2.5202 4116	2.7859 6259	3.0782 3415	3.3995 6360	21

Table 11-2
Present Value
when compounded amount is 1 $p = (1 + i)^{-n}$ [OR, $v^{n} = (1 + i)^{-n}$]

n	$\frac{2}{3}\%$	$\frac{3}{4}\%$	$\frac{7}{8}\%$	1%	n
17	0.8931 8886	0.8807 1231	0.8623 4230	0.8443 7749	17
18	0.8872 7371	0.8741 5614	0.8548 6225	0.8360 1731	18
19	0.8813 9772	0.8676 4878	0.8474 4709	0.8277 3992	19
20	0.8755 6065	0.8611 8985	0.8400 9625	0.8195 4447	20
21	0.8697 6224	0.8547 7901	0.8328 0917	0.8114 3017	21
22	0.8640 0222	0.8484 1589	0.8255 8530	0.8033 9621	22
23	0.8582 8035	0.8421 0014	0.8184 2409	0.7954 4179	23
24	0.8525 9638	0.8358 3140	0.8113 2499	0.7875 6613	24

n	$2\frac{1}{4}\%$	$2\frac{1}{2}\%$	$2\frac{3}{4}\%$	3%	n
12	0.7656 6748	0.7435 5589	0.7221 3440	0.7013 7988	12
13	0.7488 1905	0.7254 2038	0.7028 0720	0.6809 5134	13
14	0.7323 4137	0.7077 2720	0.6839 9728	0.6611 1781	14
15	0.7162 2628	0.6904 6556	0.6656 9078	0.6418 6195	15
16	0.7004 6580	0.6736 2493	0.6478 7424	0.6231 6694	16
17	0.6850 5212	0.6571 9506	0.6305 3454	0.6050 1645	17
18	0.6699 7763	0.6411 6591	0.6136 5892	0.5873 9461	18
19	0.6552 3484	0.6255 2772	0.5972 3496	0.5702 8603	19
20	0.6408 1647	0.6102 7094	0.5812 5057	0.5536 7575	20
21	0.6267 1538	0.5953 8629	0.5656 9398	0.5375 4928	21

11.9 *Equivalent Values Involving Compound Interest*

It was stated in Chapter Nine that a single obligation or a set of obligations may be replaced by another single obligation or set of obligations due at different times. In order to satisfy both the creditors and the debtors, the values of the new obligations should be equivalent to the values of the original ones. An EQUATION OF VALUE is usually arranged in order to obtain the required equivalent values. The equation gives the equivalent values of the original obligations and the new obligations on a comparison date, sometimes called the focal date, at the agreed or present investment market interest rate. The answer for a required equivalent value may vary slightly in simple interest problems depending on the selection of the comparison date. However, in compound interest problems the selection of the comparison date does not affect the answer.

The formula $S = P(1 + i)^{n}$ is an equation of value since the value of S is equivalent to the value of P after n periods with a compound interest rate i per period.

Thus, if $P = \$1$, $i = 12.5\%$ compounded annually, $n = 3$ (years), then $S = 1(1 + 12.5\%)^3 = \$1.42$. The illustration may be stated as follows: If money is worth 12.5% compounded annually (the value on the present investment market), $1 now is equivalent to $1.42 in three years.

Likewise, the formula $P = S(1 + i)^{-n}$ is an equation of value since the value of P is equivalent to the value of S for n periods before it is due when the interest rate i per period is involved. Thus, if $S = \$1$, $i = 12.5\%$ compounded annually, and $n = 3$ (years), then $P = 1(1 + 12.5\%)^{-3} = \$0.70$. Therefore, $1 due in three years at 12.5% compounded annually is equivalent to $0.70 now.

Note that a sum of money has different values at different times if interest is involved, and the amount due in the future is normally larger than its equivalent value at the present time. A person may borrow $1 now and repay $1.42 after three years. On the other hand, a creditor may agree to discharge a debt of $1 which is due in three years by having the debtor pay only $0.70 now. The values in the two transactions are equivalent to each other under the compound interest method. The following examples illustrate further problems in equivalent values involving compound interest.

Example 11.9a

A debt of $200 is due at the end of four years. If money is worth 18% compounded monthly, what is the value of the debt when is paid (a) at the end of three years? (b) at the end of four years and eight months?

SOLUTION:

According to the problem, $200 is the maturity value or the amount due at the end of four years. The interest rate, which is agreed upon by both lender and borrower to settle the debt, is 18% compounded monthly.

(a)   If the debt of $200 is paid at the end of three years, which is one year (or 12 months) before the due date, the required equivalent value is less than $200. Thus, the compound discount formula $P = S(1 + i)^{-n}$ is used to compute the required value. In other words, the value is obtained by discounting the maturity value (or the amount on the due date) by the compound discount method for the advanced time of one year.
$S = 200$, $i = 18\%/4 = 1.5\%$ (per month), $n = 12$ (months)

Substituting the values in the compound discount formula:
$P = 200(1 + 1\frac{1}{2}\%)^{-12} = 200(0.836\ 39) = \$167.28$.
If the debt is paid at the end of three years, the payment is $167.28.

(b) If the debt of $200 is paid at the end of four years and eight months, which is eight months after the due date, the required equivalent value is more than $200. Thus, the compound discount $S = P(1 + i)^n$ is used to compute the required value. In other words, the value is obtained by accumulating the amount on the due date for the extended time of eight months.

$P = 200$, $i = 1.5\%$ (per month), $n = 8$ (months)

Substituting the values in the compound amount formula:
$S = 200(1 + 1\frac{1}{2}\%)^8 = 200(1.126\ 49) = \$225.30$.
When the debt is paid at the end of four years and eight months, the payment is $225.30.

The example may be diagrammed as follows:

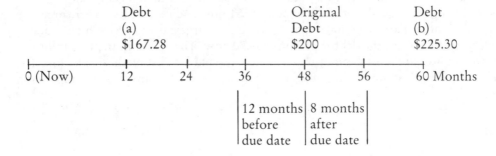

| Debt (a) $167.28 | | | | Original Debt $200 | | Debt (b) $225.30 |

0 (Now)   12   24   36   48   56   60 Months

12 months before due date | 8 months after due date

Example 11.9b
A man owes (a) $300 due in four years and six months and (b) $400 due in seven years. He and his creditor have agreed to settle the debts by two equal payments in five years and six months and six years respectively. Find the size of each payment if money is worth 12% compounded quarterly.

SOLUTION:

Let x be each payment and the comparison date be six years from now. The values on the comparison date are computed below.

1. The value of the old debt of $300 becomes $358.22 on the comparison date and is computed as follows:
    $P = 300$, $i = 12\%/4 = 3\%$, $n = (6 - 4\frac{1}{2}) \times 4 = 6$ quarters from the due date to the comparison date)

    Substituting the values in the formula $S = P(1 + i)^n$:
    $S = 300(1 + 3\%)^6$
    $\quad = 300(1.194\ 05) = \$358.22$

2. The value of the old debt of $400 becomes $355.40 on the comparison date and is computed as follows:

$S = 400$, $i = 3\%$, $n = (7 - 6) \times 4 = 4$ (quarters from the comparison date to the due date)

Substituting the values in the formula $P = S(1 + i)^{-n}$:
$P = 400(1 + 3\%)^{-4}$
$= 400(.888\ 49) = \$355.40$

3. The value of the new debt, which is the first payment due in four years and six months becomes $x(1.03)^2$ on the comparison date and is computed as follows:
$P = x$, $i = 3\%$, $n = (6 - 5\frac{1}{2}) \times 4 = 2$ (quarters from the due date to the comparison date)

Substituting the values in the formula $S = P(1 + i)^n$:
$S = x(1 + 3\%)^2 = x(1.03)^2$

4. The value of the second payment due in six years does not change and is x since the comparison date is also in six years.

The values in Example 11.9b are diagrammed in the following manner:

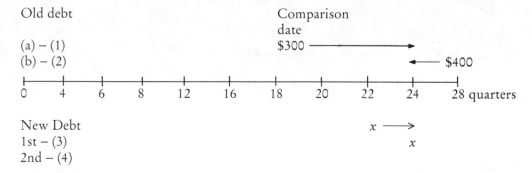

Old debt

(a) – (1)
(b) – (2)

Comparison
date
$300
$400

```
├──┼──┼──┼──┼──┼──┼──┼──┼──┼──┤
0   4   6   8  12  16  18  20  22  24  28 quarters
```

New Debt
1st – (3)
2nd – (4)

$x \longrightarrow$
x

The equation of value based on the comparison date is given below:

$\underline{\text{New Debts}}$ $\underline{\text{Old Debts}}$
$x + x(1.03)^2\ =\ 355.40 + 358.22$ Solve for x.
$x + x(1.0609)\ =\ 713.62$
$2.0609x\ =\ 713.62$
$x\ =\ \$346.27$

Example 11.9c
A man owes (a) $700 due in $1\frac{1}{2}$ years and (b) $1 000 due in four years. His creditor has agreed for him to pay the debts with a payment of $800 in six months and the remainder in $2\frac{1}{2}$ years. If money is worth 16% compounded semi-annually, what size must the second payment be?

SOLUTION:

Let x be the second payment, which is to be made on the comparison date, or $2\frac{1}{2}$ years hence. The following diagram indicates the equivalent values of the given values on the comparison date.

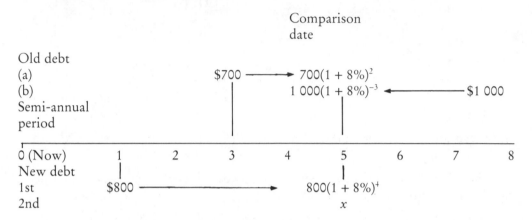

The equation of value based on the comparison date is given below:

New Debts	Old Debts

$$x + 800(1 + 8\%)^4 = 1\,000(1 + 8\%)^{-3} + 700(1 + 8\%)^2$$
$$x = 1\,000(.7938322) + 700(1.1664) - 800(1.360489)$$
$$= 793.832 + 816.48 - 1088.391$$
$$= \$521.92$$

Example 11.9d

Francine borrowed (a) $500 due in one year, and (b) $1 000 with interest at 9% compounded monthly due in $1\frac{1}{2}$ years. If money is worth 12% compounded quarterly, what single payment $3\frac{1}{2}$ years hence will be equivalent to the two original obligations?

SOLUTION:

Let x be the unknown single payment and the comparison date be $3\frac{1}{2}$ years hence. Since (b) is an interest-bearing debt, the maturity value based on a 9% interest rate compounded monthly for $1\frac{1}{2}$ years (or 18 months) should be computed first. The maturity value is then accumulated at 12% compounded quarterly for two years (or eight quarterly periods) from the due date to the comparison date. The maturity value at the end of $1\frac{1}{2}$ years is
$$\$1\,000(1 + 9\%/12)^{18} = 1\,000(1 + 0.75\%)^{18} = 1\,000(1.143\,960) = \$1\,143.96$$
and its value on the comparison date becomes
$$\$1\,143.96(1 + 12\%/4)^8 = 1\,143.96(1 + 3\%)^8 = \$1\,449.13.$$

The entire problem is diagrammed in the following manner:

Comparison
Old debt   12% for $2\frac{1}{2}$ years (10 periods)   date
(a)   \$500————————————————————→$500(1 + 3\%)^{10}$
(b) \$1 000 ——→\$1 143.96 ————————————→$1\ 143.96\ (1 + 3\%)^{8}$
      ├———————————————————————————————————————┤
      0 (Now)   2   4   6   8   10   12   14 Quarters
                                                     │
New debt x

The equation of value based on the comparison date is written below:

New Debt   Old Debts
$$x = 1\ 143.96(1 + 3\%)^{8} + 500(1 + 3\%)^{10}$$
$$= 1\ 143.96(1.266\ 77) + 500(1.343\ 92)$$
$$= 1\ 449.13 + 671.96$$
$$= \$2\ 121.09$$

EXERCISE 11.9 / REFERENCE SECTION: 11.9

Find the value of the new obligations in each of the following problems:

	Original Debts	Interest Rate Compounded	New Debts and Comparison Date
1.	\$5 000 due in 3 years	8% quarterly	All in 5 years.
2.	\$2 000 due in 5 years	12% monthly	All in 2 years.
3. (a)	\$3 000 due in 2 years	18% quarterly	Two equal payments: one in 3 years,
(b)	\$1 500 due in 9 years	18% quarterly	the other in 7 years. Comparison date: 7 years hence.
4. (a)	\$2 400 due in $1\frac{1}{2}$ years	15.5% semi-annually	Two equal payments: one in $3\frac{1}{2}$ years,
(b)	\$4 700 due in 7 years		the other in 8 years. Comparison date: $3\frac{1}{2}$ years hence.
5. (a)	\$1 000 due in 5 years	19% semi-annually	\$600 in 1 year, the remainder in 8
(b)	\$1 600 due in 10 years		years.
6. (a)	\$3 400 due in 4 years	12% monthly	\$3 000 in 5 years, the remainder in
(b)	\$4 500 due in 9 years		7 years.
7. (a)	\$1 800 due in 3 years	17.5% semi-annually	All in 9 years.
(b)	\$2 500 due in $5\frac{1}{2}$ years		
8. (a)	\$1 500 due in $3\frac{1}{2}$ years	14% quarterly	All in 4 years.
(b)	\$4 000 due in 5 years		

Statement Problems:

9. A debt of $4 200 is due in seven years. If money is worth 19.5% compounded monthly, what is the value of the debt if it is paid: (a) five years hence, (b) seven years hence, (c) ten years hence?

10. A debt of $5 200 is due in eight years. If money is worth 15% compounded quarterly, what is the value of the debt if it is paid: (a) at the end of four years, (b) at the end of eight years, (c) at the end of eleven years?

11. Aris owes (a) $2 800 due in $1\frac{1}{2}$ years, and (b) $3 600 due in 5 years. He and his creditor agree to settle the obligations by two equal payments, one in $2\frac{1}{2}$ years and the other in $7\frac{1}{2}$ years. Find the size of each payment if money is worth 17% compounded quarterly and the comparison date is $7\frac{1}{2}$ years hence.

12. Find the size of each payment in Problem 11 if the comparison date is $2\frac{1}{2}$ years hence.

13. Marisa owes (a) $2 000 due in four years and (b) $1 700 due in six years. Her creditor has agreed for her to pay the debts with a payment of $1 500 in three years and the remainder in eight years. If money is worth 19% compounded quarterly, what size must the second payment be?

14. Refer to Problem 13. If the remainder of the debt is to be paid in five years, what is the size of the second payment?

15. A man owes (a) $300 due in one year and (b) $700 in four years plus interest at 17.8% compounded semi-annually. If money is worth 22.5% compounded monthly, what single payment three years from now will be equivalent to the two debts?

16. Refer to Problem 15. What single payment made six years from now will be equivalent to the two debts?

11.10 Equivalent Rates

If a principal invested at various interest rates will accumulate to the same compound amount in a certain period of time, the rates are said to be equivalent to each other. The various interest rates are thus called equivalent rates. Equivalent rates may be obtained by the use of the effective rate method based on a one-year period as illustrated in the following examples.

Example 11.10a
At what nominal rate compounded quarterly will a principal yield an interest which is equivalent to an effective rate of 18.5%.

SOLUTION:

$m = 4$ (quarters), $f = 18.5\%$

Substituting the values in Formula 11-4:
$18.5\% = (1 + j/4)^4 - 1, (1 + j/4)^4 = 1 + 18.5\%$

Extracting the fourth root of each side of the above equation: then
$(1 + j/4) = (1 + 18.5\%)^{1/4} = 1.043\ 349$
Thus, $j/4 = 1.043\ 349 - 1 = .043\ 349$
$j = .043\ 349 \times 4 = .173\ 395\ 8$, or the nominal rate is 17.339 58%, which is
rounded to 17.34%.

The nominal rate 17.34% compounded quarterly is equivalent to an effective rate of
18.5%.

Example 11.10b
At what nominal rate compounded monthly will a principal accumulate to the same
amount as at 16% compounded quarterly?

SOLUTION:

Let the unknown nominal rate be j; then $i = j/12$ (per month). The effective rate in
the first case is:
$f = (1 + j/12)^{12} - 1.$

In the latter case, $i = 16\%/4 = 4\%$ (per quarter). The effective rate is $f = (1 + 4\%)^4 - 1.$

Since the accumulated amount in the first case is the same as the amount in the latter
case, the effective rates must be the same in both cases. Thus,
$(1 + j/12)^{12} - 1 = (1 + 4\%)^4 - 1$, or
$(1 + j/12)^{12} = (1 + 4\%)^4.$

Extracting the twelfth root on each side of the above equation; then
$(1 + j/12) = (1 + 4\%)^{4/12} = (1 + 4\%)^{1/3} = 1.013\ 159\ 4$
$j/12 = 1.013\ 159\ 4 - 1 = 0.013\ 159\ 4$
$j = .013\ 159\ 4 \times 12 = .157\ 912\ 9$, or 15.791 29%

It may be stated that 15.79% compounded monthly is equivalent to 16% compounded
quarterly. The statement holds true for any principal and for any number of periods
of investment.

From Example 11.10b note that the nominal rate of 15.791 29% is computed from the
equation
$(1 + j/12) = (1 + 4\%)^{1/3},$
which does not contain the values of S and P. Furthermore, both sides of the equation are the accumulation factors for a one-month period, which is also the conversion period of the unknown nominal rate. Thus, computation of equivalent rate
problems may be simplified by using an equation which contains only the accumulation factors of a length equal to one conversion period for the unknown nominal rate.

Example 11.10c
If a principal P, invested at 13.5% compounded quarterly for three years, will accumulate to the compound amount S, at what nominal rate compounded semi-annually will the principal accumulate to the same amount in the same period?

SOLUTION:

Let the unknown nominal rate be j, then $i = j/2$ (per semi-annual period). The accumulation factor for one conversion period (six months) is $(1 + j/2)$.

In the first case, $i = 13.5\%/4 = 3.375\%$ (per quarter). The accumulation factor for a six-month period (the conversion period for the unknown rate j) or two quarters is $(1 + 3.375\%)^2$. The equation may be written as follows: $(1 + j/2) = (1 + 3.375\%)^2$
Since $(1 + 3.375\%)^2 = 1.068\ 639\ 1$

$$1 + j/2 = 1.068\ 639\ 1$$
$$j/2 = 1.068\ 639\ 1 - 1$$
$$j = .068\ 639\ 1 \times 2 = .137\ 278\ 1, \text{ or } 13.727\ 8\%.$$

Thus, a principal P invested at 13.5% compounded quarterly will accumulate to the same amount if invested at 13.728% compounded semi-annually during a period of three years. The values of P, S, and n (three years) need not be included in the computation.

11.11 *Continuously Compounded Interest*

Although compound interest is usually computed at regularly stated intervals such as annually, semi-annually, quarterly, or monthly, it may be computed more frequently such as every minute, every second, or continuously. Continuous compounding is not commonly used in the actual investment market. However, its concept is theoretically important in analysing financial problems.

   To compute an interest at a nominal rate compounded continuously, first find the equivalent effective rate, then compute the compound interest based on the effective rate. The formula for finding the effective rate of the nominal rate j compounded continuously can be derived from Formula 11-4, which is

$$f = \left(1 + \frac{j}{m}\right)^m - 1,$$

where f = effective rate,
      j = nominal rate, and
      m = number of conversion periods for one year.

The derivation is presented below:

Let $k = \frac{m}{j}$, and $\frac{1}{k} = \frac{j}{m}$. Then, the term

$$\left(1 + \frac{j}{m}\right)^m = \left[\left(1 + \frac{j}{m}\right)^{m/j}\right]^j = \left[\left(1 + \frac{1}{k}\right)^k\right]^j.$$

The values of $\left(1 + \dfrac{1}{k}\right)^k$ can be computed as follows:

When k is	the value of $\left(1 + \dfrac{1}{k}\right)^k$ is
1	$\left(1 + \dfrac{1}{1}\right)^1 = 2$
2	$\left(1 + \dfrac{1}{2}\right)^2 = (1.5)^2 = 2.25$
10	$\left(1 + \dfrac{1}{10}\right)^{10} = (1.1)^{10} = 2.594$
100	$\left(1 + \dfrac{1}{100}\right)^{100} = (1.01)^{100} = 2.705$
1 000	$\left(1 + \dfrac{1}{1\,000}\right)^{1\,000} = (1.001)^{1\,000} = 2.717$
10 000	$\left(1 + \dfrac{1}{10\,000}\right)^{10\,000} = (1.000\ 1)^{10\,000} = 2.718$

When k approaches an infinitely large value ($k \rightarrow \infty$), the limit of $(1 + 1/k)^k$, usually denoted by the letter e, is an IRRATIONAL NUMBER and is 2.718 28 approximately. It is written

$$e = \lim_{k \to \infty} \left(1 + \frac{1}{k}\right)^k = 2.718\ 28 \text{ approximately.}$$

(An irrational number is the number which cannot be written as a fraction with numerator and denominator being integers—it is a never-ending decimal.)

When j is compounded continuously, m becomes infinitely large; the value of $k = m/j$ also becomes infinitely large, and the term $(1 + j/m)^m$ equals e^j, or

$$\left(1 + \frac{j}{m}\right)^m = \left[\left(1 + \frac{1}{k}\right)^k\right]^j = e^j.$$

When e^j is substituted into Formula 11-4, the effective rate of the nominal rate j compounded continuously is

$$\boxed{f = e^j - 1}$$ ⟵ *Formula 11-7*

The value of e^j can be obtained by use of an electronic calculator as illustrated in the following examples.

Example 11.11a
Find the effective rate if money is worth 12% compounded continuously.

SOLUTION:

Here $j = 12\% = .12$.
Use an electronic calculator:
The value of e raised to any power may be obtained by the following steps:
1. enter the power
2. press the key labelled $\underline{e^x}$

$$e^j = e^{.12} = 1.127\ 496\ 9$$

$$f = e^j - 1 = 1.127\ 496\ 9 - 1 = .127\ 496\ 9,\ \text{or } 12.749\ 69\%$$

Example 11.11b
Find the effective rate if money is worth 13.5% compounded continuously.

SOLUTION:

Here $j = 13.5\% = .135$.

$$e^j = e^{.135} = 1.144\ 536\ 8$$

Substituting e^j value in Formula 11-7,
$f = e^j - 1 = 1.1445368 - 1 = .1445368$, or 14.45368%.
    By substituting the effective rate for continuous compounding f (Formula 11-7) for i in the compound amount formula S, we have

$$S = P(1 + i)^n = P(1 + f)^n = P(1 + e^j - 1)^n$$
$$= P(e^j)^n = P(e^{jn}).$$

Thus, the formula for finding the compound amount (S) of the principal (P) at the nominal rate j compounded continuously for n years is

$$\boxed{S = P(e^{jn})} \quad \longleftarrow \textit{Formula 11-8}$$

Example 11.11c

Find the compound amount and the compound interest when $10 000 is invested at 10% compounded continuously for (a) a half year, and (b) one year.

SOLUTION:

P = $10 000, j = 10% = .10. Use Formula 11-8.
(a) $n = \frac{1}{2}$ year, and jn = .10($\frac{1}{2}$) = .05
S = 10 000($e^{.05}$) = 10 000(1.051 271 10)
   = $10 512.71 (Compound amount)
Compound interest = 10 512.71 − 10 000.00 = $512.71.

(b) n = 1 year, and jn = .10(1) = .10
S = 10 000($e^{.1}$) = 10 000(1.105 170 92)
   = $11 051.71 (Compound amount)
Compound interest = 11 051.71 − 10 000 = $1 051.71.

EXERCISE 11.11 / REFERENCE SECTIONS: 11.10 and 11.11

1. At what nominal rate compounded semi-annually will a principal yield interest which is equivalent to an effective rate of 13.5%?
2. What nominal rate compounded monthly is equivalent to an effective rate of 12.25%?
3. At what nominal rate compounded semi-annually will a principal yield interest which is equivalent to 17.5% compounded monthly?
4. What nominal rate compounded quarterly is equivalent to 12.5% compounded monthly?
5. Find the nominal rate compounded quarterly which is equivalent to 15.25% compounded semi-annually.
6. Find the nominal rate compounded monthly which is equivalent to 17.25% compounded semi-annually.
7. Find the effective rate if money is worth (a) 13.25% and (b) 20% compounded continuously.
8. Find the effective rate if money is worth (a) 12% and (b) 50% compounded continuously.
9. What is the effective rate if money is invested at 12.5% compounded continuously?
10. What is the effective rate if money is invested at 13.25% compounded continuously?
11. Find the compound amount and the compound interest if $1 000 is invested at 15.25% compounded continuously for (a) one year, and (b) two years.
12. Find the compound amount and the compound interest if $1 000 is invested at 16.25% compounded continuously for (a) one year, and (b) $1\frac{1}{2}$ years.

EXERCISE / CHAPTER REVIEW

1. What are the compound amount and the compound interest at the end of ten years if $4 000 is borrowed at 15% compounded monthly?

2. Find the compound amount and the compound interest at the end of six years if $5 000 is invested at 12% compounded monthly.

3. (a) What is the simple interest on $1 000 for five years at 22.5%? (b) What is the compound interest on $1 000 for five years at 22.5% compounded annually?

4. What is the interest on $2 500 for $4\frac{1}{2}$ years at (a) 13.5% simple interest? (b) 13.5% compounded monthly?

5. A note having a face value of $2 500 will mature in six years. The interest charged is 19.5% compounded monthly. Find the maturity value.

6. Find the compound amount if $3 000 is invested at 17.5% compounded annually for 20 years.

7. The principal is $600 and the interest rate is 22.5% compounded monthly for the first seven years and 22% compounded semi-annually for the next three years. Find the compound amount at the end of the tenth year.

8. What is the amount at the end of $3\frac{2}{3}$ years if $1 000 is invested at 12% compounded monthly for the first $1\frac{2}{3}$ years and 13.5% compounded quarterly for the next 2 years?

9. Find the amount if $2 000 is invested at 16.5% compounded monthly for $3\frac{1}{2}$ years.

10. What is the amount if $4 000 is borrowed at 22.5% compounded monthly for ten years?

11. What are the amount and the interest if $5 000 is invested for five years and two months at 17.5% compounded annually?

12. Find the amount and the interest if $300 is borrowed for ten years and one month at 15% compounded quarterly.

13. (a) Find the present value if $650 is due at the end of $5\frac{1}{2}$ years and money is worth 17% compounded quarterly. (b) What is the compound discount?

14. (a) What is the present value if $820 is due at the end of four years and money is worth 15% compounded monthly? (b) What is the compound discount?

15. A note of $500 dated April 1, 1985, plus 16% interest compounded quarterly was due in eight years. It was discounted at 15% compounded monthly on April 1, 1988. Find the proceeds and compound discount.

16. Carla had a note that would pay her $400 plus 19% interest compounded quarterly at the end of six years. She sold the note two years before it was due at 21% compounded monthly. How much proceeds did she receive?

17. A non-interest-bearing note of $800 is discounted at 12% compounded quarterly for five years and two months. Find the proceeds and the compound discount.

18. Tim received a note that would pay him $700 on the due date. He discounted the note at 18% compounded quarterly for two years and two weeks before it was due. Find the proceeds and the compound discount.

19. If $900 will accumulate to $1 500 in $3\frac{1}{3}$ years, what is the interest rate compounded monthly?

20. What is the nominal interest rate compounded monthly that will enable $1 000 to amount to $1 800 in eight years?

21. What is the effective rate if $1 is invested for one year at 18% compounded (a) annually? (b) semi-annually? (c) quarterly? (d) monthly?

22. What is the effective rate if money is worth 12% compounded monthly?

23. Alan invested his money at 15% compounded quarterly and Helen invested her money at 15.5% compounded annually. Which one of the two rates is higher?

24. Which is the higher rate: 13.5% compounded monthly or 14% compounded annually?

25. How long will it take $200 to accumulate to the amount of $340.16 at 13.5% compounded monthly?

26. How much time is needed for $350 to yield $30 interest if the interest rate is 17% compounded quarterly?

27. Bruno has two debts, one for $1 000 due in 4 years and one for $2 000 due in 12 years. He and his creditors have agreed to settle the debts by two equal payments, one due in 6 years and the other due in 9 years. If money is worth 15% compounded monthly, what is the amount of the payments? What single payment due 6 years from now will be equivalent?

28. Arnella has incurred three non-interest-bearing debts: $1 500 due immediately, $2 000 due in 2 years, and $500 due in 5 years. Arnella expects to receive an inheritance on her 21st birthday, 3 years from now. Her creditor has agreed to accept a single payment on her 21st birthday in settlement of the three debts. If the current rate of interest is 15% compounded monthly, how much must Arnella pay on her 21st birthday?

29. A debt of $500 is due at the end of 6 years. If money is worth 19.5% compounded monthly, what is the value of the debt when it is paid at the end of (a) 2 years? (b) 9 years?

30. A debt of $800 is due in 3 years. If interest is 6% compounded quarterly, what is the value of the debt when it is paid at the end of (a) 1 year? (b) $5\frac{1}{2}$ years?

31. Bob owes John $300 due in two years and $800 due in 5 years. Assume that the two debts are to be discharged by 2 equal payments in $1\frac{1}{2}$ and 4 years respectively. What is the size of each payment if money is worth 12% compounded monthly? Let 4 years from now be the comparison date.

32. Compute Problem 31 by letting 3 years hence be the comparison date.

33. Carl owes Dean $900 due in 2 years and $1 500 due in 7 years. Assume that the two debts are to discharged by a payment of $700 in 3 years and the remainder in 6 years. What is the size of the second payment if money is worth 17.5% compounded semi-annually?

34. Refer to Problem 33. (a) If the two debts are to be discharged by two equal payments in 3 years and 5 years respectively, what is the size of each payment? (b) What single payment would discharge the two debts 10 years hence?

35. Mary owes Jack $400 due in 1 year and $950 with interest at 10% compounded monthly due in 8 years. If money is worth 17.5% compounded annually, what is the single payment 10 years from now that will discharge the two debts?

36. Refer to Problem 35. If the two debts are to be discharged by a payment of $500 in 2 years and the remainder in 5 years, what is the size of the second payment?

37. Susan borrowed some money from Janet as follows: $50 due in 1 year, $200 due in 3 years, and $300 due in 5 years. If money is worth 22.5% compounded monthly, when can Susan discharge all her debts by a single payment of $550?

38. Dorothy promised to pay Bob the following amounts: $100 due in 2 years, $400 due in 5 years, and $500 plus interest at 19% compounded semi-annually due in 6 years. If money is worth 18% compounded quarterly, when can Dorothy repay her debts by a single payment of $1 000?

39. What nominal rate compounded quarterly is equivalent to a 19.5% effective rate?

40. Find the nominal rate compounded semi-annually that is equivalent to an effective rate of 17.5%?

41. What nominal rate compounded monthly is equivalent to 13% compounded semi-annually?

42. Find the nominal rate compounded semi-annually that is equivalent to 14.5% compounded quarterly.

43. Find the effective rate if money is invested at (a) 12% and (b) 13% cmpounded continuously.

44. What is the effective rate if money is invested at (a) 15% and (b) 16% compounded continuously?

45. Find the compound amount and the compound interest if $10 000 is invested at 17% compounded continuously for (a) one year, and (b) two years.

46. Find the compound amount and the compound interest if $10 000 is invested at 12.5% compounded continuously for (a) one year, and (b) four years.

Summary of Formulae

Formula 11-1	$S = P(1 + i)^n$	Used to find the compound amount.
Formula 11-2	$P = S(1 + i)^{-n}$	Used to find the present value.
Formula 11-2A	$P = \dfrac{S}{(1 + i)^n}$	A variation of Formula 11-2, used to find the present value.
Formula 11-3	$(1 + i)^n = \dfrac{S}{P}$	Used to find the interest rate and the number of conversion periods.
Formula 11-3A	$i = \left(\dfrac{S}{P}\right)^{1/n} - 1$	A variation of Formula 11-3, used to find the interest rate and the number of conversion periods.
Formula 11-4	$f = \left(1 + \dfrac{j}{m}\right)^m - 1$	Used to find the effective rate, when compounding continuously.
Formula 11-4A	$f = (1 + i)^m - 1$	A variation of Formula 11-4, used to find the effective rate, when compounding continuously.
Formula 11-5	$n = \dfrac{\ln \frac{S}{P}}{\ln (1 + i)}$	Used to find the number of conversion periods.
Formula 11-6	$(1 + i)^n = \dfrac{S}{P}$	Used to find the interest rate and the number of payments when using tables.
Formula 11-7	$f = e^j - 1$	Used to find the effective rate of the nominal rate.
Formula 11-8	$S = P(e^{jn})$	Used to find the compound amount of the principal at the nominal rate when compounding continuously.

Glossary

ACCUMULATION FACTORS when the interest
rate changes during compound accumulation, the compound amount is the product
of the principal and several different interest rates for respective given periods

COMPOUND ACCUMULATION the process of
accumulating a principal to obtain a compound amount

COMPOUND AMOUNT the final sum due at the
end of the borrowing period

COMPOUND DISCOUNT the difference between
the value of the compound amount and its
present value

COMPOUND INTEREST the difference between
the original principal and the compound
amount

CONVERSION PERIOD the period for computing
interest, usually at regularly stated intervals

DISCOUNT FACTOR the factor $(1 + i)^{-n}$ used in
discounting a compound amount

EFFECTIVE ANNUAL INTEREST RATE see *effective
rate*

EFFECTIVE RATE the ratio of the compound
interest earned for a one-year period to the
principal

EQUATION OF VALUE when a single or set of
debts is replaced by another single or set of
debts due at different times, yet equal to
the first single or set or debts

INTEREST PERIOD see *conversion period*

IRRATIONAL NUMBER a number which cannot
be written as a fraction with numerator and
denominator being integers—it is a
never-ending decimal

NOMINAL ANNUAL RATE see *nominal rate*

NOMINAL RATE the stated annual interest rate

PROCEEDS the present value of the face value
of a non-interest-bearing note; the present
value on the date of discount computed
from the maturity value on an interest-bearing note

Ordinary annuities 12

Introduction

Many transactions in personal and corporate finance involve periodic payments of a fixed amount. These periodic payments are calculated using the methods presented in this chapter.

When an individual purchases a product such as a vacuum cleaner, a car or a house on an instalment plan the periodic payments represent an annuity. Periodic payments made to or received from a pension fund or an insurance policy also fall within this category.

The operation of certain types of business involve annuities. For example, the operation of insurance companies and pension fund management are largely centred around the receipts of periodic payments.

The financial services field is a large and growing industry, therefore the concepts which are basic to this field should be studied in order to ensure the ability to communicate in this area.

A word of caution, since there are many types of annuities, it is necessary to classify an annuity according to the type before proceeding with the calculations.

Chapter Twelve covers the classification of annuities and the methods used in calculations involving a simple ordinary annuity.

12.1 Basic Concept and Classification

Generally speaking, an ANNUITY is a series of periodic payments, usually made in equal amounts. The payments are computed by the compound interest method and are made at equal intervals of time, such as annually, semi-annually, quarterly, or monthly. The word annuity originally referred only to annual payments, but it now applies to payment intervals of any length of time.

The period of time between two successive payment dates is called the PAYMENT INTERVAL. The time between the beginning of the first payment interval and the end of the last payment interval is called the TERM of the annuity.

A.   ANNUITIES CLASSIFIED BY TERM

According to their terms annuities may be classified into three groups:

1. ANNUITY CERTAIN. The term of an annuity certain begins and ends on definite dates, such as a five-year term from January 1, 1979, to January 1, 1984.

2. PERPETUITY. The term of a perpetuity begins on a definite date but never ends, such as a principal which remains forever untouched, drawing interest. The length of the term is infinite.

3. CONTINGENT ANNUITY. The term of a contingent annuity begins on a definite date but the ending date is not fixed in advance. Instead the ending date depends upon some condition happening in the future, such as life insurance premiums being paid only so long as the insured is living, the length of time therefore being uncertain.

B.   ANNUITIES CLASSIFIED BY DATES OF PAYMENT

According to the dates of payments, annuities may be classified into three groups:

1. ORDINARY ANNUITY. Periodic payments are made at the *end* of each payment interval. For example, if the term of an annuity is one year, which begins on January 1, and the payment interval is one quarter, the first payment should be made three months later, or on April 1, the end of the first quarter; the second payment should be made on July 1, the end of the second quarter; and so on.

2. ANNUITY DUE. Periodic payments are made at the *beginning* of each payment interval. For instance, in the above example the first payment is made on January 1, the beginning of the first quarter; the second payment is made on April 1, the beginning of the second quarter; and so on.

3. DEFFERED ANNUITY. Periodic payments are made at the *end* of each payment interval. However, the term of the annuity does not begin until *after* a designated period of time. For example, a man borrows $100 on April 15, 1979, and agrees to repay the loan by making a series of three equal annual payments, but the first payment is not due until two years from the date of the loan.

C.   ANNUITIES CLASSIFIED BY LENGTH OF PAYMENT INTERVAL AND INTEREST CONVERSION PERIOD

According to the *length* of payment interval and interest conversion period, annuities may be divided into two groups:

1. SIMPLE ANNUITY. The payment interval coincides with the interest conversion period. In other words, the payment date is the interest computing date. For example, when the payment interval is one month, the interest is compounded monthly. When each of the payments of an annuity is made at the end of each month, the interest is also computed and compounded at the end of each month.

2. COMPLEX ANNUITY (GENERAL ANNUITY). The payment interval does not coincide with the interest conversion period. For example, when the payment interval is one month, the interest is compounded quarterly; or when the payment interval is one quarter, the interest is compounded monthly. The formulae for a complex annuity may also be used for solving simple annuity problems. Thus, the complex annuity is considered as a general case of annuity and is also called a *general annuity*.

Hereafter, unless otherwise specified, the word *annuity* means an *ordinary annuity*, which is also an *annuity certain*. Only ordinary annuities of the simple annuity type are discussed in this chapter. Other types of annuities are presented in Chapter Fourteen.

12.2 *Amount of an Annuity*

The AMOUNT of an annuity is the final value at the end of the term of the annuity. The amount includes all of the periodic payments and the compound interest.

A. COMPUTATION IN GENERAL

The amount of an annuity is obtained by totalling the compound amounts of the individual periodic payments. Each of the compound amounts is computed by the formula $S = P(1 + i)^n$.

Example 12.2a
What is the amount of an annuity if the size of each payment is $100, payable at the end of each month for four months at an interest rate of 12% compounded monthly?

SOLUTION:

The first payment is made at the end of the first month, which is three months before the end of the term of the annuity. Thus, interest is accumulated on the first payment for three interest periods; on the second payment, for two interest periods; and on the third payment, for one interest period. The fourth payment is not entitled to interest since it is paid at the end of the term.

The entire computation is diagrammed as follows:

Term: 4 months

Month	0(Now)	1	2	3	4
Payment		First	Second	Third	Fourth
					$100
				$100 $\longrightarrow$	$100(1 + 1\%)$
			$100 \longrightarrow$		$100(1 + 1\%)^2$
		$100 \longrightarrow$			$100(1 + 1\%)^3$

(Total amount) $406.040 1

The amount of the annuity, $406.040 1, which is the final value at the end of the fourth month, is computed as follows:

$$100 = 100(1)$$
$$100(1 + 1\%) = 100(1.01)$$
$$100(1 + 1\%)^2 = 100(1.020\ 1)$$
$$\underline{100(1 + 1\%)^3 = 100(1.030\ 301)}$$
$$(\text{Total amount})\ 100(4.060\ 401) = \$406.040\ 1, \text{ or } \$406.04$$

The total of the compound interest on the four payments is
$406.04 − (100 × 4) = \$6.04.$

The preceding example may be applied in the following case:

A man deposits $100 in a bank at the end of each month for four months. If the money earns interest at 12% compounded monthly, how much does he have in his account at the end of the term after the last payment is made? Answer: He has $406.04.

EXERCISE 12.2A / REFERENCE SECTION: A

Using the method employed in Example 12.2a, find the amount of each annuity and the total interest on the payments in each of the following cases. (Assume that each payment is made at the end of each payment interval.)

	Each Payment	Payment Interval	Term	Compound Interest Rate
1.	$10 000	1 month	4 months	9% monthly
2.	800	1 month	3 months	12% monthly
3.	2 000	1 quarter	6 months	10% quarterly
4.	700	6 months	1 year	13% semi-annually
5.	3 000	1 quarter	1 year	8% quarterly
6.	600	6 months	$1\frac{1}{2}$ years	11.5% semi-annually

Statement Problems:
7. What is the amount of an annuity if the size of each payment is $1 200, payable at the end of each year for three years at an interest rate of 10% compounded annually?
8. Find the amount of an annuity if the size of each payment is $80, payable at the end of each month for four months at an interest rate of 12% compounded monthly.

B.   COMPUTATION BY FORMULA 12-1

Let R = size of each regular payment (or periodic rent)
    i = interest rate per conversion period

n = number of payments during the term of an annuity (It is also the number of payment intervals, or the number of conversion periods.)

S_n = the amount of an ordinary annuity

The formula for the amount of an ordinary annuity is:

$$S_n = R \cdot \frac{(1+i)^n - 1}{i} \qquad \longleftarrow Formula\ 12\text{-}1\ ^1$$

---

[1] *Proof–Formula 12-1, the amount of an ordinary annuity*

In Example 12.2a, since $R = \$100$, $i = 1\%$, and $n = 4$ (monthly payments), the diagram may be drawn with symbols as shown.

Term: 4 months

Month	0(Now)	1	2	3	4
Payment		First	Second	Third	Fourth
					R
				$R \longrightarrow$	$R(1+i)$
			$R \longrightarrow$	$R(1+i)^2$	
		$R \longrightarrow$	$R(1+i)^3$		

Notice that the number of interest conversion periods for the first payment is 3, which is 1 less than 4, or $(n-1)$; the number for the second payment is 2, which is 2 less than 4, or $(n-2)$; and so on. On the other hand, the number of interest conversion periods for the last payment, the fourth or nth payment, is zero; the number for the next to the last, the third or $(n-1)$th payment, is 1; the number for the second or $(n-2)$th payment is 2; and so on. Extend this idea and let n = any number of payments. The following results may be obtained:

The compound amount of the 1st payment $= R(1+i)^{n-1}$

The compound amount of the 2nd payment $= R(1+i)^{n-2}$

The compound amount of the $(n-2)$th payment $= R(1+i)^2$

The compound amount of the $(n-1)$th payment $= R(1+i)$

The compound amount of the nth (the last) payment $= R$

There are n compound amounts.

Let S_n = the sum of n compound amounts, (or the amount of the annuity).

Thus, $S_n = R + R(1+i) + R(1+i)^2 + \ldots + R(1+i)^{n-2} + R(1+i)^{n-1}$ Step (1)

Multiply both sides of the equation in Step (1) by $(1+i)$.

Then, $S_n(1+i) = R(1+i) + R(1+i)^2 + R(1+i)^3 + \ldots + R(1+i)^{n-1} + R(1+i)^n$ Step (2) $\longrightarrow$

Formula 12-1 is obtained by using the method employed in Example 12.2a. When Formula 12-1 is used, the answer to Example 12.2a may be computed as follows:

R = \$100 (per month), i = 12%/12 = 1% (per month) and n = 4 (monthly payments)

Substituting the values in Formula 12-1:

$$S_n = S_4 = 100 \cdot \frac{(1 + 1\%)^4 - 1}{1\%} = 100 \cdot \frac{1.040\ 604\ 01 - 1}{.01} = 100 \cdot \frac{.040\ 604\ 01}{.01}$$

$$= 100(4.060\ 401) = \$406.040\ 1, \text{ or } \$406.04$$

Example 12.2b
Find the amount of an annuity of \$150 payable at the end of each quarter for 3.75 years if the interest rate is 20% compounded quarterly.

SOLUTION:

R = \$150 (quarterly)
i = 20%/4 = 5% (quarterly)
n = 3.75 × 4 = 15 (quarterly payments)

Substituting the values in Formula 12-1:

$$S_n = 150\frac{(1 + 5\%)^{15} - 1}{5\%} = 150(21.578\ 563\ 59) = \$3\ 256.78$$

Example 12.2c
In order to save for a down payment on a house, Mr. and Mrs. Dan Brown opened an RHOSP account on December 1, 1983 in which they make a deposit of \$1 000 each year on December 1. (a) How much will they have in the account after their deposit on December 1, 1993 if the account earns interest at 12.5% compounded annually? (b) After the 10-year allowable deposits the fund is left to earn interest at 15% compounded quarterly. How much will be available as a down payment on a house on September 1, 1995?

Subtract the equation in Step (2) from the equation in Step (1).
Then, $S_n - S_n(1 + i) = R - R(1 + i)^n$. Factor,   Step (3)

$$S_n[1 - (1 + i)] = R[1 - (1 + i)^n], \quad S_n(-i) = R[1 - (1 + i)^n]$$

$$S_n = \frac{R[1 - (1 + i)^n]}{-i} = \frac{R[1 - (1 + i)^n]}{-i} \cdot \frac{-1}{-1}$$

$$S_n = R \cdot \frac{(1 + i)^n - 1}{i}$$

NOTE: The right side of the equation in Step (1) is a geometric progression and may also be solved by the geometric progression formula in Chapter 5, Section 5.2c, Formula 5-5.

SOLUTION:

(a) $R = \$1\ 000$ (per year)
        $i = 12.5\%$ (per year)
        $n = 10$ years (December 1, 1983 to December 1, 1993)

$$S_n = R\left[\frac{(1+i)^n - 1}{i}\right]$$

$$S_{10} = 1\ 000\left[\frac{(1 + 12.5\%)^{10} - 1}{12.5\%}\right]$$

$$S_{10} = 1\ 000\left[\frac{3.247\ 321 - 1}{.125}\right]$$

$$S_{10} = 1\ 000\left[\frac{2.247\ 321}{.125}\right]$$

$$= 1\ 000(17.978\ 568)$$

$$= \$17\ 978.57$$

(b) The principal at the end of 10 years is $S_{10} = \$17\ 978.57$.
     $P = \$17\ 978.57$
     $i = 15\%/4 = 3.75\%$ (per quarter)
     $n = 1\frac{3}{4} \times 4 = 7$ (quarters)
     $S = P(1 + i)^n$
     $S = 17\ 978.57(1 + 3.75\%)^7$
       $= 17\ 978.57(1.293\ 947\ 7)$
       $= 23\ 263.33$

The amount available as down payment on a house on September 1, 1995 is $23 263.33.

EXERCISE 12.2B / REFERENCE SECTION: B

Find the amount of the ordinary annuity in each of the following problems:

	Payment (R)	Payment Interval	Term	Compound Interest Rate
1.	$2 000	1 month	2 years	18% monthly
2.	1 500	1 month	3 years, 4 months	15% monthly
3.	600	6 months	$8\frac{1}{2}$ years	17% semi-annually
4.	1 000	6 months	15 years	13% semi-annually
5.	400	1 quarter	15 years, 6 months	16% quarterly
6.	500	1 year	5 years	17.5% annually
7.	300	6 months	10 years	16.5% semi-annually
8.	800	6 months	12 years	19% semi-annually

Statement Problems:

9. Harriett has a Registered Retirement Savings Pension fund in which she makes regular deposits of $25 at the end of each month. Her first deposit was made on her fortieth birthday. Assuming that the interest rate is 16.5% compounded monthly and is unchanged for the term of the fund, how much will she have in the fund on her sixtieth birthday?

10. Maurice de Souza has set up a fund for his son's college education. He made his first deposit of $100 one month after his son was born and will make regular monthly deposits of $100 at the end of each month, the last of which will be made on his son's eighteenth birthday. If the fund pays 13.5% compounded monthly, how much will be in the fund on his son's eighteenth birthday?

11. A condominium corporation set up a contingency fund to cover major repairs which it anticipates will be due in 8 years. If the corporation deposits $5 000 at the end of each six months in an account which pays 16% compounded semi-annually, how much will be in the fund at the end of 8 years?

12. On January 1, 1982, the city of Kensington received a non-interest-bearing loan which will fall due on January 1, 1992 and must be repaid out of taxes. If the city deposits $1 000 at the end of each month starting April 1, 1982 in a fund which pays interest at 19.5% compounded monthly, how much will be available on January 1, 1992?

13. Arlene Grant deposits $45 monthly at an interest rate of 12% compounded monthly. How much will she have in her account at the end of two years and four months?

14. At the end of each quarter, a company placed $1 500 in an account. The fund was invested at 16% compounded quarterly. (a) What will be the final value at the end of five years? (b) What will be the total interest?

15. At the end of each month during a three-year period, a business manager of a hospital invested one-sixth of her monthly salary of $3 000. How much will the amount be four years after the last investment is made if the interest rate is 16% compounded monthly?

16. Bill Morton deposited $50 every three months in a fund earning interest at 14% compounded quarterly. The first deposit was made when he was 20 years of age and the last deposit was made when he was 25. If he leaves the fund intact, how much will he have in the fund when he is 28?

12.3 Present Value of an Annuity

The PRESENT VALUE of an annuity is the value at the beginning of the term of the annuity. The methods for computing the present value are based on either of the following two different interpretations of the value:

1. It is the sum of the present values of the periodic payments of an annuity.
2. It is the single principal which, at a given compound interest rate, will accumulate to the amount of an annuity by the end of the term of the annuity.

A. COMPUTATION IN GENERAL

Example 12.3a
What is the present value of an annuity if the size of each payment is $100 payable at the end of each month for four months and the interest rate is 12% compounded monthly?

SOLUTION:

METHOD A When the present value of an annuity is considered as the *sum of the present values* of the periodic payments, each of the present values (P) is computed by the compound discount formula $P = S(1 + i)^{-n}$. In the present case, S is the payment, or $S = \$100$.

The first payment is made at the end of the first month, which is one month after the beginning of the term of the annuity. Thus, the present value of the first payment is obtained by discounting the payment for one month, or one interest period. The present value of the second payment is obtained by discounting the payment for two periods, and so on.

The computation is diagrammed as follows:

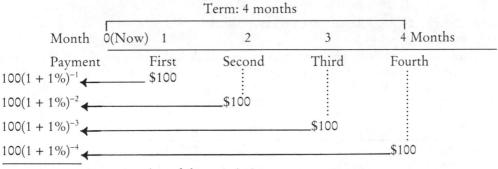

$390.20 (present value of the annuity)

The present value of the annuity, $390.20, is computed as follows:

$$100(1 + 1\%)^{-1} = 100(0.990\ 099\ 01)$$
$$100(1 + 1\%)^{-2} = 100(0.980\ 296\ 05)$$
$$100(1 + 1\%)^{-3} = 100(0.970\ 590\ 15)$$
$$100(1 + 1\%)^{-4} = \underline{100(0.960\ 980\ 34)}$$
$$100(3.901\ 965\ 55) = \$390.196\ 555,\ \text{or}\ \$390.20$$

METHOD B When the present value of an annuity is considered as the *single principal* of the amount of the annuity, the principal (P) is obtained by the compound discount formula $P = S(1 + i)^{-n}$. In the present case, S is equal to the amount of the annuity, S_n. The computation is as follows: (Also see Example 12.2a.)

STEP (1) To obtain the value of S_n, use Formula 12-1:

$R = 100, i = 12\%/12 = 1\%, n = 4$

$$S_n = R\left[\frac{(1 + i)^n - 1}{i}\right]$$

$$= 100\left[\frac{(1 + 1\%)^4 - 1}{1\%}\right] = 100(4.060\ 401)$$

$$= 406.040\ 1$$

STEP (2) The single principal $P = 406.040\ 1(1 + 1\%)^{-4}$

$$= 406.040\ 1(0.960\ 980\ 34) = \$390.196\ 55, \text{ or } \$390.20$$

The sum of compound discounts on the four payments is:
$(100 \times 4) - \$390.20 = \$9.80.$

The computation in the above example may also be applied in solving problems such as the following:

A man would like to borrow money from a bank which charges interest at 12% compounded monthly. If he agrees to pay $100 at the end of each month for four months, how much money should he receive from the bank at the time of the borrowing? Answer: He should receive $390.20.

EXERCISE 12.3A / REFERENCE SECTION: A

Find the present value of the annuity in each of the following problems. Use the methods presented in Example 12.3a: Method A for Problems 1-4, and Method B for Problems 5-8.

Payment	Payment Interval	Term	Compound Interest Rate
1. $2 000	1 year	4 years	13.25% annually
2. 1 000	1 month	3 months	12% monthly
3. 200	1 quarter	6 months	10% quarterly
4. 300	1 quarter	6 months	12% quarterly
5. 600	1 quarter	1 year	8% quarterly
6. 3 000	6 months	$1\frac{1}{2}$ years	11% semi-annually

Statement Problems:

7. What is the present value of an annuity if the size of each payment is $2 000 payable at the end of each quarter for 9 months and the interest rate is 8% compounded quarterly?

8. Find the present value of an annuity if the size of each payment is $800 payable at the end of each month for four months at an interest rate of 12% compounded monthly.

B.   COMPUTATION BY FORMULA 12-2

Let R = size of each regular payment (or periodic rent)

i = interest rate per conversion period

n = number of payments during the term of an annuity (It is also the number of payment intervals, or the number of conversion periods.)

A_n = the present value of an ordinary annuity

The formula   for the present value of an ordinary annuity is:

$$A_n = R \cdot \frac{1-(1+i)^{-n}}{i}$$ $\longleftarrow$ *Formula 12-2* [2]

---

[2] *Proof–Formula 12-2, the present value of an annuity*

The following diagram shows that the present value of an annuity of R payable at the end of each period for four periods at interest rate i per period is A_4, and the amount of the annuity is S_4.

Here, $A_4 = R(1+i)^{-4} + R(1+i)^{-3} + R(1+i)^{-2} + R(1+i)^{-1}$.

Multiply both sides of the equation by $(1+i)^4$:

$A_4(1+i)^4 = R + R(1+i) + R(1+i)^2 + R(1+i)^3 = S_4$

Extend this idea by letting n = number of periods. Then,

$A_n(1+i)^n = S_n$

$$A_n = S_n(1+i)^{-n} = R \cdot \frac{(1+i)^n - 1}{i} \cdot (1+i)^{-n}$$

$$= R \cdot \frac{1-(1+i)^{-n}}{i}$$

The proof also indicates that:

1. The present value of an annuity is the sum of the present values of the periodic payments.
2. The present value of an annuity is the single principal of the amount of the annuity.

Formula 12-2 is obtained by using the methods employed in Example 12.3a. When Formula 12-2 is used, the answer to Example 12.3a may be computed as follows:

R = $100, (per month), i = 12%/12 = 1% (per month), and n = 4 (monthly payments)

Substituting the values in Formula 12-2:

$$A_n = A_4 = 100 \cdot \frac{1 - (1 + 1\%)^{-4}}{1\%} = 100 \cdot \frac{1 - 0.960\,980\,34}{.01} = 100 \cdot \frac{0.039\,019\,66}{.01}$$

$$= 100(3.901\,966) = \$390.196\,6, \text{ or } \$390.20$$

Example 12.3b

If a man wishes to receive $2 000 at the end of each quarter for nine years from a bank which pays interest at 20% compounded monthly, how much must he deposit in the bank now?

SOLUTION:

The quarterly payment by the bank is $2 000, or R = $2 000, i = 20%/4 = 5% (per quarter), n = 9 × 4 = 36 (quarterly payments)

Substituting these values in Formula 12-2:

$$A_n = R \cdot \frac{1 - (1 + i)^{-n}}{i}$$

$$= 2\,000 \cdot \frac{1 - (1 + 5\%)^{-36}}{5\%}$$

$$= 2\,000(16.546\,852)$$

$$= \$33\,093.70$$

The present value of the annuity is $33 093.70. Thus, the man must deposit $33 093.70 in the bank now. The sum of the compound interest paid by the bank on the 36 payments is computed as follows:

Payments = 2 000 × 36 = $72 000
Compound interest = 72 000 − 33 093.70 = $38 906.30

Example 12.3c

What is the cash value of a car that can be bought for $500 down and $200 a month for 30 months if money is worth 18% compounded monthly?

SOLUTION:

Since a down payment has been made, the first of the regular payments should be made at the end of the month following the date of purchase. Thus, this is an ordinary annuity problem.

$R = \$200$ (per month)
$i = 18\%/12 = 1.5\%$ (per month)
$n = 30$ (months or payments)

Substituting the above values in Formula 12-2:

$$A_n = 200 \cdot \frac{1 - (1 + 1.5\%)^{-30}}{1.5\%}$$

$$= 200(24.015\ 838\ 01)$$

$$= \$4\ 803.17.$$

The cash value of the car is $4 803.17.

Example 12.3d

Find the present value of an annuity of $150 payable at the end of every six months for $7\frac{1}{2}$ years if the interest rate is 10% converted semi-annually.

SOLUTION:

$R = \$150$ (semi-annually)
$i = 10\%/2 = 5\%$ (semi-annually)
$n = 15$ (semi-annual periods or payments)

Substituting the values in Formula 12-2:

$$A_n = 150 \cdot \frac{1 - (1 + 5\%)^{-15}}{5\%}$$

$$= 150(10.379\ 658\ 04)$$

$$= \$1\ 556.95$$

The present value is $1 556.95.

NOTE: The relationship of magnitude among the present value, the sum of actual payments, and the amount of an annuity may be expressed as follows:

Present value < Actual payments < Amount

Using the data given in Example 12.3d, the above expression may be illustrated in the following manner:

Present value = $1 556.95; Actual payments = $150 \times 15 = \$2\ 250$;

$$\text{Amount} = 150 \cdot \frac{(1 + 5\%)^{15} - 1}{5\%} = \$3\ 236.78$$

$1 556.95 < \$2\ 250 < \$3\ 236.78$

EXERCISE 12.3B / REFERENCE SECTION: B

Find the present value of the ordinary annuity in each of the following problems:

	Payment (R)	Payment Interval	Term	Compound Interest Rate
1.	$2 000	1 month	2 years	24% monthly
2.	1 000	1 month	$3\frac{1}{2}$ years	15% monthly
3.	700	6 months	$8\frac{1}{2}$ years	17% semi-annually
4.	3 000	1 quarter	$7\frac{1}{2}$ years	12% quarterly
5.	800	1 quarter	15 years, 6 months	16% quarterly
6.	400	1 year	4 years	10% annually
7.	500	6 months	20 years	15% semi-annually
8.	600	6 months	12 years	15% semi-annually

Statement Problems:

9. Fred Grey bought a boat on which he made a down payment of $2 000 and agreed to make equal monthly payments of $800 payable at the end of each month for two years. If the interest rate charged is 12% compounded monthly, what is the cash price of the boat?

10. Ms Caluso wants to buy a stereo. Sounds Inc. has offered her the following terms: $50 down and $60 per month for one year. Stereo City has offered her the following terms: $25 down and $65 per month for one year. If the current interest rate is 18% compounded monthly, which store is offering her the better deal?

11. What is the cash price of a car which can be bought with $200 down and equal payments of $500 each at the end of the month for 24 months if the interest rate charged is 16% compounded monthly?

12. A widow as beneficiary will receive $400 at the end of each month for 20 years, or a cash settlement. If money can be invested at 12% compounded monthly, how much should she accept as a cash settlement? (Assume that interest rates will remain at 12% for the 20 years).

13. Mrs. K.G. Griffin purchased a refrigerator and made a down payment of $150. She agreed to pay $100 per month thereafter for one year. If the interest was at 18% compounded monthly, what was the cash price of the refrigerator?

14. Fred Johnson wants to buy a television. King Appliances offered him a payment plan of $70 down and $50 per month thereafter for six payments. T.V.s-To-Go offered him a payment plan of $80 down and $25 per month. Which store offered him the better plan? Why? (Assume the interest rate charged by both stores is 24% compounded monthly).

15. A house sells for $50 000 cash and $400 per month for twenty years. Find the equivalent cash price if interest is at 11% compounded monthly.

16. Bill Grant borrowed some money from his employer and agreed to repay the loan by paying $150 at the end of every quarter for $1\frac{1}{2}$ years. If money was worth 10% compounded quarterly, how much did Grant receive from his employer?

17. What is the cash value of a lot that can be bought for $1 000 down and monthly payments of $600 payable at the end of each month at 20% interest compounded monthly for 5 years?

18. Enterprise Limited must set up an account to be used to replace obsolete equipment. If $500 is deposited at the end of each month in an account which pays
15% compounded monthly, how much will be available at the end of 10 years?

12.4 Finding the Size of Each Periodic Payment (R)

Frequently the size of each periodic payment must be determined when the amount
or the present value of an annuity is known. In this type of problem the interest rate
and the term of the annuity are usually given.

A. THE PRESENT VALUE IS KNOWN

To find the size of each periodic payment when the present value is known, use the
formula

$$A_n = R\left[\frac{1-(1+i)^{-n}}{i}\right]$$

in the following form

$$\boxed{R = A_n\left[\frac{i}{1-(1+i)^{-n}}\right]} \longleftarrow Formula\ 12\text{-}3$$

Example 12.4a

The present value of an annuity for $3\frac{1}{2}$ years is $10 000. Find the size of the monthly
payment if the interest rate is 12% compounded monthly.

SOLUTION:

$A_n = \$10\ 000$
  $i = 12\%/12 = 1\%$ (per month)
  $n = 3\frac{1}{2} \times 12 = 42$ (monthly payments)

Substituting the values in Formula 12-3:

$$R = 10\ 000\left[\frac{1\%}{1-(1+1\%)^{-42}}\right]$$

$$= 10\ 000\left[\frac{1\%}{1-.658\ 418\ 9}\right]$$

$$= 10\ 000\left[\frac{.01}{.341\ 581\ 1}\right]$$

$$= 10\ 000(.029\ 275\ 6)$$
$$= \$292.76$$

$$\text{or } 10\ 000\left[\frac{.01}{.341\ 581\ 1}\right] = \left[\frac{100}{.341\ 581\ 1}\right] = \$292.76$$

The monthly payment is $292.76.

Example 12.4b
Ray purchased a lot for $65 000. He made a down payment of $5 000 and agreed to make equal payments at the end of each month for 20 years. If the interest is 18% compounded monthly, what is the size of the monthly payment?

SOLUTION:

A_n = 65 000 − 5 000 = $60 000
i = 18%/12 = 1.5% (per month)
n = 20 × 12 = 240 (monthly payments)

Substituting the values in Formula 12-3:

$$R = 60\ 000 \left[\frac{1.5\%}{1 - (1 + 1.5\%)^{-240}} \right]$$

$$= 60\ 000 \left[\frac{.015}{1 - .028\ 064} \right]$$

$$= 60\ 000 \left[\frac{.015}{.971\ 936} \right]$$

$$= 60\ 000(.015\ 433\ 1)$$
$$= \$925.99$$

Ray's monthly payments would be $925.99.

B.   THE AMOUNT IS KNOWN

To find the size of each periodic payment when the amount is known, use the formula

$$S_n = R \left[\frac{(1 + i)^n - 1}{i} \right]$$

in the following form

$$\boxed{R = S_n \left[\frac{i}{(1 + i)^n - 1} \right]} \quad \longleftarrow Formula\ 12\text{-}4$$

Example 12.4c
The amount of an annuity for $3\frac{1}{2}$ years is $10 000. Find the size of the monthly payment if the interest rate is 12% compounded monthly.

SOLUTION:

S_n = $10 000
i = 12%/12 = 1% (per month)
n = $3\frac{1}{2}$ × 12 = 42 (monthly periods)

Substituting the values in Formula 12-4:

$$R = 10\ 000 \left[\frac{1\%}{(1 + 1\%)^{42} - 1} \right]$$

$$= 10\ 000 \left[\frac{.01}{1.518\ 789\ 9 - 1} \right]$$

$$= 10\ 000 \left[\frac{.01}{.518\ 789\ 9} \right]$$

$$= 10\ 000(.019\ 275\ 6)$$

$$= \$192.76$$

$$R = 10\ 000 \left[\frac{.01}{.518\ 789\ 9} \right] = \left[\frac{100}{.518\ 789\ 9} \right] = \$192.76$$

The monthly payment is $192.76.

Example 12.4d

Fiona would like to have a $12 000 fund at the end of twenty years. If her savings can be invested at 18% compounded monthly, how much must she invest at the end of each month for twenty years?

SOLUTION:

$S_n = 12\ 000$
$\quad i = 18\%/12 = 1.5\%$ (per month)
$\quad n = 20 \times 12 = 240$ (months)

Substituting the values in Formula 12-4:

$$R = 12\ 000 \left[\frac{1.5\%}{(1 + 1.5\%)^{240} - 1} \right]$$

$$= 12\ 000 \left[\frac{.015}{(1.015)^{240} - 1} \right]$$

$$= 12\ 000 \left[\frac{.015}{35.632\ 816 - 1} \right]$$

$$= 12\ 000[.000\ 433\ 1]$$

$$= \$5.20$$

Thus, $5.20 deposited at the end of each month in an account which pays 18% compounded monthly will amount to $12 000 in 20 years.

EXERCISE 12.4 / REFERENCE SECTIONS: A-B

Find the size of the payment in each of the following ordinary annuities:

	Amount (S_n)	Present Value (A_n)	Payment Interval	Term	Compound Interest Rate
1.	$ 3 000		1 year	5 years	12.5% annually
2.		$ 4 000	6 months	8 years	16% semi-annually
3.		50 000	7 years, 1 month	7 years, 1 month	14% monthly
4.	20 000		1 quarter	10 years, 6 months	9% quarterly
5.		6 000	1 month	1 year	12% monthly
6.	10 000		1 year	4 years	13.75% annually
7.	500		1 quarter	$1\frac{1}{4}$ years	11% quarterly
8.		800	6 months	3 years	15% semi-annually

Statement Problems:

9. The amount of an annuity for $4\frac{1}{2}$ years is $5 000. What is the size of the semi-annual payment if the interest rate is 15% compounded semi-annually?

10. The present value of an annuity for 12 years is $4 200. Find the size of the semi-annual payment if the interest rate is 14% compounded semi-annually?

11. Theresa Sanders bought a truck for $9 500. She made a down payment of $500 and agreed to pay the balance in 24 equal monthly payments. If the interest charged was 18% compounded monthly, how much should she pay each month?

12. Charles Hicks bought a machine for $560. He paid $50 down and agreed to pay the balance plus interest at 16% compounded quarterly in equal quarterly payments for three years. What is the quarterly payment?

13. A debt of $2 500 was repaid in ten equal quarterly payments. If the rate of interest was 18% compounded quarterly, what was the size of each payment?

14. A woman wishes to have a $5 000 fund at the end of five years. If her money can be invested at 17% compounded monthly, how much must she invest at the end of each month during the period?

15. A store manager plans to exchange her old car at the end of four years for a new one worth $10 500. The trade-in value of the old car at that time is estimated to be $500. If money can be invested at 16% compounded quarterly, how much must she invest at the end of each quarter in order to make the exchange?

16. Ed Merrick wishes to provide a college education fund for his daughter who is now eight years old. If the fund can earn 15% compounded semi-annually and is to be used when she reaches eighteen years of age, what must be the size of each semi-annual deposit in order to provide a fund of $10 000? (Assume that Merrick wishes to make the first deposit six months from now and the last deposit on his daughter's eighteenth birthday.)

12.5 A Personal Loan as an Annuity

Personal loans are often repaid by equal monthly payments and are thus one type of annuity problem. The amount of the loan, the interest rate and the term of the loan are usually known and the size of the payment must be determined. Chartered banks, trust companies and other financial institutions frequently have computer-generated tables listing the required monthly payment for various amounts and lengths of time. Table 12-1 lists the gross interest charge and the monthly payments for loans at 15% compounded monthly.

Example 12.5a

Use Table 12-1 to find (a) the required monthly payment for a loan of $10 000 to be repaid in 24 equal monthly payments if the rate of interest is 15% compounded monthly, and (b) the amount of the gross interest charge.

SOLUTION:

(a) From Table 12-1 under the column headed *Unpaid Balance* and row labelled $10 000 headed 24 months, the regular monthly payment is shown as $484.87. This value could be found using the method of Section 12.4A.

Thus, A_n = $10 000 (amount of loan)

$i = 15\%/12 = 1.25\%$ (per month)

$n = 24$ (monthly payments)

$$R = A_n \left[\frac{i}{1 - (1 + i)^{-n}} \right]$$

$$= 10\ 000 \left[\frac{1.25\%}{1 - (1 + 1.25\%)^{-24}} \right]$$

$$= 10\ 000(.048\ 486\ 65)$$

$$= \$484.87$$

The required monthly payment is $484.87.

(b) Under the row labelled $10 000 and *Gross Interest Charge* for 24 months, the value $1 636.88 is found.

The gross interest charge is the difference between the total amount paid and the amount of the loan.

Monthly payments = $484.87

Number of payments = 24

Total amount paid = 484.87 × 24 = $11 636.88

Amount of loan = $10 000

Gross interest charge = 11 636.88 − 10 000 = $1 636.88

NOTE: The gross interest charge is the total interest charge for the loan.

Table 12-1
Personal Loans   15.00%

Unp Bal	6 MONTHS Gross Interest Charge	6 MONTHS Regular Monthly Payment	9 MONTHS Gross Interest Charge	9 MONTHS Regular Monthly Payment	12 MONTHS Gross Interest Charge	12 MONTHS Regular Monthly Payment	15 MONTHS Gross Interest Charge	15 MONTHS Regular Monthly Payment	18 MONTHS Gross Interest Charge	18 MONTHS Regular Monthly Payment	21 MONTHS Gross Interest Charge	21 MONTHS Regular Monthly Payment	24 MONTHS Gross Interest Charge	24 MONTHS Regular Monthly Payment	Unp Bal
100	4.40	17.40	6.38	11.82	8.36	9.03	10.25	7.35	12.32	6.24	14.24	5.44	16.40	4.85	100
200	8.86	34.81	12.67	23.63	16.60	18.05	20.65	14.71	24.64	12.48	28.69	10.89	32.80	9.70	200
300	13.26	52.21	19.05	35.45	24.96	27.08	30.90	22.06	36.96	18.72	42.93	16.33	49.20	14.55	300
400	17.66	69.61	25.43	47.27	33.20	36.10	41.15	29.41	49.10	24.95	57.17	21.77	65.36	19.39	400
500	22.12	87.02	31.81	59.09	41.56	45.13	51.40	36.76	61.42	31.19	71.62	27.22	81.76	24.24	500
600	26.52	104.42	38.10	70.90	49.92	54.16	61.80	44.12	73.74	37.43	85.86	32.66	98.16	29.09	600
700	30.92	121.82	44.48	82.72	58.16	63.18	72.05	51.47	86.06	43.67	100.31	38.11	114.56	33.94	700
800	35.38	139.23	50.86	94.54	66.52	72.21	82.30	58.82	98.38	49.91	114.55	43.55	130.96	38.79	800
900	39.78	156.63	57.15	106.35	74.76	81.23	92.55	66.17	110.70	56.15	128.79	48.99	147.36	43.64	900
1000	44.18	174.03	63.53	118.17	83.12	90.26	102.95	73.53	123.02	62.39	143.24	54.44	163.76	48.49	1000
1100	48.64	191.44	69.91	129.99	91.36	99.28	113.20	80.88	135.16	68.62	157.48	59.88	180.16	53.34	1100
1200	53.04	208.84	76.20	141.80	99.72	108.31	123.45	88.23	147.48	74.86	171.72	65.32	196.32	58.18	1200
1300	57.44	226.24	82.58	153.62	108.08	117.34	133.70	95.58	159.80	81.10	186.17	70.77	212.72	63.03	1300
1400	61.90	243.65	88.96	165.44	116.32	126.36	144.10	102.94	172.12	87.34	200.41	76.21	229.12	67.88	1400
1500	66.30	261.05	95.34	177.26	124.68	135.39	154.35	110.29	184.44	93.58	214.86	81.66	245.52	72.73	1500
1600	70.70	278.45	101.63	189.07	132.92	144.41	164.60	117.64	196.76	99.82	229.10	87.10	261.92	77.58	1600
1700	75.16	295.86	108.01	200.89	141.28	153.44	174.85	124.99	208.90	106.05	243.34	92.54	278.32	82.43	1700
1800	79.56	313.26	114.39	212.71	149.64	162.47	185.25	132.35	221.22	112.29	257.79	97.99	294.72	87.28	1800
1900	84.02	330.67	120.68	224.52	157.88	171.49	195.50	139.70	233.54	118.53	272.03	103.43	310.88	92.12	1900
2000	88.42	348.07	127.06	236.34	166.24	180.52	205.75	147.05	245.86	124.77	286.27	108.87	327.28	96.97	2000
2100	92.82	365.47	133.44	248.16	174.48	189.54	216.15	154.41	258.18	131.01	300.72	114.32	343.68	101.82	2100
2200	97.28	382.88	139.82	259.98	182.84	198.57	226.40	161.76	270.50	137.25	314.96	119.76	360.08	106.67	2200
2300	101.68	400.28	146.11	271.79	191.08	207.59	236.65	169.11	282.82	143.49	329.41	125.21	376.48	111.52	2300
2400	106.08	417.68	152.49	283.61	199.44	216.62	246.90	176.46	294.96	149.72	343.65	130.65	392.88	116.37	2400
2500	110.54	435.09	158.87	295.43	207.80	225.65	257.30	183.82	307.28	155.96	357.89	136.09	409.28	121.22	2500

2600	114.94	452.49	165.16	307.24	216.04	234.67	267.55	191.17	319.60	162.20	372.34	141.54	425.68	126.07	2600
2700	119.34	469.89	171.54	319.06	224.40	243.70	277.80	198.52	331.92	168.44	386.58	146.98	441.84	130.91	2700
2800	123.80	487.30	177.92	330.88	232.64	252.72	288.05	205.87	344.24	174.68	400.82	152.42	458.24	135.76	2800
2900	128.20	504.70	184.21	342.69	241.00	261.75	298.45	213.23	356.56	180.92	415.27	157.87	474.64	140.61	2900
3000	132.60	522.10	190.59	354.51	249.36	270.78	308.70	220.58	368.70	187.15	429.51	163.31	491.04	145.46	3000
3100	137.06	539.51	196.97	366.33	257.60	279.80	318.95	227.93	381.02	193.39	443.96	168.76	507.44	150.31	3100
3200	141.46	556.91	203.35	378.15	265.96	288.83	329.20	235.28	393.34	199.63	458.20	174.20	523.84	155.16	3200
3300	145.86	574.31	209.64	389.96	274.20	297.85	339.60	242.64	405.66	205.87	472.44	179.64	540.24	160.01	3300
3400	150.32	591.72	216.02	401.78	282.56	306.88	349.85	249.99	417.98	212.11	486.89	185.09	556.40	164.85	3400
3500	154.72	609.12	222.40	413.60	290.80	315.90	360.10	257.34	430.30	218.35	501.13	190.53	572.80	169.70	3500
3600	159.12	626.52	228.69	425.41	299.16	324.93	370.50	264.70	442.62	224.59	515.37	195.97	589.20	174.55	3600
3700	163.58	643.93	235.07	437.23	307.52	333.96	380.75	272.05	454.76	230.82	529.82	201.42	605.60	179.40	3700
4000	176.84	696.14	254.12	472.68	332.36	361.03	411.65	294.11	491.72	249.54	572.75	217.75	654.80	193.95	4000
4500	198.90	783.15	285.93	531.77	373.92	406.16	463.05	330.87	553.14	280.73	644.37	244.97	736.56	218.19	4500
5000	221.02	870.17	317.65	590.85	415.48	451.29	514.45	367.63	614.56	311.92	715.99	272.19	818.32	242.43	5000
5500	243.14	957.19	349.46	649.94	457.04	496.42	566.00	404.40	676.16	343.12	787.61	299.41	900.32	266.68	5500
6000	265.20	1044.20	381.18	709.02	498.60	541.55	617.40	441.16	737.58	374.31	859.02	326.62	982.08	290.92	6000
6500	287.32	1131.22	412.99	768.11	540.16	586.68	668.80	477.92	799.00	405.50	930.64	353.84	1063.84	315.16	6500
7000	309.44	1218.24	444.71	827.19	581.72	631.81	720.35	514.69	860.42	436.69	1002.26	381.06	1145.84	339.41	7000
7500	331.50	1305.25	476.52	886.28	623.28	676.94	771.75	551.45	922.02	467.89	1073.88	408.28	1227.60	363.65	7500
8000	353.62	1392.27	508.24	945.36	664.84	722.07	823.15	588.21	983.44	499.08	1145.50	435.50	1309.36	387.89	8000
8500	375.74	1479.29	540.05	1004.45	706.40	767.20	874.55	624.97	1044.86	530.27	1217.12	462.72	1391.36	412.14	8500
9000	397.86	1566.31	571.77	1063.53	747.96	812.33	926.10	661.74	1106.28	561.46	1288.74	489.94	1473.12	436.38	9000
9500	419.92	1653.32	603.58	1122.62	789.40	857.45	977.50	698.50	1167.88	592.66	1360.36	517.16	1554.88	460.62	9500
10000	442.04	1740.34	635.39	1181.71	830.96	902.58	1028.90	735.26	1229.30	623.85	1431.77	544.37	1636.88	484.87	10000

EXERCISE 12.5 / REFERENCE SECTION: 12.5

For each of the following personal loans with interest at 15% compounded monthly, find the missing item from Table 12-1:

	Amount of Loan	Term of Loan (Months)	Gross Interest Charge	Regular Monthly Payment
1.	$1 000	12	?	?
2.	3 200	24	?	?
3.	?	6	?	$348.07
4.	7 500	9	?	?
5.	?	15	?	147.05
6.	?	24	?	121.22

Statement Problems:

7. Bascalle received a $16 000 personal loan from the Bank of Montreal with interest at 16.5% compounded monthly. The loan is to be amortized by 24 equal monthly payments. (a) What is the amount of each payment? (b) How much is the gross interest charge?

8. Gabrial bought a car for $9 600 on August 5, 1985. He made a down payment of $1 000 and agreed to pay the balance in 18 equal payments on the 5th of each month. If the rate of interest charged is 18.5% compounded monthly, (a) what is the amount of each monthly payment, (b) what is the gross interest charge, and (c) when will he make his last payment?

9. Francois plans to buy a car priced at $10 500. He has $1 200 saved for a down payment and plans to pay the balance in 24 equal monthly payments. He has two payment options: (a) take a personal loan at 16.5% compounded monthly from a bank for the balance, or (b) finance the balance through the dealer at 17% compounded monthly. What is the amount of each payment if he uses option (a)? What is the amount of each payment if he uses option (b)? How much does he save in gross interest charges if he uses option (a)?

10. Ms Kaplan bought a fur coat for $6 500 and agreed to pay on the store's credit plan with 24 equal monthly payments at the rate of 18.5% compounded monthly. Ms Browne bought a similar coat for $6 500. She paid for it with a personal loan from the Toronto-Dominion Bank which she repaid in 24 equal monthly payments of $315.16. (a) What is the amount of the monthly payments made by Ms Kaplan? (b) What are the gross interest charges for Ms Kaplan? (c) What are the gross interest charges for Ms Browne? (d) How much did Ms Browne save by taking a personal loan rather than using the credit plan from the store?

12.6 Finding the Term of an Annuity (n)

Before the term of an annuity can be found, the size of the periodic payment, the interest rate per conversion period, and the amount or the present value of the annuity must be given.

A.   THE AMOUNT IS KNOWN

To find the term of annuity when the amount is known, use the formula:

$$n = \frac{\ln\left[\dfrac{S_n}{R}i + 1\right]}{\ln(1 + i)} \qquad \longleftarrow Formula\ 12\text{-}5 \ ^{3}$$

NOTE: log may be used instead of ln

Example 12.6a
If $30 is deposited at the end of each month, how many months will be required for the deposits to amount to $1 220, if the interest rate is 12% compounded monthly?

SOLUTION:

$S_n = 1\ 220$
$R = \$30$ (per month)
$\ i = 12\%/12 = 1\%$ (per month)
$\ n = ?$ (monthly payments)

$$n = \frac{\ln[\frac{1\ 220}{30}(.01) + 1]}{\ln(1.01)}$$

$$= \frac{\ln[(40.6)(0.1) + 1]}{\ln(1.01)}$$

$$= \frac{\ln 1.406}{\ln 1.01}$$

$$= \frac{.341\ 222\ 8}{.009\ 950\ 3}$$

$$= 34.292\ 607$$

---

[3] Proof $S_n = R\left[\dfrac{(1 + i)^n - 1}{i}\right]$

$$\frac{(1 + i)^n - 1}{i} = \frac{S_n}{R}$$

$$(1 + i)^n - 1 = \frac{S_n}{R}i$$

$$(1 + i)^n = \frac{S_n}{R}i + 1$$

Taking the logarithm of both sides:

$$n\ln(1 + i) = \ln\left[\frac{S_n}{R}i + 1\right]$$

$$n = \frac{\ln\left[\frac{S_n}{R}i + 1\right]}{\ln(1 + i)}$$

Therefore, 35 monthly payments will be necessary.

When $n = 34$:

$$30\left[\frac{(1 + 1\%)^{34} - 1}{1\%}\right] = \$1\,207.73.$$

When $n = 35$:

$$30\left[\frac{(1 + 1\%)^{35} - 1}{1\%}\right] = \$1\,249.81.$$

Therefore, the 35th payment will be less than \$30.

The above calculations may be illustrated as follows:

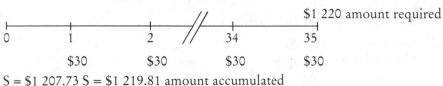

$S = \$1\,207.73 \quad S = \$1\,219.81$ amount accumulated

34   0.19 last payment

The amount of the 35th payment may be found as follows:

1. Find the amount at the 35th month if no further payment is made:
   $$S = 1\,207.73(1 + 1\%)^1 = \$1\,219.81$$

2. The final payment is the difference between the required amount and the amount found in (1).

B.   THE PRESENT VALUE IS KNOWN

To find the term of the annuity when the present value is known use the formula:

$$n = \frac{\ln\left[1 - \frac{A_n}{R}i\right]}{\ln(1 + i)} \quad \longleftarrow \textit{Formula 12-6}\,[4]$$

NOTE: log may be used instead of ln

---

[4] Proof $A_n = R\left[\dfrac{1 - (1 + i)^{-n}}{i}\right]$

$$\frac{1 - (1 + i)^{-n}}{i} = \frac{A_n}{R}$$

$$1 - (1 + i)^{-n} = \frac{A_n}{R}i$$

$$-(1 + i)^{-n} = \frac{A_n}{R}i - 1$$

$$(1 + i)^{-n} = 1 - \frac{A_n}{R}i$$

Taking the logarithm of both sides:

$$-n\ln(1 + i) = \ln\left[1 - \frac{A_n}{R}i\right]$$

$$-n = \frac{\ln\left[1 - \frac{A_n}{R}i\right]}{\ln(1 + i)}$$

$$n = -\frac{\ln\left[1 - \frac{A_n}{R}i\right]}{\ln(1 + i)}$$

Example 12.6b
Lisa borrowed $4 000 and agreed to repay the loan and interest by making equal payments of $156.93 at the end of each month. If the interest rate charged is 24% compounded monthly, how many payments must she make?

SOLUTION:

A_n = $4 000 (present value)
R = $156.93 (monthly payment)
i = 24%/12 = 2% (per month)

$$n = -\frac{\ln[1 - \frac{4\,000}{156.93}(.02)]}{\ln(1.02)}$$

$$= -\frac{\ln(1 - .509\,781\,4)}{\ln(1.02)}$$

$$= -\frac{\ln(.490\,218\,6)}{\ln(1.02)}$$

$$= -\left(\frac{-0.712\,903\,9}{0.019\,802\,6}\right)$$

$$= 36.000\,472$$

Thus, 36 monthly payments of $156.93 will settle the debt.

EXERCISE 12.6 / REFERENCE SECTIONS: A–B

Find the term in each of the following ordinary annuities:

	Amount (S_n)	Present Value (A_n)	Payment	Compound Interest Rate
1.	$2 500		$ 200 semi-annually	12% semi-annually
2.		$ 3 879	450 quarterly	11% quarterly
3.		6 000	300 monthly	18% monthly
4.	936		60 quarterly	13.75% quarterly
5.		4 092	120 monthly	15% monthly
6.	1 025		50 monthly	17% monthly
7.	5 520		300 semi-annually	14% semi-annually
8.		14 200	$1 000 quarterly	12% quarterly

Statement Problems:
9. If $150 is deposited at the end of each quarter, how much time will be required for the deposits to amount to $5 800 if the interest rate is 21% compounded quarterly?

10. The price of a boat is $10 000. The buyer made a down payment of $1 000 and agreed to pay $200 at the end of each month. If money is worth 12% compounded monthly, how long will it take the buyer to pay the balance and the interest?

11. Ms Magariety borrows $7 500 and agrees to repay it by paying $400 at the end of each quarter. If the interest rate is 16% compounded quarterly, how many payments must she make?

12. On January 1, 1984, a man decided to deposit $250 in a savings account at the end of each quarter, with the first deposit to be made on April 1. The interest rate is 17% compounded quarterly. When will $3 800 be on deposit in the man's account?

12.7 Finding the Interest Rate per Conversion Period (i) and the Nominal (Annual) Interest Rate

Sometimes an investor or borrower desires to know the interest rate of an annuity. In this type of problem, the size of each periodic payment, the term, and the amount or the present value of the annuity are usually given.

A. THE AMOUNT IS KNOWN

To find the interest rate when the amount is known, Formula 12-1

$$S_n = R \cdot \frac{(1 + i)^n - 1}{i}$$

can be reduced to an nth order equation $(1 + i)^n - \dfrac{S_n}{R} i - 1 = 0$

and the value for i which satisfies the equation can be found by the iterative process. That is, some starting value can be selected for i and the value of the equation computed successively with incremented values of i until the desired value is found.

    This approach will not be pursued in this text. A more convenient method is to express Formula 12-1 in the form

$$\boxed{\frac{(1 + i)^n - 1}{i} = \frac{S_n}{R}} \quad \longleftarrow Formula\ 12\text{-}7$$

and solve for i by trial and error.

Example 12.7a
If periodic deposits of $48.49 made at the end of each month for two years amount to $1 347.35, what rate of interest, compounded monthly, is earned?

SOLUTION:

$S_n = \$1\ 347.35$
$R = \$48.49$
$n = 24$ (monthly deposits)
$i = ?$

Using Formula 12-7:

$$S_n = R \cdot \frac{(1+i)^n - 1}{i}$$

and solving for $\frac{(1+i)^n - 1}{i}$.

Thus, $\dfrac{(1+i)^n - 1}{i} = \dfrac{S_n}{R}$

$$\frac{(1+i)^{24} - 1}{i} = \frac{1\,347.35}{48.49} = 27.786.$$

Select a starting value for i. For example, let $i = .5\%$:

$$\frac{(1 + .5\%)^{24.} - 1}{.5\%} = 25.431\,955\,24.$$

This value i is too low, so select a larger value for i. Let $i = 1.5\%$:

$$\frac{(1 + 1.5\%)^{24} - 1}{1.5\%} = 28.633\,520\,80.$$

This value is too high. It can be seen that the value of i is somewhere between .5% and 1.5%. By increasing the value of i by increments of, for example, .25% starting at $i = .5\%$, or decreasing the value of i by increments of .25%, it can be found that $i = 1.25\%$, since

$$\frac{(1 + 1.25\%)^{24} - 1}{1.25\%} = 27.788\,084\,03.$$

Thus, the annual rate is 15%, $(1.25\% \times 12) = 15\%$. This method is sometimes quite time-consuming and the exact value for i may be difficult to find by trial and error. It is sometimes convenient to use a table of values to locate the two values closest to the desired value of i. (See Section 12.9).

B.   *THE PRESENT VALUE IS KNOWN*

To find the interest rate when the present value of an annuity is known use Formula 12-2

$$A_n = R \cdot \frac{1 - (1+i)^{-n}}{i}$$

in the form

$$\boxed{\dfrac{1 - (1+i)^{-n}}{i} = \dfrac{A_n}{R}}$$
     ←——*Formula 12-8*

and select a starting value for i and find the required value by trial and error.

Example 12.7b

If a debt of $2 000 is to be repaid in 18 equal payments of $124.77 made at the end of each month, what is the rate of interest charged if interest is compounded monthly?

SOLUTION:

$A_n = 2\ 000$

$R = 124.77$

$n = 18$ (monthly payments)

$i = ?$

$$\frac{1 - (1 + i)^{-18}}{i} = \frac{2\ 000}{124.77} = 16.029\ 494$$

Select a starting value for i. For example, let $i = 2\%$:

$$\frac{1 - (1 + 2\%)^{-18}}{2\%} = 14.992\ 031\ 25.$$

Decrease the value by increments of .25%:

$$\frac{1 - (1 + 1.75\%)^{-18}}{1.75\%} = 15.326\ 862\ 72$$

$$\frac{1 - (1 + 1.50\%)^{-18}}{1.50\%} = 15.672\ 560\ 89$$

$$\frac{1 - (1 + 1.25\%)^{-18}}{1.25\%} = 16.029\ 548\ 93$$

Thus, $i = 1.25\%$ and the annual rate is 15%, $(1.25\% \times 12) = 15\%$.

As indicated in Section A, the trial and error method is sometimes time-consuming and it is often convenient to use a table of values to locate the two values closest to i. (See Section 12.9).

EXERCISE 12.7 / REFERENCE SECTIONS: A–B

Find the interest rate per conversion period (i) and the nominal interest rate in each of the following problems:

	Amount (S_n)	Present Value (A_n)	Payment	Term	Interest Conversion Period
1.	$2 680		$200 annually	10 years	1 year
2.		$6 850	500 semi-annually	10 years	6 months
3.		8 502	260 monthly	3 years	1 month
4.	926		50 quarterly	4 years	1 quarter
5.		6 642	270 monthly	$2\frac{1}{2}$ years	1 month
6.	2 520		200 monthly	1 year	1 month
7.	700		65 quarterly	$2\frac{1}{2}$ years	1 quarter
8.		530	80 semi-annually	4 years	6 months

Statement Problems:

9. At what nominal interest rate compounded semi-annually will an annuity of $220 payable at the end of every six months amount to $2 530 in five years?

10. A man deposited $80 each month in a financial association. He received $1 000 immediately after the 12th deposit was made. If the nominal interest rate was compounded monthly, what was the rate?

11. The present value of an annuity of $50 payable at the end of each quarter for $9\frac{1}{2}$ years is $1 380. What is the nominal interest rate compounded quarterly?

12. Mary borrowed $600 from her employer and agreed to repay it in 10 equal monthly payments of $65. The first payment is to be made at the end of one month after the borrowing. The monthly payment plan results in the interest rate being compounded monthly. What is the nominal interest rate?

13. Jack Davis signed a three-year non-interest-bearing note for $520. He is allowed to discharge the debt by making six equal semi-annual payments of $75 payable at the end of every six months. If he can invest his money at 10% compounded semi-annually, should he invest the money instead of paying the debt? Why?

14. The cash price of a washing machine is $370. If it can be bought by paying $25 down and $20 at the end of each month for $1\frac{3}{4}$ years, what is the nominal interest rate compounded monthly?

12.8 Using a Financial Calculator to Solve Simple Ordinary Annuity Problems

Where a financial calculator (preprogrammed is useful but not necessary) is used the task of calculating the amount, present value, interest per conversion period, and number of payments may be simplified by use of the special keys provided.

On most financial calculators, the keys used in solving simple annuity problems are:

Press Key	To Enter
2nd/FIN	financial mode
FV	future value (S_n)
PV	present value (A_n)
%i	rate per conversion period (i)
N	number of conversion periods (n)
PMT	periodic payment (R)

To retrieve a value press CPT following by one of the above (FV, PV, %i, N, PMT).

Example 12.8a

Rachel received a $5 000 loan at the Royal Bank of Canada and agreed to settle the loan and interest by making equal payments at the end of each month for 18 months. If the rate of interest charged is 18.9% compounded monthly, how much must she pay each month?

SOLUTION:

A_n = $5 000 (present value)
  i = 18.9%/12 = 1.575% (interest per month)
  n = 18 (monthly payments)

The steps are shown below:

Enter	Press	Display Shows
	2nd/FIN	FIN
5000	PV	5000
1.575	%i	1.575
18	N	18
0	FV	0
	CPT/PMT	321.17813 ANN FIN

Thus, $321.18 must be paid at the end of each month for 18 months.

NOTE: ANN appears in the display when annuity problems are computed to show that the payment value is not zero.

Example 12.8b

Mr. Hietala has set up an RRSP fund in which he deposits $100 at the end of each month. He made his first deposit on January 31, 1984. If the fund pays 12.9% interest compounded monthly, how much will he have in the account on March 31, 1991?

SOLUTION:

R = $100 (periodic payment)
i = 12.9%/12 = 1.075% (interest per month)
January 31, 1984 to March 31, 1991 is 7 years and 2 months.
n = 7 × 12 + 2 = 86 (months)

The steps are shown below:

Enter	Press	Display Shows
	2nd/FIN	FIN
100	+/−	−100 ANN FIN
	PMT	−100 ANN FIN
1.075	%i	1.075
86	N	86
0	PV	0
	CPT/FV	14029.785

Thus, there will be $14 029.79 in the fund on March 31, 1991.

NOTE: In order to obtain a present value, the way in which financial calculators are programmed the payment is subtracted to bring it down to zero. Therefore, when the amount (future value) is given or is to be computed, enter the payment as a negative number.

Example 12.8c

Ms Kerr bought a car for $10 900. She made a down payment of $1 000 and agreed to pay the balance in equal payments of $447.31 made at the end of each month. If the interest rate charged is 20.4% compounded monthly, how many payments must she make?

SOLUTION:

Balance = 10 900 − 1 000 = 9 900
A_n = 9 900 (present value)
   i = 20.4%/12 = 1.7% (interest per month)
   R = 447.31 (monthly payment)
The steps are shown below:

Enter	Press	Display Shows
	2nd/FIN	FIN
9900	PV	9900
1.7	%i	1.7
447.31	PMT	447.31 ANN FIN
0	FV	0
	CPT/N	28

Thus, 28 payments of $447.31 must be made.

Example 12.8d
Kelly loaned $10 000 to her friend Fred who agreed to repay the loan and interest by making payments of $681.30 at the end of each quarter for six years. What rate of interest did Kelly receive?

SOLUTION:

A_n = $10 000 (present value)
 $n = 6 \times 4 = 24$ (quarters)
 R = $681.30 (quarterly payments)
The steps are shown below:

Enter	Press	Display Shows
	2nd/FIN	FIN
10000	PV	10000
681.30	PMT	681.30 ANN FIN
24	N	24
0	FV	0
	CPT/%i	4.375 141

Thus, the quarterly rate of interest is 4.375 141% and the nominal rate is 4.375 141% × 4 = 17.500 564 or 17.5%.

EXERCISE 12.8 / REFERENCE SECTION: 12.8

Use a financial calculator to find the missing value in each of the following:

	Amount(S_n)	Present Value (A_n)	Payment (R)	Payment Interval	Term (years)	Interest Rate Compounded
1.	?		$1 000	1 month	$3\frac{1}{2}$	12% monthly
2.		?	500	1 quarter	5	15% quarterly
3.	$20 000		?	6 months	8	14.5% semi-annually
4.		$9 800	?	1 year	5	16.5% annually
5.		5 000	321.18	1 month	?	18.9% monthly
6.	8 499.60		250	1 quarter	24	? quarterly
7.	8 777.25		412.14	1 month	?	15% monthly
8.		5 500	266.63	1 month	2	? monthly

Statement Problems:
9. Mr. and Mrs. Rainer opened an RHOSP account in which they made a deposit of $1 000 at the end of each year for ten years. They cash in the account just after

the tenth payment. (a) How much will they have to make a down payment on a house? (b) How much interest did they receive? (The account pays interest at 12.5% compounded annually.)

10. The Isaacs bought a new car on which they made a down payment of $1 500 and promised to pay the balance in 32 equal monthly payments of $306.80. If the interest rate charged is 15.5% compounded monthly what was the cash price of the car?

11. George bought a boat for $15 000. He wants to pay for it by making 36 equal monthly payments. If the interest rate charged is 14.5% compounded monthly, how much must George pay at the end of each month.

12. What is the nominal rate of interest compounded monthly charged if a loan of $6 000 is repaid by 36 equal payments of $216.92?

13. How many monthly payments of $245.02 must be made to settle a debt of $7 500 if the rate of interest charged is 16.5% compounded monthly?

12.9 Using a Table of Values to Find S_n, A_n, R, i, n

A. FINDING THE AMOUNT

A table of values of $\frac{(1+i)^n - 1}{i}$ may be used to find the amount of an annuity. For convenience, the value of $\frac{(1+i)^n - 1}{i}$ is usually represented by the symbol $S_{\overline{n}|i}$ (which is read s angle n at i). The values of $S_{\overline{n}|i}$ for various interest rates (i) and numbers of payments (n) are provided in Table 12-2. The unit value of each entry in the table is best represented by one dollar, although it may be represented by any other unit. Therefore, each entry in the table becomes the amount of the annuity in dollars when each payment is $1, or when $R = \$1$.

When Table 12-2 is employed, the computation of the amount of an annuity is simplified. In general, Formula 12-1 is written in the following form:

$$\boxed{S_n = R\, s_{\overline{n}|i}} \qquad \longleftarrow Formula\ 12\text{-}9$$

$$\left(\begin{array}{c}\text{Amount of an}\\ \text{ordinary annuity } S_n\end{array}\right) = \left(\begin{array}{c}\text{Size of each}\\ \text{payment } R\end{array}\right) \times \left(\begin{array}{c}\text{An entry}\\ \text{in Table 12-2}\end{array}\right)$$

(The entry is at the interest rate i per conversion period for n conversion periods or payments).

Example 12.9a
Find the amount of an annuity of $150 payable at the end of every six months for $7\frac{1}{2}$ years, if the interest rate is 10% compounded semi-annually.

SOLUTION:

$R = \$150$ (semi-annually)
$i = 10\%/2 = 5\%$ (semi-annually)
$n = 15$ (semi-annual payments)

Substituting the values in Formula 12-9:
$S_n = 150s_{\overline{15}|\,5\%} = 150(21.578\ 56) = \$3\ 236.78$

Example 12.9b

If $20 is deposited at the end of each month for three years in a fund which earns 6% interest compounded monthly, what will be the final value at the end of the three-year term? What is the total interest?

SOLUTION:

$R = \$20$ (per month)
$i = 6\%/12 = \frac{1}{2}\%$ (per month)
$n = 3 \times 12 = 36$ (monthly payments)

Substituting the values in Formula 12-9:
Final value $= S_n = 20s_{\overline{36}|\,1/2\%} = 20(39.336\ 1) = \$786.72$

Total deposits $= 20 \times 36 = \$720$
Total interest $= 786.72 - 720 = \$66.72$

B. FINDING THE PRESENT VALUE

A table of values of $\frac{1-(1+i)^{-n}}{i}$ may be used to find the present value of an annuity. For convenience, the value of $\frac{1-(1+i)^{-n}}{i}$ is usually represented by the symbol $a_{\overline{n}|\,i}$ (which is read a angle n at i). The values of $a_{\overline{n}|\,i}$ for various interest rates (i) and numbers of payments (n) are provided in Table 12-3. The unit value of each entry in the table is best represented by one dollar, although it may be represented by any other unit. Therefore, each entry in the table becomes the present value of an annuity in dollars when each payment is $1, or when $R = \$1$.

  When Table 12-3 is employed, the computation of the present value of an annuity is simplified. In general, Formula 12-2 is written in the following form:

$$\boxed{A_n = R\,a_{\overline{n}|\,i}} \quad \longleftarrow Formula\ 12\text{-}10$$

$$\left(\begin{array}{c}\text{Present value of an}\\\text{ordinary annuity } A_n\end{array}\right) = \left(\begin{array}{c}\text{Size of each}\\\text{payment R}\end{array}\right) \times \left(\begin{array}{c}\text{An entry in}\\\text{Table 12-3}\end{array}\right)$$

(The entry is at the interest rate i per conversion period for n conversion periods of payments).

Example 12.9c

Josephine bought a car on which she made a down payment of $1 500 and agreed to pay the balance by equal payments of $524.21 made at the end of each month for twenty months. If the interest rate charged is 18% compounded monthly, what was the cash price of the car?

SOLUTION:

$i = 18\%/12 = 1.5\%$ (monthly rate)
$n = 20$ (months)
$R = \$524.21$ (monthly payments)

Substituting the values in Formula 12-10:
$A_n = 524.21\,a_{\overline{20}|\,1.5\%}$

$A_{20} = 524.21(17.168\ 64)$
$\quad\ = \$8\ 999.97$

The cash price of the car $= A_{20} +$ down payment
$$= 8\ 999.97 + 1\ 500$$
$$= \$10\ 499.97$$

C. FINDING THE SIZE OF EACH PERIODIC PAYMENT (R)

When a set of tables is to be used to find the periodic payment, use the formula

$A_n = R_{\,a_{\overline{n}|\,i}}$

in the form

$$R = \frac{A_n}{a_{\overline{n}|\,i}}$$ ⟵——Formula 12-11

if the present value is known.

When the amount is known, use the formula

$S_n = R_{\,s_{\overline{n}|\,i}}$

in the form

$$R = \frac{S_n}{s_{\overline{n}|\,i}}$$ ⟵——Formula 12-12

Example 12.9d
A loan of \$2 500 is to be paid off by equal payments made at the end of each quarter for eight quarters. If the interest rate is 15% compounded quarterly, what is the amount of each payment?

SOLUTION:

$A_n = 2\ 500$ (present value)
$i = 15\%/4 = 3.75\%$ (quarterly rate)
$n = 8$ (quarters)

Substituting the values in Formula 12-11:

$$R = \frac{2\ 500}{a_{\overline{8}|\ 3.75\%}}$$

$$= \frac{2\ 500}{6.802\ 796}$$

$$= \$367.50$$

Example 12.9e

Sam is saving for a vacation in Hawaii. He would like to have $6 000 three years from now. How much should be deposit in an account at the end of each month in order to have the required amount just after his 36th deposit? The account earns interest at 12% compounded monthly.

SOLUTION:

$S_n = \$6\ 000$
  $i = 12\%/12 = 1\%$ (per month)
  $n = 36$ (months)

Substituting the values in Formula 12-12:

$$R = \frac{6\ 000}{S_{\overline{36}|\ 1\%}}$$

$$= \frac{6\ 000}{43.076\ 878}$$

$$= \$139.29$$

Thus, 36 monthly deposits of $139.29 will amount to $6 000 at 12% compounded monthly.

D.   FINDING THE INTEREST RATE PER CONVERSION PERIOD (i) AND THE NOMINAL (ANNUAL) INTEREST RATE

Sometimes, an investor or borrower desires to use a table of values to find the interest rate of an annuity. In this type of problem, the size of each periodic payment, the term, and the amount or the present value of the annuity are usually given.

    To find the interest rate when the amount is known, use Formula 12-9,

$$\boxed{S_n = R\, s_{\overline{n}|\ i}}$$

Example 12.9f

At what nominal rate compounded monthly will an annuity of $150 payable at the end of each month amount to $6 600 in 32 months?

SOLUTION:

$S_n = \$6\ 600$
$R = \$150$ (per month)
$n = 32$ (monthly payments)
$i = ?$ (per quarter)

Substituting the values in Formula 12-9:

$$6\ 600 = 150 s_{\overline{32}|\,i}$$

$$S_{\overline{32}|\,i} = \frac{6\ 600}{150} = 44$$

Follow the line for $n = 32$ in Table 12-2 to find the value of 44 or the two values closest to 44. It is found that the first value greater that 44 is 44.227 029 61, which is located in the 2% column, and the first value smaller than 44 is 43.307 935 63, which is located in the $1\frac{7}{8}\%$ column. Therefore, the desired value of i is greater than $1\frac{7}{8}\%$ and is smaller than 2%, or

$$1\frac{7}{8}\% < i < 2\%.$$

When a more accurate value of i is needed, the interpolation method may be employed as follows:

	i	$S_{\overline{32}|\,i}$	
	2%	44.227 0	(1)
	x	44.000 0	(2)
	$1\frac{7}{8}\%$	43.307 9	(3)
(2) − (3)	$x - 1\frac{7}{8}\%$	= .692 1	(4)
(1) − (3)	$\frac{1}{8}\%$	.919 1	(5)

Solve for x from the proportion formed by the differences on lines (4) and (5):

$$x - 1\frac{7}{8}\% = \frac{1}{8}\%\left(\frac{.692\ 1}{.919\ 1}\right) = \left(\frac{1}{800}\right) \cdot \left(\frac{6\ 921}{9\ 191}\right) = .000\ 94$$

$$x = 1\frac{7}{8}\% + .000\ 94 = 0.187\ 5 + .000\ 94 = .019\ 69$$

The desired value of i is .019 69 or 1.969% per month.

The nominal interest rate = $.019\ 69 \times 12 = .236\ 28$, or 23.628%.

Example 12.9g

T.R. Ford signed a ten-month non-interest-bearing note for $5 000. He was offered the privilege of discharging the obligation by making 10 equal monthly payments of $488 payable at the end of each month. If he can invest his money at $5\frac{1}{2}\%$ compounded monthly, should he accept the offer?

SOLUTION:

$S_n = \$5\ 000$
$R = \$488$ (per month)
$n = 10$ (monthly payments)
$i = ?$

Substituting the values in Formula 12-9:

$5\ 000 = 488 s_{\overline{10}|\, i}$

$S_{\overline{10}|\, i} = \dfrac{5\ 000}{488} = 10.245\ 9$

Follow the line for $n = 10$ in Table 12-2 to find the value of 10.245 9 or the two values closest to it. The first value greater than 10.245 9 is 10.247 3, which is located in the $\frac{13}{24}\%$ column, and the first value smaller than 10.245 9 is 10.228 0, which is located in the $\frac{1}{2}\%$ column. Thus, the desired value of i is between $\frac{1}{2}\%$ and $\frac{13}{24}\%$, or

$$\frac{1}{2}\% < i < \frac{13}{24}\%.$$

The nominal rate $= i \times 12$, which must be greater than ($\frac{1}{2}\% \times 12$) or 6%, but smaller than ($\frac{13}{24}\% \times 12$) or $6\frac{1}{2}\%$. Since Ford can invest his money at only $5\frac{1}{2}\%$ compounded monthly, he should accept the offer to discharge his obligation by making the monthly payment. In this type of problem, use of the interpolation method is not required.

To find the interest rate when the present value is known, use Formula 12-10,

$$\boxed{A_n = R_{\,a_{\overline{n}|\, i}}}$$

Example 12.9h

The present value of an annuity of $200 payable at the end of every quarter for five years is $3 000. What is the nominal rate compounded quarterly?

SOLUTION:

$A_n = \$3\ 000$
$R = \$200$ (per quarter)
$n = 5 \times 4 = 20$ (quarterly periods or payments)
$i = ?$ (per quarter period)

Substituting the values in Formula 12-10:

$$3\ 000 = 200_{a\,\overline{20}|\,i}$$

$$a\,\overline{20}|\,i = \frac{3\ 000}{200} = 15$$

Follow the line for $n = 20$ in Table 12-3 to find the value of 15 or the two values closest to it. The first value greater than 15 is 15.227 3, which is located in the $2\frac{3}{4}\%$ column, and the first value smaller than 15 is 14.877 5, which is located in the 3% column. Thus, the desired value is

$$2\frac{3}{4}\% < i < 3\%.$$

When a more accurate value of i is needed, the interpolation method may be employed as follows: (Write the larger numbers, which are in the column of values all known, on the top lines.)

	i	$a\,\overline{20}|\,i$	
	$2\frac{3}{4}\%$	15.227 3	(1)
	x	15.000 0	(2)
	3%	14.877 5	(3)
(2) − (3)	$x - 3\%$ =	.122 5	(4)
(1) − (3)	$-\frac{1}{4}\%$	.349 8	(5)

Solve for x from the proportion formed by the differences on lines (4) and (5).

$$x - 3\% = \left(-\frac{1}{4}\%\right)\frac{.122\ 5}{.349\ 8} = 1\frac{1}{400} \cdot \frac{1\ 225}{3\ 498} = -.0009$$

The desired value of i is .029 1, or 2.91% per quarter.
The nominal interest rate = .029 1 × 4 = .116 4, or 11.64%.

Example 12.9i
T.R. Rosen bought a car and paid $400 down plus $120 at the end of each month for three years. The cash price of the car was $4 012.90. What rate of interest did he pay?

SOLUTION:

$A_n = 4\ 012.90 - 400 = \$3\ 612.90$
$R = \$120$ (per month)
$n = 3 \times 12 = 36$ (payments or months)
$i = ?$ (per month)

Substituting the values in Formula 12-10:

$3\ 612.90 = 120_{a\overline{36}|\,i}$

$$a_{\overline{36}|\,i} = \frac{3\ 612.90}{120} = 30.107\ 5$$

Follow the line for $n = 36$ in Table 12-3 to find the value of 30.107 5, or the two values closest to it. Since 30.107 5 appears in the 1% column, no interpolation is needed. The desired value of i is 1%. The nominal interest rate is $i \times 12 = 1\% \times 12 = 12\%$.

E.   FINDING THE NUMBER OF CONVERSION PERIODS (n)

To use a table of values to find the term of an annuity when the amount is known, use Formula 12-9,

$$S_n = R\,s_{\overline{n}|\,i}$$

expressed as

$$\boxed{S_{\overline{n}|\,i} = \frac{S_n}{R}} \quad \longleftarrow \textit{Formula 12-13}$$

Example 12.9j
Lillian opened a retirement savings plan (RRSP) into which she makes regular deposits of $60 at the end of each month. The plan pays 12% compounded monthly. How many deposits must she make in order to have $3 867.79 in the plan?

SOLUTION:

$R = \$60$ (monthly deposit)
$i = 12\%/12 = 1\%$ (per month)
$S_n = 3\ 867.79$

$$S_{\overline{n}|\,1\%} = \frac{3\ 867.79}{60} = 64.463\ 167$$

In the 1% column in Table 12-2, find the closest value to 64.463 167. When $n = 50$, $S_{\overline{n}|\,1\%} = 64.463\ 182\ 18$.

Thus, in order to have $3 867.79 in the plan, 50 monthly deposits must be made.

Example 12.9k

Marty bought a boat for $20 000 on the instalment plan. He has agreed to make equal quarterly payments of $1 805.17. If the rate of interest charged is 15% compounded quarterly, how many payments must he make?

SOLUTION:

$A_n = \$20\ 000$

$i = 15\%/12 = 1\frac{1}{4}\%$ (per quarter)

$R = \$1\ 805.17$ (quarterly payments)

$$a_{\overline{n}|\ 1.25\%} = \frac{20\ 000}{1\ 805.17} = 11.079\ 289$$

When $n = 12$, $a_{\overline{n}|\ 1\frac{1}{4}\%} = 11.079\ 311\ 97$

Thus, 12 quarterly payments must be made.

Table 12-2
Amount of Annuity

when periodic payment is 1 $S_{\overline{n}|\ i} = \dfrac{(1 + i)^n - 1}{i}$

n	$\frac{1}{2}\%$	$\frac{13}{24}\%$	$\frac{7}{12}\%$	$\frac{5}{8}\%$	n
1	1.0000 0000	1.0000 0000	1.0000 0000	1.0000 0000	1
2	2.0050 0000	2.0054 1667	2.0058 3333	2.0062 5000	2
3	3.0150 2500	3.0162 7934	3.0175 3403	3.0187 8906	3
4	4.0301 0012	4.0326 1752	4.0351 3631	4.0376 5649	4
5	5.0502 5063	5.0544 6086	5.0586 7460	5.0628 9185	5
6	6.0755 0188	6.0818 3919	6.0881 8354	6.0945 3492	6
7	7.1058 7939	7.1147 8249	7.1236 9794	7.1326 2576	7
8	8.1414 0879	8.1533 2090	8.1652 5285	8.1772 0468	8
9	9.1821 1583	9.1974 8472	9.2128 8349	9.2283 1220	9
10	10.2280 2641	10.2473 0443	10.2666 2531	10.2859 8916	10
11	11.2791 6654	11.3028 1066	11.3265 1396	11.3502 7659	11
12	12.3355 6237	12.3640 3422	12.3925 8529	12.4212 1582	12
30	32.2800 1658	32.4798 5241	32.6812 6164	32.8842 5766	30
31	33.4414 1666	33.6557 8494	33.8719 0233	34.0897 8427	31
32	34.6086 2375	34.8380 8711	35.0694 8843	35.3028 4542	32
33	35.7816 6686	36.0267 9341	36.2740 6045	36.5234 8820	33
34	36.9605 7520	37.2219 3854	37.4856 5913	37.7517 6000	34
35	38.1453 7807	38.4235 5738	38.7043 2548	38.9877 0850	35
36	39.3361 0496	39.6316 8498	39.9301 0071	40.2313 8168	36
37	40.5327 8549	40.8463 5661	41.1630 2630	41.4828 2782	37
38	41.7354 4942	42.0676 0771	42.4031 4395	42.7420 9549	38
39	42.9441 2666	43.2954 7391	43.6504 9562	44.0092 3359	39

Table 12-2 (Continued)
Amount of Annuity

when periodic payment is 1 $S_{\overline{n}|\,i} = \dfrac{(1 + i)^n - 1}{i}$

n	$\frac{2}{3}\%$	$\frac{3}{4}\%$	$\frac{7}{8}\%$	1%	n
34	38.0202 6443	38.5645 7819	39.3996 7085	40.2576 9862	34
35	39.2737 3286	39.8538 1253	40.7444 1797	41.6602 7560	35
36	40.5355 5774	41.1527 1612	42.1009 3163	43.0768 7836	36
37	41.8057 9479	42.4613 6149	43.4693 1478	44.5076 4714	37
38	43.0845 0009	43.7798 2170	44.8496 7128	45.9527 2361	38
39	44.3717 3009	45.1081 7037	46.2421 0591	47.4122 5085	39
40	45.6675 4163	46.4464 8164	47.6467 2434	48.8863 7336	40
41	46.9719 9191	47.7948 3026	49.0636 3317	50.3752 3709	41
42	48.2851 3852	49.1532 9148	50.4929 3996	51.8789 8946	42
43	49.6070 3944	50.5219 4117	51.9347 5319	53.3977 7936	43
44	50.9377 5304	51.9008 5573	53.3891 8228	54.9317 5715	44
45	52.2773 3806	53.2901 1215	54.8563 3762	56.4810 7472	45
46	53.6258 5365	54.6897 8799	56.3363 3058	58.0458 8547	46
47	54.9833 5934	56.0999 6140	57.8292 7347	59.6263 4432	47
48	56.3499 1507	57.5207 1111	59.3352 7961	61.2226 0777	49
49	57.7255 8117	58.9521 1644	60.8544 6331	62.8348 3385	50
50	59.1104 1837	60.3942 5732	62.3869 3986	64.4631 8218	
51	60.5044 8783	61.8472 1424	63.9328 2559	66.1078 1401	51
52	61.9078 5108	63.3110 6835	65.4922 3781	67.7688 9215	52

n	$1\frac{5}{8}\%$	$1\frac{3}{4}\%$	$1\frac{7}{8}\%$	2%	n
29	36.6731 4927	37.3632 9267	38.0695 2111	38.7922 3451	29
30	38.2690 8795	39.0171 5029	39.7833 2463	40.5680 7921	30
31	39.8909 6063	40.6999 5042	41.5292 6197	42.3794 4079	31
32	41.5391 8874	42.4121 9955	43.3079 3563	44.2270 2961	32
33	43.2142 0055	44.1544 1305	45.1199 5942	46.1115 7020	33
34	44.9164 3131	45.9271 1527	46.9659 5866	48.0338 0160	34
35	46.6463 2332	47.7308 3979	48.8465 7038	49.9944 7763	35
36	48.4043 2608	49.5661 2949	50.7624 4358	51.9943 6719	36

n	$4\frac{1}{2}\%$	5%	$5\frac{1}{2}\%$	6%	n
5	5.4707 0973	5.5256 3125	5.5810 9103	5.6370 9296	5
6	6.7168 9166	6.8019 1281	6.8880 5103	6.9753 1854	6
7	8.0191 5179	8.1420 0845	8.2668 9384	8.3938 3765	7
8	9.3800 1362	9.5491 0888	9.7215 7300	9.8974 6791	8
9	10.8021 1423	11.0265 6432	11.2562 5951	11.4913 1598	9
10	12.2882 0937	12.5778 9254	12.8753 5379	13.1807 9494	10
11	13.8411 7879	14.2067 8716	14.5834 9825	14.9716 4264	11
12	15.4640 3184	15.9171 2652	16.3855 9065	16.8699 4120	12
13	17.1599 1327	17.7129 8285	18.2867 9814	18.8821 3767	13
14	18.9321 0937	19.5986 3199	20.2925 7203	21.0150 6593	14
15	20.7840 5429	21.5785 6359	22.4086 6350	23.2759 6988	15
16	22.7193 3673	23.6574 9177	24.6411 3999	25.6725 2808	16
17	24.7417 0689	25.8403 6636	26.9964 0269	28.2128 7976	17
18	26.8550 8370	28.1323 8467	29.4812 0483	30.9056 5255	18

Table 12-3
Present Value of Annuity

when periodic payment is 1 $a_{\overline{n}|\,i} = \dfrac{1 - (1 + i)^{-n}}{i}$

n	$\frac{2}{3}\%$	$\frac{3}{4}\%$	$\frac{7}{8}\%$	1%	n
32	28.7311 5662	28.3556 5045	27.8051 6894	27.2695 8947	32
33	29.5342 6154	29.1371 2203	28.5553 0998	27.9896 9255	33
34	30.3320 4789	29.9127 7621	29.2989 4422	28.7026 6589	34
35	31.1245 5088	30.6826 5629	30.0361 2809	29.4085 8009	35
36	31.9118 0551	31.4468 0525	30.7669 1757	30.1075 0504	36
37	32.6938 4653	32.2052 6576	31.4913 6810	30.7995 0994	37
38	33.4707 0848	32.9580 8016	32.2095 3467	31.4846 6330	38
39	34.2424 2564	33.7052 9048	32.9214 7179	32.1630 3298	39
40	35.0090 3209	34.4469 3844	33.6272 3350	32.8346 8611	40
41	35.7705 6168	35.1830 6545	34.3268 7335	33.4996 8922	41
42	36.5270 4803	35.9137 1260	35.0204 4446	34.1581 0814	42
43	37.2785 2453	36.6389 2070	35.7079 9947	34.8100 0806	43

n	$1\frac{1}{8}\%$	$1\frac{1}{4}\%$	$1\frac{3}{8}\%$	$1\frac{1}{2}\%$	n
7	6.6953 3948	6.6627 2585	6.6303 5140	6.5982 1396	7
8	7.6097 3002	7.5681 2429	7.5268 5712	7.4859 2508	8
9	8.5139 4810	8.4623 4498	8.4112 0308	8.3605 1732	9
10	9.4081 0690	9.3455 2591	9.2835 5421	9.2221 8455	10
11	10.2923 1832	10.2178 0337	10.1440 7320	10.0711 1779	11
12	11.1666 9302	11.0793 1197	10.9929 2054	10.9075 0521	12
13	12.0313 4044	11.9301 8466	11.8302 5454	11.7315 3222	13
14	12.8863 6880	12.7705 5275	12.6562 3136	12.5433 8150	14
15	13.7318 8509	13.6005 4592	13.4710 0504	13.3432 3301	15
16	14.5679 9514	14.4202 9227	14.2747 2754	14.1312 6405	16
17	15.3948 0360	15.2299 1829	15.0675 4874	14.9076 4931	17
18	16.2124 1395	16.0295 4893	15.8496 1651	15.6725 6089	18
19	17.0209 2850	16.8193 0759	16.6210 7671	16.4261 6837	19
20	17.8204 4845	17.5993 1613	17.3820 7320	17.1686 3879	20
21	18.6110 7387	18.3696 9495	18.1327 4792	17.9001 3673	21
22	19.3929 0371	19.1305 6291	18.8732 4086	18.6208 2437	22
23	20.1660 3580	19.8820 3744	19.6036 9012	19.3308 6145	23
24	20.9305 6693	20.6242 3451	20.3242 3191	20.0304 0537	24
25	21.6865 9276	21.3572 6865	21.0350 0067	20.7196 1120	25
26	22.4342 0792	22.0812 5299	21.7361 2890	21.3986 3172	26

n	$2\frac{1}{4}\%$	$2\frac{1}{2}\%$	$2\frac{3}{4}\%$	3%	n
15	12.6121 6551	12.3813 7773	12.1566 9892	11.9379 3509	15
16	13.3126 3131	13.0550 0266	12.8045 7315	12.5611 0203	16
17	13.9976 8343	13.7121 9772	13.4351 0769	13.1661 1847	17
18	14.6676 6106	14.3533 6363	14.0487 6661	13.7535 1308	18
19	15.3228 9590	14.9788 9134	14.6460 0157	14.3237 9911	19
20	15.9637 1237	15.5891 6229	15.2272 5213	14.8774 7486	20
21	16.5904 2775	16.1845 4857	15.7929 4612	15.4150 2414	21
22	17.2033 5232	16.7654 1324	16.3434 9987	15.9369 1664	22
23	17.8027 8955	17.3321 1048	16.8793 1861	16.4436 0839	23
24	18.3890 3624	17.8849 8583	17.4007 9670	16.9355 4212	24
25	18.9623 3263	18.4243 7642	17.9083 1795	17.4131 4769	25
26	19.5231 1260	18.9506 1114	18.4022 5592	17.8768 4242	26

Table 12-3 (Continued)
Present Value of Annuity

when periodic payment is 1 $a_{\overline{n}|\,i} = \dfrac{1 - (1 + i)^{-n}}{i}$

n	$3\frac{1}{4}\%$	$3\frac{1}{2}\%$	$3\frac{3}{4}\%$	4%	n
1	0.9685 2300	0.9661 8357	0.9638 5542	0.9615 3846	1
2	1.9065 5981	1.8996 9428	1.8928 7270	1.8860 9467	2
3	2.8150 7003	2.8016 3698	2.7883 1103	2.7750 9103	3
4	3.6949 8308	3.6730 7921	3.6513 8413	3.6298 9522	4
5	4.5471 9911	4.5150 5238	4.4832 6181	4.4518 2233	5
6	5.3725 8994	5.3285 5302	5.2850 7162	5.2421 3686	6
7	6.1719 9994	6.1145 4398	6.0579 0036	6.0020 5467	7
8	6.9462 4692	6.8739 5554	6.8027 9553	6.7327 4488	8
9	7.6961 2292	7.6076 8651	7.5207 6677	7.4353 3161	9
10	8.4223 9508	8.3166 0532	8.2127 8525	8.1108 9578	10
11	9.1258 0637	9.0015 5104	8.8797 9494	8.7604 7671	11

EXERCISE 12.9 / REFERENCE SECTIONS: A–E

Use a table of values to find the missing value in each of the following:

	Amount (S_n)	Present Value (A_n)	Payment (R)	Payment Interval	Term (years)	Rate Compounded
1.	?		$1 000	1 month	$3\frac{1}{2}$	12% monthly
2.		?	500	1 quarter	5	15% quarterly
3.	$20 000		?	6 months	8	14.5% semi-annually
4.		$9 800	?	1 year	5	16.5% annually
5.		5 000	321.18	1 month	?	18.9% monthly
6.	6 885.29		200	1 quarter	24	?
7.	8 500		412.14	1 month	?	15% monthly
8.		5 500	266.63	1 month	2	?

Statement Problems:

9. Marlene has opened an RRSP account into which she makes regular deposits of $1 000 at the end of each year. The account pays interest at 12% compounded annually. (a) How much will she have in the account just after the 10th deposit? (b) How much interest will she have earned?

10. James received a loan and agreed to repay the loan by paying $150 at the end of each quarter for $1\frac{1}{2}$ years. If the interest rate charged is 12% compounded quarterly, how much did James borrow?

11. Celia signed a three-year non-interest-bearing note for $2 000. She is allowed to discharge the debt by making equal semi-annual payments of $406.73 at the end of each six months for three years. (a) What is the rate of interest charged? (b) She has won the lottery. If she can earn 12.5% on her money, should she pay off the debt now?

12. Charles bought a television for $850. He paid $50 down and agreed to pay the balance plus interest at 15% compounded monthly in equal monthly payments made at the end of each month for two years. What is the size of each monthly payment?

13. The price of a boat is $9 991. The buyer made a down payment of $1 000 and agreed to pay $200 at the end of each month. If money is worth 12% compounded monthly, how long will it take the buyer to pay the balance and interest?

EXERCISE/CHAPTER REVIEW

1. What is the amount of an annuity if the payment is $30 payable at the end of every quarter for 10 years at 19% compounded quarterly?

2. Find the amount of an annuity of $300 payable at the end of each year for ten years if the interest rate is 16.5% compounded annually.

3. (a) If $40 is deposited at the end of each month for $6\frac{1}{5}$ years in a bank that pays $10\frac{1}{2}$% interest compounded monthly, what will be the final value at the end of $3\frac{1}{2}$ years? (b) What is the total interest at the end of 4 years?

4. (a) If $90 is deposited at the end of each six months for six years in a fund that earns 17% interest compounded semi-annually, what will be the value of the fund at the end of nine years? (b) What is the total interest earned?

5. What is the present value of an annuity if the payment is $65 payable at the end of each month for eight years and the interest rate is 18% compounded monthly?

6. If Jerome Wilson wishes to receive $80 at the end of each month for $2\frac{1}{2}$ years from a financial company that pays 12% interest compounded monthly, how much must he deposit in the company now?

7. What is the cash price of a house that can be bought for $1 500 down and $100 a month for 20 years, if the interest is 16% compounded monthly?

8. What is the amount and the present value of an annuity of $40 payable at the end of each month for 30 years if the interest rate is 5% compounded monthly?

9. Find the amount and the present value of an annuity of $100 payable at the end of each quarter for 40 years if the interest rate is 6% compounded quarterly.

10. The present value of an annuity payable quarterly for $7\frac{1}{2}$ years is $7 500. What is the size of the quarterly payment if the interest rate is 8% compounded quarterly?

11. The price of a small lot is $8 000. The buyer made a down payment of $3 000. The balance is to be paid in monthly instalments for eight years. If the interest rate charged is 20% compounded monthly, how much should the buyer pay each month?

12. The amount of an annuity payable monthly for 4 years is $8 500. What is the size of the monthly payment if the interest rate is 15% compounded monthly?

13. Shirley Roth wishes to have $4 000 at the end of five years. If her savings can be invested at 12% compounded monthly, how much must she save at the end of each month for five years?

14. Judy Reese figures that she will have $2 790.80 in her savings account at the end of $2\frac{1}{2}$ years. She deposits $40 one month from now and $40 thereafter at the end of each month. At what nominal interest rate compounded monthly has she figured the interest?

15. Steven Kyle plans to invest $100 each month with the first investment to be made one month from now. He expects $3 993.01 at the end of $1\frac{1}{2}$ years. What must be the nominal interest rate compounded monthly?

16. Robert Oaks bought a car for $300 down with monthly payments of $500 for 20 months. The cash price was $8 884.32. What was the nominal rate charged?

17. James Allen bought a color television. The cash price was $423.32. Under the terms of his instalment purchase, he made 12 monthly payments of $40 each, with the first payment beginning on the date of purchase. What was the nominal interest rate charged?

18. If $50 is deposited at the end of each quarter, how many quarterly deposits will be needed for the deposits to amount to $1 000 if the interest rate is 16% compounded quarterly?

19. Johnson plans to invest $150 each month starting one month from now. He wishes to have at least $1 500 as the final value. If he can earn 15% interest compounded monthly on his investment, how many monthly deposits are required for the final value?

20. A company is considering the purchase of a new machine that will increase operating efficiency and thus save $2 000 each six months in labor costs. It is estimated that the machine will be used for ten years and it can then be sold for $1 000. If money is worth 19%, how much can the company afford to pay for this machine?

21. A piece of land is available at a price of $25 000. Company G is considering its purchase for future plant expansion. If the land will not be needed for 20 years and the annual taxes will be 2% of the purchase price, what must the prospective price of the land be in 20 years to make it worthwhile for the company to buy the land now? Assume that money is worth 12%.

Summary of Formulae

Formula 12-1	$S_n = R \cdot \dfrac{(1+i)^n - 1}{i}$	To find the amount of an ordinary annuity
Formula 12-2	$A_n = R \cdot \dfrac{1 - (1+i)^{-n}}{i}$	To find the present value of an ordinary annuity.
Formula 12-3	$R = A_n \left[\dfrac{i}{1 - (1+i)^{-n}} \right]$	To find the size of each periodic payment when the present value is known.
Formula 12-4	$R = S_n \left[\dfrac{i}{(1+i)^n - 1} \right]$	To find the size of each periodic payment when the amount is known.
Formula 12-5	$n = \dfrac{\ln \left[\dfrac{S_n}{R} i + 1 \right]}{\ln (1+i)}$	To find the term of an annuity when the amount is known.
Formula 12-6	$n = \dfrac{\ln \left[1 - \dfrac{A_n}{R} i \right]}{\ln (1+i)}$	To find the term of an annuity when the present value is known.
Formula 12-7	$\dfrac{(1+i)^n - 1}{i} = \dfrac{S_n}{R}$	To find the interest rate of an annuity when the amount is known.
Formula 12-8	$\dfrac{1 - (1+i)^{-n}}{i} = \dfrac{A_n}{R}$	To find the interest rate of an annuity when the present value is known.
Formula 12-9	$S_n = R\, s_{\overline{n}|\, i}$	To find the amount of an ordinary annuity with a table of values.

Formula 12-10	$A_n = R\, a_{\overline{n}|\, i}$	To find the interest rate with a table of values when the present value is known.
Formula 12-11	$R = \dfrac{A_n}{a_{\overline{n}|\, i}}$	To find the periodic payment with a table of values when the present value is known.
Formula 12-12	$R = \dfrac{S_n}{S_{\overline{n}|\, i}}$	To find the periodic payment with a table of values when the amount is known.
Formula 12-13	$S_{\overline{n}|\, i} = \dfrac{Sn}{R}$	To find the term of an annuity with a table of values when the amount is known.

Glossary

AMOUNT the final value at the end of the term of an annuity; includes all periodic payments and compound interest

ANNUITY periodic payments (usually of equal amount) made on an instalment basis

ANNUITY CERTAIN where the term of an annuity begins and ends on definite dates; see *ordinary annuity*

ANNUITY DUE where periodic payments against an annuity are made at the beginning of each payment interval

COMPLEX ANNUITY (GENERAL ANNUITY) an annuity where the payment interval does not coincide with the interest conversion period

CONTINGENT ANNUITY where the term of an annuity begins on a definite date but the ending date is not fixed in advance

DEFERRED ANNUITY an annuity where periodic payments are made at the end of each payment interval, however, the term does not begin until after a designated period of time

ORDINARY ANNUITY periodic payments of an annuity are made at the end of each payment interval

PAYMENT INTERVAL the period of time between two successive payment dates

PERPETUITY where the term of an annuity begins on a definite date but never ends, such as a principal which remains untouched forever, drawing interest; length of term is infinite

PRESENT VALUE the value at the beginning of the term of an annuity

SIMPLE ANNUITY the payment interval of an annuity which coincides with the interest conversion period; the payment date is the interest computing date

TERM the time between the beginning of the first payment interval and the end of the last payment interval

Complex (or general) ordinary annuity certain 13

Introduction

In Chapter Twelve, the special type of annuity for which the payment interval and the interest conversion period are the same was covered. However, there are many cases involving periodic payment for which the payment interval and the interest conversion period are not the same. For example, in Canada, a residential mortgage requires periodic monthly payments and the interest is converted semi-annually.

Since a home is likely to be the largest single investment an individual will make, the mortgage taken to finance the home will likely be the largest debt contracted by an individual. It is therefore essential that the individual possess the communication skills necessary to make correct decisions when negotiating a mortgage contract.

Annuities for which the payment interval and the interest conversion period are not the same are called complex or general annuities. Chapter Thirteen covers the methods used in calculations involving complex ordinary annuity certain, with special emphasis on home mortgages.

13.1 Basic Concepts and Terminology

When the length of the payment interval of an annuity is not the same as the length of the interest conversion period, the annuity is called a COMPLEX ANNUITY. Thus, if each of the payments of an annuity is made monthly and the interest is compounded or converted quarterly, or if each of the payments is made quarterly and the interest is compounded monthly, the annuity is called a complex annuity. As shown in Chapter Twelve, n represents the number of payments of an annuity, and also the number of interest periods of an annuity. However in this chapter, to avoid confusion in a complex annuity problem, n represents *only the number of payments of an annuity. The letter c will be used to represent the number of interest periods in one payment interval.* Thus, the total number of interest periods of a complex annuity is the product of n and c, or nc.

For example, assume that the payment of an annuity is made monthly and the interest is compounded semi-annually. A one-year term of this annuity consists of two payments (or $n = 2$), each payment interval consists of six interest periods (or $c = 6$), and there are twelve interest periods ($nc = 2 \times 6 = 12$) during the year.

The diagram below shows the semi-annual payments of an annuity with interest compounded monthly. In this illustration, # denotes the date for computing interest.

						R					R (Payments)
#	#	#	#	#	#	#	#	#	#	#	# (Interest Periods)
0	1	2	3	4	5	6	7	8	9	10	11	12 (Month)
(Now)						1					2 (Six Months)

If the payment of an annuity is made monthly and the interest is compounded semi-annually, a one-year term of an annuity consists of 12 payments (or $n = 12$), each payment interval consists of $\frac{1}{6}$ of an interest period (or $c = \frac{1}{6}$), and there are two interest periods (or $nc = 12 \times \frac{1}{6}$) during the year. This type of payment is diagrammed below:

						#					# (Interest Periods)
R	R	R	R	R	R	R	R	R	R	R	R (Payments)
0	1	2	3	4	5	6	7	8	9	10	11	12 (Month)
(Now)						1					2 (Six Months)

Additional illustrations of complex annuities are presented in Table 13-1:

Table 13-1
Illustrations of Complex Annuities

Payment Interval	Interest Conversion Period	Term of Annuity	Total Number of Payments (n)	Number of Interest Periods in One Payment Interval (c)	Total Interest Periods ($n \times c$)
1 quarter	1 month	2 years	8	3	24
1 month	1 quarter	2 years	24	$\frac{1}{3}$	8
6 months	1 month	1 year	2	6	12
1 year	1 quarter	1 year	1	4	4
1 quarter	6 months	1 year	4	$\frac{1}{2}$	2
1 month	1 year	1 year	12	$\frac{1}{12}$	1
1 quarter	1 quarter	1 year	4	1	4
1 month	1 month	1 year	12	1	12

When $c = 1$, the number of payments (n) is the same as the number of interest periods [$nc = n(1) = n$]. The formulae developed below may apply in any case involving simple annuity problems. Therefore, complex annuity is also referred to simply as a general case in annuity problems or as a GENERAL ANNUITY.

13.2 Ordinary Complex Annuity Problems

A.   THE AMOUNT AND THE PRESENT VALUE

The terms which have been used in Chapter Twelve are also used here with the same meanings. Thus, the word ORDINARY is used to indicate that the periodic payment of a complex annuity is made at the end of each payment interval. The AMOUNT of a complex annuity (S_{nc}) is defined as the final value at the end of the annuity. The PRESENT VALUE of a complex annuity (A_{nc}) is the value at the beginning of the term of the annuity.

Basically, as discussed in Chapter Twelve, the amount and the present value of an annuity may be found by using the following two compound interest formulas:

$$S = P(1 + i)^n \quad \text{and} \quad P = S(1 + i)^{-n}.$$

However, the two principal annuity formulae below, which are derived from the two above, offer a more convenient way to solve any type of SIMPLE annuity problem: (See Chapter Twelve).

$$S_n = R \cdot \frac{(1 + i)^n - 1)}{i}$$ ⟵ *Formula 12-1*

$$A_n = R \cdot \frac{1 - (1 + i)^{-n}}{i}$$ ⟵ *Formula 12-2*

When applying Formula 12-1 or 12-2, let f = the interest rate per payment interval. Then, convert the value of f into the given interest rate i. Thus,

$$S_n = R \left[\frac{(1 + f)^n - 1}{f} \right]$$ ⟵ *Formula 13-1*

and $$A_n = R \left[\frac{1 - (1 + f)^{-n}}{f} \right]$$ ⟵ *Formula 13-2*

Example 13.2a

Find the amount and present value of an annuity of $100 payable at the end of each quarter for ten years if the interest rate is 12% compounded monthly.

SOLUTION:

R = $100 (quarterly payment)

$n = 10 \times 4 = 40$ (quarterly payments)

$i = \frac{12\%}{12} = 1\%$ (monthly rate)

$c = 3$ (interest periods in one payment interval, $\frac{3 \text{ months}}{1 \text{ month}} = 3$)

f = interest rate for one quarter

In one payment interval, one quarter or three months, the compound amount of $1 at rate f per quarter is $1 + f$, and at rate 1% per month is $(1 + 1\%)^3$. The two amounts are equal. Thus, $1 + f = (1 + 1\%)^3$ and, $f = (1 + 1\%)^3 - 1$.

Let S_{40} = the amount of the annuity of 40 quarterly payments at the quarterly rate f. Then,

$$S_{40} = 100 \left[\frac{(1 + f)^{40} - 1}{f} \right]$$

$$= 100 \, \frac{[(1 + 1\%)^3]^{40} - 1}{(1 + 1\%)^3 - 1}$$

$$= 100 \, \frac{(1 + 1\%)^{120} - 1}{(1 + 1\%)^3 - 1}$$

$$= 100 \, \frac{(3.300\ 386\ 8 - 1)}{1.030\ 301 - 1}$$

$$= 100 \left(\frac{2.300\ 386\ 8}{.030\ 301} \right)$$

$$= 100(75.917\ 855)$$

$$= \$7\ 591.79$$

Thus, the amount is \$7 591.79.

Let A_{40} = the present value of an annuity of 40 quarterly payments at the quarterly rate f. Then,

$$A_{40} = 100 \left[\frac{1 - (1 + f)^{-40}}{f} \right]$$

$$= 100 \left\{ \frac{1 - [(1 + 1\%)^3]^{-40}}{(1 + 1\%)^3 - 1} \right\}$$

$$= 100 \left\{ \frac{1 - .302\ 994\ 8}{1.030\ 301 - 1} \right\}$$

$$= 100 \left(\frac{.697\ 005\ 2}{.030\ 301} \right)$$

$$= 100\ (23.002\ 714)$$

$$= \$2\ 300.27$$

Thus, the present value is \$2 300.27.

Example 13.2a is diagrammed as follows:

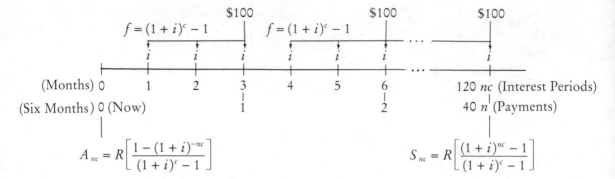

$$A_{nc} = R\left[\frac{1-(1+i)^{-nc}}{(1+i)^c - 1}\right] \qquad S_{nc} = R\left[\frac{(1+i)^{nc} - 1}{(1+i)^c - 1}\right]$$

The above calculations may be expanded by letting:

R = size of actual periodic payment
i = given interest rate per conversion period
c = number of interest periods in one payment interval, or
$\quad = \dfrac{\text{payment interval}}{\text{interest period}}$
n = number of actual payments
f = interest rate per payment interval

The formulae for a complex ordinary annuity may be obtained from the formulae:

$$\boxed{S_n = R\left[\frac{(1+f)^n - 1}{f}\right]} \quad \longleftarrow Formula\ 13\text{-}1$$

$$\boxed{A_n = R\left[\frac{1-(1+f)^{-n}}{f}\right]} \quad \longleftarrow Formula\ 13\text{-}2$$

The proofs are presented below:
$$1 + f = (1+i)^c$$
$$f = (1+i)^c - 1$$

$$S_n = R\left[\frac{(1+f)^n - 1}{f}\right]$$

$$S_{nc} = R\left\{\frac{[(1+i)^c]^n - 1}{(1+i)^c - 1}\right\}$$

$$\boxed{S_{nc} = R\left[\frac{(1+i)^{nc} - 1}{(1+i)^c - 1}\right]} \quad \longleftarrow Formula\ 13\text{-}3$$

Similarly,

$$A_n = R\left[\frac{(1+f)^n - 1}{f}\right]$$

$$A_{nc} = R\left\{\frac{1 - [(1+i)^c]^{-n}}{(1+i)^c - 1}\right\}$$

$$\boxed{A_{nc} = R\left[\frac{1 - (1+i)^{-nc}}{(1+i)^c - 1}\right]} \quad \longleftarrow \text{Formula 13-4}$$

Example 13.2b

A condominium corporation has set up a contingency fund which will be used to cover the cost of major repairs. (a) If $2 000 is deposited in an account at the end of each year and the account pays 12% compounded monthly, how much will be available to the corporation when the 8th payment is made? (b) If the corporation wants to make a single deposit now which will be equivalent to the eight annual payments, how much should they deposit?

SOLUTION:

$R = \$2\ 000$ (annual deposit)

$i = \dfrac{12\%}{12} = 1\%$ (monthly)

$n = 8$ (annual payments)

$c = 12$ (interest periods in one payment interval, $\dfrac{12 \text{ months}}{1 \text{ month}} = 12$)

$f = (1+i)^c - 1 = (1 + 1\%)^{12} - 1$

(a) $\quad S_{nc} = R\left[\dfrac{(1+i)^{nc} - 1}{(1+i)^c - 1}\right]$

$\qquad = 2\ 000\left\{\dfrac{[(1+1\%)^{12}]^8 - 1}{(1+1\%)^{12} - 1}\right\}$

$\qquad = 2\ 000\left[\dfrac{(1+1\%)^{96} - 1}{(1+1\%)^{12} - 1}\right]$

$\qquad = 2\ 000\left(\dfrac{2.599\ 272\ 9 - 1}{1.126\ 825 - 1}\right)$

$\qquad = 2\ 000(12.610\ 076)$

$\qquad = \$25\ 220.15$

Thus, $25 220.15 would be available just after the 8th deposit.

(b) $A_{nc} = R \left[\dfrac{1 - (1 + i)^{-nc}}{(1 + i)^c - 1} \right]$

$= 2\,000 \left\{ \dfrac{1 - [(1 + 1\%)^{12}]^{-8}}{(1 + 1\%)^{12} - 1} \right\}$

$= 2\,000 \left[\dfrac{1 - (1 + 1\%)^{-96}}{(1 + 1\%)^{12} - 1} \right]$

$= 2\,000 \left(\dfrac{1 - .384\,722\,97}{1.126\,825\,03 - 1} \right)$

$= 2\,000 \left(\dfrac{.615\,277}{.126\,825} \right)$

$= 2\,000(4.851\,385\,8)$

$= \$9\,702.77$

Thus, a deposit of $9 702.77 made now would be equivalent to the eight annual deposits.

These calculations are diagrammed as follows:

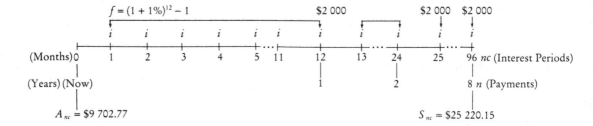

Example 13.2c
A boat can be bought with a down payment of $6 000 and $400 payable at the end of each month for ten years. If the interest rate is 18% compounded semi-annually (a) what single payment at the end of ten years would be equivalent to the monthly payments, and (b) what is the cash price of the boat?

SOLUTION:

$R = \$400$ (monthly payment)

$i = \dfrac{18\%}{2} = 9\%$ (semi-annually)

$n = 10 \times 12 = 120$ (monthly payments)

$c = \dfrac{1}{6} \left(\text{interest periods in one payment interval, } \dfrac{1 \text{ month}}{6 \text{ months}} = \dfrac{1}{6} \right)$

$f = (1 + i)^c - 1 = (1 + 9\%)^{1/6} - 1$

(a) Let S_{nc} = the amount of the annuity of 120 monthly payments at the monthly rate r. Then,

$$S_{nc} = R \left\{ \frac{[(1 + i)^c]^n - 1}{(1 + i)^c - 1} \right\}$$

$$= 400 \left\{ \frac{[(1 + 9\%)^{1/6}]^{120} - 1}{(1 + 9\%)^{1/6} - 1} \right\}$$

$$= 400 \left[\frac{(1 + 9\%)^{20} - 1}{(1 + 9\%)^{1/6} - 1} \right]$$

$$= 400 \left(\frac{5.604\ 410\ 8 - 1}{1.014\ 466\ 6 - 1} \right)$$

$$= 400(318.278\ 7)$$

$$= \$127\ 311.48$$

Thus, a single payment of \$127 311.48 at the end of ten years would be equivalent to the monthly payments.

(b) Let A^{nc} = the present value of the annuity of 120 monthly payments at the monthly rate f. Then,

$$A_{nc} = R \left\{ \frac{1 - [(1 + i)^c]^{-n}}{(1 + i)^c - 1} \right\} = R \left\{ \frac{1 - (1 + i)^{nc}}{(1 + i)^c - 1} \right\}$$

$$= 400 \left[\frac{1 - [(1 + 9\%)^{\frac{1}{6}}]^{-120}}{(1 + 9\%)^{1/6} - 1} \right]$$

$$= 400 \left[\frac{1 - (1 + 9\%)^{-20}}{(1 + 9\%)^{1/6} - 1} \right]$$

$$= 400 \left(\frac{1 - .178\ 430\ 9}{1.014\ 466\ 6 - 1} \right)$$

$$= 400 \left(\frac{.821\ 569\ 1}{.014\ 466\ 6} \right)$$

$$= 400(56.790\ 752)$$

$$= \$22\ 716.30$$

Thus, the cash value of the boat is the down payment plus the present value of the monthly payments:

Cash Value = \$6 000 + \$22 716.30 = \$28 716.30

The above calculations may be illustrated as follows:

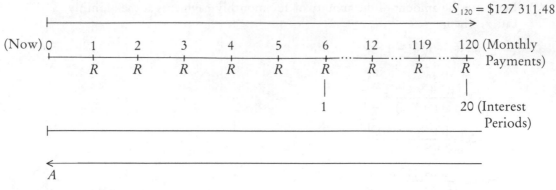

Present value = $22 716.30
Down payment = $\underline{6\ 000.00}$

Cash value = $28 716.30

EXERCISE 13.2A / REFERENCE SECTION: A

Find the amount and the present value of the complex annuity in each of the following problems:

	Payment (R)	Payment Interval	Term	Interest Rate Compounded
1.	$ 250	1 month	$3\frac{1}{2}$ years	18% semi-annually
2.	140	1 quarter	2 years	19% semi-annually
3.	70	6 months	5 years	13.5% monthly
4.	85	1 year	10 years	21% quarterly
5.	300	1 quarter	6 years	20% semi-annually
6.	460	1 month	$1\frac{1}{2}$ years	19.5% semi-annually
7.	1 000	1 year	4 years	22.5% monthly
8.	2 500	1 month	10 years	16% semi-annually

Statement Problems:

9. Find the amount and the present value of an annuity of $350 payable at the end of each month for three years if the interest rate is (a) 5% compounded annually, and (b) 5% compounded monthly.

10. What are the amount and the present value of an annuity of $500 payable at the end of each quarter for six years if the interest rate is (a) 8% compounded semi-annually, and (b) 8% compounded quarterly?

11. A man bought a store and agreed to pay $4 000 at the end of every six months for seven years. What is the equivalent cash price of the store if the interest rate is 10% compounded quarterly?

12. A company deposits $800 at the end of every nine months in a bank that pays 6% interest compounded monthly. Find the amount of the company's account at the end of $4\frac{1}{2}$ years.

13. What is the cash value of a house that can be bought for $10 000 down and monthly payments of $600 for 20 years if the mortgage contract calls for 20% interest compounded semi-annually?

14. Refer to Problem 13. What is the cash price if the rate of interest is 20% compounded quarterly?

15. Enterprise Limited must set up an account to be used to replace obsolete equipment. If $500 is deposited at the end of each month in an account which pays 15% compounded semi-annually, how much will be available at the end of 10 years?

16. Refer to Problem 15. How much will be available at the end of 10 years if the interest rate is 16% compounded quarterly.

B. THE AMOUNT AND THE PRESENT VALUE OF AN ORDINARY COMPLEX ANNUITY–USING THE EFFECTIVE RATE f

It is sometimes convenient to convert the interest rate i into the equivalent rate for one payment interval and substitute this value into the formula:

$$S_n = R\left[\frac{(1+f)^n - 1}{f}\right]$$ $\longleftarrow$ Formula 13-1

$$A_n = R\left[\frac{1-(1+f)^{-n}}{f}\right]$$ $\longleftarrow$ Formula 13-2

Here, the problem is reduced to a simple ordinary annuity with n payments and interest rate f per payment interval.

Example 13.2d
Find the amount and present value of an annuity of $1 000 payable at the end of each year for ten years if the rate is 15% compounded monthly.

SOLUTION:

$R = \$1\ 000$

$n = 10$ (payments)

$i = \dfrac{15\%}{12} = 1.25\%$

$c = 12$ (interest periods in one payment interval)

$f = (1 + 1.25\%)^{12} - 1$

$\quad = .160\ 754\ 5$

$\quad = 16.075\ 45\%$

$$S_n = R\left[\frac{(1+f)^n - 1}{f}\right]$$

$$S_{10} = 1\,000\left[\frac{(1 + 16.075\,45\%)^{10} - 1}{16.075\,45\%}\right]$$

$$= 1\,000\left(\frac{4.440\,212\,6 - 1}{.160\,754\,5}\right)$$

$$= 1\,000(21.400\,412)$$

$$= \$21\,400.41$$

Thus, the amount of the annuity is \$21 400.41.

$$A_n = R\left[\frac{1 - (1+f)^{-n}}{f}\right]$$

$$A_{10} = 1\,000\left[\frac{1 - (1 + 16.075\,45\%)^{-10}}{16.075\,45\%}\right]$$

$$= 1\,000\left[\frac{1 - .225\,214\,4}{.160\,754\,5}\right]$$

$$= 1\,000\left(\frac{.774\,785\,6}{.160\,754\,5}\right)$$

$$= 1\,000(4.819\,681\,9)$$

$$= \$4\,819.68$$

Thus, the present value of the annuity is \$4 819.68

This example is diagrammed below:

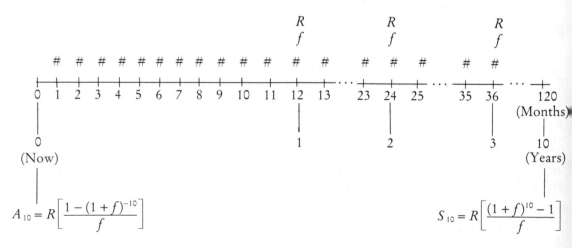

C.   THE SIZE OF PAYMENT OF AN ORDINARY COMPLEX ANNUITY

When finding the size of payment of an ordinary complex annuity, use Formula 13-3 when the amount of the annuity is known and use Formula 13-4 when the present value of the annuity is known.

Example 13.2e

A man wishes to receive $20 000 $2\frac{1}{2}$ years from now. How much must he invest at the end of every six months if the first payment starts six months from now and he can get 10% interest compounded quarterly?

SOLUTION:

S_{nc} = $20 000

$i = \dfrac{10\%}{4} = 2\frac{1}{2}\%$ (per quarter)

$n = 5$ (semi-annual payments)
$c = 2$ (interest periods in six months)
$R = ?$

Substituting the values in Formula 13-3:

$$S_{nc} = R\left[\frac{(1+i)^{nc} - 1}{(1+i)^c - 1}\right]$$

$$20\ 000 = R\left[\frac{(1 + 2\frac{1}{2}\%)^{10} - 1}{(1 + 2\frac{1}{2}\%)^2 - 1}\right]$$

$$= R\left[\frac{1.280\ 084\ 5 - 1}{1.050\ 625 - 1}\right]$$

$$= R\left(\frac{.280\ 084\ 5}{.050\ 625}\right)$$

$$= R(5.532\ 534\ 3)$$

$$R = \left(\frac{20\ 000}{5.532\ 534\ 3}\right)$$

$$= \$3\ 614.98$$

NOTE: Remember to store the values of intermediate calculations in order to obtain the values correct to 8 significant digits.

Example 13.2f

A lot which sells for $16 000 can be bought for $6 000 down with the balance payable in 24 equal monthly payments. If the interest rate is 12% compounded semi-annually, what is the size of the monthly payment?

SOLUTION:

$$A_{nc} = \$16\ 000 - \$6\ 000 = \$10\ 000$$

$$i = \frac{12\%}{2} = 6\% \text{ (semi-annually)}$$

$$c = \frac{1}{6} \text{ (interest periods in one month)}$$

$$n = 24 \text{ (monthly payments)}$$

$$R = ?$$

Substituting the values in Formula 13-4:

$$A_{nc} = R\left[\frac{1 - (1 + i)^{-nc}}{(1 + i)^c - 1}\right]$$

$$10\ 000 = R\left[\frac{1 - (1 + 6\%)^{-4}}{(1 + 6\%)^{1/6} - 1}\right]$$

$$= R\left(\frac{1 - .792\ 093\ 7}{1.009\ 758\ 8 - 1}\right)$$

$$= R\left(\frac{.207\ 906\ 3}{.009\ 758\ 8}\right)$$

$$= R\ (21.304\ 513)$$

$$R = \frac{10\ 000}{21.304\ 513}$$

$$= \$469.38$$

Example 13.2g

A lot which sells for $66 000 can be bought with $6 000 down payment and equal monthly payments, payable at the end of each month for five years. If the mortgage contract calls for 18% interest compounded semi-annually, what should be the amount of each monthly payment?

SOLUTION:

$$A_{nc} = R\left[\frac{1 - (1 + i)^{-nc}}{(1 + i)^c - 1}\right]$$

Thus, $R = A_{nc}\left[\dfrac{(1 + i)^c - 1}{1 - (1 + i)^{-nc}}\right]$

$$A_{nc} = \$60\ 000$$

$$i = \frac{18\%}{2} = 9\%$$

$$n = 60 \text{ (monthly payments)}$$

$$c = \frac{1}{6} \text{ (interest period in each month)}$$

$$R = ?$$

$$R = 60\ 000 \left[\frac{(1 + 9\%)^{1/6} - 1}{1 - (1 + 9\%)^{-10}} \right]$$

$$= 60\ 000 \left(\frac{1.014\ 466\ 59 - 1}{1 - .422\ 410\ 81} \right)$$

$$= 60\ 000 \left(\frac{.014\ 466\ 59}{.577\ 589\ 11} \right)$$

$$= \$1\ 502.79$$

Thus, the amount of each monthly payment would be $1 502.79.

EXERCISE 13.2B / REFERENCE SECTIONS: B-C

Find the payment of the ordinary complex annuity in each of the following problems:

	Amount (S_{nc})	Present Value (A_{nc})	Number of Payments (n)	Compound Interest Rate
1.	$1 000		5 annual payments	13.5% semi-annually
2.	5 400		12 semi-annual payments	16.5% monthly
3.		$3 500	24 monthly payments	22% semi-annually

Statement Problems:

4. The amount of an annuity at the end of ten years is $8 000, the payments are made at the end of each year, and the interest rate is 19% compounded quarterly. What is the size of each annual payment?

5. Don Emerson wishes to receive $6 000 four years from now. How much must he invest at the end of each quarter during the four-year period? Assume that he will make his first investment three months from now and he can earn 17.5% interest compounded semi-annually.

6. The present value of an annuity for three years is $500, the payments are made at the end of every six months, and the interest rate is 19.5% compounded monthly. How large is each payment?

7. Jane Parker wishes to receive $2 000 in cash now. She agrees to repay it by making 15 equal monthly payments with the first payment to be made one month from now. If the interest rate is 15% compounded semi-annually, how much should she pay at the end of each month?

8. How much should be deposited at the end of each month in a fund which pays 12% compounded semi-annually in order to have $60 000 after the 80th payment?

9. What is the cash price of a car which can be bought for $500 down and $200 payable at the end of each month for 24 months if the interest rate charged is 19% compounded semi-annually?

13.3 Home Mortgage Loans

A consumer usually undertakes a mortgage obligation for the purpose of buying a house. A MORTGAGE may be obtained from a bank, a trust company, a credit union, a mortgage broker or a friend or relative.

An Open or Closed Mortgage

An OPEN MORTGAGE contract provides the consumer with the right to pay off the debt at any time with a small PENALTY. The penalty imposed is usually an increase of a quarter to one percent in the interest rate. A CLOSED MORTGAGE contract is a binding agreement that the debt will not be paid off until the term of the contract ends.

Term and Amortization Period

The TERM of a mortgage is the time for which the contract will last. It is the time from the beginning of the first payment interval to the end of the last payment interval. The current trend is toward a shorter term contract. A mortgage may now be obtained for a term of from six months to five years. A shorter term usually involves a lower interest rate. The AMORTIZATION PERIOD is the period over which the debt will be paid off if the contract is renewed at the same rate of interest. The amortization period for a home mortgage is generally from twenty to thirty years. However, a mortgage may be amortized over five, ten or fifteen years. A longer amortization period results in a lower monthly payment and a higher total interest payment.

A Variable Rate Mortgage (VRM)

With the VARIABLE RATE MORTGAGE, the interest varies with the current market rate. Usually, the monthly payments remain the same for the term of the mortgage and the outstanding debt is adjusted to offset the change in rate. If the rate goes up the outstanding debt is increased while the outstanding debt is decreased if the interest rate goes down. The terms and conditions of a variable rate mortgage vary considerably among lending institutions.

Optional Clauses

When negotiating a home mortgage, the consumer should be aware of certain optional clauses which may be negotiated. It is possible to include a clause which allows the consumer to reduce or pay off the mortgage before the end of the term. This clause provides for a payment without penalty of up to ten percent of the debt on each anniversary of the mortgage. Other clauses are the RENEGOTIATION and the TRANSFERABILITY clauses. The renegotiation clause allows the consumer to renegotiate the terms upon payment of penalty equal to three months' interest. This clause will allow the consumer to negotiate a lower rate of interest if the market rate should drop significantly. The transferability clause allows the consumer to transfer the mortgage to the buyer if the property is sold.

Under the terms of the *Canada Interest Act*, any mortgage more than five years old can be paid off with a small penalty. Some lenders are requiring the consumer to waive this right by including a clause on the mortgage renewal agreement which states that this right is expressly waived. The consumer should insist on having this clause removed when signing a renewal contract.

Example 13.3a

Mr. and Mrs. DeVrai obtained a five-year term mortgage amortized over 25 years in the amount of $32 000. The rate of interest charged was 14.5% compounded semi-annually. (a) What is the amount of each monthly payment if payments are made at the end of each month? (b) What is the total amount paid by the DeVrai's after five years? (c) What is the amount of the outstanding debt after five years? (d) How much of the amount paid in the five years was interest?

SOLUTION:

(a) A_{nc} = 32 000 (present value)

$\quad n = 25 \times 12 = 300$ (monthly payments necessary to amortize the debt)

$\quad i = \dfrac{14.5\%}{2} = 7.25\%$ (semi-annually)

$\quad c = \dfrac{1}{6} \left(\dfrac{\text{interest period}}{\text{number of payments}} \right)$

$\quad nc = (300)\dfrac{1}{6} = 50$

$\quad R = A_{nc} \left[\dfrac{(1+i)^c - 1}{1 - (1+i)^{-nc}} \right]$

$\qquad = 32\ 000 \left[\dfrac{(1 + 7.25\%)^{1/6} - 1}{1 - (1 + 7.25\%)^{-50}} \right]$

$\qquad = 32\ 000 \left(\dfrac{1.011\ 733\ 7 - 1}{1 - .030\ 308\ 9} \right)$

$\qquad = 32\ 000 \left(\dfrac{.011\ 733\ 7}{.969\ 791\ 1} \right)$

$\qquad = 32\ 000(.012\ 099\ 2)$

$\qquad = \$387.17$

The amount of each monthly payment is $387.17.

(b) Number of payments made: $12 \times 5 = 60$ (monthly payments)
     Amount paid = $387.17 \times 60 = $23 230.20

(c) The amount outstanding after 60 payments is the present value of an annuity of 240 payments, (300 − 60).

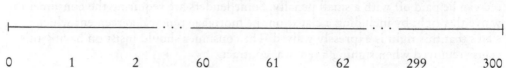

$$R = \$387.17 \text{ (monthly payment)}$$

$$i = \frac{14.5\%}{2} = 7.25\% \text{ (semi-annually)}$$

$$c = \frac{1}{6}$$

$$n = 240$$

$$nc = 240 \times \frac{1}{6} = 40$$

$$A_{nc} = 387.17\left[\frac{1 - (1 + 7.25\%)^{-40}}{(1 + 7.25\%)^{1/6} - 1}\right]$$

$$A_{40} = 387.17\left(\frac{1 - .060\ 828\ 6}{1.011\ 733\ 7 - 1}\right)$$

$$= 387.17\left(\frac{.939\ 171\ 4}{.011\ 733\ 7}\right)$$

$$= 387.17(80.040\ 512)$$

$$= \$30\ 989.29$$

The outstanding balance of the debt after five years is $30 989.29.

(d) Original amount of debt $32 000.00
     Amount owing after five years   30 989.29
     Amount of principal paid $ 1 010.71

   Amount of interest paid = Amount Paid − Amount of Principal Paid
   Amount of Interest Paid = 23 230.20 − 1 010.71 = $22 219.49

The problem may also be solved by substituting into Formula 13-2:

(a) $A_n = \$32\ 000$ (present value)

   $n = 25 \times 12 = 300$ (payments necessary to amortize the debt)

   $c = \frac{1}{6}$ (interest period in one payment interval)

   $i = \frac{14.5\%}{2} = 7.25\%$ (semi-annually)

   $f = (1 + i)^c - 1 = (1 + 7.25\%)^{1/6} - 1$

   $A_n = R\left[\frac{1 - (1 + f)^{-n}}{f}\right]$

$$R = A_n \left[\frac{f}{1 - (1 + f)^{-n}} \right]$$

$$= 32\,000 \left(\frac{.011\,733\,7}{1 - (1.011\,733\,7)^{-300}} \right)$$

$$= 32\,000 \left(\frac{.011\,733\,7}{1 - .030\,208\,9} \right)$$

$$= 32\,000 \left(\frac{.011\,733\,7}{.969\,791\,1} \right)$$

$$= 32\,000(.012\,099\,2)$$
$$= \$387.17$$

The monthly payment is $387.17.

(b) After five years the DeVrai's have made 60 payments ($12 \times 5 = 60$) of $387.17.
     Amount Paid $= 387.17 \times 60 = \$23\,230.20$.

(c) The amount outstanding after five years is the present value of an annuity of 240
     payments ($300 - 60$).

$$A_{240} = 387.17 \left[\frac{1 - (1 + .011\,733\,7)^{-240}}{.011\,733\,7} \right]$$

$$= 387.17 \left[\frac{1 - .060\,828\,6}{.011\,733\,7} \right]$$

$$= 387.17(80.040\,511)$$
$$= \$30\,989.29$$

The outstanding balance of the debt after five years is $30 989.29.

(d) Original amount of debt $32 000.00
     Amount owing after five years   30 989.29
     Amount of principal paid $ 1 010.71

     Therefore, the amount of interest paid $23 230.20
                                                 −1 010.71
                                                 $22 219.49

Example 13.3b

Ms Jenson bought a house for $80 000. She made a down payment of $4 800 and
agreed to make equal payments at the end of each month for seven years. The rate of
interest charged was 18.25% compounded semi-annually. (a) What is the amount of
each monthly payment? (b) What is the outstanding balance after the sixth payment?

SOLUTION:

(a) $A_{nc} = \$75\ 200$

$i = \dfrac{18.25\%}{2} = 9.125\%$ (semi-annually)

$n = 7 \times 12 = 84$

$c = \dfrac{1}{6}\left(\dfrac{\text{interest period}}{\text{payment interval}}\right)$

$nc = 84\left(\dfrac{1}{6}\right) = 14$

$A_{nc} = R\left[\dfrac{1 - (1 + i)^{-nc}}{(1 + i)^{c} - 1}\right]$

$R = A_{nc}\left[\dfrac{(1 + i)^{c} - 1}{1 - (1 + i)^{-nc}}\right]$

$= 75\ 200\left[\dfrac{(1 + 9.125\%)^{1/6} - 1}{1 - (1 + 9.125\%)^{-14}}\right]$

$= 75\ 200\left(\dfrac{1.014\ 660\ 4 - 1}{1 - .294\ 483\ 1}\right)$

$= 75\ 200\left(\dfrac{.014\ 660\ 4}{.705\ 516\ 9}\right)$

$= 75\ 200(.020\ 779\ 7)$

$= \$1\ 562.63$

The monthly payment is $1 562.63.

(b) After the sixth payment, 78 payments are outstanding $(84 - 6)$. The outstanding balance is the present value of an annuity of 78 payments. This is illustrated below:

$A_n = \$75\ 200$

$A_{78} = \$72\ 335.79$

$R = \$1\ 562.63$ (monthly payment)

$A_{nc} = \$75\ 200$

$i = \dfrac{18.25\%}{2} = 9.125\%$ (semi-annually)

$c = \dfrac{1}{6}\left(\dfrac{\text{interest period}}{\text{payment intervals}}\right)$

$$nc = 78 \times \frac{1}{6} = 13$$

$$A_{nc} = R\left[\frac{1 - (1 + i)^{-nc}}{(1 + i)^c - 1}\right]$$

$$A_{13} = 1\ 562.63\left[\frac{1 - (1 + 9.125\%)^{-13}}{(1 + 9.125\%)^{1/6} - 1}\right]$$

$$= 1\ 562.63\left(\frac{1 - .321\ 354\ 7}{1.014\ 660\ 4 - 1}\right)$$

$$= 1\ 562.63\left(\frac{.678\ 645\ 3}{.014\ 660\ 4}\right)$$

$$= 1\ 562.63(46.291\ 056)$$
$$= \$72\ 335.79$$

Thus, \$72 335.79 is outstanding after the sixth payment.

This example may also be solved using Formula 13-2:

(a) $A_n = \$75\ 200$

$$i = \frac{18.25\%}{2} = 9.125\% \text{ (semi-annually)}$$

$$n = 7 \times 12 = 84$$

$$c = \frac{1}{6} \text{ (interest periods in one payment interval)}$$

$$\begin{aligned}f &= (1 + i)^c - 1\\ &= (1 + 9.125\%)^{1/6} - 1\\ &= 1.014\ 660\ 4 - 1\\ &= .014\ 660\ 4 \text{ (interest rate per month)}\end{aligned}$$

$$A_n = R\left[\frac{1 - (1 + f)^{-n}}{f}\right]$$

$$R = A_n\left(\frac{f}{1 - (1 + f)^{-n}}\right)$$

$$= 75\ 200\left(\frac{.014\ 660\ 4}{1 - (1.014\ 660\ 4)^{-84}}\right)$$

$$= 75\ 200\left(\frac{.014\ 660\ 4}{.705\ 661\ 7}\right)$$

$$= 75\ 200(.020\ 779\ 7)$$
$$= \$1\ 562.63$$

Each monthly payment is \$1 562.63.

The above calculations are illustrated as follows:

$A_n = \$75\ 200$

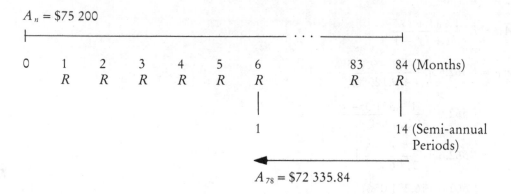

(b) After the sixth payment $(84 - 6) = 78$ payments are outstanding. The balance owing may be found by:

$n = 78$
$R = \$1\ 562.63$
$f = .014\ 660\ 4$

Finding the present value of an annuity of 78 payments:

$$A_n = R\left[\frac{1-(1+f)^{-n}}{f}\right]$$

$$A_{78} = 1\ 562.63\left[\frac{1-(1+.014\ 660\ 4)^{-78}}{.014\ 660\ 4}\right]$$

$$= 1\ 562.63\left(\frac{.678\ 645\ 4}{.014\ 660\ 4}\right)$$

$$= 1\ 562.63(46.\ 291\ 056)$$

$$= \$72\ 335.79$$

The outstanding balance is $72 335.79.

Table 13-2 is an amortization schedule showing the amount of interest, principal and outstanding balance for the first 36 payments. The difference in the values calculated for R and outstanding balance and those shown in Table 13-2 are due to rounding error.

Table 13-2
Amortization Schedule

Original Principal	Interest Rate Per Annum		Monthly Payment	Term in Years	Compounded Half-Yearly
$75 200.00	18.25		$1 562.62	7.0	—

Pay No.	Payment Date	Payment	Principal	Interest	Balance
1	MAR 31 1982	1 562.62	460.16	1 102.46	74 739.84
2	APR 30 1982	1 562.62	466.91	1 095.71	74 272.93
3	MAY 31 1983	1 562.62	473.75	1 088.87	73 799.18
4	JUN 30 1982	1 562.62	480.70	1 081.92	73 318.40
5	JUL 31 1982	1 562.62	487.74	1 074.88	72 830.74
6	AUG 31 1982	1 562.62	494.90	1 067.72	72 335.84
7	SEP 30 1982	1 562.62	502.15	1 060.47	71 833.69
8	OCT 31 1982	1 562.62	509.51	1 053.11	71 324.18
9	NOV 30 1982	1 562.62	516.98	1 045.64	70 807.20
10	DEC 31 1982	1 562.62	524.56	1 038.06	70 282.64
11	JAN 31 1983	1 562.62	532.25	1 030.37	69 750.38
12	FEB 28 1983	1 562.62	540.05	1 022.57	69 210.33
13	MAR 31 1983	1 562.62	547.97	1 014.65	68 662 36
14	APR 30 1983	1 562.62	556.01	1 006.61	68 106.35
15	MAY 31 1983	1 562.62	564.16	998.46	67 542.20
16	JUN 30 1983	1 562.62	572.43	990.19	66 969.77
17	JUL 31 1983	1 562.62	580.82	981.80	66 388.95
18	AUG 31 1983	1 562.62	589.33	973.29	65 799.62
19	SEP 30 1983	1 562.62	597.97	964.65	65 201.64
20	OCT 31 1983	1 562.62	606.74	955.88	64 594.90
21	NOV 30 1983	1 562.62	615.64	946.98	63 979.27
22	DEC 31 1983	1 562.62	624.66	937.96	63 354.60
23	JAN 31 1984	1 562.62	633.82	928.80	62 720.79
24	FEB 29 1984	1 562.62	643.11	919.51	62 077.68
25	MAR 31 1984	1 562.62	652.54	910.08	61 425.14
26	APR 30 1984	1 562.62	662.11	900.51	60 763.03
27	MAY 31 1984	1 562.62	671.81	890.81	60 091.22
28	JUN 30 1984	1 562.62	681.66	880.96	59 409.56
29	JUL 31 1984	1 562.62	691.65	870.97	58 717.90
30	AUG 31 1984	1 562.62	701.79	860.83	58 016.11
31	SEP 30 1984	1 562.62	712.08	850.54	57 304.03
32	OCT 31 1984	1 562.62	722.52	840.10	56 581.50
33	NOV 30 1984	1 562.62	733.11	829.51	55 843.39
34	DEC 31 1984	1 562.62	743.86	818.76	55 104.53
35	JAN 31 1985	1 562.62	754.77	807.85	54 349.76
36	FEB 28 1985	1 562.62	765.83	796.79	53 583.92

EXERCISE 13.3 / REFERENCE SECTION: 13.3

Find the missing item in each of the following problems involving a home mortgage:

	Amount (S_{nc})	Present Value (A_{nc})	Number of Payments	Amount of Each Monthly Payment	Interest Rate Compounded Semi-Annually
1.	$20 000		200	?	14%
2.	15 000		120	?	13.5%
3.		75 000	150	?	12.5%
4.		80 000	180	?	15%
5.	?		84	560	18%
6.	?		90	460	15%
7.		?	120	600	17%
8.		?	100	550	16.5%

Statement Problems:

9. Megan obtained a two-year term home mortgage amortized over twenty years in the amount of $40 000. The rate of interest charged is 12.5% compounded semi-annually. (a) What is the amount of each monthly payment? (b) What is the total amount paid at the end of the two-year term? (c) What is the amount of the outstanding debt? (d) How much interest was paid for the two-year term?

10. Gabrielle received a one year term home mortgage amortized over 15 years in the amount of $30 000. The rate of interest is 13.5% compounded semi-annually. (a) What is the amount of each payment? (b) What is the total amount paid at the end of one year? (c) What is the amount of the outstanding debt? (d) How much interest was paid for the year?

11. A house was purchased for $30 000 down and equal monthly payments of $500 made at the end of each month for twenty years. The interest rate is 11.75% compounded semi-annually. (a) What is the cash price of the house? (b) How much is the cost of financing? (c) If the interest rate is changed to 18% at the end of one year, what is the amount of the new monthly payment?

13.4 Use of an Electronic Calculator to Solve Problems Involving Complex Ordinary Annuity Certain

A financial calculator (preprogrammed) may be used to calculate the amount, present value, amount of each payment, interest rate per conversion period, and number of payments of a complex (general) ordinary annuity.

When a financial calculator is used, the following steps should be taken:

1. Calculate the equivalent rate for one payment interval using

$$f = (1 + i)^c - 1 \qquad \text{and enter this value as } \underline{\%i}.$$

2. Use the keys (FV, PV, %i, N) as used in Chapter Twelve.

Example 13.4a

Find the amount of an annuity of $100 deposited at the end of each quarter for ten years if the interest rate is 12% compounded monthly.

SOLUTION:

$R = \$100$

$n = 10 \times 4 = 40$ (quarterly payments)

$i = \dfrac{12\%}{12} = 1\%$ (monthly)

$c = 3$ (interest periods per payment interval)

$f = (1 + 1\%)^3 - 1$

1. Calculate f :

Enter	Press	Display Shows	
	2nd/FIN	FIN	
1	PV	1	
0	PMT	0	
1	%i	1	
3	N	3	
	CPT/FV	1.030301	⟵ $(1.01)^3$
			(The value of $(1.01)^3$ = 1.030301)
1	− =	.030301	
	X		
100	=	3.0301	⟵ 3.0301%

(The effective quarterly rate = 3.0301%, enter this value as %i)

2.

	Press	Display Shows
	%i	3.0301
0	PV	0
40	N	40
100	+/−	−100
	PMT	−100
	CPT/FV	7591.7855

The amount of the annuity is $7 591.79. This is the same answer as that obtained in Example 13.2a.

Example 13.4b

A tractor may be purchased by a down payment of $2 500 and 36 monthly payments of $1 000 each made at the end of the month. What is the cash price of the tractor if the rate of interest is 15% compounded semi-annually?

SOLUTION:

Down payment = $2 500

$R = \$1\,000$ (monthly payment)

$i = \dfrac{15\%}{2} = 7.5\%$ (semi-annually)

$c = \dfrac{1}{6}$ (interest periods per payment)

$n = 36$ (monthly payments)

1. Calculate $f = (1 + 7.5\%)^{1/6} - 1$

Enter	Press	Display Shows	
	2nd/FIN	FIN	
1	PV	1	
0	PMT	0	
7.5	%i	7.5	
6	$\frac{1}{x}$	0.1666667	
	N	0.1667	
	CPT/FV	1.0121288	$\longleftarrow (1.075)^{1/6}$
	−	1.0121288	
1	=	0.0121288	
	X		
100	=	1.21288	
(The effective rate = 1.212 88%).			
	%i	1.21288	
0	FV	0	

Enter	Press	Display Shows
1000	PMT	1000
36	N	
	CPT/PV	29029.605

(The present value is $29 029.61.)

The cash price of the tractor is the present value of the payments plus the down payment:

Cash price = $29 029.61 + $2 500 = $31 529.61

Example 13.4c

A debt of $2 500 can be settled by equal payments at the end of each month for two years. What must be the amount of each payment if the interest rate is 17% compounded quarterly?

SOLUTION:

A_n = $2 500 (present value)

$n = 2 \times 12 = 24$ (monthly payments)

$i = \dfrac{17\%}{4} = 4.25\%$

$c = \dfrac{1}{3}$ (interest periods per payment interval)

$f = (1 + 4.25\%)^{1/3} - 1$

Calculate f:

Enter	Press	Display Shows
	2nd/FIN	FIN
1	PV	1
0	PMT	0
4.25	%i	4.25
3	$\frac{1}{x}$	0.3333333
	N	0.3333
	CPT/FV	1.0139692
	$-$	
1	$=$	.0139692
	X	
100	$=$	1.39692

(The effective rate is 1.396 92%)

	%i	1.39692
2500	PV	2500
0	FV	0
24	N	24
	CPT/PMT	123.3212

The debt will be settled by 24 monthly payments of $123.32.

Example 13.4d

How many quarterly payments of $183.54 made at the end of each quarter must be made to settle a debt of $5 000 if the interest rate is 13.2% compounded monthly?

SOLUTION:

R = $183.54 (quarterly payment)

A_{nc} = $5 000 (present value)

$$i = \frac{13.2\%}{12} = 1.1\% \text{ (per month)}$$

$c = 3$ (interest periods per payment interval)

$f = (1 + 1.1\%)^3 - 1$

Calculate f:

Enter	Press	Display Shows
	2nd/FIN	FIN
1	PV	1
0	PMT	0
1.1	%i	1.1
3	N	3
	CPT/FV	1.0333643
	$=$	
1	$=$	.0333643
	X	
100	$=$	3.33643

(The effective quarterly rate is 3.336 43%)

	%i	3.33643
5000	PV	5000
0	FV	0
183.54	PMT	183.54
	CPT/N	73

Thus, 73 quarterly payments will settle the debt.

Example 13.4e

$150 is deposited in an RRSP account at the end of each month. After four years and four months, the amount in the account is $10 000. What nominal rate of interest was received if the interest is compounded semi-annually?

SOLUTION:

$S_{nc} = \$10\ 000$
$R = \$150$ (per month)
$n = 4\dfrac{4}{12} \times 12 = 52$ (months)

Enter	Press	Display Shows
	2nd/FIN	FIN
0	PV	0
10000	FV	10000
150	+/−	−150
	PMT	−150
52	N	
	CPT/%i	.940152

(The effective monthly rate is .940 152%.)

$f = (1 + i)^c − 1$
$1 + .940\ 152\% = (1 + i)^{1/6}$
$(1 + .940\ 152\%)^{1/6} − 1 = i$
$1.057\ 751\ 6 − 1 = i$
$i = .057\ 751\ 6$ (semi-annually)

Therefore, the nominal rate = .057 751 6 × 2 = .115 503 1, or 11.550 31%.

EXERCISE 13.4 / REFERENCE SECTION: 13.4

For each of the following ordinary annuity problems, use a financial calculator to find the missing item:

Amount (S_{nc})	Present Value (A_{nc})	Number of Payments (n)	Amount of Each Monthly Payment (R)	Compound Interest Rate (i)
1. ?	?	100	560	18.5% semi-annually
2. ?	?	120	420	15.4% quarterly
3.	30 000	80	?	12.8% annually
4. 60 000		150	?	16.5% semi-annually
5.	50 000	?	520	18% quarterly
6. 70 000		?	600	17.5% semi-annually

Statement Problems:

7. What cash payment is equivalent to a payment of $650 made at the end of each quarter for ten years if the interest rate is 14.7% compounded monthly?

8. Arlene expects to retire in twelve years. She opened an account into which she makes regular deposits of $100 at the end of each month. If the interest rate is 16.4% compounded quarterly, how much will she have in the account at the end of ten years?

9. A debt of $10 000 is to be amortized by making payments of $480 at the end of each month. If the interest rate is 16.8% compounded quarterly, how many payments must be made?

10. A car can be bought for $1 000 down and payments of $308 made at the end of each month for three years. If the list price is $9 600 what is (a) the effective monthly rate, and (b) the nominal rate compounded semi-annually?

13.5 Use of a Table of Values to Solve Problems Involving Complex Ordinary Annuity Certain

A. FINDING THE AMOUNT AND PRESENT VALUE

A table of the values of $\frac{(1+i)^n - 1}{i}$ and $\frac{1-(1+i)^{-n}}{i}$ may be used to find the amount and present value of a complex ordinary annuity certain. When using a table of values use the formulae[1]:

$$\boxed{S_{nc} = R\left[\frac{(1+i)^{nc} - 1}{(1+i)^c - 1}\right], \; S_{nc} = R_{\,s_{\overline{nc}|\,i}} \cdot \frac{1}{s_{\overline{c}|\,i}}} \qquad \longleftarrow \textit{Formula 13-5}$$

and,

$$\boxed{A_{nc} = R\left[\frac{1-(1+i)^{-nc}}{(1+i)^c - 1}\right], \; A_{nc} = R_{\,a_{\overline{nc}|\,i}} \cdot \frac{1}{s_{\overline{c}|\,i}}} \qquad \longleftarrow \textit{Formula 13-6}$$

---

[1] Proof:

$$S_{nc} = R\left[\frac{(1+f)^n - 1}{f}\right] \text{ and, } f = (1+i)^c - 1$$

Thus, substituting the value of f:

$$S_{nc} = R\left\{\frac{[1+(1+i)^c - 1]^n - 1}{(1+i)^c - 1}\right\}$$

$$= R\left[\frac{(1+i)^{nc} - 1}{(1+i)^c - 1}\right]$$

$$= R\left[\frac{(1+i)^{nc} - 1}{i}\right] \cdot \left[\frac{i}{(1+i)^c - 1}\right]$$

$$= R_{\,s_{\overline{nc}|\,i}} \cdot \frac{1}{s_{\overline{c}|\,i}}$$

$\longrightarrow$

Example 13.5a

What is the amount and present value of an annuity of $100 payable at the end of each quarter for ten years if the interest rate is 12% compounded monthly?

SOLUTION:

$R = \$100$ (quarterly payment)

$n = 10 \times 4 = 40$ (quarterly payments)

$i = \dfrac{12\%}{12} = 1\%$ (monthly rate)

$c = 3$ (interest periods in one payment interval)

$nc = 40 \times 3 = 120$

$$S_{nc} = R_{s_{\overline{nc}|\,i}} \cdot \frac{1}{s_{\overline{c}|\,i}}$$

$$= 100_{s_{\overline{120}|\,1\%}} \cdot \frac{1}{s_{\overline{3}|\,1\%}}$$

$$= 100(230.038\ 689\ 46)\left(\frac{1}{3.030\ 100\ 0}\right) \qquad \text{(Table 13-3)}$$

$$= \$7\ 591.79$$

$$A_n = R\left[\frac{1 - (1 + f)^{-n}}{f}\right]$$

$$= R\left\{\frac{1 - [1 + (1 + i)^c - 1]^{-n}}{(1 + i)^c - 1}\right\}$$

$$= R\left[\frac{1 - (1 + i)^{-nc}}{(1 + i)^c - 1}\right]$$

$$= R\left[\frac{1 - (1 + i)^{-nc}}{i}\right] \cdot \left[\frac{i}{(1 + i)^c - 1}\right]$$

$$= R_{a_{\overline{nc}|\,i}} \cdot \frac{1}{s_{\overline{c}|\,i}}$$

NOTE: The values of $s_{\overline{nc}|\,i}$ and $s_{\overline{c}|\,i}$ may be found in Table 13-3. If c is fractional, the value of $s_{\overline{c}|\,i}$ may be found in Table 13-3A, where $c = 1/m$ (m = the number of payments in one given interest period). The value of $a_{\overline{nc}|\,i}$ may be found in Table 13-4.

The values of nc will be read as n in the tables.

$$A_{nc} = R\, a_{\overline{nc}|\,i} \cdot \frac{1}{s_{\overline{c}|\,i}}$$

$$= 100\, a_{\overline{120}|\,1\%} \cdot \frac{1}{s_{\overline{3}|\,1\%}}$$

$$= 100(69.700\;522\;03)\left(\frac{1}{3.030\;100\;0}\right) \qquad \text{(Table 13-3 and Table 13-4)}$$

$$= \$2\;300.27$$

These are the same values as those obtained in Example 13.2a.

B. FINDING THE SIZE OF PAYMENT

When finding the size of payment of a complex ordinary annuity, use Formula 13-5 when the amount is known and Formula 13-6 when the present value is known.

Example 13.5b

A lot which sells for $66 000 can be bought for $6 000 down with the balance payable at the end of each month for five years. If the interest rate is 18% compounded semi-annually, what is the size of each monthly payment?

SOLUTION:

$A_{nc} = \$60\;000$ (balance owing)

$\quad n = 5 \times 12 = 60$ (monthly payments)

$\quad c = \dfrac{1}{6}$ (interest period in each payment interval)

$nc = 60 \times \dfrac{1}{6} = 10$

$\quad i = \dfrac{18\%}{2} = 9\%$

$nc = 60 \times \dfrac{1}{6} = 10$

$$A_{nc} = R\, a_{\overline{nc}|\,i} \cdot \frac{1}{s_{\overline{c}|\,i}}$$

Thus, $R = A_{nc} \cdot \dfrac{1}{a_{\overline{nc}|\,i}} \cdot s_{\overline{c}|\,i}$

$$= 60\;000 \frac{s_{\overline{1/6}|\,9\%}}{a_{\overline{10}|\,9\%}}$$

$$= 6\;000\left(\frac{.160\;739\;91}{6.417\;661\;4}\right)$$

$$= 60\;000(.025\;046\;5)$$

$$= \$1\;502.79$$

EXERCISE 13.5 / REFERENCE SECTIONS: A–B

For each of the following ordinary annuity problems use a table of values to find the missing item:

	Amount (S_{nc})	Present Value (A_{nc})	Number of Payments (n)	Amount of Each Monthly Payment (R)	Compound Interest Rate (i)
1.	?	?	20	100	12% quarterly
2.	?	?	40	250	16% semi-annually
3.	20 000		100	?	18% quarterly
4.		10 000	50	?	10% annually

Statement Problems:

5. What is the cash price of a car that can be bought for $1 000 and 36 monthly payments of $200 if the interest rate is 12% compounded quarterly?
6. Mr. Kline has set up a fund from which his daughter will receive $100 at the end of each month for four years. How much must Mr. Kline deposit in the fund now if it pays interest at 15% compounded semi-annually?
7. A car is listed for $9 890. A down payment of $890 is made and the balance is paid by equal monthly payments at the end of each month for three years. What is the amount of each monthly payment if the interest rate is 18% compounded quarterly?
8. Fred has opened an account into which he deposits $250 at the end of each quarter. The account pays interest at 17% compounded semi-annually. How much will he have in the account at the end of five years?

Table 13-3
Amount of Annuity

when periodic payment is 1 $s_{\overline{n}|\,i} = \dfrac{(1 + i)^n - 1}{i}$

n	$\frac{2}{3}$%	$\frac{3}{4}$%	$\frac{7}{8}$%	1%	n
1	1.0000 0000	1.0000 0000	1.0000 0000	1.0000 0000	1
2	2.0066 6667	2.0075 0000	2.0087 5000	2.0100 0000	2
3	3.0200 4444	3.0225 5625	3.0263 2656	3.0301 0000	3
4	4.0401 7807	4.0452 2542	4.0528 0692	4.0604 0100	4
5	5.0671 1259	5.0755 6461	5.0882 6898	5.1010 0501	5
6	6.1008 9335	6.1136 3135	6.1327 9133	6.1520 1506	6
115	172.0663 9075	181.5285 1468	196.9575 3168	214.0204 8860	115
116	174.2135 0002	183.8899 7854	199.6809 1009	217.1606 9349	116
117	176.3749 2335	186.2691 5338	202.4281 1805	220.3323 0042	117
118	178.5507 5618	188.6661 7203	205.1993 6408	223.5356 2343	118
119	180.7410 9455	191.0811 6832	207.9948 5852	226.7709 7966	119
120	182.9460 3518	193.5142 7708	210.8148 1353	230.0386 8946	120

Table 13-3A
For Fractional Interest Periods $s_{\frac{1}{m}\rceil\, i} = \dfrac{(1 + i)^{1/m} - 1}{i}$

m	$\frac{1}{4}\%$	$\frac{1}{3}\%$	$\frac{5}{12}\%$	$\frac{11}{24}\%$	$\frac{1}{2}\%$	m
2	.4996 8789	.4995 8403	.4994 8025	.4994 2839	.4993 7656	2
3	.3330 5594	.3329 6365	.3328 7144	.3328 2537	.3327 7932	3
4	.2497 6597	.2496 8811	.2496 1032	.2495 7146	.2495 3261	4
6	.1664 9332	.1664 3566	.1663 7805	.1663 4927	.1663 2050	6
12	.0832 3800	.0832 0629	.0831 7461	.0831 5879	.0831 4297	12

m	$\frac{13}{24}\%$	$\frac{7}{12}\%$	$\frac{5}{8}\%$	$\frac{2}{3}\%$	$\frac{3}{4}\%$	m
2	.4993 2474	.4992 7295	.4992 2118	.4991 6943	.4990 6600	2
3	.3327 3329	.3326 8728	.3326 4129	.3325 9532	.3325 0345	3
4	.2494 9379	.2494 5498	.2494 1619	.2493 7742	.2492 9994	4
6	.1662 9175	.1662 6301	.1662 3429	.1662 0558	.1661 4821	6
12	.0831 2716	.0831 1136	.0830 9557	.0830 7978	.0830 4824	12

m	$\frac{7}{8}\%$	1%	$1\frac{1}{8}\%$	$1\frac{1}{4}\%$	$1\frac{3}{8}\%$	m
2	.4989 1101	.4987 5621	.4986 0161	.4984 4719	.4982 9297	2
3	.3323 6581	.3322 2835	.3320 9109	.3319 5401	.3318 1712	3
4	.2491 8385	.2490 6793	.2489 5218	.2488 3660	.2487 2118	4
6	.1660 6226	.1659 7644	.1658 9075	.1658 0518	.1657 1975	6
12	.0830 0099	.0829 5381	.0829 0671	.0828 5968	.0828 1273	12

m	$1\frac{1}{2}\%$	$1\frac{5}{8}\%$	$1\frac{3}{4}\%$	$1\frac{7}{8}\%$	2%	m
2	.4981 3893	.4979 8509	.4978 3143	.4976 7797	.4975 2469	2
3	.3316 8042	.3315 4390	.3314 0758	.3312 7143	.3311 3548	3
4	.2486 0593	.2484 9084	.2483 7592	.2482 6117	.2481 4658	4
6	.1656 3445	.1655 4927	.1654 6423	.1653 7931	.1652 9452	6
12	.0827 6585	.0827 1904	.0826 7231	.0826 2565	.0825 7907	12

m	$2\frac{1}{4}\%$	$2\frac{1}{2}\%$	$2\frac{3}{4}\%$	3%	$3\frac{1}{4}\%$	m
2	.4972 1870	.4969 1346	.4966 0897	.4963 0522	.4960 0220	2
3	.3308 6412	.3305 9350	.3303 2362	.3300 5447	.3297 8604	3
4	.2479 1789	.2476 8985	.2474 6247	.2472 3573	.2470 0963	4
6	.1651 2531	.1649 5662	.1647 8843	.1646 2073	.1644 5354	6
12	.0824 8611	.0823 9345	.0823 0108	.0822 0899	.0821 1719	12

m	$3\frac{1}{2}\%$	$3\frac{3}{4}\%$	4%	$4\frac{1}{2}\%$	5%	m
2	.4956 9993	.4953 9838	.4950 9757	.4944 9811	.4939 0153	2
3	.3295 1834	.3292 5136	.3289 8510	.3284 5470	.3279 2714	3
4	.2467 8417	.2465 5935	.2463 3516	.2458 8868	.2454 4469	4
6	.1642 8684	.1641 2064	.1639 5492	.1636 2496	.1632 9692	6
12	.0820 2568	.0819 3445	.0818 4349	.0816 6243	.0814 8248	12

Table 13-3A (Continued)
For Fractional Interest Periods $\quad s_{\frac{1}{m}\rceil\,i} = \dfrac{(1 + i)^{1/m} - 1}{i}$

m	$5\frac{1}{2}\%$	6%	$6\frac{1}{2}\%$	7%	$7\frac{1}{2}\%$	m
2	.4933 0780	.4927 1690	.4921 2880	.4915 4348	.4909 6090	2
3	.3274 0237	.3268 8037	.3263 6113	.3258 4460	.3253 3076	3
4	.2450 0317	.2445 6410	.2441 2746	.2436 9321	.2432 6135	4
6	.1629 7080	.1626 4657	.1623 2422	.1620 0372	.1616 8505	6
12	.0813 0362	.0811 2584	.0809 4914	.0807 7351	.0805 9892	12

m	8%	$8\frac{1}{2}\%$	9%	$9\frac{1}{2}\%$	10%	m
2	.4903 8106	.4898 0392	.4892 2945	.4886 5765	.4880 8848	2
3	.3248 1960	.3243 1108	.3238 0518	.3233 0188	.3228 0115	3
4	.2428 3184	.2424 0466	.2419 7979	.2415 5721	.2411 3689	4
6	.1613 6821	.1610 5317	.1607 3991	.1604 2842	.1601 1868	6
12	.0804 2538	.0802 5286	.0800 8137	.0799 1089	.0797 4140	12

Table 13-4
Present Value of Annuity

when periodic payment is 1 $\quad a_{\overline{n}\rceil\,i} = \dfrac{1 - (1 + i)^{-n}}{i}$

n	$\frac{2}{3}\%$	$\frac{3}{4}\%$	$\frac{7}{8}\%$	1%	n
113	79.2040 3788	76.0210 7223	71.5834 3531	67.5148 5852	113
114	79.6728 8531	76.4477 1437	71.9538 3922	67.8364 9358	114
115	80.1386 2779	76.8711 8052	72.3210 3020	68.1549 4414	115
116	80.6012 8589	77.2914 9431	72.6850 3614	68.4702 4173	116
117	81.0608 8002	77.7086 7922	73.0458 8465	68.7824 1755	117
118	81.5174 3048	78.1227 5853	73.4036 0312	69.0915 0252	118
119	81.9709 5743	78.5337 5536	73.7582 1871	69.3975 2725	119
120	82.4214 8089	78.9416 9267	74.1097 5832	69.7005 2203	120

n	$8\frac{1}{2}\%$	9%	$9\frac{1}{2}\%$	10%	n
3	2.5540 2237	2.5312 9467	2.5089 0683	2.4868 5199	3
4	3.2755 9666	3.2397 1988	3.2044 8112	3.1698 6545	4
5	3.9406 4208	3.8896 5126	3.8397 0879	3.7907 8677	5
6	4.5535 8717	4.4859 1859	4.4198 2538	4.3552 6070	6
7	5.1185 1352	5.0329 5284	4.9496 1222	4.8684 1882	7
8	5.6391 8297	5.5348 1911	5.4334 3581	5.3349 2620	8
9	6.1190 6264	5.9952 4689	5.8752 8385	5.7590 2382	9
10	6.5613 4806	6.4176 5770	6.2787 9803	6.1445 6711	10
11	6.9689 8439	6.8051 9055	6.6473 0414	6.4950 6101	11
12	7.3446 8607	7.1607 2528	6.9838 3940	6.8136 9182	12
13	7.6909 5490	7.4869 0392	7.2911 7753	7.1033 5620	13
14	8.0100 9668	7.7861 5039	7.5718 5163	7.3666 8746	14
15	8.3042 3658	8.0606 8843	7.8281 7500	7.6060 7951	15
16	8.5753 3325	8.3125 5819	8.0622 6028	7.8237 0864	16
17	8.8251 9194	8.5436 3137	8.2760 3678	8.0215 5331	17
18	9.0554 7644	8.7556 2511	8.4712 6647	8.2104 1210	18
19	9.2677 2022	8.9501 1478	8.6495 5842	8.3649 2009	19

CHAPTER REVIEW

1. A washing machine can be bought for six equal monthly payments with the first payment due one month from now. If the cash price is $100, and the interest rate is 16% compounded monthly, what is the size of each payment?
2. Mr. Rogers purchased a farm on May 1, 1984, and promised to pay for it in equal monthly instalments. The cash price of the farm is $70 000. The first payment was made on the purchase date and the last payment is to be made on January 1, 1986. What is the size of each monthly payment if the interest rate is 18% compounded semi-annually?
3. What is the answer to Problem 1 if the interest rate is 16% compounded semi-annually?
4. What is the answer to Problem 2 if the interest rate is 18% compounded quarterly?
5. At what nominal rate compounded quarterly will an annuity of $300 payable at the end of each quarter for eight years amount to $12 000?
6. What is the nominal rate compounded monthly if the amount of an annuity of $60 payable at the end of each month for three years is $2 500?
7. At what nominal rate compounded quarterly does an annuity of $80 payable at the end of each quarter for nine years have a present value of $2 300?
8. What is the nominal rate compounded semi-annually if the present value of an annuity of $300 payable at the beginning of every six months for five years is $2 500?
9. If $80 is deposited at the end of each quarter at 16% compounded quarterly, how many payments will be required for the deposits to amount to at least $3 000?
10. On March 1, 1985, Mr. Bobson plans to invest $120 each month with the first investment starting one month from then. He wishes to have at least $5 000 as the final value. If he can earn 18% compounded monthly on his investment, on what date will he have the final value?
11. Carlson purchased a $6 000 car and agreed to pay for it with monthly instalments of $180 each starting one month from the date of purchase. If the interest rate is 15% compounded semi-annually, how many monthly payments are required?
12. Allison bought a house for $89 000, and made a down payment of $6 000. If the mortgage contract calls for equal payments at the end of each month for ten years with interest at 19% compounded semi-annually, what are her monthly payments?
13. Refer to Problem 12. If the payments are made at the end of each month and deposited in a fund which pays interest at 12% compounded monthly, how much will be in the fund at the end of the ten years?
14. Refer to Appendix III to generate an amortization schedule for a mortgage of $85 200 with interest at 19.25% compounded semi-annually and amortized over seven years, and answer the following questions:

(a)   How many monthly payments are required by the mortgage contract?
(b)   What is the effective monthly interest?
(c)   What is the amount of each monthly payment?
(d)   How much is the outstanding balance after the 12th payment?
(e)   If $5 000 is paid at the end of the first year how many payments will be required?

Summary of Formulae

Formula 13-1	$S_n = R\left[\dfrac{(1+f)^n - 1}{f}\right]$	When using the equivalent rate r, this formula is used to find the amount in any simple annuity problem.
Formula 13-2	$A_n = R\left[\dfrac{1-(1+f)^{-n}}{f}\right]$	When using the equivalent rate r, this formula is used to find the present value in any simple annuity problem.
Formula 13-3	$S_{nc} = R\left[\dfrac{(1+i)^{nc} - 1}{(1+i)^c - 1}\right]$	Used when finding the size of payment of an ordinary complex annuity when the amount of the annuity is known.
Formula 13-4	$A_{nc} = R\left[\dfrac{1-(1+i)^{-nc}}{(1+i)^c - 1}\right]$	Used when finding the size of payment of an ordinary complex annuity when the present value of the annuity is known.
Formula 13-5	$S_{nc} = R\,s_{\overline{nc}|\,i} \cdot \dfrac{1}{s_{\overline{c}|\,i}}$	When using a table of values to solve a complex ordinary annuity certain when the amount is known.
Formula 13-6	$A_{nc} = R\,a_{\overline{nc}|\,i} \cdot \dfrac{1}{s_{\overline{c}|\,i}}$	When using a table of values to solve a complex ordinary annuity certain when the present value is known.

Glossary

AMORTIZATION PERIOD the period over which the debt will be paid off if the mortgage contract is renewed at the same rate of interest; for a home mortgage, the average amortization period is twenty to thirty years

AMOUNT the final value at the end of the term of an annuity

CLOSED MORTGAGE a mortgage contract that includes a binding agreement that the debt will not be paid off until the term of the contract ends

COMPLEX ANNUITY where the length of the payment interval is not the same as the length of the interest conversion period

GENERAL ANNUITY see *complex annuity*

MORTGAGE a claim on property given to a person, bank, or firm that has loaned money in case the money is not repaid when due

OPEN MORTGAGE a mortgage contract which provides the consumer the right to pay off the debt at any time, with a small penalty

ORDINARY (annuity) when the periodic payment of a complex annuity is made at the end of each payment interval

PENALTY a fee imposed on an open mortgage contract, usually an increase of a quarter to one percent in the interest rate, charged against the consumer if the mortgage debt is paid off before the end of the term

PRESENT VALUE the value at the beginning of the term of an annuity

RENEGOTIATION (clause) an optional clause in a mortgage contract that allows the consumer to negotiate the terms if, say, the market rate drops; acceptable upon payment of a penalty equal to three months' interest

SIMPLE (annuity) see *ordinary* (annuity)

TERM the length of time for which a mortgage contract will last; the time from the beginning of the first payment interval to the end of the last payment interval

TRANSFERABILITY (clause) an optional clause in a mortgage contract that allows the consumer to transfer the mortgage to the buyer if the property is sold

VARIABLE RATE MORTGAGE (VRM) a mortgage contract where the interest rate varies with the current market rate; the monthly payments usually remain equal, however, the outstanding debt is adjusted to offset the change in rate

Other types of annuity *14*

Introduction

In Chapters Twelve and Thirteen, simple ordinary annuity and complex (general) ordinary annuity were covered. This chapter covers other simple annuities involving variations in the payment periods, such as annuities due, deferred annuities, and perpetuities.

It is essential, at this point, to first determine the type of annuity involved before attempting a solution.

14.1 Annuity Due

An ANNUITY DUE is an annuity for which the periodic payments are made at the *beginning* of each payment interval. The term of an annuity due begins on the date of the first payment and ends one payment interval after the last payment is made.

A.   *AMOUNT OF AN ANNUITY DUE (S_n (due))*

The *amount* of an annuity due is the value at the end of the term of the annuity. It includes all the periodic payments plus the compound interest. By a method similar to that used in finding the amount of an ordinary annuity, the amount of an annuity due may be found by totaling the individual compound amounts of the periodic payments (see Chapter Twelve). Each of the compound amounts is computed by the formula $S = P(1 + i)^n$. However, a simpler method of finding the amount of an annuity due is to use the formula for finding the amount of an ordinary annuity, Formula 12-1, $S_n = R \left[\frac{(1 + i)^n - 1}{i} \right]$. When this formula is used, the amount of an annuity due may be found in either of two ways:

METHOD A First, find the amount of the ordinary annuity of $(n + 1)$ payments. Then, subtract the additional payment from the amount obtained:

$$S_n \text{ (due)} = R\left[\frac{(1 + i)^{n+1} - 1}{i}\right] - R \qquad \longleftarrow \textit{Formula 14-1}$$

This formula may also be written in the form

$$S_n \text{ (due)} = R\left\{\left[\frac{(1 + i)^{n+1} - 1}{i}\right] - 1\right\}$$

Example 14.1a

What is the amount of an annuity due for four months if each payment is $100 payable at the beginning of each month and the interest rate is 12% compounded monthly?

SOLUTION:

$R = \$100$ (per month)

$i = \dfrac{12\%}{12} = 1\%$ (per month)

$n = 4$ (monthly payments)

$n + 1 = 4 + 1 = 5$

Substituting the values in Formula 14-1:

$$S_n \text{ (due)} = 100\left[\frac{(1 + 1\%)^5 - 1}{1\%}\right] - 100$$

$$= 100(5.101\ 005) - 100$$
$$= \$410.10$$

This example is illustrated as follows:

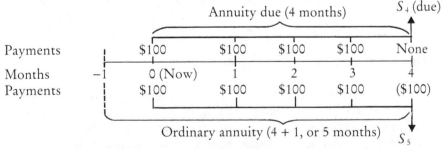

The diagram shows that if an additional payment ($100) is made at the end of the fourth month, the five (or 4 + 1) payments form an ordinary annuity. The amount of the ordinary annuity is S_5 (or S_{4+1}). The difference between the amount of the ordinary annuity of five payments and the amount of the annuity due for four payments is the additional payment ($100). Thus,

$$S_4(\text{due}) = S_{4+1} - 100 = 100\left[\frac{(1 + 1\%)^5 - 1}{1\%}\right] - 100.$$

Extending this idea, let n = number of payments (or number of interest conversion periods)

R = the size of each regular payment. Then,

$$S_n(\text{due}) = R\left[\frac{(1 + i)^{n+1} - 1}{i}\right] - R.$$

Example 14.1b
If $20 is deposited at the beginning of each month in a fund which earns interest at 15% compounded monthly, what is the final value at the end of three years?

SOLUTION:

R = $20 (per month)

$i = \dfrac{15\%}{12} = 1.25\%$ (per month)

$n = 3 \times 12 = 36$ (months or payments)

$n + 1 = 36 + 1 = 37$

Substituting the values in Formula 14-1:

$$S_{36}(\text{due}) = 20\left[\frac{(1 + 1.25\%)^{37} - 1}{1.25\%}\right] - 20$$

$$= 20(46.679\ 449) - 20$$
$$= \$933.59 - 20$$
$$= \$913.59$$

METHOD B   First, find the amount as if it were an ordinary annuity. Then, accumulate the amount obtained for one interest period.

$$S_n(\text{due}) = R\left[\frac{(1 + i)^n - 1}{i}\right](1 + i) \qquad \longleftarrow Formula\ 14\text{-}2$$

Example 14.1a may be computed in the following manner when Formula 14-2 is used:

R = $100

$i = 1\%$

$n = 4$ (monthly payments)

$$S_n(\text{due}) = 100\left[\frac{(1 + 1\%)^4 - 1}{1\%}\right](1 + 1\%)$$

$$= 100(4.060\ 401)(1.01)$$
$$= \$410.10$$

This example is diagrammed as follows:

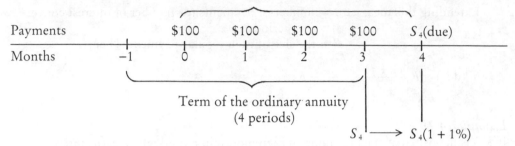

This diagram shows that the annuity due is first converted to an ordinary annuity. The amount of the ordinary annuity (S_4) is the value at the end of the third month. The required amount of the annuity due is the value at the end of the fourth month. Thus, S_4 is accumulated for one interest period, or

$$S_4(\text{due}) = S_4(1 + i) = 100 \left[\frac{(1 + 1\%)^4 - 1}{1\%} \right] (1 + 1\%).$$

Extending this idea, then,

$$S_n(\text{due}) = S_n(1 + i) = R \left[\frac{(1 + i)^n - 1}{i} \right] (1 + i).$$

Example 14.1b can be computed in the following manner when Formula 14-2 is used:

$$R = \$20$$
$$i = 1.25\%$$
$$n = 36$$

$$S_{36}(\text{due}) = 20 \left[\frac{(1 + 1.25\%)^{36} - 1}{1.25\%} \right] (1 + 1.25\%)$$

$$= 20(45.115\ 506)(1.012\ 5)$$
$$= \$913.59$$

NOTE: It is important to master the methods rather than to merely memorize the formulae. Method A is preferred in most cases since the computation is simpler than that in Method B.

B.   PRESENT VALUE OF AN ANNUITY DUE (A_n (due))

The *present value* of an annuity due is the value at the beginning of the term of the annuity. By a method similar to that of finding the present value of an ordinary annuity, the present value of an annuity due may be found by totaling the individual present values of the periodic payments (see Chapter Twelve, page 397). Each of the present values is computed by the formula $P = S(1 + i)^{-n}$. However, a simpler method of finding the present value of an annuity due is to use the formula for finding the present value of an ordinary annuity, $A_n = R_{\overline{n}\,i}$. When this formula is used, the present value may be found in either of two ways:

METHOD A First, find the present value of the ordinary annuity of $(n - 1)$ payments. Then, add the excluded payment to the present value obtained:

$$A_n(\text{due}) = R\left[\frac{1 - (1 + i)^{-(n-1)}}{i}\right] + R \qquad \longleftarrow Formula\ 14\text{-}3$$

This formula may also be written in the form

$$A_n(\text{due}) = R\left\{\left[\frac{1 - (1 + i)^{-(n-1)}}{i}\right] + 1\right\}.$$

Example 14.1c
What is the present value of an annuity due if the size of each payment is \$100 payable at the beginning of each month for four months and the interest rate is 12% compounded monthly?

SOLUTION:

$R = \$100$ (per month)

$i = \dfrac{12\%}{12} = 1\%$ (per month)

$n = 4$ (monthly payments)

$n - 1 = 4 - 1 = 3$

Substituting the values in Formula 14-3:

$$A_n(\text{due}) = 100\left[\frac{1 - (1 + 1\%)^{-3}}{1\%}\right] + 100$$

$$= 100(2.940\ 99) + 100$$

$$= \$394.10$$

This example is diagrammed as follows:

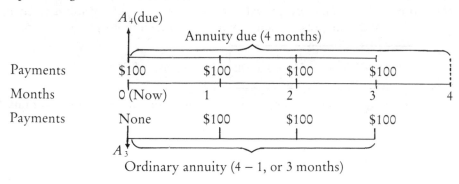

This diagram shows that if the $100 payment at the beginning of the first month is excluded, the remaining three (or 4 − 1) payments form an ordinary annuity. The present value of the ordinary annuity is A_3 (or A_{4-1}). The difference between the present value of the ordinary annuity of three payments and the present value of the annuity due for four payments is the excluded payment of $100. Thus,

$$A_4(\text{due}) = A_{4-1} + 100 = 100\left[\frac{1 - (1 + 1\%)^{-3}}{1\%}\right] + 100.$$

Extending this idea, let n = number of payments (or number of interest conversion periods)

R = size of each regular payment. Then,

$$A_n(\text{due}) = R\left[\frac{1 - (1 + i)^{-(n-1)}}{i}\right] + R.$$

Example 14.1d

What is the selling price of a television set that can be bought for $45 a month for 10 months beginning now, if money is worth 12% compounded monthly?

SOLUTION:

This is an annuity due problem since the first payment starts now, the beginning of the first payment interval.

R = $45 (per month)

$i = \dfrac{\$12\%}{12} = 1\%$ (per month)

n = 10 (months or payments)

$n - 1 = 10 - 1 = 9$

Substituting the values in Formula 14-3:

$$A_n(\text{due}) = 45\left[\frac{1 - (1 + 1\%)^{-9}}{1\%}\right] + 45$$

$$= 45(8.566\ 017\ 6) + 45$$

$$= \$430.47$$

METHOD B First, find the present value as if it were an ordinary annuity. Then, accumulate the present value obtained for one interest period:

$$\boxed{A_n(\text{due}) = R\left[\frac{1 - (1 + i)^{-n}}{i}\right](1 + i)}$$ ⟵ *Formula 14-4*

Example 14.1c may be computed in the following manner when Formula 14-4 is used:

R = $100

$i = 1\%$

n = 4 (monthly payments)

$$A_n(\text{due}) = 100\left[\frac{1-(1+1\%)^{-4}}{1\%}\right](1+1\%)$$

$$= 100(3.901\ 97)(1.01)$$
$$= \$394.10$$

This example is diagrammed as follows:

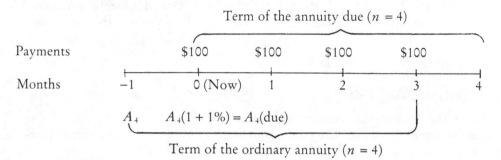

This diagram shows that the annuity due is first converted to an ordinary annuity. The present value of the ordinary annuity (A_4) is the value at the beginning of one month before the beginning of the first month. The required present value of the annuity due is the value at the beginning of the first month. Thus, A_4 is accumulated for one interest period, or

$$A_4(\text{due}) = A_4(1+i)$$

$$= 100\left[\frac{1-(1+1\%)^{-4}}{1\%}\right](1+1\%)$$

Extending this idea, then,

$$A_n(\text{due}) = A_n \cdot (1+i)$$

$$= R\left[\frac{1-(1+i)^{-n}}{i}\right](1+i)$$

Example 14.1d may be computed in the following manner when Formula 14-4 is used:
$R = \$45$
$i = 1\%$
$n = 10$

$$A_n(\text{due}) = 45\left[\frac{1-(1+1\%)^{-10}}{1\%}\right](1+1\%)$$

$$= 45(9.471\ 304\ 5)(1.01)$$
$$= \$430.47$$

C.   RELATIONSHIP BETWEEN THE AMOUNT AND THE PRESENT VALUE OF AN ANNUITY DUE

The present value of an annuity due is also the single principal which, invested at a given compound interest rate, will accumulate the amount of the annuity due by the end of the term. The relationship between the amount and the present value may be expressed by using the compound interest formula $S = P(1 + i)^n$ and the compound discount formula $P = S(1 + i)^{-n}$. Here, P is the present value, $A_n(\text{due})$; and S is the amount of the annuity due, $S_n(\text{due})$. The formulae may be written in the following manner:

$S_n(\text{due}) = A_n(\text{due})(1 + i)^n$; and

$A_n(\text{due}) = S_n(\text{due})(1 + i)^{-n}$.

When the amount of an annuity due is known, for instance, the present value of the annuity due of Example 14.1c can be computed by using the $A_n(\text{due})$ formula, as shown:

$S_4(\text{due}) = \$410.10$ (See Example 14.1a)
   $i = 1\%$
   $n = 4$

$A_4(\text{due}) = S_4(\text{due})(1 + 1\%)^{-4}$
   $= 410.10(.960\ 98)$
   $= \$394.10$

EXERCISE 14.1A / REFERENCE SECTIONS: A–C

Find the amount and the present value of the annuity due in each of the following:

	Payment (R)	Payment Interval	Term	Compound Interest Rate
1.	$ 2 000	1 month	3 years	21% monthly
2.	3 000	1 quarter	9 years	17% quarterly
3.	400	6 months	$4\frac{1}{2}$ years	16.5% semi-annually
4.	600	1 quarter	5 years	12% quarterly
5.	500	1 month	$4\frac{1}{6}$ years	15% monthly
6.	220	1 year	10 years	19% annually
7.	1 000	6 months	$12\frac{1}{2}$ years	17.5% semi-annually
8.	1 200	6 months	10 years	13.5% semi-annually

Statement Problems:
9. Find the amount of an annuity due of $700 payable at the beginning of each month for two years if the interest rate is 12% compounded monthly.

10. What is the amount of an annuity due for two years and five months if each payment is $450 payable at the beginning of each month and the interest rate is 16.5% compounded monthly?
11. Find the present value of the annuity due in Problem 9.
12. What is the present value of the annuity due in Problem 10?
13. If $600 is deposited at the beginning of each month in a bank that pays 22.5% interest compounded monthly, what is the final value at the end of three years and four months?
14. On July 1, 1984, a man deposits $150 in a savings and loan association that pays 14% compounded quarterly. The man continues to deposit $150 every quarter thereafter. How much will be in his account on July 1, 1989, immediately before the deposit on this date is made?
15. What is the cash price of a freezer that can be bought for $50 per quarter for $2\frac{1}{2}$ years if the first payment is made now and the interest rate is 18% compounded quarterly?
16. A house is rented for $300 per month, each month's rent payable in advance. If money is worth 19.5% compounded monthly, what is the cash value of the rent for one year?

D. OTHER TYPES OF PROBLEMS IN AN ANNUITY DUE

In Formula 14-1, $S_n(\text{due}) = R(s_{\overline{n+1}|\,i} - 1)$, there are four quantities: $S_n(\text{due})$, R, n and i. If any three of them are known, the one unknown may be determined by using the formula. The methods used in finding the values of $S_n(\text{due})$ and $A_n(\text{due})$ have already been discussed in this section. In the remaining portion of this section, the methods of finding the values of R, i, and n are given.

Finding the Value of R When S_n (due) Is Known

Example 14.1e
A man wishes to receive $2 000 $1\frac{1}{4}$ years from now. How much must he invest at the beginning of every quarter if the first payment starts now and the interest is 18% compounded quarterly?

SOLUTION:

$S_n(\text{due}) = \$2\ 000$

$i = \dfrac{18\%}{4} = 4.5\%$ (quarterly)

$n = 1\dfrac{1}{4} \times 4 = 5$ (quarterly periods or payments)

$R = ?$ (quarterly)

Express Formula 14-1 in the following form:

$$S_n(\text{due}) = R\left\{\left[\frac{(1+i)^{n+1}-1}{i}\right]-1\right\}$$

Substitute the values into the above expression:

$$2\,000 = R\left\{\left[\frac{(1+4.5\%)^6-1}{4.5\%}\right]-1\right\}$$

$$= R(6.716\,891\,7 - 1)$$

$$= R(5.716\,891\,7)$$

$$R = \frac{2\,000}{5.716\,891\,7}$$

$$= \$349.84.$$

Finding the Value of R When $A_n(\text{due})$ Is Known

Example 14.1f
A refrigerator which sells for $500 can be bought under terms of 20 equal monthly payments starting now. If money is worth 22.5% compounded monthly, what is the size of each payment?

SOLUTION:

$$A_n(\text{due}) = \$500$$

$$i = \frac{22.5\%}{12} = 1.875\% \text{ (per month)}$$

$$n = 20 \text{ (months or payments)}$$

$$R = ? \text{ (per month)}$$

Express Formula 14-1 in the following form, and then substitute the values into the expression:

$$A_n(\text{due}) = R\left\{\left[\frac{1-(1+i)^{-(n-1)}}{i}\right]+1\right\}$$

$$500 = R\left\{\left[\frac{1-(1+1.875\%)^{-19}}{1.875\%}\right]+1\right\}$$

$$= R(15.860\,725\,78 + 1)$$

$$R = \frac{500}{16.860\,725\,78}$$

$$= \$29.65$$

Finding the Value of i When $S_n(\text{due})$ Is Known

Example 14.1g
At what nominal rate compounded quarterly will an annuity due of $1 000 payable at the beginning of each quarter for one year amount to $4 500?

SOLUTION:

$S_n(due) = \$4\ 500$
$R = \$1\ 000$ (per quarter)
$n = 4$ (quarters or payments)
$i = ?$ (quarterly)

Substitute the values in Formula 14-1 expressed as:

$$S_n(due) = R\left\{\left[\frac{(1+i)^{n+1}-1}{i}\right]-1\right\}$$

$$4\ 500 = 1\ 000\left\{\left[\frac{(1+i)^5-1}{i}\right]-1\right\}$$

$$\frac{(1+i)^5-1}{i} = \frac{4\ 500+1\ 000}{1\ 000} = 5.5$$

The value of i for which $\frac{(1+i)^5-1}{i} = 5.5$ may be found by trial and error or by the use of a table of values or a preprogrammed calculator.

By trial and error:

$$\frac{(1+4.75\%)^5-1}{4.75\%} = 5.498\ 103\ 5$$

$$\frac{(1+5\%)^5-1}{5\%} = 5.525\ 631\ 3$$

Thus, the value of i is greater than 4.75% and smaller than 5%. It may be written:

$4.75\% < i < 5\%$
and the nominal rate j
$19 < j < 20\%$.

NOTE: A more accurate value may be obtained by using a smaller increment. For example, $4.75\% + .125\% = 4.875\%$.

$$\frac{(1+4.875\%)^5-1}{4.875\%} = 5.511\ 850\ 6$$

$4.875\% < i < 5\%$

Finding the Value of i When A_n (due) is Known

Example 14.1b
Fred bought a used car for \$5 800 and agreed to pay \$300 down now and the balance in equal monthly payments of \$300 payable at the beginning of each month for two years. What is the rate of interest compounded monthly that Fred was charged?

SOLUTION:

A_n(due) = \$5 800
R = \$300 (per month)
n = 2×12 = 24 (monthly payments)
i = ? (per month)

Substituting the values in the formula:

$$A_n(\text{due}) = R\left[\frac{1 - (1 + i)^{-(n-1)}}{i}\right] + R$$

$$5\ 800 = 300\left[\frac{1 - (1 + i)^{-23}}{i}\right] + 300$$

$$\frac{1 - (1 + i)^{-23}}{i} = \frac{5\ 800 - 300}{300}$$

$$= 18.\dot{3}$$

$$\frac{1 - (1 + 2\%)^{-23}}{2\%} = 18.292\ 204$$

$$\frac{1 - (1 + 1.875\%)^{-23}}{1.875\%} = 18.544\ 214$$

Thus, i is between 1.875% and 2%, or
1.875% < i < 2%
and the nominal rate j is between 22.5% and 24%, or
22.5% < j < 24%.

Finding the Value of n When S_n (due) is Known

Example 14.1i
If \$100 is deposited at the beginning of each month at an interest rate of 9% compounded monthly, how many months will be required for the deposits to amount to at least \$7 600?

SOLUTION:

S_n(due) = \$7 600
R = \$100 (per month)
$i = \dfrac{9\%}{12} = \dfrac{3}{4}\%$ (per month)
n = ? (months or payments)

Substituting the values in the formula:

$$S_n(\text{due}) = R\left[\frac{(1 + i)^{n+1} - 1}{i}\right] - R$$

$$7\ 600 = 100\left[\frac{(1 + \frac{3}{4}\%)^{n+1} - 1}{\frac{3}{4}\%}\right] - 100$$

By trial and error, using various values of n, it can be found that

$$\frac{(1 + \frac{3}{4}\%)^{n+1} - 1}{\frac{3}{4}\%} = \frac{7\,600 + 100}{100} = 77$$

$$\frac{(1 + \frac{3}{4}\%)^{61} - 1}{\frac{3}{4}\%} = 76.989\,818$$

$$\frac{(1 + \frac{3}{4}\%)^{62} - 1}{\frac{3}{4}\%} = 78.567\,242$$

$n + 1 = 62$, $n = 62 - 1 = 61$ months or five years, one month.

Finding the Value of n When A_n (due) is Known

Example 14.1j
A man bought a \$3 000 boat and agreed to pay for it in instalments of \$300 quarterly, starting on the date of purchase. If the interest charged is 18% compounded quarterly, how long will it take the man to pay for the boat?

SOLUTION:

A_n(due) = \$3 000
R = \$300 (per quarter)
$i = \dfrac{18\%}{4} = 4.5\%$ (per quarter)
n = ? (quarterly periods or payments)

Substituting the values in the formula:

$$A_n(\text{due}) = R\left[\frac{1 - (1 + i)^{-(n-1)}}{i}\right] + R$$

$$3\,000 = 300\left[\frac{1 - (1 + 4.5\%)^{-(n-1)}}{4.5\%}\right] + 300$$

$$\frac{1 - (1 + 4.5\%)^{-(n-1)}}{4.5\%} = \frac{3\,000 - 300}{300} = 9$$

By trial and error:

$$\frac{1 - (1 + 4.5\%)^{-11}}{4.5\%} = 8.528\,916\,9$$

$$\frac{1 - (1 + 4.5\%)^{-12}}{4.5\%} = 9.118\,580\,8$$

Since 9 is between these two values, the desired value of $n - 1$ is the greater of the two. The last payment will be less than \$300. $n - 1 = 12$, $n = 12 + 1 = 13$ quarterly payments.

EXERCISE 14.1B / REFERENCE SECTION: D

Find the unknown value in each annuity due:

	Amount	Present Value	Payment	Term (n)	Compound Interest Rate
1.	$ 2 500	$	$100 monthly	1 year	? monthly
2.	530		60 quarterly	?	18% quarterly
3.		990	60 quarterly	5 years	? quarterly
4.		5 000	? semi-annually	6 years	17% semi-annually
5.		3 800	250 semi-annually	?	14% semi-annually
6.	12 500		450 monthly	2 years	? monthly
7.		20 000	? semi-annually	$7\frac{1}{2}$ years	14% semi-annually
8.		1 800	30 monthly	?	21% monthly
9.	6 000		? quarterly	$3\frac{1}{4}$ years	19% quarterly
10.	3 000		? quarterly	$4\frac{1}{2}$ years	13.5% quarterly
11.	3 200		120 monthly	?	19.75% monthly
12.		2 400	340 annually	9 years	? annually

Statement Problems:

13. How much money must a man invest at the beginning of each quarter if he wishes to receive $1 500 six years from now? Assume that the first payment starts now and the interest rate is 15% compounded quarterly.

14. H.K. Jackson wishes to have $500 on December 1 for Christmas shopping. Starting on January 1 of this year, she will make regular monthly investments which will earn 13.5% interest compounded monthly. However, she does not plan to invest on December 1. What must be the size of each monthly investment in order to accomplish this goal?

15. A house which sells for $60 000 can be purchased under terms requiring 240 monthly payments. Assume that the first payment begins now and the interest is 12% compounded monthly. What is the size of each monthly payment?

16. Jack Newton purchased a mobile home on March 1, 1984, and agreed to pay for it in equal quarterly payments. The first payment was made on the date of purchase. The last payment will be made on March 1, 1989. The cash price of the home was $20 000. If money is worth 15% compounded monthly, how much should Newton pay each month?

17. At what nominal rate compounded monthly will an annuity due of $500 payable at the beginning of each month for one year and eight months amount to $12 772?

18. Sharon Williams invested $200 at the beginning of each quarter for ten quarters. At the end of the tenth quarter, she received $4 403.80, including principal and interest. If the interest rate was compounded quarterly, what was the interest rate?

19. What is the nominal rate compounded semi-annually if the present value of an annuity due of $80 payable at the beginning of each six months for four years is $530?

20. Brad Hunt bought a used car for $5 200 from his cousin on January 1, 1984. He agreed to pay for it by making payments of $250 each month until the last payment on November 1, 1985. The first payment was made on the date of purchase. If the interest was compounded monthly, what was the interest rate?

21. If $60 is deposited at the beginning of each month at 18% interest compounded monthly, how many months will be needed for the deposits to amount to at least $3 000?

22. Joe Kelly signed a note to his employer on March 1, 1984. The face value of $800 is to be paid in full when it is due. Assume that the note may be discharged by equal monthly payments of $100 each starting now and the interest is computed at 16.5% compounded monthly. When should the last payment be made?

23. A man buys a $54 500 farm and agrees to pay $600 at the beginning of each month until he completes his payments. The first payment is due on the date of purchase. How long will it take the man to pay for the farm if the interest rate is 12% compounded monthly?

24. If the present value of an annuity due of $200 payable semi-annually is $2 800 and interest is computed at 19.5% compounded semi-annually, what is the number of payments?

14.2 Deferred Annuity

When the term of an annuity starts on a future date, the annuity is called a DEFERRED ANNUITY. The period between now and the beginning of the term of the annuity is called the PERIOD OF DEFERMENT. The computation of a deferred annuity may be conveniently carried out if the ordinary annuity formulae are used. Hereafter, the name "deferred annuity" actually means "deferred ordinary annuity." It should be recalled that the first payment of an ordinary annuity is always made at the end of the first payment period. Thus, an annuity of $100 payable quarterly for six payments with the first payment to be made at the end of the *third* quarter is a deferred annuity. The period of deferment consists of *two* quarters, and the term of the ordinary annuity is six quarters, starting at the beginning of the third quarter and continuing to the end of the eighth quarter. (See diagram, Example 14.2b)

A. THE AMOUNT OF A DEFERRED ANNUITY

The amount of a deferred annuity is the final value at the end of the term of the annuity. The amount includes all the periodic payments plus the accumulated interest. Thus, the amount of the deferred annuity is the same as the amount of the ordinary annuity. Let S_n(defer.) = the amount of a deferred annuity. It follows that:

$$S_n(\text{defer.}) = S_n = R\left[\frac{(1+i)^n - 1}{i}\right] \qquad \longleftarrow Formula\ 14\text{-}5$$

Example 14.2a

Find the amount of an annuity of $100 payable at the end of each month for six payments. The interest rate is 18% compounded monthly. The first payment is due at the end of three months.

SOLUTION:

This example is identical to the diagram which shows that there are no payments during the period of deferment. Therefore, in computing the amount of the annuity, the portion of deferment may be disregarded.

$R = \$100$ (per month)

$i = \dfrac{18\%}{12} = 1.5\%$ (per month)

$n = 6$ (payments or months)

Substituting the values in Formula 14-5:

$$S_n(\text{defer.}) = 100\left[\frac{(1 + 1.5\%)^6 - 1}{1.5\%}\right]$$

$$= 100(6.229\ 550\ 8)$$
$$= \$622.96$$

B. THE PRESENT VALUE OF A DEFERRED ANNUITY

The present value of a deferred annuity is the value at the beginning of the period of deferment, *not* at the beginning of the term of the ordinary annuity. Let d = the number of the deferred payment intervals. The present value of a deferred annuity, denoted by $A_n(\text{defer.})$, may be found by either of the following two methods:

METHOD A First, consider that the payments were made during the period of deferment. Second, consider that there were two ordinary annuities: one, which relates to the period of deferment, consists of d payments, while the other, which relates to the period of deferment *plus* the term of the ordinary annuity, consists of $d + n$ payments. Third, subtract the present value of the annuity consisting of d payments from the present value of the annuity consisting of $d + n$ payments. The remainder is the present value of the deferred annuity. These steps may be accomplished by the formula:

$$A_n(\text{defer.}) = A_{d+n} - A_d = R\, a_{\overline{d+n}|\,i} - R\, a_{\overline{d}|\,i}, \text{ or}$$

$$A_n(\text{defer.}) = R\left[\frac{1 - (1+i)^{-(d+n)}}{i}\right] - R\left[\frac{1 - (1+i)^{-d}}{i}\right] \qquad \longleftarrow Formula\ 14\text{-}6$$

Example 14.2b
Find the present value of an annuity of $100 payable at the end of each month for six payments. The interest rate is 18% compounded monthly. The first payment is due at the end of three months.

SOLUTION:

$R = \$100$

$i = \dfrac{18\%}{12} = 1.5\%$ (per month)

$n = 6$

$d = 2$ (months)

Substituting the values in Formula 14-6:

$$A_n(\text{defer.}) = R\left[\frac{1-(1+i)^{-(d+n)}}{i}\right] - R\left[\frac{1-(1+i)^{-d}}{i}\right]$$

$A_6(\text{defer.}) = A_6 - A_2$

$$A_8 = 100\left[\frac{1-(1+1.5\%)^{-8}}{1.5\%}\right]$$

$$= 100(7.485\ 925\ 1)$$
$$= \$748.592$$

$$A_2 = 100\left[\frac{1-(1+1.5\%)^{-2}}{1.5\%}\right]$$

$$= 100(1.955\ 883\ 4)$$
$$= \$195.588$$

$A_6(\text{defer.}) = \$748.592 - \$195.588$
$\quad\quad\quad\quad\ = \$533.00$

This example is illustrated as follows:

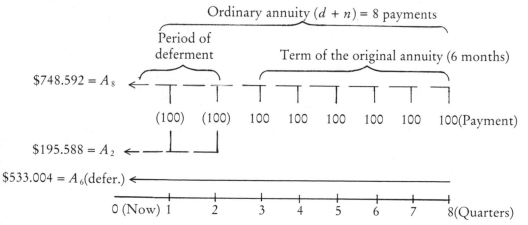

Example 14.2c

A student received a loan and agreed to make equal payments of $200 at the end of each month for two years with the first payment due at the end of four years and five months. If the interest rate is 12% compounded monthly, what is the amount of the loan?

SOLUTION:

$R = \$200$ (per month)

$i = \dfrac{12\%}{12} = 1\%$ (per month)

$n = 2 \times 12 = 24$ (monthly payments)

$d = 4 \times 12 + 4 = 52$ (months deferred)

Substituting the values in Formula 14-6:

$$A_n(\text{defer.}) = R\left[\frac{1 - (1 + i)^{-(d+n)}}{i}\right] - R\left[\frac{1 - (1 + i)^{-d}}{i}\right]$$

$$= 200\left[\frac{1 - (1 + 1\%)^{-76}}{1\%}\right] - 200\left[\frac{1 - (1 + 1\%)^{-52}}{1\%}\right]$$

$$= 200(53.056\ 487) - 200(40.394\ 194)$$

$$= 10\ 611.297 - 8\ 078.839$$

$$= \$2\ 532.46$$

The result is illustrated below:

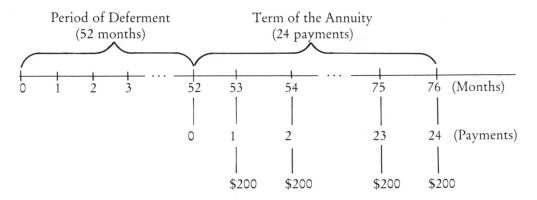

METHOD B Discount the present value of the ordinary annuity for the period of deferment. This may be computed by use of the following formula:

$$A_n(\text{defer.}) = A_n(1 + i)^{-d} = R \cdot \left[\frac{1 - (1 + i)^{-n}}{i}\right] \cdot (1 + i)^{-d} \qquad \longleftarrow \textit{Formula 14.7}$$

Example 14.2b may then be computed as follows:

$$A_n = A_6 = 100\left[\frac{1-(1+1.5\%)^{-6}}{1.5\%}\right]$$

$$= 100(5.697\ 187\ 2)$$
$$= \$569.72$$

$$A_n(\text{defer.}) = A_n\ (1+i)^{-d}$$
$$= 569.72(1+1.5\%)^{-2}$$
$$= 569.72(.970\ 661\ 7)$$
$$= \$533.00$$

Example 14.2b is diagrammed below to illustrate Method B:

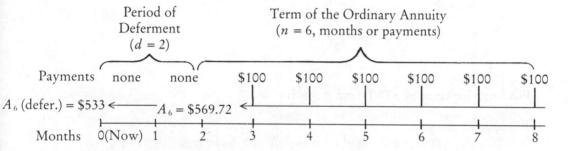

Method B may be used in computing Example 14.2c as follows:

Substituting the values in the formula:

$$A_n\ (\text{defer.}) = R\left[\frac{1-(1+i)^{-n}}{i}\right](1+i)^{-d}$$

$$= 200\left[\frac{1-(1+1\%)^{-24}}{1\%}\right](1+1\%)^{-52}$$

$$= 200(21.243\ 39)(.596\ 058\ 1)$$
$$= \$2\ 532.46$$

C.   OTHER TYPES OF DEFERRED ANNUITY PROBLEMS

Finding the Payment of a Deferred Annuity

Example 14.2d
A student received a loan of $10 000 at 12% compounded monthly, and agrees to repay it in 14 equal monthly payments. Find the size of each payment if the first payment is due at the end of 7 months.

SOLUTION:

A_n (defer.) = \$10 000

$i = \dfrac{12\%}{12} = 1\%$ (monthly)

$n = 14$ (payments or monthly periods)
$d = 7 - 1 = 6$ (months deferred)
$R = ?$

Substituting the values in Formula 14-7:

$$10\ 000 = R\left[\frac{1 - (1 + 1\%)^{-20}}{1\%}\right] - R\left[\frac{1 - (1 + 1\%)^{-6}}{1\%}\right]$$

$$= R(18.045\ 553 - 5.795\ 476\ 5)$$
$$= R(12.250\ 077)$$
$$R = \frac{10\ 000}{12.250\ 077}$$
$$= \$816.32$$

Finding the Term of a Deferred Annuity

Example 14.2e
If \$100 is deposited at the end of each month and the interest rate is 12% compounded monthly, how many months will be required for the deposits to equal a present value of \$4 500? The first deposit is made the end of six months.

SOLUTION:

A_n (defer.) = \$4 500
$R = \$100$ (per month)

$i = \dfrac{12\%}{12} = 1\%$ (monthly)

$d = 5$ (months or payments)
$n = ?$ (months or payments)

Substituting the values in Formula 14-7:

$$A_n \text{ (defer.)} = R\left[\frac{1 - (1 + i)^{-n}}{i}\right](1 + i)^{-d}$$

$$4\ 500 = 100\left[\frac{1 - (1 + 1\%)^{-n}}{1\%}\right](1 + 1\%)^{-5}$$

$$4\ 500 = 100(1.01)^{-5}\left[\frac{1 - (1.01)^{-n}}{.01}\right]$$

$$\frac{4\ 500}{100\ (1.01)^{-5}} = \frac{1 - (1.01)^{-n}}{.01}$$

$$\frac{4\ 500\ (.01)}{100\ (1.01)^{-5}} = 1 - (1.01)^{-n}$$

$$.472\ 954\ 5 = 1 - (1.01)^{-n}$$

$$-(1.01)^{-n} = .457\ 295\ 45 - 1$$

$$-(1.01)^{-n} = .527\ 045\ 5$$

$$(1.01)^{-n} = .527\ 045\ 5$$

$$-n \ln (1.01) = \ln .527\ 045\ 5$$

$$-n = \frac{\ln .527\ 045\ 5}{\ln (1.01)}$$

$$-n = \frac{-.640\ 468\ 4}{.009\ 950\ 3}$$

$$n = 64.366\ 747$$

Thus, 65 monthly payments must be made. The last payment will be less than $100.

EXERCISE 14.2/ REFERENCE SECTIONS: A–C

Find the unknown value of the deferred annuity in each of the following problems:

	Amount S_n (defer.)	Present Value A_n (defer.)	Payment (R)	Number of Payments (n)	Period of Deferment (d)	Compund Interest Rate (i)
1.	?	?	$300 semi-annually	15	5	17% semi-annually
2.		$ 750	100 annually	?	4	16% annually
3.		2 000	? semi-annually	10	3	19% semi-annually
4.	?	?	500 quarterly	7	10	15% quarterly
5.		1 600	125 quarterly	?	7	21% quarterly
6.	?	?	400 quarterly	18	8	12% quarterly
7.	?	?	600 monthly	14	12	12% monthly
8.		5 000	? quarterly	20	6	14% quarterly

Statement Problems:

9. Find the amount and the present value of an annuity of $150 payable at the end of every month for 30 payments. The first payment is due at the end of $2\frac{1}{3}$ years. The interest rate is 15% compounded monthly.

10. Find the amount and the present value of 40 monthly payments of $75 each. The first payment is due in two years. The interest rate is 13.5% compounded monthly.

11. Jane Berman purchased a theater for $80 000 on January 2, 1983. She paid $10 000 cash and agreed to pay the balance plus interest at 19% compounded

semi-annually in 14 semi-annual payments, with the first payment due on July 2, 1985. What is the size of each payment?

12. If $400 is to be paid at the end of each quarter, the first payment is to be made at the end of $1\frac{1}{2}$ years, and the interest rate is 17% compounded quarterly, how many payments will be needed to discharge a debt whose present value is $5 000?

13. A man borrowed $6 500 at 18% interest compounded quarterly, and agreed to repay the loan in quarterly payments of $500 each. The first payment is due in two years. Find the number of payments.

14. A student borrowed $250 and agreed to repay the principal and interest at 16.5% compounded monthly in 20 equal monthly payments. The first payment is due $1\frac{1}{2}$ years from now. How large is each payment?

15. If money is worth 17% compounded semi-annually, what single payment now is equivalent to 45 semi-annual payments of $350 each with the first payment due in $2\frac{1}{2}$ years?

16. Find the amount and the present value of an annuity of $1 200 payable at the beginning of each year for six years with interest at 12% compounded monthly.

17. What are the amount and the present value of an annuity of $2 800 payable at the end of every six months for 18 years with interest at 17% compounded annually?

18. What are the amount and the present value of an annuity of $130 payable monthly for 30 payments, with the first payment at the end of 19 months from the present time with interest at 12% compounded semi-annually?

19. Find the amount and the present value of an annuity of $180 payable semi-annually, for eight payments, with the first payment in $5\frac{1}{2}$ years with interest at 18% compounded quarterly.

14.3 Perpetuity

When the term of an annuity begins on a definite date but never ends, the annuity is called a PERPETUITY. In other words, the payments of a perpetuity continue forever. Since there is no end to a perpetuity, it is impossible to determine its final value. However, as will be shown in the following examples, the present value of a perpetuity can be determined.

Perpetuities may be divided into two groups: (a) simple, and (b) complex (general). Since a perpetuity is a type of annuity, the qualified words, such as ordinary, due, deferred, simple, complex, and general, used previously in annuity problems are also used within this section.

A. SIMPLE PERPETUITIES

When the payments of a perpetuity are made at the *end* of each interest period, the perpetuity is called a SIMPLE ORDINARY PERPETUITY. It will be recalled that in the method used to find the simple interest on an investment, the simple interest (I) is obtained by using the formula $I = Pin$. When $n = 1$ and i represents the rate per period, the formula becomes $I = Pi$. The formula indicates that if P is invested now at the interest rate of i per period, the periodic interest is the value of Pi. The interest may be drawn periodically as long as the principal (P) is invested. Thus, if $100 is invested now at the interest rate of 4% per quarter, the quarterly interest is $4(or $100 × 4%), which may be drawn by the investor at the end of each quarter as long as he leaves the $100 principal in the investment. The size of the investment is found by dividing both sides of the formula $I = Pi$ by i. Thus,

$$P = \frac{I}{i}.$$

This idea is used in a similar manner in the case of simple perpetuities. Let A_∞ denote the present value of a simple ordinary perpetuity. Then,

$$A_\infty = P = \frac{I}{i} \text{ or,}$$

$$\boxed{A_\infty = \frac{I}{i}} \quad \longleftarrow Formula\ 14\text{-}8$$

NOTE: The symbol "∞" represents "infinity." I is the periodic payment (or receipt, whichever the case may be) of the perpetuity made at the end of each period, and i is the interest rate per period.

Example 14.3a

Find the present value of a simple perpetuity of $500 payable at the end of each quarter if the interest rate is 4% per quarter, (or 16% compounded quarterly).

SOLUTION:

$I = \$500$
$i = 4\%$ (per quarter)

Substituting the values in Formula 14-8:

$$A_\infty = \frac{I}{i}$$

$$= \frac{500}{.04}$$

$$= \$12\ 500$$

The answer indicates that if $12 500 is invested now at 4% per quarter, the investor can draw $500 at the end of each quarter forever; that is, if the principal remains intact and the interest rate does not change. In other words, $12 500 is the cash equivalent of a perpetuity of $500 payable at the end of each quarter when the given interest rate is involved.

Example 14.3b

Find the present value of a simple annuity of $500 payable at the end of each quarter for (a) 20 years, (b) 25 years, and (c) 50 years. The interest rate is 4% per quarter.

SOLUTION:

(a) $R = 500$
$i = 4\%$
$n = 20 \times 4 = 80$ (quarters)

$$A_{80} = 500\left[\frac{1 - (1 + 4\%)^{-80}}{4\%}\right]$$

$= 500(23.915\ 392)$
$= \$11\ 957.70$

(b) $n = 25 \times 4 = 100$ (quarters)

$$A_{100} = 500\left[\frac{1 - (1 + 4\%)^{-100}}{4\%}\right]$$

$= 500(24.504\ 999)$
$= \$12\ 252.50$

(c) $n = 50 \times 4 = 200$ (quarters)

$$A_{200} = 500\left[\frac{1 - (1 + 4\%)^{-200}}{4\%}\right]$$

$= 500(24.990\ 199)$
$= \$12\ 495.10$

The answers may be compared with that given in Example 14.3a:

n (quarters)	Present Value
80	$11 957.70
100	12 252.50
200	12 495.10
∞	12 500.00

The comparison indicates that as the length of the term of an annuity increases, its present value gets closer to the present value of a perpetuity.

When the payments of a perpetuity are made at the *beginning* of each interest period, the perpetuity is called a SIMPLE PERPETUITY DUE.

Example 14.3c

Find the present value of a simple perpetuity due of $200 payable at the beginning of each month if the interest rate is 12% compounded monthly.

SOLUTION:

First, the present value of a simple perpetuity due of $200 payable at the *end* of each month is computed as follows:

$I = 200$

$i = \dfrac{12\%}{12} = 1\%$ (per month)

Substituting the values in Formula 14-8:

$$A_\infty = \frac{I}{i}$$

$$= \frac{200}{1\%}$$

$$= \$20\ 000$$

The present value of a simple perpetuity due of $200 payable at the *beginning* of each month is:

20 000 + 200 = $20 200.

Note that $200 is the first payment, whose present value is the value of the payment unchanged.

B.   COMPLEX (GENERAL) PERPETUITIES

When each of the periodic payments of a perpetuity is made at the end of several interest periods, the perpetuity is called a COMPLEX (OR GENERAL) PERPETUITY.

Example 14.3d

A man invests $1 000 now at an interest rate of 16% compounded quarterly and wants to draw interest at the end of each year forever. How much interest will he receive annually?

SOLUTION:

The compound amount of $1 000 at the end of every fourth quarter (or every year) is:

1 000(1 + 4%)⁴ = 1 000(1.169 858 6)

$$= \$1\ 169.86$$

The compound interest at the end of each year is:

1 169.86 − 1 000 = $169.86

Example 14.3d is a complex perpetuity problem and may be stated in the following manner:

> If the present value of a perpetuity is $1 000 and the interest rate is 16% compounded quarterly, the periodic payment at the end of every four interest periods (quarters) is $169.86.

Let R = the size of the periodic payment (or periodic interest)

i = interest rate per interest conversion period

c = interest conversion periods per payment interval

A_∞ = present value of a perpetuity, with payments of R made at the end of every c interest periods

The value of R is computed as follows:

$$R = A_\infty(1 + i)^c - A = A_\infty[(1 + i)^c - 1].\ \text{Thus,}$$

$$\boxed{A_\infty = \frac{R}{(1 + i)^c - 1}} \quad \longleftarrow \textit{Formula 14-9}$$

NOTE: When $c = 1$, $(1 + i)^c - 1 = i$. Then $A_\infty = \dfrac{R}{i}$ and $R = I$.

Formula 14-9 becomes identical to Formula 14-8. Thus, Formula 14-9 is a general formula for ordinary perpetuities.

The following diagram supports the above illustrations in Example 14.3d and Formula 14-9:

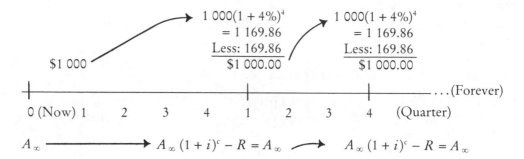

Example 14.3e
Find the present value of a perpetuity of $500 payable semi-annually if money is worth 12% compounded monthly, and (a) the first payment is due six months hence, (b) the first payment is due now.

SOLUTION:

(a) $R = \$500$ (per six months)

$i = \dfrac{12\%}{12} = 1\%$ (monthly)

$c = 6$ (interest periods in one payment interval)

Substituting the values in Formula 14-9:

$$A_\infty = \frac{R}{(1 + i)^c - 1}$$

$$= \frac{500}{(1 + 1\%)^6 - 1}$$

$$= \frac{500}{.061\ 520\ 2}$$

$$= \$8\ 127.42$$

(b)   The present value of a complex perpetuity *due* is obtained by adding one payment to the answer in (a) as follows:
500 + 352.48 = 852.48.
Note that $500 is the first payment whose present value is the value of the payment unchanged.

EXERCISE 14.3 / REFERENCE SECTIONS: A–B

Find the present value of the perpetuity in each of the following problems:

Payment	Interest Rate
1. $450 quarterly, at the end of each quarter	3% per quarter
2. $600 semi-annually, at the end of every six months	8% per six months
3. $800 semi-annually, at the end of every six months	12% compounded monthly
4. $375 annually, at the end of each year	15% compounded quarterly
5. $400 quarterly, at the beginning of each quarter	17% per quarter
6. $500 monthly, at the beginning of each month	2% per month
7. $700 annually, at the beginning of each year	21% compounded monthly
8. $200 semi-annually, at the beginning of each six months	17.5% compounded quarterly

Statement Problems:

9. Find the present value of a simple perpetuity of $1 000 payable semi-annually if the interest rate is 6.5% per six months and the first payment is due (a) six months from now, and (b) now.

10. What is the present value of a simple perpetuity of $1 200 payable quarterly if the interest rate is 4.5% per quarter, and the first payment is due (a) three months from now, and (b) now?

11. Refer to Problem 9. If the interest rate is 18% compounded quarterly, find the answers to (a) and (b).

12. Refer to Problem 10. If the interest rate is 19.5% compounded monthly, find the answers to (a) and (b).

13. The alumni of a college want to provide a scholarship fund that will permanently give $1 000 at the end of each year. If the effective interest rate is 13.5%, how large must the fund be?

14.4 Use of a Financial Calculator to Solve Problems Involving Annuities

A. ANNUITY DUE

A financial calculator (preprogrammed) may be used to calculate the amount, present value, amount of each payment, interest rate for each conversion period, and the number of payment periods for an annuity due.

When such a calculator is used, enter the values as shown in Chapter 12, Section 12.8, then press the key marked <u>DUE</u> followed by the variable to be calculated.

Example 14.4a

An account is opened on May 1, 1984 and a deposit of $500 is made. Deposits of $500 are then made at the beginning of each month for five years. If the account pays 16.8% compounded monthly, (a) how much will be in the account at the end of five years, and (b) what single deposit made on May 1, 1984 would have been equivalent to the sixty deposits?

SOLUTION:

$R = \$500$ (monthly)
$n = 5 \times 12 = 60$ (months)
$i = \dfrac{16.8\%}{12} = 1.4\%$ (monthly)

(a)   The amount in the account is the amount of an annuity due:

Enter	Press	Display Shows
	2ND/FIN	FIN
500	$^+\!/_-$	−500
	PMT	−500
60	N	60
1.4	%i	1.4
	DUE/FV	47184.019

Thus, $47 184.02 will be in the account at the end of five years.

(b)   The single deposit made on May 1, 1984 is the present value of an annuity due:

Enter	Press	Display Shows
	2ND/FIN	FIN
500	PMT	500
60	N	60
1.4	%i	1.4
	DUE/PV	20488.852

Thus, a single deposit of $20 488.85 on May 1, 1984 will be equivalent to the 60 deposits.

Example 14.4b
On August 15, 1985, House and Company signed a five-year lease for $7 000. If the obligation is settled by equal quarterly payments with the first payment made on August 15, 1985 and at the beginning of each quarter thereafter for six years, what must be the amount of each payment. The interest rate charged is 18.8% compounded quarterly.

SOLUTION:

A_n(due) = $7 000
$n = 6 \times 4 = 24$ (quarters)
$i = \dfrac{18.8\%}{4} = 4.7\%$ (quarterly)

Enter	Press	Display Shows
	2ND/FIN	FIN
7000	PV	7000
0	FV	0
24	N	24
4.7	%i	4.7
	DUE/PMT	470.48212

Thus, payments of $470.48 must be made at the beginning of each quarter.

Example 14.4c
How much must be deposited in an account at the beginning of each month in order to have $8 700 in the account at the end of seven years? The account pays interest at 12.6% compounded monthly.

SOLUTION:

S_n(due) = $8 700
$i = \dfrac{12.6\%}{12} = 1.05\%$ (monthly)
$n = 7 \times 12 = 84$ (monthly payments)

Enter	Press	Display Shows
	2ND/FIN	FIN
8700	FV	8700
0	PV	0
84	N	84
1.05	%i	1.05
	DUE/PMT	−64.35853

Thus, $64.36 must be deposited at the beginning of each month.

Example 14.4d

A lease in the amount of $10 500 is to be settled by equal payments of $1 494.81 made at the beginning of each quarter. If the interest rate charged is 15.6% compounded quarterly, how many payments must be made?

SOLUTION:

$A_n(\text{due}) = \$10\ 500$

$R = \$1\ 494.81$ (quarterly payment)

$i = \dfrac{15.6\%}{4} = 3.9\%$ (quarterly)

Enter	Press	Display Shows
	2ND/FIN	FIN
10500	PV	10500
1494.81	PMT	1494.81
3.9	%i	3.9
0	FV	0
	DUE/N	8

Thus, 8 quarterly payments, made at the beginning of each quarter, will settle the debt.

Example 14.4e

What nominal rate of interest is charged if a debt of $7 890 due in two years may be settled by 24 equal monthly payments of $287.76 made at the beginning of each month?

SOLUTION:

$S_n(\text{due}) = \$7\ 890$

$n = 2 \times 12 = 24$ (monthly payments)

$R = \$287.76$

Enter	Press	Display Shows
	2ND/FIN	FIN
7890	FV	7890
287.76	+/_	−287.76
	PMT	−287.76
24	N	24
0	PV	0
	DUE/%i	1.0499418

Thus, the monthly rate of interest is 1.049 941 8%. The nominal rate is 1.049 941 8% × 12 = 12.599 302%.

B.   DEFERRED ANNUITY

A financial calculator (preprogrammed) may be used to calculate the amount, the present value, the periodic payments, and the number of payments of a deferred ordinary annuity. When such a calculator is used the methods presented in Chapter Twelve, Section 12.8 will be used with an adjustment made to account for the period of deferment. The rate of interest for a deferred annuity may not be found directly since this value has not been preprogrammed.

Example 14.4f
Maurice Farm and Company bought a tractor and agreed to make equal quarterly payments of $1 000 at the end of each quarter for 20 quarters with the first payment to be made two years from the date of the agreement. If the rate is 14% compounded quarterly, what was the price of the tractor?

SOLUTION:

$R = \$1\ 000$ (quarterly)
$n = 20$ (quarters)
$i = \dfrac{14\%}{4} = 3.5\%$ (quarterly)
$d = 7$ (quarters)

Find the present value of the annuity of 20 payments:

Enter	Press	Display Shows
	2ND/FIN	FIN
1000	PMT	1000
20	N	20
3.5	%i	3.5
	CPT/PV	14212.403

Thus, the present value of the annuity at the end of the period of deferment is $14 212.40. The present value of the annuity at the beginning of the period of deferment is the present value of this amount:

Enter	Press	Display Shows
	2ND/FIN	FIN
14212.40	FV	14212.40
0	PMT	0
3.5	%i	3.5
7	N	7
	CPT/PV	11170.818

Thus, the price of the tractor is $11 170.82.

This example is diagrammed as follows:

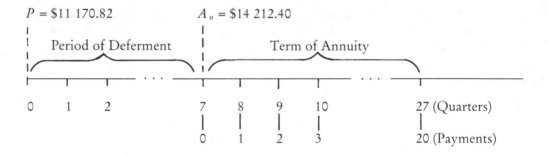

$P = \$11\ 170.82$ $A_n = \$14\ 212.40$

Example 14.4g

Brian will retire in three years. He has a trust fund which will pay $1 500 at the beginning of each month for twenty years starting on the date of his retirement. If the fund pays interest at 14.4% compounded monthly, how much is in the account now?

SOLUTION:

$R = \$1\ 500$ (monthly payment)
$n = 20 \times 12 = 240$ (months)
$i = \dfrac{14.4\%}{12} = 1.2\%$ (monthly)
$d = 35$

Find the present value of the annuity of 240 payments:

Enter	Press	Display Shows
	2ND/FIN	FIN
1500	PMT	1500
240	N	240
1.2	%i	1.2
	CPT/PV	117861.83

Thus, the amount in the fund when Brian retires is $117 861.83. The amount in the fund three years before his retirement is the present value of this amount:

Enter	Press	Display Shows
	2ND/FIN	FIN
117861.83	FV	117861.83
35	N	35
1.2	%i	1.2
	CPT/PV	77634.586

Thus, there is $77 634.59 in the fund three years before Brian's retirement.

Example 14.4b
A loan in the amount of $8 900 is to be repaid in 12 equal payments made at the beginning of each month with the first payment due seven months after the date of the loan. If the interest rate is 18.6% compounded monthly, what should be the amount of each payment?

SOLUTION:

A_n(defer.) = $8 900

n = 12 (monthly payments)

$i = \dfrac{18.6\%}{12} = 1.55\%$ (monthly)

d = 6 (months)

Find the accumulated value of the debt at the end of the period of deferment:

Enter	Press	Display Shows
	2ND/FIN	FIN
8900	PV	8900
6	N	6
1.55	%i	1.55
	CPT/FV	9760.444

Thus, the amount of the debt at the end of six months, the period of deferment, is $9 760.44. The amount of each payment is the periodic payment of an ordinary annuity with present value of $9 760.44:

Enter	Press	Display Shows
	2ND/FIN	FIN
9760.44	PV	9760.44
12	N	12
1.55	%i	1.55
0	FV	0
	CPT/PMT	897.626 88

Thus, the amount of each payment is $897.63. This result is diagrammed as follows:

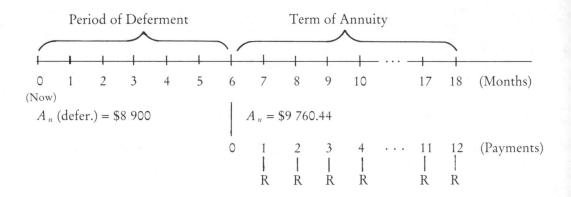

Example 14.4i

Misty bought a ski-doo for $6 500 and agreed to pay for it by equal monthly payments of $966.08 made at the end of each month, the first payment to be made three months from the date of purchase. If the rate of interest charged is 12% compounded monthly, how many payments must be made?

SOLUTION:

$A_n(\text{defer.}) = \$6\ 500$

$i = \dfrac{12\%}{12} = 1\%\ (\text{monthly})$

$d = 2\ (\text{months})$

$R = \$966.08\ (\text{monthly payment})$

Enter	Press	Display Shows
	2ND/FIN	FIN
6500	PV	6500
1	%i	1
0	FV	0
966.08	PMT	966.08
	CPT/N	7

Thus, seven payments of $966.08 will settle the debt.

EXERCISE 14.4 / REFERENCE SECTIONS: A–B

Use an electronic calculator to solve the following problems:

Find the unknown value for each of the following annuity due:

	Amount S_n (due)	Present A_n (due)	Payment R	Term n	Compound Interest Rate
1.	?	?	$2 000 monthly	2 years	15.5% monthly
2.	?	?	3 000 quarterly	3 years	17.2% quarterly
3.	5 000		? semi-annually	1½ years	18.2% semi-annually
4.		50 000	? annually	12 years	12.5% annually
5.	16 000		763.12	?	19% monthly
6.		7 500	713.32	?	10% quarterly
7.	25 000		827.13 monthly	2 years	? monthly
8.		8 000	1 475.82	1½ years	? quarterly

Find the unknown value for each of the following deferred annuity:

	Present Value A_n (defer.)	Period of Deferrment	Payment	Term	Compound Interest Rate
9.	?	5 months	$100 monthly	2 years	12% monthly
10.	?	6 months	90 quarterly	18 months	14.8% quarterly
11.	$16 000	1 year	? annually	5 years	12.8% annually
12.	28 000	1½ years	? semi-annually	6 years	13% semi-annually
13.	1 200	2 months	74.79 monthly	?	12.2% monthly
14.	20 000	6 months	2 238.83	?	14.5% quarterly

Statement Problems:

15. A television set can be bought by making equal monthly payments of $90 for $2\frac{3}{4}$ years. The first payment is due on the date of purchase and the rate of interest charged is 17.5% compounded monthly.
   (a) What is the cash price of the television set? (b) What is the total amount paid for the television set? (c) What is the cost of credit?

16. A boat can be bought by making equal monthly payments of $1 000 for 3 years. The first payment is made on the date of purchase and the rate of interest charged is 14.8%.
   (a) What is the cash price of the boat? (b) What is the total amount paid for the boat? (c) What is the cost of credit?

17. On December 1, 1984 Marlene has $60 000 in an RRSP account. She expects to withdraw equal monthly amounts from the account starting January 1, 1986. How much can she withdraw each month if she is to make her last withdrawal on January 1, 1990, when her regular pension becomes available. The account pays interest at 14.5% compounded monthly.

18. Martin Grove Limited received a loan in the amount of $20 000. The loan is to be repaid by equal monthly payments made at the end of each month for 12 months. The first payment is due six months after the date of the loan and the rate of interest is 13.5% compounded monthly. What should be the amount of each payment?

14.5 Use of Tables to Solve Problems Involving Annuity Due, Deferred Annuity, and Perpetuities

A table of values may be used to find the amount, present value, amount of each payment, interest rate per conversion period and the number of payments.

A.   ANNUITY DUE

When a table of the values of $\frac{(1+i)^n - 1}{i}$ is used to find the amount of an annuity due or $\frac{1-(1+i)^{-n}}{i}$ to find the present value of an annuity due, Formulas 14-1 to 14-4 may be written as follows:

To find the amount:

$$\boxed{S_n(\text{due}) = R\,s_{\overline{n+1}|\,i} - R} \qquad \longleftarrow Formula\ 14\text{-}10$$

$$\boxed{S_n(\text{due}) = R\,s_{\overline{n}|\,i}(1 + i)} \qquad \longleftarrow Formula\ 14\text{-}11$$

To find the present value:

$$A_n(\text{due}) = R\,a_{\overline{n-1}|\,i} + R$$ ←——*Formula 14-12*

$$A_n(\text{due}) = R\,a_{\overline{n}|\,i}(1 + i)$$ ←——*Formula 14-13*

Example 14.5a

Robert opened a Registered Retirement Savings Account into which he made a deposit of $150 at the beginning of each month. The account earns interest at 12% compounded monthly. How much will he have in the account at the end of six years?

SOLUTION:

$R = \$150$ (monthly)

$n = 6 \times 12 = 72$ (months)

$i = \dfrac{12\%}{12} = 1\%$

$S_n(\text{due}) = ?$

METHOD A Substitute into Formula 14-10:

$$S_n(\text{due}) = R\,s_{\overline{n+1}|\,i} - R$$

$$S_{72}(\text{due}) = 150\,s_{\overline{73}|\,1\%} - 150$$

$$= 150(106.757\ 030\ 52) - 150$$

$$= \$15\ 863.56$$

Robert will have $15 863.56 in the account at the end of six years.

METHOD B Substitute into Formula 14-11:

$$S_n(\text{due}) = R\,s_{\overline{n}|\,i}(1 + i)$$

$$S_{72}(\text{due}) = 150\,s_{\overline{72}|\,1\%}(1 + 1\%)$$

$$= 150(104.709\ 931\ 21)(1.01)$$

$$= \$15\ 863.55$$

The difference of 1¢ is due to rounding error.

Example 14.5b

What is the selling price of a truck that can be bought for $1 500 down and 36 equal monthly payments of $250 made at the beginning of each month, if money is worth 18% compounded monthly?

SOLUTION:

Down payment = $1 500
R = $250 (monthly)
n = 36 (monthly payments)
$i = \dfrac{18\%}{12} = 1.5\%$ (monthly)

METHOD A   Substitute into Formula 14-12:

$A_n(\text{due}) = R\,a_{\overline{n-1}|\,i} + R$

$\qquad = 250\,a_{\overline{35}|\,1.5\%} + 250$

$\qquad = 250(27.075\ 594\ 58) + 250$ (See Table 14-2.)

$\qquad = \$7\ 018.90$

The selling price of the truck is $7 018.90 + $1 500 = $8 518.90.

METHOD B   Substitute into Formula 14-13:

$A_n(\text{due}) = R\,a_{\overline{n}|\,i}(1 + i)$

$\qquad = 250\,a_{\overline{36}|\,1.5\%}(1 + 1.5\%)$

$\qquad = 250(27.660\ 684\ 31)(1.015)$

$\qquad = \$7\ 018.90$

$7 018.90 + $1 500 = $8 518.90 is the selling price of the truck.

Example 14.5c

A lease in the amount of $5 000 is to be paid in twelve equal payments made at the beginning of each month. If the interest rate is 15% compounded monthly, what should be the amount of each payment?

SOLUTION:

$A_n(\text{due})$ = $5 000
n = 12 (months)
$i = \dfrac{15\%}{12} = 1.25\%$

Substitute into Formula 14-13, and solve for R:

$R = \dfrac{A_n(\text{due})}{a_{\overline{n}|\,i}(1 + i)}$

$\quad = \dfrac{5\ 000}{a_{\overline{12}|\,1.25\%}(1 + 1.25\%)}$

$\quad = \dfrac{5\ 000}{(11.079\ 312)(1.012\ 5)}$

$\quad = \$445.72$

The lease can be settled by twelve payments of $445.72.

Example 14.5d

Megan wishes to save $5 000 for a vacation three years from now. How much must she deposit into an account at the beginning of each quarter starting now if the account earns 14% compounded quarterly?

SOLUTION:

$S_n(\text{due}) = \$5\ 000$

$n = 3 \times 4 = 12$ (quarters)

$i = \dfrac{14\%}{4} = 3.5\%$ (quarterly)

Substitute into Formula 14-11, and solve for R:

$$R = \frac{S_n(\text{due})}{s_{\overline{n}|\,i}(1 + i)}$$

$$= \frac{5\ 000}{s_{\overline{12}|\,3.5\%}(1 + 3.5\%)}$$

$$= \frac{5\ 000}{(14.601\ 961\ 64)(1.035)}$$

$$= \$330.84$$

Thus, twelve quarterly deposits of $330.84 made at the beginning of each quarter will amount to $5 000 in three years.

Example 14.5e

A man bought a boat for $10 500 and agreed to pay for it in monthly instalments of $589.25 starting on the date of purchase. If the interest charged is 15% compounded monthly, how many payments must he make?

SOLUTION:

$A_n(\text{due}) = \$10\ 500$

$R = \$589.25$

$i = \dfrac{15\%}{12} = 1.25\%$ (monthly)

Substituting the values in Formula 14-12:

$$A_n(\text{due}) = R\,a_{\overline{n-1}|\,i} + R$$

$$10\ 500 = 589.25\,a_{\overline{n-1}|\,1.25\%} + 589.25$$

$$a_{\overline{n-1}|\,1.25\%} = \frac{10\ 500 - 589.25}{589.25}$$

$$a_{\overline{n-1}|\,1.25\%} = 16.819\ 262$$

From Table 14-1, the entry for $a_{\overline{19}|\,1.25\%}$ is 16.819 307 59.

$n - 1 = 19$ and $n = 20$.

Thus, 20 monthly payments of $589.25 will settle the debt.

B. DEFERRED ANNUITY

When a table of values of $\frac{(1+i)^n - 1}{i}$ is used to find the amount of a deferred annuity, or $\frac{1-(1+i)^{-n}}{i}$ to find the present value of a deferred annuity, Formulas 14-5 and 14-7 may be written as follows:
To find the amount:

$$\boxed{S_n(\text{defer.}) = S_n = R\,s_{\overline{n}|\,i}} \qquad \longleftarrow Formula\ 14\text{-}14$$

To find the present value:

$$\boxed{A_n(\text{defer.}) = A_n(1 + i)^{-d} = R\,a_{\overline{n}|\,i}(1 + i)^{-d}} \qquad \longleftarrow Formula\ 14\text{-}15$$

Example 14.5f
Find the amount of an annuity of $100 payable at the end of each month for six payments. The interest rate is 18% compounded monthly. The first payment is due at the end of three months.

SOLUTION:

$R = \$100$
$n = 6$ (payments)
$i = \dfrac{18\%}{12} = 1.5\%$ (per month)

Substituting the values in Formula 14-14:
$S_6(\text{defer.}) = 100\,s_{\overline{6}|\,1.5\%}$
$\qquad\qquad = 100(6.229\ 55)$
$\qquad\qquad = \$622.96$
This is the same value obtained in Example 14.2a.

Example 14.5g
A trust fund is to be set up for Fran on her 11th birthday from which she may withdraw $2 000 at the end of each quarter for twelve years starting on her 21st birthday. If the fund pays 10% compounded quarterly, how much must be deposited in the fund on Fran's 11th birthday?

SOLUTION:

$R = \$2\ 000$ (quarterly payments)

$n = 12 \times 4 = 48$ (quarters)

$i = \dfrac{10\%}{4} = 2.5\%$ (quarterly)

$d = 10 \times 4 - 1 = 39$ (quarters)

Substituting the values into Formula 14-15:

$A_n(\text{defer.}) = R_{a\overline{n}|_i}(1 + i)^{-d}$

$A_{48}(\text{defer.}) = 2\ 000_{a\overline{48}|\ 2.5\%}(1 + 2.5\%)^{-39}$

$\qquad\qquad\quad = 2\ 000(27.773\ 154)(.381\ 741\ 4)$

$\qquad\qquad\quad = \$21\ 204.34$

Thus, \$21 204.34 should be deposited in the fund.

Example 14.5h

A debt of \$10 000 is to be settled by 16 equal quarterly payments with the first payment to be made $1\frac{3}{4}$ years from the date of the debt. What should be the amount of each payment if the interest rate is 14% compounded quarterly?

SOLUTION:

$A_n(\text{defer.}) = \$10\ 000$

$i = \dfrac{14\%}{4} = 3.5\%$ (quarterly)

$n = 16$ (quarterly payments)

$d = 1\dfrac{1}{2} \times 4 = 6$ (quarters)

$R = ?$

Substituting into Formula 14-15:

$A_n(\text{defer.}) = R(a_{\overline{n}|_i})(1 + i)^{-d}$

$\qquad R = \dfrac{A_n(\text{defer.})}{a_{\overline{16}|\ 3.5\%}(1 + 3.5\%)^{-6}}$

$\qquad\quad = \dfrac{10\ 000}{(12.094\ 117)(.813\ 500\ 64)}$

$\qquad\quad = \$1\ 016.41$

Thus, \$1 016.41 would be the amount of each payment.

Example 14.5i

A debt of \$4 500 is to be settled by equal payments of \$99.32 made at the end of each month with the first payment to be made at the end of six months. If the interest rate charged is 12% compounded monthly, how many payments must be made?

SOLUTION:

A_n(defer.) = $4 500

R = $99.32 (monthly)

$i = \dfrac{12\%}{12} = 1\%$ (monthly)

d = 5 (months)

n = ?

Substituting into Formula 14-15:

A_n(defer.) = $R \, a_{\overline{n}|\,i}(1 + i)^{-d}$

$$4\ 500 = 99.32 \, a_{\overline{n}|\,1\%}(1 + 1\%)^{-5}$$

$$= 99.32(.951\ 465\ 7) \, a_{\overline{n}|\,1\%}$$

$$a_{\overline{n}|\,1\%} = \frac{4\ 500}{(99.32)(.951\ 465\ 7)}$$

$$= 47.619\ 263$$

From Table 14-1, $a_{\overline{65}|\,1\%}$ = 47.626 607 77, thus 65 payments will be necessary.

Table 14-1
Amount of Annuity

when periodic payment is 1 $s_{\overline{n}|\,i} = \dfrac{(1 + i)^n - 1}{i}$

n	$\frac{2}{3}\%$	$\frac{3}{4}\%$	$\frac{7}{8}\%$	1%	n
61	74.9667 0195	76.9898 1795	80.1555 1519	83.4863 6656	61
62	76.4664 7997	78.5672 4159	81.8568 7595	85.3212 3022	62
63	77.9762 5650	80.1564 9590	83.5731 2362	87.1744 4252	63
64	79.4960 9821	81.7576 6962	85.3043 8845	89.0461 8695	64
65	81.0260 7220	83.3708 5214	87.0508 0185	90.9366 4882	65
66	82.5662 4601	84.9961 3353	88.8124 9636	92.8460 1531	66
67	84.1166 8765	86.6336 0453	90.5896 0571	94.7744 7546	67
68	85.6774 6557	88.2833 5657	92.3822 6476	96.7222 2021	68
69	87.2486 4867	89.9454 8174	94.1906 0957	98.6894 4242	69
70	88.8303 0633	91.6200 7285	96.0147 7741	100.6763 3684	70
71	90.4225 0837	93.3072 2340	97.8549 0671	102.6831 0021	71
72	92.0253 2510	95.0070 2758	99.7111 3714	104.7099 3121	72
73	93.6388 2726	96.7195 8028	101.5836 0959	106.7570 3052	73
74	95.2630 8611	98.4449 7714	103.4724 6618	108.8246 0083	74
75	96.8981 7335	100.1833 1446	105.3778 5025	110.9128 4684	75
76	98.5441 6118	101.9346 8932	107.2999 0644	113.0219 7530	76

Table 14-1 (Continued)

Amount of Annuity

when periodic payment is 1 $s_{\overline{n}|i} = \dfrac{(1+i)^n - 1}{i}$

n	$1\frac{1}{8}\%$	$1\frac{1}{4}\%$	$1\frac{3}{8}\%$	$1\frac{1}{2}\%$	n
1	1.0000 0000	1.0000 0000	1.0000 0000	1.0000 0000	1
2	2.0112 5000	2.0125 0000	2.0137 5000	2.0150 0000	2
3	3.0338 7656	3.0376 5625	3.0414 3906	3.0452 2500	3
4	4.0680 0767	4.0756 2695	4.0832 5885	4.0909 0338	4
5	5.1137 7276	5.1265 7229	5.1394 0366	5.1522 6693	5
6	6.1713 0270	6.1906 5444	6.2100 7046	6.2295 5093	6
7	7.2407 2986	7.2680 3762	7.2954 5893	7.3229 9419	7
8	8.3221 8807	8.3588 8809	8.3957 7149	8.4328 3911	8
9	9.4158 1269	9.4633 7420	9.5112 1335	9.5593 3169	9
10	10.5217 4058	10.5816 6637	10.6419 9253	10.7027 2167	10
11	11.6401 1016	11.7139 3720	11.7883 1993	11.8632 6249	11

n	$3\frac{1}{4}\%$	$3\frac{1}{2}\%$	$3\frac{3}{4}\%$	4%	n
1	1.0000 0000	1.0000 0000	1.0000 0000	1.0000 0000	1
2	2.0325 0000	2.0350 0000	2.0375 0000	2.0400 0000	2
3	3.0985 5625	3.1062 2500	3.1139 0625	3.1216 0000	3
4	4.1992 5933	4.2149 4288	4.2306 7773	4.2464 6400	4
5	5.3357 3526	5.3624 6588	5.3893 2815	5.4163 2256	5
6	6.5091 4665	6.5501 5218	6.5914 2796	6.6329 7546	6
7	7.7206 9392	7.7794 0751	7.8386 0650	7.8982 9448	7
8	8.9716 1647	9.0516 8677	9.1325 5425	9.2142 2626	8
9	10.2631 9401	10.3684 9581	10.4750 2503	10.5827 9531	9
10	11.5967 4781	11.7313 9316	11.8678 3847	12.0061 0712	10
11	12.9736 4212	13.1419 9192	13.3128 8241	13.4863 5141	11
12	14.3952 8548	14.6019 6164	14.8121 1550	15.0258 0546	12
13	15.8631 3226	16.1130 3030	16.3675 6983	16.6268 3768	13

Table 14-2

Present Value of Annuity

when periodic payment is 1 $a_{\overline{n}|i} = \dfrac{1 - (1+i)^{-n}}{i}$

n	$\frac{2}{3}\%$	$\frac{3}{4}\%$	$\frac{7}{8}\%$	1%	n
61	49.9851 9868	48.8073 1863	47.1125 9198	45.5000 3803	61
62	50.6475 4836	49.4365 4455	47.6952 5846	46.0396 4161	62
63	51.3055 1161	50.0610 8640	48.2728 7084	46.5739 0258	63
64	51.9591 1749	50.6809 7906	48.8454 7296	47.1028 7385	64
65	52.6083 9486	51.2962 5713	49.4131 0826	47.6266 0777	65
66	53.2533 7238	51.9069 5497	49.9758 1984	48.1451 5621	66
67	53.8940 7852	52.5131 0667	50.5336 5039	48.6585 7050	67
68	54.5305 4158	53.1147 4607	51.0866 4227	49.1669 0149	68

Table 14-2 (Continued)

Present Value of Annuity

when periodic payment is 1 $a_{\overline{n}|\,i} = \dfrac{1 - (1 + i)^{-n}}{i}$

n	$1\frac{1}{8}\%$	$1\frac{1}{4}\%$	$1\frac{3}{8}\%$	$1\frac{1}{2}\%$	n
7	6.6953 3948	6.6627 2585	6.6303 5140	6.5982 1396	7
8	7.6097 3002	7.5681 2429	7.5268 5712	7.4859 2508	8
9	8.5139 4810	8.4623 4498	8.4112 0308	8.3605 1732	9
10	9.4081 0690	9.3455 2591	9.2835 5421	9.2221 8455	10
11	10.2923 1832	10.2178 0337	10.1440 7320	10.0711 1779	11
12	11.1666 9302	11.0793 1197	10.9929 2054	10.9075 0521	12
13	12.0313 4044	11.9301 8466	11.8302 5454	11.7315 3222	13
14	12.8863 6880	12.7705 5275	12.6562 3136	12.5433 8150	14
15	13.7318 8509	13.6005 4592	13.4710 0504	13.3432 3301	15
16	14.5679 9514	14.4202 9227	14.2747 2754	14.1312 6405	16
17	15.3948 0360	15.2299 1829	15.0675 4874	14.9076 4931	17
18	16.2124 1395	16.0295 4893	15.8496 1651	15.6725 6089	18
19	17.0209 2850	16.8193 0759	16.6210 7671	16.4261 6837	19
20	17.8204 4845	17.5993 1613	17.3820 7320	17.1686 3879	20
21	18.6110 7387	18.3696 9495	18.1327 4792	17.9001 3673	21
30	25.3424 1766	24.8889 0623	24.4468 2540	24.0158 3801	30
31	26.0493 6233	25.5692 9010	25.1016 7734	24.6461 4582	31
32	26.7484 4236	26.2412 7418	25.7476 4719	25.2671 3874	32
33	27.4397 4522	26.9049 6215	26.3848 5543	25.8789 5442	33
34	28.1233 5745	27.5604 5644	27.0134 2089	26.4817 2849	34
35	28.7993 6460	28.2078 5822	27.6334 6080	27.0755 9458	35
36	29.4678 5127	28.8472 6737	28.2450 9080	27.6606 8431	36
37	30.1289 0114	29.4787 8259	28.8484 2496	28.2371 2740	37
38	30.7825 9692	30.1025 0133	29.4435 7579	28.8050 5163	38
39	31.4290 2044	30.7185 1983	30.0306 5430	29.3645 8288	39

n	$2\frac{1}{4}\%$	$2\frac{1}{2}\%$	$2\frac{3}{4}\%$	3%	n
42	26.9879 0390	25.8206 0683	24.7769 2069	23.7013 5920	42
43	27.3720 3316	26.1664 4569	25.0383 6563	23.9819 0213	43
44	27.7477 0969	26.5038 4945	25.3414 7507	24.2542 7392	44
45	28.1151 1950	26.8330 2386	25.6364 7209	24.5187 1254	45
46	28.4744 4450	27.1541 6962	25.9235 7381	24.7754 4907	46
47	28.8258 6259	27.4674 8255	26.2029 9154	25.0247 0783	47
48	29.1695 4777	27.7731 5371	26.4749 3094	25.2667 0664	48
49	29.5056 7019	28.0713 6947	26.7395 9215	25.5016 5693	49
50	29.8343 9627	28.3623 1168	26.9971 6998	25.7297 6401	50

n	$3\frac{1}{4}\%$	$3\frac{1}{2}\%$	$3\frac{3}{4}\%$	4%	n
10	8.4223 9508	8.3166 0532	8.2127 8725	8.1108 9578	10
11	9.1258 0637	9.0015 5104	8.8797 9494	8.7604 7671	11
12	9.8070 7639	9.6633 3433	9.5226 9392	9.3850 7376	12
13	10.4669 0207	10.3027 3849	10.1423 5558	9.9856 4785	13
14	11.1059 5842	10.9205 2028	10.7396 1984	10.5631 2293	14
15	11.7248 9920	11.5174 1090	11.3152 9623	11.1183 8743	15
16	12.3243 5758	12.0941 1681	11.8701 6504	11.6522 9561	16
17	12.9049 4681	12.6513 2059	12.4049 7835	12.1656 6885	17

Table 14-2 (Continued)
Present Value of Annuity

when periodic payment is 1 $a_{\overline{n}|\,i} = \dfrac{1 - (1 + i)^{-n}}{i}$

n	$3\frac{1}{4}\%$	$3\frac{1}{2}\%$	$3\frac{3}{4}\%$	4%	n
18	13.4672 6083	13.1896 8173	12.9204 6106	12.6592 9697	18
19	14.0118 7490	13.7098 3742	13.4173 1187	13.1339 3940	19
20	14.5393 4615	14.2124 0330	13.8962 0421	13.5903 2634	20
21	15.0502 1419	14.6979 7420	14.3577 8719	14.0291 5995	21

EXERCISE 14.5 / REFERENCE SECTIONS: A–B

Use a table of the values of $\dfrac{(1 + i)^n - 1}{i}$ or $\dfrac{1 - (1 + i)^{-n}}{i}$ to solve the following problems:

	Amount S_n (due)	Present A_n (due)	Payment R	Term n	Compound Interest Rate
1.	?	?	$2 000 monthly	2 years	15% monthly
2.	?	?	3 000 quarterly	3 years	18% quarterly
3.	$ 5 000		? semi-annually	$1\frac{1}{2}$ years	12% semi-annually
4.		50 000	? annually	12 years	10% annually
5.	16 000		763.12	?	18% monthly
6.		7 500	713.32	?	12% quarterly
7.	25 000		827.13 monthly	2 years	? monthly
8.		8 000	1 475.82	$1\frac{1}{2}$ years	? quarterly

Find the unknown value for each of the following deferred annuity:

	Present Value A_n (defer.)	Period of Deferment	Payment	Term	Compound Interest Rate
9.		5 months	$100 monthly	2 years	12% monthly
10.		6 months	90 quarterly	18 months	14% quarterly
11.	$16 000	1 year	? semi-annually	5 years	13% semi-annually
12.	28 000	$1\frac{1}{2}$ years	? semi-annually	6 years	14% semi-annually
13.	1 200	2 months	74.79 monthly	?	18% monthly
14.	20 000	6 months	2 238.83	?	16% quarterly

Statement Problems:

15. A television set can be bought by making equal monthly payments of $90 for $2\frac{3}{4}$ years. The first payment is due on the date of purchase and the rate of interest charged is 18% compounded monthly.
    (a) What is the cash price of the television set? (b) What is the total amount paid for the television set? (c) What is the cost of credit?

16. A boat can be bought by making equal monthly payments of $1 000 for 3 years. The first payment is made on the date of purchase and the rate of interest charged is 14% quarterly,.
    (a) What is the cash price of the boat? (b) What is the total amount paid for the boat? (c) What is the cost of credit?

17. On December 1, 1984 Marlene has $60 000 in an RRSP account. She expects to withdraw equal monthly amounts from the account starting January 1, 1986. How much can she withdraw each month if she is to make her last withdrawal on January 1, 1990, when her regular pension becomes available. The account pays interest at 12% compounded monthly.

18. Martin Grove Limited received a loan in the amount of $20 000. The loan is to be repaid by equal monthly payments made at the end of each month for 12 months. The first payment is due six months after the date of the loan and the rate of interest is 12% compounded monthly. What should be the amount of each payment?

19. A lease in the amount of $15 000 is to be settled by equal quarterly payments made at the beginning of each quarter for two years. The rate of interest charged is 15% compounded quarterly. What should be the amount of each payment?

20. How much must the equal monthly payments be to settle a debt in the amount of $10 000 if payments are made at the beginning of each month for 18 months? The first payment is due six months from the date the debt was contracted and the interest rate is 15% compounded monthly.

EXERCISE / CHAPTER REVIEW

1. What are the amount and the present value of an annuity of $140 payable at the beginning of each month for 30 months if the interest rate is 15% compounded monthly?

2. What are the amount and the present value of an annuity of $60 payable at the beginning of each quarter for 10 years if the interest rate is 16% compounded quarterly?

3. In Problem 1, if payments are payable at the end of each month, what are the amount and the present value?

4. Find the amount and the present value in Problem 2 if the payments of $60 each are payable at the end of each quarter.

5. Refer to Problem 1. What are the amount and the present value if the payments of the annuity are payable at the end of each month and the interest rate is 15% compounded (a) quarterly, (b) semi-annually?

6. Refer to Problem 2. What are the amount and the present value if the payments are payable at the end of each quarter and the interest rate is 8% compounded (a) monthly, (b) quarterly?

7. Refer to Problem 1. What are the amount and the present value if the interest rate is 15% compounded semi-annually?

8. Refer to Problem 2. Find the amount and the present value if the interest rate is 16% compounded (a) monthly, (b) annually.

9. Tom plans to deposit $30 now and $30 hereafter every month for a total of 36 deposits. If his deposits can earn 15% compounded monthly, what is the final value at the end of three years?

10. Assume that $80 is deposited now and hereafter for 26 additional monthly deposits of $80 each. What is the final value if the interest rate is 16% compounded monthly?

11. Refer to Problem 9. What is the cash equivalent of the annuity?

12. Refer to Problem 10. What is the cash equivalent of the annuity?

13. On April 1, 1984, Jane Taylor deposits $120 in a bank that pays 12% interest compounded monthly. She plans to deposit the same amount every month thereafter until the last deposit on September 1, 1985. How much money will be in her account on October 1, 1985?

14. A suite of living room furniture can be bought for $40 per month for 12 monthly payments, with the first payment due now. If money is worth 18% interest compounded monthly, what is the cash price of the suite?

15. A house can be bought for $5 350 down plus $450 per month payable at the end of each month. The last monthly payment will be 14 years and 11 months from the date of purchase. The mortgage is computed at 17% interest compounded semi-annually. What is the cash price of the house?

16. Refer to Problem 15. If the house can be rented for $500 per month payable in advance each month and the house is expected to have a value of $70 000 at the end of 15 years, should a man who wishes to occupy the house for 15 years only buy or rent the house? Assume that the man can invest his money at 16% interest compounded monthly.

17. A scholarship fund is set up to award $1 000 to a community college student at the end of each year. How large should the fund be if the money can be invested at (a) 15% interest compounded annually, and (b) 15% interest compounded monthly?

18. Frank Swartz would like to ensure that each year the top student in the graduating class of his high school will be able to afford at least one year of college. He estimates that a fund which generates $4 000 each year should make this possible. How much must he deposit in the fund today if (a) the fund can be invested at 18% interest compounded annually, and (b) 18% interest compounded quarterly?

19. Johnson wishes to have $3 000 three years from now. How much must he invest every month if the first investment starts now and the interest is 10% compounded semi-annually? He will not make an investment at the end of the three years.

20. Davy's father wishes to have $5 000 when Davy reaches 18 years of age. How much must the father invest now and each month thereafter at a 12% interest rate compounded semi-annually? Davy is 14 years old now. His father does not wish to make an investment on Davy's 18th birthday.

21. A man wants to have $3 000 at the end of six years. His investment can earn 12% interest compounded monthly. How much must he invest each year if the first investment starts (a) now, and (b) at the end of one year?

22. Compute Problem 20 assuming the interest rate is 13.5% compounded semi-annually. Also, find the size of the semi-annual investment if Davy's father makes the first investment six months from now and the last investment on Davy's 18th birthday.

23. A washing machine can be bought for 18 equal monthly payments with the first payment due now. If the cash price is $400 and the interest rate is 16% compounded monthly, what is the size of each payment?

24. Mr. Rogers purchased a farm on May 1, 1984, and promised to pay for it in equal monthly instalments. The cash price of the farm is $70 000. The first payment was made on the purchase date and the last payment is to be made on January 1, 1986. What is the size of each monthly payment if the interest rate is 18% compounded semi-annually?

25. What is the answer in Problem 23 if the interest rate is 16% compounded semi-annually?

26. What is the answer in Problem 24 if the interest rate is 18% compounded monthly?

27. At what nominal rate compounded quarterly will an annuity of $300 payable at the beginning of each quarter for eight years amount to $12 000?

28. What is the nominal rate compounded monthly if the amount of an annuity of $60 payable at the beginning of each month for three years is $2 500?

29. At what nominal rate compounded quarterly does an annuity of $80 payable at the beginning of each quarter for nine years have a present value of $2 300?

30. Mabel bought a stereo for $2 300. She paid $100 down and agreed to pay $200 one month from now and thereafter for a total of 12 payments. What was the interest rate charged?

31. If $80 is deposited at the beginning of each quarter at 12% interest compounded quarterly, how many payments will be required for the deposits to amount to at least $3 000?

32. On March 1, 1985, Bobson plans to invest $120 each month with the first investment starting then. He wishes to have at least $5 000 as the final value. If he can earn 15% interest compounded monthly on his investment, on what date will he have the final value?

33. Carlson purchased a $6 000 car and agreed to pay for it with monthly instal-

ments of $180 each, starting on the date of purchase. If the interest rate is 15.25% compounded monthly, how many monthly payments are required?

34. The present value of an annuity of $60 payable at the beginning of each month is $2 500. What is the number of payments of the annuity if the interest rate is 14.7% compounded monthly?

35. What are the amount and the present value of an annuity of $120 payable at the end of each quarter for 15 payments, with the first payment to be made one year from now? Assume that the interest rate is 15.75% compounded quarterly.

36. Find the amount and the present value of an annuity of $50 per month for 30 payments if the first payment is due $1\frac{1}{2}$ years from now and money is worth 11.75% interest compounded monthly.

37. Smith borrows $8 000 at 18.8% interest compounded monthly and agrees to repay it in 20 equal monthly payments. What is the size of each payment if the first payment is due at the end of two years?

38. Thomas borrows $600 at 10.6% interest compounded monthly and agrees to repay it in 16 monthly payments. Find the size of each monthly payment if the first payment is due at the end of one year.

39. If $100 is deposited at the end of each month and the interest rate is 13% compounded monthly, how many monthly payments will be needed for the deposits to have a present value of $3 600? Assume that the first deposit is made at the end of eight months.

40. If a man will deposit $25 at the end of ten months and $25 every month thereafter, how many monthly deposits will be required for a value which now is equivalent to $800? Assume that the interest rate is 17.2% compounded monthly.

Summary of Formulae

Formula 14-1	$S_n(\text{due}) = R\left[\dfrac{(1+i)^{n+1}-1}{i}\right] - R$	Used to find the amount of an annuity due. (METHOD A).
Formula 14-2	$S_n(\text{due}) = R\left[\dfrac{(1+i)^n-1}{i}\right](1+i)$	Used to find the amount of an annuity due. (METHOD B).
Formula 14-3	$A_n(\text{due}) = R\left[\dfrac{1-(1+i)^{-(n-1)}}{i}\right] + R$	Used to find the present value of an annuity due. (METHOD A).

Formula 14-4

$$A_n(\text{due}) = R\left[\frac{1 - (1 + i)^{-n}}{i}\right](1 + i)$$

Used to find the present value of an annuity due. (METHOD B).

Formula 14-5

$$S_n(\text{defer.}) = S_n = R\left[\frac{(1 + i)^n - 1}{i}\right]$$

Used to find the amount of a deferred annuity.

Formula 14-6

$$A_n(\text{defer.})$$

$$= R\left[\frac{1 - (1 + i)^{-(d + n)}}{i}\right] - R\left[\frac{1 - (1 + i)^{-d}}{i}\right]$$

Used to find the present value of a deferred annuity for the period of deferment. (METHOD A).

Formula 14-7

$$A_n(\text{defer.}) = A_n(1 + i)^{-d}$$

$$= R\left[\frac{1 - (1 + i)^{-n}}{i}\right]$$

Used to find the present value of a deferred annuity for the period of deferment. (METHOD B).

Formula 14-8

$$A_\infty = \frac{I}{i}$$

Used to find the present value of a simple perpetuity.

Formula 14-9

$$A_\infty = \frac{R}{(1 + i)^c - 1}$$

Used to find the present value of ordinary perpetuities. A general formula for ordinary perpetuities.

Formula 14-10 $S_n(\text{due}) = R\,s_{\overline{n+1}|\,i} - R$

Used to find the amount of an annuity due when using a table of values. (METHOD A).

Formula 14-11 $S_n(\text{due}) = R\,s_{\overline{n}|\,i}(1 + i)$

Used to find the amount of an annuity due when using a table of values. (METHOD B).

Formula 14-12 $A_n(\text{due}) = R\,a_{\overline{n-i}|\,i} + R$

Used to find the present value of an annuity due when using a table of values. (METHOD A).

Formula 14-13 $A_n(\text{due}) = R\,a_{\overline{n}|\,i}(1 + i)$

Used to find the present value of an annuity due when using a table of values. (METHOD B).

Formula 14-14 $S_n(\text{defer.}) = S_n = R\,s_{\overline{n}|\,i}$

Used to find the amount of a deferred annuity when using a table of values.

Formula 14-15 $A_n(\text{defer.}) = A_n(1 + i)^{-d}$
$\qquad\qquad\qquad = R\,a_{\overline{n}|\,i}(1 + i)^{-d}$

Used to find the present value of a deferred annuity when using a table of values.

Glossary

ANNUITY DUE an annuity for which the periodic payments are made at the beginning of each payment interval

COMPLEX (OR GENERAL) PERPETUITY a perpetuity whose payments are made at the end of several interest periods

DEFERRED ANNUITY an annuity whose term begins on a future date

PERIOD OF DEFERMENT the period between now and the beginning of the term of a deferred annuity

PERPETUITY an annuity whose term begins on a definite date but never ends

SIMPLE ORDINARY PERPETUITY a perpetuity whose payments are made at the end of each interest period

SIMPLE PERPETUITY DUE a perpetuity whose payments are made at the beginning of each interest period

15

Extinction of debts

Introduction

The word "debt" in this chapter refers to a long-term obligation. Long-term debts are normally in the form of long-term notes or bonds with a maturity date which is more than one year. Generally, notes are issued to a *single source* from which a loan is obtained, whereas bonds are issued to a *group* of creditors. Long-term debts usually involve large sums of money. A borrower may promise to discharge his debt either by making periodic partial payments under the AMORTIZATION method or by establishing a sinking fund into which periodic deposits are made in order to pay a single sum on the date of maturity.

The amortization method broadly refers to the discharging of a debt by means of a set of regular or irregular and equal or unequal payments. The methods for irregular and unequal payments were presented in Chapter Eight (Section 8.4, partial payments; the declining-balance method). In this chapter only a debt discharged by a sequence of *equal* payments at *equal* intervals of time is considered. *The original principal of the debt, therefore, is the present value of an annuity of the equal payments*. In order to discharge a debt, each payment must be greater than the periodic interest, so that a part of the payment applies to the interest and the remainder applies to the principal until the principal becomes zero.

The following discussion first treats long-term debts other than bonds. Amortization of bonded debts is discussed later in this chapter.

15.1 Debt Extinction by Amortization–Simple Annuities

A. *FINDING THE SIZE OF THE PERIODIC PAYMENT*

The size of the periodic payment for amortizing a debt may be found by using the method discussed in Section 12.4 of Chapter Twelve. The method shows how to find the size of each periodic payment of an ordinary annuity when the present value is known. In applying this method, consider the value of the debt as the present value of the annuity.

Example 15.1a

Kaline Simonds borrowed $5 000 and signed an agreement to make equal payments at the end of each month for one year. If the interest rate charged is 21% compounded monthly, how much must she pay at the end of each month?

SOLUTION:

$A_n = \$5\ 000$

$i = \dfrac{21\%}{12} = 1.75\%$

$n = 1 \times 12 = 12$

$A_n = \$5\ 000$

$$\begin{array}{c}\vdash\quad\vdash\quad\vdash\ \cdots\ \vdash\\ 0\quad 1\quad 2\qquad\quad 12\\ \qquad\qquad\qquad R\end{array}$$

$R = A_n\left[\dfrac{i}{1 - (1 + i)^{-n}}\right]$

$\quad = 5\ 000\left[\dfrac{.017\ 5}{1 - (1.017\ 5)^{-12}}\right]$

$\quad = 5\ 000\left[\dfrac{.017\ 5}{1 - .812\ 079}\right]$

$\quad = 5\ 000\left[\dfrac{.017\ 5}{.187\ 942\ 1}\right]$

$\quad = \dfrac{87.5}{.187\ 942\ 1}$

$\quad = \$465.57$

Or, $R = 5\ 000(.093\ 113\ 8)$

$\qquad = \$465.57$

Thus, $465.57 must be paid at the end of each month.

B.   FINDING THE OUTSTANDING PRINCIPAL (SIMPLE ANNUITIES)[1]

Often both the creditor and the borrower must know the amount of the *outstanding principal* or the *unpaid balance* on a certain date. The information may be needed for

---

[1] Some banks and finance companies use the Rule of 78, also known as the Sum-of-the-Digits Rule, to determine the outstanding principal after a payment. The outstanding principal computed by this method is usually greater than the outstanding principal computed by the methods presented in this section. The Rule of 78 is covered in Section 10.6. The outstanding balance by the Rule of 78 is usually determined from a precomputed table. The borrower should determine the method used by the lending institution.

various reasons: it may be necessary for accounting purposes; the creditor may want to sell the unpaid balance; or the creditor and the borrower may agree to settle the balance on an earlier date. The outstanding principal may be determined under two types of arrangements: (a) all periodic payments are equal, or (b) all periodic payments, except the final payment, are equal.

1. All Periodic Payments are Equal

When it is necessary for all the periodic payments to be the same size, the method given in Example 15.1a should be used to find the size of the payments. The outstanding principal on a certain date is the present value of an annuity formed by the remaining unpaid payments, as shown below.

Example 15.1b

Refer to Example 15.1a. Find the outstanding principal after each payment has been made.

SOLUTION:

$A_n = \$5\ 000$
$\quad i = 1.75\%$
$\quad n = 12$
$\quad R = \$465.57$

Amortization Schedule (Example 15.1b)

(1) Period (monthly interval)	(2) Outstanding Principal (2) − (5)*	(3) Interest due at End of Period (2) × 1.75%	(4) Equal Payment at End of Period	(5) Portion of Payment Applied to Principal (4) − (3)
1	$5 000.00	$ 87.50	$ 465.57	$ 378.07
2	4 621.93	80.88	465.57	384.69
3	4 237.24	74.15	465.57	391.42
4	3 845.82	67.30	465.57	398.27
5	3 447.55	60.33	465.57	405.24
6	3 042.31	53.24	465.57	412.33
7	2 629.98	46.02	465.57	419.55
8	2 210.44	38.68	465.57	426.89
9	1 783.55	31.21	465.57	434.36
10	1 349.19	23.61	465.57	441.96
11	907.23	15.88	465.57	449.69
12	457.54	8.01	465.55	457.54
Total		**$ 586.81**	**$5 586.82**	**$5 000.01**

* Of the previous period. For example, 4 621.93 = 5 000.00 − 387.07.

Observe the amortization schedule of Example 15.1b. Column (2) shows the outstanding principal after each payment is made. For example, the outstanding principal after the fourth payment is $3 447.55. The fourth payment is made at the end of the fourth period. Thus, $3 447.55 is also the principal at the beginning of the fifth payment period. The discharged portion of the original principal after the fourth payment is $1 552.45 ($5 000 − $3 447.55, or $378.07 + $384.69 + $391.42 + $398.27, see Column (5) of the schedule).

Each outstanding principal shown in Column (2) may be checked by using the formula method, $A_n = R\left[\dfrac{1 - (1 + i)^{-n}}{i}\right]$. For example, the outstanding principal after the fourth payment is made is the present value of an annuity formed by the eight remaining unpaid payments.

Example 15.1c
Refer to Example 15.1a. Find the outstanding principal after Kaline has made four monthly payments.

SOLUTION:

After four payments have been made, eight payments are still outstanding. Thus, what is required here is the present value of these eight remaining payments.

Debt	$5 000								
Month	0	1	2	3	4	9	10	11	12
Payment		R	R	R	R	R	R	R	R

$A_8 \blacktriangleleft \text{———————————}$

$$A_n = \$5\ 000$$
$$R = \$465.57$$
$$i = 1.75\%$$
$$n = 12 - 4 = 8 \text{ (remaining payments)}$$

$$A_n = R\left[\frac{1 - (1 + i)^{-n}}{i}\right]$$

$$A_8 = 465.57\left[\frac{1 - (1.017\ 5)^{-8}}{.017\ 5}\right]$$

$$= 465.57\left[\frac{1 - .870\ 411\ 6}{.017\ 5}\right]$$

$$= 465.57\left[\frac{.129\ 588\ 4}{.017\ 5}\right]$$

$$= 465.57(7.405\ 053)$$
$$= \$3\ 447.57$$

The two-cent difference is due to rounding error.

The last figures in Columns (2) and (5) should be the same. The total for Column (5) should be equal to the original principal, $5 000. Theoretically speaking, all the payments should be equal. However, the schedule shows that the twelfth payment is $465.55. Any discrepancies result from rounding all computations to the nearest cent. For example, interest due at the end of the twelfth period is computed as follows:

457.54 × .0175 = $8.00695 which is rounded to $8.01.

The size of the twelfth payment therefore is $457.54 + $8.01 = $465.55. The final payment covers the outstanding principal at the beginning of the last payment interval and the interest due thereon.

Here, the interest for each period is computed by the simple interest method. It should be observed that *when a debtor makes each of the simple interest payments on the interest date, the simple interest method is actually a compound interest method*. Also, note that as the principal is gradually reduced, the periodic interest becomes smaller after each payment is made. Thus, a greater portion of each equal payment is used in reducing the principal.

EXERCISE 15.1A / REFERENCE SECTION: A–B (1)

Find the size of the periodic payment and the outstanding principal at the indicated time in each of the following problems, without constructing an amortization schedule: (Payments are assumed to be made at the end of each period.)

	Debt	Number of Payments by Amortization	Compound Interest Rate	Required Outstanding Principal
1.	$ 2 000	10, annually	10% annually	after 5th payment
2.	1 000	12, quarterly	20% quarterly	after 5th payment
3.	4 000	4, monthly	18% monthly	after 3rd payment
4.	6 000	8, semi-annually	19% semi-annually	after 1st payment
5.	8 000	20, quarterly	14% quarterly	after 7th payment
6.	20 000	45, monthly	21% monthly	after 18th payment
7.	200	5, quarterly	18% quarterly	after 2nd payment
8.	500	10, quarterly	16% quarterly	after 6th payment

Statement Problems:

9. A debt of $6 000 is to be amortized with four equal quarterly payments. If the interest rate is 18% compounded quarterly, what is the size of each payment? Construct an amortization schedule.

10. A loan of $2 000 is to be amortized with five equal semi-annual payments. The interest rate is 21% compounded semi-annually. Find the semi-annual payment and construct an amortization schedule.

11. A man bought an $8 000 tractor and made a $1 000 down payment. He agreed to pay the balance by making equal payments at the end of every month for a

period of two years. The interest charged is 16% compounded quarterly. Find the outstanding principal after the fourth payment by constructing a partial amortization schedule.

12. A $42 000 boat was purchased with a down payment of $2 000 and monthly payments for 20 years. The interest rate is 16% compounded monthly. (a) Find the size of the monthly payment. (b) Construct a partial amortization schedule to find the outstanding principal after the third payment.

2. All Periodic Payments, Except the Final Payment, Are Equal

Sometimes the size of each payment is not obtained by the method explained in Section 1 above. Instead, it is specified by the agreement between the creditor and the debtor, and a more convenient or rounded figure, such as $50 or $100, is decided upon as the size of each payment. The exact size of the final payment is not known. It may or may not equal the size of other payments. Under such a condition, when an amortization schedule is not constructed, the outstanding principal on a certain date is computed by a method different from that discussed above. The following example is used to illustrate the methods of computation for this type of problem.

Example 15.1d
A debt of $6 000 is to be discharged by payments of $1 000 at the end of every month. Interest charged is 12% compounded monthly. Find (a) the number of payments, (b) the outstanding principal after each payment is made, (c) the interest included in each payment, (d) the principal included in each payment, (e) the size of the final payment and (f) the total of the payments.

SOLUTION:

Amortization Schedule (Example 15.1d)

(1) Period (1-month interval)	(2) Outstanding Principal at Beginning of Each Period (2) − (5)	(3) Interest Due at End of Period (2) × 1%	(4) Payment at End of Each Period	(5) Portion of Principal Reduced by Each Payment (4) − (3)
1	$6 000.00	$ 60.00	$1 000.00	$ 940.00
2	5 060.00	50.60	1 000.00	949.40
3	4 110.60	41.11	1 000.00	958.89
4	3 151.71	31.52	1 000.00	968.48
5	2 183.23	21.83	1 000.00	978.17
6	1 205.06	12.05	1 000.00	987.95
7	217.11 +	2.17 =	219.28	217.11
Total		219.28	$6 219.28	$6 000.00

(a) Seven payments must be made.
(b) See Column (2).
(c) See Column (3).
(d) See Column (5).
(e) The final payment is $219.28.
(f) The total of the payments is $6 219.28.

Example 15.1e

Refer to Example 15.1d. Find the size of the final payment without setting up an amortization schedule.

SOLUTION:

The amount of the final payment may be found by either of the following methods:

$$A_n = \$6\ 000$$
$$i = \frac{12\%}{12} = 1\% \text{ (per month)}$$
$$R = \$1\ 000$$
$$n = ? \text{ (months)}$$

METHOD A   Compute the value of n and determine the value of the payment for the fractional part of n. Add the applicable interest.

$$(1 + i)^{-n} = \left[1 - \frac{A_n}{R}i\right]$$

$$-n \ln(1 + i) = \ln\left[1 - \frac{A_n}{R}i\right]$$

$$-n \ln(1 + 1\%) = \ln\left[1 - \frac{6\ 000}{1\ 000}(.01)\right]$$

$$-n \ln(1.01) = \ln .94$$
$$-n(.009\ 950\ 3) = -.061\ 875\ 4$$
$$n = \frac{.061\ 875\ 4}{.009\ 950\ 3} = 6.218\ 446 \text{ (months)}$$

The outstanding principal is the present value of an annuity of $1 000 for the fractional part of a payment interval of .218 446 (months).

$$A_{.218446} = 1\ 000\left[\frac{1 - (1 + 1\%)^{-.218\ 446}}{1\%}\right]$$

$$= 1\ 000\ (.217\ 124\ 9)$$
$$= \$217.12$$

The balance owing after the sixth payment of $1 000 is $217.12. If the payment is made at the end of the interest period then interest for the last payment interval will have to be included and the amount of the final payment is

$217.12 + Interest

$I = \$217.12 \,(.01)$

$ = \$2.17$

The final payment $= \$217.12 + \$2.17$

$ = \$219.29$

METHOD B Compute the outstanding principal after the last equal payment and add any applicable interest. Here, finding the outstanding principal at the beginning of the last payment interval involves two steps:

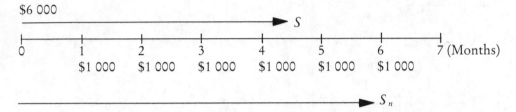

STEP (1) Find the amount of the debt of $6 000 at 12% compounded monthly at the end of six months.

$S = \$6\ 000\ (1 + 1\%)^6$

$ = \$6\ 000\ (1.061\ 520\ 2)$

$ = \$6\ 369.120\ 9$

STEP (2) Find the amount of the annuity of the six payments of $1 000 each.

$$S_n = 1\ 000 \left[\frac{(1 + 1\%)^6 - 1}{1\%} \right]$$

$ = 1\ 000\ (6.152\ 015\ 1)$

$ = \$6152.015\ 1$

The outstanding principal after the sixth payment is the difference between S and S_n.

$S - S_n = 6\ 369.120\ 9 - 6\ 152.015\ 1$

$ = \$217.105\ 9$

$ = \$217.11$

The final payment is the outstanding principal plus interest for one month.

$I = \$217.11\,(.01)$

$ = \$2.17$

Final payment $= \$217.11 + \$2.17$

$ = \$219.28$

Example 15.1f
Refer to Example 15.1d. Find the outstanding principal after the fifth payment
Here Method B is used.

STEP (1) Find the amount of the debt at the fifth payment.

$P = \$6\ 000$

$$S = 6\ 000\ (1 + 1\%)^5$$
$$= 6\ 000\ (1.051\ 010\ 1)$$
$$= \$6\ 306.06$$

STEP (2) Find the amount of the annuity of five payments of $1 000 each.

$$S_5 = 1\ 000 \left[\frac{(1 + 1\%)^5 - 1}{1\%} \right]$$

$$= 1\ 000\ (5.101\ 005)$$
$$= \$5\ 101.01$$

The outstanding principal after the fifth payment is
$$S - S_5 = 6\ 306.060 - 5\ 101.005$$
$$= \$1\ 205.06$$

The outstanding principal after any payment n is the difference between the
value of the debt and the value of the payments at time n.

EXERCISE 15.1B / REFERENCE SECTIONS: A–B

In each of the following problems, find (a) the number of payments, (b) the outstanding principal at the indicated time, (c) the interest and the principal
included in the next payment after the indicated time in (b), (d) the size of the
final payment and (e) the total of the cash payments: (Do not construct an amortization schedule in finding your answers.)

	Debt	Payment (made at end of each period)	Compound Interest Rate	Required Outstanding Principal
1.	$ 4 000	$ 220 every 3 months	20% quarterly	after 20th payment
2.	6 000	600 every month	18% monthly	after 3rd payment
3.	5 000	1 000 every quarter	16% quarterly	after 3rd payment
4.	800	100 every 6 months	17% semi-annually	after 4th payment
5.	1 400	150 every year	10% annually	after 6th payment
6.	25 000	2 500 every 6 months	19% semi-annually	after 11th payment

Statement Problems:

7. A debt of $8 000 is to be amortized with $2 500 being paid at the end of every six months. The interest rate is 17% compounded semi-annually. Construct an amortization schedule.

8. A debt of $4 000 is to be amortized with $800 being paid at the end of each semi-annual period. The interest rate is 18% compounded semi-annually. Construct an amortization schedule.

15.2 Debt Extinction by Amortization–Complex (General) Annuities

When the payment interval and the interest conversion period are not the same, the periodic equal payments represent a general annuity.

Example 15.2a
A debt of $75 200 is to be repaid by equal payments at the end of each month for 7 years. Interest is charged at 18.25% compounded semi-annually. (a) Find the size of the monthly payments. (b) Set up an amortization schedule for the first six payments. (c) Find the outstanding balance after the 10th payment.

SOLUTION:

(a) $A_{nc} = \$75\ 200$

$n = 7 \times 12 = 84$ (monthly payments)

$i = \dfrac{18.25\%}{2} = 9.125\%$

$c = \dfrac{1}{6}$ (interest period per payment interval)

$f = (1 + i)^c - 1$
$= (1.091\ 25)^{1/6} - 1$
$= .014\ 660\ 4$

$R = A_{nc}\left[\dfrac{f}{1 - (1 + f)^{-n}}\right]$

$= 75\ 200\left[\dfrac{.014\ 660\ 4}{1 - (1.014\ 660\ 0)^{-84}}\right]$

$= 75\ 200[.020\ 779\ 7]$

$= 1\ 562.63$

(b) $A_{nc} = \$75\ 200$

$n = 7 \times 12 = 84$ (monthly payments)

$R = \$1\ 562.63$

$f = .014\ 660\ 4$

Amortization Schedule (Example 15.2a)

(1)	(2)	(3)	(4)	(5)
Payment No. (1 month interval)	Payment	Interest due at end of period	Amount applied to Principal	Balance
		(5) × 1.46604%	(2) − (3)	*(5) − (4)
0	...	...	...	75 200.00
1	1 562.63	1 102.46	460.17	74 739.83
2	1 562.63	1 095.72	466.91	74 272.92
3	1 562.63	1 088.87	473.76	73 799.16
4	1 562.63	1 081.93	480.70	73 318.46
5	1 562.63	1 074.88	487.75	72 830.65
6	1 562.63	1 067.73	494.90	72 335.75

* Of the previous period. For example, 74 739.83 = 75 200 − 460.17

In the amortization table for Example 15.2a the entry in Column (3) is the amount of interest due at the end of the time period, the entry in Column (4) is the difference between the entry in Column (2) and Column (3) and the entry in Column (5) is the balance at the end of the previous period less the entry in Column (4). At the end of the first month the entries are:

Column (2): Amount of payment
Column (3): 75 200 × 1.466 04% = $1 102.46
Column (4): 1 562.63 − 1 102.46 = $460.17
Column (5): 75 200 − 460.17 = $74 739.83

(c) After the tenth payment there are 84 − 10 = 74 payments remaining. The outstanding principal after the tenth payment has been made is given by the present value of the annuity of the remaining 74 payments. This value is calculated below:

A_{nc} = $75 200

$$A_{74} = 1\ 562.63 \left[\frac{1 - (1 + .014\ 660\ 4)^{-74}}{.014\ 660\ 4} \right]$$
$$A_{74} = 1\ 562.63\ (44.977\ 093)$$
$$= \$70\ 282.56$$

The outstanding principal after the tenth payment is $70 282.56.

Example 15.2b
A mortgage for $80 000 with interest at 22% compounded semi-annually is amortized by equal monthly payments over twenty-five years and is renewable at the end of one year. (a) What is the amount of the monthly payments? (b) What is the outstanding balance at the end of one year? (c) If the mortgage is renewed for a further three years at 18.5% compounded semi-annually at the end of the first year what is the size of the new monthly payment? (For part (c), assume the mortgage is amortized over 24 years.)

SOLUTION:

(a) $A_{nc} = \$80\ 000$

$$i = \frac{22\%}{2} = 11\% \text{ (semi-annually)}$$

$n = 25 \times 12 = 300 \text{ (monthly payments)}$

$c = \frac{1}{6} \text{ (interest period per payment interval)}$

$f = (1 + i)^c - 1$
$= (1 + 11\%)^{1/6} - 1$

$= .017\ 545\ 5$

$$R = A_{nc}\left[\frac{f}{1 - (1 + f)^{-n}}\right]$$

$$= 80\ 000\left[\frac{.017\ 545\ 5}{1 - (1 + .017\ 545\ 5)^{-300}}\right]$$

$= 80\ 000\ [.017\ 641\ 1]$

$= \$1\ 411.29$

(b) At the end of one year there are $300 - 12 = 288$ payments outstanding.

$$A_{288} = R\left[\frac{1 - (1 + f)^{-n}}{f}\right]$$

$$A_{288} = \$1\ 411.29\left[\frac{1 - (1 + .017\ 545\ 5)^{-288}}{.017\ 545\ 5}\right]$$

$= 1\ 411.29\ (56.614\ 194)$

$= \$79\ 899.05$

Amortization Schedule (Example 15.2b)

(1)	(2)	(3) Interest Due at the End of Period	(4) Amount Applied to Principal	(5)
Payment No.	Payment			Balance
0	...	...	...	$80 000.00
1	$1 411.29	$1 403.64	7.65	79 992.35
2	1 411.29	1 403.50	7.79	79 984.56
3	1 411.29	1 403.37	7.92	79 976.64
4	1 411.29	1 403.23	8.06	79 968.58
5	1 411.29	1 403.09	8.20	79 960.38
6	1 411.29	1 402.94	8.35	79 952.03
7	1 411.29	1 402.80	8.49	79 943.54
8	1 411.29	1 402.65	8.64	79 934.90
9	1 411.29	1 402.50	8.79	79 926.11
10	1 411.29	1 402.34	8.95	79 917.16
11	1 411.29	1 402.19	9.10	79 908.06
12	1 411.29	1 402.03	9.26	79 898.80

(c) $A_{nc} = \$79\ 899.05$

$i = 18.5\% = 9.25\%$ (semi-annually)

$c = \dfrac{1}{6}$

$n = 24 \times 12 = 288$ (monthly payments)

$f = (1 + 9.25\%)^{1/6} - 1$

$ = .014\ 854$

$$R = A_{nc} \left[\frac{f}{1 - (1 + f)^{-n}} \right]$$

$$= 79\ 899.05 \left[\frac{.014\ 854}{1 - (1.014\ 854)\ 288} \right]$$

$$= 79\ 899.05\ (.015\ 069\ 7)$$

$$= \$1\ 204.06$$

Thus, the new monthly payment is $1 204.06.

Example 15.2c
Abbotsford Variety Store signed an agreement to repay a loan of $16 000, by equal quarterly payments for 3 years. The interest rate charged is 18% compounded monthly. How much should they pay each quarter?

SOLUTION:

$A_{nc} = \$16\ 000$

$i = \dfrac{18}{12} = 1.5\%$ (per month)

$c = 3$ (interest periods per payment interval)

$n = 3 \times 4 = 12$ (quarters)

$f = (1 + 1.5\%)^3 - 1$

$\quad = .045\ 678\ 4$

$$R = A_{nc}\left[\frac{f}{1 - (1 + f)^{-n}}\right]$$

$$= 16\ 000\left[\frac{.045\ 678\ 4}{1 - (1.045\ 678\ 4)^{-12}}\right]$$

$= 16\ 000\ (.110\ 092\ 2)$

$= \$1\ 761.48$

EXERCISE 15.2 / REFERENCE SECTION: 15.2

Find the size of the periodic payment and the outstanding principal at the indicated time in each of the following problems, without constructing an amortization schedule: (Payments are assumed to be made at the end of each period.)

	Debt	Number of Payments by Amortization	Compound Interest Rate	Required Outstanding Principal
1.	$ 2 000	12, monthly	22% semi-annually	after 5th payment
2.	1 000	12, quarterly	18% semi-annually	after 5th payment
3.	4 000	24, monthly	20% quarterly	after 23rd payment
4.	6 000	8, semi-annually	17.5% quarterly	after 1st payment
5.	8 000	20, quarterly	16% annually	after 7th payment
6.	20 000	45, monthly	15% semi-annually	after 18th payment
7.	200	5, quarterly	19% semi-annually	after 2nd payment
8.	85 500	200, monthly	22.5% semi-annually	after 16th payment

Statement Problems:

9. A debt of $6 000 is to be amortized with four equal quarterly payments. If the interest rate is 22% compounded monthly, what is the size of each payment? Construct an amortization schedule.

10. A loan of $2 000 is to be amortized with five equal monthly payments. The interest rate is 18% compounded semi-annually. Find the semi-annual payment and construct an amortization schedule.

11. A man bought an $8 000 tractor and made a $1 000 down payment. He agreed to pay the balance by making equal payments at the end of every month for a period of two years. The interest charged is 19% compounded semi-annually. Find the outstanding principal after the fourth payment by constructing a partial amortization schedule.

12. A $95 000 house was purchased with a down payment of $5 000 and monthly payments for 20 years. The interest rate is 22% compounded semi-annually. (a) Find the size of the monthly payment. (b) Construct a partial amortization schedule to find the outstanding principal after the third payment.

13. A mortgage for $60 000 is to be amortized over twenty years and is renewable after two years. The interest is 20.5% compounded semi-annually. (a) What is the size of the monthly payments? (b) What is the balance at the end of the two-year term? (c) If the mortgage is renewed at the end of the two years at 18.5% compounded semi-annually what is the size of the new monthly payment? (d) Construct a partial amortization schedule for the first six payments of the two-year term.

15.3 Debt Extinction by Sinking Fund

In some cases, the principal of a long-term investment may be repaid on the maturity date, but the interest is paid periodically when it is due. Since a long-term debt is usually for a large amount, debtors often periodically deposit a sum of money in a fund, known as a SINKING FUND, in order to retire the principal on the maturity date. The periodic deposits need not be of equal amount nor made at equal intervals of time.

However, in this chapter, only examples of periodic deposits made at equal intervals and in equal amounts are considered. The deposits may be made either at the end or at the beginning of each period. The deposits thus form an annuity problem, *and the amount of the annuity is the value of the principal of the debt on the maturity date*. The size of the periodic deposit can be obtained from the ordinary annuity formula $S_n = R_{s\overline{n}|i}$ if the periodic deposit (R) is made at the end of each period.

Since the sinking fund is established for the purpose of paying the principal of the debt at maturity, the periodic interest on the debt should not be paid out of the fund. The interest rate on the debt may or may not equal the rate used for the sinking fund investment. The interest on the debt is called INTEREST EXPENSE, whereas the interest from the sinking fund investment is called sinking fund INTEREST INCOME. It should be emphasized here that in the following discussion *the interest date is also regarded as the date for making the periodic deposit to the fund*. The debtor thus is making two payments on each payment date–one for interest on the debt and the other as a deposit in the fund.

Example 15.3a

A \$4 000 debt is to be repaid at the end of three years. Interest charged is 14% payable at the end of every six months. The debtor establishes a sinking fund which earns 12% interest compounded semi-annually. (a) Find the interest payment on the debt for each six-month period. (b) Construct a sinking fund accumulation schedule.

SOLUTION:

(a) The semi-annual interest payment for the debt is

$\qquad$ 4 000 (14%) $(\frac{1}{2})$ = \$280.00.

(b) The sinking fund accumulation schedule is constructed as follows:

First, the size of each semi-annual deposit in the sinking fund should be found. Here, we have the problem of finding the periodic payment of an ordinary annuity when the amount is known.

$\qquad S_n = \$4\ 000$

$\qquad i = \dfrac{12\%}{2} = 6\%$ (per six months)

$\qquad n = 3 \times 2 = 6$ (semi-annual periods)

$\qquad R = ?$ (per six months)

$\qquad$ Thus, $R = S_n \left[\dfrac{1}{(1 + i)^n - 1} \right]$

$\qquad\qquad = 4\ 000 \left[\dfrac{6\%}{(1 + 6\%)^6 - 1} \right]$

$\qquad\qquad = 4\ 000\ (.143\ 362\ 6)$

$\qquad\qquad = \$573.45$

Sinking Fund Accumulation Schedule (Example 15.3a)

(1)	(2)	(3)	(4)	(5)	(6)
At End of Period (6-month interval)	Interest Income on Sinking Fund	Periodic Deposit in Fund	Periodic Increase in Fund	Sinking Fund Accumulated	Book Value
	$6\% \times (5)^*$		$(2) + (3)$	$(4) + (5)^*$	$\$4\ 000 - (5)$
1	...	$ 573.45	$ 573.45	$ 573.45	$3 426.55
2	$ 34.41	573.45	607.86	1 181.31	2 818.69
3	70.88	573.45	644.33	1 825.64	2 174.36
4	109.53	573.45	682.98	2 508.63	1 491.37
5	150.52	573.45	723.97	3 232.60	767.40
6	193.96	573.45**	767.41	4 000.00	...
Total	559.30	3440.70	4 000.00		

* Of the previous period. For example, $34.41 = 573.45(6\%)$; and $70.88 = 1\ 181.31(6\%)$.
** Correction for one cent discrepancy.

The information in the columns of the sinking fund schedule can be obtained directly as illustrated in the following example.

Example 15.3b
Refer to Example 15.3a. Find (a) the amount in the sinking fund at the end of the fourth period, (b) the sinking fund interest income for the fifth payment period, and (c) the book value of the debt at the end of the fourth period, without constructing a schedule.

SOLUTION:

(a) The amount in the sinking fund at the end of the fourth period.
It is the amount of an annuity of $573.45 payable semi-annually at 12% compounded semi-annually for four periods.
$R = \$573.45$
$i = 6\%$
$n = 4$

$$S_4 = 573.45\left[\frac{(1 + 6\%)^4 - 1}{6\%}\right]$$

$$= 573.45(4.374\ 616)$$
$$= \$2\ 508.62$$

(b) The sinking fund interest income for the fifth payment period.

The principal at the beginning of the fifth payment period is the amount in the sinking fund at the end of the fourth period, $2 508.62.
$I = 2\ 508.62\ (6\%)$
$ = \$150.52$

(c) The book value of the debt at the end of the fourth period.

The BOOK VALUE is the net obligation, which equals the original debt less the accumulated amount in the fund at that time.
$4\ 000 - 2\ 508.62 = \$1\ 491.38$
(one cent difference is due to rounding error)

Example 15.3c
Refer to Example 15.3a. Assume that the debt bears 12% interest. What is the total cost to the debtor at the end of every six months?

SOLUTION:

The periodic (semi-annual) interest for the debt is $4\ 000\ (12\%)\ (\frac{1}{2}) = \$240$.

The periodic deposit in the sinking fund is the same as that in Example 15.3a, $573.45 since the interest rate on the debt does not affect the interest rate of the sinking fund. The total cost = 573.45 + 240 = $813.45.

Note that the cost is the same as the size of the periodic payment by the amortization method of Example 15.1c.

In Example 15.3a, the rate of interest is assumed to be unchanged throughout the three-year period. However, in practice, the interest rate on the sinking fund investment does sometimes change. When it changes, the periodic deposits are adjusted for the difference between the scheduled interest income and the actual interest income.

Example 15.3d
In Example 15.3a assume that the interest rate on the sinking fund was 6% per six-month period during the first and second periods, 7% during the third and fourth periods, and 5% during the fifth and sixth periods. Construct a sinking fund accumulation schedule as a guide for the periodic deposits.

SOLUTION:

Sinking Fund Accumulation Schedule (Example 15.3d)

(1)	(2)	(3)	(4)	(5)	(6)
At End of Period (6 months)	Scheduled Interest Income (See Example 15.3a)	Actual Interest Income (See below)	Interest Discrepancy (2) − (3)	Adjusted Deposit Schedule $ 753.45 + (4)	Periodic Increase in Fund (3) + (5)
1	...	...	...	$ 573.45	$ 573.45
2	$ 34.41	$ 34.41	...	573.45	607.86
3	70.88	82.69	$−11.81	561.64	644.33
4	109.53	127.79	−18.26	555.19	682.98
5	150.52	125.43	25.09	598.54	723.97
6	193.96	161.63	32.32	605.78	767.41*
Total	**$559.30**	**$531.95**	**$ 27.34**	**$3 468.05**	**$4 000.00**

* Corrected for one-cent discrepancy.

The interest in Column (3) is based on the following expression:
    Actual Interest income = Sinking fund accumulated × Interest rate
(See Column (5) of Example 15.3a.)

Thus, the interest for each period is computed as follows:

First period   = 0 (6%) = 0
Second period = 573.45 (6%) = $34.41
Third period   = 1 181.31 (7%) = $82.69
Fourth period   = 1 825.64 (7%) = $127.79
Fifth period   = 2 508.63 (5%) = $125.43
Sixth period   = 3 232.60 (5%) = $161.63

Notice that the values in Column (6), periodic increase in fund, of the above schedule are the same as the values in Column (4) of the sinking fund accumulation schedule of Example 15.3a. The sum of the periodic increases in the fund equals the sum of the actual interest income plus the sum of the adjusted (actual) deposits:

531.95 + 3 468.05 = $4 000.00.

EXERCISE 15.3 / REFERENCE SECTION: 15.3

1. A debt of $7 000 is to be amortized in five equal quarterly payments. Construct an amortization schedule assuming 20% interest compounded quarterly for the debt.

2. A loan of $10 000 is to be discharged by paying $2 000 at the end of each six-month period. The interest rate is 19% compounded semi-annually. Construct an amortization schedule.

3. A debt of $6 000 is to be amortized with payments of $1 500 at the end of every quarter. The interest rate is 15% compounded quarterly. Construct an amortization schedule.

4. White bought a house for $53 000 and made a down payment of $3 000. The balance is to be amortized with payments of $1 020 at the end of each month. The interest rate is 24% compounded semi-annually. What is the outstanding principal after the 55th payment?

5. A debt of $30 000 is to be repaid by making a $1 500 payment at the end of each month. The interest rate is 18% compounded monthly. What is the outstanding principal after the 12th payment?

6. In Problem 4, what are the interest and the principal included in the 56th monthly payment?

7. In Problem 5, find the interest and the principal included in the 13th quarterly payment.

8. A debt of $5 000 is to be repaid at the end of $1\frac{1}{4}$ years under the sinking fund plan with the fund earning 18% interest compounded quarterly. The interest rate on the debt is 10% payable quarterly. (a) Find the interest payment on the debt, and (b) construct a sinking fund schedule.

9. A $7 000 loan will be repaid at the end of two years by a sinking fund which earns 17% compounded semi-annually. The interest on the loan is payable semi-annually at 19%. (a) Find the interest payment on the loan for each semi-annual period, and (b) construct a sinking fund schedule.

10. In Problem 8, assume that the debt bears 18% interest compounded quarterly. (a) What is the total of the interest payment and the sinking fund deposit that must be made by the debtor at the end of every quarter? (b) If each deposit is to be amortized by equal quarterly payments at 18% compounded quarterly, what is the size of each payment?

11. In Problem 9, assume that the interest on the loan is 19% payable semi-annually. (a) What is the total payment, including the interest on the loan and the deposit in the sinking fund, made by the borrower at the end of each semi-annual period? (b) If the loan is to be amortized by equal semi-annual payments at 19% compounded semi-annually, what is the size of each payment?

12. In Problem 8, assume that the interest rate on the sinking fund was $4\frac{1}{2}$% per quarter during the first six months, 5% per quarter during the second six months, and 3% for the last quarter of the borrowing time. Construct a sinking fund accumulation schedule.

13. In Problem 9, assume that the nominal interest rate on the sinking fund was 12% for the first six months, 10% for the second six months, and 14% for the remaining year during the loan period. Construct a sinking fund accumulation schedule.

14. A $15 000 debt is to be discharged at the end of ten years by a sinking fund which is invested at 18% compounded quarterly. Find (a) the amount in the sinking fund and the book value of the debt at the end of six years, and (b) the sinking fund interest income for the first quarter of the seventh year.

15. A man borrowed $5 000 and agreed to repay the principal at the end of three years but to pay interest periodically. He established a sinking fund which earns 24% compounded monthly. Find (a) the amount in the sinking fund and the book value of the debt at the end of two years, and (b) the sinking fund interest income for the first month of the third year.

Glossary

AMORTIZATION method of discharging a debt by making periodic partial payments

BOOK VALUE the net obligation of a debt, which equals the original debt less the accumulated amount in a sinking fund at that time

INTEREST EXPENSE the interest on a debt; may or may not equal the rate used for a sinking fund investment

INTEREST INCOME the interest from a sinking fund investment

SINKING FUND method of discharging a debt by establishing a fund into which periodic deposits are made in order to pay a single sum on the date of maturity

Investment in bonds 16

Introduction

Investors frequently purchase stocks and bonds in an investment market to make profits. STOCK, also called CAPITAL STOCK, represents ownership in a corporation and is divided into shares. Those who purchase a share of stock acquire not only a share of the ownership of the corporation but also the right to receive income in the form of DIVIDENDS. Unlike stocks, BONDS are generally issued by corporations or governmental units for the purpose of *borrowing* funds from a group of creditors. Those who purchase bonds expect the issuing party to repay the principal on a future date, as well as to provide a periodic income in the form of interest during the life of the investment.

The prices of both stocks and bonds fluctuate frequently on the investment market, although the price of bonds fluctuates within a much smaller range than that of stocks. An investor should have the ability to investigate the possibility of making a fair profit and the safety of such investments. An extensive study of stocks and bonds is beyond the scope of this text. The following studies are limited to the mathematical operations peculiar to the investment in bonds.

Note that when an investor purchases or sell stocks through a broker, he usually has to pay a commission or brokerage fee for the broker's services. On the *Toronto Stock Exchange*, for example, the charges for the commissions and fees are based on the market value of each stock, but the rate is different for 100-share lots than for a lot consisting of less than 100 shares. The method of computing the charges is basically the same as the method of computing the commissions and fees for buying and selling merchandise presented in Chapter Seven, Section 7.5.

16.1 Basic Concepts and Terminology

A. TERMS FREQUENTLY USED

Certain terms frequently used in computing various problems concerning the investment in bonds are explained below:

1. FACE VALUE or PAR VALUE. The value stated on the bond, usually called the denomination, such as $1 000.

2. REDEMPTION VALUE. The value that the issuing party pays to the bondholder when the bond is surrendered. A bond is usually redeemed at the maturity date and is paid according to the face value, or is said to be redeemable at par. However, some bonds may be called prior to the date of maturity. The redemption values of some bonds may also be set above par to make the bonds more attractive.

3. BOND RATE or CONTRACT RATE. The interest rate stated on the bond. This rate is used as a basis for computing the interest payment.

4. YIELD RATE or INVESTOR'S RATE. The actual interest rate that is expected by the purchaser of the bond. The yield rate is usually the prevailing rate on the investment market when the bond is purchased and is often not equal to the bond rate.

5. INTEREST DATES. The interest on most bonds is payable semi-annually on the first day of the payable month. Sometimes the interest payment dates are indicated by the initial letters of the months. Thus, if the interest is payable semi-annually on January 1 and July 1, the dates may be abbreviated as J-J; on February 1 and August 1, the initials F-A may be used; etc.

6. PURCHASE PRICE. The purchase price is computed at the yield rate. The purchase price is also the value quoted on the bond market plus accrued interest on the bond, if any.

7. BOND ABBREVIATIONS. The name of the issuing party, the bond rate, and the redemption date of a bond are usually abbreviated in publications. Thus, Gen Cdn Tran 8s 85 means that the bond was issued by General Canadian Transportation Corp., it bears 8% interest, and the date of maturity is 1985.

8. ACCRUED INTEREST. The amount of interest that has been earned on the bond since the last bond interest was paid.

9. FLAT PRICE. The bondholder's selling price.

10. QUOTED PRICE. The flat price of the bond less the accrued interest. The quoted price is often called the "and interest price."

16.2 The Purchase Price of a Bond

An investor may purchase bonds on the interest payment dates or between the interest payment dates. The methods of computing the purchase prices at different times are presented below.

A.   PURCHASE PRICE ON INTEREST DATE

When an investor purchases a bond, he acquires two items:

1. The redemption value which will be realized at a future date; that is, at the redemption or maturity date.
2. The periodic interest payment according to the interest rate contracted on the bond.

Therefore, the purchase price of a bond is the sum of the present values of the two items above. The first item, the redemption value, is computed by use of the compound discount formula $P = S(1 + i)^{-n}$; where P is the present value of the redemption value, S is the redemption value, i is the yield rate (or investor's interest rate), and n is the number of interest periods between the date of purchase and the date of redemption.

The second item, the periodic interest payment is computed by use of formula $A_n = R\left[\dfrac{1 - (1 + i)^{-n}}{i}\right]$; where A_n is the present value of all interest payments, n and i mean the same as n and i in the first item above and R is the periodic interest payment according to the bond contract.

The interest conversion period for the yield rate (investor's rate) is assumed to coincide with the interest payment period for the bond. When the purchase is made on an interest date, the bond interest payment on that date is not included in the purchase price. In summary,

> Purchase Price $= P + A_n$, or
>
> Purchase Price $= S(1 + i)^{-n} + R\left[\dfrac{1 - (1 + i)^{-n}}{i}\right]$ ⟵ *Formula 16-1*

B. CANADA SAVINGS BONDS

Canada Savings Bonds differ from the bonds which are generally traded on the market. This type of bond was first issued during World War II as "Victory Bonds" and has since become an important method of encouraging Canadians to save.

The principal characteristics of these bonds are:
1. They can be cashed at any time for the face value plus accrued interest.
2. They do not rise and fall in price as other bonds do.
3. Although the terms may change (for example, increase in interest rate) the redemption price is the face or par value plus any outstanding interest.
4. They are fully registered and are not transferable or assignable.

The bonds discussed below are bonds which are traded on the market. The price of these bonds is affected by the interest rate at the time of trading.

C. *READING BOND QUOTATIONS*

A bond quotation in a newspaper may be shown as follows:

XYZ Company	bid	ask
12 April 1 – 83 – 90	97.50	98.75

This means that the bond

(a) pays 12% interest per year

(b) matures on April 1, 1990 but the XYZ Company may redeem it any time after April 1, 1983

(c) can be sold for $97.50

(d) can be bought for $98.75.

The price of a bond is usually quoted on the market in terms of bid and ask prices. BID is the highest price any buyer wanted to pay and ASK is the lowest price any seller wanted to take.

In the listings shown the price is the average of the *bid* and *ask* prices and yield is the investor's rate.

Bond prices

TORONTO (CP) - Selected bond quotes on actively traded issues Wednesday provided to the Investment Dealers Association of Canada. Price is the midpoint between the bid and ask quotation.

	Price	Yld	Ch'ge
GOVERNMENT OF CANADA			
Canada 10 Jun 1-84	100.18	9.19	- -
Canada 13 May 1-85-90	106.87	11.42	- -
Canada 15 Mar 15-87	110.00	11.07	- -
Canada 10½ Mar 15-88	98.37	11.00	- -
Canada 11¼ Feb 1-93	97.62	11.68	- -
Canada 9½ Oct 1-01	84.25	11.62	+ ⅛
Canada 11¼ Dec 15-02	94.00	12.06	+ ⅛
Canada 11¾ Feb 1-03	97.50	12.09	+ ⅛
Canada 10¼ Feb 1-04	88.12	11.81	+ ⅛
Canada 12 Mar 1-05	99.12	12.11	- -
PROVINCIALS AND GUARANTEED			
Alta Mun 12¼ Dec 15-02	97.87	12.54	- -
BC Hy 13½ Jan 15-11	104.25	12.87	- -
Man 11¾ Mar 15-93	98.75	11.98	- -
NB Ele 11¾ Feb 8-93	98.00	12.12	- -
Nfld 12⅞ Apr 6-03	99.00	13.01	- -
NS Pow 13½ Dec 1-02	104.00	12.88	- -
Ont Hy 10½ Feb 8-88	97.62	11.24	- -
Ont Hy 12½ Nov 30-02	100.12	12.48	- -
Ont Hy 13 Jan 29-11	102.25	12.70	- -
Quebec 12 Apr 7-93	99.25	12.13	+ ¼
Quebec 13 Apr 7-03	99.37	13.08	+ ⅛
Sask 12¼ Mar 30-03	97.75	12.56	+ ⅛
CORPORATES			
Bell 10½ Jul 15-85	100.25	10.31	- -
Bell 11 Oct 15-04	89.00	12.49	- -
Cdn Util 12 Jul 15-00	95.62	12.63	+ ⅛
IMO 12 Mar 31-93	99.50	12.09	+ ⅛
Shell 11¾ Jan 15-88	101.25	11.34	- -
Transalta 13 Dec 16-97	101.50	12.76	+ ⅛
Westcst 12½ Apr 1-93	100.12	12.10	- -

Example 16.2a

Fred Beilai owns a $1 000, 16% bond redeemable March 1, 1995. Interest is payable semi-annually on March 1 and September 1. How much should an investor pay for the bond on March 1, 1983 if he wishes to earn 17% compounded semi-annually on his investment? The bond is redeemable (a) at par (b) at 105%.

SOLUTION:

(a) The present value of the redemption value is computed as follows:
The redemption value is at par, $1 000, which is due in 12 years (from March 1, 1983 to March 1, 1995).

$$S = \$1\,000$$

$$i = \frac{17\%}{2} = 8\frac{1}{2}\% \text{ (yield rate per six months)}$$

$$n = 12 \times 2 = 24 \text{ (semi-annual interest periods)}$$

$$P = 1\,000\left(1 + 8\frac{1}{2}\%\right)^{-24}$$

$$= 1\,000\,(.141\,151\,8)$$

$$= \$141.151\,8$$

The present value of the interest payments is computed as follows:

$$b = \frac{16\%}{2} = 8\% \text{ (bond rate for six months).}$$

The periodic interest payment according to the bond (or contract) rate is

$$R = 1\ 000\ (.08)$$
$$= \$80 \text{ (per six months).}$$

Thus, $A_n = 80\left[\dfrac{1-(1+i)^{-n}}{i}\right]$

$$= 80\left[\frac{1-(1+8.5\%)^{-24}}{8.5\%}\right]$$

$$= 80\left(\frac{1-.141\ 151\ 8}{.085}\right)$$

$$= 80\left(\frac{.858\ 848\ 2}{.085}\right)$$

$$= 80\ (10.104\ 097)$$
$$= \$808.327\ 76$$

The purchase price is

$$P + A_n = 141.151\ 8 + 808.327\ 76$$
$$= \$949.48.$$

The solution to Example 16.2a may be diagrammed as follows:

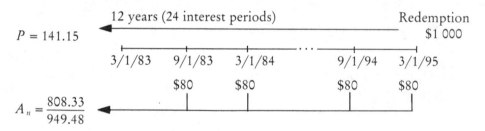

(b)   The present value of the redemption value is computed as follows:
The redemption value is 105% of the face value, or

$$S = 1\ 000\ (1.05)$$
$$= \$1\ 050.$$

The other values are the same as above

$$P = 1\ 050\ (1 + 8.5\%)^{-24}$$
$$= 1\ 050\ (.141\ 151\ 8)$$
$$= \$148.209\ 39$$

The present value of the bond interest payments is the same as above. Thus, the purchase price is

$$148.209\ 39 + 808.327\ 76 = \$956.54.$$

Example 16.2b
The investor's interest rate is 16% compounded semi-annually. Find the purchase price of a $10 000 bond with 17% interest payable semi-annually, and redeemable in six years (a) at par, and (b) at 98%.

SOLUTION:

(a) $S = \$10\ 000$ (at par)

$i = \dfrac{16\%}{2} = 8\%$ (investor rate per six months)

$n = 6 \times 2 = 12$ (semi-annual periods)

$b = \dfrac{17\%}{2} = 8\frac{1}{2}\%$ (bond rate per six months)

$R = 10\ 000\ (.085)$
   $= \$850$

The purchase price

$= 10\ 000\ (1 + 8\%)^{-12} + 850\left[\dfrac{1 - (1 + 8\%)^{-12}}{8\%}\right]$

$= 10\ 000\ (.397\ 113\ 8) + 850\ (7.536\ 078)$
$= 3971.138 + 6405.666$
$= \$10\ 376.80$

(b) $S = 10\ 000\ (98\%)$
     $= \$9\ 800$

The purchase price

$= 9\ 800\ (1 + 8\%)^{-12} + 850\left[\dfrac{1 - (1 + 8\%)^{-12}}{8\%}\right]$

$= 9\ 800\ (.397\ 113\ 8) + 850\ (7.536\ 078)$
$= 3\ 891.715 + 6\ 405.666$
$= \$10\ 297.38$

Example 16.2c
An investor wishes to earn 12% compounded monthly on her investment. How much must she pay for a $100, 11% bond redeemable at par in six years with interest payable semi-annually.

SOLUTION:

$S = \$100$

$i = \dfrac{12\%}{12} = 1\%$ (investor rate per month)

$\quad = 6 \times 2 = 12$ (six month periods)

$b = \dfrac{11\%}{2} = 5.5\%$ (semi-annual bond rate)

$R = \$100\,(.055)$

$\quad = \$5.50$ (semi-annual bond interest)

$r = (1 + 1\%)^6 - 1$

$\quad = 6.152\,02\%$ (yield rate per six months)

The purchase price

$$= 100\,(1 + 6.152\,02\%)^{-12} + 5.50\left[\frac{1 - (1 + 6.152\,02\%)^{-12}}{6.152\,02\%}\right]$$

$$= 100\,(.488\,495\,9) + 5.50\left(\frac{1 - .488\,495\,9}{.061\,520\,2}\right)$$

$$= 48.849\,59 + 5.50\left(\frac{.511\,504\,2}{.061\,520\,2}\right)$$

$$= 48.849\,59 + 5.50\,(8.314\,410\,3)$$

$$= 48.849\,59 + 45.729\,257$$

$$= \$94.58$$

EXERCISE 16.2A / REFERENCE SECTIONS: A–C

Find the purchase price of the bond in each of the following problems:

	Par Value	Redemption Value	Bond Rate	Bond Interest Dates	Time Before Redemption	Yield (Investor's) Rate, Compounded Semi-Annually
1.	$1 000	at par	12%	J–J	5 years	15%
2.	1 000	110%	8%	F–A	$4\frac{1}{2}$ years	$6\frac{1}{2}\%$
3.	2 000	95%	15%	M–S	6 years	12%
4.	4 000	at par	8%	A–O	8 years	16%
5.	600	105%	15%	M–N	$7\frac{1}{2}$ years	17%
6.	5 000	98%	11%	J–D	8 years	14%
7.	6 000	at par	12%	A–O	12 years	11%
8.	400	at par	8%	M–N	7 years	$6\frac{1}{2}\%$

Statement Problems:

9. A $10 000, 12% bond will be redeemed on January 1, 1997. Interest is payable semi-annually on January 1 and July 1. Find the purchase price of the bond if the date of purchase is July 1, 1983, the yield rate is 15% compounded semi-annually, and the bond is redeemable (a) at par, and (b) at 108%.

10. Find the purchase price of $1 000, 11% bond, if it is bought to yield 13% compounded semi-annually. The bond interest is payable semi-annually, and the bond is redeemable at par in (a) $4\frac{1}{2}$ years, (b) 8 years.

11. The investor's interest rate is 15% compounded semi-annually. Find the purchase price of a $2 000 bond with 11% interest payable semi-annually, and redeemable at par in (a) 4 years, (b) 8 years.

12. An $8 000, 12% bond will be redeemed on April 1, 1990. Interest is payable semi-annually on April 1 and October 1. Find the purchase price of the bond if the date of purchase is April 1, 1983, the yield rate is 15% compounded semi-annually, and the bond is redeemable (a) at par, and (b) at 95%.

D.   PURCHASE PRICE BETWEEN INTEREST DATES

When a bond is purchased between interest dates, the purchase price on the interest date that immediately precedes the purchase date is first computed. The interest at the yield rate for the period between the interest date and the purchase date is then added to obtain the purchase price on the purchase date. *Hereafter, unless otherwise specified, the bond is assumed to be redeemable at par, the face value*. This assumption is made in order to simplify the computation and to meet most practical situations.

Example 16.2d
Refer to Example 16.2a. If the bond is bought on April 30, 1983 what is the purchase price of the bond?

SOLUTION:

The purchase price on the interest date, March 1, 1983 which immediately precedes the purchase date is $949.48. See the solution for Example 16.2a(a). The interest at the yield rate for the period between the interest date (March 1, 1983) and the purchase date (April 30, 1983) is computed as follows:
The period is 60 days, yield rate is 17%, the principal for computing the interest is $949.48. Thus

$I = 949.48 \ (17\%) \ (60/365) = \$26.53.$

The purchase price on April 30, 1983 is

$949.48 + 26.53 = \$976.01.$

On the other hand, the purchase price is the bondholder's selling price. The price should include the incurred, yet not paid, bond interest, called *accrued interest*, for the period from March 1, 1983 to the purchase date (or for 60 days). The accrued interest at the bond rate is computed as follows:

$1 \ 000 \ (16\%) \ (60/365) = \$26.30.$

The accrued interest is the seller's income since he owns the bond during the 60 days. Thus, the selling price of $976.01 may be considered to include two items: (1) the accrued interest at the bond rate, $26.30 and (2) the net price for the bond $949.71 (or 976.01 − 26.30).

The purchase price (or the bondholder's selling price) of $976.01 is frequently referred to by a bond house as the *flat price*, and the net price of the bond, $949.71, without including the accrued interest, as the *quoted price*.

The above illustration is diagrammed as follows:

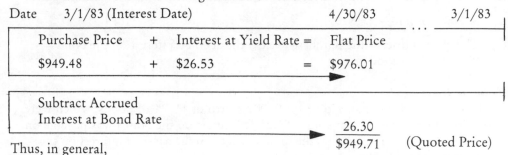

Thus, in general,

Flat price (purchase price) = Quoted price + Accrued interest on a bond.

However, if the bond is purchased on an interest date, there is no accrued interest. Thus,

Flat Price (purchase price on the interest date) = Quoted price.

Example 16.2e
A $1 000, 6% bond, redeemable in six years and two months, interest payable semi-annually, is bought to yield 7% compounded semi-annually. What are (a) the purchase price, (b) the accrued interest on the bond, and (c) the quoted price?

SOLUTION:

(a) The interest date immediately preceding the purchase date is six years and six months (13 semi-annual periods) before redemption. The purchase price on the interest date is computed as follows:

Yield rate $(i) = \dfrac{7\%}{2} = 3\dfrac{1}{2}\%$ (per six months)

$R = 1\,000 \times 6\% \times \dfrac{1}{2}$

$\quad = \$30$

$n = 6\dfrac{1}{2} \times 2 = 13$ (semi-annual periods)

The purchase price

$= 1\,000 \left(1 + 3\dfrac{1}{2}\% \right)^{-13} + 30\,a_{\overline{13}|\,3\frac{1}{2}\%}$

$= 1\,000\,(0.639\,404) + 30\,(10.302\,7)$

$= 639.404 + 309.081$

$= 948.485$, rounded to $948.49

For the four months after the last interest date, the interest on the purchase price based on the yield rate is $948.49(7\%)\left(\dfrac{4}{12}\right) = \$22.13.$

The purchase price on the purchase date, six years and two months before redemption is $948.49 + 22.13 = \$970.62.$

(b) According to the bond contract, the accrued interest for the four-month period
is $1\ 000\ (6\%)\left(\dfrac{4}{12}\right) = \$20$.

(c) The quoted price = the purchase price – the accrued interest on the bond =
970.62 – 20 = \$950.62.

Example 16.2f
On February 9, 1984 a man acquired \$10 000 worth of 11.5% of bonds, which were
quoted on the market on that date at 92.25%. Interest on the bonds was payable on
May 1 and November 1. Find (a) the quoted price, (b) the accrued interest on the
bonds, and (c) the purchase price (or flat price).

SOLUTION:

(a) The quoted price is at 92.25% of the face value.
Thus, the quoted price
= 10 000 (92.25%)
= 10 000 (.9225)
= \$9 225.

(b) The accrued interest on the bonds at the bond rate for the period from November 1, 1983 to February 9, 1984, or 100 days (during which time the seller owns
the bonds) is computed as follows:
$$10\ 000\ (11.5\%)\left(\frac{100}{365}\right) = \$315.07.$$

(c) The purchase price
= the quoted price + the accrued interest
= 9 225 + 315.07 = \$9 540.07.

EXERCISE 16.2B / REFERENCE SECTION: D

In each of the following problems find (a) the purchase price, (b) the accrued
interest on the bond, and (c) the quoted price:

	Par Value	Bond Rate Payable Semi-annually	Time Before Redemption	Yield Rate, Compounded Semi-annually
1.	\$ 4 000	16%	5 years and 1 month	15%
2.	2 000	12%	4 years and 9 months	11%
3.	5 000	9%	6 years and 4 months	10%
4.	6 000	11%	8 years and 2 months	13%
5.	900	8%	7 years and 5 months	9%
6.	700	8%	10 years and 4 months	10%
7.	10 000	11%	12 years and 3 months	12%
8.	25 000	13%	3 years and 5 months	15%

Statement Problems:

9. A $3 000, 15% bond, redeemable in five years and three months, interest payable semi-annually, is bought to yield 17% compounded semi-annually. What are (a) the purchase price, and (b) the quoted price?

10. A $3 500, 16% bond will be redeemed on May 1, 1993. Interest is payable semi-annually on May 1 and November 1. Find the purchase price of the bond if the date of purchase is July 1, 1983, and the yield rate is 17% compounded semi-annually.

11. A $7 000, 15.5% bond, interest payable semi-annually on March 1 and September 1, redeemable on March 1, 1990 is bought to yield 16.25% compounded semi-annually on November 15, 1986. Find the purchase price.

12. Refer to Problem 11. What would be the purchase price of the bond if the yield rate were 14.5% compounded semi-annually?

13. On May 31, a man purchased a $2 500 bond. The interest rate on the bond was 12% payable semi-annually on April 1 and October 1. The bond was quoted on the market at 80%. Find (a) the quoted price, (b) the accrued interest, and (c) the purchase price of the bond.

14. Refer to Problem 13. If the bond were quoted on the market on May 31 at 110%, what are the new answers to (a), (b), and (c)?

16.3 Bond Premium and Discount

A.   GENERAL COMPUTATION

In Example 16.2a, it was found that a $1 000, 16% bond, interest payable semi-annually, redeemable on March 1, 1995, was sold on March 1, 1983 for $949.48 to give the purchaser a yield rate of 17% compounded semi-annually. The purchase price is $50.52 less than the face value (which is now assumed to be equal to the redemption value) as shown below:

1 000 − 949.48 = $50.52 (discount).

When the purchase price is smaller than the face value, the difference is called the DIS-COUNT on the bond. A bond is purchased at a discount when the bond interest rate is smaller than the yield rate. The deficit interest for the above example is computed as follows:

Periodic bond interest payment
= bond face value × bond interest rate per interest period
= 1000 (16%) ($\frac{1}{2}$) = $80
Periodic bond interest based on yield rate
= bond face value × yield rate per interest period
= 1 000 (17%) ($\frac{1}{2}$) = $85
The deficit per interest period
= $85 − $80 = $5.00

According to the face value, the investor will sustain a $5.00 loss each interest period for twelve years, or a total of 24 losses of $5.00 each. The present value of the annuity which is formed by the periodic deficits is computed by use of the formula

$$A_n = R\left[\frac{1-(1+i)^{-n}}{i}\right] \quad \text{(at yield rate)}$$

$n = 12 \times 2 = 24$ (losses)

$$A_{12} = 5.00\left[\frac{1-(1+8\tfrac{1}{2}\%)^{-24}}{8\tfrac{1}{2}\%}\right]$$

$$= \$5.00 \,(10.104\ 097)$$

$$= \$50.52$$

Thus, the *discount is the present value of an annuity which is formed by the periodic deficit income*. The discount must be subtracted from the face value to obtain the purchase price, as shown below:

Purchase = face value − discount = 1 000 − 50.52 = $949.48

On the other hand, it was found that a $10 000, 17% bond, interest payable semi-annually, redeemable in six years, was sold at $10 376.80 to give the purchaser a yield rate of 16% compounded semi-annually. (See Example 16.2b in Section 16.2.) When the purchase price is larger than the face value, the difference is called the PRE-MIUM on the bond. A bond is purchased at a premium when the bond interest rate is larger than the yield rate. The excess interest for the above example is computed as follows:

Periodic bond interest payment
= bond face value × bond interest rate per interest period
= 10 000 (.085) = $850
Periodic bond interest based on yield rate
= bond face value × yield rate per interest period
= 10 000 (.08) = $800

The excess per interest period = 850 − 800 = $50.00. According to the face value, the investor will gain $50.00 excess each interest period for six years, or a total of 12 excess gains of $50.00 each. The present value of the annuity which is formed by the periodic excess gains is computed by use of the formula

$$A_n = R\left[\frac{1-(1+i)^{-n}}{i}\right], \quad \text{where}$$

$R = \$50$ (the periodic excess)

$i = \dfrac{16\%}{2} = 8\%$ (yield rate)

$n = 6 \times 2 = 12$ (excess gains)

$$A_{12} = 50\left[\frac{1-(1+8\%)^{-12}}{8\%}\right]$$

$$= 50(7.536\ 078)$$

$$= \$376.80$$

Thus, *the premium is the present value of an annuity which is formed by the periodic excess income*. The premium must be added to the face value to obtain the purchase price, as shown below:

Purchase price = face value + premium = 10 000 + 376.80 = $10 376.80

In summary, let i = yield rate per interest period
b = bond rate per interest period
F = face value of bond

When b is greater than i:

$$\text{Premium} = (Fb - Fi)_{a_{\overline{n}|i}} = F(b - i)_{a_{\overline{n}|i}} \qquad \longleftarrow \textit{Formula 16-2}$$

When b is smaller than i:

$$\text{Discount} = (Fi - Fb)_{a_{\overline{n}|i}} = F(i - b)_{a_{\overline{n}|i}} \qquad \longleftarrow \textit{Formula 16-3}$$

When b is equal to i, there is no premium or discount, and the purchase price = the face value.

Example 16.3a
A $10 000, 13% bond, redeemable in 10 years, interest payable semi-annually, is bought to yield 12% interest compounded semi-annually. Find (a) the premium, and (b) the purchase price.

SOLUTION:

$b = \dfrac{13\%}{2} = 6\dfrac{1}{2}\%$ (per six months)

$i = \dfrac{12\%}{2} = 6\%$ (per six months)

$n = 10 \times 2 = 20$ (semi-annual payments)
$F = \$10\ 000$

Since the bond rate is greater than the yield rate, there must be a premium.

(a) Premium = $10\ 000\ (6.5\% - 6\%) \left[\dfrac{1 - (1 + 6\%)^{-20}}{6\%} \right]$

$= 10\ 000\ (.5\%)\ (11.469\ 921) = \$573.50$

(b) Purchase price = $10\ 000 + 573.50 = \$10\ 573.50$

Example 16.3b
A $10 000, 17% bond, redeemable in 10 years, interest payable semi-annually, is bought to yield 18% interest compounded semi-annually. Find (a) the discount, and (b) the purchase price.

SOLUTION:

$$b = \frac{17\%}{2} = 8.5\%$$

$$i = \frac{18\%}{2} = 9\%$$

$$n = 10 \times 2 = 20$$

$$F = \$10\ 000$$

Since the bond rate is smaller than the yield rate, there must be a discount.

(a)   Discount $= 10\ 000\ (9\% - 8.5\%)\left[\dfrac{1 - (1 + 9\%)^{-20}}{9\%}\right]$

   $= 10\ 000\ (.5\%)\ (9.128\ 545\ 7) = \$456.43$

(b)   Purchase price $= 10\ 000 - 456.43 = \$9\ 543.57$

Example 16.3c

Refer to Example 16.3b. If the bond is bought to yield 17% interest compounded semi-annually, find (a) the premium or the discount, and (b) the purchase price.

SOLUTION:

(a) $b = 8.5\%$
   $i = 8.5\%$
   Since the bond rate is equal to the yield rate, there is no premium or discount.

(b)   The purchase price is the face value, \$10 000.

NOTE: When the redemption value is not at par, the following expressions may be obtained by a method of reasoning similar to that in the illustrations above:

$$\boxed{\text{Premium} = (\text{Face value} \times b) - (\text{Redemption value} \times i)_{a_{\overline{n}|\,i}}}\qquad \longleftarrow Formula\ 16\text{-}4$$

   Purchase Price = Redemption value + premium

The premium may be thought of as a positive figure, whereas the discount may be thought of as a negative premium. In other words, when the premium becomes a negative figure, it is a discount. Or,

   – Premium = Discount

   Example 16.2a(b) of Section 16.2 may be computed as follows:

$$\text{Premium} = [1\ 000\ (8\%) - 1\ 050\ (8.5\%)]\left[\frac{1 - (1 + 8.5\%)^{-24}}{8.5\%}\right]$$

   $= (80 - 89.25)(10.104\ 097) = -\$93.46$

– Premium = Discount

Purchase price $= 1\ 050 - 93.46 = \$956.54$

Example 16.2b(b) of Section 16.2 may be computed as follows:

Premium $= [10\ 000\ (8.5\%) - 9\ 800\ (8\%)]\left[\dfrac{1 - (1 + 8\%)^{-12}}{8\%}\right]$

$\quad\quad = (850 - 784)(7.536\ 078)$

$\quad\quad = 66\ (7.536\ 078)$

$\quad\quad = \$497.38$

Purchase price $= \$9\ 800 + \$497.38 = \$10\ 297.38$

EXERCISE 16.3A / REFERENCE SECTION: A

Find (a) the premium or the discount, and (b) the purchase price in each of the following problems:

	Par Value	Bond Rate Payable Semi-Annually	Time Before Redemption	Yield Rate Compounded Semi-annually
1.	$ 4 000	15%	5 years	17%
2.	2 000	11%	$4\frac{1}{2}$ years	13%
3.	5 000	14%	6 years	15%
4.	6 000	13%	8 years	12%
5.	900	10%	7 years	9%
6.	700	9%	10 years	8%
7.	10 000	15%	12 years	14%
8.	25 000	14%	7 years	11%

Statement Problems:

9. A $3 000, 15% bond, redeemable in eight years, interest payable semi-annually, is bought to yield 14% interest compounded semi-annually. Find (a) the premium or the discount, and (b) the purchase price.

10. Refer to Problem 9. If the yield rate is 16% compounded semi-annually, find the answers to (a) and (b).

11. Compute Problems 2, 3, 5, 6 of Exercise 16.2A by the method used in Section 16.3A, (Formula 16-4).

B. AMORTIZATION OF PREMIUM

When an investor purchases a bond at premium, he should be aware that the premium is not redeemable on the maturity date of the bond. The premium is recovered periodically, through the interest receipts on the bond. Thus, the book value of the bond investment should be reduced accordingly in the investor's record, until the premium becomes zero on the maturity date. The process of reducing the book value of a bond investment to par by periodic deductions is called *amortization of the bond premium*.

Example 16.3d

A $10 000, 14% bond, interest payable semi-annually, redeemable in $3\frac{1}{2}$ years, is bought to yield 13% interest compounded semi-annually. Find the purchase price and construct a schedule for amortization of the premium.

SOLUTION:

$$b = \frac{14\%}{2} = 7\%$$

$$i = \frac{13\%}{2} = 6\frac{1}{2}\%$$

b is greater than i

$$n = 3\frac{1}{2} \times 2 = 7 \text{ (semi-annual payments)}$$

$$\text{Premium} = 10\ 000 \left(7\% - 6\frac{1}{2}\% \right) \left[\frac{1 - (1 + 6\frac{1}{2}\%)^{-7}}{6\frac{1}{2}\%} \right]$$

$$= 50 (5.484\ 519\ 8)$$
$$= \$274.23$$

Purchase price = 10 000 + 274.23 = $10 274.23

The following schedule shows that the periodic premium amortization is in the excess of the interest receipt from the bond over the investor's yield. An investor is willing to purchase a bond at a premium because he can recover the premium through the high periodic interest receipts from the bond.

Amortization Schedule for Bond Premium (Example 16.3d)

(1)	(2)	(3)	(4)	(5)
At End of Interest Period	Interest Receipt from Bond	Yield Investor's Interest	Premium Amortization	Bond Book Value
	$10 000 × 7%	(5) × $6\frac{1}{2}\%$	(2) − (3)	(5) − (4)
0	...	...	...	$10 274.23
1	$ 700	$ 667.82	$ 32.18	10 242.06
2	700	665.73	34.27	10 207.79
3	700	663.51	36.49	10 171.30
4	700	661.13	38.87	10 132.43
5	700	658.61	41.39	10 091.04
6	700	655.92	44.08	10 046.95
7	700	653.05	46.95	10 000.00
Total	$4 900	$4 625.77	$274.23	

NOTE:

1. The investor receives:

	$ 4 900.00	(interest)
	10 000.00	(redemption value)
	14 900.00	

    The investor paid: 10 274.23   (purchase price)

    The investor's net gain: 4 625.77   (see Column (3))

2. According to the purchase price and the yield rate, the excess income of the first period is \$32.18. It is computed as follows:
   The investor's expected interest for the first period is
   $$10\ 274.23 \times 6\tfrac{1}{2}\% = \$667.82.$$
   However, the actual interest receipt for the first period from the bond is
   $$10\ 000 \times 7\% = \$700.$$
   The first period excess income is
   $$700 - 667.82 = \$32.18.$$

The excess income is subtracted from the original purchase price to obtain the book value of the bond at the end of the first period.
$$10\ 274.23 - 32.18 = 10\ 242.05$$

C. ACCUMULATION OF DISCOUNT

When an investor purchases a bond at discount, he should know that the entire face value of the bond is redeemable to the bondholder on the maturity date. The investor receives a smaller periodic interest from the bond than he would receive if the interest rate on the bond were equal to the current market interest rate. However, the periodic deficits are recovered through receipt of the full redemption value. Each of the periodic deficits is added to the original purchase price listed in the investor's records. The book value increases periodically and will be equal to par on the maturity date. The process of increasing the book value of a bond investment to par by periodic additions is called ACCUMULATION of the bond discount.

Example 16.3e
A \$10 000, 14% bond, interest payable semi-annually, redeemable in $3\tfrac{1}{2}$ years, is bought to yield 15% interest compounded semi-annually. Find the purchase price, and construct a schedule for accumulation of the discount.

SOLUTION:

$$i = \frac{15\%}{2} = 7.5\%$$

$$b = \frac{14\%}{2} = 7\%$$

i is greater than b

$$n = 3\frac{1}{2} \times 2$$

= 7 (semi-annual interest periods)

$$\text{Discount} = 10\ 000\left(7\frac{1}{2}\% - 7\%\right)\left[\frac{1 - (1 + 7.5\%)^{-7}}{7.5\%}\right]$$

$$= 50(5.296\ 601\ 3) = \$264.83$$

Purchase price = 10 000 − 264.83 = \$9 735.17

Accumulation Schedule for Bond Discount (Example 16.3e)

(1) At End of Interest Period	(2) Interest Receipt from Bond $10\ 000 \times 7\%$	(3) Yield Investor's Interest $(5) \times 7.5\%$	(4) Discount Accumulation $(3) - (2)$	(5) Bond Book Value $(5) + (4)$
0	...	...	...	\$ 9 735.17
1	\$ 700	\$ 730.14	\$ 30.14	9 765.31
2	700	732.40	32.40	9 797.71
3	700	734.83	34.83	9 832.53
4	700	737.44	37.44	9 869.97
5	700	740.25	40.25	9.910.22
6	700	743.27	43.27	9 953.49
7	700	746.51	46.51	10 000.00
Total	\$4 900	\$5 164.84	\$264.84	

NOTE:

1. According to the purchase price and the yield rate, the deficit of the first period is \$30.14. It is computed as follows:

   The investor's expected interest for the first period is
   9 735.17 × 7.5% = \$730.14.

   However, the actual interest receipt for the first period from the bond is only
   10 000 × 7% = \$700.00.

The first period deficit is
    730.14 − 700.00 = $30.14.
The deficit is added to the original purchase price to obtain the book value of the bond at the end of the first period:
    9 735.17 + 30.14 = $9 765.31.

2. The book value of a bond on any interest date is the purchase price of the bond on that date. Thus, the book value may be checked by the method used in finding the purchase price. (See Section 16.2A or 16.3A.) For example, the book value at the end of the 5th period in Example 16.3e may be computed as follows: $n = 2$, which represents the number of interest periods from the end of the 5th period to the redemption date.

$$\text{Discount} = 10\ 000(7.5\% - 7\%)\left[\frac{1 - (1 + 7.5\%)^{-2}}{7.5\%}\right]$$

$$= 50\ (1.795\ 565\ 2)$$
$$= \$89.78$$

Book value (= Purchase price) = 10 000 − 89.78 − $9 910.22

It can be determined from the above schedule that the periodic discount accumulation is the deficit of the interest receipt from the bond in relation to the investor's yield. An investor is willing to purchase a bond that offers smaller periodic interest payments than those offered on the prevailing investment market, because he knows that the deficits may be accumulated to an amount equal to the discount and may be recovered through redemption of the bond on the maturity date.

EXERCISE 16.3B / REFERENCE SECTIONS: B–C

1. A $4 000 bond, interest at 11% payable semi-annually, redeemable in $2\frac{1}{2}$ years, is purchased to yield 15% interest compounded semi-annually. Find the purchase price, and construct a schedule for amortization of the premium.
2. A $3 000 bond, interest at 9% payable semi-annually, redeemable in three years, is bought to yield 11% interest compounded semi-annually. Find the purchase price, and construct a schedule for amortization of the premium.
3. Refer to Problem 1. If the yield rate is 10% compounded semi-annually, find the purchase price and construct a schedule for accumulation of the discount.
4. Refer to Problem 2. If the yield rate is 8% compounded semi-annually, find the purchase price and construct a schedule for accumulation of the discount.
5. An $8 000, 16% bond will be redeemed on April 1, 1986. Interest is payable semi-annually on April 1 and October 1. The bond was bought on April 1, 1976, to yield an interest rate of 15% compounded semi-annually. Find the book value of the bond on April 1, 1979. (A schedule is not required).
6. Refer to Problem 5. If the yield rate were 17% compounded semi-annually, what would be the book value of the bond on April 1, 1984? (A schedule is not required.)

16.4 Approximate Yield Rate on Bond Investment

When an investor purchases a bond on the market, the bond is usually listed at a quoted price. If the yield rate is not indicated, it should be determined by the investor so that he can decide which one of several bonds is the best investment, or know if the interest payment is what he had expected. This information may be found *approximately* as discussed below.

A. AVERAGE INVESTMENT METHOD

Under the *average investment method*, the yield rate is obtained by dividing the annual income by the average annual investment.

$$\text{Yield rate (approximate)} = \frac{\text{Annual income}}{\text{Average annual investment}}$$

Here,

$$\text{Average annual investment} = \frac{\text{Beginning investment} + \text{Ending investment}}{2}, \text{or,}$$

$$= \frac{\text{Quoted price} + \text{Redemption value}}{2}$$

$$\frac{\text{Average income}}{\text{per interest period}} = \frac{\text{Total Interest receipts} - \text{Premium}}{\text{Number of interest periods}}$$

$$\text{Discount} = -\text{Premium}$$

Example 16.4a
A $1 000, 16% bond, redeemable in five years, interest payable annually, is bought at the quoted price of $1 063. What is the nominal yield rate?

SOLUTION:

The annual income is computed first:

Annual interest receipts = 1 000 (.16) = $160 (a gain)

$$\text{Annual premium amortization} = \frac{(1\ 063 - 1\ 000)}{5} = \$12.60 \text{ (a loss)}$$

The annual income = 160 − 12.60 = $147.40 (a gain)

$$\text{The average annual investment} = \frac{(1\ 063 + 1\ 000)}{2} = \$1\ 031.50$$

$$\text{The nominal yield rate} = \frac{147.40}{1\ 031.50} = .142\ 898\ 7, \text{ or } 14.289\ 87\%$$

NOTE: The average annual investment may be computed as follows:

$$\frac{(1\ 063.00 + 1\ 050.40 + 1\ 037.80 + 1\ 025.20 + 1\ 012.60 + 1\ 000.00)}{6} = \frac{6\ 189}{6} = \$1\ 031.50$$

The annual investments form an arithmetic progression, whose common difference is the annual premium amortization $12.60.

Example 16.4b

A $1 000, 15% bond, redeemable in eight years, interest payable semi-annually, is bought at the quoted price of $970. What is the nominal yield rate?

SOLUTION:

The average income per interest period is first computed.

$$\text{Interest each 6 months} = \$1\ 000\ (.15) \left(\frac{1}{2}\right)$$

$$= \$75 \text{ (a gain)}$$

Number of interest periods = 8 × 2 = 16
Total interest receipts = $75 × 16 = $1 200 (a gain)
Total discount accumulation = 1000 − 970

$$= \$30 \text{ (a gain)}$$

$$\text{Average income per interest period} = \frac{1\ 200 + 30}{16}$$

$$= \$76.88$$

$$\text{Average annual investment} = \frac{970 + 1\ 000}{2}$$

$$= \$985$$

$$\text{Approximate yield per six months} = \frac{76.88}{985}$$

Nominal yield = .078 050 8 × 2
$$= .156\ 101\ 5 \text{ or } 15.610\ 15\%$$

EXERCISE 16.4 / REFERENCE SECTION: A

Find the approximate nominal yield rate in each of the following problems:

	Par Value	Bond Rate Payable Semi-Annually	Time Before Redemption	Quoted Price
1.	$1 000	17%	15 years	$1 240
2.	2 000	16%	10 years	2 300
3.	2 500	12%	7 years	2 360
4.	3 000	13%	6 years	2 820
5.	4 000	18%	14 years	4 350
6.	5 000	11%	5 years	4 780
7.	3 500	12%	4 years	3 380
8.	500	15%	12 years	560

Statement Problems:

9. A $1 000, 12% bond, interest payable semi-annually, redeemable on August 1, 1987, is bought at the quoted price of $920 on August 1, 1979. What is the nominal yield rate?

10. A $2 000, 13% bond is to be redeemed on September 1, 1989. Interest is payable semi-annually on March 1 and September 1. If the bond is quoted at 96(%) on March 1, 1979, what is the nominal yield rate?

11. Refer to Problem 9. If the bond were bought at the quoted price of $1 080 on August 1, 1979, what would be the nominal yield rate compounded semi-annually?

12. Refer to Problem 10. If the bond were quoted at 104(%) on March 1, 1979, what would be the nominal yield rate compounded semi-annually?

16.5 Other Types of Bonds

A. ANNUITY BONDS

An ANNUITY BOND is a contract in which the issuer promises to pay both the principal and the interest periodically until the entire debt is paid.

Example 16.5a

An annuity bond of $5 000 is to be repaid in ten equal semi-annual payments, principal and interest included. The bond interest rate is 16% compounded semi-annually. Assume that the yield rate is 18% compounded semi-annually. Find the purchase price (a) now, and (b) after the sixth payment is made.

SOLUTION:

(a) First, the size of the ten semi-annual payments should be determined. The method to follow is the same as the one used in finding the size of the payments in an ordinary annuity problem when the present value ($5 000 in this example) is known. (See Chapter Twelve, Section 12.4.)

$A_n = \$5\ 000$

$b = \dfrac{16\%}{2} = 8\%$ (*bond interest rate* per six months)

$n = 10$ (semi-annual payments)

$R = ?$ (per six months)

(Note: Substitute the value of b for i in this formula.)

Substituting the values in the formula

$$R = A_n \left[\frac{i}{1 - (1 + i)^{-n}} \right]$$

$$= 5\ 000 \left[\frac{8\%}{1 - (1 + 8\%)^{-10}} \right]$$

$$= 5\ 000\,(.149\ 029\ 5)$$

$$= \$745.15$$

Second, find the present value of an annuity of $745.15 payable (to the purchaser) at the end of every six months, for ten payments, at the *yield rate* of 18% compounded semi-annually.

$A_n = ?$

$R = \$745.15$

$i = \dfrac{18\%}{2} = 9\%$ (*yield rate* per six months)

$n = 10$(semi-annual payments)

Substituting the above values in the formula:

$$A_n = R\left[\frac{1-(1+i)^{-n}}{i}\right]$$

$$A_{10} = 745.15\left[\frac{1-(1+9\%)^{-10}}{9\%}\right]$$

$$= 745.15\,(6.417\ 657\ 7)$$

$$= \$4\ 782.12$$

(b) Since the bond is purchased after the sixth payment, the annuity is formed by the remaining four semi-annual payments of $745.15 each. The present value of the annuity is computed as follows:

$n = 4$

$i = 9\%$ (yield rate)

$$A_4 = 745.15\left[\frac{1-(1+9\%)^{-4}}{9\%}\right]$$

$$= 745.15\,(3.239\ 719\ 9)$$

$$= \$2\ 414.08$$

B. SERIAL BONDS

When the bonds in an issue are redeemable periodically on a series of specified due dates, the bonds are called SERIAL BONDS. According to the different due dates, a serial bond may be thought of as several groups of bonds combined in one issue. Thus, the purchase price of a serial bond is obtained by totalling the purchase prices of the individual groups of bonds.

Example 16.5b

A three-year, 8% bond for $15 000 provides that the bond is to be redeemed at the end of each year by payments of $5 000 each and that the interest is to be paid semi-annually. If the bond is purchased now to yield 7% compounded semi-annually, what is the purchase price?

SOLUTION:

$b = \dfrac{8\%}{2} = 4\%$ (per six months)

$i = \dfrac{7\%}{2} = 3\dfrac{1}{2}\%$ (per six months)

Since b is greater than i, there must be a premium. The excess of the periodic bond interest payment over the semi-annual yield for a \$5 000 bond is

$$5\ 000\ (4\%) - 5\ 000\ (3\tfrac{1}{2}\%) = 5\ 000\ (4\% - 3\tfrac{1}{2}\%)$$
$$= 5\ 000(\tfrac{1}{2}\%)$$
$$= \$25\ (\text{per six months}).$$

Use the premium method, Formula 16-2, as follows:

The purchase price for the \$5 000 bond which is due in one year is

$$5\ 000 + 25\,a_{\overline{2}|\,3\frac{1}{2}\%} = 5\ 000 + 25(1.899\ 7)$$
$$= 5\ 000 + 47.493 = \$5\ 047.493.$$

The purchase price for the \$5 000 bond which is due in two years is

$$5\ 000 + 25\,a_{\overline{4}|\,3\frac{1}{2}\%} = 5\ 000 + 25(3.673\ 1)$$
$$= 5\ 000 + 91.828 = \$5\ 091.828.$$

The purchase price for the \$5 000 bond which is due in three years is

$$5\ 000 + 25\,a_{\overline{6}|\,3\frac{1}{2}\%} = 5\ 000 + 25(5.328\ 6)$$
$$= 5\ 000 + 133.215 = \$5\ 133.215.$$

The total purchase price is

$$5\ 047.493 + 5\ 091.828 + 5\ 133.215 = \$15\ 272.54.$$

EXERCISE 16.5 / REFERENCE SECTIONS: A–B

1. A \$3 000 annuity bond is to be repaid in eight equal semi-annual payments, principal and interest included. The bond rate is 15% compounded semi-annually. Find the purchase price (a) now, and (b) after the fifth payment is made. Assume that the yield rate is 16% compounded semi-annually.

2. A \$4 000 annuity bond is to be repaid by twelve equal semi-annual payments, principal and interest included. The bond rate is 17% compounded semi-annually. Assume that the yield rate is 15%. Find the purchase price (a) now, and (b) after the ninth payment is made.

3. Refer to Problem 1. Assume that the yield rate is 14% compounded semi-annually. What are the answers to (a) and (b)?

4. Refer to Problem 2. Assume that the yield rate is 18% compounded semi-annually. What are the answers to (a) and (b)?

5. A 12% serial bond of \$18 000, interest payable semi-annually, is to be redeemed in three annual instalments of \$6 000 each. The bond is bought on the interest date, which is one year before the first redemption date. If the yield rate is 14% compounded semi-annually, what is the purchase price?

6. A 15% bond for \$16 000 is to be redeemed by a series of four annual payments of \$4 000 each. The first redemption date is April 1, 1980, the bond interest is payable on April 1 and October 1 each year. If the bond is purchased to yield 12% compounded semi-annually, what is the purchase price on April 1, 1979?

7. In Problem 5, if the bond is bought on the interest date, which is seven years before the first annual redemption date, what is the purchase price?

8. In Problem 6, if the first redemption date is October 1, 1988, what is the purchase price on April 1, 1983?

EXERCISE / CHAPTER REVIEW

1. A $1 000, 12% bond is bought five years before redemption to yield 11% compounded semi-annually. The interest on the bond is payable semi-annually. Find the purchase price if the bond is redeemable at (a) par, (b) 103(%), and (c) 97(%).

2. A $500, 13% bond is purchased on February 1, 1979 to yield 14% compounded semi-annually. The interest on the bond is payable on February 1 and August 1 each year. Find the purchase price by assuming that the bond is redeemable on August 1, 1988, at (a) par, (b) 104(%), and (c) 96(%).

3. Refer to Problem 1(a). If the bond is bought four years and ten months before redemption, what is (a) the purchase price? (b) the accrued interest on the bond? and (c) the quoted price?

4. Refer to Problem 2(a). Assuming that the bond is purchased on May 1, 1979, what is (a) the purchase price? (b) the accrued interest on the bond? and (c) the quoted price?

5. On April 30, 1984 a man purchased $2 000 of 16% bonds. Bonds were quoted on the market on that date at 96(%). Interest on the bonds was payable on March 1 and September 1. Find (a) the quoted price, (b) the accrued interest on the bonds, and (c) the purchase price.

6. A 15% bond of $5 000 was quoted on the market at $96\frac{1}{2}$(%) on April 21, 1980. Interest on the bond was payable semi-annually on April 1 and October 1. Find (a) the quoted price, (b) the accrued interest on the bond, and (c) the purchase price.

7. A $7 000, 11% bond, redeemable in eight years, interest payable semi-annually, is purchased to yield 12% interest compounded semi-annually. Find (a) the discount and (b) the purchase price.

8. A $5 000, 13% bond, redeemable in 10 years, interest payable semi-annually, is bought to yield 12% interest compounded semi-annually. Find (a) the discount and (b) the purchase price.

9. Refer to Problem 7. What is the purchase price if the yield rate is (a) 16% compounded semi-annually? (b) 15% compounded monthly?

10. Refer to Problem 8. What is the purchase price if the yield rate is (a) 12% compounded semi-annually? (b) 13% compounded quarterly?

11. A $6 000, 11% bond, interest payable semi-annually, is bought two years before the redemption date to yield 13% compounded semi-annually. (a) Find the purchase price. (b) Construct a schedule showing the periodic changes of the book value to par.

12. A $2 000, 15% bond, interest payable semi-annually, redeemable in $2\frac{1}{2}$ years, is purchased to yield 12% compounded semi-annually. (a) Find the purchase price. (b) Construct a schedule showing the periodic changes of the book value to par.

13. Work Problem 11, using a yield rate of 10% compounded semi-annually.

14. Work Problem 12, using a yield rate of 16% compounded semi-annually.

15. A $3 000, 14% bond, redeemable in seven years, interest payable semi-annually is bought at the quoted price of $3 420. What is the approximate nominal yield rate?

16. A $5 000, 11% bond, redeemable in 12 years, interest payable semi-annually, is bought at the quoted price of $4 640. What is the approximate nominal yield rate?

17. An annuity bond of $10 000 is to be retired in eight semi-annual payments, including principal and interest. The bond interest rate is 15% and the yield rate is 16%, both compounded semi-annually. What is the purchase price (a) now, and (b) after the fifth payment is made?

18. A 16% annuity bond of $6 000 is to be repaid in twelve semi-annual payments, principal and interest included. Assume that the yield rate is 15% compounded monthly. Find the purchase price (a) now, and (b) after the eighth semi-annual payment.

19. An 11% bond of $21 000 is to be redeemed by three payments of $7 000 each at the end of every two years. The interest on the bond is payable semi-annually. If the bond is purchased now to yield 12% compounded quarterly, what is the purchase price?

20. A 12% bond of $12 000 is to be redeemed by a series of four annual payments of $3 000 each with the first payment on August 1, 1990. Interest on the bond is payable on February 1 and August 1 each year. If the bond is bought to yield 11% compounded monthly, find the purchase price on August 1, 1984.

Summary of Formulae

Formula 16-1	Purchase Price $= S(1 + i)^{-n} + R \left[\dfrac{1 - (1 + i)^{-n}}{i} \right]$	Used to find the purchase price of a bond.
Formula 16-2	Premium $= (Fb - Fi)_{a_{\overline{n}\,i}} = F(b - i)_{a_{\overline{n}\,i}}$	Used to find the premium of a bond.
Formula 16-3	Discount $= (Fi - Fb)_{a_{\overline{n}\,i}} = F(i - b)_{a_{\overline{n}\,i}}$	Used to find the discount of a bond.
Formula 16-4	Premium $=$ (Face value $\times b$) $-$ (Redemption value $\times i)_{a_{\overline{n}\,i}}$	Used to find the premium of a bond when the redemption value is not at par.

Glossary

ACCUMULATION the process of increasing the book value of a bond investment to par by periodic additions of the bond discount

ANNUITY BOND a contract in which the issuer promises to pay both the principal and the interest periodically until the entire debt is paid

ASK the lowest price any seller will take for a bond

BID the highest price any buyer will pay for a bond

BOND RATE the interest rate stated on a bond

BONDS generally issued by corporations or governmental units for the purpose of borrowing funds from a group of creditors; purchasers expect the issuing party to repay the principal on a future date, as well as to provide a periodic income in the form of interest during the life of the investment

CAPITAL STOCK see *stock*

CONTRACT RATE see *bond rate*

DISCOUNT when the purchase price of a bond is smaller than the face value, the difference is the discount

DIVIDENDS profits divided among the shareholders of a corporation

FACE VALUE the value stated on a bond

PAR VALUE see *face value*

PREMIUM when the purchase price of a bond is larger than the face value, the difference is the premium

REDEMPTION VALUE the value that the issuing party pays to a bondholder when the bond is surrendered

SERIAL BONDS when the bonds in an issue are redeemable periodically on a series of specified due dates

STOCK ownership in a corporation that has been divided into shares; entitles the owner of the stock to receive income in the form of dividends

17 Depreciation, depletion and capitalization

Introduction

The tangible assets of a business, excluding land, usually have limited useful lives. Buildings, machines, and various types of equipment, after being used for a number of years, eventually come to the end of their lives. They must be retired from the business regardless of efforts to maintain and repair them. At the time of retirement, the assets may have a small trade-in or scrap value, or may be worthless. In either case, there is a loss in the value of the property. This loss is called DEPRECIATION EXPENSE, or simply DEPRECIATION.

Depreciation expense should be periodically charged to business operating expenses or to the cost of goods manufactured during the useful life of the asset. The total of the periodic depreciation charges is limited to the cost of the property. Thus, the computation of the periodic depreciation is actually a process of allocating the cost of the property as an expense or a cost of goods manufactured to the proper business operating periods. The allocation is necessary in order to calculate the periodic net income from business operations. The place of depreciation expense on an income statement is explained in Chapter Seven.

An account, which generally bears the name *accumulated depreciation*, or *allowance for depreciation*, is often used by accountants to record the amount of accumulated depreciation. The difference between the original cost of an asset and its total amount in the accumulated depreciation account is its book value. The book value is not necessarily the same as the market value or the resale value. Rather, it indicates the unallocated cost of the asset.

Retirement of assets is caused by various factors, such as wear and tear, decay, damage, inadequacy, and obsolescence. These factors may operate gradually at one time and drastically at another time. Thus, the value of property may decrease more at one time than at another. However, the allocation of the cost of property is usually gradual and is done in a systematic and rational manner.

There are many methods of estimating the depreciation charges for each business operation period. The methods listed below are generally known and are illustrated in this chapter:

1. *Methods of Averages* (Section 17.1)
   A. Straight line method
   B. Service hours method
   C. Product units method

2. *Reducing Charge Methods* (Section 17.2)
   A. Diminishing rate on fixed depreciation–sum of the years-digits method
   B. Fixed rate on diminishing book value

3. *Compound Interest Methods* (Section 17.3)
   A. Annuity method
   B. Sinking fund method

The following symbols are used in illustrating the depreciation methods listed above:

C = original cost of an asset
T = estimated trade-in value or scrap value
$C - T$ = total depreciation charges or expenses
n = useful life of the asset estimated in years, service-hours, or product-units
r = rate of depreciation expense per year, per service-hour, per product-unit or per dollar

17.1 Depreciation–Methods of Averages

A. STRAIGHT LINE METHOD

The *straight line method* is based on the assumption that the depreciation charges are equal for each year. In other words, the depreciable asset contributes its services equally to each year's operation. The formula for this method is

$$r = \frac{C - T}{n}$$ ⟵ *Formula 17-1*

r = depreciation expense per year, and n = number of years

Example 17.1a
A machine which was purchased for \$1 100 has an estimated useful life of five years and a trade-in value of \$120. Use the straight line method to find the depreciation charges for each year, and construct a depreciation schedule.

SOLUTION:

C = 1 100
T = 120
n = 5 (years)

Substituting the values in Formula 17-1

$$r = \frac{C - T}{n}$$

$$= \frac{1\ 100 - 120}{5}$$

$$= \$196 \text{ (per year)}$$

Depreciation Schedule–Straight Line Method (Example 17.1a)

(1) End of Year	(2) Annual Depreciation Expense	(3) Accumulated Depreciation from (2)	(4) Book Value of Machine $1 100 – (3)
0	. . .	. . .	$1 100
1	$196	$196	904
2	196	392	708
3	196	588	512
4	196	784	316
5	196	980	120
Total	**$980**		

NOTE: The annual depreciation expense is a constant amount, $196. If the above data are plotted on graph paper, the accumulated depreciation forms a straight line. Thus, this method is known as a "straight line" method.

B.   SERVICE HOURS METHOD

The *service hours method* relates depreciation to estimated productive capacity of the asset in terms of its hours of useful service. Under this method, first the depreciation rate per service hour (r) is found by using Formula 17-1, $r = \frac{C-T}{n}$. For this method, n = number of service hours. Next, the depreciation charges for a given year are determined by multiplying the actual number of service hours used in the year by r.

Example 17.1b
Refer to Example 17.1a. Assume that the useful life of the machine is estimated to be 20 000 service hours and the actual number of hours spent in production each year is as follows:
  1st year: 5 000 service hours
 2nd year: 4 500 service hours
 3rd year: 4 200 service hours
 4th year: 3 400 service hours
 5th year: 2 900 service hours

Use the service hours method to find the depreciation charges for each year. Construct a depreciation schedule.

SOLUTION:

$C = 1\ 100$
$T = 120$
$n = 20\ 000$ (service hours)

Substituting the values in Formula 17-1

$$r = \frac{1\ 100 - 120}{20\ 000}$$

$$= \$.049 \text{ (per service hour)}$$

The annual depreciation charges are computed as follows:
  1st year: $5\ 000 \times .049 = \$245.00$
2nd year: $4\ 500 \times .049 = \$220.50$
3rd year: $4\ 200 \times .049 = \$205.80$
4th year: $3\ 400 \times .049 = \$166.60$
5th year: $2\ 900 \times .049 = \$142.10$

Depreciation Schedule–Service Hours Method (Example 17.1b)

(1) End of Year	(2) Annual Depreciation Expense	(3) Accumulated Depreciation from (2)	(4) Book Value of Machine $1\ 100 - (3)$
0	. . .	. . .	$1 100.00
1	$245.00	$245.00	855.00
2	220.50	465.50	634.50
3	205.80	671.30	428.70
4	166.60	837.90	262.10
5	142.10	980.00	120.00
Total	$980.00		

C.   PRODUCT UNITS METHOD

Under the *product units method*, depreciation is related to the estimated number of units that will be produced by each asset during its useful life. To determine the amount of depreciation, first, the depreciation rate per unit of product (r) is found by using Formula 17-1, $r = \frac{C-T}{n}$. For this method, $n =$ number of product units. Then, the depreciation charges for a given period are determined by multiplying the number of units produced in the period by r.

Example 17.1c

Refer to Example 17.1a. Assume that the useful life of the machine is estimated to be 70 000 product units and the number of units produced each year is estimated as follows:

1st year: 14 000units
2nd year: 15 000 units
3rd year: 16 500 units
4th year: 17 000 units
5th year: 7 500 units

Use the product units method to find the depreciation charges for each year. Construct a depreciation schedule.

SOLUTION:

$C = 1\ 100$
$T = 120$
$n = 70\ 000$ (units)

Substituting the values in Formula 17-1

$$r = \frac{1\ 100 - 120}{70\ 000}$$

$$= \$.014 \text{ (per unit)}$$

The annual depreciation charges are computed as follows:

1st year: 14 000 × .014 = $196
2nd year: 15 000 × .014 = $210
3rd year: 16 500 × .014 = $231
4th year: 17 000 × .014 = $238
5th year: 7 500 × .014 = $105

Depreciation Schedule–Product Units Method (Example 17.1c)

(1) End of Year	(2) Annual Depreciation Expense	(3) Accumulated Depreciation from (2)	(4) Book Value of Machine $1 100 − (3)
0	. . .	. . .	$1 100.00
1	$196	$196	904
2	210	406	694
3	231	637	463
4	238	875	225
5	105	980	120
Total	$980		

EXERCISE 17.1 / REFERENCE SECTIONS: A–C

1. A building which was constructed for $50 000 has an estimated useful life of twenty years and a salvage value of $5 000. Use the straight line method to find the depreciation charges for each year.

2. A piece of equipment which was purchased for $800 has an estimated useful life of seven years and a scrap value of $30. Use the straight line method to compute the depreciation charges for each year.

3. The cost of a machine purchased by the Gordon Company is $2 650. It is estimated that the machine will have a $250 trade-in value at the end of its useful life, which is estimated at five years. Use the straight line method to find the depreciation charges for each year, and construct a depreciation schedule.

4. The Kent Company has a machine costing $5 400 with an estimated useful life of six years and a trade-in value of $300. Use the straight line method to find the depreciation charges for each year, and construct a depreciation schedule.

5. Refer to Problem 3. Assume that the useful life of the machine is estimated to be 30 000 service hours and that the actual number of hours spent in production for each year is as follows:

    1st year: 5 500 hours
    2nd year: 7 400 hours
    3rd year: 6 200 hours
    4th year: 5 800 hours
    5th year: 5 100 hours

    Use the product units method to find the depreciation charges for each year. Construct a depreciation schedule.

6. Refer to Problem 3. Assume that the useful life of the machine is estimated to be 100 000 units of production, and that the number of units produced each year is estimated as follows:

    1st year: 24 000 units
    2nd year: 23 000 units
    3rd year: 19 000 units
    4th year: 18 000 units
    5th year: 16 000 units

    Use the product units method to find the depreciation charges for each year. Construct a depreciation schedule.

7. Refer to Problem 4. Assume that the useful life of the machine is estimated to be 17 000 service hours and the actual number of hours spent in production for the first year is 2 800 hours. Use the service hours method to compute the depreciation charges for the first year.

8. Refer to Problem 4. Assume that the useful life of the machine is estimated to be 50 000 units of production and the number of units produced during the first year is 8 500 units. Use the product units method to compute the depreciation charges for the first year.

17.2 Depreciation–Reducing Charge Methods

Generally, the maintenance and repair expenses for new equipment are less than those for older equipment. Therefore, larger amounts of depreciation expense are often charged to the earlier years of the useful life of certain equipment than are charged to the later years. When this is done, the sum of the depreciation expenses and the maintenance and repair costs for each year during the useful life is equalized.

A.   DIMINISHING RATE ON FIXED DEPRECIATION–SUM OF THE YEARS-DIGIT METHOD

Under the *sum of the years-digit method*, the depreciation expense for the earlier years is greater than that of later years. The total depreciation is fixed and is the difference between the original cost and the trade-in or scrap value $(C - T)$. The rate of depreciation is expressed in a changing fraction which becomes smaller each year. In this changing fraction, the numerator is the number of remaining years of life. The denominator is the sum of the digits that represent the years of life.

Example 17.2a
A machine which was purchased for $1 100 has an estimated useful life of five years and a trade-in value of $120. (The information is the same as that in Example 17.1a) Use the sum of the years-digit method to find the depreciation charges for each year and construct a depreciation schedule.

SOLUTION:

The sum[1] of the five years digits is
$1 + 2 + 3 + 4 + 5 = 15.$

---

[1] The sum of the years-digits may be obtained by using the sum of the arithmetic progression formula given in Chapter Five, Section 5.2,
$S_n = \frac{n}{2}(a + L),$
where S_n is the sum
      n is the number of years in the life of the asset
      a is the first number in the series of numbers
      L is the last number in the series.

In Example 17.2a
  $n = 5$
  $a = 1$
  $L = 5$
The sum of the years-digits $= \frac{5}{2}(1 + 5)$
                    $= 2.5 \times 6 = 15$

In Example 17.2b
  $n = 5$
  $a = 8$
  $L = 12$
The sum of the years-digits $= \frac{5}{2}(8 + 12)$
                    $= 2.5 \times 20 = 50$

The total depreciation charge is 1 100 − 120 = $980. The annual depreciation charges are computed as follows:

1st year: $980 \times \dfrac{5}{15} = \$326.67$

2nd year: $980 \times \dfrac{4}{15} = 261.33$

3rd year: $980 \times \dfrac{3}{15} = 196.00$

4th year: $980 \times \dfrac{2}{15} = 130.67$

5th year: $980 \times \dfrac{1}{15} = \dfrac{65.33}{}$

 Total: **$980.00**

Depreciation Schedule–Sum of the Years-Digits Method (Example 17.2a)

(1)	(2)	(3)	(4)
End of Year	Annual Depreciation Expense	Accumulated Depreciation from (2)	Book Value of Machine $1 100 − (3)
0	. . .	. . .	$1,100.00
1	$326.67	$326.67	773.33
2	261.33	588.00	512.00
3	196.00	784.00	316.00
4	130.67	914.67	185.33
5	65.33	980.00	120.00
Total	**$980.00**		

When the rates based on the sum of the years-digits method are considered too extreme, the rates may be modified by adding the same number to each of the numbers of the years.

Example 17.2b

Refer to Example 17.2a. Find the annual depreciation charges by adding 7 to each of the numbers of the years.

SOLUTION:

The sum of the five years-digits becomes
$(1 + 7) + (2 + 7) + (3 + 7) + (4 + 7) + (5 + 7)$
$= 8 + 9 + 10 + 11 + 12 = 50.$

Thus, the annual depreciation charges are as follows:

1st year: $980 \times \dfrac{12}{50} = \$235.20$

2nd year: $980 \times \dfrac{11}{50} =\ \ 215.60$

3rd year: $980 \times \dfrac{10}{50} =\ \ 196.00$

4th year: $980 \times \dfrac{9}{50} =\ \ 176.40$

5th year: $980 \times \dfrac{8}{50} =\ \ \underline{156.80}$

Total: **$980.00**

The difference between each successive year in Example 17.2b is $980 \times \frac{1}{50}$, or \$19.60; whereas, the difference between each successive year in Example 17.2a is $980 \times \frac{1}{15}$, or \$65.33. Thus, the rates in this example are more moderate than those in Example 17.2a.

B.   *FIXED RATE ON DIMINISHING BOOK VALUE*

Under this method, the depreciation expense for earlier years is higher than that of later years. The depreciation expense for each year is obtained by multiplying the fixed (or constant) annual rate by the diminishing book value of an asset as of the beginning of each year. As shown below, there are two ways to compute the fixed annual depreciation rate.

The Declining-Balance Method. The declining-balance method provides a steadily declining depreciation charge over the estimated life of the asset. The annual rate of depreciation must not exceed twice the straight line rate for the depreciable asset. The maximum rate may be obtained as follows:

First, find the annual depreciation rate by dividing 100% by the number of years of useful life of the property (straight line method).

Second, find the maximum annual depreciation rate by multiplying the annual depreciation rate obtained above by 2.

This method is the basis of the capital allowance which is used for income tax purposes. However, capital cost allowance is applied on a group basis to each class of asset. New assets are added to the group and disposals are deducted.[2]

---

[2] *Depreciation for Tax Purposes.* Under the *Income Tax Act* capital allowances may be deducted from income in order to arrive at taxable income. It is necessary to make a clear distinction between capital cost allowance and depreciation. Depreciation allocates the cost of an asset over its estimated useful life, and the depreciation allowance per period may be calculated using any of the methods described in this chapter, applied on a consistent basis. Capital cost allowance is calculated using the declining-balance method only, and the maximum rates allowable for each class of asset are specified by tax regulations. Although these rates may not be exceeded, a company may adopt a lower rate in any given year if it is advantageous to do so.

The scrap value or the trade-in value under this method is not deducted from the cost of the property prior to the rate application. As shown in the following example, the scrap value often is not equal to the original estimation when using this maximum rate.

Example 17.2c
Refer to Example 17.2a. Use the declining-balance method to find the maximum depreciation charges for each year, and construct a depreciation schedule.

SOLUTION:

The annual depreciation rate based on the straight line method is $\frac{100\%}{5}$ = 20% (per year).
The maximum annual depreciation rate is 20% × 2 = 40%.
The annual depreciation charges are computed in the following schedule:

Depreciation Schedule–Declining-Balance Method (Example 17.2c)

(1) End of Year	(2) Annual Depreciation Expense (4)* × 40%	(3) Accumulated Depreciation	(4) Book Value of Machine $1 100 – (3)
0	. . .	. . .	$1 100.00
1	$ 440.00	$ 440.00	660.00
2	264.00	704.00	396.00
3	158.40	862.40	237.60
4	95.04	957.44	142.56
5	57.02	1 014.46	85.54
Total	$1 014.46		

* The diminishing book value as of the beginning of each year, which is also the value at the end of each preceding year. For example, the book value as of the beginning of third year is $396, which is also the book value at the end of second year. The depreciation charges for the third year are computed as follows:
    396 × 40% = $158.40.
Note that in Example 17.2c the book value at the end of fifth year is $85.54, which is not equal to the original estimated amount of $120.[3]

---

[3] The book value at the end of fifth year can be checked by using the nth term formula of a geometric progression (see Section 5.2C) as follows:
$L = ar^{(n-1)}$
    $= 1\ 100\ (1 - 40\%)^{6-1}$
    $= 1\ 100\ (.6)^5$
    $= 1\ 100\ (.077\ 76)$
    $= 85.536$ or 85.54

According to the Fixed Rate Formula. When the following fixed rate formula is used, the book value at the end of the life of the asset is equal to the scrap or trade-in value. The formula for the rate of annual depreciation charges (r) is as follows:

$$r = 1 - \sqrt[n]{\frac{T}{C}}$$

←——*Formula 17-2*[4]

Example 17.2d

Refer to Example 17.2a. Use the fixed rate formula to find the depreciation charges for each year, and construct a depreciation schedule.

---

[4] *Proof Formula 17-2*

C = the original cost
T = the trade-in value or scrap value
n = the number of years of useful life
r = the annual depreciation rate based on the original cost

The depreciation charges and the book value at the end of each year are as follows:

	Depreciation Charges	Book Value
At the end of the 1st year:	Cr	$C - Cr = C(1 - r)$
At the end of the 2nd year:	$Cr(1 - r)$	$C(1 - r) - Cr(1 - r)$ $=C(1 - r)(1 - r)$ $=C(1 - r)^2$
At the end of the 3rd year:	$Cr(1 - r)^2$	$C(1 - r)^2 - Cr(1 - r)^2$ $=C(1 - r)^2(1 - r)$ $=C(1 - r)^3$
At the end of the nth year:	$Cr(1 - r)^{n-1}$	$C(1 - r)^n$

Since the book value at the end of the nth year is also the trade-in or scrap value (T) then
　　$C(1 - r)^n = T$.
Divide both sides by C

$$(1 - r)^n = \frac{T}{C}$$

Extract the nth root of each side

$$1 - r = \sqrt[n]{\frac{T}{C}}$$

Then,

$$r = 1 - \sqrt[n]{\frac{T}{C}}.$$

$C = 1\ 100$
$T = 120$
$n = 5(\text{years})$

Substituting the values in Formula 17-2

$$r = 1 - \sqrt[5]{\frac{120}{1000}}$$

The value of $\sqrt[5]{\dfrac{120}{1\ 100}}$ may be obtained by using logarithms as follows:

$$\log \sqrt[5]{\frac{120}{1\ 100}} = \left(\frac{1}{5}\right) \log\left(\frac{120}{1\ 100}\right)$$

$$= \left(\frac{1}{5}\right)(\log 120 - \log 1\ 100)$$

$$= \left(\frac{1}{5}\right)(2.079\ 181 - 3.041\ 393)$$

$$= \left(\frac{1}{5}\right)(-.962\ 212)$$

$$= -.192\ 442\ 4$$

Find the antilog,

$$\sqrt[5]{\frac{120}{1\ 100}} = 0.642\ 033$$

$$r = 1 - 0.642\ 033$$

then, $= 0.357\ 967, \text{or } 35.796\ 7\%$

The annual depreciation charges are computed in the following schedule:

Depreciation Schedule–Based on the Fixed Rate Formula (Example 17.2d)

(1) End of Year	(2) Annual Depreciation Expense (4)* × .357 967	(3) Accumulated Depreciation	(4) Book Value of Machine $1 100 − (3)
0	. . .	. . .	$1 100.00
1	$393.76	$393.76	706.24
2	252.81	646.57	453.43
3	162.31	808.88	291.12
4	104.21	913.09	186.91
5	66.91	980.00	120.00
Total	**$980.00**		

* Of the preceding year. For example, 393.76 = 1 100.00 × .357 967; 252.81 = 706.24 × .357 967.

EXERCISE 17.2 / REFERENCE SECTIONS: A–B

1. A car, which was bought for $8 500 has an estimated useful life of six years and a trade-in value of $200. Use the sum of the years-digits method to find the depreciation charges of each year, and construct a depreciation schedule.

2. The Johnson Steel Company has a machine costing $28 000 with an estimated useful life of five years and a scrap value of $1 000. Use the sum of the years-digits method to find the depreciation charges for each year, and construct a depreciation schedule.

3. Refer to Problem 1. Find the annual depreciation charges if 8 is added to each of the numbers of the six years.

4. Refer to Problem 2. What are the annual depreciation charges if 6 is added to each of the numbers of the five years?

5. Refer to Problem 1. Construct a depreciation schedule using the two fixed rate methods: (a) according to declining-balance method, and (b) according to the fixed rate formula.

6. Refer to Problem 2. Construct a depreciation schedule using the two fixed rate methods: (a) according to declining-balance method, and (b) according to the fixed rate formula.

17.3 *Depreciation–Compound Interest Methods*

In the previous methods, no consideration is given to the interest, which could accrue on either the original cost or its diminishing book value. The following two methods are used in finding the depreciation charges when interest is involved, and therefore take into account the cost of the funds which are tied up in these depreciable assets. Both methods will give the same *net* annual depreciation charges.

A.   ANNUITY METHOD

The annuity method resembles the method of amortizing a debt. Under the annuity method, the periodic depreciation charges are equal and include not only a part of the cost of the asset but also the interest on the book value for each operating period. The periodic book value is assumed to be earning the same interest as the amount would earn if it were invested elsewhere.

Before computing the periodic depreciation charges, find the present value of the total depreciation charges. Let

i = the interest rate per period (year), and

n = the estimated number of years of the useful life of the asset.

The present value of the trade-in value if $P = T (1 + i)^{-n}$, which is obtained by using the compound discount formula. The present value of the total depreciation charges is the difference between the original cost (C) and the present value of the estimated trade-in or scrap value (P). It may be expressed as follows:

Present value of total depreciation charges = $C - P = C - T(1 + i)^{-n}$.

The annual depreciation charges are required to be equal. Thus, the present value may be thought of as the present value of an annuity (A_n) with payments consisting of equal depreciation charges, or

$$C - T(1 + i)^{-n} = A_n = R\, a_{\overline{n}|\,i}$$

where, $a_{\overline{n}|\,i} = \dfrac{1 - (1 + i)^{-n}}{i}$.

Here, R represents the annual depreciation charges. Thus, the annual depreciation charges (R) may be obtained as follows:

$$R = \frac{A_n}{a_{\overline{n}|\,i}} = \frac{C - T(1 + i)^{-n}}{a_{\overline{n}|\,i}} \qquad \longleftarrow \text{Formula 17-3}$$

Example 17.3a

A machine which was purchased for $1 100 has an estimated useful life of five years and a trade-in value of $120. (The information is the same as that in Example 17.1a.) Use the annuity method to find the depreciation charges for each year and construct a depreciation schedule. Assume that the effective interest rate is 12%.

$C = 1\ 100$
$T = 120$
$i = 12\%$
$n = 5(\text{years})$

The present value of the trade-in or scrap value is
$P = 120(1 + 12\%)^{-5}$
  $= \$68.09.$

The present value of the total depreciation charges is
$A_n = C - P$
  $= 1\ 100 - 68.09$
  $= \$1\ 031.91.$

$a_{\overline{5}|\,12\%} = \dfrac{1 - (1 + 12\%)^{-5}}{12\%}$
$= 3.604\ 776\ 2$

The annual depreciation charges are
$R = \dfrac{A_n}{a_{\overline{n}|\,i}}$

$= \dfrac{1\ 031.91}{3.604\ 776\ 2}$

$= \$286.26.$

Depreciation Schedule–Annuity Method (Example 17.3a)

(1)	(2)	(3)	(4)	(5)	(6)
End of Year	Annual Depreciation Charges	Interest Income	Net Depreciation Charges to be Accumulated	Accumulated Depreciation	Book Value
	(R)	(6) × 12%	(2) − (3)	from (4)	$1 100 − (5)
0	...	...	...	...	$1 100.00
1	$ 286.26	$132.00	$154.26	$154.26	945.75
2	286.26	113.49	172.77	327.03	772.97
3	286.26	92.76	193.50	520.53	579.47
4	286.26	69.54	216.72	737.25	362.75
5	286.27*	43.53	242.75	980.00	120.00
Total	**$1 431.30**	**$450.83**	**$980.00**		

* Corrected for one-cent discrepancy.

When an accountant uses the annuity method in computing annual depreciation charges, he keeps two accounts:

1. Depreciation charges (or expense) [See Column(2)].

2. Interest income [See Column (3)].

Only the difference between the annual depreciation charges and the interest income is used in reducing the book value of the investment. For example, although the total depreciation charges for the operation of the asset during the first year are $286.26, the net loss is only $154.26 (or $286.26 − $132.00). Thus, the book value at the end of the first year is reduced by $154.26 to obtain a new book value of $945.74 (or $1 100 − $154.26).

B.   SINKING FUND METHOD

Under the sinking fund method, it is assumed that a sinking fund is established for the purpose of replacing an asset at the end of its useful life. The periodic depreciation charges are exactly the same as the periodic increases (including the periodic deposit and the interest) in the sinking fund. Thus, the depreciation charges for each year are not equal. However, the total of the depreciation charges is equal to the amount in the sinking fund (S_n) at the end of the useful life of the asset. The size of each deposit (R) made in the sinking fund can be obtained by using the annuity formula

$$S_n = R \, s_{\overline{n}|\,i}, \text{ or}$$

$$\boxed{R = \frac{S_n}{s_{\overline{n}|\,i}} = \frac{C-T}{s_{\overline{n}|\,i}}} \quad \longleftarrow \textit{Formula 17-4}$$

where, $S_{\overline{n}|\,i} = \dfrac{(1+i)^n - 1}{i}$.

Example 17.3b

Assume that the effective interest rate is 12%. Use the data in Example 17.3a to find the annual depreciation charges by the sinking fund method. Construct a depreciation schedule.

SOLUTION:

$C = 1\ 100$
$T = 120$
$\quad i = 12\%$
$\quad n = 5\text{(years)}$
The total depreciation at the end of the fifth year is
$C - T = 1\ 100 - 120$
$\qquad = \$980$
which should be equal to the final amount in the sinking fund. Thus,
$\qquad S_n = \$980,$

$$S_{\overline{5}|\,12\%} = \frac{(1 + 12\%)^5 - 1}{12\%}$$
$$= 6.352\ 847\ 4.$$

Substituting the values in Formula 17-4,

the annual deposit $R = \dfrac{980}{S_{\overline{5}|\,12}}$

$$= \frac{980}{6.352\ 847\ 4}$$

$$= \$154.26.$$

The annual depreciation charges are shown in Column (4) in the depreciation schedule.

Note that the values in Columns (4), (5), and (6) in the schedule are the same as the values in the same columns of the depreciation schedule in Example 17.3a by the annuity method. Also, the actual establishment of a sinking fund for replacement purposes is unnecessary. The depreciation schedule may be used as a standard or a guide for charging the periodic depreciation expense, regardless of whether or not a sinking fund has been established.

Depreciation Schedule–Sinking Fund Method (Example 17.3b)

(1)	(2)	(3)	(4)	(5)	(6)
End of Year	Periodic Deposit in Fund	Interest Income from Sinking Fund	Periodic Increase in Fund = Annual Depreciation Charges	Accumulated Sinking Fund = Accumulated Depreciation	Book Value
	(R)	(5) × 12%	(2) + (3)	from (4)	$1 100 − (5)
0	...	...	...	...	$1 100.00
1	$154.26	...	$154.26	$154.26	945.74
2	154.26	$ 18.51	172.77	327.03	772.97
3	154.26	39.24	193.50	520.53	579.47
4	154.26	62.46	216.72	737.25	362.75
5	154.27*	88.47	242.75	980.00	120.00
Total	**$771.32**	**$208.68**	**$980.00**		

* Corrected for one cent discrepancy.

EXERCISE 17.3 / REFERENCE SECTIONS: A–B

1. A piece of equipment which was bought for $2 400 has an estimated useful life of four years and a scrap value of $300. Use the annuity method to find the annual depreciation charges, and construct a depreciation schedule. Assume that the effective interest rate is 15.5%.

2. The Regina Sales Company has a machine costing $5 000 with an estimated useful life of six years and a scrap value of $800. Use the annuity method to find the annual depreciation charges, and construct a depreciation schedule. Assume that the effective interest rate is 14.2%.

3. Refer to Problem 1. Use the sinking fund method to find the depreciation charges for each year, and construct a depreciation schedule.

4. Refer to Problem 2. Use the sinking fund method to find the depreciation charges for each year, and construct a depreciation schedule.

5. Find the book value at the end of the third year in Problem 1 without referring to a depreciation schedule.

6. Find the book value at the end of the fourth year in Problem 2 without referring to a depreciation schedule.

7. A robot used in materials handling costs $250 000 and has an estimated life of 20 years with scrap value of $10 000. Compute the depreciation charge in the 10th year using:
   (1) the straight line method
   (2) the sum of the years-digits method

(3) the declining-balance method
(4) the fixed rate formula
(5) the annuity method with 15.5% interest compounded annually
(6) the sinking fund method with 15.5% interest compounded annually.
8. Garvey and Sons Limited bought farm equipment costing $150 000 with an esti-
    mated life of 10 years and scrap value of $5 000. Compute the depreciation
    charge in the 5th year using:
    (1) the straight line method
    (2) the sum of the years-digits method
    (3) the declining-balance method
    (4) the fixed rate formula
    (5) the annuity method using 12.5% compounded annually
    (6) the sinking fund method using 12.% compounded annually.

17.4 *Depletion*

After a period of removal operations, some natural resources, such as minerals, oil,
gas, and timber, are eventually exhausted in the areas of the deposits and cannot be
replaced in the near future. Such natural resources are frequently called WASTING
ASSETS. The reduction in the value of such a wasting asset resulting from exhaustion is
called DEPLETION.

A.   METHOD OF COMPUTING DEPLETION

In general, TOTAL DEPLETION is the difference between the cost and the salvage value
of the property. The *annual depletion deduction* is obtained by multiplying the number of units sold during the year by the depletion rate per unit. The depletion rate per
unit is derived by dividing the total depletion by the number of units estimated to be
in the reserve of the property.

Example 17.4a
Jameson invested $200 000 in a coal mine. The mine is estimated to have a reserve of
264 000 tonnes of coal. The land can be salvaged for $2 000. Assume that during the
first year $\frac{1}{5}$ of the reserve, or 52 800 tonnes of coal, was mined and sold. Find the total
depletion and the depletion deduction for the first year of operation.

SOLUTION:
Total depletion = 200 000 − 2 000
                = $198 000

Depletion rate per unit
= 198 000 ÷ 264 000
= $0.75 (per tonne)

Depletion deduction for the first year
= 0.75 × 52 800
= $39 600

Example 17.4b

Refer to Example 17.4a. Assume that Jameson receives $50 000 as his income before depletion at the end of the first year. What is his net income after depletion?

SOLUTION:

Net income = Income before depletion − Depletion
$$= 50\ 000 - 39\ 600$$
$$= \$10\ 400$$

B.   SINKING FUND FOR DEPLETION

An investor who invests in a wasting asset is entitled to (a) periodic interest on his capital investment (b) the recovery of his investment less any residual value. The investor may wish to withdraw his capital investment at the end of the term of his investment rather than through periodic recovery. Thus the owner of a wasting asset may deposit a portion of his annual receipt (income before depletion) at the end of each year in a sinking fund, which will eventually accumulate to an amount equal to the total depletion. Then, his net annual income from the property is the difference between the income before depletion and the annual deposit in the sinking fund.

Annual net income = Income before − Annual deposit in
  from investment   depletion   sinking fund

The amounts of the annual deposits in the sinking fund are all equal and the size of each annual deposit can be obtained by using the formula $R = \dfrac{S_n}{S_{\overline{n}|i}}$, where

R = annual deposit in the sinking fund
S_n = total depletion (or cost − salvage value)
n = number of interest periods (or deposits)
i = interest rate per period for sinking fund
$$S_{\overline{n}|i} = \frac{(1+i)^n - 1}{i}.$$

Example 17.4c

Use the information given in Examples 17.4a and 17.4b. Assume that annual sales and annual income before depletion are expected to be equal each year and the mine is estimated to be exhausted at the end of the five years. If Jameson wishes to withdraw his original investment ($200 000) at the end of the fifth year and he can invest a portion of his annual income in a sinking fund earning 12% effective interest, what are (a) the size of each annual deposit? (b) the net income from the investment for each year? and (c) the rate of the annual net income on the investment?

SOLUTION:

(a)   Jameson's original investment, $200 000, may be recovered at the end of five years from two sources: the salvage value of the mine ($2 000), and the savings from the annual receipts in the sinking fund, which will accumulate to $198 000 in five years. Since the fund earns 12% interest annually, the annual deposit (R) should be:

$$s_{\overline{5}|\,12\%} = \frac{(1 + 12\%)^5 - 1}{12\%}$$

$$= 6.352\ 847\ 4$$

$$R = \frac{S_n}{s_{\overline{5}|\,12\%}}$$

$$= \frac{198\ 000}{6.352\ 847\ 4}$$

$$= \$31\ 167.13$$

Thus, if Jameson receives $50 000 income annually for five years, he should deposit $31 167.13 in the sinking fund each year in order to draw $198 000 at the end of the fifth year.

(b) The net income from the investment after the deposit in the sinking fund is the same for each year.

Annual net income = 50 000 − 31 167.13
          = $18 832.87

(c) The rate of the annual net income on the investment is

$$\frac{18\ 832.97}{200\ 000} = .094\ 164\ 47 \text{ or } 9.416\ 44\%.$$

The sinking fund schedule is constructed as follows:

Sinking Fund Schedule (Example 17.4c)

(1)	(2)	(3)	(4)	(5)	(6)
End of Year	Deposit in Sinking Fund	Sinking Fund Interest Income	Periodic Increase	Accumulated Sinking Fund	To Be Recovered
		$(5) \times 12\%$	$(2) + (3)$	from (4)	$\$200\ 000 - (5)$
0	...	...	...	...	$200 000.00
1	$ 31 167.13	...	$ 31 167.13	$ 31 167.13	168 832.87
2	31 167.13	$ 3 740.04	34 907.17	66 074.30	133 925.70
3	31 167.13	7 928.92	39 096.05	105 170.35	94 829.65
4	31 167.13	12 620.44	43 787.57	148 957.92	51 042.08
5	31 167.13	17 874.95	49 042.08	198 000.00	2 000.00
Total	$155 835.65	$42 164.35	$198 000.00		

NOTE:

1. The accumulated sinking fund at the end of the operating period is the same as the total depletion. However, the periodic increase in the sinking fund is *not* intended to be a guide for the periodic depletion deduction from income. The periodic depletion deductions should be based on the actual quantities that are sold. In our example, the units sold each year are assumed to be equal during the five-year period. The depletion deduction for each year is a constant amount (see Example 17.4a), but the periodic increases in the sinking fund are not the same each year (see the sinking fund schedule). The periodic depletion deductions and the periodic increases in the sinking fund are separate transactions.

2. In Example 17.4c, since the units sold each year are assumed to be equal, the amount of $10 400 (see Example 17.4a) is the annual net income (after depletion) from the mine operation during the five years. The amount of $18 832.87 is the average annual net income when the sinking fund interest income is included. The actual annual net income is not the same for each year during the five years and may be computed as follows: (See Column (4).)

Sinking Fund Schedule–Net Income (Example 17.4c)

(1) End of Year	(2) Income from Operation After Depletion	(3) Interest Income from Sinking Fund	(4) Total Net Income (2) + (3)
1	$10 400	...	$10 400.00
2	10 400	$ 3 740.04	14 140.04
3	10 400	7 928.92	18 328.92
4	10 400	12 620.44	23 020.44
5	10 400	17 874.95	28 274.95
Total	**$52 000**	**$42 164.35**	**$94 164.35**

The average annual net income $= \dfrac{94\ 164.35}{5}$

$= \$18\ 832.87$

which is the same as the answer in Solution (b).

In summary, let D = annual income before depletion (or dividend)

C = cost of original investment (or purchase price of the wasting asset)

T = salvage value (or trade-in value)

R = annual deposit to sinking fund

I = annual net income after sinking fund deposit

r = rate of the annual net income on the cost of the original investment, or I/C

i = interest rate per period for sinking fund

n = number of years of the life of depletion

$$s_{\overline{n}|\,i} = \frac{(1 + i)^n - 1}{i}$$

Then, $D = I + R$, or

$$D = Cr + \frac{C - T}{s_{\overline{n}|\,i}} \qquad \longleftarrow \textit{Formula 17-5}$$

Here $Cr = I$, since

$r = I/C$; and

$C - T = S_n$.

If there is no salvage value (T), the formula becomes

$$D = Cr + \frac{C}{s_{\overline{n}|\,i}} = C\left(r + \frac{1}{s_{\overline{n}|\,i}}\right) \qquad \longleftarrow \textit{Formula 17-6}$$

Any quantity in the above formulae may be solved if the other quantities are known.

Example 17.4c may be computed by using Formula 17-5 in the following manner:

C = 200 000

T = 2 000

D = 50 000

n = 5(years)

i = 12% (per year)

(a) $R = ?$

(b) $I = ?$

(c) $r = ?$

The computations are shown as follows:

(a) $R = \dfrac{C - T}{s_{\overline{n}|\,i}}$

$ = \dfrac{(200\ 000 - 2\ 000)}{s_{\overline{5}|\,12\%}}$

$ = \dfrac{198\ 000}{6.352\ 847\ 4}$

$ = \$31\ 167.13$

(b) $I = D - R$
    $= 50\ 000.00 - 31\ 167.13$
    $= \$18\ 832.87$

(c) $r = \dfrac{I}{C}$

$\quad = \dfrac{18\ 832.87}{200\ 000}$

$\quad = .094\ 164\ 4 \text{ or } 9.416\ 44\%$

Example 17.4d

A timberland is estimated to yield an annual income before depletion of $30 000 for the next 30 years. At the end of that time, the land can be sold for $1 000. What is the purchase price of the timberland if the purchaser wants to secure a yield of 15% on his investment and if he can invest the sinking fund at 13%?

SOLUTION:

$$D = 30\ 000$$
$$T = 1\ 000$$
$$r = 15\%$$
$$i = 13\%$$
$$n = 30$$
$$C = ?$$
$$s_{\overline{30}|\ 15\%} = 293.199\ 22$$

Substituting the values in Formula 17-5

$$D = Cr + \frac{C - T}{s_{\overline{n}|\ i}}$$

$$30\ 000 = C\ (15\%) + \frac{C - 1\ 000}{s_{\overline{30}|\ 13\%}}$$

$$30\ 000 = .15C + \frac{C - 1\ 000}{293.199\ 22}$$

$$30\ 000 = .15C + (C - 1\ 000)\ (.003\ 410\ 7)$$
$$30\ 000 = .153\ 410\ 7C - 3.4107$$
$$30\ 0003.4107 = .153\ 410\ 7C$$

$$C = \frac{30003.410\ 7}{.153\ 410\ 7}$$

$$= \$195\ 575.73 \text{ (purchase price)}$$

Example 17.4e
Refer to Example 17.4d. Assume that the land at the end of the 30th year will be worthless. What is the purchase price of the timberland?

SOLUTION:

$T = 0$

Substituting the other values (in Example 17.4d) in Formula 17-6

$$D = C\left(r + \frac{1}{s_{\overline{n}|\,i}}\right)$$

$$30\ 000 = C\left(15\% + \frac{1}{s_{\overline{30}|\,13\%}}\right)$$

$$= C(.15 + .003\ 410\ 7)$$

$$30\ 000 = .153\ 410\ 7C$$

$$C = \frac{30\ 000}{.153\ 410\ 7}$$

$$= \$195\ 553.50\ \text{(purchase price)}$$

EXERCISE 17.4 / REFERENCE SECTIONS: A–B

1. Baxter bought a mine for $300 000 and expected to operate it for four years. At the end of the period, the mine will be exhausted and the salvage property can be sold for $20 000. Assume that the mine is estimated to have a reserve of 400 000 units and that during the first year of operation, $\frac{1}{4}$ of the reserve was mined and sold. The income before depletion is $19 000 for this year. Find (a) the total depletion, (b) the depletion rate per unit, (c) the depletion deduction for the first year, and (d) the net income for the first year of operation.

2. A company purchased a piece of land containing oil wells for $100 000. The total reserves of crude oil in the wells are estimated at 200 000 barrels and are expected to be removed in ten years. The salvage land can be sold for $4 000 at the end of the operation. Assume that during the first year of operation 1/10 of the reserve was removed and sold, and the income before depletion was $14 000. Find (a) the total depletion, (b) the depletion rate per barrel, (c) the depletion deduction for the first year, and (d) the net income for the first year of operation.

3. Refer to Problem 1. Assume that the annual sales and income before depletion are equal for each year during the four years. Baxter wishes to keep his cost of investment intact until the end of the period, and he can invest part of the income in a sinking fund at 12%. Find (a) the size of each deposit in the sinking fund, (b) his net income for each year, and (c) the rate of the annual net income on his cost of investment.

4. Refer to Problem 2. Assume that the sales and income before depletion are equal every year during the ten years. The company wants to have the cost of investment recovered when the wells become completely exhausted in ten years so that the company may use the fund to purchase new wells. If the company can invest a part of its income in a sinking fund earning 10% effective interest, what are (a) the size of each annual deposit in the sinking fund? (b) the net annual income for each year? and (c) the rate of the annual net income on the cost of investment?

5. Refer to Problem 3. What are answers to (a), (b) and (c) if the salvage property would be worthless at the end of four years?

6. Refer to Problem 4. What are answers to (a), (b), and (c) if the salvage land would be worthless at the end of ten years?

7. A piece of land with natural resources is estimated to yield an annual income before depletion of $6 000 for the next fifteen years. At the end of that time, the land can be sold for $300. What should be the purchase price of the land if the purchaser wants a yield of 15% on his investment and he can invest the sinking fund at 13% effective interest?

8. A silver mine is estimated to yield an annual income before depletion of $25 000 for the next twenty years. The salvage land is expected to be worth $900 at the end of the period. If the purchaser wishes a yield of 14.25% on his investment and he can invest the sinking fund at 12% effective interest, what should be the purchase price of the mine?

9. Refer to Problem 7. If the land were worthless at the end of fifteen years, what should be the purchase price?

10. Refer to Problem 8. Find the purchase price if the mine were worthless at the end of twenty years.

17.5 Capitalization

CAPITALIZATION is the process of converting an unlimited number of periodic payments into a single present value or cash equivalent. In other words, if the single sum were invested now at a given interest rate, the periodic interest would be payable forever. Thus, the single sum is the present value of a perpetuity which is formed by the periodic payments.

A. ASSET AND LIABILITY VALUATIONS

Capitalization is a very useful method for evaluating assets and liabilities.

Income-producing properties (tangible or intangible) and liabilities are often capitalized as standards for estimating their values.

Example 17.5a
What is the cash equivalent of one hectare of land if the land yields a net rental of $7 200 per year and money is worth (a) 12% effective interest rate, and (b) 12% compounded quarterly?

SOLUTION:

(a) I = $7 200 (per year)
   i = 12% (per year)

   Substituting the values in Formula 14–8

   $$A_\infty = \frac{I}{i}$$

   $$= \frac{7\ 200}{.12}$$

   $$= \$60\ 000$$

(b) R = $7 200 (per year)

   $$i = \frac{12\%}{4} = 3\% \text{ (per quarter)}$$

   $c = 4$ (quarters in a yearly payment interval)
   $f = (1 + i)^c - 1$

   Substituting the values in Formula 14–9

   $$A_\infty = \left[\frac{R}{(1 + i)^c - 1} \right]$$

   $$= \frac{7\ 200}{(1 + 3\%)^4 - 1}$$

   $$= \frac{7\ 200}{.125\ 508\ 8}$$

   $$= \$57\ 366.49$$

Example 17.5b
Capitalize an obligation of $600 payable at the end of each year forever if the effective interest rate is 15%.

SOLUTION:

   I = $600 (per year)
   i = 15% (per year)

$$A_\infty = \frac{600}{.15}$$

   $$= \$4\ 000 \text{ (present value of the obligation)}$$

Thus, if a debtor has $4 000 now, he may use the money to pay off his obligation.

B.　CAPITALIZED COST

An asset, such as a building, a machine, or a piece of equipment, often needs to be renewed or replaced periodically after it is constructed or bought. The cost of the asset may be capitalized so that a sufficient sum of money can be invested now and the accumulated interest will become available for an unlimited number of future renewals or replacements. The CAPITALIZED COST is generally defined as the sum of the original cost and the present value of the future renewals. The future renewals form a perpetuity.

Let K = capitalized cost

　　F = first (or original) cost

　　i = interest rate per interest conversion period

　　c = number of interest periods in one renewal interval

　　R = each renewal cost if $c > 1$

　　I = each renewal cost if $c = 1$

　　$f = (1 + i)^c - 1$

　　　　= the effective rate for one renewal interval

The computations for capitalized cost (K) are as follows:

　　If the *interest period coincides with the renewal interval (or $c = 1$)*, the value of K is the sum of the first cost and the present value of the simple ordinary perpetuity, or

$$K = F + \frac{I}{i}$$ ◄——— *Formula 17-7*

Example 17.5c

The first cost of a new car is \$10 500. Thereafter, the purchaser wants to trade his car for a new one every year. Assume that he has to pay \$1 000 for each trade-in. If interest is 13.5%, find the capitalized cost for the car.

SOLUTION:

　F = \$10 500

　I = \$1 000 (per year)

　i = 13.5% (per year)

　$K = 10\ 500 + \dfrac{1\ 000}{13.5\%}$

　　= 10 500 + 7 407.41

　　= \$17 907.41

If the *number of interest periods in one renewal interval is more than 1 (or $c > 1$)*, the value of K is the sum of the first cost and the present value of the complex ordinary perpetuity. In general,

$$K = F + \frac{R}{f}$$ ◄——— *Formula 17-8*

Example 17.5d

The original cost of a warehouse was $300 000. The warehouse must be completely rebuilt every 25 years. If money can be invested at 15% compounded semi-annually what is the capitalized cost of the warehouse? Assume that the cost of each replacement will be $270 000.

SOLUTION:

$F = \$300\ 000$

$R = \$270\ 000$ (every 25 years)

$i = \dfrac{15\%}{2} = 7.5\%$ (per quarter)

$c = 25 \times 2 = 50$ (semi-annual periods in a 25-year payment interval)

The capitalized cost of the warehouse is equal to the first cost added to the present value of the future replacement costs.

$f = (1 + 7.5\%)^{50} - 1 = 36.189\ 746$

$K = 300\ 000 + \dfrac{270\ 000}{f}$

$\quad = 300\ 000 + \dfrac{270\ 000}{36.189\ 746}$

$\quad = 300\ 000 + 7\ 460.676\ 8$

$\quad = \$307\ 460.68$

However, when the *cost of replacement (R) is the same as the first cost (F)* the value of K may be computed by using the following formula:

$$\boxed{K = \dfrac{R}{1 - (1 + i)^{-c}}} \quad \longleftarrow \textit{Formula 17-9}[5]$$

---

[5] Proof–Formula 17-9

When $F = R$, Formula 17-8 may be written as follows:

$K = R + \dfrac{R}{f} = R\left[1 + \dfrac{1}{f}\right]$

$\quad = R\left[1 + \dfrac{1}{(1 + i)^c - 1}\right]$

$\quad = R\left[\dfrac{(1 + i)^c - 1 + 1}{(1 + i)^c - 1}\right]$

$\quad = R\left[\dfrac{(1 + i)^c}{(1 + i)^c - 1}\right]$

$\quad = R\left[\dfrac{1}{1 - (1 + i)^{-c}}\right]$

$\quad = \dfrac{R}{1 - (1 + i)^{-c}}$

Example 17.5e

In Example 17.5d, assume that the cost of replacement will be $300 000, the same as the original cost. What is the capitalized cost of the warehouse?

SOLUTION:

$F = \$300\ 000$

$R = \$300\ 000$

$i = 7.5\%$

$c = 50$ (semi-annual periods)

$K = \dfrac{300\ 000}{1 - (1 + 7.5\%)^{-50}}$

$= \dfrac{300\ 000}{.973\ 110\ 9}$

$= \$308\ 289.64$

CHECK:

The present value of the investment is $308 289.64. After the original cost of $300 000 has been used, the remaining principal is $8 289.64. The principal $8 289.64 is invested at 15% compounded semi-annually. At the end of 25 years, when the warehouse will be replaced for the first time, the compound amount will be as follows:

$P = \$8\ 289.64$

$i = \dfrac{15\%}{2} = 7.5\%$ (semi-annually)

$n = 25 \times 2 = 50$ (semi-annual periods)

$S = \$8\ 289.64\ (1 + 7.5\%)^{50}$

$\quad = \$8\ 289.64\ (37.189\ 746)$

$\quad = \$308\ 289.61$ (the difference is due to rounding error)

Therefore, another $300 000 is available for the first replacement. The remaining part is intact and becomes the new principal to be invested for the next 25 years.

Example 17.5f

Refer to Example 17.5e. Assume that 20 years after the warehouse was built, there is a need for a major repair which will prolong the useful life for 3 years; that is, the warehouse will become useless and must be replaced at the end of 28 years. How much of the capitalized cost can the owner afford to pay for repair costs?

SOLUTION:

At the end of 20 years, the remaining capitalized cost, $8 289.64, will have accumulated to the following amount: (n = 20 × 2 = 40 semi-annual periods).

$$S = 8\ 289.64\ (1 + 7.5\%)^{40}$$

$$= 8\ 289.64\ (18.044\ 239) = \$149\ 580.25$$

At the end of 28 years, the required capitalized cost is $308 289.64, the same as the cost when the first warehouse was constructed. The principal, which is required to accumulate to the amount of $308 289.64 from the end of the 20th to the end of the 28th year (8 years, or 16 semi-annual periods) is computed as follows:

$$P = 308\ 289.64\ (1 + 7.5\%)^{-16}$$

$$= 308\ 289.64\ (.314\ 387) = \$96\ 922.25$$

After deducting the required principal, the remaining portion of the capitalized cost investment at the end of the 20th year may be used for the major repair, as shown below:

The repair cost = 149 580.25 − 96 922.25 = $52 658.00.

Example 17.5f is diagrammed as follows:

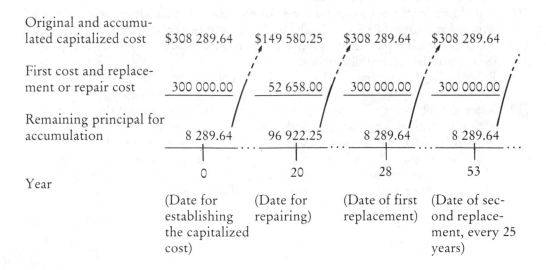

Original and accumu-lated capitalized cost	$308 289.64	$149 580.25	$308 289.64	$308 289.64
First cost and replace-ment or repair cost	300 000.00	52 658.00	300 000.00	300 000.00
Remaining principal for accumulation	8 289.64	96 922.25	8 289.64	8 289.64
Year	0	20	28	53
	(Date for establishing the capitalized cost)	(Date for repairing)	(Date of first replacement)	(Date of second replacement, every 25 years)

EXERCISE 17.5 / REFERENCE SECTIONS: A–B

1. What is the cash equivalent of a lot if the lot can be rented for $8 000 per year and money is worth (a) 12%, and (b) 16% compounded monthly?

2. Capitalize an obligation of $600 payable at the end of each month forever if interest is (a) 12% compounded monthly, and (b) 16% compounded semi-annually.

3. The annual income from a piece of property is $20 000. If a man wishes a return on his investment of 14% compounded semi-annually, what should be the purchase price of the property?

4. The annual future earnings of a store are conservatively estimated at $75 000. (a) At what price will a person purchase the store if he wishes a return on his investment of 15% compounded monthly? (b) Assume that the net assets of the store are valued at $60 000. What is the price of goodwill (the excess payment over the value of the net assets)?

5. A factory bought a machine for $25 000. The machine is to be exchanged every year. The net cost of each exchange is estimated to be $7 000. If interest is 14%, what is the capitalized cost of the machine?

6. A man purchased a truck for $10 000. He wishes to trade his truck for a new one every year. Assume that he has to pay $1 000 for each trade-in. If interest is 18%, find the capitalized cost of the truck.

7. Refer to Problem 5. Compute the capitalized cost of the machine if the interest is 16% compounded semi-annually.

8. Refer to Problem 6. Compute the capitalized cost of the truck if the interest is 22% compounded semi-annually.

9. The original cost of a library was $2 000 000. The library must be completely rebuilt every 20 years. If money can be invested at 15% compounded semi-annually, what is the capitalized cost of the library? Assume that the cost of each replacement will be $1 800 000.

10. A building for the School of Business Administration in a college was constructed at a cost of $5 500 000. The building must be replaced every 40 years and the cost of each replacement is estimated to be $5 700 000. Compute the capitalized cost if the interest rate is 16%.

11. Refer to Problem 9. Assume that the cost of replacement will be $2 000 000, the same as the original cost. What is the capitalized cost of the library?

12. Refer to Problem 10. Compute the capitalized cost, assuming that the cost of each replacement is estimated at $5 500 000.

13. Refer to Problem 11. Assume that 15 years after the library was built, there is a need for a major repair which will prolong the useful life for 4 years; that is, the library will become useless and must be replaced at the end of 24 years. How much of the capitalized cost can the owner afford to pay for repair cost?

14. Refer to Problem 12. Assume that 30 years after the building was constructed, the building is demolished and must be rebuilt. How much can the college afford to spend for rebuilding from the capitalized cost investment if the new type of construction must be replaced thereafter at the same cost every 30 years?

17.6 Comparison of Buying Costs

The method for determining capitalized cost is also useful in selecting equipment (or service) from a number of different types or brands. If the various types of equipment give the same service, the buyer can choose the type with the lowest capitalized cost and thus save money. (See Example 17.6a.) The method is also useful in figuring the replacement cost for a different grade or type of equipment (or service) from the same capitalized cost. (See Example 17.6b and 17.6c.)

Example 17.6a

The cost of machine A is $20 000 and the machine must be replaced every ten years at the same cost. The cost of machine B is $19 000 and the machine must be replaced every eight years at a cost of $18 000. If money is worth 12% compounded annually, which machine is a better buy?

SOLUTION:

The capitalized cost of machine A is:

$$K = \left[\frac{20\,000}{1 - (1 + 12\%)^{-10}} \right]$$
$$= \$29\,497.36$$

The capitalized cost of machine B is:

$$K = \left[19\,000 + \frac{18\,000}{(1 + 12\%)^8 - 1} \right]$$
$$= \$19\,000 + \$12\,195.43$$
$$= \$31\,195.43$$

Since machine A has a lower capitalized cost, it is a better buy.

Example 17.6b

A piece of equipment which now needs to be replaced was purchased for $2 500 with a guaranteed life of 10 years. If new equipment is guaranteed for a useful life of 12 years, how much can the buyer afford to pay with the same capitalized cost which is invested at 16%?

SOLUTION:

Since no replacement costs are stated for either piece of equipment, the replacement costs are considered the same as the original costs in computing the value of the capitalized costs of both items.

The capitalized cost of the old equipment is

$$K = \left[\frac{2\,500}{1 - (1 + 16\%)^{-10}} \right]$$

$$= \frac{2\,500}{.773\,316\,4}$$

Let R = the cost of the new equipment.
The capitalized cost of the new equipment is

$$K = \left[\frac{R}{1 - (1 + 16\%)^{-12}} \right]$$

$$= \frac{R}{.831\ 537\ 2}$$

Equate the right sides of the two equations above since the capitalized cost is the same. Then, solve for R as follows:

$$\frac{R}{.831\ 537\ 2} = \frac{2\ 500}{.773\ 316\ 4}$$

$$R = \left(\frac{2\ 500}{.773\ 316\ 4} \right)(.831\ 537\ 2)$$

$$= \$2\ 688.22$$

Example 17.6c
Refer to Example 17.6b. Assume that the cost of the new piece of equipment is the same as the cost of the old piece. If an attachment had been added to the new equipment to prolong the guaranteed life to 12 years, how much money can the buyer afford to pay for the additional attachment from the same capitalized cost?

SOLUTION:

R = the entire cost of the replacement, or
R = the cost of the new equipment + the cost of the attachment
   = \$2 688.22
Since the cost of the new equipment is the same as that of the old, or \$2 500, the cost of the attachment = 2 688.22 − 2 500 = \$188.22.

EXERCISE / REFERENCE SECTION: 17.6

1. The cost of one type of garage is \$8 000. It has to be replaced every eight years at the same cost. The cost of another type of garage is \$10 000. It has to be replaced every ten years at the same cost. If money is worth 16% compounded annually, which type of garage is less expensive?
2. A typewriter worth \$850 has to be replaced every five years. Another typewriter worth \$800 has to be replaced every four years. If money is worth 18%, which typewriter is the better buy?
3. Refer to Problem 1. If the \$10 000 garage must be replaced every ten years at a cost of \$9 000, which type of garage is less expensive?
4. Refer to Problem 2. If the typewriter worth \$800 can be replaced every four years at a net cost of \$760, which typewriter is the better buy?
5. A machine which now needs to be replaced was purchased for \$1 000 with a guaranteed life of 15 years. If a new machine is guaranteed for a useful life of

18 years, how much can the buyer afford to pay with the same capitalized cost which is invested at 14%?

6. A house which was painted three years ago for $700 now needs to be repainted. If a better type of paint is used, it will last four years. How much can the owner afford to pay for the better paint with the same capitalized cost which is invested at 18%?

7. Refer to Problem 5. Assume that the price of the new machine is the same as that of the old machine. However, the purchaser wishes to buy a special service so that the new machine will last 20 years. How much can he afford to pay for the service from the same capitalized cost?

8. Refer to Problem 6. (a) If a type of paint that will last five years is used for the repainting job, how much can the owner afford to pay? (b) What is the difference between the prices of the three-year paint and the five-year paint?

EXERCISE / CHAPTER REVIEW

1. A garage which was constructed for $10 000 has an estimated scrap value of $1 000 at the end of five years. Use the following methods to find the depreciation charges for each year and construct depreciation schedules for methods (d) and (e):
   (a) Straight line method
   (b) Sum of the years-digits method
   (c) Fixed rate: 1. Tax method
                    2. Formula method (use percent rate including three decimals)
   (d) Annuity method (based on 15% effective interest)
   (e) Sinking fund method (based on 12% effective interest).

2. A typewriter which was bought for $320 has an estimated useful life of four years and a trade-in value of $20. Use the following methods to find the depreciation charges for each year and construct depreciation schedules for methods (d) and (e):
   (a) Straight line method
   (b) Sum of the years-digits method
   (c) Fixed rate: 1. Tax method
                    2. Formula method
   (d) Annuity method (based on 12% effective interest)
   (e) Sinking fund method (based on 12% effective interest).

3. The cost of a bookbinding machine is $1 200. It is estimated that the machine will have a $200 trade-in value at the end of its useful life. Assume that the useful life of the machine is estimated to be 25 000 service-hours and the actual number of hours spent in production for the first year is 2 200, and for the second year, 2 000. Find the depreciation expense for each of the two years.

4. Refer to Problem 3. Assume that the useful life of the machine is estimated to be 300 000 copies of books, and the number of copies bound for the first year is 25 000 and for the second year, 24 000. What is the depreciation expense for each of the two years?

5. Find the composite rate of the group assets in the following table:

Asset	Original Cost	Scrap Value	Estimated Life
Tables	$90 000	$2 000	11 years
Chairs	8 000	600	8 years
Cabinets	5 000	500	15 years

6. Refer to Problem 5. Find the composite life of the group of assets by (a) the straight line method, and (b) the sinking fund method, based on 13.5% effective interest.

7. A man invested $500 000 in a zinc mine. The mine is estimated to have a reserve of 10 000 tonnes of zinc. The salvage land can be sold for $4 000. Assume that during the first year $\frac{1}{4}$ of the estimated reserve was mined and sold. Find (a) the total depletion and the depletion deduction for the first year of operation, and (b) the net income if the man receives $165 000 as the income before depletion at the end of the first year.

8. A man invested $800 000 in land containing wasting assets. It is estimated to have a reserve of 5 million units. The salvage land can be sold for $2 500. Assume that during the first year, 600 000 units were mined and sold. (a) What are the total depletion and the depletion deduction for the first year of operation? (b) What is the net income if the man receives $180 000 as the income before depletion at the end of the first year?

9. Refer to Problem 7. Assume that the mine is estimated to be exhausted at the end of four years and that the sales and the income before depletion in each year are expected to be equal. If the man wishes to invest a portion of his annual income in a sinking fund which will earn 16.25% compounded annually so that he may recover his original investment at the end of the fourth year of operation, find (a) the size of each annual deposit in the fund, (b) the net income from the investment in the mine, and (c) the rate of the annual net income on the original investment.

10. A $200 000 mine is scheduled for 15 years of operation. Assume that the operation for each year is the same, the income before depletion for each year is $30 000, and the salvage land of the mine can be sold for $2 000 at the end of operation. The owners wish to recover their original investment by means of a sinking fund, (b) the net income from the mine investment, and (c) the rate of the annual net income to the original mine investment.

11. A copper mine is estimated to yield an annual income before depletion of $50 000 for 20 years. The salvage land can be sold for $1 500 at the end of 20 years. Find the purchase price of the mine if the purchaser wishes a 16% yield on his investment and he can invest the sinking fund at 15% compounded annually.

12. Some land containing oil wells is estimated to yield an annual income before depletion of $600 000 for ten years. The land can be sold for $2 000 at the end of the tenth year. What is the purchase price of the land if the investor wants a 12%

yield on his investment and he can invest part of the annual income in a sinking fund earning 14% annually?

13. Refer to Problem 11. If the land becomes worthless at the end of 20 years, what should the purchase price be?

14. Refer to Problem 12. If the land becomes worthless at the end of 10 years, what should the purchase price be?

15. What is the cash equivalent of a piece of property if the income from it for every month is $550 and money is worth (a) 18% compounded monthly? and (b) 16% compounded quarterly?

16. Capitalize a debt of $10 000 payable at the end of each year forever if interest is (a) 12% compounded annually, and (b) 21% compounded monthly.

17. A highway bridge is constructed at a cost of $1 000 000. The bridge must be completely rebuilt every 30 years. If money can be invested at 17% compounded semi-annually, find the capitalized cost of the bridge. Assume that the cost of each rebuilding will be $900 000.

18. The original cost of a bus station is estimated at $5 000 000. Thereafter, it should be constructed every 15 years, and the reconstruction cost is estimated to be $3 000 000 each time. If money can be invested at 15% compounded monthly, what is the capitalized cost of the station?

19. Refer to Problem 17. Assume that the cost of each rebuilding is $1 000 000. What is the capitalized cost?

20. Refer to Problem 18. Assume that the remodelling cost is estimated at $5 000 000 each time. Find the capitalization cost.

21. Refer to Problem 19. Assume that 22 years after the bridge was constructed, a major repair is needed and the bridge will have a useful life of another 15 years after the repairing. At the end of the life of that bridge, it is to be rebuilt and will be rebuilt thereafter every 30 years. How much of the capitalized cost is available for the repairing?

22. Refer to Problem 20. Assume that twelve years after the station was built, a major repair is necessary. It is estimated that eight years after the repair, the station will then be in need of reconstruction and thereafter every fifteen years. How much of the capitalized cost can be spent for the repair?

23. The cost of television set X is $400 and the set must be replaced every eight years at a cost of $390. The cost of television set Y is $360 and the set must be replaced every six years at the same cost. If money is worth 17% compounded semi-annually, which of the two sets is the cheaper one?

24. The cost of washing machine G is $300 and the machine must be replaced every 10 years at a cost of $280. The cost of washing machine F is $350 and the machine must be replaced every 12 years at a cost of $315. If money is worth 17% compounded annually, which machine is comparatively lower in cost?

25. A machine which now needs to be replaced was bought for $800 with a guaranteed life of six years. If a new machine is guaranteed for a useful life of eight years, how much can the buyer afford to pay with the same capitalized cost which earns 18% interest compounded quarterly?

26. A truck was purchased five years ago for $8 000. The capitalized cost of the truck was established for replacement every five years at the same cost and invested at 20% compounded quarterly. If a new truck has an estimated useful life of six years, how much can the owner afford to pay for the new truck from the capitalized cost?

27. Refer to Problem 25. Assume that the cost of the new machine which has a useful life of eight years is also $800, the same as the cost of the old one. How much can the buyer afford to pay from the capitalized cost for an attachment to the new machine?

28. Refer to Problem 26. Assume that the cost of the new truck with a useful life of six years is $8 000, the same as the cost of the old truck. How much can the owner afford to pay from the capitalized cost for an extra piece of equipment?

Summary of Formulae

Formula 17-1	$r = \dfrac{C - T}{n}$	Use to find the depreciation expense per year on the assumption that the depreciation charges are equal for each year.
Formula 17-2	$r = 1 - \sqrt[n]{\dfrac{T}{C}}$	Use to find the rate of annual depreciation charges.
Formula 17-3	$R = \dfrac{A_n}{a_{\overline{n}|i}} = \dfrac{C - T(1 + i)^{-n}}{a_{\overline{n}|i}}$	Use to find the annual depreciation charges using the annuity method.
Formula 17-4	$R = \dfrac{S_n}{s_{\overline{n}|i}} = \dfrac{C - T}{s_{\overline{n}|i}}$	Use to find the size of each deposit made in a sinking fund to cover annual depreciation charges using the sinking fund method.
Formula 17-5	$D = Cr + \dfrac{C - T}{s_{\overline{n}|i}}$	Use to find the annual income before depletion using the sinking fund method.

Formula 17-6	$D = Cr + \dfrac{C}{s_{\overline{n}\,i}} = C\left(r + \dfrac{1}{s_{\overline{n}\,i}}\right)$	Use to find the annual income before depletion using the sinking fund method when there is no salvage value.
Formula 17-7	$K = F + \dfrac{I}{i}$	Use to find the capitalized cost if the interest period coincides with the renewal interval.
Formula 17-8	$K = F + \dfrac{R}{f}$	Use to find the capitalized cost if the number of interest periods in one renewal interval is more than one.
Formula 17-9	$K = \dfrac{R}{1 - (1 + i)^{-c}}$	Use to find the capitalized cost when the cost of replacement is the same as the first cost.

Glossary

CAPITALIZATION the process of converting an unlimited number of periodic payments into a single present value or cash equivalent

CAPITALIZED COST the sum of the original cost and the present value of the future renewals; the future renewals form a perpetuity

DEPLETION the reduction in the value of wasting assets resulting from exhaustion

DEPRECIATION a loss in the value of property

DEPRECIATION EXPENSE see *depreciation*

TOTAL DEPLETION the difference between the cost and the salvage value of property

WASTING ASSETS natural resources which are eventually exhausted and cannot be replaced in the near future

Appendix I

Use CalcStar to solve a simplex problem. (See Chapter 6, Exercise 6.7, Problem 19.)

NOTE: CR is used to indicate *carriage return*.

Step 1

Turn on your microcomputer and insert the appropriate disk according to the requirements of your system.

Step 2

When you receive the system prompt type CS and press carriage return (CR).

VIEWING THE CALCSTAR WINDOW

As you can see, the CalcStar window has three unique sections. For clarity's sake, let's refer to them as the top, center, and bottom of the screen.

```
^CURSOR MOVEMENT- |        -COMMANDS-   ; FOLLOWED BY              | -MISC-
  <CR> RIGHT       | A AUTO   F FORMAT   M MERGE  R RECALC * EXTEND |@ CURS POS
 ^S LEFT ^D RIGHT  | C COPY   H HELP     O ORDER  S SAVE   = LOCK   | ? EVALUATE
 ^E UP    ^X DOWN  | D DELETE I INSERT   P PRINT  W WHAT   ? SPACE  | ^ DATA TOGL
 ^Z COL A NEXT NOW | E EDGE   L LOAD     Q QUIT   G OR <TAB> GOTO   | <ESC> CANCEL
COL>| A        | B        | C       | D        | E       | F           |
ROW
  1 |
  2 |
  3 |
  4 |
  5 |
  6 |
  7 |
  8 |
  9 |
 10 |
[   FILENAME]  CURSOR:    A1    CURRENT:    A1    L-R
CURRENT ||        TYPE:
DATA    ||     CONTENTS:
                  EDIT:
```

PROBLEM 19(a)

Step 3

Set the column width and decimal precision required. CalcStar is formatted to a width of ten spaces and decimal precision of two places. CalcStar also truncates instead of rounding decimal numbers. To change the column width and decimal precision use the FORMAT command as follows:

Prompt Shows	Position of Cursor	Type
	A1	;F
P)RECISION)2) OR W)IDTH(10)	A1	W
COLUMN A WIDTH (3...63)	A1	12
	A1	;F
P)RECISION(2) OR W)IDTH(10)	A1	P
PRECISION (0...12)	A1	8

The above operations will change the width of column A to 12 spaces and the decimal precision to 8 places. Repeat this for each column to be used in the problem. Problem 19(a) will require columns A to H .

Step 4

Enter the first row of the matrix using the cursor movement shown in the window of CalcStar to move from column to column.

Position of Cursor	Type
A1	8 CR
B1	3 CR
C1	4 CR
D1	1 CR
E1	1 CR
F1	0 CR
G1	0 CR
H1	7 CR

Move the cursor to row two and enter the respective values in columns A2 to H2 . Repeat this step for rows three and four. The matrix should appear as shown in rows one to four in the solution schedule at the end of this appendix.

Step 5

Select the pivot element.

Column	Ratios	Minimum
1	7/8, 3/2, 8/1	7/8
2	7/3, 3/6, 8/4	3/6
3	7/4, 3/1, 8/5	8/5
4	7/1, 3/5, 8/2	3/5

Arbitrarily select column four as the pivot column. The pivot element is therefore 5 . Any of the first four columns could have been selected. However, some columns will require more operations in order to arrive at the final matrix.

Step 6

Write the formulae necessary for the elementary row operations which will result in a zero in row one, column four. (Subtract $\frac{1}{5}$ row two from row one.)

Prompt Shows	Position of Cursor	Type
	A6	+A1 - A2*.2 CR
		; C
FROM COORD (>COORD):		A6 CR
TO COORD (>COORD):		B6>H6 CR
R)ELATIVE OR N)O ADJUSTMENT		R CR

The first row of the new matrix has now been entered in row six. Next, copy row two into row seven.

Prompt Shows	Position of Cursor	Type
	A7	;C
FROM COORD (>COORD):		A2 > H2 CR
TO COORD (>COORD):		A7 > H7 CR
R)ELATIVE OR N)O ADJUSTMENT		R CR

The second row of the new matrix is now entered in row A7. Now enter rows three and four of the new matrix. To enter row three subtract $\frac{2}{5}$ row two from row three. To enter row four subtract $\frac{7}{5}$ row two from row four. This is illustrated below:

Prompt Shows	Position of Cursor	Type
	A8	+A3-A2*.4 CR
FROM COORD (>COORD):		A8 CR
TO COORD (>COORD):		B8 > H8 CR
R)ELATIVE OR N)O ADJUSTMENT	A9	+A4-A2*1.4 CR
		; C
FROM COORD (>COORD):		A9 CR
TO COORD (>COORD):		B9 > H9 CR
R)ELATIVE OR N)O ADJUSTMENT		R CR

The second matrix should now appear as shown in rows six to eight in the solution schedule.

Step 7

Select the next pivot element. Column one is the only column with an element in row four greater than zero. The ratios are $\frac{6.4}{7.6}, \frac{3}{2}, \frac{6.8}{.2}$. The minimum ratio is $\frac{6.4}{7.6}$, therefore 7.6 is the pivot element and row one is the pivot row. To complete the next matrix in rows eleven to fourteen set the cursor position, type in the formula then copy the formula to the other entries in that row.

Cursor Position	Type in Formula	Then
A11		COPY A6 > H6 INTO A11 > H11
A12	+A7 - (A6*2/7.6)	COPY A12 INTO B12 > H12
A13	+A8 - (A6*.2/7.6)	COPY A13 INTO B13 > H13
A14	+A9 - (A6*.2/7.6)	COPY A14 INTO B14 > H14

The third matrix will appear as shown in rows eleven to fourteen in the schedule. Since all the elements in column four are now zero or less, the value for which the function is at a maximum may now be read from column eight, row fourteen. The variables in the solution are X_1 and X_4. The value of $X_1 = \frac{6.4}{7.6}$ and $X_4 = \frac{1.315\,789\,47}{5}$.

Thus $P = 3X_1 + 7X_4 = 3(\frac{6.4}{7.6}) + 7(\frac{1.315\,789\,47}{5}) = 4.368\,4$.

PROBLEM 19(b)

Step 1

Express the problem as a maximization problem:

Maximize: $P = 7y_1 + 6y_2 + 9y_3 + 7y_4$

Subject to $\begin{cases} y_1 + y_2 + y_3 + y_4 \leq 15 \\ 5y_1 + 5y_2 + 4y_3 + 3y_4 \leq 90 \\ 3y_1 + 4y_2 + 10y_3 + 12y_4 \leq 100 \end{cases}$

Step 2

Enter the values as shown for Problem 19(a). See rows one to four of the matrix in the solution schedule.

Step 3

Select pivot element.

Column	Ratios	Minimum
1	$\frac{15}{1}, \frac{90}{5}, \frac{100}{3}$	$\frac{15}{1}$
2	$\frac{15}{1}, \frac{90}{5}, \frac{100}{4}$	$\frac{15}{1}$
3	$\frac{15}{1}, \frac{90}{4}, \frac{100}{10}$	$\frac{100}{10}$
4	$\frac{15}{1}, \frac{90}{3}, \frac{100}{12}$	$\frac{100}{12}$

Hint: If the maximum of the minimum ratio is selected and the divisor used as the pivot element the number of operations will usually be reduced. Columns one and two would both qualify. Arbitrarily select column one. The pivot element is therefore 1 and the pivot row one.

Step 4

Carry out the following operations.

Cursor Position	Type in Formula	Then
A6		COPY A1 > H1 INTO A6 > H6
A7	+A2 - A1*5	COPY A7 INTO B7 > H7
A8	+A3 - A1*3	COPY A8 INTO B8 > H8
A9	+A4 - A1*7	COPY A8 INTO B8 > H8

The second matrix should now appear as shown in rows six to nine of the matrix in the schedule.

Step 5

Select the next pivot element.
Column three is the only column with an element greater than zero in row four. Row three is the pivot row and the pivot element is 7. Carry out the following operations:

Cursor Position	Type in Formula	Then
A11	+A6 - A8/7	COPY A11 INTO B11 > H11
A12	+A7 + A8/7	COPY A12 INTO B12 > H12
A13		COPY A8 > H8 INTO A13 > H13
A14	+A9 - A8*(2/7)	COPY A14 INTO B14 > H14

The third matrix will appear as shown in rows eleven to fourteen in the schedule. The solution of the minimization problem is found in row four of columns five to eight.

$$-X_1 = -6.142\ 857\ 14$$
$$X_2 = 0$$
$$-X_3 = 0.285\ 714\ 28$$

Cost $= 15(6.142\ 857\ 14) + 100(.285\ 714\ 28) = 120.714\ 285\ 7$

SIMPLEX PROBLEM (SOLUTION SCHEDULE)
CHAPTER 6, EXERCISE 6.7, PROBLEM 19

ROW								
1	8.00000000	3.00000000	4.00000000	1.00000000	1.00000000	0.00000000		7.00000000
2	2.00000000	6.00000000	1.00000000	5.00000000*	0.00000000	1.00000000		3.00000000
3	1.00000000	4.00000000	5.00000000	2.00000000	0.00000000	0.00000000		8.00000000
4	3.00000000	4.00000000	1.00000000	7.00000000	0.00000000	0.00000000		0.00000000
6	7.60000000*	1.80000000	3.80000000	0.00000000	1.00000000	-0.20000000		6.40000000
7	2.00000000	6.00000000	1.00000000	5.00000000	0.00000000	1.00000000		3.00000000
8	0.20000000	1.60000000	4.60000000	0.00000000	0.00000000	-0.40000000		6.80000000
9	0.20000000	-4.40000000	-0.00000000	0.00000000	0.00000000	-1.40000000		-4.20000000
11	7.60000000	1.80000000	3.80000000	0.00000000	1.00000000	-0.20000000	0.00000000	6.40000000
12	0.00000000	5.52631578	0.00000000	5.00000000	-0.26315789	1.05263157	0.00000000	1.31578947
13	0.00000000	1.55263157	4.50000000	0.00000000	-0.02631578	-0.39473684	1.00000000	6.63157894
14	0.00000000	-4.44736842	-0.50000000	0.00000000	-0.02631578	-1.39473684	0.00000000	-4.36842105

*PIVOT ELEMENT

Appendix II

Use CalcStar to set up a worksheet to be used to calculate a repayment schedule. (See Chapter 10, Review Problem 8.)

NOTE: `CR` is used to indicate *carriage return*.

Step 1

Turn on your microcomputer and insert the appropriate disk according to the requirements of your system.

Step 2

When you receive the system prompt type `CS` and press return. CalcStar's Main Screen will be displayed.

Step 3

Type in the following column headings:

`PAYMENT NUMBER, BALANCE BEFORE PAYMENT, PAYMENT, INTEREST, PRINCIPAL AND BALANCE AFTER PAYMENT.`

CalcStar is formatted to a width of ten spaces so it will be necessary to change the width of column `B` and column `F` with the `FORMAT` command.

 With the cursor at `A1` type in `/R PAYMENT` and press the carriage return (`CR`). Next, using the cursor movement shown in the CalcStar window type in the remainder of the first column heading.

Position of Cursor	Type
A1	/R PAYMENT CR
A2	/R NUMBER CR
A3	/R ------ CR

Move the cursor to `B1`, change the column width to 15, then type in the column heading.

Prompt Shows	Position of Cursor	Type
	B1	; F
	B1	W
P)RECISION (2) OR W)IDTH	B1	15 CR
COLUMN B WIDTH (3...63)	B1	/R BALANCE BEFORE CR
	B2	/C PAYMENT CR
	B3	/R ------- CR

The column heading for column B is now complete in this way until all headings are entered as below:

```
COLUMN  A          B               C         D         E          F

        PAYMENT    BALANCE BEFORE  PAYMENT   INTEREST  PRINCIPAL  BALANCE AFTER
        NUMBER         PAYMENT                                       PAYMENT
ROW   1
      2
      3
```

Step 4

Move the cursor to F4 and enter the initial balance of 5000 in column F4. (Do not use the $ sign as CalcStar will treat the entry as text.)

Step 5

Change the decimal precision of column A to zero so that payment number one will appear as 1 instead of 1.00.

Prompt Shows	Position of Cursor	Type
	A5	;F
P)RECISION (2) OR W)IDTH (10)	A5	P
PRECISION 0...12	A5	0 CR

Step 6

For each column, enter the first value or the formula to be used to calculate the value.

Position of Cursor	Type	
A5	1+A4 CR	payment number
B5	+F4 CR	balance before payment
C5	250.83 CR	amount of payment
D5	+B5*(.185/12) CR	amount of interest
E5	+C5-D5 CR	amount credited to principal
F5	+F4 - E5 CR	balance after payment

Step 7

The remaining rows may now be completed by use of the COPY command.

Prompt Shows	Position of Cursor	Type
	A5	;C
FROM COORD (>COORD):		A5 > E5
TO COORD (>COORD):		A6 > E6
R)ELATIVE OR N)O ADJUSTMENT		R CR

The entries for row six have now been completed. To complete the entries for row seven repeat the above steps, adjusting for the change in the row.

Prompt Shows	Position of Cursor	Type
	A6	;C
FROM COORD (>COORD):		A6 > E6
TO COORD (>COORD):		A7 > E7
R)ELATIVE OR N)O ADJUSTMENT		R CR

Repeat the above steps until the balance after payment is reduced to zero. The first twelve payments are shown in the following amortization table. Note that CalcStar does not round, it truncates. Thus the 1st digit in row one under PRINCIPAL is shown as 173.74 instead of 173.75 .

AMORTIZATION TABLE
CHAPTER 10, REVIEW PROBLEM 8

PAYMENT NUMBER	BALANCE BEFORE PAYMENT	PAYMENT	INTEREST	PRINCIPAL	BALANCE AFTER PAYMENT
0					5000.00
1	5000.00	250.83	77.08	173.746	4826.25
2	4826.25	250.83	74.40	176.425	4649.82
3	4649.82	250.83	71.68	179.145	4470.68
4	4470.68	250.83	68.92	181.90	4288.77
5	4288.77	250.83	66.11	184.71	4104.06
6	4104.06	250.83	63.27	187.55	3916.50
7	3916.50	250.83	60.37	190.45	3726.05
8	3726.05	250.83	57.44	193.38	3532.66
9	3532.66	250.83	54.46	196.36	3336.30
10	3336.30	250.83	51.43	199.39	3136.90
11	3136.90	250.83	48.36	202.47	2934.43
12	2886.07	250.83	45.24	205.59	2728.84
.	.	.	.	.	.
.	.	.	.	.	.
.	.	.	.	.	.

Appendix III

Use CalcStar to set up a worksheet to solve Chapter 13, Review Problem 14.
Refer to Appendix II, Chapter 10, Review Problem 8.

Step 1

Enter the following headings in rows one to four and formulae in row five.

Column	Heading	Formula
A	NUMBER OF PAYMENTS	7 X 12
B	SEMI-ANNUAL RATE	.1925/2
C	EFFECTIVE MONTHLY INTEREST	(1 + B5)**(1/6)-1
D	BALANCE	85000
E		D5**C5
F		1-((1+E**(-84))
G	MONTHLY PAYMENT	E5/F5

(a) Number of payments = 84
(b) Effective monthly interest = 0.15 433 7
(c) Amount of monthly payment = $1 812.54

PROBLEM 14(d)

Step 1

Extend column A so that the following entries may be made. (Use the format command ;F.)

Row

```
1 BALANCE: $85000
2 NUMBER OF PAYMENTS: 84
3 MONTHLY INTEREST: (1.09625)**(1/6)-1=.0154337
4 PAYMENT: (85 000*.0154337)/(1-(1.0154337)**(-84)) = 1812.54
```

Step 2

Enter the column headings as shown in Appendix II.

Step 3

Enter 0 under payment number in row eight (A8) and 85000. Balance after payment (H8).

Step 4

Enter the formulae required to calculate the entries:

Cursor Position	Type Formula
A9	1 + A8 CR
B9	+ F8 CR
C9	1812.54 CR
D9	+ B9*.0154337 CR
E9	+C9 - D9 CR
F9	+F8 - E9 CR

Step 5

Use the |COPY function to calculate the entries in all succeeding columns until payment number 12 has been completed.

Prompt	Cursor Position	Type
	A9	;C
FROM COORD (>COORD)		A9 > F9
TO COORD (>COORD)		A10 > F10
R)ELATIVE OR N)0 ADJUSTMENT		R CR

Step 6

Copy A9 to F9 into A11 > F11 and repeat the process until A20 > F20 is completed (payment number 12).

The outstanding balance after payment number 12 is $78 454.72. Use the save function to save the program for part (e).

PROBLEM 14(e)

Step 1

Load the partial program saved in 14(d).
Enter 5000 under principal and use the |COPY function to calculate the balance after payment.

Step 2

Use the COPY function to calculate succeeding payments. After payment number 76 the balance is $218.16.

Total amount due (84 × 1 812.54)		152 253.36
Amount paid (76 × 1 812.54):	137 753.04	
Principal paid after payment #12:	5 000.00	
Final payment	218.16	142 971.20
Saving due to prepayment of principal (assume no penalty)		9 282.16

Payments one to fifty-four are listed in the amortization schedule at the end of this appendix.

Balance after payment #12	78 454.72		
Principal paid	5 000.00		
	73 454.72		
Balance after payment 76:	218.16		
Reduction in # of payments: 84 − 76 = 8			
Reduction in amount paid:	1 812.54 × 8	=	14 500.32
Saving: 14 500.32 − 218.16		=	14 282.16
Total amount due:	84 × 1 812.54	=	152 253.36
Total amount paid:	76 × 1 812.54	=	137 753.04
			5 000.00
			142 753.04
$i = .015\ 433\ 8$			
			9 500.32
		−	218.16
Saving:			9 282.16

AMORTIZATION SCHEDULE
CHAPTER 13, REVIEW PROBLEM 14

BALANCE: $85000
NUMBER OF PAYMENTS: 7*12=84
MONTHLY INTEREST: (1.09625)* *(1/6)-1 = .0154337
PAYMENT: 85000.00*.0154337/((1-(1.0154338)**(-84)) = $1812.54

PAYMENT NUMBER	BALANCE BEFORE PAYMENT	PAYMENT	INTEREST	PRINCIPAL	BALANCE AFTER PAYMENT
0					85000.00
1	85000.00	1812.5400	1311.8645	500.67	84499.32
2	84499.32	1812.5400	1304.1372	508.40	83990.92
3	83990.92	1812.5400	1296.2906	516.24	83474.67
4	83474.67	1812.5400	1288.3230	524.21	82950.45
5	82950.45	1812.5400	1280.2324	532.30	82418.14
6	82418.14	1812.5400	1272.0169	540.52	81877.62
7	81877.62	1812.5400	1263.6746	548.86	81328.75
8	81328.75	1812.5400	1255.2036	557.33	80771.42
9	80771.42	1812.5400	1246.6019	565.93	80205.48
10	80205.48	1812.5400	1237.8673	574.67	79630.81
11	79630.81	1812.5400	1229.80	583.54	79047.27
12	79047.27	1812.5400	1219.9918	592.54	78454.72
				5000.00	73454.72
13	73454.72	1812.5400	1133.6781	678.86	72775.85
14	72775.85	1812.5400	1123.2007	689.33	72086.51
15	72086.51	1812.5400	1112.5617	699.97	71386.54
16	71386.54	1812.5400	1101.7584	710.78	70675.75
17	70675.75	1812.5400	1090.7884	721.75	69954.00
18	69954.00	1812.5400	1079.6491	732.89	69221.11
19	69221.11	1812.5400	1068.3379	744.20	68476.91
20	68476.91	1812.5400	1056.8521	755.68	67721.22

n					
21	66953.87	767.35	1045.1890	1812.5400	67721.22
22	66174.68	779.19	1033.3460	1812.5400	66953.87
23	65383.46	791.21	1021.3201	1812.5400	66174.68
24	64580.03	803.43	1009.1087	1812.5400	65383.46
25	63764.19	815.83	996.7088	1812.5400	64580.03
26	62935.77	828.42	984.1175	1812.5400	63764.19
27	62094.56	841.20	971.3319	1812.5400	62935.77
28	61240.37	854.19	958.3489	1812.5400	62094.56
29	60373.00	867.37	945.1656	1812.5400	61240.37
30	59492.24	880.76	931.7788	1812.5400	60373.00
31	58597.88	894.35	918.1854	1812.5400	59492.24
32	57689.73	908.15	904.3822	1812.5400	58597.88
33	56767.55	922.17	890.3659	1812.5400	57689.73
34	55831.14	936.40	876.1334	1812.5400	56767.55
35	54880.29	950.85	861.6812	1812.5400	55831.14
36	53914.75	965.53	847.0059	1812.5400	54880.29
37	52934.32	980.43	832.1041	1812.5400	53914.75
38	51938.75	995.56	816.9724	1812.5400	52934.32
39	50927.82	1010.93	801.6071	1812.5400	51938.75
40	49901.28	1026.53	786.0047	1812.5400	50927.82
41	48858.90	1042.37	770.1614	1812.5400	49901.28
42	47800.44	1058.46	754.0737	1812.5400	48858.90
43	46725.63	1074.80	737.7376	1812.5400	47800.44
44	45634.01	1091.39	721.1494	1812.5400	46725.63
45	44526.01	1108.23	704.3052	1812.5400	45634.24
46	43400.67	1125.33	687.2011	1812.5400	44526.01
47	42257.96	1142.70	669.8329	1812.5400	43400.67
48	41097.62	1160.34	652.1967	1812.5400	42257.96
49	39919.37	1178.25	634.2883	1812.5400	41097.62
50	38722.93	1196.43	616.1036	1812.5400	39919.37
51	37508.03	1214.90	597.6381	1812.5400	38722.93
52	36274.38	1234.65	578.8877	1812.5400	37508.03
53	35021.68	1252.69	559.8479	1812.5400	36274.38
54	33749.66	1272.02	540.5142	1812.5400	35021.68

ANSWERS TO ODD-NUMBERED QUESTIONS

Chapter 1

EXERCISE 1.1A

1. −12
3. −30
5. −47
7. −31
9. +31
11. +45
13. +22
15. +25
17. −11.23
19. −24.37
21. +12.736
23. +23.057 0
25. −23
27. +7
29. −27

31. +2
33. +27
35. +45
37. +5
39. −26
41. −17.367 8
43. −31.361
45. +6.79
47. +14.83
49. −32
51. +23
53. +42
55. +90
57. +18
59. +35

61. −24
63. −72
65. −14
67. −2 108
69. −6
71. −5
73. −12
75. −21
77. +18
79. +23
81. +15
83. −14
85. +11

EXERCISE 1.1B

1. 8
3. 4
5. 7
7. 1 152
9. 18
11. −24

13. 118
15. 39
17. 26
19. 65
21. 309
23. −8

25. −68
27. 4
29. 4
31. −146
33. 12.5
35. 3

EXERCISE 1.2

1. $\frac{7}{3}$
3. $\frac{91}{8}$
5. $\frac{47}{12}$
7. $\frac{48}{5}$
9. $\frac{275}{6}$
11. $40\frac{319}{325}$
13. $4\frac{1}{4}$
15. $1\frac{3}{8}$

17. $5\frac{1}{8}$
19. $8\frac{2}{5}$
21. $6\frac{28}{31}$
23. $37\frac{29}{124}$
25. $\frac{1}{2}$
27. $\frac{2}{3}$
29. $\frac{4}{7}$
31. $\frac{7}{11}$

33. $\frac{3}{8}$
35. $\frac{14}{17}$
37. $\frac{3}{4} > \frac{5}{7}$
39. $\frac{4}{9} > \frac{7}{16}$
41. $\frac{5}{6} > \frac{3}{4} > \frac{2}{5}$
43. $\frac{3}{5} > \frac{1}{2} > \frac{2}{7}$
45. $\frac{3}{4} > \frac{3}{5} > \frac{3}{6} > \frac{3}{7} > \frac{3}{8}$
47. $\frac{21}{32} > \frac{19}{30} > \frac{23}{40} > \frac{25}{48}$

EXERCISE 1.3A

1. $\frac{1}{2}$

3. $1\frac{1}{20}$

5. $9\frac{2}{3}$

7. $6\frac{5}{12}$

9. $\frac{101}{40} = 2\frac{21}{40}$

11. $17\frac{1}{8}$

13. $\frac{19}{21}$

15. $1\frac{7}{16}$

17. $\frac{97}{100}$

19. $11\frac{13}{30}$

21. $22\frac{19}{33}$

23. $67\frac{3}{20}$

25. $\frac{3}{20}$

27. $\frac{2}{21}$

29. $\frac{13}{100}$

31. $\frac{3}{7}$

33. $2\frac{1}{3}$

35. $7\frac{2}{3}$

37. $7\frac{7}{9}$

39. $5\frac{74}{99}$

41. $2\frac{1}{4}$

43. $\frac{1}{6}$

45. $\frac{3}{20}$

47. $7\frac{11}{45}$

49. $\frac{1}{15}$

51. $\frac{7}{26}$

53. $\frac{1}{3}$

55. $\frac{25}{84}$

57. $\frac{49}{225}$

59. $3\frac{21}{44}$

61. $\frac{10}{171}$

63. $\frac{8}{27}$

65. $8\frac{1}{15}$

67. $152\frac{11}{14}$

69. $3\,468\frac{9}{40}$

71. 845

EXERCISE 1.3B

1. 8

3. $1\frac{1}{4}$

5. $1\frac{1}{5}$

7. $\frac{110}{339}$

9. 3

11. $\frac{17}{28}$

13. $7\frac{14}{23}$

15. $\frac{7}{9}$

17. $\frac{4}{15}$

19. $\frac{17}{18}$

21. $16\frac{2}{5}$

23. $6\frac{3}{7}$

25. $1\frac{3}{5}$

27. $1\frac{7}{20}$

29. $\frac{14}{45}$

31. $\frac{25}{42}$

33. $5\frac{9}{31}$

35. $\frac{1}{8}$

37. $1\frac{1}{7}$

39. $\frac{7}{11}$

41. $\frac{15}{32}$

43. $1\frac{1}{15}$

45. $8\frac{31}{37}$

47. $\frac{38}{51}$

EXERCISE 1.4

1. $.2$

3. $.353$

5. $.923$

7. $.575$

9. 3.077

11. 3.789

13. 3.350

15. 42.538

17. $\frac{8}{25}$

19. $\frac{17}{25}$

21. $\frac{19}{250}$

23. $1\frac{3}{4}$

25. $3\frac{1}{500}$

27. $11\frac{7}{200}$

29. $4\frac{71}{200}$

31. $5\frac{501}{1000}$

33. $.\dot{1}42\,85\dot{7}$

35. $.41\dot{6}$

37. $.38\dot{3}$

39. $.\dot{5}1\dot{8}$

41. $.8\dot{6}$

43. $.11\dot{3}$

45. $.\dot{5} = \frac{5}{9}$

47. $\frac{12}{45}$

49. $\frac{23}{99}$

51. $\frac{39}{900}$

53. $4\frac{35}{90}$

55. $1\frac{4\,563}{9\,990}$

57. 32.75

59. 432.44

61. 2.58

63. $7\,362.06$

65. 1.37

67. 21.01

EXERCISE 1.5

1. .002 4
3. .063
5. .14
7. 1.48
9. 45.0
11. $\frac{2}{25}$
13. $3\frac{3}{4}$

15. $\frac{3}{250}$
17. $\frac{3}{12\,500}$
19. $\frac{21}{500\,000}$
21. 38%
23. 4.7%
25. .35%
27. 7 200%

29. 146%
31. 2%
33. 371%
35. 92%
37. 1 647%
39. 55%

Chapter 2

EXERCISE 2.2

1. $26a$
3. $-18c$
5. $-58et$
7. $-68f$
9. $43h$
11. $28w$

13. $2cd - 2c$
15. $9ab - a$
17. $10a + 10b + 3$
19. $7xy + 28x + 7y$
21. $22xy$
23. $26ab$

25. $-5bc$
27. $-2b$
29. $-5a + 6d$
31. $12f$
33. $9h$
35. $a - b + 1$

EXERCISE 2.3

1. 32
3. 15 625
5. a^6
7. c^4
9. 144
11. $(xy)^3$

13. $(mn)^a$
15. 15 625
17. p^{10}
19. y^{ab}
21. $b^{y/x}$
23. 64

25. 31.093 697
27. 1.007 132 6
29. 20.607 148
31. 5.614 366 2
33. 9.211 541 8

EXERCISE 2.4

1a. 2.58×10^{-4}
1b. 3
3a. $2.158\,61 \times 10^{-1}$
3b. 6
5a. $6.321\,8 \times 10^1$

5b. 5
7. 2 040 000
9. 21 630 000 000
11. 164 800

EXERCISE 2.5

1. $-18xy$
3. $392xy$
5. $30x^3y^2$
7. $-21p^5q^3$
9. $8a + 6$
11. $20c - 15$

13. $4ta + 4tb$
15. $-21bc + 14b^2$
17. $a^2 - b^2$
19. $a^2 - 2ab + b^2$
21. $4y^2 + 14y - 6$
23. $6t^5 + 12t^2 - 6at^3 - 12a$

25. $3x + 5$
27. $3x^2 - 2x + 1 + \frac{37}{8x + 5}$
29. $5x + 3 + \frac{-6x - 11}{5x^2 - 2x + 3}$
31. $4x + \frac{14x + 4}{7x^2 - 3}$

EXERCISE 2.6

1. $3x - 3$
3. $7x - 4$
5. $-42x + 9y$

7. $6x - 15y$
9. $7aw + 31a$
11. $5ax - 13ay$

EXERCISE 2.7

1. $5(2a + b)$
3. $6(x + 1)$
5. $6(-3x + y - z)$
7. $(a + 2c)(3x - y)$
9. $(a - b)(x + y)$
11. $(14c - 2d)(2a + b)$
13. $(3x - y^2)(3x + y^2)$
15. $(5x - 4y)(5x + 4y)$
17. $(x^2 - 7)(x^2 + 7)$

19. $(x + 3)^2$
21. $(2x + 6)^2$
23. $(6y - 5)^2$
25. $(3a + 4b)^2$
27. $(x + 2)(x + 1)$
29. $(2y + 3)(y + 1)$
31. $(a + 1)(2a - 3)$
33. $(x + 3)(7x - 1)$
35. $(7b - 5)(3b + 4)$

Chapter 3

EXERCISE 3.1

1. $x = 3\frac{1}{2}$
3. $x = 5$
5. $x = 4$
7. $x = 3$
9. $x = 12$
11. $x = 0.11$
13. $x = 2a$

15. $x = 2d$
17. $x = \frac{5n - d}{3c}$
19. $x = -\frac{7a}{26}$
21. 142 and 78
23. 18
25. $14\frac{1}{3}$ years
27. $\$1\ 247$

29. 32 quarters, 20 dimes
31. $54.67 and $27.33
33. 2.5 hours, 240 km
35. 64 km/hr
37. $250
39. 6
41. 9 dimes, 3 quarters, 18 half-dollars

EXERCISE 3.2

1. $x = 3, y = -1$
3. $x = 11, y = 2$
5. $x = 5, y = 1$
7. $x = 2, y = -3$
9. $x = 5, y = 6$
11. $x = -4, y = 2$
13. $x = 10, y = 5$
15. $x = -5, y = 12$
17. $x = \frac{1}{2}, y = \frac{1}{3}$
19. $x = 2, y = 3$

21. $x = -1, y = 2$
23. $x = -2, y = -3$
25. $x = 2, y = 3$
27. $x = -3, y = 4$
29. $x = 4, y = -2$
31. $x = 2, y = -5$
33. $x = 4, y = -3$
35. $x = 5, y = -2$
37. dependent

39. inconsistent
41. dependent
43. inconsistent
45. hat, $15.50; coat, $48.50
47. 5 and 7
49. 10 children, 30 adult
51. girl's age, 13; brother's age, 7
53. 98
55. 52.5 kg Grade A and 37.5 kg Grade B

EXERCISE 3.3

1. $\frac{4}{5}$

3. $\frac{1}{a-b}$

5. $\frac{1}{a(x+y)+b}$

7. $\frac{1}{4x-y^2}$

9. $\frac{5}{(x^2-7)}$

11. $\frac{4}{(x+3)}$

13. $\frac{19x}{20}$

15. $\frac{13}{6x}$

17. 2

19. $\frac{3(4x+1)}{2(2x+1)(3x+1)}$

21. $\frac{x}{15}$

23. $-\frac{7}{12x}$

25. $\frac{c}{a+c}$

27. $\frac{21x-8}{(-5x+6)(3x-2)}$

29. $\frac{3a^2b^3x}{4y^2}$

31. $\frac{4n^2}{3ym^2}$

33. $\frac{1}{xy(x+y)}$

35. $\frac{x(2x+3)}{(2x-1)(2x+1)}$

37. $\frac{1}{2}$

39. $\frac{2x(6x^2-y^2)}{(2x-y)(x-y)}$

41. $\frac{2x-1}{5x-2}$

43. $\frac{xy^2+2}{2+x}$

45. $x = 42$

47. $x = 16$

49. $x = 10$

51. $x = -6$

53. $x = -9$

55. $x = 7$

57. $x = 3\frac{1}{5}$

59. $x = \frac{a^2-b^2}{b-c}$

61. 35 and 45

63. 15 hours

65. 15 km

67. 2 hours

EXERCISE 3.4

1.

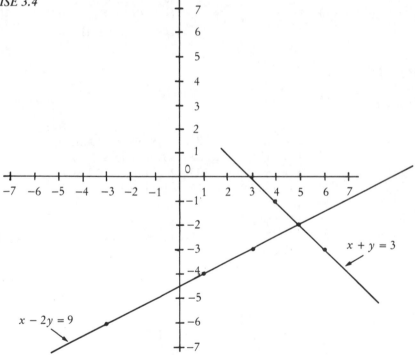

$x + y = 3$

$x - 2y = 9$

x - 2y = 9	
x	y
-3	-6
1	-4
3	-3

x + y = 3	
x	y
4	-1
5	-2
6	-3

Answer: $x = 6$, $y = 2$.

3.

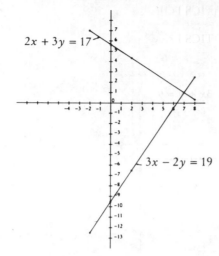

2x + 3y = 17

x	y
−2	7
0	$5\frac{2}{3}$
+2	$4\frac{1}{3}$
+8	$\frac{1}{3}$

3x − 2y = 19

x	y
−2	$-12\frac{1}{2}$
0	$-9\frac{1}{2}$
+2	$-6\frac{1}{2}$
+8	$2\frac{1}{2}$

Answer: $x = 7, y = 1$.

5.

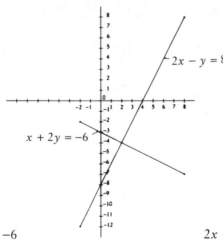

x + 2y = −6

x	y
−2	−2
0	−3
2	−4
8	−7

2x − y = 8

x	y
−2	−12
0	−8
2	−4
8	8

Answer: $x = 2, y = -4$.

7.

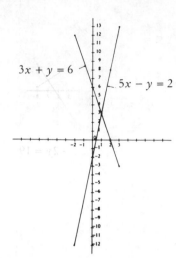

$3x + y = 6$

x	y
-2	12
0	6
2	0
3	-3

$5x - y = 2$

x	y
-2	-12
0	-2
2	8
3	13

Answer: $x = 1$, $y = 3$.

9.

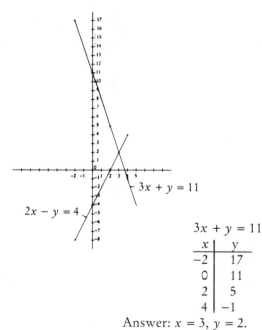

$2x - y = 4$

x	y
-2	-8
0	-4
2	0
4	4

$3x + y = 11$

x	y
-2	17
0	11
2	5
4	-1

Answer: $x = 3$, $y = 2$.

11.

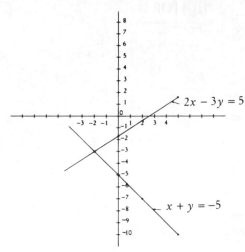

$x + y = -5$

x	y
-2	-3
0	-5
2	-7
5	-10

$2x - 3y = 5$

x	y
-2	-3
0	$-\frac{5}{3}$
2	$-\frac{1}{3}$
5	$\frac{5}{3}$

Answer: $x = -2$, $y = -3$.

EXERCISE 3.5

1a. Total Cost $= \$52\,000 + \$8\,(x)$
1b. Total Revenue $= \$12\,(x)$
3a. Total Cost $= \$62\,000 + \$11.25\,(x)$
3b. Total Revenue $= \$15.50\,(x)$

5a.

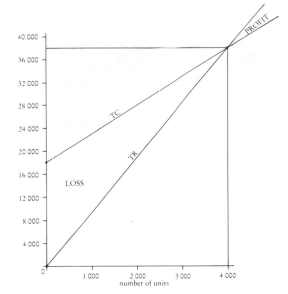

5b. Break-even $= \frac{\text{F.C.}}{\text{S.P.} - \text{V.C.}}$

5c. Break-even $= 4\ 000$ units

7a.

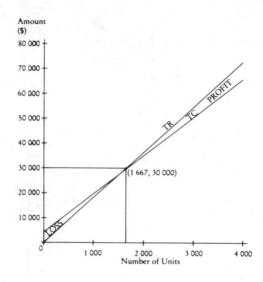

7b. Break-even $= \frac{\text{F.C.}}{\text{S.P.} - .6(\text{S.P.})}$

7c. Break-even $= 1\ 667$ units

9. Total Cost $= \$82\ 000 + \$16.95\ (x)$

11a. Total Cost $= \$12\ 500 + \$6\ (2\ 000)$, assuming the company produced its plant's capacity.

11b. Total Revenue $= \$15\ (2\ 000)$, assuming the company sold the plant's capacity.

13. Break-even $= 1\ 500$ units

15. Break-even $= 2\ 273$ units

17. Break-even $= 667$ units

Chapter 4

EXERCISE 4.1

1. $\frac{6}{1}$

3. $\frac{21}{32}$

5. $1\frac{41}{63}$

7. $\frac{53}{305}$

9. $32\frac{1}{2}$ km

11. $4/day
13. Company A, $\frac{39}{24}$; Company B, $\frac{32}{24}$; Therefore, Company A has a higher ratio.
15a. $\frac{5}{8}$
15b. $\frac{1}{8}$
15c. $\frac{1}{4}$
17. 60, 180
19. 108, 162, 378
21. 120, 180, 300, 420
23. 3 080, 800, 3 808
25. $15 000, $10 000, $7 500, $6 000, respectively
27. Dept. A, $4 325.15; Dept. B, $3 410.72; Dept. C, $2 350.89; Dept. D, $3 058.24
29. Bloor Street, $40 854.33; Sherway Gardens, $53 602.11; Yorkdale Plaza, $33 543.56

EXERCISE 4.2

1. $x = 3.5$
3. $x = 3.7\dot{3}$
5. $x = 160$
7. $x = 40$
9. $x = 2.571$
11. $x = 6.4$
13. $x = 41.16\dot{6}$

15. $x = \frac{1}{3}$
17. 157.5 km
19. $175
21. 2 366 cm
23. $222
25. 100 minutes
27. 64 men

EXERCISE 4.3

1. $y = 3.819$ (direct)
3. $y_1 = 12.015$ (indirect)
5. 46.4 hours
7. decrease by 16.6%
9. decrease by 9.0$\dot{9}$%
11. $59.94

EXERCISE 4.4A

1. 168.25
3. 24.09
5. 31.104
7. 35.5
9. 10.771 2
11. 20.0
13. 6.39

15. 6.0
17. 67.2
19. 50.0
21. $191.25
23a. $7
23b. 80%
25. $1 296

EXERCISE 4.4B

1. 75%	27. 600
3. 300%	29. 4 600
5. 14.1%	31. 7 000
7. 130%	33. 500
9. 40%	35. 80
11. 8%	37. 182.5
13. 16.7%	39. 200
15. 30%	41. 120
17. 25%	43. 215
19. 30.6%	45. 40
21. 36.5%	47. $2 500
23. 20%	49. $4.65
25a. 10%	51. 180 cm
25b. $14.50	

EXERCISE 4.4C

1. 10 937.5 kg	19. 150%
3. 345.6 litres	21. $360
5. 28.5, 47.5	23. A's Profit = $1 980
7. 98,245,343	B's Profit = $3 168
9. Dean's share = $994; Mesk's share = $710	C's Profit = $4 224
11. 5, 10, 22, 31	25. $276.59 for one cow; $248.41 for
13. 29.75	the other cow
15. 460	27. $12
17. $120	29. 1 100 units

Chapter 5

EXERCISE 5.1

1. $x = \frac{-5}{2}$ and $x = \frac{5}{2}$	17. $x = \frac{4}{3}$ and $x = \frac{1}{2}$
3. $x = \frac{-7}{4}$ and $x = \frac{7}{4}$	19. $x = 7$ and $x = \frac{3}{4}$
5. $x = \frac{2}{5}$ and $x = \frac{-4}{3}$	21. $x = \frac{7}{6}$ and $x = \frac{2}{3}$
7. $x = \frac{1}{4}$ and $x = \frac{3}{2}$	23. $x = \frac{7}{3}$ and $x = \frac{-7}{3}$
9. $y = \frac{4}{3}$ and $x = -7$	25. $x = 3$ and $x = \frac{-2}{7}$
11. $y = \frac{1}{4}$ and $y = \frac{5}{3}$	27. $x = \frac{4}{3}$ and $x = \frac{3}{8}$
13. $x = 2$ and $x = 3$	29. $x = \frac{6}{5}$ and $x = \frac{3}{7}$
15. $x = \frac{1}{3}$ and $x = 4$	31. $x = \frac{-9}{4}$ and $x = \frac{1}{3}$

EXERCISE 5.2

1. $L = 28, S_n = 144$
3. $L = 14, S_n = 56$
5. $L = 3.8, S_n = 20$
7. $L = -32, S_n = -272$
9. $a = 13, S_n = 7$
11. $L = 25, d = 3$
13. $a = \frac{1}{3}, L = 1$
15. $n = \frac{-11}{13}$ and $n = 8, L = -16$
17. $L = 6\ 144, Sn = 12\ 285$
19. $L = 81, Sn = 121$
21. $L = 1\ 458, Sn = 2\ 186$
23. $L = \frac{9}{50\ 000\ 000}, Sn = 18.181\ 818\ 18$

25. When $r = 5, L = -75$
     When $r = -6, L = -108$
27. $n = 6, L = 243$
29. $r = 2, Sn = 62$
31. $a = 3, n = 6$
33. The A.P. is: $2, 4\frac{1}{2}, 7, 9\frac{1}{2}, 12, 14\frac{1}{2}$.
35. The A.P. is: 1, 3, 5, 7, 9, 11, 13, 15.
37. The G.P. is: 2, 4, 8, 16, 32, 64.
39. The G.P. is: 1, 2, 4, 8, 16, 32, 64, 128.
41. $3\ 172
43. $395.81

EXERCISE 5.4

1. $\log 58 = 1.763\ 428$
3. $\ln 0.003\ 25 = -5.729\ 100\ 3$
5. $\log 5\ 683 = 3.754\ 578$
7. $\ln 10\ 253 = 9.235\ 325\ 6$
9. $10.6 = 10^{1.025\ 306}$
11. $2\ 452 = e^{7.804\ 659\ 9}$
13. $.003\ 559 = 10^{-2.448\ 672}$
15. $.005\ 42 = e^{-5.217\ 659\ 5}$
17a. $\log 285 = 2.454\ 844\ 9$
17b. $\ln 285 = 5.652\ 489\ 2$
19a. $\log 3.823 = 0.582\ 404\ 3$
19b. $\ln 3.823 = 1.341\ 035\ 5$
21a. $\log 4\ 328 = 3.636\ 287\ 2$
21b. $\ln 4\ 328 = 8.372\ 860\ 8$
23a. $\log 0.000\ 395\ 2 = 6.596\ 817\ -10$
23b. $\ln 0.000\ 395\ 2 = 7.836\ 118\ 6$
25a. $\log 2\ 374 = 3.375\ 480\ 7$

25b. $\ln 2\ 374 = 7.772\ 331\ 6$
27a. $\log 10.452 = 1.019\ 199\ 4$
27b. $\ln 10.452 = 2.346\ 793\ 3$
29. $x = 159.099\ 93$
31. $x = 2.789\ 998\ 7$
33. $x = 0.003\ 985$
35. $x = 49\ 099.944$
37. $x = 1.453\ 998\ 6$
39. $x = 5\ 366.626\ 9$
41. $x = 151\ 232.73$
43. $x = 9.040\ 097\ 9$
45. $x = 1.561\ 433$
47. $x = 0.090\ 756\ 8$
49. $x = 108.970\ 91$
51. $x = 1.176\ 523\ 6$
53. $x = 0.024$
55. $x = 0.005\ 63$

EXERCISE 5.5

1. $i = 1.250\ 25\%$, or 1.25%
3. $i = 2.012\ 02\%$, or 2%
5. $i = 6.000\ 08\%$, or 6%
7. $i = 1.984\ 25\%$, or 2%
9. $n = 99.999\ 969$, or 100%
11. $n = 29.999\ 984$, or 30%

Chapter 6

EXERCISE 6.2

1. $u + v = [10, 7]$

3. $x - y = \begin{bmatrix} -1 \\ 3 \\ 2 \end{bmatrix}$

5. $y - x = \begin{bmatrix} 1 \\ -3 \\ 2 \end{bmatrix}$

7. $5u = [30, 10]$

9. $3w = \begin{bmatrix} 9 \\ 21 \end{bmatrix}$

11. $4x = \begin{bmatrix} 4 \\ 24 \\ 20 \end{bmatrix}$

13. $u \cdot w = 32$

15. $z \cdot x = 97$

17. $A + B = \begin{bmatrix} 8 & 15 \\ 3 & 11 \end{bmatrix}$

19. $C - D = \begin{bmatrix} -4 & 1 \\ 1 & 2 \\ 5 & -2 \end{bmatrix}$

21. $3A = \begin{bmatrix} 9 & 27 \\ 6 & 12 \end{bmatrix}$

23. $\frac{1}{4}C = \begin{bmatrix} \frac{1}{4} & \frac{1}{2} \\ \frac{3}{4} & \frac{9}{4} \\ \frac{1}{8} & 1 \end{bmatrix}$

25. $A \cdot B = \begin{bmatrix} 11 & 81 \\ 14 & 40 \end{bmatrix}$

27. $A \cdot E = \begin{bmatrix} 21 & 63 & 81 \\ 12 & 32 & 40 \end{bmatrix}$

29. $A \cdot F = \begin{bmatrix} 51 & 39 & 30 \\ 24 & 20 & 18 \end{bmatrix}$

31. $E \cdot C = \begin{bmatrix} 46 & 74 \\ 80 & 79 \end{bmatrix}$

33. $C \cdot A = \begin{bmatrix} 7 & 17 \\ 27 & 63 \\ 32 & 88 \end{bmatrix}$

35. $F \cdot C = \begin{bmatrix} 70 & 68 \\ 22 & 41 \end{bmatrix}$

37. $C \cdot E = \begin{bmatrix} 6 & 16 & 19 \\ 21 & 63 & 81 \\ 36 & 93 & 56 \end{bmatrix}$

39. $C \cdot F = \begin{bmatrix} 15 & 23 & 36 \\ 39 & 29 & 21 \\ 36 & 30 & 27 \end{bmatrix}$

EXERCISE 6.3

1. -22
3. -14
5. 240
7. 6
9. -22
11. 240

EXERCISE 6.4

1. $\begin{bmatrix} (5 \times 1) + (-2 \times 0) & (5 \times 0) + (-2 \times 1) \\ (3 \times 1) + (4 \times 0) & (3 \times 0) + (4 \times 1) \end{bmatrix}$

$= \begin{bmatrix} 5 & -2 \\ 3 & 4 \end{bmatrix} \qquad \therefore A \cdot I = A$

and

$\begin{bmatrix} (1 \times 5) + (0 \times 3) & (1 \times -2) + (0 \times 4) \\ (0 \times 5) + (1 \times 3) & (0 \times -2) + (1 \times 4) \end{bmatrix}$

$= \begin{bmatrix} 5 & -2 \\ 3 & 4 \end{bmatrix} \qquad \therefore I \cdot A = A$

3. A^{-1} does not exist.

5. $A^{-1} = \begin{bmatrix} -\frac{7}{17} & \frac{5}{17} \\ \frac{9}{17} & \frac{-4}{17} \end{bmatrix}$

7. $A^{-1} = \dfrac{1}{240} \begin{bmatrix} 93 & 42 & -3 \\ -78 & -12 & 18 \\ -3 & -22 & 13 \end{bmatrix}$

CHECK: $\begin{bmatrix} 1 & -2 & 3 \\ 4 & 5 & -6 \\ 7 & 8 & 9 \end{bmatrix} \cdot \dfrac{1}{240} \begin{bmatrix} 93 & 42 & -3 \\ -78 & -12 & 18 \\ -3 & -22 & 13 \end{bmatrix} = \begin{bmatrix} 1 & 0 & 0 \\ 0 & 1 & 0 \\ 0 & 0 & 1 \end{bmatrix}$

EXERCISE 6.5

1. $x = 6, y = 2$
3. $x = 2, y = -3$
5. $x = 2, y = -13, z = 6$
7. $x = 1, y = -3, z = 26$

EXERCISE 6.6

1a. $x \geq 2$

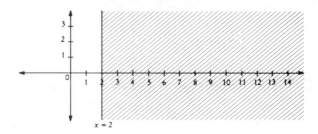

1b. $y \geq 3$

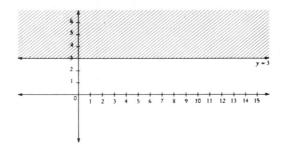

1c. $4y + 3x \le 12$

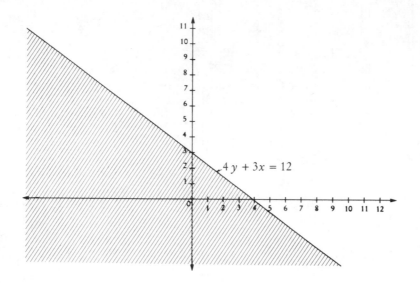

$4y + 3x = 12$

1d. $5y + 2x \le 10$

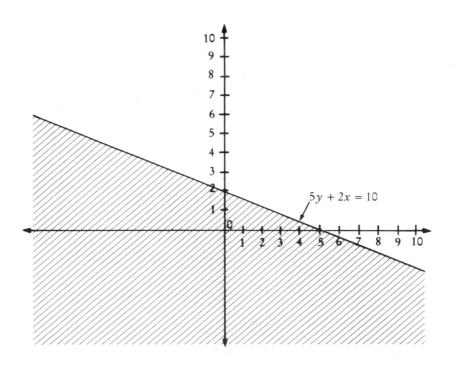

$5y + 2x = 10$

3. Restraints:
   ① $x + y \leq 7$
   ② $2x + 5y \leq 20$
   ③ $x \geq 0$
   ④ $y \geq 0$

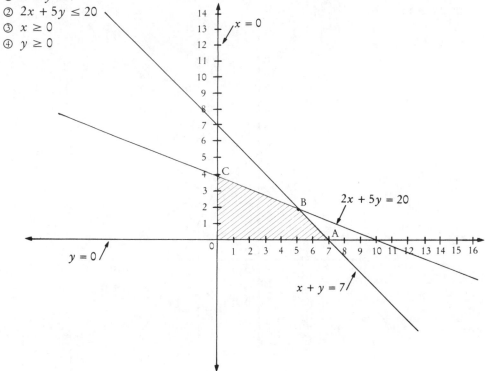

3a. Objective Function: $F = 3x + 8y$

   Point $O \longrightarrow x = 0$ and $y = 0 : F = 3(0) + 8(0) = 0$
   Point $A \longrightarrow x = 7$ and $y = 0 : F = 3(7) + 8(0) = 21$
   Point $B \longrightarrow x = 5$ and $y = 2 : F = 3(5) + 8(2) = 31$
   Point $C \longrightarrow x = 0$ and $y = 4 : F = 3(0) + 8(4) = 32$

   Thus, Point C is the optimum solution which maximizes the Objective Function F.

3b. Objective Function: $F = 3x + 4y$

   Point $O \longrightarrow x = 0$ and $y = 0 : F = 3(0) + 4(0) = 0$
   Point $A \longrightarrow x = 7$ and $y = 0 : F = 3(7) + 4(0) = 21$
   Point $B \longrightarrow x = 5$ and $y = 2 : F = 3(5) + 4(2) = 23$
   Point $C \longrightarrow x = 0$ and $y = 4 : F = 3(0) + 4(4) = 16$

   Thus, Point B is the optimum solution which maximizes the Objective Function F.

5. Restraints:

① $x + \frac{1}{2}y \leq 6$

② $2x + 3y \leq 24$

③ $x \geq 0$

④ $y \geq 0$

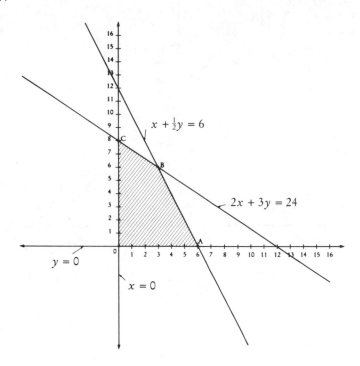

5a. Objective Function: $F = 8x + 7y$

Point $O \longrightarrow x = 0$ and $y = 0 : F = 8(0) + 7(0) = 0$

Point $A \longrightarrow x = 6$ and $y = 0 : F = 8(6) + 7(0) = 48$

Point $B \longrightarrow x = 3$ and $y = 6 : F = 8(3) + 7(6) = 66$

Point $C \longrightarrow x = 0$ and $y = 8 : F = 8(0) + 7(8) = 56$

Thus, Point B is the optimum solution which maximizes the Objective Function F.

5b. Objective Function: $F = 16x + 6y$

Point $O \longrightarrow x = 0$ and $y = 0 : F = 16(0) + 6(0) = 0$

Point $A \longrightarrow x = 6$ and $y = 0 : F = 16(6) + 6(0) = 96$

Point $B \longrightarrow x = 3$ and $y = 6 : F = 16(3) + 6(6) = 84$

Point $C \longrightarrow x = 0$ and $y = 8 : F = 16(0) + 6(8) = 48$

Thus, Point A is the optimum solution which maximizes the Objective Function F.

7. Objective Function: $P = 5(x) + 10(y)$

    Where: P = Profit
               x = Number of Chairs
               y = Number of Tables

Restraints: ① $(x) + 3(y) \le 9$ (Machine Restraint)
           ② $2(x) + 1(y) \le 8$ (Labor Restraint)

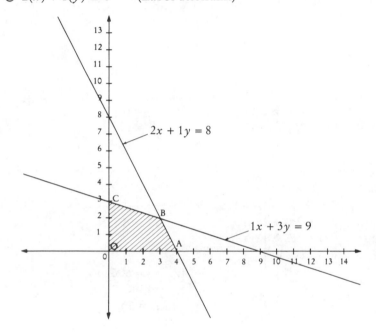

Objective Function: $P = 5x + 10y$

Point $O \longrightarrow x = 0$ and $y = 0$: Profit $= 5(0) + 10(0) = \$0$
Point $A \longrightarrow x = 4$ and $y = 0$: Profit $= 5(4) + 10(0) = \$20$
Point $B \longrightarrow x = 3$ and $y = 2$: Profit $= 5(3) + 10(2) = \$35$
Point $C \longrightarrow x = 0$ and $y = 3$: Profit $= 5(0) + 10(3) = \$30$

Thus, the Smith Company may produce 3 chairs and 2 tables to realize the highest profit.

Objective Function: $P = 5x + 15y$

Point $O \longrightarrow x = 0$ and $y = 0$: Profit $= 5(0) + 10(0) = \$0$
Point $A \longrightarrow x = 4$ and $y = 0$: Profit $= 5(4) + 15(0) = \$20$
Point $B \longrightarrow x = 3$ and $y = 2$: Profit $= 5(3) + 15(2) = \$45$
Point $C \longrightarrow x = 0$ and $y = 3$: Profit $= 5(0) + 15(3) = \$45$

Thus, the Smith Company may produce either 3 chairs and 2 tables (indicated by point B) or 3 tables (indicated by point C) to realize highest profit of $45.

Objective Function: $P = 5x + 20y$

Point $O \longrightarrow x = 0$ and $y = 0$: Profit $= 5(0) + 20(0) = \$0$
Point $A \longrightarrow x = 4$ and $y = 0$: Profit $= 5(4) + 20(0) = \$20$
Point $B \longrightarrow x = 3$ and $y = 2$: Profit $= 5(3) + 20(2) = \$55$
Point $C \longrightarrow x = 0$ and $y = 3$: Profit $= 5(0) + 20(3) = \$60$

Thus, the Smith Company may produce 3 tables (as indicated by point C) to realize highest profit of $60.

EXERCISE 6.7

1. Maximize: $12z_1 + 6z_2 + 8z_3$
   Subject to $\begin{cases} z_1 + z_2 + 0z_3 \leq 1 \\ 2z_1 + 0z_2 + z_3 \leq 1 \\ z_1, z_2, z_3 \geq 0 \end{cases}$

3. Minimize: $8z_1 + 10z_2 + 15z_3$
   Subject to $\begin{cases} 2z_1 + 0z_2 + 3z_3 \geq 3 \\ 3z_1 + 2z_2 + 2z_3 \geq 5 \\ 0z_1 + 5z_2 + 4z_3 \geq 4 \\ z_1, z_2, z_3 \geq 0 \end{cases}$

5. Minimize: $5z_1 + 3z_2 + 0z_3$
   Subject to $\begin{cases} 2z_1 + 1z_2 + 1z_3 \geq 3 \\ 1z_1 + 1z_2 + 1z_3 \geq 2 \\ z_1, z_2, z_3 \geq 0 \end{cases}$

7. $x_1 = 1.052\ 631\ 6$
   $x_2 = 2.368\ 421$
   $P = 12.368\ 421$

9. $x_1 = .941\ 176$
   $x_2 = .823\ 529\ 3$
   $x_3 = .470\ 588$
   $C = 162.352\ 93$

11. $x_1 = 8$
    $x_2 = 0$
    $P = 88$

13. $x_1 = 4$
    $x_2 = 0$
    $P = 12$

15. $x_1 = 0$
    $x_2 = 9$
    $x_3 = 0$
    $P = 90$

17. $x_1 = 600$
    $x_2 = 0$
    $P = 150$

19a. $x_1 = \dfrac{6.4}{7.6}$

   $x_4 = \dfrac{1.315\ 789\ 47}{5}$

   $P = 4.368\ 4$

19b. $-x_1 = -6.142\ 857\ 14$
   $x_2 = 0$
   $-x_3 = 0.285\ 714\ 28$
   Cost $= 120.714\ 285\ 7$

EXERCISE 6.8

1. 14
3. 13
5. 23
7. 61
9. 125
11. 239
13. 1 110
15. 11 010
17. 101 010
19. 110 001
21. 1 001 110
23. 101 010 000

25a. 101
25b. 5
27a. 1 001
27b. 9
29a. 11 001
29b. 25
31a. 1 000 000
31b. 64
33a. 110
33b. 6
35a. 1 001
35b. 9

37a. 101 100
37b. 44
39a. 110
39b. 6
41. 42
43. 130
45. 200
47. 372
49. 3
51. 4
53. 5
55. 10

Chapter 7

EXERCISE 7.2A

1. $30.80
3. $8.77
5. $25.76
7. $80.00
9. $53.50
11. $324.50
13. $16.03
15. $218.00

17. $243.50
19. $14.40
21. $28.83
23. $120.34
25a. $202.50
25b. $652.50
27. $118.75
29. $38.85

31. $35.00
33a. $30.00
33b. $9.00
35. $56.00
37a. $2.24
37b. $2.74
39. $43.20

EXERCISE 7.2B

1a. $20.00
1b. 25%
1c. 33.3%
3a. $9.15
3b. 24.56%
3c. 32.56%
5a. $.70
5b. 10.77%
5c. 12.07%
7a. $23.10
7b. 26.19%
7c. 35.48%

9a. $42.30
9b. 32.92%
9c. 49.07%
11a. $275.00
11b. $250.00
13a. $39.00
13b. $37.05
15a. $69.30
15b. $52.50
17a. $25.42
17b. $12.71
19a. $2 145.82

19b. $1 384.40
21a. $3 291.70
21b. $2 304.19
23a. $229.60
23b. 38.89%
23c. 28%
25a. 31.31%
25b. 23.85%
27a. $14 000
27b. $19 600
29. $3 000

EXERCISE 7.2C

1. 9.09%	15. 42.86%	27. 50%
3. 20.00%	17. 127.27%	29. 10.5%
5. 31.03%	19. 300.0%	31. 18.9%
7. 39.39%	21. 900%	33. 52.50%
9. 44.44%	23. 11.11%	35. 26.47%
11. 60.00%	25. 20.63%	37. 81.81%
13. 17.65%		

REVIEW EXERCISE

1. $30	17. $5.50	27a. $5.00
3. $61.44	19. $3.00	27b. $2.90
5a. $87	21a. $389.66	29. 25.93%
5b. $27	21b. $487.07	31. 16.67%
7. $40	21c. $19.99 or $20.00	33. 45.5%
9. $18	23a. 20%	35. 61.29%
11. $3.00	23b. 16.67%	37. 7.59%
13. $192.31	25a. $240	39. 56.7%
15. $4.08	25b. $300	

EXERCISE 7.3

1a. $342	19b. $30.05
1b. $158	21a. $5.82
1c. 31.6%	21b. $119.88
3a. $200.81	23. $60
3b. $99.19	25. $2 000
3c. 33.062 5%	27. $620
5a. $500	29. 42.4%
5b. $500	31. 31.6%
5c. 50%	33. 66.52%
7a. $6.48	35a. Manufacturer X
7b. $23.52	35b. $.85
7c. 78.4%	37. increase by $12.82
9a. $14.75	39. $800
9b. $.45	41. $650
9c. 2.98%	43. $270
11. $6.29	45a. 25%
13. $10.20	45b. 32.5%
15. $2 513.70	47. $537.23
17a. $39.76	49a. $27.07
17b. $10.24	49b. $35.19
19a. $17.95	

EXERCISE 7.4

1a. $11
1b. $539
3a. $9.12
3b. $447.08
5a. $1.95
5b. $63.21
7a. $0.00
7b. $24.30
9a. $.59
9b. $29.06
11. $1 550.36
13a. $824.50

13b. $833
13c. $850
15a. $567.75
15b. $579
17a. July 10
17b. $332.30
19a. $20.31
19b. $84.70
21a. 23.5%
21b. $8 314.62
21c. $646.43 each

EXERCISE 7.5

1. $2 441.40
3. $9 209.38
5. January, $180; February, $288; March, $249
7. $4 793.60
9. $381.36

EXERCISE 7.7

1. $.03
3. $.03
5. $.15
7. $.33
9. $.39
11. $.43
13a. $.54

13b. $5.92
15a. $13.48
15b. $.94
17a. $3.20
17b. $2.27
19a. $90.75
19b. $600.00

EXERCISE 7.8

1a. (1) $146.90
    (2) $17.10
    (3) $21.85
1b. $914.15
1c. (1) $34.20
    (2) $52.44
1d. $1 147.69

1e. Employee's Net Pay $914.15
Employer and Employee's Pension Plan Contribution 34.20
Employer and Employee's Unemployment Insurance Premium 52.44
Employee's Federal Income Tax 146.90

3a. (1) $144.20
(2) $13.28
(3) $16.97

3b. $632.55

3c. (1) $26.56 (from employer and employee)
(2) $40.73

3d. $844.04

3e. Employee's Net Pay $632.55
Employer and Employee's Pension Plan Contribution 26.56
Employer and Employee's Unemployment Insurance Premium 40.73
Employee's Federal Income Tax 144.20

5a. (1) $89.80
(2) $11.53
(3) $14.74

5b. $593.93

5c. (1) $23.06 (from employer and employee)
(2) $35.38

5d. $742.17

5e. Employee's Net Pay $593.93
Employer and Employee's Pension Plan Contribution 23.06
Employer and Employee's Unemployment Insurance Premium 35.38
Employee's Federal Income Tax 89.80

7a. (1) $172.75
(2) $15.58
(3) $19.90

7b. $691.77

7c. (1) $31.16 (from employer and employee)
(2) $47.76

7d. $943.44

7e. Employee's Net Pay $691.77
Employer and Employee's Pension Plan Contribution 31.16
Employer and Employee's Unemployment Insurance Premium 47.76
Employer's Federal Income Tax 172.75

9a. (1) $123.20
(2) $16.47
(3) $21.05

9b. $904.28

9c. (1) $32.94 (from employer and employee)
    (2) $50.52
9d. $1 110.94
9e. Employee's Net Pay $904.28
    Employer and Employee's Pension Plan contribution   32.94
    Employer and Employee's Unemployment Insurance Premium   50.52
    Employee's Federal Income Tax   123.20
11. UI = $21.74; CPP = $17.01; Income Tax = $117.45
13a. $223.60
13b. $4.35
15a. $86 956.52
15b. $17 000

Chapter 8

EXERCISE 8.1

1. $55.37	11a. 157 days
3. $172.21	11b. $223.78
5. $48.33	13a. 158 days
7. $143.01	13b. $49.42
9a. 125 days	15a. 306 days
9b. $171.17	15b. $44.99

EXERCISE 8.2

1. $I = \$48.08$; $S = \$3\ 048.08$	13b. $73 024.82	25. 75.26%
3. $n = 26.06$ days; $S = \$4\ 556.25$	15. $679.79	27. 37.24%
5. $n = 4$ months; $I = \$19.20$	17. $710.10	29. 2 years
7. $i = 4\%$; $I = \$7.60$	19a. $984.36	31a. 182.5 days
9. $n = .524\ 6$; $S = \$1\ 296$	19b. November 7, 1979	31b. 60.83 days
11. $i = 5\%$; $S = \$3\ 979$	21. 15%	33. $5 000
13a. $624.82	23. 11%	

EXERCISE 8.3

1. $328.40	11. $5 172.92	19a. $1 480.72
3. $5 500	13. $388.89	19b. $319.28
5. $188.18	15. $1 918.80	21. $587.41
7. $3 265.79	17a. $743.49	23. $5 082.44
9. $869.05	17b. $256.51	25. $1 013.56

EXERCISE 8.4

1. $242.81
3. $371.83
5. $474.19
7. $1 338.44
9. $985.09
11. $1 230.81
13. $646.30

EXERCISE 8.5

1. $2 085
3. $2 883.79
5. $7 766.67
7. $1 369.21
9a. $966.18
9b. $1 000

9c. $1 023.33
11. $1 532.53
13. $836.76
15. $4 347.54
17. $4 865.35

REVIEW EXERCISE

1a. $300
1b. $18.75
3. 136 days
5. 513 days
7a. $9.86
7b. $10
9a. $20.56
9b. $6.78
11. $2 270
13. $1 317.99

15a. $11.84
15b. $611.84
15c. August 29, 1984
17. 10%
19. 15.64%
21. 1.875 months
23. 7.09 months
25. $1 666.67
27. $4 147.29
29a. $785.45

29b. $24.55
31a. $848.39
31b. $82.01
33. $2 587.43
35a. $564.71
35b. $600
35c. $615
37. $763.49
39. $2 031.60

Chapter 9

EXERCISE 9.1

1. $I = \$62.67$, $S = \$5\ 062.67$
3. $i = 17.25\%$, $I = \$24.81$
5. $331
7. $203.16
9. $95.44

EXERCISE 9.2

1. $I' = \$1\ 479.45$, $P' = \$58\ 520.55$
3. $S = \$800$, $d = 3.75\%$
5. $n = 73$ days, $I' = \$57.60$
7. $d = 12.17\%$, $P' = \$8\ 775$
9. $S = \$866.94$, $I' = \$41.99$
11. $3 339.48
13. $66 391.49
15. 12.82%
17. 55 days
19. Alternative B

EXERCISE 9.4

1a. February 8, 1983	5c. 63 days	9e. $1 670.54
1b. $2 021.70	5d. $122.90	11. $1 461
1c. 23 days	5e. $4 259.02	13. $4 546.08
1d. $12.74	7a. December 4, 1985	15. $I = \$12.90$, $P' = \$967.10$
1e. $2 008.96	7b. $2 563.56	17a. June 7
3a. June 21, 1983	7c. 33 days	17b. June 4
3b. $1 800	7d. $35.35	17c. 83 days
3c. 53 days	7e. $2 528.21	17d. $81.81
3d. $42.34	9a. August 24, 1986	17e. $2 399.21
3e. $1 757.66	9b. $1 735.44	19. $I' = \$122.91$, $P' = \$2\ 142.79$
5a. November 6, 1984	9c. 78 days	21. $12 912.74
5b. $4 381.92	9d. $64.90	23. $3 420.53

REVIEW EXERCISE

1. Method (b) generates less interest expense by $369.86.
3. $492 910.96
5. 16.25%
7. 73 days
9. $605.96
11. $803.51
13a. $I' = \$88.77$, $P' = \$1\ 911.23$
13b. $I' = \$84.99$, $P' = \$1\ 915.01$
    The difference = $3.78.

Chapter 10

EXERCISE 10.2

1a. $1.99	5b. $426.63
1b. $86.99	7a. $15.70
3a. no finance charge	7b. $692.91
3b. $290.61	7c. $16.63
5a. $6.63	

EXERCISE 10.3

1. $166.24
3. $394.88
5. $32.30
7. $89.07
9. Fred's finance charge is lower by $68.17.

EXERCISE 10.4

1. Balance	Monthly Payment	Interest (15%/12)	Amount Credited to Principal	Outstanding Balance
$1 500	$261.05	$18.75	$242.30	$1 257.70
$1 257.70	$261.05	$15.72	$245.33	$1 012.37
$1 012.37	$261.05	$12.65	$248.40	$763.97
$763.97	$261.05	$9.55	$251.50	$512.47
$512.47	$261.05	$6.41	$25 .64	$257.83
$257.83	$261.05	$3.22	$257.83	$0.00

3. Balance	Monthly Payment	Interest (12%/12)	Amount Credited to Principal	Outstanding Balance
$2 500	$263.96	$25	$238.96	$2 261.04
$2 261.04	$263.96	$22.61	$241.35	$2 019.69
$2 019.69	$263.96	$20.20	$243.76	$1 775.93
$1 775.93	$263.96	$17.76	$246.20	$1 529.73
$1 529.73	$263.96	$15.30	$248.66	$1 281.07
$1 281.07	$263.96	$12.81	$251.15	$1 029.92
$1 029.92	$263.96	$10.30	$253.66	$776.26
$776.26	$263.96	$7.76	$256.20	$520.06
$520.06	$263.96	$5.20	$258.76	$261.30
$261.30	$263.96	$2.61	$261.34	Refund $.04

5.	Balance	Monthly Payment	Interest (15.25%/12)	Amount Credited to Principal	Outstanding Balance
	$2 000	$348.32	$25.42	$322.90	$1 677.10
	$1 667.10	$348.32	$21.31	$327.01	$1 350.09
	$1 350.09	$348.32	$17.16	$331.16	$1 018.93
	$1 018.93	$348.32	$12.95	$335.37	$683.56
	$683.56	$348.32	$8.69	$339.63	$343.93
	$343.93	$348.32	$4.37	$343.95	Refund $.02

7a.	Balance	Monthly Payment	Interest (18.5%/12)	Amount Credited to Principal	Outstanding Balance
	$2 500	$229.80	$38.54	$191.26	$2 308.74
	$2 308.74	$229.80	$35.59	$194.21	$2 114.53
	$2 114.54	$229.80	$32.60	$197.20	$1 917.33
	$1 917.33	$229.80	$29.56	$200.24	$1 717.09
	$1 717.09	$229.80	$26.47	$203.33	$1 513.76
	$1 513.76	$229.80	$23.34	$206.46	$1 307.30
	$1 307.30				

7b. The outstanding balance after the 6th payment is $1 307.30.

EXERCISE 10.5

1a. 8.03%
1b. 14.82%
3a. 8.99%
3b. 15.41%
5a. 13.92%

5b. 27.08%
7a. $204.88
7b. 45.57%
9a. $290
9b. 46.56%

EXERCISE 10.6

1. balance owed = $13 125; finance rebate = $897.44
3. balance owed = $5 833.33; finance rebate = $366.67
5. amount of debt = $21 960; finance rebate = $923.08
7. $1 283.33
9. $4 089.56

REVIEW EXERCISE

1a. $4.34   3. $584.38
1b. $277.61   5. $937.50
1c. $5.20   7a. $4 789.94

7b.	Balance	Monthly Payment	Interest (12%/12)	Amount Credited to Principal	Outstanding Balance
	$10 000	$222.44	$100	$122.44	$9 877.56
	9 877.56	$222.44	$98.78	$123.66	$9 753.90
	9 753.90	$222.44	$97.54	$124.90	$9 629.00
	9 629.00		$96.29	$126.15	$9 502.85
	9 502.85		$95.03	$127.41	$9 375.44
	9 375.44		$93.75	$128.69	$9 246.75
	9 246.75		$92.47	$129.97	$9 116.78
	9 116.78		$91.17	$131.27	$8 985.51
	8 985.51		$89.86	$132.58	$8 852.93
	8 852.93		$88.53	$133.91	$8 719.02
	8 719.02		$87.19	$135.25	$8 583.77
	8 583.77		$85.84	$136.60	$8 447.17
	8 447.17		$84.47	$137.97	$8 309.20
	8 309.20		$83.09	$139.35	$8 169.85
	8 169.85		$81.70	$140.74	$8 029.11
	8 029.11		$80.29	$142.15	$7 886.96
	7 886.96		$78.87	$143.57	$7 743.39
	7 743.39		$77.43	$145.01	$7 598.38
	7 598.38		$75.98	$146.46	$7 451.92
	7 451.92		$74.52	$147.92	$7 304.00
	7 304.00		$73.04	$149.40	$7 154.60
	7 154.60		$71.55	$150.89	$7 003.71
	7 003.71		$70.04	$152.40	$6 851.31
	6 851.31		$68.51	$153.93	$6 697.38
	6 697.38		$66.97	$155.47	$6 541.91
	6 541.91		$65.42	$157.02	$6 384.89
	6 384.89		$63.85	$158.59	$6 226.30
	6 226.30		$62.26	$160.18	$6 066.12
	6 066.12		$60.66	$161.78	$5 904.34
	5 904.34		$59.04	$163.40	$5 740.94
	5 740.94		$57.41	$165.03	$5 575.91
	5 575.91		$55.76	$166.68	$5 409.23
	5 409.23		$54.09	$168.35	$5 240.88
	5 240.88		$52.41	$170.03	$5 070.85
	5 070.85		$50.71	$171.73	$4 899.12
	4 899.12		$48.99	$173.45	$4 725.67

Chapter 11

EXERCISE 11.2

1. compound amount = $1 286.14; compound interest = $286.14
3. compound amount = $10 341.32; compound interest = $341.32
5. compound amount = $4 305.63; compound interest = $305.63
7. compound amount = $510.05; compound interest = $10.05
9a. $300
9b. $5.63
11a. $10
11b. $0.05

EXERCISE 11.3

1. $1 822.55
3. $6 653.14
5. $12 797.56
7. $2 377.17
9. $5 767.74
11. $2 313.33
13a. $1 160.75
13b. $1 158.65
13c. $1 155.63
13d. $1 150.00
15. $3 058.09
17. $5 297.08
19. Method A: $70 400.69 with $45 400.69 interest;
    Method B: $70 345.17 with $45 345.17 interest
21. $1 747.38
23. Liberty Bank pays more interest by $0.05.

EXERCISE 11.4A

1. $1 560.02
3. $79.74
5. $903.87
7. $96.80
9a. P = $157.87; compound discount = $1 242.13
9b. P = $189.53; compound discount = $1 210.47
11. $811.76
13. P = $1 483.65; compound discount = $2 116.35
15. $2 729.03
17. $1 182.75

EXERCISE 11.4B

1a. $572.23
1b. $427.77
3a. $1 311.56
3b. $1 188.44
5a. $1 240.93
5b. $2 739.02
7a. $2 443.40

7b. $603.96
9. $143.01
11. $4 629.37
13. $4 532.89
15. $11 861.20
17. $6 044.31

EXERCISE 11.5

1. 1.12%
3. 8.75%
5. 8.13%
7. 4.45%
9. 6.38%
11a. 13.5%

11b. 13.96%
11c. 14.20%
11d. 14.37%
13a. 17.81%
13b. Harry receives the better interest rate.

EXERCISE 11.6

1. 11 months
3. 4 semi-annual periods, or 2 years
5. 10 months
7. 14 semi-annual periods, or 7 years
9. 2 years
11. 6 semi-annual periods, or 3 years
13. $2 447.11 on November 1, 1987

EXERCISE 11.7

1. $4 272.42
3. $4 171.09
5. 2 years, 6 months
7. $9 027.44

9. $5 016.50
11. 60 months, or 5 years
13. 11.76%

EXERCISE 11.8A

1. $5 117.75
3. $50 955.41
5. $13 729.44
7. $13 016.35
9. $45 769.70

EXERCISE 11.8B

1. $1 569.97
3. $650.63
5. $1 148.46
7. $3 142.61
9. $1 368.11

EXERCISE 11.8C

1. $1 169.41
3. $1 016.24
5. $5 811.26

EXERCISE 11.8D

1. 6%
3. 15.99%
5. 8.56%

EXERCISE 11.8E

1. 22 monthly periods, or 1 year and 10 months
3. 6 semi-annual periods, or 3 years

EXERCISE 11.9

1. $5 858.30
3. $2 742.85
5. $699
7. $9 422.43
9a. $2 852.57

9b. no change
9c. $7 503.60
11. $3 959.29
13. $2 871.95
15. $1 576.46

EXERCISE 11.11

1. 13.07%
3. 18.15%
5. 14.97%
7a. 14.17%
7b. 22.14%
9. 13.31%
11a. compound amount = $1 164.74; compound interest = $164.74
11b. compound amount = $1 356.63; compound interest = $356.63

REVIEW EXERCISE

1. compound amount = $17 760.85; compound interest = $13 760.85
3a. simple interest = $125
3b. compound interest = $1 758.55
5. $7 979.58
7. $5 342.81
9. $3 549.17
11. amount = $11 503.56; interest = $6 503.56
13a. $260.16
13b. $389.84
15. proceeds = $832.41; compound discount = $921.62
17. proceeds = $434.30; compound discount = $365.70
19. 56.52%
21a. 18%
21b. 18.81%
21c. 19.25%
21d. 19.56%
23. Alan invested at a higher rate.
25. 48 months, or 4 years
27. 2 equal payments of $1 320.62; single payment of $2 165.04
29a. $230.64
29b. $893.29
31. $464.63
33. $1 871.08
35. $4 617.01
37. 16 months before year 5
39. 18.22%
41. 12.66%
43. 13.88%
45a. compound amount = $14 049.48; compound discount = $4 049.48
45b. compound amount = $11 331.48; compound discount = $6 487.21

Chapter 12

EXERCISE 12.2A

1. amount of the annuity = $40 452.25; total interest = $452.25
3. amount of the annuity = $4 050; total interest = $50
5. amount of the annuity = $12 364.82; total interest = $364.82
7. $3 972

EXERCISE 12.2B

1. $57 267.04
3. $21 192.44
5. $103 780.29
7. $14 114.74

9. $46 381.64
11. $151 621.42
13. $1 445.81
15. $26 857.75

EXERCISE 12.3A

1. $5 918.17
3. $385.48
5. $2 284.63
7. $5 767.77

EXERCISE 12.3B

1. $37 827.85
3. $6 177.63
5. $18 242.23
7. $6 297.20
9. $18 994.71

11. $10 411.77
13. $1 240.75
15. $88 752.62
17. $23 646.74

EXERCISE 12.4

1. $467.56
3. $930.49
5. $533.09
7. $94.65

9. $408.84
11. $449.32
13. $315.95
15. $458.20

EXERCISE 12.5

1. gross interest charge = $83.12; regular monthly payment = $90.26
3. amount of loan = $2 000; gross interest charge = $88.42
5. amount of loan = $2 000; gross interest charge = $205.75
7a. $787.24
7b. $2 893.76
9. option (a), $457.58; option (b), $459.81; option (a) saves $53.52

EXERCISE 12.6

1. 10 semi-annual periods, or 5 years
3. 24 monthly periods, or 2 years
5. 45 monthly periods, or 3 years, 9 months
7. 13 semi-annual periods, or $6\frac{1}{2}$ years
9. 22 quarterly periods, or 5 years, 2 months
11. 36 payments

EXERCISE 12.7

1. $i = 6.25\%$; nominal interest rate $= 6.25\%$
3. $i = \frac{25}{48}\%$; nominal interest rate $= 6.25\%$
5. $i = 1\frac{11}{32}\%$; nominal interest rate $= 16.125\%$
7. $i = 1\frac{5}{8}\%$; nominal interest rate $= 6.5\%$
9. 6.25%
11. 7%
13. Jack should invest his money at 10% instead of paying the debt because the value of i decreases by 0.2%.

EXERCISE 12.8

1. $Sn = \$51\ 878.99$
3. $R = \$702.36$
5. $n = 18$ months, or $1\frac{1}{2}$ years
7. $n = 19$ months, or 1 year, 7 months
9a. $\$17\ 978.57$
9b. $\$7\ 978.57$
11. $\$516.31$
13. 40

EXERCISE 12.9

1. $Sn = \$51\ 878.99$
3. $R = \$717.15$
5. $n = 18$ months, or $1\frac{1}{2}$ years
7. $n = 18$ months, or $1\frac{1}{2}$ years
9a. $\$17\ 548.74$
9b. $\$7\ 548.74$
11a. 12%
11b. She should pay off the debt now because the debt's interest rate is $\frac{1}{2}\%$ lower than 12.5%.
13. 60 monthly periods, or 5 years.

REVIEW EXERCISE

1. $\$3\ 410.35$
3a. $\$2\ 019.72$
3b. $\$453.41$
5. $\$3\ 295.61$
7. $\$8\ 687.75$
9. amount $= \$65\ 523.08$;
   present value $= \$6\ 051.01$

11. $\$104.77$
13. $\$48.98$
15. 103.8%
17. 13.39%
19. 10
21. $\$60\ 000$

Chapter 13

EXERCISE 13.2A

1. amount = $14 309.50; present value = $7 827.79
3. amount = $964.54; present value = $492.95
5. amount = $13 143.00; present value = $4 187.99
7. amount = $5 763.30; present value = $2 362.79
9a. amount = $13 541.33; present value = $11 697.52
9b. amount = $13 563.56; present value = $11 418.23
11. $39 436.82
13. $46 644.19
15. $133 916.54

EXERCISE 13.2B

1. $189.69
3. $179.94
5. $268.74
7. $146.63
9. $4 494.90

EXERCISE 13.3

1. payment = $26.56
3. payment = $976.06
5. S_{nc} = $90 647.92
7. A_{nc} = $35 255.50
9a. $445.64
9b. $10 695.36

9c. $38 934.28
9d. $9 629.64
11a. $76 969.68
11b. $43 030.32
11c. $672.34

EXERCISE 13.4

1. S_{nc} = $127 025.71; A_{nc} = $29 067.42
3. R = $548.23
5. n = 99
7. $13 418.84
9. 25

EXERCISE 13.5

1. S_{nc} = $2 321.57; A_{nc} = $1 887.65
3. R = $90.29
5. $7 031.73
7. $324.18

REVIEW EXERCISE

1. $17.45
3. $17.05
5. 5.59%
7. 5.08%
9. 38
11. 34
13. $347 590.76

Chapter 14

EXERCISE 14.1A

1. amount = $100 867.07; present value = $54 014.50
3. amount = $5 463.87; present value = $2 677.01
5. amount = $34 871.41; present value = $18 737.77
7. amount = $88 764.98; present value = $10 902.10
9. $19 070.24
11. $15 019.07
13. $35 936.59
15. $413.44

EXERCISE 14.1B

1. $\frac{1}{4}\% < i < \frac{1}{3}\%$
3. $2\% < i < 2\frac{1}{4}\%$
5. $n = 77$ semi-annual periods, or $38\frac{1}{2}$ years
7. $2 052.24
9. $328.55
11. 23 monthly periods, or 1 year, 11 months

13. $38.20
15. $654.11
17. $18\% < j < 19.5\%$
19. $11\% < j < 12\%$
21. 38
23. 19 years, 3 months

EXERCISE 14.2

1. $S_n = \$8\ 469.68$; $A_n = \$1\ 656.81$
3. $R = \$418.21$
5. $n = 64$
7. $S_n = \$8\ 968.45$; $A_n = \$6\ 924.07$
9. amount = $5 419.36; present value = $2 669.51
11. $14 553.47
13. 37
15. $2 895.57
17. amount = $544 865.98; present value = $32 243.62
19. amount = $1 999.75; present value = $410

EXERCISE 14.3

1. $15 000
3. $13 003.87
5. $2 752.94
7. $3 724.55
9a. $16 384.62

9b. $15 384.62
11a. $10 866.61
11b. $11 866.61
13. $7 407.41

EXERCISE 14.4

1. S_n(due) = $56 574.59; A_n(due) = $41 577.57
3. R = $1 396.70
5. n = 18 monthly payments
7. interest = 1.80% (monthly), 21.60% (nominal)
9. A_n(defer.) = $2 021.24

11. R = $5 106.29
13. n = 18 months, or $1\frac{1}{2}$ years
15a. $2 378.34
15b. $3 834.99
15c. $1 456.65
17. $1 612.31

EXERCISE 14.5

1. amount = $56 270.87;
   present value = $41 764.07
3. $888.99
5. 18 months, or $1\frac{1}{2}$ years
7. $1\frac{7}{8}$%
9. $2 021.24
11. $2 370.34

13. 19
15a. $2 364.04
15b. $3 863.98
15c. $1 499.94
17. $1 485.92
19. $2 125.28

REVIEW EXERCISE

1. amount = $5 121.30; present value = $3 528
3. amount = $5 058.07; present value = $3 484.45
5a. amount = $5 046.29; present value = $3 492.14
5b. amount = $5 029.37; present value = $3 503.25
7. amount = $5 090.36; present value = $3 545.74
9. $1 370.38
11. $876.24
13. $2 377.31
15. $35 338.91
17a. $6 666.67
17b. $6 220.66
19. $71.44
21a. $322.46
21b. $363.36
23. $24.81

25. $24.73
27. $5\% < j < 5\frac{1}{2}\%$
29. $5\% < j < 5\frac{1}{2}\%$
31. 25
33. 43
35. amount = $2 391.70;
    present value = $1 193.46
37. $670.63
39. 29

Chapter 15

EXERCISE 15.1A

1. size of payment = $325.49; outstanding principal = $1 233.86
3. size of payment = $1 037.78; outstanding principal = $1 022.44
5. size of payment = $562.89; outstanding principal = $5 799.31
7. size of payment = $45.56; outstanding principal = $125.24

9. size of payment = $1 672.46

(1) Period (quarterly interval)	(2) Outstanding Principal (2) − (5)	(3) Interest due at End of Period (2) × 4.5%	(4) Equal Payment at End of Period	(5) Portion of Payments Applied to Principal (4) − (3)
1	6 000.00	270.00	1 672.46	1 402.46
2	4 597.54	206.89	1 672.46	1 465.57
3	3 131.97	140.94	1 672.46	1 531.52
4	1 600.45	72.02	1 672.47	1 600.45
Total		689.85	6 689.85	6 000.00

11.

(1) Period (monthly interval)	(2) Outstanding Principal (2) − (5)	(3) Interest due at End of Period (2) × 1.315 940 38%	(4) Equal Payment at End of Period	(5) Portion of Payment Applied to Principal
1	7 000	92.12	342.04	249.92
2	6 750.08	88.83	342.04	253.21
3	6 496.87	85.49	342.04	256.55
4	6 240.32	82.12	342.04	259.92
5	5 980.40			

The outstanding principal after the fourth payment is $5 980.40

EXERCISE 15.1B

1a. 49
1b. $3 338.63
1c. interest = $166.93; principal = $53.07
1d. $33.04
1e. $43 686.91
3a. 6
3b. $2 502.72
3c. interest = $110.11; principal = $899.89

3d. $693.62
3e. $6 109.94
5a. 28
5b. $1 322.85
5c. interest = $132.29; principal = $17.71
5d. $63.69
5e. $20 195.18

7.

(1) Period (6-month interval)	(2) Outstanding Principal at Beginning of each Period (2) − (5)	(3) Interest Due at End of Period (2) × 8.5%	(4) Payment at End of each Period	(5) Portion of Principal Reduced by each Payment (4) − (3)
1	8 000	680	2 500	1 820
2	6 180	525.30	2 500	1 974.70
3	4 205.30	357.45	2 500	2 142.55
4	2 062.75	175.33	2 238.08	2 062.75
Total		1 738.08	9 738.08	8 000.00

EXERCISE 15.2

1. size of payment = $186.28; outstanding principal = $1 217.06
3. size of payment = $202.95; outstanding principal = $199.68
5. size of payment = $577.25; outstanding principal = $5 843.64
7. size of payment = $45.74; outstanding principal = $125.40
9.

(1) Payment Number (3-month interval)	(2) Payment	(3) Interest Due at End of Period (5) × 0.056 014 495	(4) Amount Applied to Principal (2) − (3)	(5) Balance (5) − (4)
0				6 000
1	1 715.77	336.09	1 379.68	4 620.32
2	1 715.77	258.80	1 456.97	3 163.35
3	1 715.77	177.19	1 538.58	1 624.77
4	1 715.77	91.01	1 624.77	0

Each payment is $1 715.77.

11.

(1) Payment Number (1-month interval)	(2) Payment	(3) Interest Due at End of Period (5) × 0.015 240 7	(4) Amount Applied to Principal (2) − (3)	(5) Balance (5) − (4)
0				7 000
1	350.45	106.68	243.77	6 756.23
2	350.45	102.97	247.48	6 508.75
3	350.45	99.20	251.25	6 257.50
4	350.45	95.37	255.08	6 002.42

The outstanding principal after the fourth payment is $6 002.42.

13a. $1 004.04   13b. $59 410.09

13c. $920.58

13d.

(1) Payment Number (1-month interval)	(2) Payment	(3) Interest Due at End of Period (5) × 0.016 396 356	(4) Amount Applied to Principal (2) − (3)	(5) Balance (5) − (4)
0				60 000
1	1 004.04	983.78	20.26	59 979.74
2	1 004.04	983.45	20.59	59 959.15
3	1 004.04	983.11	20.93	59 938.22
4	1 004.04	982.77	21.27	59 916.95
5	1 004.04	982.42	21.62	59 895.33
6	1 004.04	982.07	21.97	59 873.36

EXERCISE 15.3

1.

(1) Period (3-month interval)	(2) Outstanding Principal (2) − (5)	(3) Interest Due at End of Period (2) × 5%	(4) Equal Payment at End of Period	(5) Portion of Payment Applied to Principal (4) − (3)
1	7 000	350	1 616.82	1 266.82
2	5 733.18	286.66	1 616.82	1 330.16
3	4 403.02	220.15	1 616.82	1 396.67
4	3 006.35	150.32	1 616.82	1 466.50
5	1 539.85	76.99	1 616.84	1 539.85
Total		1 084.12	8 084.12	7 000.00

3.

(1) Period (3-month interval)	(2) Outstanding Principal (2) − (5)	(3) Interest Due at End of Period (2) × 3.75%	(4) Equal Payment at End of Period	(5) Portion of Payment Applied to Principal (4) − (3)
1	6 000	225	1 500	1 275
2	4 725	177.19	1 500	1 322.81
3	3 402.19	127.58	1 500	1 372.42
4	2 029.77	76.12	1 500	1 423.88
5	605.89	22.72	628.61	605.89
Total		628.61	6 628.61	6 000

5. $16 306.73
7. interest = $244.60; principal = $1 255.40
9a. $665

9b.

(1) At end of Period (6-month interval)	(2) Interest Income on Sinking Fund (5) × 8.5%	(3) Periodic Deposit in Fund	(4) Periodic Increase in Fund (2) + (3)	(5) Sinking Fund Accumulated (4) + (5)	(6) Book Value 7 000 − (5)
1		1 542.02	1 542.02	1 542.02	5 457.98
2	131.07	1 542.02	1 673.09	3 215.11	3 784.89
3	273.28	1 542.02	1 815.30	5 030.41	1 969.59
4	427.58	1 542.02	1 969.60		
Total	831.93	6 168.08	7 000.01		

11a. $2 207.02
11b. $2 184.44

13.

(1) At End of Period (6-month interval)	(2) Scheduled Interest Income	(3) Actual Interest Income	(4) Interest Discrepancy (2) − (3)	(5) Adjusted Deposit Schedule 1 542.02 + (4)	(6) Periodic Increase in Fund (3) + (5)
1				1 542.02	1 542.02
2	131.07	154.20	−23.13	1 518.89	1 673.09
3	273.28	225.06	48.22	1 590.24	1 815.30
4	427.58	352.13	75.45	1 617.47	1 969.60
Total	831.93	731.39	100.54	6 268.62	7 000.01

15a. $2 074.63
15b. $58.51

Chapter 16

EXERCISE 16.2A

1. $897.03
3. $2 201.82
5. $559
7. $6 394.55
9a. $8 283.79
9b. $8 397.31
11a. $1 712.67
11b. $1 557.43

EXERCISE 16.2B

1a. $4 405.45
1b. $266.67
1c. $4 138.78
3a. $4 844.58
3b. $75
3c. $4 769.58
5a. $858.06
5b. $6
5c. $852.06

7a. $9 641.67
7b. $275
7c. $9 366.67
9a. $2 909.54
9b. $2 797.04
11. $7 093.10
13a. $2 000
13b. $49.32
13c. $2 049.32

EXERCISE 16.3A

1a. $262.45
1b. $3 737.55
3a. $193.38
3b. $4 806.62
5a. $46

5b. $946
7a. $573.47
7b. $10 573.47
9a. $141.70
9b. $3 141.70

11a. Question 2, $1 132.71; Question 3, $2 201.82; Question 5, $559; Question 6, ·
     $4 257.63

EXERCISE 16.3B

1. purchase price = $3 676.33

(1) At End of Interest Period	(2) Interest Receipt From Bond $4\ 000 \times 5.5\%$	(3) Yield Investor's Interest $(5) \times 7.5\%$	(4) Discount Accumulation $(3) - (2)$	(5) Bond Book Value $(5) + (4)$
0				3 676.33
1	220	275.72	55.72	3 732.05
2	220	279.90	59.90	3 791.95
3	220	284.40	64.40	3 856.35
4	220	289.23	69.23	3 925.58
5	220	294.42	74.42	4 000.00
Total	1 100	1 423.67	323.67	

3. purchase price = $4 086.59

(1) At End of Interest Period	(2) Interest Receipt From Bond $4\ 000 \times 5.5\%$	(3) Yield Investor's Interest $(5) \times 5\%$	(4) Premium Amortization $(2) - (3)$	(5) Bond Book Value $(5) - (4)$
0				4 086.59
1	220	204.33	15.67	4 070.92
2	220	203.55	16.45	4 054.47
3	220	202.72	17.28	4 037.19
4	220	201.86	18.14	4 019.05
5	220	200.95	19.05	4 000.00
Total	1 100	1 013.41	86.59	

5. $8 339.57

EXERCISE 16.4

1. 14%
3. 13%
5. 17%
7. 13%
9. 13.54%
11. 10.58%

EXERCISE 16.5

1a. $2 943.31
1b. $1 319.94
3a. $3 058.38
3b. $1 344.12
5. $17 402.30
7. $16 304.92

REVIEW EXERCISE

1a. $1 037.69   5b. $52.60
1b. $1 055.25   5c. $1 972.60
1c. $1 020.13   7a. $353.71
3a. $1 056.71   7b. $6 646.29
3b. $20   9a. $5 451.01
3c. $1 036.71   9b. $5 589.64
5a. $1 920   11a. $5 794.45

11b.

(1) At End of Interest Period	(2) Interest Receipt from Bond 6 000 × 5.5%	(3) Yield Investor's Interest (5) × 6.5%	(4) Discount Accumulation (3) – (2)	(5) Bond Book Value (5) + (4)
0				5 794.45
1	330	376.64	46.64	5 841.09
2	330	379.67	49.67	5 890.76
3	330	382.90	52.90	5 943.66
4	330	386.34	56.34	6 000.00
Total	1 320	1 525.55	205.55	

13a. $6 106.38

13b.

(1) At End of Interest Period	(2) Interest Receipt From Bond 6 000 × 5.5%	(3) Yield Investor's Interest (5) × 5%	(4) Premium Amortization (2) − (3)	(5) Bond Book Value (5) − (4)
0				6 106.38
1	330	305.32	24.68	6 081.70
2	330	304.09	25.91	6 055.79
3	330	302.79	27.21	6 028.58
4	330	301.42	28.58	6 000
Total	1 320	1 213.62	106.38	

15. 11%
17a. $9 811.06
17b. $4 399.80
19. $20 257.09

Chapter 17

EXERCISE 17.1

1. $2 250/year
3. $480/year

(1) End of Year	(2) Annual Depreciation Expense	(3) Accumulated Depreciation (from (2))	(4) Book Value of Machine $2 650 − (3)
0	0	0	$2 650
1	$480	$480	$2 170
2	$480	$960	$1 690
3	$480	$1 440	$1 210
4	$480	$1 920	$730
5	$480	$2 400	$250
Total	$2 400		

5.   1st year, $440; 2nd year, $592; 3rd year, $496; 4th year, $464; 5th year, $408

(1) End of Year	(2) Annual Depreciation Expense	(3) Accumulated Depreciation	(4) Book Value of Machine $2 650 − (3)
0	0	0	$2 650
1	$440	$440	$2 210
2	$592	$1 032	$1 618
3	$496	$1 528	$1 122
4	$464	$1 992	$658
5	$408	$2 400	$250
Total	$2 400		

7. $840

EXERCISE 17.2

1.   1st year, $2 371.43; 2nd year $1 976.19; 3rd year, $1 580.95; 4th year $1 185.71; 5th year, $790.48; 6th year, $395.24

(1) End of Year	(2) Annual Depreciation Expense	(3) Accumulated Depreciation	(4) Book Value of Car $8 500 − (3)
0	0	0	$8 500
1	$2 371.43	$2 371.43	$6 128.57
2	$1 976.19	$4 347.62	$4 152.38
3	$1 580.95	$5 928.57	$2 571.43
4	$1 185.71	$7 114.28	$1 385.72
5	$790.48	$7 904.76	$595.24
6	$395.24	$8 300.00	$200.00
Total	$8 300.00		

3.   1st year, $1 082.61; 2nd year, $1 202.90; 3rd year, $1 323.19; 4th year, $1 443.48; 5th year, $1 563.77; 6th year, $1 684.06

5a. *Declining-Balance Method*

(1) End of Year	(2) Annual Depreciation Expense (Book Value × $33\frac{1}{3}$%)	(3) Accumulated Depreciation	(4) Book Value of Car $8 500 − (3)
0	0	0	$8 500
1	$2 833.33	$2 833.33	$5 666.67
2	$1 888.89	$4 722.22	$3 777.78
3	$1 259.26	$5 981.48	$2 518.52
4	$839.52	$6 821.00	$1 679.00
5	$559.68	$7 380.68	$1 119.32
6	$373.12	$7 753.80	$746.20
Total	$7 753.80		

5b. *Fixed Rate Formula*

(1) End of Year	(2) Annual Depreciation Expense (Book Value × .464 694 3)	(3) Accumulated Depreciation	(4) Book Value of Car $8 500 − (3)
0	0	0	$8 500
1	$3 949.90	$3 949.90	$4 550.10
2	$2 114.40	$6 064.30	$2 435.70
3	$1 131.85	$7 196.15	$1 303.85
4	$605.89	$7 802.04	$697.96
5	$324.34	$8 126.38	$373.62
6	$173.62	$8 300.00	$200.00
Total	$8 300.00		

EXERCISE 17.3

1. annual depreciation charges = $789.51

(1)	(2)	(3)	(4)	(5)	(6)
End of Year	Annual Depreciation Charges	Interest Income (6) × 15.5%	Net Depreciation Charges to Be Accumulated (2) − (3)	Accumulated Depreciation from (4)	Book Value $2 400 − (5)
0	0	0	0	0	$2 400
1	$789.51	$372	$417.51	$417.51	$1 982.49
2	$789.51	$307.29	$482.22	$899.73	$1 500.27
3	$789.51	$232.54	$556.97	$1 456.70	$943.30
4	$789.51	$146.21	$643.30	$2 100.00	$300.00
Total	$3 158.04	$1 058.04			

3. annual depreciation charges: 1st year, $417.51; 2nd year, $482.22; 3rd year, $556.97; 4th year, $643.30

(1)	(2)	(3)	(4)	(5)	(6)
End of Year	Periodic Deposit in Fund	Interest Income from Sinking Fund (5) × 15.5%	Periodic Increase in Fund = Annual Depreciation Charges (2) + (3)	Accumulated Sinking Fund = Accumulated Depreciation from (4)	Book Value $2 400 − (5)
0	0	0	0	0	$2 400
1	$417.51	0	$417.51	$417.51	$1 982.49
2	$417.51	$64.71	$482.22	$899.73	$1 500.27
3	$417.51	$139.46	$556.97	$1 456.70	$943.30
4	$417.51	$225.79	$643.30	$2 100.00	$300.00
Total	$1 670.04	$429.96	$2 100.00		

5. $943.30

7. (1) $12 000
   (2) $12 571.43
   (3) $9 685.53
   (4) $8 730.95
   (5) $40 957.71
   (6) $8 075.68

EXERCISE 17.4

1a. $280 000	3a. $58 585.64	5b. $12 229.67
1b. $.70	3b. $16 474.36	5c. 4.08%
1c. $70 000	3c. 5.47%	7. $34 378.85
1d. ($51 000) loss	5a. $62 770.33	9. $34 336.38

EXERCISE 17.5

1a. $66 666.67	5. $50 000	11. $2 117 341.80
1b. $46 438.65	7. $67 067.31	13. $451 300.85
3. $138 026.22	9. $2 105 607.53	

EXERCISE 17.6

1. The $8 000 garage is less expensive.   5. $1 052.95
3. The $8 000 garage is less expensive.   7. $78.30

REVIEW EXERCISE

1a. $1 800/year
1b. 1st year, $3 000; 2nd year, $2 400; 3rd year, $1 800; 4th year, $1 200; 5th year, $600
1c. (1) 1st year, $4 000; 2nd year, $2 400; 3rd year, $1 440; 4th year, $864; 5th year, 518.40
    (2) end of 1st year, $3 690; end of 2nd year, $2 328.39; end of 3rd year, $1 469.21; end of 4th year, $927.07; end of 5th year, $584.98
1d. annual depreciation charges = $2 834.84

(1) End of Year	(2) Annual Depreciation Charges (R)	(3) Interest Income (6) × 15%	(4) Net Depreciation Charges to be Accumulated (2) − (3)	(5) Accumulated Depreciation from (4)	(6) Book Value $10 000 − (5)
0					10 000
1	2 834.84	1 500	1 334.84	1 334.84	8 665.16
2	2 834.84	1 299.77	1 535.07	2 869.91	7 130.09
3	2 834.84	1 069.51	1 765.33	4 635.24	5 364.76
4	2 834.84	804.71	2 030.13	6 665.37	3 334.63
5	2 834.82*	500.19	2 334.63	9 000	1 000
Total	14 174.18	5 174.18	9 000		

*Corrected for two-cent discrepancy.

1e. annual depreciation charges: 1st year, $1 416.69; 2nd year, $1 586.69; 3rd year, $1 777.10; 4th year, $1 990.35; 5th year, $2 229.17

(1) End of Year	(2) Periodic Deposit in Fund (R)	(3) Interest Income from Sinking Fund $(5) \times 12\%$	(4) Periodic Increase in Fund = Annual Depreciation Charges $(2) + (3)$	(5) Accumulated Sinking Fund = Accumulated Depreciation from (4)	(6) Book Value $10\,000 - (5)$
0					10 000
1	1 416.69		1 416.69	1 416.69	8 583.31
2	1 416.69	170.00	1 586.69	3 003.38	6 996.62
3	1 416.69	360.41	1 777.10	4 780.48	5 219.52
4	1 416.69	573.66	1 990.35	6 770.83	3 229.17
5	1 416.67*	812.50	2 229.17	9 000	1 000
Total	7 083.43	1 916.57	9 000		

*Corrected for two-cent discrepancy.

3. 1st year, $88; 2nd year, $80
5. 8.96%
7a. $124 000
7b. $41 000
9a. $97 543.40
9b. $67 456.60
9c. 13.49%
11. $294 617.16
13. $294 530.91
15a. $33 739.20
15b. $38 855.85
17. $1 006 787.68
19. $1 007 541.90
21. $185 971.69
23. television X is less expensive
25. $926.58
27. $167.54

Index

Summary of Formulae

Supplemental Algebraic Operations

$x = \dfrac{-b \pm \sqrt{b^2 - 4ac}}{2a}$ root of any quadratic equation / 128

$L = a + (n - 1)d$ nth term of an arithmetic progression / 130

$S_n = \dfrac{n}{2}(a + L)$ sum of an arithmetic progression / 131

$L = ar^{n-1}$ nth term of a geometric progression / 133

$S_n = \dfrac{a(1 - r^n)}{1 - r}$ sum of a geometric progression / 133

Business Applications of Percents

PERCENTAGE = BASE × RATE   formula used in finding selling price or cost of an item / 208

$S = L(1 - r_1)(1 - r_2)(1 - r_3)\ldots(1 - r_n)$ selling price when a chain discount is involved / 223

$S = L(1 - r)$ selling price with a single equivalent discount rate / 224

$r = 1 - (1 - r_1)(1 - r_2)(1 - r_3)\ldots(1 - r_n)$ single equivalent discount rate / 224

Simple Interest and Simple Discount

$I = Pin$ simple interest / 258

$S = P(1 + in)$ amount / 263

or $S = P + I$ / 269

where P = principal (269); i = simple interest rate (265); n = time (266)

Discounted Loans

$I' = Sdn$ bank discount or the interest in advance / 294

$P' = S(1 - dn)$ proceeds / 294

Consumer Credit

$i = \dfrac{C}{Pn}$ simple annual interest rate on a loan with a single payment / 326

$i = \dfrac{2MC}{P(N + 1)}$ interest rate on an instalment loan / 327

$\text{Sum} = \dfrac{N}{2}(N + 1)$ sum-of-the-digits / 329

$\text{Rebate} = \dfrac{\text{Sum-of-the-digits of oustanding payments}}{\dfrac{N}{2}(N + 1)} \times C$ unearned finance charge / 330

Compound Interest

$S = P(1 + i)^n$ compound amount / 340

where P = present value (347); i = interest rate (355); n = number of conversion periods (355)

$f = \left(1 + \dfrac{j}{m}\right)^m - 1$ effective rate when compounding continuously / 357

where m = number of conversion periods in one year and j = nominal rate

$n = \dfrac{\ln \frac{S}{P}}{\ln(1 + i)}$ number of conversion periods / 360

$(1 + i)^n = \dfrac{S}{P}$ interest rate using a table of values / 372

$f = e^j - 1$ effective rate of the nominal rate / 387

$S = P(e^{jn})$ compound amount of the principal at the nominal rate when compounding continuously / 388

Ordinary Annuities

$S_n = R \cdot \dfrac{(1 + i)^n - 1}{i}$ amount / 399

$A_n = R \cdot \dfrac{1 - (1 + i)^{-n}}{i}$ present value / 405

$S_n = R \, s_{\overline{n}|\,i}$ amount using a table of values / 427

$A_n = R \, a_{\overline{n}|\,i}$ present value using a table of values / 428

where R = size of each periodic payment (409, 410); n = term (417, 418); i = interest rate (420, 421)

Complex (or General) Ordinary Annuity Certain

$S_n = R\left[\dfrac{(1 + f)^n - 1}{f}\right]$ amount of simple annuity / 446

$A_n = R\left[\dfrac{1 - (1 + f)^{-n}}{f}\right]$ present value of simple annuity / 446

$S_{nc} = R\left[\dfrac{(1 + i)^{nc} - 1}{(1 + i)^c - 1}\right]$ amount of ordinary complex annuity / 448

$A_{nc} = R\left[\dfrac{1 - (1 + i)^{-nc}}{(1 + i)^c - 1}\right]$ present value of ordinary complex annuity / 449

$S_{nc} = R \, s_{\overline{nc}|\,i} \cdot \dfrac{1}{s_{\overline{c}|\,i}}$ amount of ordinary complex annuity using a table of values / 472